A BIOGRAPHICAL DICTIONARY
OF OLD ENGLISH MUSIC

Da Capo Press Music Reprint Series
GENERAL EDITOR
FREDERICK FREEDMAN
VASSAR COLLEGE

A BIOGRAPHICAL DICTIONARY OF OLD ENGLISH MUSIC

By Jeffrey Pulver

*With a New Introduction and a Bibliography
of the Writings of Jeffrey Pulver By
Gilbert Blount, University of Texas*

DA CAPO PRESS • NEW YORK • 1973

Library of Congress Cataloging in Publication Data

Pulver, Jeffrey, 1884-
A biographical dictionary of old English music.
(Da Capo Press music reprint series)
Reprint of the 1927 ed.
Includes bibliographies.
1. Composers, English. I. Title.
ML106.G7P9   1973   780'.92'2 [B]   69-16666
ISBN 0-306-71103-6

This Da Capo Press edition of
A Biographical Dictionary of Old English Music
is an unabridged republication of the first
edition published in London and New York in
1927. It is reprinted by special arrangement
with Routledge & Kegan Paul Ltd.

JEFFREY PULVER

Biographical data on Jeffrey Pulver is not readily available, and though his birthdate of June 22, 1884 in London is well documented, little else seems generally known about this English violinist-musicologist.[1] Born of parents with interests in music, he began studying the violin at the early age of seven, and started frequenting Queen's Hall symphony concerts with his father in 1896. His more illustrious violin instructors include the noted Czech violinist Otakar Ševčik (Prague, 1904/5), the German violinist Hugo Heermann (Frankfurt, 1906), the French violinist-composer Henri Marteau (Geneva, 1907/8), and the German violinist and music scholar Andreas Moser (Berlin, 1908/9). Pulver's first violin recital was held at Steinway Hall (London) in 1910, and was followed by other concerts in the same hall and in the Broadwood Rooms. That he became a violinist of no slight ability is attested in several issues of *The Strad*,[2] and from reviews of his performances it is clear that his concert repertory embraced a broad historical latitude. His preference for teaching to public performances, however, enabled him to concentrate on developing a technique of instruction compromising the purely mechanical approach of Ševčik and the interpretative emphasis of Moser and Heermann.

In 1912 Pulver joined the Royal Musical Association, and gave before its members a series of lectures on a variety of musical subjects.[3] Contact

---

1 Though brief articles on Pulver are found in *Thompson's International Cyclopedia of Music and Musicians,* the 12th edition of Riemann's *Musik Lexikon, MGG, Baker's Biographical Dictionary of Musicians,* etc., his name is curiously omitted from all editions of *Grove's Dictionary.* A substantial portion of the biographical information presented here, has been acquired from the author directly, to whom the present writer is deeply indebted.

2 See *The Strad,* XX [No. 239] (Mar 1916), 394; XXI [No. 242] (Jun 1910), 47; XXI [No. 252] (Apr 1911), 423; XXIV [No. 278] (Jun 1913), 47; etc.

3 The Royal Musical Association membership lists, published in its annual *Proceedings,* carry no entry for Pulver until the 1918/19 issue (Volume 45, page vi). However, since the author's lectures before that body begin in 1912, it would appear that he is correct in marking that year as the beginning of his association. His more important lectures are published in the *Proceedings of the Royal Musical Association* and/or abstracted in *The Musical Times* (consult the Bibliography for listings).

there with the composer, conductor, and organist, Sir John Frederick Bridge (1844–1924), developed into a personal and scholarly relationship. As a result, Pulver undertook research for Bridge—then Gresham Professor at Gresham College, London, and King Edward Professor of Music at the University of London—at times illustrating the professor's lectures on a viola d'amore and a six-string seventeenth century tenor viol. World War I stimulated a redirection of Pulver's energies, and he worked from 1914 to 1918 in military hospitals on behalf of the Red Cross.

The nineteen-twenties and thirties were very active periods for Pulver —rich both in lectures and publications. One of the more memorable occasions during these two decades was his report on "The Viols in England," presented to the International Musicological Society at its 1933 Congress in Cambridge, in which his own musical illustrations on the tenor viol were accompanied by Otto Kinkeldey at the harpsichord. World War II found Pulver in Civil Defence Corps uniform working first at the Royal Sussex County Hospital in the Casualty Department and later in a First Aid post in Brighton. Musical research continued to occupy his attention until his sight began to fail in the early nineteen-fifties. When he was placed on the British register of the blind in 1958, his literary career ended and he was forced to abandon his projected writings. Currently residing in London, he now lives in quiet retirement.[4]

To describe Pulver as less than a prolific writer about matters musical would be to lean toward understatement. In the three decades between 1910 and 1940, Pulver contributed eight books and over one hundred and fifty articles to the literature of music, and, while many of his articles are only two or three pages in length, he normally manages to communicate something of substance and interest.[5] He rarely indulges in the kind of triviality that one occasionally associates with some of the periodicals for which he was writing.[6]

---

4 Pulver married in 1920 and he has two children: a son, John, now an electronic engineer, and a daughter, Rhoda Thelma, married to Joe Henry Mendoza, producer, director and script-writer of documentary films for the British armed forces.

5 It is curious that while most dictionary articles contain a reference to Pulver's contributions to *The Musical Quarterly*, none could be located by the present author, and none are listed in the Goodkind indices. That the attribution is erroneous is all but confirmed by Pulver's request that no similar reference be made here.

6 For example, "Music on the Lake of Geneva," *The Strad*, XXV [No. 292] (Aug 1914), 134–5.

His authorship of books on Brahms, Paganini, violin technique, medieval stringed instruments, and Machiavelli, not to mention three dictionaries, makes clear that Pulver was a man of wide interests. His articles
also cover a wide range of subjects, including music theorists (primarily
English), early instruments, dance music, opera, music in Egypt, violin
technique, and various composers. Many of his articles are serialized,
and, though they initially give the appearance of brevity, quite a number are full-length feature articles when all installments are gathered
together, a few amounting to book-length studies.[7]

While most of Pulver's books survived the critical eye of the reviewer
unscathed, *Paganini,* published in 1936, was received with mixed criticism.[8] Pulver's *Brahms* (1926) was reviewed neutrally, and his *Aids to
Elementary Violin Playing* (1926), favorably. His two major dictionaries, the *Dictionary of Old English Music and Musical Instruments*
(1923) and the *Biographical Dictionary of Old English Music* (1927)
were favored with laudatory reviews as well they should have been.

Dictionaries in the field of music assume a variety of sizes, shapes, and
formats.[9] Some are all-inclusive in scope and broad in dimension; others,
in the majority, are self-limiting in one way or another. Some restrict
themselves to a particular geographical area, others to a specific musical
period, genre, or occupation. Pulver's *Dictionary of Old English Music
and Musical Instruments* is a profuse work stressing musical terms
commonly found in writings both literary and musical (Chaucer,
Shakespeare, Jonson, Playford, Simpson, etc.) up through the seventeenth century, generally omitting terms adequately treated in other
dictionaries or textbooks.

---

7 To cite an extreme case, Pulver's series of articles on "Aids to Left Hand
Technique" appeared in *The Strad* in eighty-three consecutive installments
over a period of seven years beginning with volume XXX [No. 354] Oct
1919), 163–5, and ending with volume XXXVII [No. 436] (Aug 1926),
219/22.

8 One review of interest is by Richard Capell, *Music & Letters* XVIII/2 (Apr
1937), 191–3.

9 For a fairly comprehensive survey of the literature see James B. Coover's
A Bibliography of Music Dictionaries (Denver: Bibliographical Center for
Research, 1952) or its revision, *Music Lexicography* (Denver: Bibliographic
Center for Research, 1958); Vincent Duckles' *Music Reference and Research
Materials,* rev. ed. (New York: Free Press, 1967), 1–71; Richard Schaal's
"The Fore-Runners of the Grove-Blom: A Bibliography of Musical Diction-
aries in Chronological Order," in *Hinrichsen's Musical Year Book* VII (Lon-
don: Hinrichsen Editions, Ltd., 1952), 594–601.

His *Biographical Dictionary of Old English Music* is, as the title suggests, a dictionary of musical biographies, designed in part to comple-
ment the earlier dictionary of musical terms, to whose articles it refers
for additional information. Pulver's biographical dictionary embraces
the period from the thirteenth through the seventeenth centuries treating principally insular composers, theorists, printers, performers, and
instrument makers, though some additional coverage is granted foreign
nationalists believed to have exerted some influence on English music
and musicians. Despite Pulver's prefatory comment that the quantity
of information contained in an entry is normally proportional to the
difficulty with which that information is obtainable, he often succumbs
to the course more common to pragmatic biographers and lexicogra-
phers. Nonetheless, the quantity of information presented in this volume
is immense, and, considering the date of its completion, this dictionary
withstands remarkably well the test of comparison with products of a
more recent vintage.

Based on a substantive random sample, Percy Scholes[10] in 1938 totally
neglected about sixty-five percent of the entries included by Pulver more
than a decade earlier, and the data presented in the remaining entries
is meager when compared to the *Biographical Dictionary.* Even Scholes'
ninth edition, which the author claims is "completely revised and
reset," does little to rectify this situation. In the same random sample,
Slonimsky[11] manages to include in his volume less than twenty percent
of Pulver's entries. The only dictionary which substantially overlaps
Pulver is the latest edition of *Grove's Dictionary.*[12] In its treatment of
major composers, *Grove's* articles are more complete, and, where the
identity of a composer is of a more recent discovery, *Grove's* may carry
an entry not found at all in Pulver (such as Bedingham or Frye).
Furthermore, it is not too difficult to identify composers excluded from
both Pulver and *Grove's* (e.g., Byttering, John Cooke, Damett, Pycard,
Sandley). Nevertheless, both do contain information on a significant
number of English musicians active up to the death of Purcell, and,

---

10 Percy A. Scholes, *The Oxford Companion to Music* (London: Oxford University Press, 1938); 9th edition, 1955.

11 *Baker's Biographical Dictionary of Musicians,* 5th edition, Nicolas Slonimsky,
ed. (New York: G. Schirmer, 1965). A supplement was issued in 1971.

12 *Grove's Dictionary of Music and Musicians,* 5th edition, Eric Blom, ed.
(London: Macmillan; New York: St. Martin's Press, 1954), 9 vols. A tenth
Supplementary Volume, edited by Eric Blom and Denis Stevens, appeared in
1961.

when an article concerns a relatively minor composer, the information contained in the two dictionaries is about equal, even when the *Grove's* article is of greater length. Moreover, it is important that even where they are of nearly equal length, the articles often differ in factual detail. Finally, some musicians appearing in both dictionaries are given more comprehensive treatment in Pulver (e.g., Goodgroome, Robert Cooper), and some found in Pulver do not appear at all in *Grove's* (e.g., Amery, Ellis, Forest).

For a single-volume dictionary of the nineteen twenties, Pulver's *Biographical Dictionary* contains a significant number of references to manuscript and early print sources.[13] In addition, all data included is rendered more accessible by a comprehensive index which cross-references information under a number of headings:

     1. Listing of literary and musical works by title: e.g., *Ars Musica* (Hothby), *Dido and Aeneas* (Purcell, Henry II), *Songs and*

---

13 For additional information consult James D. Brown and Stephen S. Stratton, *British Musical Biography* (Birmingham: S.S. Stratton, 1897) [Reprint, New York: Da Capo Press, 1971]; Henry Cart De Lafontaine, *The King's Musick* (London: Novello, 1909); Edmund Horace Fellowes, *Organists and Masters of the Choristers of St. George's Chapel in Windsor Castle* (Windsor: Oxley, 1939); Walter L. Woodfill, *Musicians in English Society from Elizabeth to Charles I* (Princeton: Princeton University Press, 1953) [Reprint, New York: Da Capo Press, 1969]; Hugh Baillie, "Some Biographical Notes on English Church Musicians Chiefly Working in London (1485–1569)," *Royal Musical Association Research Chronicle* II (1962), 18–57; Alan Smith, "Parish Church Musicians in England in the Reign of Elizabeth I (1558–1603): An Annotated Register," *Royal Musical Association Research Chronicle* IV (1964), 42–92; Alan Smith, "The Gentlemen and Children of the Chapel Royal of Elizabeth I: An Annotated Register," *Royal Musical Association Research Chronicle* V (1965), 13–46; Edward F. Rimbault, ed., *The Old Cheque-Book, or Book of Remembrance, of the Chapel Royal, from 1561 to 1744* (London: Camden Society, 1872) [Reprint, with a new introduction by Elwyn A. Wienandt, New York: Da Capo Press, 1966; unaltered reprint, New York: Johnson Reprint, 1966]; Peter Le Huray, *Music and the Reformation in England, 1549–1660* (London: Jenkins, 1967). A new source catalogue of English sacred vocal music co-authored by Peter Le Huray and Ralph T. Daniel, is expected to be issued as part of the *Early English Church Music* series. Some of the listings in this bibliography identify choristers, organists, choirmasters, organ builders and repairers, singing teachers, Royal minstrels, etc., all of which Pulver would not reasonably have been expected to include in the *Biographical Dictionary*. However, some are composers, and though they might have been intentionally excluded by the author, they nevertheless form, collectively, an important part of the tradition.

Psalms (Mundy, John, 1594), *Volpone* (Jonson, Ben).

2. Listings by musical genre: e.g., anthems; canons; catches; court ayres; dramatic music; fancies; hymns; *In Nomines;* motets; part-songs; *Te Deum.*

3. Composer listings under various spellings: e.g., Hugh Aston (Aystoun), Thomas Farthing (Farding, Faredinge, Ferthing).

4. Editor listings: e.g., G. E. P. Arkwright, Dr. E. H. Fellowes, J. S. Fuller-Maitland, Dr. E. F. Rimbault.

5. Library listings: e.g., Bologna, Liceo Communale, British Museum, Euing Library, Hamburg Municipal Library, Lambeth Palace Library.

6. Publisher listings: e.g., Breitkopf und Härtel, Curwen and Sons, Novello & Co.

7. Cathedral listings: e.g., Bristol, Chapel Royal, Chester, Chichester, Canterbury, Durham, Ely, Exeter, Gloucester, Hereford, Lichfield, Lincoln, Norwich.

8. Listings by city: e.g., Cambridge, Dublin, Oxford, Windsor.

9. Listings by monarch: e.g., Charles I, II; Edward IV, VI; Queen Elizabeth; Henry VI, VII, VIII; James I; Mary Tudor; William & Mary; William III.

10. Listings by instruments: e.g., cittern music, cornets, flageolet music, flute music, harpsichord music, lute music, organ music, recorder music, sackbut, viol music, violin music, virginal music.

11. Listings by manuscript: e.g., Dijon MSS, Fayrfax Book, Forrest-Heather Part Books, Mulliner's Book, Old Hall MS, Pepys MSS, Trent MSS.

12. Degree listings: e.g., Bachelors of Music, Doctors of Music.

13. College listings: e.g., Dulwich College, Eton College, Magdalen College, Royal College of Music, Trinity College, Winchester College.

In addition to these, Pulver's index also carries some topical headings rarely found elsewhere: e.g., English musicians abroad, Foreign musicians in England, Italian influence, Keepers of the King's instruments, Masters of the King's music.

Though Pulver appears to be in part motivated by a desire to glorify his national heritage, and while much of the *Biographical Dictionary* has been duplicated or supplanted by more recent efforts, a reprint of the volume seems both justified and worthwhile because a considerable amount of information contained herein is not readily available in any other single source.

Gilbert Blount

University of Texas
Austin, Texas

JEFFREY PULVER: A BIBLIOGRAPHY
By Gilbert Blount

A. ARTICLES ABOUT PULVER: DICTIONARIES

1. *Dictionary of Modern Music and Musicians,* Arthur Eaglefield-Hull, ed. (London: Dent, 1924), 400. [Reprint, NY: Da Capo Press, 1971.]
2. *Dizionario Universale dei Musicisti,* Carlo Schmidl, ed. (Milan: Sonzogno, 1929), II, 324.
3. *Diccionario de la Música Labor,* Joaquín Peña & Higinio Anglés, eds. (Barcelona: Labor, 1954), II, 1813.
4. *Riemann Musik Lexikon,* 12th ed, Wilibald Gurlitt, ed. (Mainz: Schott, 1961), II, 448.
5. Allan, Jean Mary. "Pulver, Jeffrey," in: *Musik in Geschichte und Gegenwart,* Friedrich Blume, ed. (Kassel: Bärenreiter, 1962), X, col. 1757.
6. *Enciclopedia della Musica,* Claudio Sartori, et al, eds. (Milan: Ricordi, 1964), III, 503.
7. *Thompson's International Cyclopedia of Music and Musicians,* 9th ed, Robert Sabin, ed. (NY: Dodd, Mead, 1964), 1707.
8. *Baker's Biographical Dictionary of Musicians,* 5th ed, with 1971 supplement, Nicolas Slonimsky, ed. (NY: G. Schirmer, 1971), 1291.
9. *La Musica: Parte Seconda, Dizionario,* Guido M. Gatti & Alberto Basso, eds. (Turin: Unione Tipografico, 1971), II, 733.

B. WORKS BY PULVER

I. BOOKS

1. *A Dictionary of Musical Terms.* London: Cassell & Co., 1913.
2. *A Dictionary of Old English Music and Musical Instruments.* London: Kegan Paul, 1923. Reviews in: *Music & Letters* V/1 (Jan 1924), 93; *Musical Times* LXIV (Dec 1923), 844–5. Reprint, NY: Burt Franklin, 1969.
3. *Johannes Brahms.* London: Kegan Paul, 1926. Review in: *Music & Letters* VII/3 (July 1926), 274.

4. *Aids to Elementary Violin Playing.* London: The Strad, 1926. *(Strad Library, No. 28).* Review in: *Musical Times* LXVII (Aug 1926), 713.

5. *A Biographical Dictionary of Old English Music.* London: Kegan Paul, 1927. Reviews in: *Music & Letters* VIII/4 (Oct 1927), 482; *Musical Times* LXVIII (May 1927), 441–2.

6. *Paganini, the Romantic Virtuoso.* London: Herbert Joseph, 1936. Review in: *Music & Letters* XVIII/2 (Apr 1937), 191. Reprint, with a new bibliography by Frederick Freedman, NY: Da Capo Press, 1970.

7. *Machiavelli: the Man, His Work and His Times.* London: Herbert Joseph, 1937.

8. Panum, Hortense. *The Stringed Instruments of the Middle Ages: Their Evolution and Development,* English edition revised and edited by Jeffrey Pulver. London: William Reeves, [1939]. Reprint, NY: Da Capo Press, 1971.

II. ARTICLES

(MMR=Monthly Musical Record; MT=Musical Times; S=The Strad)

9. "Heinrich Johann Franz von Biber," *S* 21 (Feb 1911), 373–5. [First of four installments].

10. "Köchel," *MT* 52 (Mar 1911), 169–70.

11. "The Origin of the Violin Solo," *S* 22 (Dec 1911), 320–2.

12. "Philipp Spitta," *MT* 53 (Feb 1912), 92–4.

13. "Franz Benda," *S* 23 (May 1912), 31–3. [First of six installments].

14. "Friedrich Wilhelm Marpurg," *MT* 53 (June 1912), 375–7.

15. "Music at the Court of Frederick the Great," *MT* 53 (Sep 1912), 599–601.

16. "The Ancient Dance Forms," *MT* 53 (Dec 1912), 794. [Abstract of a Musical Association lecture].

17. "The Ancient Dance-Forms," *Proceedings of the [Royal] Musical Association* 39 (1912–1913), 1–25.

18. "Leopold Mozart," *S* 23 (Jan 1913), 327–8. [First of five installments].

19. "King Henry VIII–Musician," *MMR* 43 (Feb 1913), 37–8.

20. "Otto Jahn," *MT* 54 (Apr 1913), 237–9.

21. "Viol and Violin in Merrie England," *S* 24 (Aug 1913), 140–3; (Sept 1913), 166–70.
22. "Paganini in the Goethe-Zelter Correspondence," *S* 24 (Oct 1913), 199–200.
23. "Johann Mattheson," *MT* 54 (Nov 1913), 723–5.
24. "John Bannister the Elder," *S* 24 (Nov 1913), 241–2. [First of five installments].
25. "The Gigue," *Proceedings of the [Royal] Musical Association* 40 (1913–14), 73–94.
26. "Ancient Dance Forms," *S* 24 (Mar 1914), 389–90. [Abstract of Musical Association lecture].
27. "The Tromba Marina, or Trumscheidt," *S* 25 (May 1914), 15–7; (June 1914), 56–7.
28. "Twixt Euphrates and Tigris," *MMR* 44 (Aug 1914), 212–3.
29. "Dr. D. F. Scheurleer: His Writings and Collections," *MT* 55 (Aug 1914), 521–2.
30. "Music on the Lake of Geneva," *S* 25 (Aug 1914), 134–5.
31. "Daniel Farrant," *S* 25 (Sep 1914), 166–7.
32. "Illustrations on the History of Music Printing in the Library of Mr. Alfred H. Littleton," *MT* 55 (Nov 1914), 650–1; 56 (Jan 1915), 21–2; (Feb 1915), 84–6.
33. "The Hornpipe," *MMR* 45 (Jan 1915), 13–4.
34. "Claudio Monteverde," *S* 25 (Jan 1915), 297–9. [First of twelve articles].
35. "English Influence on Continental Music," *MMR* 45 (June 1915), 163–4.
36. "Israel's Music-lesson in Egypt," *MT* 56 (July 1915), 404–7.
37. "Carl Guhr's *What Paganini Played and How He Played It*," *S* 26 (Sep 1915), 157. [Book review].
38. "The Bourrée," *MMR* 45 (Sep 1915), 257–9.
39. "Native and Foreign Music in Seventeenth Century England," *MMR* 45 (Nov 1915), 316–8.
40. "Canary (Dance)," *Musical Opinion* 39 (Dec 1915).
41. "La Guerre des Bouffons," *MT* 57 (Jan 1916), 18–9; (Feb 1916), 87–9.
42. "Christopher Simpson," *Musical News* (Feb 1916), 434.
43. "The Barber's Cittern," *MMR* 46 (Feb 1916), 45–6; (Mar 1916), 76–7.
44. "Joseph Joachim," *S* 26 (Mar 1916), 347–8. [First of seven articles].

45. "Prefaces to Old Musical Publications," *Musical Opinion* 40 Mar 1916).

46. "The Intermezzi of the Opera," *Proceedings of the [Royal] Musical Association* 43 (1916–1917), 139–63.

47. "The Bachs as Violinists," *S* 27 (Mar 1917), 305–6; (Apr 1917), 350–2; 28 (May 1917), 16.

48. "The Intermezzi of the Opera," *MT* 58 (July 1917), 312. [Abstract of a Musical Association paper].

49. "Aids to Elementary Violin Playing," *S* 28 (Sep 1917), 123–5. [First of twenty-five articles; collected and published as B.I.4].

50. "The Passacaglia," *Musical Opinion* 41 (Nov–Dec 1917).

51. "The First Public Concerts in London," *MMR* 47 (Oct 1917), 226–7.

52. "The Chaconne," *Musical Opinion* 41 (Nov–Dec 1917).

53. "The Gaillarde and its Successors," *MMR* 48 (Feb 1918), 35–6; (Apr 1918), 80–2.

54. "Music in the Diary of John Evelyn," *Musical Opinion* 42 (Jan: Feb 1919); *Sackbut* 4 (Dec 1923).

55. "Music in England during the First Half of the 16th Century," *MT* 60 (Aug 1919), 411–2; (Oct 1919), 534–6.

56. "The Allemande," *Musical Opinion* 42 (July 1919).

57. "Roger the Fiddler," *MMR* 49 (Oct 1919), 222–3.

58. "Aids to Left Hand Technique," *S* 30 (Oct 1919), 163–5. [First of 83 articles].

59. "On 'Viol and Violin in Merrie England'," *MT* 60 (Nov 1919), 637. [Abstract of lecture to Amherst Musical Club].

60. "Salamone Rossi," *Musical Opinion* 43 (Dec 1919–Jan 1920).

61. "Folies d'Espagne," *MMR* 50 (Feb 1920), 32–3; (May 1920), 103–4.

62. "The Secular Music of Ancient Egypt," *MT* 61 (June 1920), 408–10; (July 1920), 459–60.

63. "The Discipline of the King's Musick," *MMR* 50 (Nov 1920), 245–7.

64. "The Viols of England," *Proceedings of the [Royal] Musical Association* 47 (1920–1921), 1–21.

65. "The Viols in England," *MT* 62 (Jan 1921), 59. [Abstract of Musical Association paper].

66. "Curtals and Double Curtals," *MMR* 51 (June 1921), 128–9.

67. "Peter Philip," *Musical Opinion* 45 (Sep 1921–Jan 1922).

68. "The Music of Ancient Egypt," *Proceedings of the [Royal] Musical Association* 48 (1921–1922), 29–55.
69. "Peter Philips," *Musical Opinion* 45 (Jan 1922), 365.
70. "The Fancy," *MT* 63 (June 1922), 396–8.
71. "Playford's *Introduction to the Skill of Musick*," *MMR* 52 (July 1922), 154–5.
72. "The Literary Works of Guiseppe Tartini," *MMR* 52 (Sep 1922), 215-6.
73. "Music by Wireless," *MT* 63 (Oct 1922), 697–8.
74. "The Music of Ben Jonson," *MMR* 53 (Feb 1923), 39–41; (Mar 1923), 71–2.
75. "The Sackbut," *Sackbut* 3 (Mar 1923).
76. "The Lute in England," *Musical Opinion* 46 (Apr–Sep 1923).
77. "Solmization and the Hexachord System," *MMR* 53 (May 1923), 136–7.
78. "Frets," *MMR* 53 (June 1923), 166–8.
79. "Seventeenth Century Ornaments," *MMR* 53 (Sep 1923), 264–5.
80. "Should the Teacher Tell," *MMR* 53 (Oct 1923), 296–7.
81. "Violin Tutors of the 17th Century," *MT* 64 (Oct 1923), 695–7.
82. "Violin Methods Old and New," *Proceedings of the [Royal] Musical Association* 50 (1923–1924), 101–27.
83. "Did Shakespeare Understand Music?" *MMR* 54 (Jan 1924), 5–6.
84. "The English Revival," *MMR* 54 (Feb 1924), 37–9.
85. "What is Wrong with Welsh Music?" *MT* 65 (Mar 1924), 225–6.
86. "Violin Methods Old and New," *MT* 65 (July 1924), 645–6. [Abstract of a Musical Association paper].
87. "Musical Instruments of Henry VIII," *Musical Opinion* 48 (Oct 1924).
88. "Brahms and the Influence of Joachim," *MT* 66 (Jan 1925), 25–8.
89. "The Dead Intruder," *Sackbut* 5 (Jan 1925), 156–61.
90. "H. J. F. von Biber," *MMR* 55 (Feb 1925), 40–1.
91. "North's Memoires of Musick," *MT* 66 (July 1925), 594–6.
92. "Bach as Violinist," *MMR* 56 (Feb 1926), 35–6.
93. "The Teachers of Johannes Brahms," *Sackbut* 6 (Apr 1926), 251–3.
94. "The Language of the Lutenist," *Sackbut* 6 (July 1926), 333–6.

95. "Bach's Solo Sonatas and Partitas for Violin," *S* 37 (Sep 1926), 270–2, through 41 (Mar 1931), 588–90. [Fifty-five installments].
96. "The English Abroad," *MT* 67 (Oct 1926), 902–4; (Nov 1926), 990–2.
97. "The First Violin Virtuoso in England," *Sackbut* 7 (Nov 1926), 96–9.
98. "Giovanni Coperario alias John Cooper," *MMR* 57 (Apr 1927), 101–2.
99. "An Evening with Cromwell," *MMR* 57 (July 1927), 196–8.
100. "The English St. Cecilia Celebrations of the Seventeenth Century," *Sackbut* 7 (July 1927), 345–9.
101. "The Leckingfield 'Proverbs'," *The Organ* 7 (July 1927), 23–31.
102. "Chilston," *MT* 68 (Aug 1927), 699–701; (Nov 1927), 1026.
103. "The Music of Mary Tudor," *Sackbut* 8 (Sep 1927), 44–50.
104. "An Evening with Pepys," *MMR* 57 (Nov 1927), 324-7.
105. "Brahms and England," *MMR* 58 (Jan 1928), 3–4.
106. "Hugh Aston and the Early History of Keyboard Music in England," *Sackbut* 8 (Jan 1928), 169–73.
107. "The Early History of the Chapel Royal," *The Organ* 7 (Apr 1928), 209–15.
108. "The School of Nations," *S* 39 (July 1928), 144–6.
109. "An Evening in Clerkenwell," *MMR* 58 (Aug 1928), 231–3.
110. "Our Debt to the Dance," *Sackbut* 9 (Sep 1928), 53–8.
111. "Walter Odington: The Consonance of the Third and the Common Chord," *MT* 69 (Dec 1928), 1086–9.
112. "Music in Malory's 'Arthur'," *MMR* 59 (Jan 1929), 3–4.
113. "Reformed Characters," *Sackbut* 9 (May 1929), 340–4.
114. "Burney in Berlin," *MMR* 59 (June 1929), 169–70.
115. "Temperament," "Tone: (a) Stringed Instruments," in: *Cobbett's Cyclopedic Survey of Chamber Music,* compiled & edited by Walter Willson Cobbett (London: Oxford University Press, 1929–30), II, 501–4; 512–3.
116. "The Siege of Rhodes," *Sackbut* 10 (Jan 1930), 159–63.
117. "William Blade's Tercentenary," *MMR* 60 (Nov 1930), 333–4.
118. "Thomas Bateson," *Sackbut* 11 (Feb 1931), 190–2.
119. "The Other Schubert," *MMR* 61 (Mar 1931), 77.
120. "Changes of Position," *S* 41 (Apr 1931), 644–6. [First of three articles].

121. "The Menuet," *Sackbut* 11 (Apr 1931), 236–41.
122. "Trilling Studies," *S* 42 (July 1931), 144–6. [First of six installments].
123. "Technical Study and the Musical Soul," *S* 42 (Sep 1931), 260–4.
124. "John Banister the Elder," *MT* 72 (Oct 1931), 891–3.
125. "The Marvellous Adventures of an Organ Builder," *The Organ*, 11 (Oct 1931), 93–9.
126. "Position Work," *S* 42 (Jan 1932), 478–9. [First of four installments].
127. "Finger Independence," *S* 43 (May 1932), 30–2; (June 1932), 68–9.
128. "Psychological Phenomena," *S* 43 (July 1932), 115–6.
129. "Physical Phenomena," *S* 43 (Aug 1932), 166–8.
130. "Violin Music in the Steingraeber Edition," *S* 43 (Sep 1932), 203–4.
131. "After the Holidays," *S* 43 (Oct 1932), 241–2.
132. "Octaves and Tenths," *S* 43 (Nov 1932), 287–8.
133. "The String Music of Johannes Brahms," *S* 43 (Apr 1933), 536–8. [First of four installments].
134. "Brahms: A Short Biographical Sketch," *MT* 74 (May 1933), 419–22.
135. "Remenyi, the 'Hungarian'," *MT* 74 (July 1933), 634.
136. "Chamber Music by Brahms in the Breitkopf Edition," *S* 44 (Aug 1933), 144–6.
137. "International Society for Musical Research: Congress at Cambridge," *S* 44 (Sep 1933), 182–4.
138. "Beethoven and the Violinist," *MMR* 63 (Sep 1933), 145–6.
139. "Brahms's Violinists and Cellists," *S* 44 (Oct 1933), 224–6; (Nov 1933), 258–9.
140. "The English Theorists: I. John Cotton," *MT* 74 (Oct 1933), 892–3.
141. "English Organists Abroad," *The Organ*, 13 (Oct 1933), 97–101.
142. "The English Theorists: II. The Two Garlandias," *MT* 74 (Nov 1933), 984–5.
143. "Nathaniel Giles," *MMR* 63 (Nov 1933), 204–5.
144. "Brahms and the Doctorate," *Sackbut* 14 (Dec 1933), 127–9.
145. "The Use and Abuse of Research," *MMR* 64 (Jan 1934), 9–11.

146. "The English Theorists: III. Robert de Handlo," *MT* 75 (Jan 1934), 26.

147. "The English Theorists: IV. Simon Tunsted," *MT* 75 (Jan 1934), 26–7.

148. "The English Theorists: V. Theinred," *MT* 75 (Jan 1934), 27–8.

149. "Brahms's Contemporary Singers," *MMR* 64 (Feb 1934), 35–6.

150. "The English Theorists: VI. John Hanboys," *MT* 75 (Mar 1934), 220–1.

151. "The English Theorists: VII. John Hothby," *MT* 75 (May 1934), 408–10.

152. "Music and Greek Civilizaion," *MMR* 64 (July–Aug 1934), 131–3.

153. "A Useful Aid to Left-Hand Technique," *S* 45 (Aug 1934), 159–60.

154. "The English Theorists: VIII. Lionel Power," *MT* 75 (Aug 1934), 709–10.

155. "The English Theorists: IX. Guilelmus Monachus," *MT* 75 (Sep 1934), 804–5.

156. "The English Theorists: X. William Bathe," *MT* 75 (Oct 1934), 900–2.

157. "Fanny Davies and Her Contemporaries," *MMR* 64 (Oct 1934), 174–5.

158. "Music in England during the Commonwealth," *Acta Musicologica* 6 (Oct–Dec 1934), 169–81.

159. "The Music Lessons of Samuel Pepys," *MMR* 64 (Nov 1934), 203–4.

160. "The English Theorists: XI. Thomas Campion," *MT* 75 (Dec 1934), 1080–2.

161. "The English Theorists: XII. Thomas Ravenscroft," *MT* 76 (Feb 1935), 124–6.

162. "Personal Contacts with Brahms," *MMR* 65 (Feb 1935), 35–6; (Mar–Apr 1935), 57–8.

163. "Margaret H. Glyn's *Theory of Musical Evolution*," *MT* 76 (Feb 1935), 130–1. [Book review].

164. "The English Theorists: XIII. Thomas Morley," *MT* 76 (May 1935), 411–4.

165. "The English Theorists: XIV. Elway Bevin," *MT* 77 (Aug 1936), 703–4.

166. "The Violin Solo," *MMR* 66 (Mar–Apr 1936), 57–8.
167. "Beethoven in the Goethe-Zelter Correspondence," *Music & Letters* 17 (Apr 1936), 124–30.
168. "Music in Mantua," *MMR* 66 (Sep 1936), 145–7.
169. "The Organist's Post," *The Organ* 16 (Apr 1937), 244–50; 17 (July 1937), 50–4.
170. "The English Theorists: XV. Thomas Mace," *MT* 78 (July 1937), 601–4.
171. "The English Theorists: XVI. Christopher Simpson," *MT* 80 (Feb 1939), 112, 117–8.
172. "Personal Contacts with Paganini and Spohr," *MT* 80 (Aug 1939), 579–80.

Pulver has contributed other articles to *Musical Opinion, Musical News, English,* and *Schoolmaster,* but the appropriate volumes were not readily available to the compilor.

A BIOGRAPHICAL DICTIONARY
OF OLD ENGLISH MUSIC

HENRY PURCELL.

(From the portrait by Sir Godfrey Kneller).

[*Front.*

A
BIOGRAPHICAL DICTIONARY
OF
OLD ENGLISH MUSIC

BY
JEFFREY PULVER
Author of *A Dictionary of Old English Music
and Musical Instruments, Johannes Brahms*, etc.

ἄνθρωπος μέτρον παντῶν

LONDON
KEGAN PAUL, TRENCH, TRUBNER & CO., LTD.
NEW YORK: E. P. DUTTON & CO.
1927

Printed in Great Britain by Stephen Austin & Sons, Ltd., Hertford.

To

SIR W. HENRY HADOW

in admiration
and esteem

ABBREVIATIONS

Add.   Additional Manuscripts (British Museum).

Ambros.   August Wilhelm Ambros, *Geschichte der Musik.*

Annalen.   Dr. W. Nagel, *Annalen der Englischen Hofmusik* (Breitkopf and Haertel, 1894 ; Supplement to Vol. 26 of the *Monatshefte für Musikgeschichte.*

Ar.   Arundel Manuscripts (British Museum).

Bale.   Bale, *Scriptorum Catalogus.*

B.M.   British Museum.

Bodl.   Bodleian Library, Oxford.

Brewer.   Brewer, *Letters and Papers of Henry VIII.*

Cal. Pat. Rolls. Calendar of Patent Rolls (Various Editors).

Cal. S.P.   Calendar of State Papers (Various Editors).

C.B.C.R.   *Cheque Book of the Chapel Royal* (Edition Dr. E. A. Rimbault, Camden Society's Publications).

Chamberlayne. Chamberlayne, *Magnae Britanniae Notitia.*

Chr. Ch. Oxf. Library of Christ Church, Oxford.

Coussemaker. C. E. H. de Coussemaker, *Scriptores de Musica Medii Aevi.*

Dic. Nat. Biogr. Dictionary of National Biography, *Reprint.*

Dic. O. E. Mus. Jeffrey Pulver, *Dictionary of Old English Music and Musical Instruments.* 1923.

Dom. Ser.   Domestic Series, State Papers.

Eg.   Egerton Manuscripts (British Museum).

Harl.   Harleian Manuscripts (British Museum).

Lans.   Lansdowne Manuscripts (British Museum).

L.C.R.	The Lord Chamberlain's Records (A useful guide and calendar to these records is provided by H. C. de Lafontaine's *The King's Musick*, Novello and Co.).
Mus. Ant. Soc.	Publications of the Musical Antiquarian Society.
Mus. School.	Music School Collection in the Bodleian Library, Oxford.
P.R.O.	Public Record Office (London).
q.v. inf.	which see below.
q.v. sup.	which see above.
Sloane.	Sloane Manuscript (British Museum).
S.P. Dom. Ser.	State Papers, Domestic Series.
s.v.	under the heading.
Tudway.	Manuscript Collection of Ecclesiastical Music scored by Thomas Tudway (*B.M.*, *Harl.* 7337–7342, six vols.).

PREFACE

THE history of music in England, dealing with the five centuries that lie between the period which made the Reading rota possible and the death of Purcell, is a story of unimaginable fascination. Yet in spite of the labours of a few faithful workers who fought, with weak weapons, to win their merited place for the musicians of England in the affection and regard of their countrymen, it was only comparatively recently that we awoke to the fact that our musical history is as glorious a one as that possessed by any other country of Europe. We can produce medieval writers of treatises whose knowledge was sufficiently profound to command the respect of their Continental colleagues, and whose experience was great and varied enough to cause instruction to go forth from these islands to the Low Countries and Paris. We can enumerate the names of early writers of polyphonic music whose achievements, whether regarded from the point of view of mere workmanship or the higher ones of taste, feeling, and melodic charm—have made foreign historians point the condemning finger of scorn at us for our indifference in making our musical heritage accessible to all. We have had madrigalists who, encouraged by the activities of the Netherlanders and the Italians, took a charming form to their hearts and—bettered their instruction. In short, we are descended from a race which has produced Dunstable, Odington, Power, and Fayrfax ; Tallis, Tye, and Robert Whyte ; Byrd, Orlando Gibbons, Thomas Morley, Wilbye, and Weelkes ; a host of others— and Henry Purcell. The state of English music in the past was such that Italian ambassadors wrote enthusiastically in their dispatches on its excellence, foreigners came hither to learn what we had to teach in instrumental music while English virginallists and violists opened the eyes of the Continent to huge possibilities. At the same time organists and writers like Bull and Philips, lutenists like Dowland, Robinson, and Cutting, violists like Thomas Simpson and many others, went abroad and spread the knowledge of English methods and manners. In those days, truly, art was international because the teaching and borrowing were reciprocal.

It is no part of my task in the present volume to discuss the reasons for the change of attitude in the English musicians of the dawning eighteenth century. But having already drawn the faintest possible outline suggesting the picture of our past glories, it may be as well to go one step farther and just as superficially hint at the causes that arrested the further development of an art possessing at least some national characteristics at the graveside of Henry Purcell. These causes, it seems to me, were the exile of Charles II and—George Frederick Handel. The former because his sojourn abroad during the Interregnum taught him to love the lighter touch of France better than his father loved the " incomparable fantasies " of John Cooper, and the latter because he rather than Purcell was followed by the English composers—or those who composed for the English. Thus it came about that instead of the post-Purcellian writers continuing the newly-developed style which Purcell had founded and settled by grafting certain French and Italian buds upon the old English stock, " they preferred to be the imitators of an imitator ". Such a procedure could lead only into a *cul-de-sac* ; for an imitator, even though he be as great as Handel himself (which his imitators were not) remains only—as far as future developments go—sufficient for himself.

In the writing of this book, I have made little attempt to produce a History of English Music—much less a History of Music in England. Even the more interesting narrative-form has been rejected in favour of the dictionary-form. My object has been to render the biographies and bibliographies of the more important of the musicians active in England as easy of reference as possible, and all artistic and literary considerations have been made subservient to that object. Manuscript numbers, for this reason, have been quoted only when they have been absolutely necessary to the searcher after examples of the work of the men treated, or when a reference to a manuscript will afford some historical information. In one respect I have reversed the usual procedure : I have given as full a list of sources as possible when dealing with the lesser-known writers, for I have found that very little difficulty is experienced in locating specimens of the music of the more celebrated composers. And though my recital of modern reproductions may appear to some readers to be unnecessary and tedious, it has been my experience that for every one research-worker who possesses the necessary opportunities, leisure, and knowledge to score from the original manuscripts, the music he requires, there are hundreds of students, singers, instrumentalists and choirmasters who have to depend upon the modern reprint. To serve the last-named, I have mentioned as many of the new editions of old works as was practicable. Happily the interest that is now being taken in the revival of our ancient music is stimulating patriotic publishers to greater activity in this direction, with the result that my lists will probably be incomplete before these words appear in print.

My greatest difficulty in the preparation of this volume has been, not to discover enough musicians to fill it, but rather to decide which to omit in order to keep the book of manageable size. The inclusion of men like those already named in this preface needs no explanation or apology. The admission of lesser men to their company was permitted in order to show that the musical landscape of England was not composed only of some half-dozen lofty but isolated peaks which stood majestic though lonely in a level plain, but rather to demonstrate that the average height was at least as considerable as that observable on the continent of Europe. In some cases the value of the subject treated has been gauged, not so much by the worth of the music he has left, as by the amount of light that an account of his life throws upon the musical manners and customs of his period. To choose an example of this kind of musician at random I should exhibit, say, Nicholas Staggins as useful in illuminating the page of history on which he stands. Similarly Henry Eveseed would deserve a place nowhere but in a police gazette were it not for the information on the discipline prevailing in the Chapel Royal which a consideration of his life affords. Foreign names like Ferrabosco, Lanier, and others appear because their owners settled here, became naturalized in their art, and left descendants who were English in every respect. Visitors like Baltzar and Nicola Matteis are included because by their art, as they practised it in this country, they influenced the native artists. Indeed, the two men just cited were of the greatest importance in the history of the music for the stringed instruments; Baltzar, because it was most probably he who opened the eyes of the English violinists to the possibilities of the higher ranges of that instrument's compass by demonstrating the more extended uses of the shift, and Matteis because he perhaps more than anyone else showed Purcell to what lengths the technics of the instrument could be developed.

The length of an article must never be taken to be indicative of the importance of the subject. Unfortunately the material available for the construction of Tudor and Stuart biographies is not always in direct ratio to the stature of the musician. A work of this kind can therefore never be complete. Fresh discoveries are being made daily ; and any moment a document may be brought to light that will prove one or other of my theories—where I have indulged in speculation—to be either sound or otherwise.

Neither I in writing this book, nor the reader in perusing it, can in justice omit to express gratitude to the able and tireless workers who have made some invaluable contributions to this branch of knowledge ; and I, for one, am happy to acknowledge my indebtedness to those gentlemen who have permitted me to use the information with which they have been accredited in the following pages. In this connexion my thanks must be tendered especially to Mr. W. Barclay Squire, Dr. E. H. Fellowes, and Mr. G. E. P. Arkwright. Frequent reference has been made to my *Dictionary of Old English Music and Musical Instruments* (1923, Kegan Paul and Co., and Curwen) and all the obsolete terms, forms, and instruments mentioned in the present volume will be found explained and sometimes illustrated in that work. Only such musicians as were active up to the death of Purcell have been included.

JEFFREY PULVER.

A

ABELL (John): A celebrated singer and lutenist of the late seventeenth century, John Abell attracts attention as much on account of his adventurous life as for his excellent voice. Born near the middle of the century, we meet him first in the Lord Chamberlain's Records, where a later addition to a list of 1674 gives him in the place of Alphonso Marsh. How much later this alteration was made it is impossible to say; nor does the life of Marsh afford any clue since his name occurs so frequently in the records and is so often confused with that of his son, that it cannot be decided with certainty when Abell succeeded him. The first trustworthy piece of information appears in the Cheque-Book of the Chapel Royal : " 1679. Mr. John Abell sworn Gentleman of his Majesties Chappell Extraordinary the first of May, 1679." On the 31st of the same month he was appointed to the private music of the king "with fee, in the place of Anthony Roberts, deceased," the salary being 40*l.* a year (*L.C.R.*). On December 15th, 1679, he received " as a free gift and bounty " the sum of 100*l.* from the king (" Moneys received and paid on Secret Services, *etc.*" *Camden Soc. Publ.*, 1851), and it was at about this time that he was sent to Italy to study. We cannot follow his movements at all closely, for we meet with many pieces of evidence that appear to be contradictory. Thus on March 9th, 1681, he received 20*l.* " for the charge of his journey to Scotland," and five days later another 100*l.* On December 20th, 1681, he was appointed as " musician for the violin in the place of Richard Dorneys, deceased ", and also as " musician for the lute and voice in the place of Alphonso Marsh, deceased." These appointments seem to suggest that Abell was a great favourite at Court, for he enjoyed the salaries belonging to these posts, plus his Chapel Royal fees and the bounty money which, according to the book cited above, amounted to a very considerable sum. It is possible that he was given the two posts just mentioned while still in Italy. At all events he must have returned soon after New Year, 1681–2, for on January 27th Evelyn entered in his diary : " After supper, came in the famous treble, Mr. Abel, newly returned from Italy ; I never heard a more excellent voice ; one would have sworn it had been a woman's, it was so high, and so well and skilfully managed, being accompanied by Signor Francesco on the harpsichord ". On October 22nd, 1683, he received a " bounty " of 50*l*. 10*s*. 6*d*., and on October 29th, 1684, the sum of 200*l*. to defray the charge of his journey into Italy. The manuscript from which these particulars were taken contains entries no later than 1688, but before coming to a close it gives information respecting a further sum of 300*l*. paid to Abell.

On August 31st, 1685, John Abell was sworn in as private musician " with fee and salary " to James II, and on October 10th of that year the certificate of appointment was made out. In 1686 (October 15th) he received the sum of 10*l*. " for a guytar bought for his Majesty's service in his Bedchamber " (*L.C.R.*), it being quite likely that Abell sang to the king at *levées*, accompanying himself on the guitar. His name appears in the records until the very end of 1688, when he is supposed to have been dismissed on account of his leanings towards Roman Catholicism. Whether the Revolution was responsible for his departure from court service or not, cannot be decided ; but two facts stand out. The first is that on March 25th, 1689, his name appears in a list of " the King's servants as receive their salaries in the treasury of the Chamber's office ", and the other is the circumstance that he was travelling on the Continent shortly after this date. At the same time, an account of a concert which Abell arranged to celebrate the birth of the prince in 1688 certainly shows him to have been a loyal supporter of James II, a contemporary publication saying : " Mr. Abel, the celebrated Musician, and one of the Royal Band, entertained the publick, and demonstrated his loyalty on the evening of 18th June, 1688, by the performance of an aquatic concert. The barge prepared for this purpose was richly decorated, and illuminated by numerous torches . . . and the performers, vocal and instrumental, amounted to one hundred and thirty, selected as the greatest proficients in the science. . . . The musick being ended, all the nobility and company that were upon the water gave three shouts to express their joy and satisfaction ; and all the gentlemen of the musick went to Mr. Abell's house, which was nobly illuminated and honoured with the presence of a great company of the nobility ".

Abell's adventures abroad make entertaining reading. With his voice and his lute he need have suffered no want ; but his improvident manner of living often brought him into awkward situations. At one time earning enough to enable him to travel from town to town in his own equipage, at another being forced by his extravagance to tramp on foot with his lute at his back. Sometimes performing in private houses or noblemen's halls,—cultivating his art in peripatetic fashion,—sometimes (as at Cassel) occupying a fixed post for a time, he passed the years until the end of the century. The oft-told story of Abell's adventures in Poland may bear one more repetition (v. Thomas Brown's *Works*, ii, 189). It appears that for some reason

or other he had refused to sing when invited to do so by the king of Poland, but that monarch had a ready though unpleasant method of overcoming the scruples of pampered vocalists, and as soon as Abell was seated, he was hoisted gallery high. King and courtiers facing him in the gallery and a few unsociable bears let loose into the hall below completed the picture. Rather than risk a bear's closer attentions, Abell sang forthwith,—and, as he said, never so well in his life. This story is so bound up with accounts of Abell's activity, that it would be a pity if it were ever proved false.

A letter written from Zell by Mr. Cressett, our resident at Hanover, and prefixed to the British Museum copy of Abell's *Collection of Songs in Several Languages* (1701), contains some very illuminating phrases referring to the singer's life abroad : " 1695, July 12. Abel the musician who is very poor and comes to sing and beg . . . is gone to Hanover to offer his services . . . July 15. Abel diverts the Princesses at Hanover . . . Sept. 3. Abel has been at Berlin, but is come back as far as Brunswick and will be here in a few days. So soon as he comes, I will be sure to tell him how favourable you are to him, and if I obtain by your kindness the permission of coming to Loo myself, I believe he will be glad to have a Cart (?) so far on his way with me, though he is tempted to stay the carnival at Hanover, and is offered a considerable sum . . . 6th. Abel is now with me, and his Catholicity does not hinder him from singing Victoria for us . . . Abel with Cressett to Loo in Holland on the rejoicings for the taking of Namur . . . Oct. 9. The Harmonious Vagabond Abel is now here. He tells me he will hasten to England, but I think his crotchets make it uncertain. He maintains the character of the Vertuose Canaglia . . ." The book of songs which contains this letter was dedicated to William III, and in the address Abell speaks of the king's kindness " in permitting my return to my native country . . ." In 1701, also, he published " a Collection of Songs in English " (R.C.M.), an introductory poem containing the lines :—

" After a twelve years' industry and toil,
    Abell, at last has reached his native soil ".
Congreve (*Literary Relics*, 1792, p. 322), writing from London on December 10th, 1700, said : " Abell is here ; has a cold at present, and is always whimsical, so that when he will sing or not upon the stage are things very disputable, but he certainly sings beyond all creatures upon earth ".

Besides the two collections of songs already mentioned, Abell wrote : *Dissembled Love*, printed by Playford in 1684 ; " A Song on Queen Ann's Coronation, the words by Mr. (Nahum) Tate, set and sung by Mr. Abell " (1702, the Ode commencing, " Alowd proclaim ") ; *A Choice Collection of Italian Ayres for all sorts of Voices, Violin or Flute* (1703), containing fifteen songs to Italian words ; besides other single songs. In 1716 he was still alive, for in that year he gave a concert at Stationers' Hall (Rimbault, Notes to *C. B. C. R.*), but how long after this date he died, is not known.

ABINGDON (Henry) : An important figure in the history

of fifteenth-century English music, since he appears to have been the first " Master of the Children of the Chapel Royal ". Having been succentor of Wells Cathedral in 1447 (following John Bernard on November 24th) he must have been born about 1425. He died in 1497 having held the succentorship all his life (Beckington and Oliver King, *Register at Wells*). There is no authentic information regarding Abingdon's activity from his appointment at Wells until 1463 when we read of him as a Bachelor of Music at Cambridge : " 1463. Item. Admissus fuit Henricus Abyngton in musica bachalaureus, 22 die Febr. cuius communa 20*d*." (*Cambridge Grace Bk. A. p.* 28*a*). It was permitted him to proceed after a year's residence, but there is no evidence of his having done so ; " 1463. Concessa est gracia Henrico Habyngton quod post admissionem ad gradum bachalarii in Musica, possit admitti ad incipiendum in eadem sic quod continuet hic ante admissionem per annum " (*Id. A. p.* 30*b*). His appointment as " Master of the Song " in the London Chapel Royal dates from 1465 (May 5th), his salary being forty Marks per annum. This salary was granted him by an Act of Parliament and was " for the fyndyng, instruction, and governaunce of the Children of the Chapelle of our Householde " (Rimbault, *Introduction* to *C.B.C.R.*, p. iv. Beyond his appointment as master of the music at St. Catherine's Hospital, Bristol, in 1478, this is all of any importance that is known of him. A couple of Latin epitaphs written by Sir Thomas More describe him as a superb singer and organist, the lines
" Millibus in mille cantor fuit
    optimus ille,
Praeter et haec ista fuit
    optimus orgaquenista,"
serving as a specimen. Rimbault (*Introduction* to the Mus. Ant. Soc. edition of Purcell's *Bonduca*) speaks of a book which contains an English epitaph by More (who was nineteen years of age when Abingdon died) :—
" Here lyeth old Henry, no
    freend to mischievous envy,
Surnam'd Abyngdon, to all
    men most heartily welcom ;
Clerck he was in Wellis,
where tingle a great many
    bellis,

Also in the Chappell he was not counted a moungrel," which seemed to delight the person who asked for it. Henry Abingdon died on September 1st, 1497, and was followed as succentor at Wells by Robert Wydow (or Wydewe). He does not appear to have left any examples of his skill as a composer; at any rate, I have found none.

ABYNGDON (Henry), *see* ABINGDON.

ADSON (John) : A performer on the flute and cornet active during the first half of the seventeenth century. Absolutely nothing is known of his early life, except that in 1621 he issued *Courtly Masquing Ayres, Composed to 5 and 6 Parts, for Violins, Consorts, and Cornets, by John Adson* (Altus part in *B.M.*). The cornet was still a very popular wind-instrument, and a full account of its English use may be seen in the Dictionary of Old English Music (*Dic. O.E.M.*).

The last six and a half years of Adson's life were spent in the royal service. On November 4th, 1633, we read : " Warrant to swear John Adson a musician for the flute and cornet in ordinary in the place of Henry Lanier,

deceased " (*L.C.R.*), the entry for December of the same year showing that he was also required to wait in the chapel. The State Papers under date January 7th, 1634–5 (Nagel, *Annalen*) give the information that at this period Adson succeeded Henry Litmer at the permanent salary of twenty pence per day, acting as music teacher to the king. On January 18th, 1635–6, he was paid 4*l.* 15*s.* for " a treble cornet and a treble recorder " which he provided for use in the royal band (*L.C.R.*). In the year of his death his salary is given as 46*l.* per annum (MS. in the *P.R.O.*). He was evidently dead by the middle of 1640, for on July 6th, of that year, we read : " Warrant to swear William Lanier one of his Majesty's musicians for the wind instruments in ordinary in the room of John Adson deceased " (*L.C.R.*). In this entry the salary attached to the post was still twenty pence a day, plus 16*l.* 2*s.* 6*d.* for livery.

Add. MS. 10444 (*B.M.*) contains a composition called " Adson's Masque " and another " Mr. Adson's Masque " (two tunes).

AKEROYDE (Samuel) : A composer of songs who was

active during the last quarter of the seventeenth century, but of whose biography next to nothing is ascertainable. The dates of his birth and death are alike unknown. He appears to us in his works as one of those writers,—present in all ages,—who in spite of mediocrity of talent achieve tremendous popularity. Beyond the assumption that he was a native of Yorkshire, we know nothing of his life until 1687, when his name appears in the Lord Chamberlain's Records (April 25th) : " Warrant to swear and admit Samuel Akeroyde musician in ordinary to his Majesty in the place of John Twist, deceased." Since John Twist is described in all the entries that refer to him as a " Violin ", we can only suppose that Akeroyde served in a similar capacity. In the entry dated March 7th, 1687–8, dealing with the payment of members of the band who " attended his Majesty during his residence at Windsor Castle " (L.C.R.) he is given as a " musician ". On March 25th, 1689, his salary again as a " musician " is noted as being 30l. per annum. In 1689 (July 20th) he was appointed " for the private musick ".

The entry dated November 29th, 1690, shows that Samuel " Akroyd " attended his sovereign to Newmarket. The amount allowed for " riding charges " on such occasions was generally five shillings a day. For the King's journey to Holland William Hall was named in the first list of musicians to accompany the royal party, but his name was afterwards erased and Akeroyde's substituted. On December 24th, 1690, a warrant was issued authorizing the payment of travelling expenses for this journey to a number of musicians, including Akeroyde.

Examples of his work may be seen in D'Urfey's *Third Collection of Songs* (1685), in *The Theater of Music* (Bk. i, 1685, four pieces ; Bk. ii, 1685, two pieces ; Bk. iii, 1685, ten pieces ; Bk. iv, 1687, two pieces) ; in *Apollo's Banquet* (1690, Pt. iii, No. 48) ; and in other contemporaneous publications. A few separately issued songs became very popular,—e.g., " The Passions " (Playford, 1685), " The Law of Nature " (*Id.* 1684, " sung to the King at Windsor "), " Give me Kind Heaven " and " The Rays

of dear Clarinda's Eyes "
(Thomas Cross), " 'Twas
Sunday in the Morn,—The
Fight at Sea " (*Id.*, cele-
brating a victory of
Rodney's), " A Scotch Song
sung at Tunbridge—Wully
and Georgy " (*Id.*). Copies
of all these songs are preserved in the British
Museum. Between 1692 and
1694 a number of Akeroyde's
vocal pieces appeared, *passim*,
in the *Gentleman's Journal.*

For the stage Akeroyde
wrote a good deal of music.
Three songs used in John
Crowne's *Sir Courtly Nice*,
were published in 1685, two
of them (a Dialogue between
two Indians, and a Scotch
Song) are signed with
Akeroyde's name ; the third
is not signed, but most probably also his. Rimbault
mentions some music by this
composer to the play *The
Commonwealth of Women*
(1685). But Akeroyde was
probably never in better company than when he con-
tributed a Dialogue to the
Third Part of D'Urfey's
Comical History of Don Quixote
(published in 1696). In this
work, which was " the
last Piece set to Musick
by the late Famous Mr.
Henry Purcell ", Courte-
ville, Akeroyde, and " other
eminent Masters of the age "
collaborated.

ALAIN (John) : A com-
poser belonging to the era
of Dunstable and Power, but
of whose life nothing is
known. He was the author of
a poem which mentions
several otherwise unknown
musicians by name, and
which speaks of the
musical methods of the time
in very enigmatical fashion.
Work of his is contained in
a manuscript at the *Liceo
Comunale* of Bologna.

ALDRICH (Henry) : A
remarkable figure in academic
England during the second
half of the seventeenth
century, noticeable perhaps
more for his versatility than
for his genius. Although he
was in the first place a
theologian, — and his biography is in the main that of
a churchman,—he found time
to act as pedagogue, architect,
and musician. If for no other
reason than that of having
written and collected a huge
musical library which he bequeathed to his *alma mater*, he
deserves the gratitude of
musicians to-day ; for his
bequest made of the library
of Christ Church, Oxford,
one of the finest in this
country.

Born at Westminster in

1647, he was educated at Westminster School and Christ Church. His academic distinctions were B.A. (1666), M.A. (1669), and B.D. and D.D. (1681). From the moment he took holy orders he advanced steadily, becoming a Canon (Christ Church) in 1681 and Dean in 1689. Combining a geniality rarely found in men of his position and attainments with intense enthusiasm for whatever he undertook, he produced a variety of works that ranged from treatises on logic, classical literature, and theology, to the plans for the building of the Peckover Quadrangle (Christ Church), All Saints' Church, and the Chapel of Trinity College, besides sacred music of all kinds. While active at Oxford he maintained a very high standard of excellence in the choir, and was continually mindful of its requirements. He died on December 14th, 1710. A portrait of Aldrich (by Kneller) graces the hall at Christ Church.

In character Aldrich was genial and jovial and his secular compositions give an illustration of his temperament. An inveterate smoker, he celebrated the weed in a "Catch on Tobacco" (printed by Hilton in *Catch that Catch Can*, 1682), in which the writing allowed the four men singing it to take puffs at their pipes during the rests arranged for the purpose. It was, indeed, "not more difficult to sing than diverting to hear". The story is told of an undergraduate losing a wager—that he should discover Aldrich smoking by ten o'clock in the morning—by meeting the Dean in the act of filling, and not smoking his pipe. Aldrich remained a bachelor all his life. Another Catch of his that was, and is, very popular, is that on the Christ Church bells. Henry Davey was not far wrong when he asserted that these two catches are the only two "of the Restoration period endurable at the present day." His serious ecclesiastical music is sound enough, and occasionally it rises above the general level of monotony ; but taken all together, it is more noticeable on account of its suitability for congregational use and understanding than because of any great musicianship displayed. The Anthem reprinted by Professor Granville Bantock (Curwen) exhibits Aldrich as a better composer than do most of his works.

The compositions of this musical divine are too numerous, and for the most part, not sufficiently meritorious to justify our space being occupied by a list of manuscripts. In the case of a less-known man, a complete bibliography might be welcomed ; but Aldrich has seen to it that his works be well preserved, and they are quite easy of access. The catalogue of the manuscripts in the Christ Church library (by Mr. G. E. P. Arkwright) gives a long list, and other compositions (or duplicates) are present at Ely, the Fitzwilliam Museum (Cambridge), the Royal College of Music (London), and the British Museum. Boyce and Arnold included examples of Aldrich's work in their collections, and his Catches are contained in several printed works (such as Playford's *Pleasant Musical Companion*, 1726). A Service and an Anthem by Henry " Alldridg " were transcribed into the books of the London Chapel Royal (*L.C.R.*, August 1st, 1676).

In the clauses of his Will, which made over to his college the collection of books he had formed, Alldrich said : " I make it my request to the Dean and Chapter of the said Church that they will be pleased to take such care of my Prints and books of Musick that they may not be exposed to common usage nor to any man without their leave and appointment, because they are things of value in themselves, and to be found in very few libraries ". There are, indeed, a number of books and manuscripts in that collection which are of the greatest value to the musical historian, and for having secured their safety Aldrich merits our recognition.

ALDRIG (Henry) : *see* ALDRICH (Henry).

ALFORD (John) : A lutenist of the sixteenth century of whom nothing is known beyond the fact that in 1568 he published a translation (from the French) of Adrien le Roy's treatise : " A Briefe and Easye Instruction to learne the tableture, to conduct and dispose the hande unto the Lute, Englished by John Alford ". The original appeared in 1557 as *Instruction de partir toute musique . . . en tableture de luth.*

ALISON (Richard) : *see* ALLISON (Richard).

ALLISON (Richard) : A composer who was active in London at the end of the sixteenth century and the beginning of the seventeenth. In two of his publications he calls himself a " Gentleman Practitioner " in the art of music, and from this most writers deduce that he was a teacher. Beyond this, and what can be gleaned from his prefaces, nothing is known of his life. His first work was *The Psalms of Dauid in Meter*, The Plaine Song beeing the common tunne to be sung and plaide upon the Lute, Orpharyon, Citterne, or Base Violl, severally or together, the singing part to be either Tenor or Treble to the Instrument, according to the nature of the voyce, or for foure voyces. With tenne Short Tunnes in the end, to which for the most part all the Psalmes may be usually sung, for the use of such as are of mean skill ", or for those " whose leysure least serueth " them for practice. The work was to be sold at the author's house " in the Dukes place neere Alde-gate, London ", and was issued in 1599 by William Barley as the assignee of Thomas Morley. It was dedicated to Lady Anne, Countess of Warwick, . . . " whose fauours to me in the dayes of your H(onourable) husband, sometimes my good Lord and Master, have beene so great that I may not forget them : and hauing no way to shewe a thankful mind, but by presenting this simple work unto your H(onour), I humbly crave pardon for my boldness in offering it . . . " John Dowland contributed a complimentary sonnet, as did William Leighton (then Esq.), " in praise of the author ". Cantus, Altus, Tenor, Bassus, Lute, and Cittern parts were all printed on the page, facing various ways, so that all could perform from a single copy. His other work was "*An Howres Recreation in Musicke*, apt for Instrumentes and Voyces. Framed for the Delight of Gentlemen and others, which are well affected to that qualitie, All for the most part with two trebles, necessarie for such as teach in priuate families, with a prayer for the long preservation of the King and his posteritie, and a thanksgiving for the deliuerence of the whole estate from the late conspiracie. By R. Alison,

Gentleman and Practitioner in this Arte. London, 1606." The "late conspiracie" was the gunpowder plot of the previous year. The work is dedicated "to the right worthily honored and most free Respecter of all vertue, his chiefly esteemde and singular good Patrone Sir John Scudamore, Knight", and contained "the fruites of your bounties and the effect of those quiet dayes which by your goodnes, I have enioyed ". The book contains ten four-part and fourteen five-part compositions.

In addition to writing the two books already mentioned, Allison contributed to Thomas East's *Whole Book of Psalmes* (1592). Isolated specimens of his work are to be found reprinted in later collections. In 1598 he wrote a complimentary verse in Giles Farnaby's *Canzonets*.

In manuscripts Allison is represented in the British Museum *Add.* 31392, which contains four Pavans by "Maister Allison " in tablature for the lute. *Add.* 31420 includes the " 81st Psalm " tune, and *Add.* 31421 the four-part hymn-tune " Rochester ". *Add.* 30478, 9 has " Behoulde, nowe

praise ", signed " Allinsonne ", which may be by Richard Allison. *Add.* 33933 gives the Counter-Tenor part of two pieces from *An Howres Recreation.* Printed book 3437 g. 19 (*B.M.*) contains, interleaved, manuscript tunes to the Sternhold and Hopkins Psalter (1712), and includes among others, five tunes by Allison. Further manuscripts containing work of his are in Cambridge (University Library), Oxford (Christ Church and the Music School Collections).

ALLWOOD (Richard) : *see* ALWOOD (Richard).

ALWOOD (Richard) : A composer who flourished at the middle of the sixteenth century. He probably took holy orders, for in a manuscript at Oxford he is described as " priest ". His work is not distinguished by any particularly noteworthy features, and is typical of the ordinary writing of the period. The working out in his compositions is not marked by any great individuality, and his contrapuntal skill not up to the standard of the best writers of his time. British Museum manuscript *Add.* 30513 (Thomas Mulliner's Book, late Henry VIII) contains a " Voluntarye " by " All-wood " (printed by Hawkins) " Claro pascali gaudio ", and another composition with the same title ; also an " In Nomine " and a piece without a title. All these are arrangements for organ or virginal. *Add.* 30485 also containing virginal music, includes work by Alwood. A Mass, " Praise Him Praiseworthy " is preserved at Oxford (Forrest-Heyther part-books).

AMBROSE, *or* AMBROSIO DE MILAN : *see* LUPO (*Family*).

AMERY (John) : A Gentleman of the Chapel Royal of whom practically nothing is known biographically. The only traceable information as to his place of origin is that afforded by the Cheque-Book of the Chapel Royal, which states that in 1595 " Jo. Amery from Norwiche was sworn the 4th of December in Mr. Madoxe place ". In 1598 (April 19th) he is again mentioned in the same records. The Cheque-Book contains references to him from time to time, and the Lord Chamberlain's Records similarly contain his name. Thus in 1603 we meet with it in a list of Gentlemen receiving an allowance of mourning livery

for the funeral of Queen Elizabeth (*L.C.R.*), and in 1604 (December 5th, *C. B. C. R.*) it appears in an order increasing the salary of the Gentlemen from 30*l.* to 40*l.* per annum. In 1612 (Funeral of Henry, Prince of Wales, *L.C.R.*), he is entered as " Mr. Emerie ". None of the further entries throw any more light upon his activities, and the last refers to his death : " 1623 : John Amery died the 18th daye of July, and Ralphe Amner, Clark, a basse from Winsore, was sworn in his place the 16th of December following . . . " (*C.B.C.R.*).

AMNER (John) : An organist and composer of sacred music who appears to have passed all his active life in Ely. Following George Barcroft, he held the offices of organist at the Cathedral and Master of the Choristers from 1610 until his death in 1641. The only other biographical detail is that he became a Bachelor of Music at Oxford in 1613, incorporating at Cambridge a year before his death. Very little is known of this musician, and several writers have apparently confused him in some particulars with Ralph Amner.

John Amner's only printed work is " Sacred Hymnes of 3, 4, 5, and 6 parts, for Voyces and Vyols, Newly Composed by John Amner, Bachelor of Musique, Master of the Choristers, and Organist of the Cathedral Church of Ely " (London, 1615 ; copy in the B.M. six part-books bound in one volume). The work is dedicated to " The Right Honourable my singular good Lord and Maister William Earle of Bath ; Lord Lieftenant of the Countye of Deuon " ; and in the address to this nobleman he says : " I shall ever acknowledge that your most noble disposition and countenance hath both held me up, and bred me to that little learning and living, which I now enjoy ". Exactly in what relationship the musician stood to the Earl is not clear, but it would appear that the latter had at some time or other acted as a patron. The work contains six three-part pieces, six four-part, six five-part, and eight six-part.

In the manuscripts preserved in various libraries Amner is fairly well represented. The Christ Church (Oxford) collection has six verse-anthems of his ;

services and anthems are contained in the Ely library ; the Peterhouse collection includes specimens of his composition ; while the British Museum has : Services in Harl. 7337, 7339, 7340, and Add. 34203 ; anthems in Add. 17792–6 (three from the 1615 collection), Harl. 7337 and 7340, and Add. 30478–9 and 31415 ; Harl. 6346 (containing words only of an anthem) ; and Add. 34608 one number from the 1615 Sacred Hymnes. Add. 30826–8 contains a Pavan and Galliard by " Amner ", possibly John.

AMNER (Ralph) : A bass-singer and member of the Chapel Royal, who was evidently in holy orders, since he is to be met with as a " Vicar " (fulfilling the office of a Minor Canon), and " Minister ". Officially he first appears as a lay clerk at Ely Cathedral in 1604, surrendering the position to Michael East (or Este) in 1609. Exactly what happened immediately after this is not to be determined with certainty. When he came to London it was from Windsor, where he had been officiating as a Minor Canon. He was appointed to the London Chapel Royal at the end of

1623 (*C.B.C.R.* ; *see* also *Amery, John*). He did not sever all connection with Windsor, for he was permitted to keep his old post, the Prince of Wales interesting himself on Amner's behalf. Although the official swearing-in took place in 1623, there is evidence of Amner having been employed occasionally (probably as a deputy) at the London Chapel Royal before that date. The Cheque-Book contains an entry of 1621, dealing with the disposal of money accumulated by a post having remained vacant for a time: " To Mr. Amner, for attending in the . . . Vacacion, xxs." Early in the year of his permanent appointment he appears as a witness at the swearing-in of another member of the Chapel (March 24th). For ten years we find no further trace of him, until in May, 1633, his name is included among those of the basses " appointed to wayte on his Majesty in- his Scottish journey, 1633, as it was signed by his Majesty, 1632 " (*L.C.R.*). Following this entry there is another great gap in the history of the man. He probably continued his work at the Chapel Royal until the Commonwealth, when the establishment was disbanded. At the Restoration he reappears, being named with the " Musitians " at the coronation of Charles II (*C.B.C.R.*, April 23rd, 1661). In 1663 he is mentioned in the Cheque-Book and in the Lord Chamberlain's Records as being exempted from paying the subsidies voted by Parliament to the king, and the same year he died at Windsor : " 1663. Mr. Ralphe Amner, Clarke, one of the Gentlemen of his Majesties Chappell Royall, dyed at Windsor, the third day of March, 1663 " (*C. B. C. R.*).

Ralph Amner must have been a very popular man and well liked : Dr. Child (with whom he must have come into contact very frequently at Windsor) wrote a " Catch in stead of an Epitaph upon Mr. Ralph Amner of Windsor, commonly called the Bull Speaker, who died 1664 " (Hilton, *Catch that Catch Can*, 1667). The date of Amner's death as here given is not wrong, for March 3rd in the old reckoning was 1663–4. This Epitaph, " Let poets ne'er puzzle," is also given in *Add.* 29291 (*B.M.*).

Most authorities seek to establish some relationship between Ralph and John Amner, several stating that they were father and son. It seems unlikely to me that this should have been the case,—although, of course, not impossible. Still, if Ralph was a lay clerk in 1604 he could not have been born later than 1584, while John, to have been Master of the Choristers in 1610 would probably have been born round about 1570. The latter date would make him forty years of age at his appointment, so that an earlier date for his birth is not likely to be correct. The two men were more probably cousins, or, still more likely brothers.

APPELBYE (Thomas) : see APPLEBY (Thomas).

APPLEBY (Thomas) : A celebrated organist and composer of ecclesiastical music belonging to the sixteenth century. He appears to have been born at Lincoln where most of his active life was spent. Educated at Lincoln Cathedral and Oxford, his first appointment was that of organist at Lincoln (1536). Two years later he is given in the Chapter Acts of Lincoln as Master of the Choristers as well as organist.

His association with that city was broken for a short time between 1539 and 1541 when he acted as organist at Magdalen College (Oxford). In the latter year he was reinstated at Lincoln and given a room " over the outer gate of the Choristers' House " (Chapter Act). Thence onwards he seems to have remained at Lincoln until he was succeeded by the youthful William Byrd. The date of his death must therefore be placed at shortly before February, 1562–3. A good many references to him are given in the Chapter records of Lincoln (recently issued, edited by Canon Cole) ; indeed, as far as I have been able to discover, these Acts form the only source of information on the subject. His works include Masses, Motets, and other Church compositions, and he is represented in manuscripts preserved at the British Museum (*Add*, 17802–5 ; a Mass *a* 4 *voc.*), and in the Peterhouse (Cambridge) partbooks. All his known works were written for the older service.

APPULBY (Thomas) : see APPLEBY (Thomas).

ASHTON (Hugh) : see ASTON (Hugh).

ASHWELL (Thomas) : A composer, chiefly of sacred music, belonging to the firſt half of the sixteenth century. Biographically nothing is known of him, but his reputation seems to have laſted until the end of the century, for Thomas Morley mentions him in the liſt of good musicians (*Plaine and Easie Introduction*, 1597). Ashwell's skill was the average for the period ; he did not attain to the ſtature of his greater contemporaries, but he is, nevertheless, by no means negligible. His only printed composition, as far as I have been able to discover, is a four-part song, " She may be callyd ", contained in Wynkyn de Worde's Song-Book published Oċtober 10th, 1530 (probably during Ashwell's lifetime). This book is of excessive rarity, the Triplex and Bassus parts being preserved at the British Museum (K. 1. e. 1.).

The manuscript works of Thomas Ashwell are fairly numerous. Among the British Museum manuscripts, *Add.* 30520 contains " Sanċte Cuthberte ", two parts of " Gloria in excelsis " and the treble and firſt tenor parts of the " Credo ". *Add.* 34191 has work of Ashwell's, but unfortunately it is only a bass part. The medius part of a " Stabat Mater " and " Te Matrem " is included in *Harl.* 1709. The Oxford Music School possesses in the Forreſt-Heyther set of six part-books the Masses " Ave Maria " and " Jesu Criſti ", while the Cambridge part-books (University and St. John's College libraries) provide a Mass by Ashwell headed " God save King Herry " (evidently Henry VIII).

ASSHETON (Hugh) : *see* ASTON (Hugh).

ASTON (Hugh) : A composer of vocal church-music and secular inſtrumental works who flourished at the beginning of the sixteenth century. A good deal of confusion exiſts concerning his biography and with the materials at present available it is not yet possible to give any details of his life with absolute certainty. If the Hugh Aſton who became Canon and Prebendary of St. Stephen's, Weſtminſter, on May 28th, 1509, was the composer of the virginal Hornpipe in the British Museum manuscript, then his identification with the Archdeacon of York bearing

c

the same name is rendered impossible, for the latter was ſtill living when the former is known to have been dead (November 23rd, 1522). An exhauſtive article on Hugh Aſton, Archdeacon of York, is given in the *Dictionary of National Biography*, but all things considered, there seems to be little reason for supposing him to have been the composer, though the dates of the two men coincide so closely that there is every excuse for the earlier confusion. How closely the chronology runs will be realized when it is remembered that the Will of Hugh Aſton, Canon of St. Stephen's, was proved in December, 1522, while that of Hugh Aſton, Archdeacon of York, was made on December 7th, 1522, and proved in the March following. But the difference, slight as it is, becomes sufficient to separate the two men.

Apart from this consideration, a good deal of nonsense has been written on the subject of his ſtatus. As an early writer of music diſtinctly conſtructed for use on the keyboard inſtruments, Hugh Aſton possesses a certain hiſtorical importance ;

but to call him the "inventor" of inſtrumental music is to make too extravagant a claim. There can be little doubt that inſtrumental music developed with the inſtruments, and although in their earlier use the latter merely accompanied the voice or duplicated the voice-parts, players of imagination muſt early have seen the possibility of elaborating their part with florid virtuose work. Out of such beginnings undoubtedly grew the art of Blitheman, Bull, and Byrd, and in this development Hugh Aſton was an outſtanding figure— no less, and certainly no more. He deserves recognition (as he receives it at the hands of M. van den Borren) for his early use of variations on a "ground",— which ground was used by many later writers for their own variations,—and in this form of composition Aſton was moſt assuredly in advance of all the contemporary Continental composers.

The much-discussed Hornpipe is contained in MS. *Royal App.* 58 (*B.M.*). This is the only piece in the book that is signed with Aſton's name, and there is no reason for supposing, as some do, that "My Lady Carey's Dompe", which follows it, is by him also. Specimens of Aston's Masses, Motets, *etc.*, are to be seen (in most cases incomplete) in the British Museum (*Harl.* 7578 and *Add.* 34191), in the Forrest-Heyther collection (Oxford), in Sadler's Part-Books (Bodleian, Oxford), in the Peterhouse Part-Books (Cambridge), in the University and St. John's College libraries (*ibid.*), etc. In the library of Christ Church, Oxford, is a manuscript containing "H. Ashton's Maske", written by Whytebroke on Aston's celebrated "ground". This ground has also been used in the Fitzwilliam Virginal Book ("Treg[ian's] Ground", called in Lady Nevell's Virginal Book "Hughe Aston's Grownde").

ATTEY (John) : The composer of a book of part-songs with lute accompaniment which appeared in 1622. Practically nothing is known of his life. The title-page of his book describes him as "Gentleman and Practicioner of Musicke", and the dedication to the Earl and Countess of Bridgewater shows that he was a member of this household when he was writing the fourteen pieces that make up his publication. He was music master to the daughters of the Earl. All the authorities I have consulted give *ca.* 1640 as the date of Attey's death, and Ross as the place ; but so far the source of this information has eluded me. The full title of his book, quoted from the British Museum copy is : *The First Booke of Ayres of Foure Parts, with Tableture for the Lute : So made, that all the parts may be plaide together with the Lute, or one voyce with the lute and Base-Vyoll. 1622.* It will be seen that the pieces contained could be played on instruments as well as sung, and that the four-part accompanied songs could be converted at will into solo songs with lute and bass-viol obligato. Naturally, the moment instrumental accompaniment was added to a part-song; the indispensability of each vocal part ceased to be so absolute ;— gradually the voices would give place to instruments, and the madrigal was doomed.

AUSTEN (Hugh) : *see* ASTON (Hugh).

AVERIE or AVERY : *see* BURTON (Davy).

AYSTOUN (Hugh) : *see* ASTON (Hugh).

B

BACHELOR (Daniel) : A prominent lutenist and composer for the lute who flourished in the reign of Queen Elizabeth, though the only specimens of his music that were printed did not appear until after her death. In Robert Dowland's publications Bachelor is described as a "Groome of her Majesties Privie Chamber", and beyond this we know nothing of his life. To Dowland's *Musical Banquet* of 1610 he contributed a song with lute accompaniment, and for the same editor's *Varietie of Lute-Lessons*, also 1610, he wrote a Pavane ("by the right perfect Musitian, Daniel Bachelor") and an Almain "commonly knowne by the name of Mounsier's Almaine". He must have enjoyed a considerable reputation in this branch of the art, for Robert Dowland was an expert lutenist and composer for the instrument, and would not have included Bachelor's music had he not been aware of the attraction it would be. He is represented by a Pavane and a Galliard in Jane Pickering's Lute-Book (*B.M. Egerton MS.* 2046, *anno* 1616).

BACHLER (Daniel) : *see* BACHELOR (Daniel).

BALDWIN (John) : (*of Windsor*). A gentleman of the Chapel Royal who deserves recognition more on account of the fact that his conscientious copying of a good deal of the older music saved much that might otherwise have been lost to us, than for any other reason. He is mentioned first in an official manner when the Lord Chamberlain ordered the Subdean of the Chapel Royal to "sweare John Baldwin . . . gent, in ordinary (without pay) in her Majesty's Chapel, and until a tenor's place be voyde ; and then he to have and be sworne into wages for the first and nexte tenor that shalbe admitted and placed in her Highnes Chapel, noe man whatsoever to prevent him . . ." (March 23rd, 1594–5). He waited for over three years before he could claim wages ; but in 1598 we read : " Roberte Tallentire died the 15th of August and Jo. Baldwin sworne in his place the 20th of the same, from Winsore " (*C.B.C.R.*). He is mentioned several times in that entry-book. In 1612 he was one of the " Gentlemen of the King's Chappell " to receive mourning livery for the funeral of Prince Henry (*L.C.R.*). In 1615 he died, the Cheque-Book entry reading : " John Baldwin died the 28th August, and Martin Otto was sworne in his place . . . by the procurement of our gracious Ladie Queene Ann ".

Examples of Baldwin's composition may be seen in the library of Christ Church (Oxford), where four works of his are preserved : " Pater Noster ", " Redime domine ", an instrumental Fancy in three parts, and a Fancy based on the cry of the " Coockow ", —all wanting the tenor part. The Forrest-Heyther Part-Books (Oxford) contain examples in his own handwriting. A good deal of William Byrd's virginal music has been preserved in Baldwin's manuscript Virginal-Book written for Lady Nevill and " Ffinished and ended the leventh of September in the yeare of our Lorde God 1591 and in the 33 yeare of the raigne of our Sofferaine ladie Elizabeth by the grace of God queene of Englande . . .

By me Jo. Baldwine of Windsore. Laudes Deo ". The volume is owned by the Marquess of Abergavenny (*de luxe* edition announced by Messrs. J. Curwen and Sons, Ltd., 1926). Baldwin's other great piece of copying is the volume of sacred music in the possession of His Majesty the King, containing music by such writers as John Dygon, Parsons, Shepherd, Tallis, John Thorne of Yorke, Giles, the two Mundys, Taverner, Bevin, Tye, *etc.*, as well as examples of his own work. This collection was copied round about the turn of the century.

BALTZAR (Thomas) : One of the most celebrated violinists of the seventeenth century who came to England during the Commonwealth and became Charles the Second's private violinist. Although a German, he must be included in this volume because his influence upon the art of violin-playing in England was very great, and there can be little doubt that he introduced many technical devices until then unknown, or at least little known, here. Anthony Wood is not always trustworthy, but in the case of Baltzar we may safely accept his statements, since he came into personal contact with the famous violinist. In the Diary of his life he enters under date 1658 : " Tho. Balsar, or Baltzar, a Lubecker borne, and the most famous artist on the Violin that the world had yet produced was now in Oxon, and this day (July 24th) A(nthony) W(ood) was with him and Mr. Edw. Low, lately organist of Christ Church, at the Meeting house of Will. Ellis. A. W. did then and there to his very great astonishment, heare him play on the Violin. He then saw him run up his fingers to the end of the Finger-board of the violin, and run them back insensibly, and all with alacrity and in very good tune, which he nor any in England saw the like before. A. W. entertained him with Mr. Low with what the house could then afford, and afterwards he invited them to the Tavern ; but they being engaged to other company, he could no more heare him play or see him play at that time. Afterwards he came to one of the weekly meetings at Mr. Ellis's house, and he played to the wonder of all the auditory ; and exercising his fingers and instrument several wayes to the utmost of his power, Wilson thereupon the public Professor (the greatest judge of musick there ever was) did after his humoursome way, stoop downe to Baltzar's feet to see whether he had a huff (hoof) on, that is to say, to see whether he was a devil or not, because he acted beyond the parts of Man. About that time it was, that Dr. Joh. Wilkins, Warden of Wadham College, the greatest curioso of his time, invited him and some of the musitians to his lodgings in that College purposely to have a Consort, and to see and heare him play. The instruments and books were carried thither, but none could be perswaded there to play against him in consort on the violin. At length, the company perceiving A. W. standing behind in a corner neare the dore, they haled him in among them, and play, forsooth, he must against him. Whereupon he being not able to avoid it, he took up a violin and behaved himself as poor Troylus did against Achilles. He was abashed at it, yet honour he got by playing with and against such a grand master as Baltzar was ".

Wood adds that " being much admired by all lovers of musick his (Baltzar's) company was therefore desired ; and company, especially musical company, delighting in drinking, made him drink more than ordinary, which brought him to his grave ". The remark of the diarist referring to Baltzar's running his fingers to the end of the fingerboard and back again, shows how slight was the knowledge of shifting in those days in England. The best players of the time scarcely climbed higher than the third position, and then only in a very vague manner (v. my paper, " Violin Methods, Old and New ", read before the *Musical Association*, April 8th, 1924, printed in the *Proceedings* of that Society). Roger North (*Memoires of Musick*), who calls Baltzar a Swede, said that he " did wonders " on the violin " by swiftness and doubling of notes, but his hand was accounted hard and rough, though he made amends for that by using often a lyra-tuning ". It is clear, then, that Baltzar was first and foremost to be regarded as an amazing technician rather than a profound musician.

Thomas Baltzar was born at Lübeck *ca*. 1630, and must have come to England before 1656, for in that year he played in the production of Davenant's *Siege of Rhodes*. On March 4th, 1656–7, John Evelyn heard him play at the house of Roger L'Estrange, and said of him that " his variety on a few notes and plain ground, with that wonderful dexterity, was admirable. Though a young man, yet so perfect and skilful, that there was nothing, however cross and perplexed, brought to him by our artists, which he did not play off at sight with ravishing sweetness and improvements, to the astonishment of our best masters, *etc*." At the Restoraion Baltzar was marked down for the private music of the king in " a new place " (*L.C.R., Vol.* 479) ; in 1661 (September 5th) he was paid 34*l*. 3*s*. 4*d*. for two violins " bought by him for his Majesty's service " ; on November 30th he was appointed " to bee one of our musitians in Ordinary for the Vyolin in our Privy Musick, *etc*." at a " yearly Fee or Sallary of 110*l*. . . . the first payment to begin from St. John Baptist last past and further " (*Dom. Entry Bk.*

Vol. V, quoted in Nagel, *Annalen, Appendix*) ; on December 23rd, 1661, a similar entry is made in the Lord Chamberlain's Records (*Vol.* 741) ; on October 9th, 1662, he was paid 6*l.* 13*s.* 4*d.* for strings. But in none of the State Papers do we find any mention of Baltzar having been leader or Master of the Band of Twenty-Four Violins, as so many authorities state. His work seems to have been quite distinct from that of the court orchestra, and he probably played only solos for the king's private entertainment. Moreover, we do not find him receiving a livery allowance. He died in 1663 and was buried in the Cloisters of Westminster Abbey on July 27th, having been in the royal service for less than two years.

One can hardly expect that the few pieces of violin-music now extant should give us any idea of his powers as a performer. Virtuosi of Baltzar's stature,—especially in the seventeenth century,—never played anything exactly as it was written, and no idea can be formed from their written music of their executive powers. Playford's *Division Violin* (1685) contains a couple of slight com-positions of his, these being all I can find of his printed music. Isolated short pieces of no great value are preserved in manuscript at Oxford (Christ Church Library and the Music School). Hugo Wehrle edited for Breitkopf and Haertel as Allemande by Baltzar.

BANASTER, BANASTIR, BANESTER, BANESTIR, *see* BANESTRE (Gilbert).

BANESTRE (Gilbert) : Poet, composer and master of the Chapel boys in the last quarter of the fifteenth century. In early Tudor days it seems to have been the general rule for the " Master of Song " to be a poet and writer of interludes. What is probably his earliest work is a metrical version of the Legend of Sisimond, dating from the middle of the century. This follows a copy of Chaucer's *Legend of Ladies*, also in Banestre's handwriting, the whole forming *Add.* 12524 (*B.M.*). Another literary work of Banestre's dating from a few years later (1467), was the *Miracle of St. Thomas.* Biographically hardly anything is known of him. In 1482 he appears to have succeeded Henry Abyngdon as " Master of the Song ", and was appointed for "the exhibition, instruction, and governaunce of the children of the Chapelle ", at a salary of forty Marks per annum guaranteed by the Act of 22 Edw. IV (1482–3). For the rest we know nothing more of him than can be gleaned from one or two entries in the State Papers. In 1486 (August 22nd) one Robert Colet was granted a corrody in the monastery of St. Oswald (Bodney, Lincs.), Gilbert Banestre having surrendered it. In another manuscript of the Rolls Series of State Papers, the same corrody is mentioned on September 1st, 1487, as being "vacant by the death of Gilbert Banestre ", which occurred in August.

A few compositions of a strictly formal nature are preserved. The *Fayrfax Book* (*B.M. Add.* 5465) contains " My feerfull dreme " (three-part) in five sections ; the Eton College manuscript includes the hymn " O Maria et Elizabeth " ; while the only other work by Banestre known to me is in *MS. Pepys.* 1236 (Magdalen College, Cambridge). His chief duties would have been, as were those of his immediate predecessor and successor, to train and direct the Chapel-singers, compose music for special occasions, and write (and sometimes perform) interludes, with or without music, for the entertainment of the king and his court.

BANISTER (James) : A member of Charles the Second's band of twenty-four violins. He was admitted to his post by warrant dated May 8th, 1676 " in the place and upon the surrender of Henry Comer, with all rights and profits " (*L.C.R.*), and in 1679 (December 13th), his salary is given in the Wardrobe Accounts as 46*l.* 12*s.* 3*d.* per annum (*L.C.R.*). He seems to have been a very improvident man and there were numerous petitions against him for debt. On November 28th, 1681, a certain John Smith made such a claim and in the August of that year already William Cooke petitioned that James Banister (" late a tennant to the petitioner and refuseth to pay rent ") be compelled to settle the account. The Lord Chamberlain issued the order, " Let James Banister have notice of this petition and appear before mee upon the 30th August instant " (*L. C. R.*). In 1684 (December 8th) " James

Mercy, joyner, against James Banister, musician, 41*l.* 10*s.* debt for meat, drink, and lodging of plaintiff in Maypole Alley, Newmarket" (*L.C.R.*). This debt was incurred on one of the royal visits to Newmarket, when part of the band accompanied the king. The musicians always received an allowance for their expenses, and James Banister either spent the money on something else, or probably never received what the treasurer was ordered by warrant to pay (see also article on John Banister I for the chaotic state of affairs that existed in Charles II's money matters). In 1684–5 (January 26th) the same order to attend practice at the Theatre Royal was issued to James Banister as was received by John Banister, junior (*q.v.*). Another sidelight is thrown on the probable causes of James Banister's insolvency in the letter he sent (March 19th, 1685–6) appointing his wife, Mary, his "true and lawful attorney, . . . to demand and receive all sums of money due to him as salary";—the violinist was evidently not to be trusted with money. After 1685–6 he vanishes from the

official records, and nothing further is known of him. As a member of the celebrated band of twenty-four violins he must have been an excellent performer, and it is possible that he was some relative to John Banister,—perhaps a younger brother, son, or nephew.

BANISTER (Jeffrey; Jeoffery *or* Jeoffrye): A violinist of distinction who flourished in the seventeenth century. It is possible that he belonged to the same family as the two Johns Banister, but there is no proof of this. We meet him first at the re-establishment of the royal music after the Restoration of the House of Stuart, and in a list of "Violins" dated 1660 and later we read his name (*L.C.R.*). Over two years later,—on October 27th, 1662,—he was still waiting for a salaried post: "Jeoffrey Bannister appointed musician in ordinary for the violin without fee" (*Id.*), but on December 24th, 1663, a warrant was issued admitting him "musician in ordinary . . . in the place of Edward Strong, deceased, with the wages of 46*l.* 12*s.* 8*d.* per annum, to commence at Michaelmas last past" (*Id.*).

At this period he, with others, was also assisting the orchestra of his Majesty's theatre ; for on December 20th, 1664, the Lord Chamberlain gave him leave to attend at the playhouse " whenever Mr. Thomas Killigrew shall desire " it. On July 10th, 1665, Jeffrey Banister was selected as one of the famous " twenty-four " who were " made choyce of by Mr. (John) Bannister " (*L.C.R., Vol.* 479). He is referred to a great many times is these records, and it will not be necessary to quote from all the entries. But in 1668–9 (February 21st) an interesting document was issued. This was at the time when Charles II was requested to be a little more economical in the management of his household, and he showed his desire to conform by giving a list of the twenty-four violins and saying that they " should be continued and theire sellerys paid them as formerly . . . any orders of retrenchment to the contrary notwithstanding ". From the entry of November 4th, 1671, we learn that these violinists also served in turn (for a month at a time) in the Chapel Royal, Jeffrey Banister's period of duty for the last

quarter of 1671 being in October. We gather from one of the assignments (June 28th, 1672) that this Banister lived in the parish of St. Clement Danes, and that he was rich enough to be able to lend money to others (*L.C.R., Vol.* 195). In 1674 he resided at St. Dunstan's-in-the-West (*Id.*). Two years later he, like many of the other musicians at court, indulged in a little gambling;— selling his chances of receiving the wages due to him to one William Parkes " in consideration of the sum of 150*l.* paid by the said Parkes ". On July 4th, 1676, a similar assignment was made in respect of his salary of 46*l.* 12*s.* 8*d.* to Thomas Bates of Westminster. It is not known when Jeoffrey Banister died; his name is to be seen for the last time in a list of salaries dated December 13th, 1679, but it is by no means certain that he was still active. The only composition bearing his name that I have been able to locate is a " Tune " in Thomas Greeting's *Pleasant Companion* (for the Flageolet) of 1682. Now, John Banister the Elder was an expert performer on the flageolet, and since the only known music by Jeffrey Banister is for that instrument, it is just possible that the two men were father and son.

BANISTER (John) (I.). Sometimes called "the Elder" to distinguish him from his son, John Banister was an interesting and important figure in seventeenth century musical England; more perhaps as an excellent executant violinist and as the originator of the public concert in this country, than for his achievements as a creative musician. Born in London in 1630, Banister was the son of one of the waits of the Parish of St. Giles-in-the-Fields. There can be little doubt that he received his earliest training from his father, for the waits were far better artists than is generally supposed (v. Dic. Old Engl. M., article "Waits"), although Hawkins contemptuously designates them as "that low class of musician". Beyond this we know nothing of his early life. We first meet with him as a violinist in the orchestra that produced the music for Sir William Davanent's *Siege of Rhodes* (1656), having as co-workers such famous men as Christopher Gibbons and

Thomas Baltzar. From this date until his appointment to the royal service the only reference to him that I have been able to trace is the entry of Pepys under date January 21st, 1659–60: "Thence to the Mitre; where I drank a pint of wine, the house being in fitting for Banister to come thither from Paget's".

His reputation as a performer must have been known in court - circles, for immediately after the Restoration we find him among the royal musicians. In the Lord Chamberlain's Records his name is included in a list of musicians receiving the usual allowance for livery of 16l. 2s. 6d. (St. Andrew, 1660). John Banister's name is crossed out and "vacatur" written against it; this probably on account of his journey to France as will be seen later. But in the list of violinists who were to attend in the Chapel Royal and at Westminster Hall for the Coronation, he appears again (April 12th, 1661, L.C.R.). In the list made up at St. Andrew of the same year, however, his name is once more crossed out. It appears that although he was appointed to the royal service he was not yet to be the recipient of the livery allowance. At the end of the year he was sent to France; whether on a diplomatic mission or to observe the constitution of the French king's orchestra, is not clear. His passport (*Cal. S.P.*, *Ent. Bk. V. p.* 62, December 2nd, 1661) reads: " Pass for Mr. Bannaster, the King's Servant, to go into France on Special Service, and return with expedition ". That he returned with expedition is evident from the fact that on May 3rd, 1662, he was back in England; for under that date we read in *Entry Book VII*, p. 36: " Warrant for a grant to John Banaster of the place of one of the Violins in Ordinary for the King's private Music, in place of David Mell, deceased; fee 110*l.* a year ". On September 26th, 1662, a warrant was issued assuring him of the yearly allowance for livery (*L.C.R.*). These entries show that Banister succeeded Mell in the first place, and not Baltzar as many authorities state; but it will be seen later that he filled the offices held by both of these violinists. On October 24th, 1662, he received 40*l.* for two Cremona violins " bought

by him for his Majesty's service, and also 10*l.* for strings for two years ending June 4th, 1662 " (*L.C.R.*). Thence onward his name appears continuously in the records until his death. In a warrant dated July 10th, 1663, he is given as a " composer for the violins ".

Charles II was a great admirer of the French style in music and sought to imitate the court of France in many ways. He began by ordering a special band of violins to be trained on the lines of the 24 *Violons du Roi,* and had twelve of his orchestra selected for the purpose.

Under the same date as that of his appointment we find the entry: " Order that John Banaster have full power to instruct and direct twelve persons mentioned, chosen by him out of the twenty-four of the band of violins, for better performance of service, without being mixed with the other Violins, unless the King orders the twenty-four " (*Ent. Bk. VII,* p. 37). The salary of this exquisite dozen is given in the State Papers: " July 1663. Order for a warrant to pay to John Banaister, appointed to choose twelve of the king's violins as a select band, 600*l.* a year, to be divided amongst them ; with proviso of dismissal of any who neglect practice, or engage in any other service ". Scarcely eleven days after the nomination of the twelve players, Banister received orders to parade them; and Charles no doubt influenced by the circumstances of the occasion, allowed his extravagance to run in the right direction for once and ordered their expenses to be paid. " May 14th, 1662, Warrant to Sir Edward Griffin, Treasurer of the Chamber, to advance 23*l*. 10*s*. each to the twelve violinists in ordinary and to John Banister, towards their expenses, in attending the king on his journey to Portsmouth to receive the Queen " (*Ent. Bk. VII*, p. *53*). On August 19th, 1663, an entry appears which shows that the 600*l*. mentioned earlier was " an augmentation for himself and twelve of the violins "; and this sum, or Banister's share of it was to be considered as additional to his ordinary salary. The original 110*l*. a year might still have been paid, or at least owed, him. *Add. MS.* *5750* (*B.M.*) gives a warrant ordering the payment of 40*l*. per annum. It is possible that one sum represented Banister's salary in the Private Music of the king, and the other his wage as a member of the State orchestra. At any rate, he must have enjoyed a very lucrative position, supposing he were paid regularly, which is very much open to doubt.

But in 1666 clouds began to form on Banister's horizon. On December 24th, 1666, we read: " Order that Mr. Bannister and the twenty-four violins appointed to practice with him . . . doe, from tyme to tyme, obey the directions of Louis Grabu, master of the private musick ". (*L.C.R.*). This may have caused jealousy, and several writers state that Banister lost favour at court through tactlessly saying in the king's hearing that he considered the English violinists superior to the French. If this story be true, he was probably justified; but the real reason is to be sought elsewhere. The band complained that the monies voted them were not honestly divided, and that several sums given them were entirely or in part withholden. The major portion, they said, went into Banister's own pocket. The charge is contained in a petition to

Lord Arlington, which stated that Banister kept the greater portion of the money for himself, forcing the twelve to submit by what was in effect common blackmail. The remonstrance says that several had already been turned away without the pleasure of the king having been consulted. In the matter of payments for the music made on the occasion of the Queen's birthday, the petitioners asked the Lord Chamberlain to interest himself in their behalf. The Queen, when she heard of it, expressed surprise, saying that they had already had great sums. The suspicion therefore remained that Banister had kept it all for himself. Out of 50*l.* given the violinists by the Queen at Bath, Banister had kept 20*l.*; out of 10*l.* presented by a high personage, he had appropriated 4*l.*; the whole 20*l.* which the Duke of Buckingham gave the violinists, had gone into Banister's purse. They asked Arlington to clear up the matter, and expressed their willingness " to answer any objection that Banister may make " (*S.P. Dom. Ser.*, 1666–7). This remonstrance, of course, looks exceedingly damning on the face of it,

but we cannot be certain that Banister actually received the money stipulated. Respecting the small presents there is naturally no documentary evidence, and it is quite possible that Banister may have kept a large percentage of this money in order to compensate himself somewhat for his own salary, which was by then hopelessly in arrears. Concerning the 600*l.* we have evidence for the defence. Already in 1665 Banister had to petition the king for the money : " Petition of John Banister to the king, for payment of the increased allowance of 600*l.* a year promised to the twelve violinists over whom he is director . . ." It is evident that he could not divide what he did not receive; and the proviso that any of the twelve who neglected his practice or engaged in any other service could be dismissed, may account for some of the " turnings away " mentioned in the remonstrance. On July 4th, 1665, a warrant was issued ordering the treasurer to pay 350*l.* for the charges incurred by the musicians in attending the king on his journeys. No mention is made of the 600*l.* due, and Banister must have had anything but a happy time between answering the clamouring violinists on the one hand, and begging for money with which to satisfy their demands on the other. On August 4th, 1667, the reins were given over into Grabu's hands, the same allowance of 600*l*. was made, and he was ordered to see that "the whole establishment . . . be made over again".

Banister did not leave the band of violins after the directorship had been taken from him. On April 29th, 1668, we find his name in the list of the "twenty-four" ordered "to wayte, twelve each month". In 1668–9 his salary is given as 46*l*. 10*s*. per annum (*L.C.R.*), but in a list dated January 9th, 1668–9 the sum named is still 110*l*. for "John Banister, private musick". It is clear that he still occupied two distinct positions. On May 6th, 1670 (*L.C.R.*) he is among the "musitians to attend in the Chappell", and in that year we find that the king owed him four years' livery money. On February 11th, 1670–1, at length, we meet with a rare document,— a receipt of Banister's for *one* year's livery. How much longer he remained at court

cannot be determined with certainty, for orders for the payment of livery continue to appear until his death. But on May 20th, 1674, an assignment appears among the Lord Chamberlain's papers which makes over two and a half years' salary of Banister's in arrears to one William Parkes. This may show that Banister had left court service and had appointed someone to collect what was still due to him out of the Treasury. This assignment describes Banister as "of St. Dunstan's-in-the-West". Warrants for the payment of the livery allowance are often to be seen long after the resignation or death of the royal musicians, and refer to arrears left owing, which were, in some cases, collected by the executors of the creditors. Nevertheless, we find the name of a Banister once more in an order dated July 4th, 1674, directing twelve of the violins to meet at "his Majesty's Theatre in the palace of Whitehall on Wednesday morning next by 7 of the clock, to practise after such manner as Monsr. Combert shall enforme them. . . . " (*L.C.R.*), while on October 31st, 1674, he was to receive five shillings a day for his expenses while in attendance, with others, on the king at Windsor. It is possible that some of these later entries may refer to John Banister, junior, and it is likely that the elder Banister left the royal band about 1672, though we find his name (always in connection with payments for livery) until the records contain the remark " obiit ". It should be remarked, however, before we leave Banister's court activities, that in 1675, there was owing to him 55*l.* for strings supplied by him " for the space of eleven years ".

Whether Banister left the court in 1672 or not, it must be assumed that the placing of the special band of violins under the direction of Grabu rendered Banister exempt from the proviso which prevented him from being engaged in any other occupation, for from this year onward we find him controlling a Music-School and a series of public concerts (the first of the kind). Our chief source of information on these points is the *London Gazette*. The first announcement is to be found in No. 742 (December 26th—30th,

1672) : " These are to give Notice, that at Mr. *John Banister's* House, now called the Musick School, over against the *George* Tavern in White Fryers this present Monday, will be Musick performed by excellent Masters, beginning precisely at four of the Clock in the afternoon, and every afternoon for the future, precisely at the same hour ". From Roger North's *Memoires of Musick* and his *Musicall Gramarian* (*Add.* 32533, *B.M.*) we can gather some account of the environment of these concerts. It appears that Banister hired " an obscure (' large ' in the *Memoires*) room in a publik hous (*MS.*) neer the Temple back gate (*Memoires*) filled it with tables and seats, and made a side box with curtains for the musick " (*MS.*). The *Memoires* gives this as " . . . . and made a large raised box for the musicians, whose modesty required curtains ". The charge was a shilling a head " call for what you pleas ". The *MS.* further tells us that here came the best performers in town " and much company to hear "; " there was very good musick " and " . . . divers musicall curiositys were pre-

D

sented, as for instance, Banister himself upon a flageolett in Consort, wch. was never heard before nor since " (*MS.*). The flageolet was quite a fashionable instrument in those days, and Banister, besides playing upon it and the violin, also performed well on the theorbo. The *London Gazette* advertisements kept the public acquainted with all details connected with the concerts. In 1674–5 Banister removed to a more central *locale* (to Chandos Street), and in 1676 another change was made to the Holborn district (Little Lincoln's Inn Fields). The concerts were given until shortly before Banister's death, the last being held in Essex Street, Strand.

The celebrated violinist was a personal friend of Pepys, and a few entries in the latter's *Diary* referring to Banister are interesting. In the entry for March 26th, 1668, we find him called " the great master of musique ", and on March 29th, 1668, we read: " Most extraordinary company . . . for musick of all sorts . . . we sang and Banister played on the theorbo, and afterwards on his flageolet ". On April 26th of the same year Banister was a guest at Pepys' house and dined with him ; afterwards they had music, singing " all the afternoon ".

One of the features of Metropolitan musical life at this period was the Corporation of Musicians, a body having considerable power and influence, and of this company Banister was a member. *Harl.* 1911 (" Orders of a Musical Corporacion ", 1661–79), gives information of his election " November 24th, 1663. Whereas Symon Hopper, one of the assistants to the Corporacion of Musique, having to surrender his Interest in the same, it is ordered that John Banister be and is hearby clothed in his Roome and plase. Signed, Nicholas Lanier, Marshall ". Of Banister's last years we know nothing; in 1678 he was still giving concerts at his last address in Essex Street ; in 1679 (October 3rd) he died, and his remains lie interred in the Cloisters of Westminster Abbey.

The written works of the elder Banister are neither particularly numerous nor of great magnitude; but such as they are they appear as typical examples of the art of this kind of composer at that period. They include pieces for the viols and the violin, for the lute, and for the flageolet. His vocal music consists chiefly of comparatively simple songs and the lyrics to two or three dramatic works. Specimens of his composition may be seen in many of Playford's publications, but it is not always possible to decide which are to be attributed to the elder Banister and which belong to his son. Playford's *Courtly Masquing Ayres* (1662) contains work of the father, and John Hilton's *Catch that Catch Can* (1667 and 1672) includes the two-part ballad " Sweet Jane, I love thee wondrous well ". More important was Banister's work in collaboration with Pelham Humphrey (1670): this was the setting of the lyrics to the Dryden and Davenant version of Shakespeare's *Tempest*. Banister's share consisted of " Come unto these yellow sands ", " Dry those eyes ", " Eccho Song, 'twixt Ferdinand and Ariel,—Go thy Way ", and " Full Fathom Five thy Father lies ". A couple of songs are contained in *Add.* 29396 (*B.M.*), a Gavotte represents him in Lock's *Melothesia*

(1673), and Playford's *Choice Songs and Ayres* (1673 and 1675) includes half a dozen of songs for one voice with theorbo or Gamba accompaniment. His most considerable effort (if indeed he wrote it all) was the music he supplied for Dr. Charles Davenant's tragedy of *Circe*. This play was first given at the Duke of York's Theatre in 1677, and was the work of Sir William Davenant's eldest son. Downes (1708) who calls it an " Opera ", tells us that all the music " was set by Mr. Banister, and being well-performed, it answered the expectations of the company ". The Fitzwilliam Museum (Cambridge) and the library of the Royal College of Music contain the music to the first act in manuscript, and one of the numbers was given in *Choice Ayres and Songs* (Second Book). Rimbault (*Ancient Vocal Musick of England, No.* 15) issued the opening scene of *Circe* (*v.* also article on Henry Purcell II).

In 1678 Banister published in conjunction with Thomas Low, *New Ayres and Dialogues composed for Voices and Viols,* etc. His chief work in connection with the publication of this book was editorial; only a couple of pieces being from his pen. " Sundry Authors " contributed, including Henry Purcell (I), the two Lawes, Blow, and Jenkins. Nos. 4 and 11 in the section headed " New Lessons for Viols or Violins " are by Banister. He also contributed an " Ayre " and a " Tune " to *Musick's Recreation on the Viol, Lyraway* (Edition of 1682) and in Thomas Greeting's *Pleasant Companion* (1682) we find some flageolet music by the elder Banister. The five pieces in the *Division Violin* (1685 and 1688) may not all be by the father. Here " Mr. John Banister " can mean the younger man. The fact that one of the pieces is labelled " Mr. John Banister, *senior* " helps to make the other four doubtful. Three airs in *The Banquet of Musick* (1688) complete the tale of his printed works.

Several short pieces of John Banister's exist in manuscript. *Add.* 18940 (middle of the seventeenth century) has a " Ground in D " consisting of sixteen sections for three viols with added Basso Continuo for the harpsichord; *Add.* 15118 has a piece for the Treble-Viol, and *Harl.*

3187-8 has " Mr. Banister's tune in D-Solra ". Further compositions (some possibly by the younger Banister) may be seen in *Add.* 30957, 33234, 19759 (*B.M.*). Other manuscripts containing specimens of his work are preserved in the Oxford Music School collection, and in the library of Christ Church. Pepys names a song by Banister: " May 7th, 1668. Here took up Knapp into our Coach, and all of us with her to her lodgings, and thither comes Banister with a song of her's, that he hath set in Sir Charles Sidley's play for her, which is, I think, but very meanly set; . . . but I did get him to prick me down the notes of the Echo in *The Tempest*, which pleases me mightily ".

BANISTER (John) (II). One of the best violinists at the end of the seventeenth century, a member of the king's private band, and the writer of a tutor for the violin (now lost). He was the son of John Banister I (*v. sup.*), and he no doubt received his musical education in his father's " Musick-School . . . in White-Fryers ". In *Add.* 18958 (*B.M.*) there is a reference to a Mr. John Bannister as music-master to the Lady Anne (*Establishment of wages* . . . *of the Duke of York*, for 1677), but it is not certain whether the son or the father was meant. Banister the elder would have been near his end in 1677, while his son could have been about twenty-five years of age at the time. I think the younger Banister is indicated. In 1679 (November 6th) a warrant was issued admitting him " as musician in ordinary for the violin, with fee, in the place of his father . . . deceased " (*L.C.R.*), and on December 13th of the same year his salary is given in the Wardrobe accounts as 46*l.* 10*s.* 10*d.* per annum (*Id.*). On January 26th, 1684–5, he was ordered, with the rest of the king's violins, to attend " at his Majesty's Theatre Royal to practice music for a ball, which is to be before his Majesty there " (*Id.*). In 1685 (August 31st) he was officially appointed to the " Private Musick in ordinary with fee and salary " to James II (*Id.*), the certificate of appointment following on September 10. In 1689 (July 22nd) he was received in a similar post under William and Mary. His salary in 1697 is given as 40*l.* a year. He was still in court service in the reign of Queen Anne, and played as leader in the orchestra when Italian opera was first performed in London. He was a member of Thomas Britton's music-club, and was one of the first violinists in England to popularize Corelli. The *London Gazette* (July 8th–11th, 1700) contains the advertisement: " The new Sonatas of the Famous . . . Corelli curiously engraven on seventy copper Plates . . . being now brought from Rome will be ready to be delivered to Subscribers on Monday next at Mr. Banister's in Brownlow Street in Drury Lane ". He died at this address in 1735. A mezzotint portrait was made by J. Smith and is reproduced in E. van der Straeten's *Romance of the Fiddle* (1911).

Which of the pieces contained in Playford's publications under the name " John Banister " are to be attributed to the father and which to the son, is often very difficult to decide ; and the same applies to those still in manuscript. In addition to these short instrumental compositions, the younger Banister issued *The Compleat Tutor to the Violin : Containing plain and easie Directions for Beginners, with the newest Tunes now in use, and a Flourish in every key* (1698). The work was advertised in the *London Gazette*, but no copy of it is known to exist. This is especially unfortunate, since it might have given us some idea of the methods of violin-teaching which he obtained presumably from his more celebrated father. In 1691 appeared *Ayres, Chacones, Divisions, and Sonatas, for Violins and Flutes, by G. Finger. To which is added a set of Ayres in Four Parts by Mr. John Banister.* This also was advertised in the *London Gazette* (November 5th, 1691). Banister was the author also of *The Gentleman's Tutor for the Violin*; but whether this was a different edition of the tutor mentioned above, or an earlier work for amateurs, cannot be determined until copies of the two works come to light.

BARCROFT (George) : An organist and composer of ecclesiastical music of whom very little is known. He matriculated at Cambridge as a sizar of Trinity College in 1574 (December 12th), and became a Bachelor of Music in 1577–8. His appointment as a Minor Canon and organist at Ely Cathedral dates from 1579. His death is generally placed in 1610, but there is no proof forthcoming as to the accuracy of this. All we know is that he was organist until 1609. The two compositions given by Tudway in the Harleian collection (*Harl.* 7337 and 7340, *B.M.*) are merely headed " Mr. Barcroft ", but the dates inserted by the writer—1532 for the " Morning Service " and 1535 as that of Barcroft's being organist at Ely,—show that Tudway confused the composer of the Full Anthem in four parts, " O Almighty God ", and of the Service already alluded to, with a Thomas Barcroft who belonged to an earlier generation. There is no confirmation in the Ely Cathedral records of a Thomas Barcroft having been organist there in 1535 (J. E. West, *Cathedral Organists*), and the dates given by Tudway are clearly too early for the compositions to which they are attached. The only alternative, then, is to ascribe these two compositions to George Barcroft, the later bearer of the surname. The Anthem " O Almighty God " has been issued by Messrs.

Novello and Co. under the editorship of Mr. J. E. West. The Motett Society (Rimbault) published the Anthem and the service.
BARCROFT (Thomas) : *see* BARCROFT (George).
BARNARD (John) : Beyond the fact that he was a Minor Canon of St. Paul's Cathedral, London, in the first half of the seventeenth century, we know nothing of the life of this industrious editor. His fame rests upon one work which has been of the greatest value to Church musicians, and to which many later editors have gone for their materials. There can be no doubt that the modern world owes a deep debt of gratitude to the Rev. John Barnard for having by these means rescued from total loss many very fine examples of early English ecclesiastical music. The work in question was issued in 1641 with the title: "*The First Book of Selected Church Musick*, consisting of Services and Anthems, such as are now used in the Cathedrall and Collegiate Churches of this Kingdome. Never before printed. Whereby such Bookes as were heretofore with much difficulty and charges, transcribed for the use of the

Quire, are now to the saving of much Labour and expence, publisht for the general good of all such as shall desire them either for publick or private exercise. Collected out of divers approved Authors ". The collection appeared in ten separate partbooks, and contained the works of no composer then living. It was Barnard's intention to issue another work with the compositions of his contemporaries, but this intention was never realized. Until the middle of the nineteenth century no complete set of part-books belonging to the 1641 work existed. The best set then known was the one at Hereford Cathedral, which was short only of two parts. In 1862 the Sacred Harmonic Society purchased an incomplete set of eight parts, but containing the two parts missing at Hereford. With the two sets it was possible to make a complete transcript; a manuscript of Adrian Batten's came to the rescue with organ-parts, and from all of these Mr. John Bishop of Cheltenham reconstructed Barnard's work in score. This was never published, and the manuscript is in the British Museum. The date of the original publication was an unfortunate one for Cathedral music, and it is possible that the majority of the copies were destroyed by the Republicans in the first flush of their misguided zeal. Besides the published set, Barnard had copied a further collection of more than six score Services and Anthems, seven parts of which now belong to the Royal College of Music. The use of the words " First Book " on the title-page in 1641 shows that he meant to publish further volumes. The composers represented in the printed set are: Tallis, Strogers, Bevin, Byrd, Orlando Gibbons, Mundy, Parsons, Morley, Giles, Ward, Woodson, Edmund Hooper, Richard Farrant, Shepheard, Adrian Batten, Tye, Robert White, Weelkes, and Bull. The Hereford set, made complete by a duplicate Bassus Decani part from the Sacred Harmonic Society's purchase and a manuscript copy of the tenth part, has been sold to the Christ Church (Oxford) library.

BARTLET (John) : A composer of Ayres, and possibly also a lutenist, of the early seventeenth century. Nothing is known of his life except for the hint,—contained in the dedication of his published work,—that he was in the service of " his singular good Lord and Maister, Sir Edward Seymore " (Seymour). He became a Bachelor of Music at Oxford in 1610. In Mr. C. F. Abdy Williams' *Musical Degrees* the entry referring to this degree is made under the name Thomas Bartlet, clearly a slip of the pen on someone's part. The work by which he is chiefly known was issued in 1606: " *A Booke of Ayres with a Triplicitie of Musicke*. Whereof the First Part is for Lute or Orpharion, and the Viole de Gambo, with four Partes to sing, The Second part is for two Trebles to sing to the Lute and Viole, the third part is for the Lute and one Voyce, and the Viole de Gambo ". The four-part Ayre, " All my Wits ", from this collection was reprinted by Mr. C. K. Scott in *Euterpe* (*Vol.* 11, *No.* 3). This Ayre is also contained in *Add.* 29291, and two more (" When from my love I look't for love " and " Unto a fly transformed ") from the same publication are included in *Add.* 24665, both manuscripts being in the British Museum.

BASSANO FAMILY: Several members of this celebrated family of Italian musicians settled in England, and for about a century (from 1538 onwards) their names figure in the lists of royal musicians. One, Anthony Basson is mentioned in *Ar. Ms.* 97 (1538) as having received 12*d.* a day as instrument-maker, and in 1541 John de Basson appears. *Lans. Ms.* 2 (1547) gives several members of the family as musicians in the royal service (*v. Annalen*), and in the Lord Chamberlain's Records we meet with Agostino, John Baptista, Jasper, John, Mark Anthony, Andrea, Edward, Henry, and Jerome Bassano, in some cases more than one musician bearing the same Christian name. It is often impossible to follow the careers of these musicians, so many were there and so carelessly were their names entered. They performed on a variety of instruments, including among their number lutenists, sackbuttists, players on the recorders, hautboys, flutes, violin, as well as singers. They appear to have been executant artists rather than composers, and very little music by them is to be found in English collections. Four five-part Fancies by Hieronymo (Jerome) Bassano are preserved in the Christ Church (Oxford) library, and the British Museum collections of manuscripts include several compositions by Giovanni Battista. Musicians in Italy at the same period, and bearing the same surname were prolific and popular composers, and these were in all probability related to their namesakes who settled in England. As far as their creative work is concerned, none of the English Bassanos merit inclusion in a book of this kind; but the influence they exercised upon the English performers must have been considerable, inasmuch as they imported Italian methods at a period when we still had much to learn in the domain of instrumental music.

BATCHELAR (Daniel): *see* BACHELOR (Daniel).

BATES (Thomas) : A well-known violist and teacher of that instrument as well as of singing. According to Playford (*Musical Banquet*, 1651), he was one of the eminent London professors during the Commonwealth, but beyond this nothing is known of his early life. He probably served in one of the armies,—most likely in that of the royal party, — since he is occasionally referred to in the State Papers as "Captain" Thomas Bates. At the Restoration he joined the king's musical establishment, and his appointment is entered in the Lord Chamberlain's Records under date January, 1660–1: "Thomas Bates in the place of Alphonso Ferabosco, junior, deceased, which his father Alphonso Ferabosco enjoyed as instructor to his late Majesty when Prince of Wales, 50*l*. per annum, and in the place of Henry Ferabosco, 40*l*. more". From this date until 1683 his name appears very frequently in the State records. In 1662 (September 26th) the usual allowance for livery (16*l*. 2*s*. 6*d*.) was made him, and on October 22nd of the same year he received 12*l*. for a bass-viol "bought by him for his Majesty's service, also the sum of 5*l*. for strings . . ." (*L.C.R.*). On November 12th, 1663, Bates, in common with the rest of the royal musicians, was excused the payment of the subsidies granted to the king by Parliament. On May 23rd, 1664, a Richard Benyon petitioned the Lord Chamberlain to redress some wrong done him by Bates : all parties concerned were summoned before that official, but with what result is not known. In 1670 an attempt was made to clear up the financial muddling of the period, and in a list of musicians to whom four years' livery allowance was owing, we find the name of Thomas Bates (*L.C.R.*). In the same year also we find his name in a petition to the Earl of Sandwich, "Master of his Majesty's great Wardrobe, praying that" the livery due for the previous year be paid. On November 4th, 1671, he is distinctly entered as "Captain Bates, Violl", in a list of musicians receiving payment of their expenses in attending the king at Windsor, at the rate of 8*s*. per day. The great Masque of 1674 employed almost every musician at court, in addition to outside artists,—and among the Bass-Viols we find "Mr. Bates". The entry in the Lord Chamberlain's Records for July 4th, 1676, shows that Bates was something of a speculator, and likewise tells us where he lived : "Assignment by Jeffery Banister . . . in consideration of the sum of

150*l.* paid by Thomas Bates, of the parish of St. Margaret's Weſtminſter, of all wages of 46*l.* 12*s.* 8*d.* per annum due to him to the said Thomas Bates ". How many years' salary was due to Baniſter is not known,—but Bates muſt have possessed the gambler's spirit to have risked 150*l.* in the hopes of collecting the debt from his extravagant Majeſty. The laſt time Thomas Bates's name appears in the Lord Chamberlain's Records is in 1683, and it is not clear whether he retired or died.

Examples of his slight compositions may be seen in Playford's *Musick's Recreation on the Viol, Lyra-way* (1669), where there are three Ayres, three Corants, one Country Dance, two Sarabands, one Almain, and one Jig. In Part II of the 1682 edition there are an Ayre and a Jig signed " T. B." which may also be by him.

BATESON (Thomas) : A musician who muſt be included among the foremoſt half-dozen of the late Elizabethan madrigaliſts. His work is marked by a certain polish and care, and his madrigals are, generally, lighter in ſtyle than the work of the majority of his contemporaries. Beauty and charm are always present in his secular music, and the only known specimen of his sacred music is diſtinguished by dignity and serenity. The occurrence of consecutive fifths, *etc.*, in his madrigals need not be attributed to lack of technical knowledge or of care;—rather the contrary. The Elizabethan madrigaliſts frequently produce ſtartling effects by daring experiments, and it was undoubtedly due to this desire to break with the more academic of the rules of composition that led Bateson deliberately to ignore the breaches of the harmonic canons alluded to.

Of his biography we know very little. Taking into consideration the fact that he was organiſt of Cheſter Cathedral in 1599, we cannot suppose that he was born later than 1575—78, and it is possible that 1570 may not be too early. The dedication of his firſt set of madrigals (1604) to his " moſt respected and good friend ", Sir William Norres, suggeſts that he was ſtill young at the time of publication. In this dedication he calls himself a " practitioner in the Art of Musicke ". The accounts kept by the treasurer of Chester Cathedral mention him several times between 1601 and 1608. In March, 1608–9, he went to Dublin as a vicar-choral in the Cathedral of the Holy Trinity, and in April, 1609, he is given as "vicar-choral and organist". His degree of Bachelor of Music dates from 1615 (Trin. Coll., Dublin). In the second set of madrigals (1618) he calls himself "Master of the Children of the Cathedral Church of the Blessed Trinitie" as well as organist. This book is dedicated to Arthur, Lord Chichester, and in the address to his lordship Bateson uses the words: ". . . to grace me with your Honourable service, and to call me to a more immediate dependency upon your lordship . . ."; which proves that if he was not employed in some way by that peer, he was at least patronized by him. He made his Will on March 2nd, 1629–30, and must have died before the end of that month. The Chester registers mention the baptism of three children,—one son (Thomas) and two daughters; and we know of another son (John). The fullest account of Bateson's Chester activity is

that given by Dr. J. C. Bridge in *Grove* (1912).

Bateson's first published work was *The First Set of English Madrigals to* 3, 4, 5, *and* 6 *voices* (*B.M.* K. 3, h. 3), which appeared in 1604. This set contains the madrigal "When Oriana walkt to take the Ayre" intended for the *Triumphes of Oriana*, but which was delivered too late for inclusion in the first edition of that work. Another "Oriana" madrigal, perhaps intended for use in a later edition of Morley's collection, —*Oriana's Farewell*,—is also printed in Bateson's First Set. His other book was *The Second Set of Madrigals to* 3, 4, 5, *and* 6 *Parts. Apt for Viols and Voyces* (1618, *B.M.* K. 3, g. 7). Modern reprints of his works include the first set of madrigals, edited by Rimbault (*Mus. Ant. Soc.*, 1845–6), and Dr. E. H. Fellowes (*English Madrigal School, Vol. XXI*), the Second Set by Dr. Fellowes (*Id., Vol. XXII*), a madrigal— "Sister awake"—issued by Mr. W. Barclay Squire, and some of the madrigals published by Novello and Co. Hawkins printed the three-part "Your shining eies and golden haire". In the nineteenth century the

Musical Antiquarian Society published the Anthem " Holy, Lord God Almighty" (Bateson's only surviving sacred composition), and Novello and Co. re-issued it under the editorship of Mr. James F. Fitzgerald.

Manuscript music by Bateson may be seen in the British Museum (*Eg.* 995 and *Add.* 31398), while *Add.* 17792–6 contain the anthem " Holie, Lorde God All-mightie ".

BATHE (William) : The writer of two treatises of great historical value. The first was *Brief Introduction to the true art of Musicke* (1584), and the second *A Briefe Introduction to the skill of Song, etc. . . . set forth by William Bathe, Gentleman* (date given in the British Museum catalogue as 1590 queried). He was, as far as can be ascertained, the earliest writer of such treatises in English, and his ideas were very advanced. He gives instructions for the discarding of the Hexachord (*v. Dic. Old Eng. Mus.*), and favours the scale system based upon a series lying between a tonic and its octave. Such an innovation would naturally bring the full use of accidentals in its train. In the address " To the Reader "

which prefaces his second book, Bathe protests strongly against the unnecessary difficulties of the hexachord series, and explains how the latter may be converted into terms of octave-scales.

Under Queen Elizabeth he acted as a diplomatic agent. In 1591 he went abroad, became a Jesuit in the Low Countries, studied in Padua, and took holy orders in that city. In 1604 he became Director of the Irish College in the Portuguese capital, went to Salamanca in 1606, and died at Madrid in 1614.

BATTEN (Adrian) : Organist of St. Paul's Cathedral, London, and composer of ecclesiastical music typical of the early seventeenth century. Although by no means comparable with the work of the greatest of the English church musicians, Batten's music possesses charms of its own. It is serious and somewhat sad, but not altogether devoid of more joyous touches. His artistic sense was perhaps in excess of his technical powers, and his self-restraint makes of his work something very suitable to certain occasions. His counterpoint is skilful, and the atmosphere created by his music is a pure and devotional one. And although Burney may have been right when he condemned Batten for "the errors in accent .with which former times abounded", he was wrong in thus implying that the music of that period was so bound to the bar as was the case later on. The faults in this direction, which become apparent only when the bar-line is inserted, were not nearly so noticeable when the unbarred music was sung by skilful singers. There is one virtue in Batten's sacred music which was possessed by only a few composers; and that is his constant endeavour to think of music as the servant of divine worship and not as the central figure of that service.

Adrian Batten began his connection with church-music as a chorister at Winchester Cathedral, where he enjoyed the instruction of John Holmes. The date of his birth is not to be fixed with certainty: but since John Holmes left that post in 1602 when his chorister pupil would have been about twelve years of age, we may suppose that the latter was born about 1590. He became a vicar-choral of Westminster in 1614, and ten years later

went to St. Paul's Cathedral, where he was also organist. But at the funeral of James I he is still styled "singing-man of Westminster" (*L.C.R.*, 1625). From this date until his death we hear no more of him. Letters of administration for the disposal of his estate were granted to John Gilbert of Salisbury (with the consent of Batten's three brothers) on July 22nd, 1637, and we can thus take it that he died at about the middle of that year,—and all the works of reference (probably influenced by Boyce and Burney) which give later dates for his death must clearly be wrong.

Quite a fair amount of church music by him is available and easily accessible. Barnard (1641) published six Full Anthems *à* 4, and one with verses. Boyce included three Full Anthems (one *à* 5 and two *à* 4) in Vol. II of his collection. "Hear my prayer, O God" was copied into the books of the Chapel Royal in 1676 (*L.C.R.*). Modern reprints include "Hear my prayer" (Curwen ; edited by Professor Granville Bantock), and "Deliver us, O Lord", "Lord, we beseech Thee", "Sing, we

merrily unto God", "Let my complaint come before Thee, O Lord" (Novello ; edited by J. E. West). Clifford gives the words of thirty-four anthems by Batten, and the total number of compositions of this class number over half a hundred. In manuscript there are preserved in Christ Church library (Oxford) a "Morning and Evening Service in the Dorian Mode", a "Long Service" Preces and Psalms (Bass-part only). In a volume of manuscript music in Purcell's handwriting (in the Fitzwilliam Museum, Cambridge) Batten is represented. The British Museum has "Hear my prayer" (*Harl.* 7337; Tudway *MS.*), and work by Batten is contained in the libraries at Ely Cathedral, Peterhouse (Cambridge), and the Music School (Oxford). In his own handwriting there is an organ book which he wrote in 1635 (*v.* HOLMES, John).
BAWDWINE (John) : *see* BALDWIN (John).
BECKET (Philip): A well-known violinist of the later Stuart period, appointed to the king's band at the Restoration. Later, as was common in the royal orchestra, he occupied a second post in the "wind consort", afterwards surrendering this extra work to another. As a writer for his own instrument he is quite advanced for his time, and examples of his "Divisions" may be seen in Playford's *Division Violin* (1685). Twelve "Airs" by him in four parts (Treble only preserved) are in the Christ Church (Oxford) library.
BENET (John): Although absolutely nothing is known of the life of this early musician, he is too important historically to ignore. He founded, with Dunstable, Power, and their other contemporaries, an English school of composers who applied the new art of the period to sacred music. The only speculation that might be allowed us in regard to his biography, is to suggest that he spent most of his active life abroad, since most, if not all, of his work is to be found in foreign manuscripts. A Sanctus and Agnus Dei from *Codex* 37 in the Bologna *Liceo Musicale* were reproduced in *facsimile* (photographically) in H. E. Wooldridge's *Early English Harmony* (1897), signed in the manuscript " Jo. benet de anglia ". The Agnus Dei

is printed in the same historian's volume of the *Oxford History of Music* (II, 162, 3). Manuscripts in Modena (*Bibl. Estense*, VI, H. 15), and from Trent (now in Vienna, 87 and 92), contain further specimens of Benet's art. It is possible that some of the anonymous compositions in the last-named manuscript (signed " Anglicus " or " de Anglia ") may be his also. Similarly the Old Hall manuscript (collection of St. Edmund's, near Ware) might enshrine, among its unnamed works, pieces by Benet (*v.* also BENNET, John).

BENNET (John): One of the greatest of the Elizabethan madrigalists, whose beautiful, though perhaps by some slightly overrated, work ranks with all but the very best produced at that period. Nothing is known of his life. In his *Madrigalls to Foure Voyces* (1599), which he calls his " first works ", he says that Ralph Assheton (Receiver of the Duchy of Lancaster) was " in many ways a principal patron of my good "; and on the strength of this it has been supposed that he was from Lancashire. The evidence is flimsy enough, but we possess none better. He enjoyed a high reputation even among his contemporaries, for Ravenscroft (1614) introduces him in this strain: " Maister Iohn Bennet, a Gentleman admirable for all kinds of composures, either in Art, or Ayre, Simple or Mixed, of what Nature soever . . . he had somewhat more than Art, even some natural instinct or better inspiration, by which, in all his works, the very life of that passion, which the ditty sounded, is so truly expressed, as if he had measured it alone by his own Soul, and invented no other harmony, than his own sensible feeling in that affection did afford him ". None of this eulogy need be altered to-day. His work shows great diversity of style, his characterization is just, and his musical language always truly poetical. The fact that his madrigals continue to afford pleasure at the present-day proves how permanent true art can be even when expressed in an obsolete form.

Besides the book of madrigals already mentioned John Bennet wrote the madrigal " All creatures now are merry minded " for the *Triumphes of Oriana* (1601), five hymn-tunes for Barley's Psalter, and five vocal pieces for Ravenscroft's *Brief Discourse* (1614). The Musical Antiquarian Society reprinted the 1599 publication in 1845 (under the editorship of E. J. Hopkins), and three of the hymns from Barley's issue were used again by Ravenscroft in 1621. Isolated vocal pieces appeared from time to time in the eighteenth and nineteenth centuries (the *Oriana* madrigal in several editions), Mr. W. Barclay Squire giving a very full list in the 1912 edition of *Grove*. Volume XXIII of the *English Madrigal School* (Dr. E. H. Fellowes) contains the latest reprint of the madrigals of 1599, the *Oriana* madrigal and two four-part songs from Ravenscroft's *Brief Discourse*.

In manuscript there are a fine Anthem, " O God of Gods and King of Kings " (*Add.* 29372, *etc.*, Myriell's *Tristitiae Remedium*, 1616), and " Venus' Birds " (a five-part instrumental arrangement in *Add.* 17786, *etc.*), in the British Museum. The libraries of Christ Church, Oxford, has " O God of Gods " (wanting the bass part), the *Oriana* madrigal (without the words), " Venus' Birds " for a treble solo with

bass, and " Ye restless Thoughts " (two treble parts only; from the 1599 collection). Further examples of Bennet's work in manuscript may be seen at the Fitzwilliam Museum and Peterhouse (Cambridge).

Care must be taken that John Bennet the madrigalist be not confused with the John Bennet, or Benet (*q.v.*), of the fifteenth century.

BERKENSHAW (John): *see* BIRCHENSHA (John).

BEVIN (Elway): Organist of Bristol Cathedral from 1589 to 1637 (Anthony Wood), and a Gentleman Extraordinary of the Chapel Royal. It is supposed that he was relieved of both posts in 1637, when it came to light that he adhered to the orthodox faith. Wood derived his information from the Bristol Chapter books, which were destroyed in the riots of 1831. Thus the only means of verifying these statements are lost. But there should be no reason for doubting that Bevin, — though by descent probably a Welshman,—was connected with Bristol, for his book of 1631 is dedicated to the Bishop of Gloucester to whom he had been " much bound for many favours ", and

E

heralded by some verses by a Bristol gentleman, Thomas Palmer. The Cheque-Book of the Chapel Royal contains no mention of his expulsion from that institution for the reason advanced by Wood or for any other. Legend fostered by the gossip of Oxford has made Bevin a pupil of Tallis. His swearing-in as a Gentleman Extra-ordinary of the Chapel Royal dates from June 3rd, 1605, but there is no reason for supposing that he ever acted in any capacity in the Royal Chapels. In the visitation of Laud to Bristol, the organist there is given as a " verie old man " in 1634 (Davey).

Bevin's first important work was his " *Briefe and Short Instruction of the Art of Musicke*, to teach how to make Discant, of all pro-portions that are in use: very necessary for all such as are desirous to attaine to knowledge in the Art; . . . And also to compose all sorts of Canons that are usuall, by these directions of two or three parts in one, upon the Plain-Song " (1631). This work is chiefly of use as a treatise on the Canon, to which he was extremely partial, and which was a form of composition

then very much in fashion. The manuscript written by John Baldwin (the property of the King; now in *B.M.*) contains some examples of his work in this form. A Service of his is contained in Barnard's collection, and also printed by Boyce (in score). An arrangement of this service is to be found in Benjamin Cosyn's Virginal Book (Royal Collection; now *B.M.*). The Christ Church library (Oxford) possesses an incomplete three-part com-position of Bevin's called *Browninge*, and he is also represented among the " In Nomines " of the Oxford Music School. Several manu-scripts in the British Museum contain work by this com-poser, including one in twenty parts — " Hark, Jolly Shep-herds ". *Add.* 31403 con-tains Bevin's explanation of some of the ornaments then in use.

BIRCHENSHA (John): A teacher of composition and writer on music as a science of numbers. Some of his theories are rather far-fetched and none of his works achieved lasting success. He is remembered chiefly as the writer of the Preface to Thomas Salmon's *Essay*, some treatises on music, and as the teacher of Samuel Pepys. From the fact that he is first to be met with in Dublin (in the service of the Earl of Kildare), most authorities suppose him to have been an Irishman ; but he is more probably to be connected with a Welsh family. We find him active in London during the Commonwealth as a teacher " for the Voyce or Viol " (Playford *Musical Banquet*), and as an instructor in the art of composition we see him engaged by Pepys. On January 13th, 1661–2, the diarist entered : " All the morning at home, with Mr. Berkenshaw (whom I have not seen a great while, came to see me), who staid with me a great while talking of musique, and I am resolved to begin to learn of him to compose, and to begin to-morrow, he giving me so great hopes that I shall soon do it . . ." The following day he wrote that he had commenced lessons. On the 15th he had another lesson. The tuition of " Mr. Berkenshaw " must have produced rapid results, for on February 24th Pepys said: " Long with Mr. Berkenshaw in the morning at my musique practice, finishing my song of ' Gaze not on swans ', in

two parts, which pleases me well, and I did give him 5*l*. for this month or five weeks that he hath taught me, which is a great deal of money, and troubled me to part with it ". Pepys also mentions Birchensha's " Great card of the body of musique which he cries up for a rare thing, and I do believe it cost much pains but is not so useful as he would have it ". This was probably Birchensha's single-sheet of the rules of composition. On February 26th Birchensha was with him " all the morning composing of musique to ' This cursed jealousy, what is it ', a song of Sir W. Davenant's ". But on February 27th the pair parted company on bad terms: " This morning came Mr. Berkenshaw to me and in our discourse, I, finding that he cries up his rules for most perfect (though I do grant them to be very good, and the best I believe that ever yet were made), and that I could not persuade him to grant wherein they were somewhat lame, we fell to angry words, so that in a pet he flung out of my chamber, and I never stopped him, having intended to put him off to-day, whether this had happened or no, because I think I have all the rules that he hath to give " ; which was quite in keeping with the cunning diarist's character. Nevertheless, on October 15th, 1665, he confesses that he " tried to compose a duo of counterpoint, and I think it will do very well, it being by Mr. Berkenshaw's rule ". John Evelyn thought very highly of Birchensha's executive talents, for on August 3rd, 1664, he wrote: " . . . a concert of excellent musicians, especially one Mr. Berkenshaw, that rare artist, who invented a mathematical way of composure very extraordinary, true as to the exact rules of art, but without much harmony ".

In 1664 Birchensha issued a translation of Alstedius's *Templum Musicum* of which Pepys said : " I took Berkenshaw's translation of Alsted his *Templum* but the most ridiculous book as he has translated it, that ever I saw in my life. I declare that I understand not three lines together from one end of the book to the other." In 1672 Birchensha published Salmon's *Essay to the Advancement of Musick* which gave rise to much controversy, and to which he supplied a

Preface. In it he said that the existing system of notation was difficult to understand because it was composed of a " confused chaos of impertinent characters with insignificant signs ". But by Salmon's " happy contrivance, the Cliffs, which were many, are reduced into an Universal character, the various shifting of notes in a systeme, or staff of lines are fixed : the necessity of their Transpositions taken away; so that he that can sing or play any one part, may sing and play all parts; and he that shall know his distances in any one part, may know them in all Parts. . . . This I was willing to premise, lest the out-crys of some shall prepossess the Reader with a Practical impossibility notwithstanding the Proposal is most evident and plain " (*v.* also SALMON, Thomas).

The British Museum possesses a few manuscripts concerning theoretical treatises by Birchensha (*Add.* 4388, 4921, and 4910), some examples of his music are present in the Oxford Music School library, and a few violin pieces are in the Christ Church collection. The Pepysian library contains some of Birchensha's music which Pepys was very proud to possess (*v. Diary*, March 14th, 1661–2). The dates of his birth and death are unknown. Mr. W. Barclay Squire (*Dic. of Nat. Biog.*) mentions a J. Birchensha who was buried in the cloisters of Westminster Abbey on May 14th, 1681, but it is not certain whether he can be identified with the musician under consideration. The spelling of his name adopted throughout this article (except in the Pepysian quotations) is the one he used himself in the signature to the Preface of 1672.

BIRD (Thomas): *see* BYRD (Thomas).

BIRD (William): *see* BYRD (William).

BISHOP (John): Organist and composer of sacred music, born in 1665. At the age of 22 we meet with him as a lay-clerk at King's College, Cambridge, and in 1688 he became choir-trainer there. His appointment as organist at Winchester College dates from 1695, and at the Cathedral he succeeded Vaughan Richardson in the organ-loft in 1729. He died on December 19th, 1737, and was buried at Winchester in the cloisters of the college, where his epitaph informs the reader that he was a man of singular piety and irreproachable morals, and that he had served the college for forty-two years. Hawkins' information relating to this musician is not reliable. A " Morning and Evening Service " in D, by John Bishop, is preserved in the Christ Church library (Oxford), while further examples of his work may be seen in the manuscript collections at the British Museum (*Add.* 17841, *Harl.* 7341, *etc.*), and the Royal College of Music. *Harmonia Wiccamica* (Philip Hayes) contains further compositions by Bishop, notably some music set to Latin words, and some few anthems of his have been printed.

BLAGRAVE (Richard): A celebrated performer on the instruments of the hautboy family (*v. Dic. Old Engl. Mus.*) who flourished in the first half of the seventeenth century. The earliest reference to him is to be found in the Lord Chamberlain's Records, where he is entered in 1625 as a musician for the wind instruments attending the funeral of James I. On July 15th, 1628, he is stated to have been a player upon the "hoboies and sackbuts" (*L.C.R.*, *Vol.* 738). From an entry dated December, 1633, we learn that he performed on the wind instruments in the Chapel also. By 1638 he appears to have needed a deputy to share his work,— either through infirmity or because it was thought politic to train young students to replace the older men as the latter fell out of the royal service. On October 17th of that year we read that a warrant was issued to swear in Thomas Blagrave (*q.v.*) as assistant to his father Richard. Blagrave, senior, died in 1641, his son succeeding him in his posts (1641–2; *L.C.R.*, *Vol.* 740). Richard was the son of Anthony Blagrave of Norwich (*L.C.R.*, Will of John Godwin, *Vol.* 196).

BLAGRAVE (Robert): A performer on the violin and the instruments of the hautboy family, and possibly related to Richard and Thomas Blagrave. Since he is not to be met with before the Restoration, it may be supposed that he was another son of Richard (and brother of Thomas). In 1660 we find him as a player on the wind instruments in the private music of the king (*L.C.R.*, *Vol.* 482), appearing in the same list with Thomas Blagrave. In the royal service he occupied the position held by Anthony Bassano before the Commonwealth. On July 2nd, 1660, he is entered as "musician in ordinary", receiving 58*l.* 14*s.* 2*d.* as salary. The last entry relating to him is contained in an Exchequer document once in the possession of Dr. Rimbault, and dated 1674. Beyond this nothing is known of his life.

BLAGRAVE (Thomas): A well-known Stuart musician and member of the king's band and of the Chapel Royal. He is already mentioned in the Lord Chamberlain's Records on December 22nd, 1637, and on October 17th of the following year was appointed "a musician to his Majesty for the Sagbutts and hautboyes who is also to attend as assistant to his father Richard Blagrave, to come in ordinary in the same place upon vacancy thereof" (*L.C.R.*, *Vol.* 739). In February, 1641, we read in the same records: "Thomas his (Richard's) son, in reversion, now admitted". On January 17th, 1641–2, his wages were fixed at 1*s*. 8*d*. per day plus the usual livery allowance of 16*l*. 2*s*. 6*d*. a year. During the interregnum he married Margaret Clarevell (otherwise Clairvox) at St. Margaret's, Westminster. At the Restoration he is entered among the musicians " that do service in the Chappell Royall " (*L.C.R.*, *Vol.* 482) in the company of such men as Thomas Purcell, Dr. Wilson, Dr. Christopher Gibbons, Dr. Child, and Pelham Humfrey. In the same year (1660) he is given as one of the musicians for the wind instruments. On June 16th he was appointed to a second place, to serve among the violins. On September 30th, 1661, he was given extra pay for playing the violin at Windsor. In the following year (November 8th) he was sworn in as Clerk of the Cheque of the Chapel Royal, " voyd by the death of Mr. Henry Lawes " (*Ch. Bk. C. R.*). In 1665 he was appointed to John Banister's band of select violins (*L.C.R.*, *Vol.* 479). In 1668–9 his salary amounted to 40*l*. 9*s*. 2*d*. per annum, but in another entry of 1668 and 1669 there is mentioned the salary of 46*l*. 10*s*. 10*d*. with the note

that he played among the violins although his patent was for the flutes. In this way many entries could be quoted from, but they vary very little. In 1688 he died: " Thomas Blagrave Clerk of the Check departed this life the 21 day of November, 1688 . . ." (*Ch. Bk. C. R.*), being buried in the cloisters of Westminster Abbey three days later. His will is dated May 14th, 1686. He appears to have been in high repute as a good musician, and Pepys mentions him more than once. Short pieces by him are to be seen in many of the contemporary publications.

BLANCKS (Edward) : A composer of sacred music who flourished in the latter part of the Elizabethan era, being enumerated by Francis Meres among the great Englishmen mentioned in *Palladis Tamia* (1598). Absolutely nothing is known of his biography. Work by him may be seen in Thomas East's *Whole Booke of Psalmes* (1592), and in its typographically inferior successor published by William Barley. A couple of compositions by Blancks are contained in *Add.* 31390 (*B.M.*) and in the Peterhouse (Cambridge) collection there is a Service by " Blanke ".

BLANKE: see BLANCKS (Edward).

BLITHEMAN (William): A sixteenth-century composer who is far more interesting and important from the historical point of view than from any other. Being distinguished as a writer of music for the keyboard instruments that abounds in great technical difficulties and tricks of digital dexterity, he is an exception in an age at which most composers devoted themselves almost exclusively to ecclesiastical music. In his compositions for the Virginal he shows how far his pupil John Bull was influenced by his teachings, and remembering the high position occupied by England in the history of keyboard music, we shall be compelled to accord William Blitheman one of the foremost places among the men who foresaw the possibilities of this class of music. It needed only the mechanical improvement of the instruments in question fully to develop the ideas formulated by Blitheman. Like his pupil, he was also an able executant on the organ; and Francis Meres, only seven years after Blithe-

man's death, names him as one of the great musicians of his age (*Palladis Tamia*). It is a pity that Rimbault should have selected the uninteresting arrangement of a *Gloria tibi* as representative of Blitheman's work (*History of the Pianoforte*, 1860).

The earliest reference to the name is that made by Bishop Tanner, who mentions a John Blitheman as a member of the Christ Church choir or master of the choristers there. But whether this John Blitheman was the father, brother, or other relative of William Blitheman,—or the latter himself (through an error in the Christian name), —cannot be decided to-day with the materials at hand. Wood says that William was organist of Queen Elizabeth's chapel, and he certainly was in the Chapel Royal when he died " much lamented " in 1591. He was awarded the degree of Mus. Bac. at Cambridge in 1586. The only other biographical detail known of him is the date of his death, which occurred on Whit-Sunday in the year given by Wood. He was interred at St. Nicholas Olave, Queenhithe, where an epitaph was engraved on a plate " in the north wall of the chancel "

(Stow, *Survey Book*). This epitaph was very quaint and read as follows :—
" Here Blytheman lies, a worthy wight
Who feared God above;
A friend to all a Foe to none,
Whom Rich and Poore did love.
Of Princes Chappell, Gentleman,
Unto his dying day;
Whom all took great delight to heare
Him on the Organs play.
Whose passing Skill in Musick's Art,
A Scholar left behind;
John Bull (by name) his Master's veine,
Expressing in each kinde.
But nothing here continues long,
Nor resting Place can have;
His Soule departed hence to Heaven,
His Body here in Grave."
The appointment of his successor was entered in the Cheque-Book of the Chapel Royal: " 1591. Jo. Hewlett sworne the 23rd of Maye in Mr. Blitheman's place . . ."
Examples of Blitheman's composition may be seen in manuscripts preserved in the British Museum: *Add.* 17802–5 (Motets), 31403, 29384, 30513 (the Virginal Book of Thomas Mulliner),

30485 (*ff. 58b.* and 59, " In Nomine "); and in the Fitzwilliam Virginal Book (Cambridge). The " In Nomine " included in the Fitzwilliam manuscript may be seen in the Breitkopf and Haertel reprint; it is constructed on the same plain-song as is used in *Add.* 31403 and 30485. Hawkins (*History*) prints an organ piece.

BLOW (John): Organist, Master of the Children of the Chapel Royal, and voluminous composer of sacred and secular music, flourishing in the second half of the seventeenth century. Eliminating his pupil Henry Purcell, John Blow is certainly the most considerable musician of the period, and he has left a large quantity of music marked by real nobility, depth of feeling and sincerity. Indeed, his feeling was greater than his technical skill,—though the shortcomings in his work belong rather to the age in which he wrote than to the individual. Purcell had the greatest possible admiration for his master, both as man and as musician, and said (in his treatise on composition in Playford's *Introduction*) that Blow's " character is sufficiently known by his

Works, of which this very Instance (a Canon) is enough to recommend him as one of the Greatest Masters in the World ". But, curiously enough, he was more esteemed by his contemporaries as an executant organist than as a composer. As far as concerns Burney's opinion of Blow's harmonic shortcomings,—" crudities " inseparable from the transitional period, — it is sufficient to say that most of the faults exposed by the eighteenth-century historian have become part and parcel of our modern system, and that far from being a condemnation of Blow's work, this censure is really a confession of his advanced ideas. In his attempt to avoid the stereotyped conventionalities of the age, he showed the experimenting spirit of the Elizabethan madrigalists, although his methods were so different. Like all the men who were as boys in Captain Cooke's Chapel, he showed distinct dramatic power, and his Masque of *Venus and Adonis* stands to his credit as an exceedingly interesting piece of work. In addition to this varied work he also wrote some harpsichord music of great value. Taken all in

all, John Blow remains one of the most important figures in the history of English music at the end of the seventeenth century, and there can be little doubt that he prepared the way for the greater genius of his pupil Purcell.

The date of Blow's birth is not to be fixed with absolute certainty; but all the most recent research seems to prove that the son of a certain Henry Blow, baptized at Newark on February 23rd, 1648–9, was the composer. Tradition says that he was born at North Collingham (Notts.), but there is no confirmation forthcoming (*v.* also *Athenaeum* for December 7th, 1901, and the late Dr. W. H. Cummings' paper read before the *Mus. Assoc.* on March 16th, 1909, printed in the *Proceedings*). Wood says that " Dr. Rogers tells me that John Blow was borne in London "—but like many of his remarks, this is also probably only based on hearsay. We find no dated information regarding Blow until 1660, when he was a member of the first Chapel organized by Captain Cooke at the Restoration. He was a precocious boy, and while still a chorister he composed anthems (*v.*

PELHAM HUMFREY). He is said to have received in- struction from John Hingston and Christopher Gibbons. The former could easily have been his teacher, but the latter could not have had anything to do with Blow until after the Restoration. Anthems were certainly written by Blow before he was fourteen years of age, as Clifford's *Divine Services and Anthems* (1663) contains the words of three com- positions by him,—" I will magnifie ", " Lord, Thou hast been our refuge ", and " Lord, rebuke me not ". In 1665 (May 17th) Henry Cooke received 30*l.* yearly " for the maintenance of John Blow. . . late child of his Majesty's Chappell . . . whose voice is changed and is to go from his Majesty's Chappell " (*L.C.R.*) ; but he must have been employed in some other capacity, for in 1668–9 he is in a list of musicians headed, " Private Musick for lutes and voyces, theorboes and virginalls " (*L.C.R., Vol.* 478). On January 15th of the same year the records contain notice of the " Appointment of John Blow in place of Giles Tompkins, as one of his Majesty's musicians for the virginalls " (with a salary of 40*l.* per annum). He was only 20 years of age when he became organist of Westminster Abbey in 1668. He was appointed by warrant to be Master of the Children of the Chapel Royal and com- poser in the king's " Private Musick for voyces in ordinary, in the place of Pelham Humphreyes ", on July 23rd, 1674 (*L.C.R.*), having been sworn in as a Gentleman of the Chapel on March 16th, 1673–4 (*C.B.C.R.*) in the place of Roger Hill). In 1674, too, he witnessed the Will of his friend Pelham Humfrey. This was altogether an event- ful year in Blow's life, for in it he married Elizabeth, the daughter of Edward Brad- dock, a Gentleman of the Chapel Royal. In 1675 a warrant fixed Blow's salary as Master at 40*l.* per annum, in addition to 24*l.* a year for " keeping and instructing " each of two boys " for his Majesty's Private Musick ". In 1676 the organistship of the Chapel was added to that of the Abbey, and Blow must by then have been a very busy man. Not only had he to see that the boys were taught singing, lute and viol- playing, *etc.*, but was expected to accept responsibility for their care in illness. On December 5th, for example, he was paid a large sum for various purposes, including something "for the cure of a broaken legg of one of the Children" (*L.C.R.*). On December 10th, 1677, he was honoured with the Degree of Doctor of Music by the Archbishop of Canterbury, the actual conferring of the degree proceeding from the Dean, with the note "Sede vacante" (*Lambeth Registers*). The entry in the Lord Chamberlain's Records for March 8th, 1678–9 is worth quoting, because it gives a very good idea of the duties of a master of the choristers at the Chapel Royal in those days. The entry refers to the payment of 124*l*. made up as follows: "For the Children learning on the lute, 30*l*.; For those learning on the violin, 30*l*.; For those learning on the theorbo, 30*l*.; For fire and strings in the musick room in the Chappell, 20*l*.; For ruled paper, penns, and inke, 2*l*. 10*s*.; For strings for the lutes and theorboes, 5*l*. 10*s*.; For eight days going to Salisbury and bringing a boy from thence, 5*l*. 10*s*." (*Vol.* 747). He was probably quite busy enough at this period of his career to relinquish one of his posts without reluctance; and in 1680 Henry Purcell took his master's place in the organloft of the Abbey. For the famous competition at the Temple Church between the rival organ-builders, Father Smith and Harris, the former retained the services of Blow and Purcell for the purpose of exhibiting the virtues of his instrument. Although pitted against so redoubtable an organist as Harris's player,—Giovanni Baptista Dragi,—Blow and Purcell secured the victory for Smith's organ. On September 10th, 1685, a certificate appointing Blow to the service of King James II was issued, and he continued as before under the new ruler, with the difference that much of the arrears of pay and of livery allowance was paid (*cf.* WILLIAM CHILD). The Lord Chamberlain's Records for 1686, for example, contain an order for the payment of arrears of 193*l*. 10*s*. to Blow, out of the new imposition on tobacco and sugar, and another on September 21st, 1686, for 230*l*. to be paid from the same source. In

1687 he became Master of the Choristers at St. Paul's Cathedral, as well as almoner, holding these posts until 1693 when he gave them over to another of his pupils, Jeremiah Clarke. On the death of Henry Purcell in 1695, Blow resumed his work at the Westminster organ, and on November 30th, of that year was appointed, together with " Mr. Bernard Smith, as tuners of the regalls, organs, virginalls, flutes, and recorders, and all other kind of wind instruments in ordinary to his Majesty in the place of Mr. Henry Purcell, deceased. The place between them and the survivor to enjoy the whole place " (*L.C.R.*). In 1689 he had already been appointed as " Composer in the private musick", and ten years later he became composer to the Chapel Royal with the salary of 40*l.*, later increased to 73*l.* The authority for the latter appointment is the Cheque-Book of the Chapel Royal: " 1699. Upon a new establishment of a composer's place for the Chapel Royal, Dr. John Blow was admitted into it by a warrant from the R. R. the Dean ". Near the end of James the Second's

reign, a hasty remark of Blow's was like to have cost him his post. The story runs that the king having heard an Italian anthem in the Chapel, asked Blow if he could equal it. His reply was the performance, on the following Sunday of his " I beheld and lo ! " At its conclusion Father Petre was charged by the king to convey his expressions of approval to the composer. This self-satisfied prelate added as his own finding that the work was too long ; whereupon Blow hastily replied that " that is the opinion of one fool,—I heed it not ". The father rendered angrier by this than his cloth should have permitted, appears to have used all his influence with the king to bring about Blow's dismissal. The Revolution, following closely upon this affair, saved the composer's place. The story is given on the authority of Blow's pupil Samuel Weeley, a Vicar-Choral at St. Paul's Cathedral. The death of John Blow is entered in the Cheque-Book as follows : " 1708. Dr. John Blow, Organist, Composer, and Master of the Children, dyed the first of October, 1708, and had his full pay for both places to Christ-mas ". He was buried on the seventh of the month in Westminster Abbey. He made his will on January 3rd, 1707, and from his bequests we gather that he was rather wealthy. He left eight houses in London to his three daughters, besides a good deal of money; his servant Elizabeth Luddington receiving 110*l.* His wife died at the birth of his last child in 1683 (October 29th), and by her he had five children: Henry (who was buried on September 1st, 1676), John (died 1693 at the age of fifteen), Elizabeth (died 1719), Katherine (died 1730), and Mary (died 1738). Blow was buried near the old entrance to the organ-loft in the Abbey, not far from Purcell's grave. A contemporary engraving of him is prefixed to the *Amphion Anglicus*; another portrait was in the possession of the late Dr. W. H. Cummings; and a half-length painting belongs to Mr. Algernon Ashton.

A good deal of Blow's music was written for special occasions. While a chorister he shared the writing of the " Club-Anthem " with Pelham Humfrey and William Turner, all three being boys together in the choir. It was not written to celebrate a naval victory over the Dutch, as Tudway says, because Humfrey left the Chapel a year before that event. There can be little doubt that the composition owes its origin to the friend-ship of the three boys. A similar anthem was written jointly by Blow, Clarke, and Croft to celebrate the union with Scotland (" Behold, how good and joyful "). To his chorister-days belongs also " Goe, perjur'd man " (words by Herrick), written at the request of Charles II in imitation of a composition by Carissimi. In 1681 he wrote the ode " Great Sir, ye joy of all our hearts " (for New Year's Day); in 1684 he composed the second of the St. Cecilia odes; for the coronation of James II he wrote two anthems, and in memoriam for Purcell he set Dryden's words " Mark how the lark and linnet sing ". For the re-opening of St. Paul's Cathedral in 1697 he set " I was glad when they said " (October 15th), and the Treaty of Ryswick being signed in the same year, he wrote " Praise the Lord, O my soul ", in thanksgiving for the peace. In addition to these he wrote over a hundred anthems, fourteen services, the masque "Venus and Adonis", besides shorter songs and harpsichord music. "Venus and Adonis", produced at Court between 1680 and 1687, is in three acts and a prologue, and contains some very interesting work. The part of Venus was played by Mary Davis, a favourite of Charles II, and that of Cupid was sung by the daughter of that royal mistress,—Lady Mary Tudor. The original manuscript is in the Chapter Library of Westminster where the late Sir Frederick Bridge found it. Copies are in manuscripts in the British Museum and in the library of Christ Church, Oxford. It has been printed by Mr. G. E. P. Arkwright as No. XXV of the *Old English Edition*. In 1700 Blow published *Amphion Anglicus*, a collection of secular vocal music, from which Mr. Arkwright has issued six songs as No. XXIII of the same series (Jos. Williams). "The self-banished", from the same work was reprinted by Rimbault in his series *Ancient Vocal Music of England* (No. 9). Several contemporary publications contained pieces by Blow. Examples of his songs are to be seen in the *Theater of Music* which he edited in collaboration with Henry Purcell (Books I-III, 1685; Book IV, 1687). *Harmonia Sacra* (1688) contains eight compositions by Blow, a "Penetential Hymn" is included in the second book of the same (1693), and the second edition of Book II (1714) has an anthem not included in the first edition. Short pieces are also to be seen in *Musick's Hand-Maid* (*Pt. II*, 1689). Playford published "Bartholomew Fair, a Catch" and "The Perfection, a new Song to the Dutchess" (of Grafton), in 1685, and Thomas Cross issued "Thou Flask once fill'd with glorious red" (sung by Mr. Leveridge), besides two more songs for the stage. In 1698 appeared his *Choice Lessons for the Harpsichord*, a collection to which Henry Purcell also contributed. A tremendous amount of Blow's music remains in manuscript, and may be seen in the British Museum, Christ Church library, and the Music School, Oxford, the Fitzwilliam Museum, Cambridge (ten anthems in a volume copied by Purcell), and in the Royal College of Music. In 1676 nine of his anthems were copied into the books of the Chapel Royal, besides two services (in A and G), his " Benedicite ", and his " Te Deum to the Benedicite " (*L.C.R.*). About a dozen of his anthems have been published by Novello and Co. A complete list of Blow's printed and manuscript works is impossible in a work of this magnitude without doing injustice to others.

BLYTHEMAN (William): *see* BLITHEMAN(William).

BOWER (Richard): Master of the Children of the Chapel Royal under four Tudor sovereigns. According to the inscription on his tomb- stone, he was master during the reign of Henry VIII, having been appointed in succession to William Crane (*q.v.*). Rymer's *Foedera* (XV, 517) gives his salary as 40*l.* per annum (probably Marks). The list of Gentle- men of the Chapel receiving livery for the coronation of Edward VI (*L. C. R.* February 20th, 1546–7) in- cludes the name of Richard Bower, and the Household Book of that prince contains the entry " To Richard Bower, for playing before the King's Majestie with the Children of the Chappell, in rewarde VI. *li.* xiij*s.* iiij*d.*", showing that like Crane and Cornyshe he added the super- vision of the Court entertain- ments to his duties in the Chapel. The sum mentioned was the usual " reward " for such service. The practice was then in vogue of " pressing " into the Chapel any boys with suitable voices, and in 1552 Bower received a warrant to commandeer children as necessity arose " to supply vacancies as they might occur ". The plight of these children was not a very terrible one; they were clothed, fed, and otherwise well cared for, and their education, both while in the Chapel and after their voices broke, was at the charge of the sovereign. In 1557 Mary Tudor granted Bower and Tallis a lease for twenty-one years of a manor in Thanet, out of the proceeds of which the two musicians augmented their incomes. More than this has not been discovered concerning Bower. He died in 1563 (*C.B.C.R.*) and was buried in old Greenwich Church.

BOWMAN (Henry): Both Henry Davey and the *Dictionary of National*

Biography mention Bowman as organist of Trinity College, Cambridge, but Mr. West's *Cathedral Organists* does not include his name in this connection. All that is known of him is that he published a small volume of *Songs for one, two, and three Voyces to the Thorow-Bass*, etc., at Oxford in 1677 (second edition two years later); but the title-page describes him merely as " Philo-Musicus " and makes no allusion to his having occupied any official post. The Oxford Music School library has a few songs of his and " 15 Ayres first performed in the Schooles 5th February, 1673–4 ". In the library of Christ Church (Oxford) there are a " Miserere mei Deus " in score (*MS.*) and a manuscript copy of one of the three part-songs from the published book of songs. He is represented in the British Museum MSS. *Add.* 30382 (autograph motets, the " Miserere " for two trebles and bass, an anthem, and songs), *Add.* 33234 (a copy of the same MS.), and *Add.* 35043. A John Bowman was appointed as " musician in ordinary to the king for the private musick " on Novem-

ber 26th, 1684, and it was this musician who was probably appointed organist of Trinity College, Cambridge, in 1709.

BOWMAN (John):   *see* BOWMAN (Henry).

BOWYER (Richard):   *see* BOWER (Richard).

BRADE (William): A celebrated violist who was active at the end of the sixteenth century and the beginning of the seventeenth. His influence upon English music could have been only very slight, for he passed most of his musical life abroad. He was born in England in 1560 (Riemann, Edition 1922), and his first appointment appears to have been at the court of Christian IV of Denmark, from 1594 to 1596; dates provided by the dedications prefixed to his works. Before 1594 and after 1596 he was in the employ of the Markgraf of Brandenburg. In 1599 he returned to Copenhagen and remained there until 1606. Concerning the years 1606–9 we have no information, but from the latter year until 1614 he was superintendent of the municipal music of Hamburg (*v.* dedication to the publication of that year, dated August 19th). In

F

1614 he moved to the court of Holstein (Schleswig). In 1618 he was in Halle-on-the-Saale, but could not have remained long, for in 1619-20 he was again in Brandenburg. His final appointment at the court of Berlin was that of chapel-master, and he appears to have been treated as a musician enjoying a great reputation. His salary was five hundred thalers a year with board-wages, and wine in addition, all his expenses paid, and two " liveries of honour ". In 1620 he returned to Denmark and in 1622 he was still living there. In that year, however, he renewed acquaintance with the Hamburg municipality, and died in that city on February 26th, 1630.

His chief publications were *Musicalische Concerten* (Hamburg, 1609, in five parts); *Neue Ausserlesene Paduanen, Galliarden, etc.* (*Ib.* 1609), another book of a similar nature for six instruments (*Ib.* 1614), *Newe Ausserlesene liebliche Branden, Intraden, etc.* (Lübeck, 1617, five parts), *Newe lustige Volten, Couranten, etc.* (Berlin, 1621, five parts). Some dance forms by him are included in the collections of Füllsack

and Hildebrand (1607–9). Authorities are much at variance concerning Brade's published works, and a considerable amount of uncertainty exists in the matter of dates, etc. Perhaps Möller's *Cimbria Literata* (1744) is the most trustworthy source of bibliographical knowledge in the case of Brade (*v.* L. Schneider, *Geschichte der Churfürstlich - Brandenburgischen und Kgl. Preussischen Capelle*).

BRAMSTON (Richard): An organist of Wells Cathedral who flourished in the early part of the sixteenth century. He commenced his musical career in that Cathedral as a chorister, and on July 23rd, 1507, he was admitted as a Vicar-Choral on probation (Wells, *Chapter Acts*). He evidently gave satisfaction, for on January 25th, 1508, he was appointed permanently. At the same date he took some of the work off the hands of the organist, Hygons: " Master Hygons, with the consent of the Chapter, promised to pay Richard Bramston, Vicar Choral, 40s. per annum to teach Choristers to sing well and faithfully as Richard Hygons had done in times paſt, and that Richard Bramſton would take care of and play at the Organs in the Great Choir and also in the Lady Chapel " (*Chapter Aɛs*). He served as organiſt in Hygon's place until May, when he resigned. He appears then to have ſtudied with the objeɛ of taking holy orders, the Chapter inſiſting that he should become a sub-deacon. The great hiatus that occurs in the Chapter Aɛs between the beginning of the second decade of the century until 1534 prevents us from following Bramſton closely. He appears in a document of 1531, when he was granted leave of absence " from Matins during his lifetime ". He was also a full Maſter of the Choriſters by that date, since he received an annuity of 4*l.* on his surrender of that poſt. While he held it his salary had been 26*s.* 8*d.* per annum. His signature appears appended to the latter documents as " Ryc. Bramſton " (*Chapter MSS., Wells, Vol.* II).

A motet of his, " Recordare, Domine, teſtamenti ", is preserved in *Add.* 17802–5 (*B.M.*), and he is represented by another motet in the Peterhouse (Cambridge) Part-Books.

BREWER (Thomas): A famous violiſt who flourished in the seventeenth century, and who wrote a good deal of music of a popular type. Born in 1611 he was placed in Chriſt's Hospital at the age of three and received all his education there. He was taught the viol by a teacher in the Hospital, and left that inſtitution in 1626. Next to nothing further is known of his life. That he was of a jovial disposition may be gathered from the ſtory told of him in Sir Nicholas L'Eſtrange's *Merry Passages and Jeſts* (*Harl.* 6395; *B.M.*), where we read: " Thom: Brewer, my musical servant, through his Proneness to good fellowship, having attained to a very rich and rubicund nose; being reproved by a friend for his too frequent use of ſtrong drinks and sack; as very pernicious to that diſtemper and inflammation of his nose. Nay, faith, says he, if it will not endure sack, it's no nose for me ". John Jenkins was sponsor for this anecdote. It is not known when Brewer died.

Music by him is included in Hilton's *Catch that Catch*

Can (1658) and the *Musical Companion* (1672); also in Playford's *Select Musical Ayres and Dialogues* (1653 and 1659). A large number of British Museum manuscripts contain vocal compositions of his (*Add.* 10337, *Add.* 11608, *Add.* 29382–5, *Add.* 29386, *Add.* 31462, *Add.* 31811, *Add.* 31813), and *Add.* 31423 (in the hand of John Jenkins) has a trio for three viols by Brewer. A few of his catches and glees were reprinted during the eighteenth century, " Turn Amaryllis " being a great favourite. According to Rimbault he composed music to Shirley's *Love's Tricks* (1631). Messrs. Novello re-issued " Turn Amaryllis " in Tonic Sol-fa (1851). The only evidence of Brewer having written any ecclesiastical music is provided in Clifford's *Divine Services and Anthems, etc.*, where the words only of a " Psalm of Thanksgiving " are printed.

BRIAN (Albertus): *see* BRYAN (Albertus).

BRITTON (Thomas): One of the most interesting figures in London musical life in the last quarter of the seventeenth century and the beginning of the eighteenth. Born at Wellingborough or Higham Ferrers (Northamptonshire) at about the middle of the seventeenth century, Britton came to London as a dealer in coal or charcoal and became known as the " musical small-coal man ". He was an individual of cultured tastes, and by association with clever men and the constant use of a large library, he amassed considerable knowledge of chemistry, astrology, old books, and music. Over his small place of business in Clerkenwell, he arranged a music-room and held weekly concerts which quickly attracted all that was fashionable and musical in the metropolis. The concerts which he instituted in 1678 became a well-known fixture and his patrons formed themselves into a club for the hearing and practice of music of the highest class. Among the performers were such well-known musicians as John Banister, Handel, and Pepusch; while among the audience were the most famous artists and poets of the day. These concerts were free at the outset, but, the audience probably becoming too great for the limited accommodation, a subscription of ten shillings a year was charged later. Coffee was served at a penny a dish, and such men as the Earl of Pembroke, the Earl of Sunderland, and the Earl of Oxford were not above partaking of this refreshment to the accompaniment of excellent music. The Earl of Winchelsea, also, often called to chat with the coal-man on old books. So great became Britton's reputation in these matters that he even assisted in the formation of Lord Harley's wonderful library. Indeed, so great was the number of eminent men who foregathered in his music-room, that he soon obtained the reputation, among the ignorant, for being either a magician or a political agent of some sort or other. Ned Ward's description of the meeting place of these amateurs and professionals is very diverting: " His Hut wherein he dwells, which has long been honoured with such good company looks without side as if some of his Ancestors had happened to be executors to old Snorling Diogenes and that they had carefully transplanted the Athenian Tub into Clerken-well; for his House is not much higher than a Canary-pipe, and the Windows of

his State Room, but very little bigger than the Bunghole of a Cask ". But better than this the accommodation could scarcely have been. Britton's place of business (situate on the site where the Bull's Head Tavern now stands) was nothing more than a stable of which the rent was 4l. per annum. The lower part of this shed was used for storing coals, while the upper storey, reached by a ram-shackle ladder (it was hardly to be dignified by the name of staircase), served as the music-room of the club. Mr. W. Barclay Squire in the *Dictionary of National Biography* says that the in-formation concerning the sub-scription of ten shillings was given by Walpole, but that it was rendered doubtful by an entry in Thoresby's Diary: " June 5th, 1712. In our way home called at Mr. Britton's the noted small-coal man, where we heard a noble con-cert of music the best in town, which for many years past he has had weekly for his own entertainment, and of the gentry . . . gratis, to which most foreigners of dis-tinction, for the fancy of it, occasionally resort ". Britton died in 1714 in most peculiar circumstances. An habitue of the club, a magistrate named Robe, brought the celebrated blacksmith-ventriloquist Honeyman with him on one occasion; and as a practical joke the latter, in a feigned voice, told the small-coalman that unless he knelt down at once and recited the Lord's prayer he would not live many hours. Britton was much affected and complied. For the rest of the party the joke probably ended there. But the thing played upon Britton's mind and he died within a few days of the occurrence. He was buried on October 1st, 1714, at St. James's, Clerkenwell, and his funeral was attended by all the members of the club. His instruments and music, and his library of nearly fifteen hundred books, were sold for the benefit of his widow. His portrait by Wollaston is in the National Portrait Gallery (London). A second portrait was painted by the same artist showing Britton tuning his harpsichord (a fine instrument by Ruckers) on which Pepusch used to play when he came to Clerkenwell.

BROWNE (John): A composer of undoubted talent who flourished in the fifteenth century ; and although not much is known of his life, a good deal of his music has been preserved, and from it a just appreciation of his merits may be gained. Dr. W. H. Grattan Flood, in one of the examples of his painstaking work (*Mus. Times*), is the only writer who has taken the trouble to discover something of the biography of this musician. He it was who first named the records from which some information could be obtained. If the John Browne who entered King's College (Cambridge) in 1445 at the age of nineteen, was the composer, he must have been born in 1426; but there is nothing to connect this student with the musician, and the name was not uncommon. On the other hand, there is nothing to prevent the entry from referring to the same man. He was rector of West Tilbury Church in 1480, and in 1490 he gave up that position in favour of one Thomas Clerk. On leaving Tilbury Browne entered St. Stephen's, Westminster. He was mentioned on the Patent Rolls of 1489 (July) together with the Archbishop of Canterbury ; but here again, although the dates fit so nicely, we cannot be at all certain that the musician

John Browne is meant in each case. The Browne of the Westminster records died in 1498, for in that year (February 19th) Stephen Beworth, a royal chaplain, succeeded him at St. Stephen's.

The British Museum manuscripts contain some examples of Browne's work. *Add.* 5465 (The Fayrfax Book) has the carol " Jhesu, mercy, how may this be ", with a second part " Crist that was ", a third part " He that wrought ", a fourth part " Ah, Jhesu, whi suffyred thou ", and a fifth part " So, man ". The same manuscript contains the secular composition " Margarit make " (second part, " That goodly las "; third part, " Her lusty chere "; and fourth part, " My Margarit I can not mete "), a very interesting composition. Other works by him are in the Eton College manuscript (" O Mater venerabilis " *à* 5; " O Maria Salvatoris mater " *à* 8; " Salve Regina " *à* 5; " O Maria plene gracie " and " O Regina mundi clare " *à* 6).

A reason for doubting that the Browne of Tilbury Parish Church and he of St. Stephen's were identical is the fact that a John Browne was mentioned in a list of 1483 in the Lord Chamberlain's Records. According to the Tilbury evidence, Browne did not resign his post there until 1490. But whether there were two men of the same name active contemporaneously or not, the fact remains that someone of that name wrote some music that is exceedingly good for its comparatively early period.

BRYAN (Albertus): A celebrated organist and composer of sacred music as well as of popular dance-tunes for instruments. Since he was appointed organist of St. Paul's Cathedral at the age of seventeen in 1638, it follows that he was born in 1621. He was a pupil of John Tomkins, organist of St. Paul's, and it was on the death of his master that Bryan became organist. His reputation must then already have been great, and his touch undoubtedly noted for a certain softness, for in the Life of Susanna Perwick (*The Virgin's Pattern*, 1661) he is described as " velvet-fingered ". He held the post until the suppression of the Cathedral services during the Commonwealth, when, like so many other musicians, he turned to teaching for a livelihood (Playford, *Musical Banquet*). At the Reſtoration he was reinſtated. At the same time the king was petitioned to appoint him as organiſt of the Chapel Royal of Whitehall, since he had " so induſtriously practised that science that he hath very much augmented his skill and knowledge therein ". This petition was printed from the State Papers in *Musical Standard* for April 11th, 1868, and reprinted by Mr. Weſt (*Cathedral Organiſts, ed.* 1921), while Rimbault alluded to it in *Notes and Queries (Vol.* X, p. 182, *ser.* III). There is no information forthcoming to show that the petition was granted and Nagel (*Annalen*) is incorrect when he says that Bryan was given the poſt asked for. The Great Fire of London once more robbed him of the St. Paul's position, and in the interim he played at Weſtminſter Abbey (1666–8) until succeeded by Blow. He appears to have been connected with St. Paul's until 1670. It is doubtful whether the organiſt of Dulwich College (1671–7) was the musician under consideration, for Archbishop Sheldon, in recommending

him for the poſt, described him as a " young man, one Albertus Bryan ". This Bryan may have been a son of the St. Paul's organiſt. It is hardly likely that a man who had played on the St. Paul's and the Abbey organs would have accepted the poſt at All Hallows', Barking, at 18*l.* per annum, which is what the Dulwich organiſt did. The date of the elder Bryan's death is not known, but Wood says that he was buried in the Cloiſters of Weſtminſter Abbey.

A " Whole Service " in G with Jubilate inſtead of Benedictus by Bryan is contained in the Tudway manuscript (*Harl.* 7338, *B.M.*) and again in *Add.* 31443 (*B.M.*). The Verse Anthem " I heard a Voyce " is included in *Add.* 30478–9 and 30931 (*B.M.*). The Service in G is again present among the Chriſt Church (Oxford) manuscripts. The Anthem mentioned was printed by Barnard in 1641, and the Service by Arnold. Inſtrumental music by Bryan is contained in Playford's *Musick's Hand-Maid,* 1678 (two Ayres, two Sarabandes, and a Corant), and three harpsichord pieces are in manuscript in the Christ Church collection.

BRYNE (Albertus): *see* BRYAN (Albertus).

BULL (John): Perhaps the most celebrated virginalist, organist, and writer of music destined for these instruments that this country has ever possessed. His influence upon the development of the music for the keyboard instruments was very great, and there can be no doubt as to his importance in the history of this class of composition. Judging by the esteem in which he was held by his musical contemporaries, John Bull must have been a performer of amazing ability, and the technical difficulties—great as they are —of some of his virginal music, probably give only a faint idea of his skill as an executant. As a composer his one aim,—in the major part of his work at any rate,— seems to have been at brilliant virtuosity. There can be no doubt that his knowledge was very profound; but he did not hesitate to make depth of feeling and musical beauty step into the background in favour of the technicalities of his instrument, when the latter required them to do so. The result was the raising of the mechanical standard of keyboard music, and the paving of the way to the many improvements that followed here and on the Continent. Like most of the Elizabethans, Bull was a daring experimentalist, and among other innovations we already see in some of his work the attempt to use the whole-tone scale. His preference for instrumental music is perhaps traceable to the influence of his teacher, William Blytheman; and, indeed, so amazing was his technical dexterity in such music, that his sacred vocal work is apt to be overlooked. In the latter he possessed sufficient self-restraint to avoid the devices that made his virginal and organ music so surprisingly anticipatory. In one or two of his Motets there is real beauty and a power of expression not to be expected if he were judged solely by his instrumental work. At an age when the majority of the great musicians were devoting almost the whole of their energies to the service of the church, Bull came as a welcome force that helped to preserve the balance between the two classes of composition.

Born in 1563 John Bull is supposed by Anthony Wood to have come "of the same family as it seems, with those of his name in Somersetshire" (MS. in Bodleian library, Oxford). There was a family named Bull in that county with more than one John in it, but the musician's connection with it cannot be proved conclusively. He certainly visited the West Country, and it may be that he went to see his relatives. There is a record in the Cheque-Book of the Chapel Royal referring to the election of one William Phelps of Tewkesbury, as an extraordinary member of the Chapel in recognition of his "most rare kyndnes to Mr. Doctor Bull in his great distresse, being robbed in those parts". His musical education was derived in the Chapel Royal under the eye of William Blytheman, and the latter must have discovered great talent in his pupil as well as adaptability to the organ. Wood says that Blytheman "spared neither time nor labour to advance his natural gifts". The result of this training was Bull's appointment to

Hereford Cathedral as organist in 1582 (December 24th), when he was barely twenty years of age. To this work the mastership of the choristers was added later. He remained at Hereford only two years, for in January, 1585, he re-entered the Chapel Royal. The entry in the Cheque-Book reads: "1585. Jo. Bull sworne the (blank) of Januarie in Mr. Bodinghurst place. Childe there". In 1586 he became a Bachelor of Music at Oxford, having "practised the faculty of music for fourteen years". He proceeded Doctor at Cambridge, incorporating at Oxford in 1592. According to Wood (*Fasti Oxon.*) he did not proceed Doctor at Oxford in the usual way on account of "rigid Puritans there that could not endure Church music". In 1591 he became organist of the Chapel Royal in succession to his teacher. On April 20th of the same year he addressed a petition to the Queen, begging for a lease valued at 30*l.* per annum in order "to relieve his great poverty which altogether hinders his studies" (Salisbury MSS. at Hatfield to which attention has been drawn by Mr. W. Barclay Squire). The result of the petition was the granting of a lease of about half the value asked for. Bull muſt have ſtood well with the Queen, for it was on her recommendation in 1596 that he was appointed the firſt Gresham lecturer in music (Letter from Elizabeth to the Mayor and Aldermen, November 30th, 1596; *S.P., Dom. Ser.*). So high was his reputation also,—or so powerful was the Court influence behind him,—that, though he was the firſt professor, exceptions to the prescribed rules were made in his favour. The lectures were to have been delivered alternately in English and Latin, but owing to Bull's scanty knowledge of the latter language, he was permitted to speak altogether in English. His initial lecture at the College was printed, but no copy of it is known to exiſt. The title-page read: " The oration of Maiſter Iohn Bull, Doctor of Musicke and one of the Gentlemen of hir Maieſties Royall Chappell, as hee pronounced the same beefore diuers worshipfull persons . . . with a great Multitude of other people the 6. day of October, 1597, In the New erected Colledge of Sir Thomas Gresham. Imprinted

at London by Thomas Eaſte " (*v. Harl. 5936. B.M.*).

In 1601 Bull travelled on the Continent and aroused a good deal of enthusiasm by his playing wherever he went. During his absence his chair at the Gresham College was occupied by Thomas Byrd, the son of the more celebrated William Byrd. His journey took him through the Low Countries, France, and Germany, and it was at St. Omer that he performed the feat described by Anthony Wood. At that city Bull was shown " a lesson or song of forty parts . . . and challenged to add one more part to them ". The composer allowed himself to be locked in a room with paper and pens, and added — another forty parts. And to make the ſtory more impressive, Wood deliciously adds: " The musician . . . swore by the Great God that he that added those forty parts muſt either be the devil or Dr. Bull . . . Whereupon Bull making himself known, the musician fell down and ador'd him ". Indeed, the admiration Bull aroused on the Continent caused the Queen some uneasiness, and she ordered him home before some ambitious foreign court secured his services. The Lord Chamberlain's Records give the name of Dr. Bull in the lił of musicians receiving mourning livery for the funeral of Queen Elizabeth in 1603. His salary in that year was 40*l*. ("Fees granted to sondry persons in the several offices and places", granted by Elizabeth; the lił written after her death; *Cotton MS. Tib. B.* III, *fol.* 248; cited by Nagel, *Annalen*). This was the increased salary mentioned in several entries in the Cheque-Book of the Chapel Royal. Bull was a freeman of the Merchant Taylors' Company, and when King James I dined at their Hall, the musician "in a citizen's gowne, cappe, and hood, played mołt excellent melodie upon a small payre of organes placed there for that purpose onely" (Stowe, *Chron.*). He appears to have given his services to the Company for nothing on this occasion, — "Whereas the musicians in the Greate Hall exaćted unreasonable somes of the Company for the same" (*Id.*). In recognition of this, Bull was the next day made a liveryman of the Merchant Taylors (*v.* also Giles, Nathaniel). At the end of 1607 he married Elizabeth Walter, of the Strand, London, and two days before his license was issued he resigned the Gresham professorship (December 20th) since a condition of the founder direćted that only bachelors could hold the poł. In 1612 he is described as "Dočtor of Musicke to the Kinge" (*L.C.R.*).

The circumłances that brought about the next great change in Bull's life,—his self-banishment from England,—are to some extent mylterious. Charges were made againł him that no member of the Chapel could face unless he had a complete defence. Whether the accusations made againł him were true or not, can hardly be decided to-day. It is juł possible that he might have preferred service at a Catholic court and went to Brussels without permission because he knew that he would not receive a licence to travel for that purpose. A petition of his to Sir M. Hicks, Secretary to the Earl of Salisbury (April, 1613), asks that his child's name be subłituted for his own in a patent, and may have foreshadowed his departure: an attempt to

leave some means of subsistence for his son. It reads: "Sir, I have bin many times to have spoken with you, to desire your favor to my Lord and Mr. Chancellor, to graunte me theire favors to chaunge my name, and put in my childes, leaving out my owne: It is but 40*l.* by yeare for my service heretofore, the matter is not greate, yet it will be some reliefe for my poor childe, having nothinge ells to leave it". An entry in the Cheque-Book of the Chapel Royal says: "1613. John Bull, Doctor of Musicke, went beyond the seas without licence and was admitted into the Archduke's service, and entered into paie there about Michaelmas . . ." Trumbull, the English ambassador to the Low Countries, was instructed to lodge a protest with the Archduke. Trumbull's report (together with Bull's letter to Hicks) can be seen in the British Museum (*Add.* 6194), and in his account of what passed he says: " . . . and I told him plainly, that it was notorious to all the world, the said Bull did not leave your Majesty's service for any wrong done unto him, or for matter of religion, under which fained pretext he now sought to wrong the reputation of your Majesty's justice, but did in that dishonest manner steal out of England through the guilt of a corrupt conscience, to escape the punishment which notoriously he had deserved, and was designed to have inflicted on him by the hand of justice, for his incontinence, fornication, adultery, and other grievous crimes". Whether these grievous crimes were to be preferred against Bull or not, the fact remains that the Archduke kept the organist in Brussels. In 1617 he succeeded the celebrated Waelrent at the Cathedral of Antwerp, staying there until his death in March, 1628. He was interred in the Cathedral on the fifteenth of the month. A portrait of John Bull hangs in the Music School, Oxford, showing him in his twenty-seventh year ; it is dated 1589. Round the frame appear the oft-quoted lines:—
"The Bul by force In field
  doth raigne;
But Bull by skill Good will
  doth gayne".
This picture has been reproduced in Hawkins' *History*, in Sir Frederick Bridge's *Twelve Good*

Musicians, in Mr. Abdy Williams' *Story of Organ Music, etc.* The late Dr. W. H. Cummings possessed another, and later, portrait.

Bull's works are not very numerous when we take into consideration his reputation and the length of his active life. To *Parthenia* (1611) he contributed a Prelude, two Pavanes, and four Galliards for the Virginals; in Leighton's *Teares, etc.* (1614) there are three works of his (two settings of " Attend unto my tears " and " In the departure of the Lord "); and he is represented in Barnard's and Boyce's collections. One or two foreign publications of the seventeenth century contain work of Bull's. In more modern reprints several pieces are available: in the re-issue of *Parthenia* (1847 and 1908), in the Fitzwilliam Virginal Book (J. A. Fuller-Maitland and W. Barclay Squire, 1894–99; over two score of virginal pieces); a good example of his sacred music has been published by Curwen and Sons (" Fraile man despise the treasures of this life "); and a number of virginal pieces arranged as pianoforte solos, by Professor Granville Bantock (1912), in the *Early*

English Musical Magazine (1891), in the *École de Piano* of A. Dupont (1884–91), and a couple of organ solos edited by Mr. J. E. West for Novello (1906). A larger amount of his music exists in manuscript. He is represented in the Virginal Books of William Forster and Benjamin Cosyn (in the possession of his Majesty the King; now in *B.M.*), in the collection of " In Nomines " in the Oxford Music School, in the Christ Church library (Oxford), in the Peterhouse library (Cambridge), in the library of the Royal College of Music, in at least eight different manuscripts at the British Museum, and in a few Continental collections.

That the National Anthem, —" God Save the King ",— was based upon an air by John Bull is the theory held by several investigators and denied by others. No conclusive proofs are yet available, and those willing to accept the arguments of the pro-Bull camp may claim that the virtuose doctor's air first suggested the tune of the anthem. But so many variants of the melody have been discovered that it is quite impossible to fix even the

century of the hymn's inception with any degree of certainty.
BURNETT (Davy): see BURTON (Davy).
BURTON (Avery): see BURTON (Davy).
BURTON (Davy): A member of the Chapel Royal and composer of sacred music under Henry VII and VIII. A good deal of confusion has been occasioned by the fact that his name is sometimes given as Davy Burton and sometimes as Avery Burton. It is also to be found as merely " Burton " or " Averie ", and the official records make it highly probable that all these names refer to the same man. Even " Burnett " is most likely only another of the many forms of his patronymic. Such looseness of orthography and nomenclature was not at all uncommon in early Tudor times. In 1494 (November 29th) we find his name in Henry the Seventh's book of expenses: " To Burton for making a Mass . . . 20s.", a sum large enough to justify us in the belief that Burton enjoyed a high reputation already so early. In 1509 he appears as a Gentleman of the Chapel, and on February 27th, 1511, he received an allowance for mourning livery to be used at the funeral of Prince Henry (L. C. R.). It frequently happened in those days that outside appointments were granted to the gentlemen of the Chapel Royal to augment their income, and in the same year Burton was given a post as keeper of Chestenwood (Kent). In 1518 he surrendered this post in favour of one John Copynger (Brewer, Catalogue of Patent Rolls). His salary as gentleman of the Chapel (in 1526) was sevenpence-halfpenny per day. Further signs of royal favour followed in 1526 when a sixty years' lease of land at Lewisham and Lee (Co. Kent) was granted him; and again in 1527 when he shared the lease of fee farms at Camberwell and Peckham. In 1542 the first lease was granted in reversion to Henry Byrd (Patent Rolls), and in the document the musician is described as " David Burton of the King's Chapel ". He must have been an old man by then if he composed a Mass in 1494, and it is probable that he died shortly after the entry of 1542. A certain amount of doubt exists regarding the biography of

this musician, and the identification of Davy Burton with Avery, although probably fully justified, cannot be accepted with absolute certainty.

A Mass by him (probably the one for which he received 20s.) is contained in the Forrest-Heyther part-books (Oxford); and in British Museum manuscript *Add.* 29996 (in John Redford's hand), is preserved a " Te Deum " signed " Avere ". According to Henry Davey there was an old pensioner at the time of Elizabeth's accession named Thomas Avery, and it is not outside the bounds of possibility that this was a different man, and that the composition in *Add.* 29996 may have been his. Thomas Morley (*Introduction*, 1597) gives " Avarie " as one of his celebrated men.

BYRD (Thomas): There were at least three musicians of this name, probably all belonging to the family of William Byrd. One of them was William's son (baptized at Lincoln in 1569) and the godson of Thomas Tallis (mentioned in Tallis's will). Another was a son of William's eldest son Christopher. One of these two acted as Bull's deputy at Gresham College during the absence abroad of the Professor (*v.* Bull, John). A third Thomas Byrd (probably the father of William) is mentioned in the Lord Chamberlain's Records as a Gentleman of the Chapel Royal at the coronation of Edward VI (February 20th, 1546–7; *L.C.R.* Vol. 426), and again in the list of gentlemen receiving mourning livery for the funeral of Henry VIII (list made out February 21st, 1547–8). This Thomas Byrd died in 1561 as appears from the Cheque-Book of the Chapel Royal: " 1561. Thomas Byrd died in Februarie, Clarke of the Checke, and Morcocke made Clarke Checke, Anno 3." (Eliz.). Neither of the other bearers of this Christian name are to be confused with the gentleman of the chapel just mentioned, for both of them lived well into the seventeenth century. The probability is strongest that Bull's deputy at Gresham College was William's son (*cf.* Pedigree in *Add.* 33274A.).

BYRD (William): Undoubtedly the most imposing figure in the whole history of English music, William Byrd stands out by reason of the versatility of his genius, and the dignity and intrinsic worth of all his achievements. That the productions of some of his successors should have equalled, and have proved even superior to, his work as a writer of madrigals, can be explained by the very circumstance that the later madrigalists enjoyed the advantage of knowing his pioneer work in this field of art. He himself was new to this class of writing; and except for very little earlier music of this sort (*cf.* Whythorne's part-songs) nothing of a similar nature had appeared until Byrd's madrigals formed the foundation upon which the English school of madrigalists built. His skill as a performer on the keyboard instruments was considerable, and here again it is only among his successors that we find his peers. It is in his sacred music that William Byrd appears as an isolated monument to the art of the Elizabethan age. Here his nobility and grandeur, associated with ingenuity, personality, feeling, and an admirable sense of fitness, make of him what he has been called figuratively by foreigners,—the Palestrina or the Orlando Lassus of the

English,—though he was not directly influenced by any of the newer methods then employed on the Continent. It is gratifying to know that his was one of the rare examples of genius recognized during his own lifetime. Byrd remains as the greatest musical ornament of the Elizabethan era, just as surely as Henry Purcell marked the culmination of the next great age in English music nearly a century later.

The date of his birth may be fixed as 1543, or, perhaps, 1542, for his will (made in 1622) gives him as having then been in his eightieth year. We possess no certain knowledge of his descent or training. Thomas Tallis has been selected by many writers as his teacher, but beyond two lines in the *Cantiones Sacrae*:—

" Tallisius magno dignus honore senex
Et Birdus tantem natus decorare magistrum,"

and Anthony Wood's note that " he was bred up to musick under Thomas Tallis ", there is no evidence to support the supposition. The use of the word " magister " need not connote " teacher " here, and Wood is not always dependable. It is not known whether Tallis and Byrd met before they came into contact with each other in the Chapel Royal. There is no trustworthy information concerning Byrd until we learn that he was appointed as organist of Lincoln Cathedral in 1563 or thereabouts. After five years of activity in this capacity he married a Lincolnshire lady, Ellen (or Julian) Birley, on September 14th, 1568,—the union being blessed by six children. Upon the tragic death of Robert Parsons by drowning, Byrd was " sworne Gentleman in his place . . . the 22d of Februarie " (1569, *C.B.C.R.*). Whether he left for London immediately is not clear. His son Christopher was baptized at Lincoln in 1569, and his daughter Elizabeth in 1571–2 ; but these facts need not have prevented him from being active in the Chapel Royal and journeying to Lincoln to have his children baptized in the church where his work lay. But the probability is that he did not take up his duties at the Chapel Royal (or, at any rate, remove permanently to London with his family) until the end of 1572, after he had recommended Thomas Butler for the organist's post at

Lincoln (December 7th, 1572). Thence onwards, until the death of the older man, Byrd and Tallis were constantly in touch with each other, sharing the organist's post at the Chapel Royal, and later working together in other directions. Thus, in 1575 a patent was granted jointly to the two musicians to print and sell music and ruled paper, the monopoly to stand in their favour for twenty-one years. Mr. W. Barclay Squire, whose account of Byrd in the 1912 edition of *Grove* is probably the fullest and most reliable of all that had hitherto appeared, mentions a petition addressed by Tallis and Byrd to the Queen, for a twenty-one years' lease in 1577 (*Cal. of MSS.* at Hatfield, *v. Grove*, 1912, I, 429). In this petition Byrd says that " being called to Her Majesty's service from Lincoln Cathedral, where he was well settled, is now, through great charge of wife and children, fallen into debt and great necessity. By reason of his daily attendance in the Queen's service he is letted from reaping such commodity by teaching as heretofore he did. Her grant two years ago of a licence for printing music has fallen out to their loss and hindrance to the value of 200 marks at least ". This petition was granted.

From 1578 we find Byrd resident at Harlington (Middlesex); and his stay there is interesting chiefly on account of the light thrown by the local records upon his religion. He lived and died a Roman Catholic, and, according to the text of his will, believed that there would be no salvation for him unless he died " a true and perfect member of his holy Catholicke Church ". This being the case, no surprise need be felt when we find him and his family in frequent trouble for non-attendance at divine service under the Elizabethan *régime*. Thus, his wife and servant were often proceeded against for this crime, and he himself was honoured with a true bill as late as 1592 (*County of Middlesex*, Sessions Rolls). But he seems to have suffered no serious consequences; the Cheque-Book of the Chapel Royal (which mentions all sorts of trivialities) does not give any information that could be regarded as indicative of his religion having cost him his post. We may suppose that Elizabeth's love for music outweighed her religious scruples, or that Byrd was then already so popular that an indulgent eye was cast upon his recusancy. The fact remains that at his death the composer was spoken of with the greatest reverence by the writer of the Cheque-Book. The *Autobiography of Father Weston* would lead one to believe that Byrd " who had been formerly in the Queen's Chapel, and held in the highest estimation; but for his religion he sacrificed everything, both his office and the court and all those hopes " which holders of royal appointments harbour. This was written at the time when a true bill was found against the whole Byrd household, and there may have been, for a short time, some doubt as to the issue. But, as has been noticed, neither the Cheque-Book of the Chapel Royal nor any other source of authentic information proves that Byrd sacrificed anything. He was only one of many members of the Chapel Royal who still practised the older religion in the privacy of their homes, while conforming to the requirements of the newer cult when in the Chapel. It is quite conceivable that Byrd preferred to live in the Home Counties rather than be nearer his work, and the eyes of officialdom, for this very purpose.

An interesting petition sent through the Earl of Northumberland to Lord Burghley in 1579 shows that Byrd taught music, and that statesmen of high rank near the person of the sovereign were not afraid to recommend the musician to one another. The letter containing the suit has the following pertinent sentences: " I am the more importunate . . . for that he is my friend and chiefly that he is schoolmaster to my daughter in his art. The man is honest and one whom I know your lordship may command " (February 28th, 1579–80; spelling modernized). In 1585 the well-beloved Tallis died, and Byrd continued to work the publishing monopoly single-handed.

In 1593 Byrd secured an interest in the estate of Stondon Place, near Ongar (Essex), with its rich two hundred acres of good land; and the owner, William Shelley, being apprehended for adhesion to plotting

Papists, the place was sequestrated and Byrd became the holder of the lease. A good deal of litigation followed, which dragged through the first decades of the seventeenth century. The widow of the original owner died in 1609 and Byrd eventually secured peaceful possession by purchasing all rights from her son. The ecclesiastical authorities of Essex were no more benevolent to Byrd than those of Middlesex had been, for he had the same petty annoyances to cope with, and, indeed, since 1598, had actually been excommunicated by the Archdeacon's Court of Essex. We cannot suppose that these things affected the musician's London work very seriously, for we find him continuously active in the Chapel Royal, and in 1603 we read that an allowance for mourning livery was made (*L.C.R.*). In 1618 we find Byrd's name again mentioned in the records, when it is entered as that of a Gentleman of the Chapel, the organists then being Edmund Hooper and Orlando Gibbons.

In 1622 (November 15th) Byrd made his will (printed *in extenso* in *The Musician* for June 2nd, 1897), and in it he directs that his "body ... be honourably buried in that parish or place where it shall please God to take me out of this life, which I humbly desyre (if it shall please God) may be in the parish of Stondon where my dwellinge is, and ... be buried near unto the place where my wife lyeth buryed ". He died on July 4th, 1623. The Cheque-Book of the Chapel Royal noted the occurrence in official manner as follows : " 1623. William Byrd, a Father of Musick, died the fourth of July, and John Croker, a counter tenor of Westminster was admitted ... for a yeare of probacion ..."

The musical stature of William Byrd was fully recognized by his contemporaries. His pupil Thomas Morley wrote that he was " never without reverence to be named of musicians "; and there is no reason for altering this to-day. Peacham (*Compleat Gentleman*, 1622) said that "in Motets and Musick of piety and devotion, as well for the honour of our nation, as the merit of the man, I preferre above all other our Phoenix, Mr. William Byrd, whom, in that kind, I know not whether any may equall, I am sure none excell, even by the judgment of France and Italy ". Indeed, it was in music of piety and devotion that Byrd stood second to none in England. His work for the Roman ritual exhibits a dignity and a charm, a feeling of true devotion and loving tenderness, nowhere else so happily united. And if an abundance of examples of false relation,—so common at the period,—disfigures, from the modern point of view, some of his sacred music, his three superb Masses (perhaps the finest examples of English composition) should be sufficient to gain for him the highest place in the annals of native art. His work in the field of secular vocal music is not of so uniformly high a standard, though some of his songs are magnificent. Judging his achievements from the majority of his compositions in each branch of the art, there can be no doubt that his average sacred work is finer than his average secular writing. It may be that, as Peacham says, " beinge of himselfe naturally disposed to Gravitie and Pietie, his veine is not so much for light madrigals or

Canzonets "; still, we find bright and optimistic examples among his sacred compositions as well as among his secular pieces.

The first work to be published during his lifetime was: *Cantiones, quae ab argumento sacrae vocantur, quinque et sex partium* (1575), by himself and Tallis, Byrd's share consisting of eighteen numbers. In 1588 the first work entirely by Byrd appeared : *Psalmes, Sonets, and Songs of sadnes and Pietie* (five-part), the publisher being Thomas Este, " the assigne of William Byrd ". The work is dedicated to Sir Christopher Hatton and Byrd's entertaining " Reasons briefly set downe by th' Auctor, to perswade every one to learne to singe " are given by way of introduction. These " reasons " are quoted at length by Mr. Barclay Squire in *Grove*, and by the late Sir Frederick Bridge in *Twelve Good Musicians* (1920). In the same year Byrd contributed two madrigals to Nicholas Yonge's *Musica Transalpina*,—" the first and second parts of *La Virginella* made by Maister Byrd upon two stanzas of Ariosti, and brought to speak English

with the rest ". The publication of the three masses (one each in three, four, and five parts) would appear to belong to the same period as Yonge's collection, Mr. Barclay Squire thinking the date of their appearance, by typographical evidence, to have been about 1588. They were not supplied with title-pages, and in view of the circumstance that the Harlington local authorities were at that period subjecting the composer to petty persecution on religious grounds, we can see in their omission a probable proof of their date. In 1589 Byrd issued *Songs of Sundrie Natures, some of gravitie, and others of mirth, fit for all companies and voyces* (second edition, 1610). In 1589 also appeared the *Liber Primus Sacrarum Cantionum quinque vocum*, and two years later, the *Liber Secundus* followed. Byrd wrote two versions of " This Sweet and Merry Month of May " for Thomas Watson's first set of *Italian Madrigals Englished*. The next dated publication in which he had a hand appeared during his residence at Stondon. This was " Medulla Musicke Sucked out of the Sappe of Two of the most famous Musitians that ever were in this land, namely Master Wylliam Byrd and Master Alfonso Ferabosco . . . either of whom have made fortie severall waies (without contention), shewing most rare and intricate skill in two partes in one upon the playne songe ' Miserere ' ". This work is known to us only from the entry in the Registers of the Stationers' Company, where it is dated 1603. The two musicians were clearly on good terms and Morley (*Introduction*, Edition 1608) says that each judged the other's performance. Byrd's two books of *Gradualia* were issued in 1607 (a second edition of both in 1610). The last published work entirely by William Byrd appeared in 1611 : " *Psalmes, Songs, and Sonnets*: some solemne, others joyfull, framed to the life of the Words: Fit for Voyces or Viols ". Sir William Leighton's *Teares or Lamentacions*, etc. (1614) contained four anthems by Byrd, the last compositions of " the father of music " to appear in print before he died.

Manuscripts containing work by William Byrd are preserved in many libraries, a large proportion of the pieces being copies from his published compositions. A good deal of his music is to be seen in the library of Christ Church, Oxford,— particularly in a set of part-books written in 1581. This library possesses several manuscript works of Byrd's that have not yet been printed. British Museum manuscripts *Add.* 17802–5 and 30480–4 include sacred music of his. A small book of canons in his own handwriting, every page signed with the initials " W. B.", is also in the Museum (*Add.* 31391). The Fitzwilliam Museum, Cambridge, has his " Bow Thine Ear " in Purcell's autograph, and he is also represented in Sadler's part-books (Bodleian, Oxford). Further examples of his work are in the Music School (Oxford), Peterhouse (Cambridge), and Lambeth Palace. Byrd's only contributions to stage-music is contained in *Harl.* 2412 (*B.M.*), a Latin play, *Richardus Tertius*, by Dr. Thomas Legge (1579). This is a very short three-part song written at the end of the text, commencing " Preces Deo fundamus ", and signed " Mr. Bird ".

From another point of view William Byrd is an intensely

interesting composer. As a writer for the virginal he is of the utmost importance in the history of keyboard music. He probably was a very brilliant performer himself, and his writing for the clavier exhibits, for the period, great virtuosity. There can be no doubt that Byrd deserves much honour for his pioneer work in this field. His versatility is remarkable ; contrapuntal devices, fugato, and, above all, variation, are used with the happiest results. Indeed, he has been hailed as the "inventor" of the Fugue and the Variation-form,—so far as these perfectly natural developments can be said to have been "invented"; but whether he can claim so peculiar a title or not, the fact remains that he was a very early writer in these forms. The *Fitzwilliam Virginal Book* alone contains no fewer than seventy-one pieces, mostly variations on popular tunes or on original themes. *My Ladye Nevell's (Virginal) Book* (in the possession of the Marquess of Abergavenny, and written by John Baldwin) contains forty-two numbers all by Byrd,—including a set of descriptive pieces representing a battle,

one of the earliest attempts at "programme-music." The writing of the manuscript was completed in September, 1591, so that all the pieces contained were composed long enough anterior to this date for them to have become popular. Baldwin signed most of the compositions with Byrd's name, sometimes adding "Gentleman of the Chappell", "Organiste of Her Majesties' Chappell", and so on, No. 17 having "Homo memorabilis" written after Byrd's name. *Will. Forster's Virginal Book* (in the possession of His Majesty the King) contains thirty-five examples of Byrd's music. *Benjamin Cosyn's Virginal Book* (also belonging to the King) gives an instrumental version of the popular Elizabethan song, "Goe from my window" and of the "Morning and Evening Service in D" by Byrd. The last two MSS. are now in the British Museum. In *Parthenia* (published probably 1611 ; second edition, 1655) Bull, Orlando Gibbons, and Byrd collaborated, the last-named being represented by eight compositions,—two Preludes, two Pavanes, and four Galliards. *Add.* 31392 (*B.M.*) contains four Pavanes and four Galliards arranged in pairs. It should be noted that many of the pieces are duplicated in the various manuscripts, some of the more popular compositions appearing in several manuscripts.

Similarly Byrd devoted his talents to music for the ſtringed inſtruments, and some In Nomines and Fantasias (Fancies) are preserved in manuscript,— notably in the Music School (Oxford). A couple of Fantasias for the ſtring consort were included in the *Psalms, Songs, and Sonnets, etc.* In this music for the viols Byrd certainly shows better work than had appeared before for these inſtruments, — as diſtinct from vocal music arranged for ſtrings.

A fair amount of Byrd's work is now available in modern editions. Apart from the compositions included in Barnard's work of 1641, and by Boyce in *Cathedral Music,* the following have appeared: The three-part mass (*ed.* G. F. Graussent, 1904; W. Barclay Squire, 1901); the four-part

mass (Rockſtro; W. Barclay Squire, 1890); and the five-part mass (W. Barclay Squire and Sir Richard R. Terry, 1899; Musical Antiquarian Society, 1841); one of Byrd's madrigals in *Musica Transalpina* (1588) is included in Dr. Fellowes' *English Madrigal School (Vol.* XVI); the 1588 "Psalms, Sonnets, and Songs", in *Vol.* XIV, of Dr. Fellowes' edition, *Liber Primus sacrarum cantionum, etc.,* published by the Musical Antiquarian Society (1842); several isolated numbers from the laſt-named work by various editors; "Songs of Sundrie Natures, *etc.*" (1589) edited by Dr. Fellowes in *Vol.* XV of *The English Madrigal School,* and nearly all the pieces in this work by G. E. P. Arkwright in his *Old English Edition;* "Psalmes, Songs, and Sonnets" (1611) has appeared as *Vol.* XVI of Dr. Fellowes' moſt praiseworthy series; the *Fitzwilliam Virginal Book,* with its large number of pieces by Byrd, has been printed under the editorship of J. A. Fuller-Maitland and W. Barclay Squire; some isolated inſtrumental and sacred compositions by Byrd have been edited by Professor Granville Bantock; and the firm of Novello and Co. have issued a number of examples of his sacred music, the editors of which have, in some cases, taken liberties with Byrd's text, and in others done their work admirably.

C

CAESAR: see SMEGER-GILL (William).
CAMPIAN (Thomas): see CAMPION (Thomas).
CAMPION (Thomas): A physician, poet, and composer who flourished in the late Elizabethan era and during the reign of James I. But although he was professionally a physician, his achievements as a poet and a musician are far too important to allow us to look upon him as an amateur in the ordinary accepted sense of this much-misinterpreted word. In his solo-songs with instrumental accompaniment he was one of the first in England to develop his style along the lines suggested by Caccini in his work which culminated in the publication of the *Nuove Musiche* in the year after Campion's solo-songs appeared (*v.* also Rosseter, Philip; and Jones, Robert). In masque-music he was considered an authority at the beginning of the seventeenth century, and he found time to write a treatise on Counterpoint which was accepted as a standard work for many years. His music cannot be called ambitious in scope nor

profound in conception; but it has the charm of unaffected simplicity, and it must have appealed very strongly to the poet-musicians of the period. An exception among the composers of that era, Campion avoided the daring experiments that were being made on every side; and his outlook was described in a verse of his own:—

" Strive not yet for curious ways,
Concord pleaseth more the less 'tis strained;
Zeal affects not outward praise,
Only strives to show a love unfained."

He wrote a large number of lyrics, not only for his own setting, but also for others. Many composers availed themselves of his words, and for the purpose to which they were to be put they may be taken as some of the very finest of their class.

As far as I have been able to check the only authority to give the date of Thomas Campion's birth is Dr. E. H. Fellowes (*English Madrigal Composers*) who says it took place on February 12th, 1567, adding that the future musician was baptized at St.

Andrew's, Holborn. His first intention was probably to study law, and in 1586 he entered Gray's Inn, but left before 1595. In the latter year his first work appeared, —a volume of Latin verses and epigrams under the title, *Thomae Campiani Poemata*. It should be noted in passing that he often used the spelling " Campian ". In 1602 he issued *Observations on the arte of Poesie*. He was educated at Cambridge, and probably also studied medicine on the Continent. He was forty years of age before he is first called a " doctor of Phisicke " (1606–7), and, indicative of the fact that his studies in music and stage-craft were already far advanced, we find him devising a masque in honour of Lord Hay's wedding in the same year,— he, Thomas Lupo, and Giles, sharing the task of providing the music for it. In 1617 the Earl of Cumberland was in correspondence with his son regarding a masque which was being prepared, and he recommended the calling in of Dr. Campion for consultation in the matter. It must be clear, from this circumstance alone, that Campion was at that time considered a high authority on the subject. We do not come across him very often in the pursuit of his calling, but in January, 1616, we know that he visited Sir Thomas Monson in the Tower " on matters relating to his health ". He died in 1619–20 and was buried at St. Dunstan's - in - the - West (Fleet Street, London). Campion was an intimate friend of Philip Rosseter, the lutenist and composer; and on his deathbed left all his estate by verbal will to his friend, saying that he wished he had more to leave. Three years after Campion's death, Rosseter rejoined him at St. Dunstan's.

The first musical work published by Campion seems to have been the *Booke of Ayres* which he issued in collaboration with Rosseter (*q.v.*). This appeared in 1601, and something more on the work will be found in the article on Philip Rosseter. In 1607 he prepared the masque performed at Whitehall and wrote two of the songs. The same year saw the publication of " *The Description of a Maske* presented before the Kinges Majestie at White Hall on Twelfth Night last, in honour of the Lord Hayes and his Bride . . . Invented and set forth by Thomas Campion, Doctor of Physicke . . . 1607 ". The music used in this masque (two pieces by Campion, two by Thomas Lupo, and one by Thomas Giles) was reprinted by Mr. G. E. P. Arkwright in his *Old English Edition* (1889). While on the subject of masques, it may be mentioned that Campion devised entertainments of this kind for two more weddings. On February 14th, 1612–13, when the Elector Frederick of the Palatinate married Princess Elizabeth, " The Lord's Masque " was performed, the " invention ", the text, and one of the songs being by Campion. The other occasion was the marriage of the " Earle of Somerset and the . . . Lady Frances Howard ", and for this function Campion wrote a masque, in the music for which he, Coperario, and Nicholas Lanier collaborated. Campion's authorship of the " Masque of Flowers ", performed by the gentlemen of Gray's Inn on Twelfth Night, 1613, is doubtful. But he wrote the masque produced before Queen Anna at " Lord Knowles " (Knollys) place near Reading, when Her Majesty was on the road to Bath (April 27th and 28th, 1613).

More important from the musical point of view was the publication of Campion's " *Two Bookes of Ayres*. The first contayning Diuine and Morall Songs, the Second, Light Conceits of Louers; To be sung to the Lute and Viols, in two, three, and foure parts: or by one voyce to an Instrument ". The British Museum Catalogue gives the date 1611 (queried) for this work, but internal evidence would place it after the death of Prince Henry of Wales, in 1612 or 1613. Upon this death Campion wrote the words of " the Songs of Mourning bewailing the untimely death of Prince Henry " which Coperario set to music. " *The Third and Fourth Booke of Ayres*. Composed by Thomas Campion. So as they may be expressed by one Voyce with a Violl, Lute, or Orpharion ", appeared *ca.* 1617 (certainly not earlier). At about the same time or a little later (perhaps in 1618) Campion wrote a theoretical treatise: " A new way of making Foure parts in Counter-point, by a most familiar, and infallible Rule. Secondly a necessary discourse on Keyes, and their proper Closes. Thirdly, the allowed passages of All Concords, are declared. Also by way of Preface, the nature of the Scale is expressed, with a briefe method teaching to Sing ". This little work was of great importance, since it was a long ſtride towards the modern syſtem of keys and harmony. It formed the basis of the second edition, which was published with Chriſtopher Sympson's annotations in 1655: *The Art of Setting or composing of Musick in Parts*, etc. In this form the treatise was included in Playford's *Introduction to the Skill of Musick*, and remained there for several editions until replaced by Purcell's work. A three-part song, " If Love love Truth ", was included in the *Musical Companion* (1672), and " Ev'ry Dame effects good fame " was reprinted by Rimbault in *Ancient Vocal Music of England* (*No*. 2). In 1889 Mr. A. H. Bullen collected all Campion's writings (except the treatise on Descant) into his *Works of Thomas Campion*, a volume that makes very intereſting reading on account of the complete descriptions it gives of the masques; but none of the music is reproduced.

Several compositions by Campion are preserved in the British Museum, and a couple of pieces from the printed works are in manuscript in the Chriſt Church library (Oxford).

CARLETON (Nicholas): *see* CARLTON (Nicholas).

CARLETON (Richard): *see* CARLTON, Richard.

CARLTON (Nicholas): A composer of inſtrumental music of whose biography absolutely nothing is known. He is represented in two British Museum manuscripts, —in *Add*. 30513 (Thomas Mulliner's Book) by an arrangement of a " Gloria Tibi Trinitas " for a keyboard inſtrument, and in *Add*. 29996 by " a Verse for two to play on one Virginall or Organ " (score) and another " upon the Sharpe ". In both manuscripts his name is spelled " Carleton " (in one Nicholas, and in the other Nycholas).

CARLTON (Richard): A madrigaliſt of whom very little is known. That he belonged to a Norfolk family seems almost certain; and that the Church was to be his main vocation, and not music, appears to be eſtablished. He was trained at Clare College, Cambridge, and took the *B.A.* degree in 1577, and the *B.Mus.* later on. In 1597 he was vicar at Norwich and teacher of the choristers at the Cathedral there. His last clerical appointment was that of rector of Bawsey and Glosthorp in the County of Norfolk. The date of his death is not known; but since a locum tenens was selected in 1627 and a new rector installed in 1638, it is safe to assume that failing health caused the former and his death the latter, appointment.

The work of Carlton, though not of the very first quality when compared with that of the great men of his own period, is, nevertheless, interesting and shows that he was by no means devoid of talent. In 1601 he issued *Madrigals to Five Voyces, etc.*, a set of twenty-one numbers, the title-page of which describes him as " Preist " and " Batchelor in Musique ". This collection has been reprinted by Dr. E. H. Fellowes in *Vol.* XXVII of *The English Madrigal School*, which also contains the madrigal contributed by Carlton to the *Triumphes of Oriana* in the same year (" Calm was the Air and Clear the Sky " *à* 5).

Beyond these compositions the only other pieces by Carlton that I have been able to trace are a five-part arrangement for instruments of a madrigal,—" If women could (can) be courtious " (1601),—in *Add.* 37402–6; and a Pavane for five instruments in *Add.* 17792–6 (*B.M.*).

CARR (John): A music publisher of the mid-seventeenth century who issued, either alone or in association with John Playford, several important works of that period. His son Richard was a violinist employed in the court-orchestra in post-Restoration days, and who also became a publisher of music, joining forces with Henry Playford.

One Robert Carr, whether or not related to the above is unknown, was active in the royal band from December 22nd, 1683, when he was " appointed musician for the Violl in the place of Mr. Hingston, deceased ", at a salary of 50*l.* per annum (*L.C.R.*) His name figures in the official lists until the close of the century. Work by Robert Carr may be seen in *The Delightful Companion, or Choice New*

Lessons for the Recorder or Flute (Edition 2, 1686).
CARR (Richard), CARR (Robert): *see* CARR (John).
CASE (John): A lecturer on Philosophy at Oxford who had been a chorister in his youth. Flourishing in the second half of the sixteenth century (he died January 23rd, 1599–1600), he is of interest to musicians only as the writer of two tracts on the art: *The Praise of Musicke* (1586) and *Apologia Musice tam vocalis tam instrumentalis et mixtae* (1588), a copy of each being in the British Museum collection.
CAUSTON (Thomas): A gentleman of the royal chapel and composer of sacred music perfectly representative of the Mid-Tudor period. The date of his birth is unknown; but since he is known to have been in the Chapel Royal in 1552 it could not have been much later than 1525. The date of his death (1569) would not make 1500 too early for his birth. How long anterior to 1552 he was active in the Chapel is not known, but in this year he is mentioned in *Stowe MS.* 571 (*B.M.*). His death is recorded in the Cheque-Book of the Chapel Royal as follows : " 1569.

Mr. Causton died the 28th of October and Richard Farrant (*q.v.*) was sworne in his place ".
Examples of his printed music may be seen in John Day's *Certaine Notes, etc.* (1560) and in the same publisher's *Whole Psalmes* (1563). Jebb printed a " Venite " and a Communion Service (1862), and in a " Magnificat and Nunc Dimittis ", published by Novello and edited by Royle Shore and Francis Burgess, use is made of music by Causton. The British Museum possesses a Morning Service consisting of Venite, Te Deum, Benedictus, and Gloria in Excelsis (*cf.* Day's *Certaine Notes, etc.*), in *Add.* 30480–3; while some really splendid music is contained in the Morning Service (commencing " Wee knowledge thee to be the Lord ") in *Add.* 31226.
CAVENDISH (Michael): A composer of considerable ability who was much esteemed by his contemporaries, since he contributed to East's *Whole Book of Psalms* (1592) and to the *Triumphes of Oriana* (1601; *Come gentle swains, etc., à* 5). His part-writing is distinguished by freshness and

spontaneity, and one or two of his madrigals might very well be revived to-day. Practically all we know of his life is to be gathered from his published work of 1598. A copy of this is now in the British Museum and the title-page gives the contents as: " 14 Ayres in Tabletorie to the Lute expressed with two voyces with the base violl or the voice and Lute only. 6 more to 4 Voyces and in Tabletorie, And, 8 Madrigalles to 5 voyces by Michael Cavendish, Gentle-man." The work is dedicated " to the Honourable Pro-tection of the Ladie Arbella " and is dated " From Cavendish this 24 of July ". At the end of the book is a coat of arms with three stags' heads. The information that this writer was " of Cavendish " would naturally cause us to suspect him to have belonged to the family which still flourishes with the Dukes of Devonshire at its head. Anthony Wood knew him to have been one of the ancient family of the Cavendishes. All this would naturally direct the enquirer to pedigrees of that family, and in *Add.* 19122 (*B.M. fol.* entitled " Barretts *MS.*" *fol.* 96) we find the family

traced back to the earliest known " Cavendish of Cavendish ". Michael, designated in the manuscript as " Servant in the Bed-chamber to Prince Charles ", was the third son of William Cavendish and Ann Cocks daughter of John Cocks. This William Cavendish was the eldest son of George Cavendish of Cavendish, and so back to the early four-teenth century. The " Ladie Arbella " of the dedication was without doubt Lady Arabella Stuart, James the First's cousin; and since the book was published in 1598 it is plain that Michael Cavendish was in some way connected with the Scottish royalty before the death of Elizabeth. Prince Charles was born in 1600 and came to the throne of England in 1625, and between these two dates must be the period of the composer's court service. The will of one Michael Cavendish, proved on July 11th, 1628, is most likely that of the composer. I have found no trace of any other Michael Cavendish at this period, and there is no valid argument to dissociate the Michael Cavendish of the will (and the pedigree mentioned above) from the musician who published the book of " Tabletorie " from Cavendish in 1598.

Modern reprints of his compositions include the " Oriana " madrigal in 1895 (also contained in Benson's edition of the Orianas, 1905, and in Dr. Fellowes' *Vol.* XXXII (*English Madrigal School*). " Every Bush new Springing " was issued in 1840 and 1891. Manuscript music is preserved in the Christ Church library, Oxford, and in *Add.* 31811 at the British Museum.

CHARLTON (Richard): *see* CARLTON (Richard).

CHILD (William): An organist and composer of the transitional period. His great age enabled him to see the Elizabethan methods changed,—for although he was almost twenty years of age when Orlando Gibbons died, he lived long enough to bury Henry Purcell. He was brought up in the old traditions and would possibly have risen to considerable heights had the fashion in music not changed. This will be clear when his earlier work is compared with the post-Restoration music. Had the style of the motets written before the return of Charles II been maintained, Child would have remained a greater figure in English music than is actually the case. Some of his music is undoubtedly very fine indeed ; but the lowering of his ideals and the diminution in his capacity for taking pains later on, just prevented him from rising to the higher levels attained by others. It must not be forgotten that he was no longer a young man when Charles the Second's more superficial tastes brought from France many ingredients which a musician of the older school could only use at his peril.

William Child was born at Bristol in 1606 or 1607, eventually singing as a chorister in the Cathedral there at a time when Elway Bevin was instructor. His long connection with Windsor began in 1630 when he became a lay clerk at St. George's Chapel, soon afterwards receiving the appointment of organist,— sharing the post with Nathaniel Giles. From the early part of 1634, however, Child filled the organist's post alone. He was already known as a composer at that time, for the Services that pleased Charles I so much and his published volume of

Psalms date from before the civil war. In 1631 he obtained the degree of *Mus. Bac.* at Oxford. On the outbreak of the Revolution, of course, all the musicians connected with the Chapels Royal found themselves without employment, and how some of them managed to live is somewhat of a mystery. Child, according to tradition, retired to a farm and devoted himself to composition. We hear nothing of him during the Commonwealth, and it is quite likely that he did withdraw to the seclusion of some rural retreat.

As soon as the Royal music began to be re-organized in 1660, we find Child's name prominent. On June 16th of that year, for example, he is noted for appointment in the " Private Musick " in Ferrabosco's place as " composer of wind musick ". It is possible that Child was an expert authority on wind-instruments, and he appears as a " musician for the cornets", being a per-former on the instruments of that class. On November 20th, 1660, a warrant was issued for the delivery of the materials required for his livery: " Fourteen yards of Chamblett for a gowne, three yards of black velvet to gare the same gown, one furre of Budge for the same, price 4*l.*, eight yards of damask for a jaquet and three yards of velvet for a doublet . . . the making also to be paid for out of the Great Ward-robe " (*L.C.R.*). In 1663 he proceeded *Mus. Doc.* at Oxford, the Anthem which he composed as his exercise having been performed at St. Mary's Church. The following year he added Henry Ferrabosco's place to his list of appointments (July 11th, 1664; *L.C.R.*). With all these varied posts to fill Child could not have led a lazy life. At this period of his career he played the Cornet (*v. Dict. Old Engl. Mus.* for this instrument), composed for the wind-consort, and did service in the Chapel Royal (*L.C.R.*, 1668). A curious document crops up in the Lord Chamberlain's Records under date May 4th, 1670: a petition from " Dr. Child, musician for the wind instru-ments, against the rest of his fellows, for deteyning six years and a half of board wages upon the pretence of his not attending the service ". Child was then sixty-four years of age, and since he received an allowance of 8*s*. a day for attending at Windsor, we may suppose that he was generally attached to the Chapel Royal in London. The organiſt named in the same entry was John Blow. We do not find Child's name as organiſt in the Chamberlain's Records until 1674, and between his two periods as a performer on that inſtrument a considerable number of years muſt have elapsed. The Chapter Aɛts of Windsor give the amusing ſtory of how St. George's Chapel there came to be paved: " Ld. Clarendon paved the floor all about the altar in our chapel, and that the occasion of Dr. Child ye organiſts paving the reſt of the Choir in like manner, was this: Dr. Child having been organiſt for some years to the King's Chapel in K. Charles the Second's time, had great arrears of his salary due to him to the value of about 500*l*., which he and some of our canons discoursing of, Dr. Child slited, and said he would be glad if anybody would give him 5*l*. and some bottles of wine for ; which the canons accepted of, and accordingly had articles made

hand and seal. After this K. James II coming to the crown, paid off his Brs. arrears wch. much affeɛting Dr. Child, and he repining at, the canons generously released his bargain, on condition of his paving the body of the church with marble, wch. was accordingly done, as is commemorated on his Grave-ſtone ". In 1690 Dr. Child was assessed for taxation by poll at a shilling, and " for 300*l*. in ready money and debts " at another 30*s*. He died on March 23rd, 1696–7 (date on tombſtone), and was buried at Windsor. On the twenty-fourth of the month Francis Piggot was sworn in as organiſt in Child's place (*C.B.C.R.*). A full-length portrait of him in his doɛtor's robes hangs in the Oxford Music School.

Child's firſt published work appeared in 1639: " The firſt set of Psalmes of three voyces, fitt for private Chappells, or other private meetings with a continuall Base, either for the organ or Theorbo . . ." It re-appeared in 1650, and was advertised in Book I of Henry Lawes's *Ayres and Dialogues* of 1653, in which Dr. Child is described as " late organiſt of Windsor ". In 1656 a third edition appeared as *C h o i s e   M u s i c k   t o   t h e   Psalmes   of   Dauid*, etc. Among other contemporary publications Playford's *Court Ayres* (1655) and *Catch that Catch Can* (1658) contain examples of his lighter pieces. Specimens of his ecclesiastical music may be seen in the works of Arnold and Boyce. Novello and Co. have issued a number of Child's compositions, while almost every library of any importance has manuscript music of his; the Fitzwilliam Museum (Cambridge) having interesting copies of some of Child's compositions made by Purcell and Blow, and the Christ Church library (Oxford) possesses what is perhaps the best of his unpublished music.

CHILSTON. The writer of a treatise on music from the arithmetical aspect. Nothing is known of the life of this theoretician beyond the fact that he flourished during the first half of the fifteenth century,—perhaps a little earlier. His treatise, contained in *Lansdowne MS.* 763 (*B.M.*) was transcribed by one John Wylde, precentor of Waltham Abbey (Herts), *ca.* 1460. This manuscript was brought away from Waltham Holy Cross at the dissolution by Thomas Tallis. The work is written in English,—an unusual thing, —and deals with the ratios of different intervals. An important section from the historical point of view gives the rules of the " Sights " in descant and " Faburden " (Faux-Bourdon). Hawkins printed this tract almost in its entirety (*Hist.*).

CLARKE (Jeremiah): An organist, composer of vocal music for church and stage, and writer of many interesting instrumental works,—chiefly for the harpsichord. Flourishing during the latter part of the seventeenth century and the opening decade of the eighteenth, Clarke may be looked upon as a connecting link between the musicians who still showed traces of the older methods and the newer writers who already looked towards the mode of the eighteenth century. It cannot be said that his talent was exceptionally great, though he wrote some very charming vocal music of a sentimental nature and some excellent pieces for the keyboard instruments. But he lived in a difficult period musically, and further was overshadowed by the brilliant genius of Purcell. At the same time he is a musician worthy of consideration,— especially from the point of view of the historian who seeks examples of the music belonging to the era during which the remnants of the late Tudor and early Stuart methods were dropped and a new one marked by a more superficial melody and greater artificiality was adopted. Jeremiah Clarke was essentially a product of his period.

The date of Clarke's birth is not to be determined with certainty,—most authorities fix upon *ca.* 1669 and a few add "probably much earlier". But "much earlier" it could not have been. Clarke was a chorister under Blow; and the probability is that he did not come under the direct influence of that musician until the latter became Master of the Children (1674). If this was the case, Clarke's birth cannot be placed earlier than *ca.* 1665. But in 1691 (April 26th) an entry in the Lord Chamberlain's Records (Bundle 8) speaks of Clarke as " late Child of the Chappell whose voice is changed ". A later entry (1696) is admittedly erroneous, but

there is no reason for supposing that the one of 1691 is the result of a mistake. Supposing his voice to have broken at the age of seventeen, his birth would have to be placed somewhere in 1673. This being so, he could have come under Blow *ca.* 1682 or 1683 (aged 9 or 10); he would have been nineteen years of age when appointed as organist to Winchester College (1692); aged twenty when Almoner and Master of the Children at St. Paul's Cathedral; aged twenty-two when organist there; Gentleman of the Chapel Royal at the age of twenty-seven (1700); aged thirty-one when organist there (1704); thirty-two years old when Vicar-Choral of St. Paul's ; and thirty-four when he shot himself in despair through, it is said, unrequited love (1707). The only date which seems to be open to argument is 1693 when he was Master of the Children of St. Paul's. It is true that a man of twenty would be very young to hold such a post; but he had it on the resignation of Blow, and it is probable that his master still kept an eye on him. If he had been born as early as 1660, as some say, he would have been fourteen years old when Blow became Maſter of the Children of the Chapel Royal and forty-seven when he committed suicide for a hopeless love affair. The reason that the dates I have suggeſted above were not accepted earlier was probably due to the belief that because Clarke's name was inserted in error in a Lord Chamberlain's entry of 1696, it was assumed that the entry of 1691 muſt be equally wrong, which need not be the case.

Clarke's music is of a very varied charaĉter. British Museum manuscripts contain Catches, Odes, Songs, and incidental music to plays, Anthems, Hymns. He was the firſt to set Dryden's " Alexander's Feaſt " as an ode to St. Cecilia (1697). Music by him is included in *Harmonia Sacra* (1693 and 1714), and a large number of songs were published separately between 1698 (?) and 1700, as well as numerous later reprints. In 1700 he collaborated with Croft, Blow, and two others in a book of *Ayres for the Harpsichord or Spinett*, and in conjunĉtion at different times, with such men as Daniel Purcell, Leveridge, *etc.*, he supplied the music to a number of plays popular between 1699 and 1706. Three of his anthems,—" How long wilt Thou forget me ", " I will love Thee, O Lord ", and " Praise the Lord, O Jerusalem ", — have been issued by Novello and Co. CLIFFORD (James): A clergyman who is important to musicians, only on account of his " *Divine Services and Anthems*, usually sung in the Cathedrals and Collegiate Choires in the Church of England ", a volume containing the words of a large number of anthems, which otherwise might not have been preserved. Two editions appeared in 1663 and 1664. Clifford was born at Oxford in 1622 (baptized May 2nd), and became successively a choriſter at Magdalen College, Minor Canon of St. Paul's Cathedral, and senior cardinal. For a time he held the curacy of St. Gregory by St. Paul's. He died after the middle of September, 1698, for on the 26th of that month his will (by which he bequeathed his music-books to the minor canons of St. Paul's) was proved by his widow. COBB (John): An organiſt of the Chapel Royal who appears to have enjoyed high favour. John Playford and Henry Lawes were among his friends and the present writer has it from the late Henry Davey that Archbishop Laud left Cobb all his instruments and 50*l.* In his *History of English Music* Davey adds that Cobb was probably Laud's household musician. Whether this was so or not cannot be determined. His appointment to the Chapel Royal dates from 1638 when " John Clarke dyed the (space blank) July, and John Cobb was sworne in his place " (*C.B.C.R.*). Playford (*Musical Banquet*) includes Cobb among the eminent teachers for organ and virginal during the Commonwealth. To the *Choice Psalmes* (1648) of the brothers Lawes he contributed an elegy to the memory of William Lawes. For Henry Lawes's *Ayres and Dialogues* (1653) he wrote some verses and referred to that musician as his " ever honoured Friend and Father ". Other examples of his work may be seen in *Select Ayres and Dialogues* (Book III), *Catch that Catch Can* (1658), and the *Musical Companion* (1672). British Museum manuscripts contain a Catch, a part-song, and a Trio, *Harl.* 6346 con-

tains six Verse Anthems by him, while the Christ Church collection (Oxford) has two Almaines and two Corants *à* 3.

COBBOLD (William): A madrigalist of considerable repute, born at Norwich (St. Andrew's Parish) on January 5th, 1559–60. The first we learn of his activities is that he was appointed organist of Norwich Cathedral not later than 1599, holding the post until 1608 when a new organist took his place. He then became a singer in the Cathedral. In 1630 his wife died, and was buried at Norwich; and in his will, made on August 4th, 1637, he desired to lie interred in the Cathedral with her. On November 7th, 1639, however, he died at Beccles, and was buried in the Parish Church there (*v.* J. E. West, *Cathedral Organists*).

His best-known work is the contribution to the *Triumphes of Oriana* (1601),— " With Wreaths of Rose and Laurel " (*à* 5),—which, though perhaps not meriting the praise given it by Burney, is, nevertheless, well worthy of revival. It was reprinted by Novello, Ewer, and Co. (edited by A. H. Mann) in 1892, and by L. Benson in 1905. He assisted in the harmonizing of the Psalm-tunes in East's *Whole Booke of Psalmes* (1592), and some sacred music of his remains in manuscript. He also (like Weelkes, Orlando Gibbons, and Richard Dering) wrote in the so-called " Humorous Fancy " form. Manuscripts containing examples of his work are in the Royal College of Music, and the British Museum (*Add.* 18936–9, *New Fashions, à* 4, containing many popular songs of the seventeenth century, a motet, " Sub diuersis specibus ", an " Anome "— probably " In Nomine "— apparently for five instruments though only four parts remain; *Add.* 31421, " O God, my strength and fortitude ").

COCK (Arthur): A famous organist active near the end of the sixteenth century. Very little is known of his life, and the date and place of his birth are alike unknown. He is first to be met with as organist of Canterbury Cathedral from 1584 to 1590 (West, *Cathedral Organists, Ed.* 1921). In 1591 he went to Exeter in a similar capacity, being there when he supplicated for, and was granted, the degree of Bachelor of Music (1593). He left Exeter in 1601 and must have gone directly to the Chapel Royal in London, for on March 3rd, 1600–1, the Lord Chamberlain ordered the deputy of the Sub-Dean " to sweare Arter Cocke gentleman in ordinary and organiste (without pay) in his Majeste's saide Chapple, untill an organiste place shal become voyde, and the saide Arter Cocke (by his Honor's appointment) to geve his attendaunce, and to supplye the wantes of organistes which may be throughe sicknes or other urgent causes, and that at the commandment of the sub-deane . . . and at his owne proper costes and charges " (*C.B.C.R.*), which shows that a deputy organist on the waiting-list was none too well off. But Cocke had not long to wait. " George Water-house died the 18th of Februarie and Arthur Cock from Exon. was sworne the eighth of Marche following " (*Id.*). In 1603 he is mentioned among the members of the Chapel receiving mourning liveries for the funeral of Queen Elizabeth (*L.C.R., Vol.* 554). Shortly afterwards he died: " 1604. Arthur Cock died the 26th of Januarie, and Orlando Gibbons sworne in his room "

(*C.B.C.R.*). The only known music by him is in the "In Nomine" form (Music School, Oxford).

COLEMAN: *see* COLMAN.

COLMAN (Catherine): The wife of Edward Colman, she was introduced to the music-drama of the Commonwealth by her husband. She enjoys the distinction of having been the first woman to appear on the stage in England, though she does not seem to have sung in any other production than Davenant's *Siege of Rhodes* (1656), in which she took the part of Ianthe. Pepys was on friendly terms with the Colmans, and from his *Diary* we obtain an idea of Mrs. Colman's powers as a vocalist, though she was probably past her prime when the entry was made on October 31st, 1665: " . . . . and anon comes Mrs. Colman and her husband, and she sang very finely ; though her voice is decayed as to strength, but mighty sweet though soft, and a pleasant jolly woman, and in a mighty good humour . . . But . . . we got Mrs. Coleman to sing part of the Opera, though she would not own she did get any of it without book in order to the stage; but above all her counterfeiting of Captain Cooke's part . . . she do it most excellently ",— Captain Cooke having sung the part of Solyman in the *Siege of Rhodes.* It is interesting to note that Davenant's patent contained a clause permitting the female rôles in the opera to be sung by women.

COLMAN (Charles) (I): A popular composer of instrumental music and an able violist who flourished during the seventeenth century. He contributed large quantities of light music to the collections of his day, and favoured the Lyra-viol; having been, as Wood remarks, " an improver of it by his excellent inventions ". The date of his birth is not known. Mr. W. Barclay Squire (*Dic. Nat. Biog.*) mentions a Charles Colman who played the part of Hymen in a masque in 1617. He cannot have been very old when he joined the consort of the King, for in 1625 he is already. mentioned in that capacity. Three years later he is entered in the Lord Chamberlain's Records among the " lutes and voices ". On the outbreak of the civil war, of course,

he lost his court appointment, but does not seem to
have been idle. According to
Playford's *Musical Banquet*
he taught singing and viol-
playing during the Commonwealth. Living at Richmond,
Colman had the famous
Puritan commander, Col.
Hutchinson, living with him.
It is known that the latter
" had a great love to music "
and performed well upon the
gamba. It is not at all unlikely that he was a pupil
of Colman. At all events,
the musician must have had
some friends at the republican
headquarters, for one of the
recommendations of the Committee appointed to reform
the University of Cambridge
was that Charles Colman be
admitted a Doctor of Music.
The conferring of the degree
dates from July 2nd, 1651.
In 1656 he shared with Cooke,
Lawes, and Hudson, the task
of providing the music for
" The First Day's Entertainment ", and in the same year
collaborated with George
Hudson in the writing of the
entr'actes to the *Siege of
Rhodes*.

At the Restoration Henry
Cooke obtained Colman's
" composer's " place, and the
latter was appointed " for
the viall, among the lutes

and voices " in the place of
Thomas Ford (*L.C.R.*, *Vol.*
477). This appointment
Colman shared with his son
Charles (*Id.*, *Vol.* 181). His
salary was 40*l.* per annum,
with 20*l.* for strings. In
1662 Henry Lawes died and
Colman received back his
appointment as composer
with a further 40*l.* a year. In
the same year he joined the
Corporation of Music. On
July 8th, 1664, he is given
as " deceased " in the Lord
Chamberlain's Records, his
death having taken place a
few days before this date at
his house just off Fetter Lane,
London. He must have died
within the first week of July,
for his will was dated in that
month, and before the eighth
he certainly was dead. His
will was proved on the 16th
by his widow, Grace.

So far as I know all the
music of Charles Colman was
of a secular nature. He wrote
the music to a masque presented to the King and Queen
at Richmond in 1636 (some
portions of it being in the
Music School collection at
Oxford) and he contributed
to several of the Common-
wealth publications. In 1652,
1653, and 1659 he supplied
pieces for Playford's *Select
Ayres and Dialogues* and *Court*

Ayres, appearing in 1655, contains no fewer than six dozen short pieces in two parts. *Musick's Delight on the Cithren* (1666) and *Musick's Recreation on the Viol, Lyra-way* (1669) both contain work by Colman. He contributed some verses to Henry Lawes's second book of *Ayres and Dialogues* (1655) and gave the interpretation of the musical terms in Edward Phillip's *New World of Words* (1658). Manuscript music by Colman is preserved in the collections at the British Museum, the Music School and Christ Church (Oxford), the Fitzwilliam Museum (Cambridge), *etc.* Later works headed " Charles Colman " (without the prefix "Dr.") must be examined carefully before it can be determined whether they are not to be attributed to Charles Colman II (*q.v.*).

COLMAN (Charles) (II): A son of Charles Colman (I), and a court musician during the second half of the seventeenth century. Like his father he was celebrated as a performer on the Viola da Gamba. We meet with him first as a royal musician on the restoration of King Charles II, having been appointed musician " in ordinary amongst the lutes and voices in the King's private music ". He was sworn in before April 20th, 1661, and shared his first post with his father, probably assisting the latter and deputising for him. On May 4th, 1665, a warrant was issued allowing Charles, junior, the livery " as Dr. Charles Colman formerly enjoyed " (*L.C.R., Vol.* 742), and on June 27th he is called " musician in ordinary for the Violls, in the place of . . . his father, deceased " (*Id., Vol.* 814). In 1668–9 his salary is given as 60*l.* per annum (*Id., Vol.* 482). In 1674 he was one of the three gambists who performed in the great masque of that year (*Id., Vol.* 745). In 1685 he was sworn in as a performer on the same instrument to James II (*Id.*), and in the following year it was ordered that 129*l.* in arrears on his livery account from the time of Charles II be paid him out of the tobacco and sugar imposition (*Id., Vol.* 805). He died in or before June, 1694, for on the 22nd of that month Robert Lewis was appointed in his place, Colman being given as " deceased " (*Id., Vol.*

183). News of a Charles Colman was advertised for in the *London Gazette* in 1697, but it is quite clear from at least two entries in the Lord Chamberlain's Records that he died in 1694.

COLMAN (Edward): Like his father Dr. Charles Colman and his brother Charles Colman II, Edward was a musician active at the Stuart court, and well known as a violist, singer, and teacher. We meet with him during the Commonwealth as the composer of Shirley's *Contention of Ajax and Ulysses* (1653), as a singer and actor in Davenant's *Siege of Rhodes* (1656) taking the part of Alphonso, and as one of the eminent teachers in London " for Voyce or Viol " (*Musical Banquet*). At the Restoration he was appointed to a post in the private music of the king " for a Voyce ", in the place of John Lanier at a salary of 40*l.* and the usual livery allowance (*L.C.R., Vol.* 180; November 9th, 1660), and also as a gentleman of the Chapel Royal. He died in 1669, the Cheque Book of the Chapel Royal containing the entry: " Mr. Edward Colman . . . departed this life at Green-wich on Sunday the 29th of August ".

Specimens of Edward Colman's writing can be seen in the *Select Musicall Ayres and Dialogues* (1653 and 1659) and in the *Musical Companion* (1672). In the latter is to be found " The Glories of our Birth and State ", a very popular song, from Colman's setting of Shirley's work mentioned above. It is also present in British Museum manuscripts *Add.* 31462 and 31463, and was printed in the *European Magazine* (*Vol.* III, 297). *Add.* 29396 (*B.M.*) contains another song of his,—" A Chine of Beefe ",—also contained in the *Musical Companion*. He is represented in manuscripts at Lambeth Palace and the Fitzwilliam Museum (Cambridge).

COOKE (Henry): A post-Restoration Master of the Children of the Chapel Royal who exercised considerable influence upon the succeeding generation of musicians. Among the boys who formed the juvenile section of the choir, Cooke had such pupils to instruct as John Blow, Michael Wise, Tudway, Pelham Humfrey, and Henry Purcell,—to name only five, —and his gifts as a teacher muſt have been very great to have produced such uniformly good results. Already during the Commonwealth he enjoyed a high reputation as a teacher, and he was probably one of the laſt to base a method of inſtruction upon the traditions of the Elizabethan era. Perhaps he was particularly fortunate in having exceptional talent to deal with in the firſt set of boys at the Chapel;—but there can be little doubt that the dramatic school of the rising generation owed much of its success to the training derived from Henry Cooke. As a singer he was held to be the moſt " transcendent in England in that art ", and John Evelyn entered in his Diary (November 28th, 1654) that he had a visit from " one Captain Cooke, eſteemed the beſt singer, after the Italian manner, of any in England; he entertained us with his voice and theorbo ". Cooke's military rank dated from the civil war, when he served with the royal forces. At the performance of Davenant's *Siege of Rhodes* (1656) Cooke sang the part of Solyman, and his great fame as a vocaliſt was probably founded on that occasion. Besides singing in this epoch-making work, he also supplied some of the music. Captain Cooke was a very great man during the period at which he was active and it should not be forgotten that after the Commonwealth there was scarcely " one lad . . . capable of singing his part readily " (*v. Dic. Old Engl. Mus. s.v.* " Cornet "), and it was Cooke who brought out the music that was in the younger generation,—a labour which culminated in the productions of the younger Purcell. The dramatic tendencies of so many of Cooke's pupils may perhaps be traced to the Captain's experiences on the ſtage during the interregnum. It is a pity that so conscientious and industrious a man should have been saddled poſthumously with a reputation for vanity and jealousy that he perhaps never merited. Possibly it was Pepys who set the ſtory going that Cooke was a " vain coxcomb ", or it may have been Anthony Wood who ſtarted the legend that he " died in discontent and with grief " because of the success of his pupil Pelham Humfrey. But, I think, neither of these scraps of information merit the seriousness with which they have been treated. Pepys could be very biassed on occasion, and the cause for his remark may lay in the circumstance that " Captain Cooke had the arrogance to say that he was fain to direct Sir W. Davenant in the breaking of his verses into such and such lengths, according as would be fit for musick " (Pepys, *Diary*, February 13th, 1666–7). As to the other tale, Cooke was too old a man when he died to have suffered much through jealousy at the success of a pupil. He was possibly annoyed at the Gallic methods and manners affected by his quondam scholar,— but that such puerilities caused the death of an aged and honoured master, only an Anthony Wood would care to suggest.

Except for the information already given nothing is known of Cooke's life until we meet with him after the Restoration of the house of Stuart, engaged upon re-organizing the Chapel Royal. In 1660 we find him appointed to a multiplicity of posts. In that year he was engaged as " a base in Mons. Du Vall's place " (*L.C.R.*), probably as a singer accompanying himself on the lute as did Duval; as " Composer in the private Musick in the place of Dr. Coleman "; and as " Master of the boyes in the private Musick " (*L.C.R.*, June 29th). The entry for November 9th, 1660, gives the salaries he received: " Warrant to admit . . . to his Majesty's private Musick in ordinary: Henry Cooke in the place of Mons. Du Vall for a lute and voyce, 60*l.* per annum and 20*l.* for strings. Also 24*l.* per annum for breeding a boy for vocall musick which Thomas Day lately enjoyed " (*L.C.R.*). For the year commencing at Michaelmas, 1660, we find Cooke's account " for shoes and gloves provided by him for the said children " (*L.C.R. Papers, Bundle* 21), and warrants for the payment of his expenses " for the keep of two boys and for teaching them ", and for sums of 10*l.* quarterly paid to Cooke " for keeping and teaching two singing boys ". Such entries as these are very frequent indeed in the State Papers, and no useful purpose will be served by quotations from all of them; the reader is referred to H. C. de Lafontaine's *The King's*

Musick (Novello), where all allusions to musicians from 1460 to 1700 are calendarized. Cooke's duties, as will be seen from these records, were very varied; and in addition to those mentioned, it was part of his business to see that the boys of the Chapel were properly fed, clothed, and housed, and also nursed in case of sickness. Likewise he had to keep the supply adequate so that the losses occasioned by the " going off " of choristers when their voices broke could be made good. Thus on July 4th, 1661, he received 23*l.* 16*s.* 9*d.* " for fetching five boys from Newarke and Lincolne for his Majesty's service " (*L.C.R.*, *Vol.* 741). An interesting entry is that made under date September 16th, 1661: " Warrant for the following payment to Henry Cooke . . . 19*l.* 10*s.* being extraordinary charges for himself and twelve children, commanded to attend upon his Majesty at Windsor for the space of six days, at the rate of 5*s.* a day to each, and 2*l.* 16*s.* for torches and lights for practising the musick against his Majesty's coronation " (*L.C.R.*). In Bundle 4 of the Lord Chamberlain's papers is preserved one of the rarest of Stuart documents, — a *receipt* for 50*l.* 1*s.* paid to Henry Cooke (May, 1662). In the autumn of 1662 Cooke was elected an assistant of the Corporation of Musick,—an influential guild that controlled the activities of all the professional musicians of the metropolis, and in 1663 he was steward at the annual Chapel Feast, though he did not think such an office " meete or convenient " for " the Master of the Children to have ". On May 31st, 1664, he, in association with John Lilly, John Hingston, and Hudson, met " fower of the musique of the cittie of London to treat upon such matters and things as concerne the good of the said Corporation ", for no musician was allowed to practise in town without the licence of that body. In 1665 (April 11th) he was paid for " nursing of three boys that were sick of the small pox ". On January 9th, 1668–9 a list was made up giving the salaries of all the musicians at court, Henry Cooke receiving 40*l.* with further sums of 40*l.* as composer, 48*l.* as master of the boys, 40*l.* for training two boys for the private music, and 20*l.* for strings,—a total of 188*l.*, a very respectable sum in those days,—and when not too far in arrears. The entry for April 9th, 1669, shows that Cooke dwelt at the " further end of the Old Bowleing Alley at Hampton Court ", for on that date an order was issued for the repair of his lodgings there and for the erection of " Chymneyes there necessary and convenient " (*L.C.R., Vol.* 771). Payment of the sums due to him for the maintenance of the boys must have been very irregular towards the end of Cooke's life, since he had to petition for new clothes for them as they were not " fit at present to attend upon your Majesty's service nor to walke in the streets " (*Annalen*).

Henry Cooke died on July 13th, 1672, his place as master of the boys at the Chapel Royal being filled by his pupil Pelham Humfrey (*C.B.C.R.*). His last illness could not have been of long duration, for it was not until June 24th that he asked the Corporation of Music to choose his successor (he had been Marshall of the Corporation since 1670), " he

being by reason of sickness unable to attend the buysinesse of the said Corporation ". In another of his posts at the Chapel he was followed by Burges Howe on September 11th, 1672 (*C.B.C.R.*), and as musician for the lute and voice he was succeeded by another of his pupils,—William Turner,— on September 29th (*L.C.R.*). His will (*Id., Vol.* 198) was dated July 6th, 1672, and in it he desires to be buried in the cloisters of Westminster, near his daughter Mary, a grave to be left between for his wife. He left land in Kent to be divided between his daughters after the death of his wife. The king's Treasury, on various accounts, owed him a round thousand pounds, not to mention other sums due to him. He bequeathed this money owing to him to his daughters Katherine and Amy in unequal shares, and to Katherine 120 " broad pieces of gold now in the house ". The Lord Chamberlain's Records also include a " Certificate of the burial of Captain Henry Cooke . . . in the Cloyster belonging to the Collegiate Church of St. Peter's, Westminster, on the 17th July, 1672 ".

I

The music of Henry Cooke, interesting though it may be, was not so excellent as his instruction, and as a composer he left nothing of really outstanding merit. He collaborated with others in *The First Day's Entertainment* and *The Siege of Rhodes* (1656), wrote short dance-forms which are included in Playford's *Court Ayres* of 1655, and music for the coronation of Charles II. He is represented in manuscripts preserved in the libraries of Christ Church (Oxford), the Music School (*Ibid*), and the British Museum (*Add.* 29396, " Margarita first "; *Add.* 14399, " Where shall my troubled soul " with echo; *Add.* 33234, " Morning song —Awake my soul "; *Add.* 31460, " Sleep, downy sleep " ; and *Harl.* 6346, words only of anthems by him). *Harl.* 1911, being the Minutes of the Corporation of Music, contains Henry Cooke's signature as deputy Marshall of the Company.

COOPER (John): *see* COPERARIO (Giovanni).

COOPER (Robert), COPER (Robert): *see* COWPER (Robert).

COPERARIO (Giovanni): An English musician who flourished in the first quarter of the seventeenth century, and who changed his name from John Cooper to Giovanni Coperario after a visit to Italy. Generally looked upon as merely a popular lutenist, violist, and writer of fancies and masque music, Coperario is, in fact, a personage of much greater importance. The reason for this lies not so much in the circumstance that he was the music-master of the children of King James I, or in that Charles I was exceedingly fond of playing " those incomparable Phantasies of Mr. Coperario to the Organ " (Playford *Introduction, Ed.* 1697), as in the date at which Coperario visited Italy. He was there at the time when the seed of dramatic music was germinating; when the form of composition that was to develop into the Oratorio was being experimented with; when the cult of homophonic music (the solo-song with instrumental accompaniment) was gaining a hold upon the imagination of the more serious musicians. The late Sir Frederick Bridge, told me that a friend of his,— the Rev. Spooner Lillington, —discovered a record of the production of the first Opera in Italy, and found among the names of the performers that of an Englishman,—Giovanni Coperario. The importance of this is evident when we remember that Coperario became the teacher of the brothers Lawes; and there can be no doubt that he was one of the small number of composers active at the turn of the century who formed the connecting link between the Italian innovators and the English school of writers. Compared with this, his having been one of the three first English musicians to set music for Viols Lyraway (*v. Dic. Old Engl. Mus.*) fades into insignificance.

Of the biography of Coperario we know comparatively little. His visit to Italy must have taken place before the end of the sixteenth century, and he could have returned to England not later than about 1604 or 1605. In these early years of the century we meet with him chiefly as a teacher and composer. In 1607 (July 16th) a magnificent feast was prepared for James I by the Merchant Taylor's Company, and John Bull and Nathaniel Giles were responsible for the music. For this function Coperario wrote songs and was paid 12*l*.

for his labour. Most of his masque-music was produced between 1612 and 1614, but whether he wrote all the music of this nature that has been attributed to him is open to question. It is on the authority of Rimbault that we suppose Beaumont's *Masque of the Inner Temple and Gray's Inn* (1612) to have been set by him. He collaborated with Campion and Nicholas Lanier in the celebrated masque presented on the occasion of the marriage of the Earl of Somerset in 1613–14; but whether he had anything to do with the production of the music for the *Masque of Flowers*, written for the same festivities, is open to doubt (*cf.* article on Wilson, John). It is possible that these performances secured a permanent post for him, —though he did not hold it for long,—in the royal music. From the list of musicians headed *The Chamber of King Charles* (1625) we learn that Coperario was, in that year, in the king's establishment (*L.C.R.*). In a list of those exempt from paying the subsidies voted by Parliament (December 22nd, 1625) we find the name of "John Caprario" among the

" musicians for the Lute and Voices " (*Annalen*). In July, 1626, we read that Alphonso Ferrabosco was appointed " Composer of Music to the King " with a salary of 40*l.* per annum, in the place of " John Coprario ",—and at about this time the latter muſt have died.

His firſt printed work was "*Funeral Teares For the death of the Right Honorable the Earle of Deuonshire,* Figured in seaven songes, whereof sixe are so set forth that the wordes may be expreſt by a treble voice alone to the Lute and Base Viole, or else that the meane part may be added, if any shall affeĉt more fulnesse of parts. The Seaventh is made in forme of a Dialogue, and cannot be sung without two voyces " (1606). The death of Prince Henry in 1612 called forth: "*The Songs of Mourning*, bewailing the untimely death of Prince Henry . . . set forth to be sung with one voice to the Lute or Viol " (the words were by Campion and the work was published in 1613). Sir William Leighton's *Teares or Lamentacions* (1614) included two pieces by Coperario. He is also represented in a Dutch colleĉtion:

XX. Konincklyche Fantasien op 3 Fiolen (Amſterdam, 1648). Inſtrumental music by Coperario is to be seen in the British Museum (*Add.* 23779, and—in autograph— *Add.* 31416). *Royal Appendix* 63 (*B.M.*) contains copies of the two contributions to Leighton's *Teares, etc.*, " Ile lye me downe to sleepe in peace ", and " O Lord how do my woes increase " (Cantus with Viol and Lute accompaniment). The firſt of the two is to be seen again in *Add.* 11587, the latter in *Add.* 29372–7, and both in *Add.* 31418 (another copy of Leighton's *Teares*). The Chriſt Church Library (Oxford) possesses a manuscript copy of six songs from the 1613 *Songs of Mourning* and a large number of inſtrumental fancies and danceforms.

COPRARIO (Giovanni): *see* COPERARIO (Giovanni).

CORKINE (William): A composer of vocal and inſtrumental music who flourished early in the seventeenth century. Of his life absolutely nothing is known. In 1610 he published: *Ayres to Sing and Play to the Lute and Basse Violl. With Pauins, Galliards, Almaines, and Corantes for the Lyra-Violl,* and in 1612 *The*

Second Booke of Ayres. Some to Sing and Play to the Base-Viall alone; Others to be sung to the Lute and Base Violl. With new Corantoes, Pauins, Almaines, as also diuers new Descants upon old Grounds, set to the Lyra-Violl. A copy of each of these books is in the British Museum. The Chriſt Church library (Oxford) has in manuscript a full anthem, " Prayse the Lord " (wanting the bass part).

CORNISH (William): *see* CORNYSHE (William).

CORNYSHE (William): A famous poet, deviser of pageants and plays, gentleman of the Chapel Royal, and Maſter of the Children, active during the reign of Henry VII and the early part of that of Henry VIII. In moſt of the accounts of the royal revels of this period we find Cornyshe mentioned, and, as was common in those days, there is evidence of his having been occupied in many directions other than in that of music. The Maſters of Song in early Tudor times were expected to write and produce the plays performed before the court, and in this pursuit Cornyshe was no exception to the rule. The date of his birth is not

known, but would probably fall shortly after the middle of the fifteenth century. In 1493 we find that 13s. 4d. was paid " to one Cornyshe for a prophecy "; but whether this entry in the Privy Purse expenses of Henry VII refers to the musician is not at all certain. There were several musicians with this surname at the period, and the fact that he is described as " junior " in some manuscripts points to the fact that more musicians of the name were in the public eye. All references to Cornyshes before the laſt three or four years of the century muſt be looked upon with suspicion; and we know nothing certainly of the William Cornyshe in whom we are at present intereſted, until almoſt the end of the fifteenth century. In 1502 (October 26th) he received payment for preparing three pageants (at the rate of 10l. each), and in the same year was paid 13s. 4d. " for setting of a Carrall upon Criſtmas day ". The facile pen which made him so popular a writer of plays for the court's recreation soon led him into serious trouble. Naturally gifted with a biting wit and a satirical mode of expression, he allowed his opportunities to beguile him into liberties of speech that could not be tolerated in high circles. The result was that he was incarcerated in the Fleet prison for alleged libel. Stow (*Annals*) tells us that he wrote a ballad againſt the well-hated lawyer Empson, and it may have been this composition that secured his imprisonment in 1503-4. While a prisoner he wrote *A Treatise bitweene Trouth and Enformacion,* — a copy of which is in the British Museum (*Roy.* 18 *D.* 11) being superscribed: "In the flete made by me Willm. Cornysshe, otherwise called Nyssewhete Chapelman wth the mooſt famoſt and noble Kyng Henry the VIIth, his raigne the XIXth yere the moneth of July". His *alias* of Nyssewhete is clearly made up of the laſt syllable of his name (Nyshe) and "Whete" or Wheat for "Corn". He was released juſt before the end of the reign of Henry VII, and immediately returned to the Chapel. In December, 1508, he was paid the usual sum of 6*l.* 13*s.* 4*d.* for performing a play before the King at Richmond with "others of the Chapell".

In 1509 Cornyshe's name appears in the liſt of "Gentil-men of the King's Chapel" attending the funeral of Henry VII, where he was in such company as that of Newark, Fayrfax, Crane, *etc.* Moſt works of reference say that Cornyshe became Maſter of the Children on the death of William Newark in 1509, but in an Exchequer account of 1510 (June 5th), he is ſtill described as "one of the gentlemen of the chapel", and in February, 1510-11, at the funeral of Prince Henry, he is also mentioned merely as a "Gentleman" (*L.C.R.*). Not until 1513 (December) do we find the King's Book of Payments designating him as "Maſter of the Children of the Chapel", when he received 20*s.* "for singing *Audivi* on Allhallows day". In 1511 (with Crane and others) he played in the "Golldyn Arber" and also in the Greenwich pageant of "The Dangerous Fortress". On April 9th, 1514, Cornyshe received 66*s.* 8*d.* as a half-yearly allowance "for teching, fynding and thapparyng of Robert Philip, child of the kingis chapel". At Chriſtmas of the same year he took part in the performance (and probably also in the writing) of "The Triumph of Love and Beauty", receiving "a ryche rewarde out of his (*i.e.* the King's) owne hand, to be dyvyded with the rest of his felows" (Cornyshe's autograph account of the expenses). In 1515 (April) he was paid 6*l.* 13*s.* 4*d.* "for Mr. Gyles who played on the organs in the Chapel" (*King's Book of Payments*). In that and the following year he is again mentioned as having played in the entertainments provided for the king. In 1516 he received 36*l.* 10*s.* for paving, providing gutters, *etc.*, at Greenwich, and in July of the same year he was paid 100*l.* for various repairs at that palace as well as for providing conveniences of an even less aesthetic nature. The authority for supposing that Cornyshe followed Newark as Master before Henry VII died, is provided in a Record Office list (1516) of the "Fees and Annuities paid by Henry VII", in which we read: "W. Cornyshe, master of the Children of the Chapel, *vice* W. Newark, during pleasure, 26*l.* 13*s.* 4*d.*" A good deal of the master's time must have been occupied in

teaching the choristers, for we find several entries similar to the following: "Cornyshe for finding and teaching William Saundres, late child of the Chapel, one quarter, 33*s.* 4*d.*, this to be paid quarterly, besides 20*d.* a week for his board when the King keepeth no household" (*King's Bk. of Payments*, July, 1517).

In 1518 an interesting correspondence was exchanged between Pace and Wolsey, the original letters being in the Public Record Office. On March 25th Wolsey received the following: "My Lord, if it were not for the personal love that the King's highness doth bear unto your grace, surely he would have out of your Chapel, not children only, but also men; for his grace hath plainly shown unto Cornysche that your Grace's Chapel is better than his". On the following day Pace wrote again,—this time somewhat enigmatically: "Sufficient provision has been made at Abingdon of horse meat for the King. Cannot tell how other poor men will do, insomuch that Cornysche hath made a merry supplication unto the King's grace for a bottle of hay and an horse-loaf ". It appears that bluff Hal had borrowed or commandeered a child from the Cardinal's chapel, for on March 29th he commanded Pace to write to Wolsey and thank him for the child ; Pace saying that he had spoken to Cornyshe to treat the child honestly, " *i.e.* otherwise than he doth his own ". From a letter of April 1st we learn that Cornyshe " doth greatly laud and praise the child of your chapel sent hither, not only for his sure and cleanly singing but also for his good and crafty descant and doth in like manner extol Mr. Pygote for the teaching of him ". These letters are given in summary in Brewer's *Letters and Papers . . . of . . . Henry VIII.*

At the famous " Field of the Cloth of Gold " (1520) Cornyshe was occupied with the preparations connected with the pageants and the necessary music for the banquet. On August 12th, 1520, he was paid the expenses of " the diette of ten children, every of theim at 2*d.* the day for sixty-two dais at the King's journey to Calais " (*Annalen*). Thence onwards the records give particulars of the

granting of corrodies and similar small favours, and towards the end of 1523 Cornyshe died. Of his domestic affairs we know nothing beyond the facts that his wife's name was Jane and that he had a son called Henry.

Cornyshe has left a few written works by which his style may be judged. In the British Museum the Fayrfax Book (*Add. 5465*) contains " Woffully araid " with a second part, " Behold me, I pray ", a third part, " Thus nakyd am I nailed ", and a fourth part, " Off sharpe thorne ". These pieces are signed " William Cornyssh. Junior " (*fol. 63b*). *Harl.* 1709 has a setting of " Salve Regina mater misericordia " by " W. Cornysshe ". He is further represented in the Eton College manuscript and in another preserved in the Gonville and Caius College collection. In Wynkyn de Worde's Song-Book of 1530 there are printed three songs by Cornyshe in four parts and one in three (*Triplex* and *Bassus* parts in the *B.M.— K. 1, e* 1). A " Provincial Song, both quaint and gay " (3 *voc.*, words by Skelton) was published by Rimbault in 1847.

COSYN (Benjamin): An organist and virginalist active during the first half of the seventeenth century. All that is known of his life is that he was organist at Dulwich College between 1622 and 1624, and at the Charter-house from 1626 until his death in 1643. He is remembered to-day as the owner, and possibly the writer, of a volume of virginal music known as *Benjamin Cosyn's Virginal-Book*, a valuable collection of compositions by the best-known writers of that and the preceding generation. Represented among the writers of the ninety-eight pieces contained are Orlando Gibbons, John Bull, Thomas Tallis, William Byrd, Elway Bevin, Thomas Weelkes, Cosyn himself, and others, and the book (now deposited in the British Museum) is the property of H.M. the King. It is not at all certain that all the compositions bearing Cosyn's name in this book were his own work; many if not all of these may have been merely arranged for the virginal by him. The Christ Church (Oxford) library has a five-part anthem, " O praise God in his holiness " (without the words) by Cosyn, and eight virginal pieces in the same collection signed " B. C. " are probably also by him.

An Altus part of " Musicke of Six and Fiue partes, made upon the common tunes used in singing of the Psalmes " by John Cosyn, is in the British Museum, left from a set published in 1585. Whether this John Cosyn was related to Benjamin is not known.

COSYN (John): *see* COSYN (Benjamin).

COTTO (Joannes): *see* COTTON (John).

COTTON (John) (*also* Cotto *and* Cottonius): Although there is no conclusive proof that this important theoretician was an Englishman, the probability is so great — judging from the character of the contents of his manuscript " De Musica " and the fact that an " Epistola ad Fulgentium " says " Domino et parti suo venerabili Anglorum antistiti Fulgentio "—that we shall be quite justified in ranking him with the native musicians. Cotton's celebrated treatise exists in six copies (Rome, Vatican ; Paris ; Antwerp ; Leipzig ; and Vienna, two copies). The example from which Martin Gerbert prepared his issue of the work (in his *Scriptores*) was burnt in the fire of St. Blasius (1768). Two of the manuscripts (those at Antwerp and Paris) give the author's name as Cotton (Cottonius), but in two of the others the Christian name only is given ("Joannis Musica"). The fact that a monk of Melk (quoted by Gerbert) mentions an English writer called Joannes need not prove that Cotton was an Englishman on account of the number of people—musicians included—named John. But I know of no other English writer of such treatises whose name was John and who lived at the period of the work. Beyond the knowledge that the treatise was written at the turn of the eleventh century into the twelfth, we are ignorant of all other details concerning the man and his work. "De Musica" is advanced in its tendency; it advocates the dropping of the older parallel movement; contrary motion is given as a good point; and parts cross frequently, a trifling point that helps to give the music of that period one of its distinguishing features. Cotton must have been active very near to the time when

mensurable music became developed, though he does not mention it (*v. Dic. Old. Engl. Mus. s.v. Mensurable Music*).

COUPAR (Robert): *see* COWPER (Robert).
COURTEVILE (Raphael), COURTEVILLE (John): *see* COURTEVILLE (Raphael).
COURTEVILLE (Raphael): I. A gentleman of the Chapel Royal, mentioned in the Lord Chamberlain's Records (December 10th, 1663, November 4th, 1671, and again in 1674), and who died on December 28th, 1675, his place being filled by Michael Wise (*Ch. Bk. C.R.*).

II. Raphael Courteville, son of the above, was also a chorister in the Chapel Royal, but is better known as a secular composer. He wrote a number of short pieces for the popular collections of his day, and a good deal of music for the stage. He was considered good enough a musician to contribute work to Part III of D'Urfey's *Don Quixote* in which Henry Purcell also participated (1695). In 1691 he became the first organist of St. James's Church (Piccadilly), a post he held until well into the eighteenth century. The exact date of his death is unknown. His published works include six sonatas for two flutes, another six for two violins, a set of airs in the Violin Tutor of Thomas Cross and an "excellent Solo" in Walsh's *Self-Instructor on the Violin* (1695). The psalm - tune "St. James's", named after his church, was also his work. The Christ Church library (Oxford) has two parts only of an Overture, and six pieces for strings, in manuscript, probably by this Courteville.

III. Raphael Courteville, the son of II, succeeded his father as organist of St. James's, but he occupied himself chiefly with political pamphleteering (gaining only the punned name of "Court-Evil"), and, moreover, his period of activity falls quite outside the scope of this volume.

A John Courteville is represented in Playford's *Theater of Music* (*Bk.* III, 1685, and *Bk.* IV, 1687), but nothing more seems to be known of him.

COWPER (Robert): An early Tudor musician who, though perhaps not the possessor of exceptional talent was quite up to the average for the period. He was a well-educated man and enjoyed a fairly high reputation during his lifetime. This reputation survived him by a full century, for we still find Francis Meres (*Palladis Tamia*, 1598) including him amongst the "excellente musitions" of England. The first we hear of him is the information concerning the " Grant to Robert Couper of the free Chapel within Snodhill Castle in the diocese of Hereford void by the surrender of Robert Fayrefax . . . resigned " (*Cal. of Pat. Rolls*, *Hy.* VII; November 16th, 1498). In 1502 we learn from the Cambridge Grace Book (*Gamma*, p. 3*a*) that he became Doctor of Music, the entry running: " 1502. Item, conceditur magistro Roberto Cowper ut studium quinque annorum cum practica totidem annorum citra introitum suum in eadem sufficiat sibi ad incipiendum in musica " (*v.* C. F. Abdy Williams, *Musical Degrees*). He held the chapel of Snodhill Castle for sixteen years when he resigned: " Robert Geffrey. Presentation of the free Chapel . . . of Snodhill . . . void by the resignation of Robert Cowper, clerk, doctor of music " (November

4th, 6 *Hen.* VIII, *Cal. Pat. Rolls*). Two years later (1516) he was given two benefices by the Archbishop of Canterbury: "21 Ap. 1516. Mgr. Robertus Coper Musices Doctor ad ecclesiam de Est Aersley in Decm. de Croydon, ex Coll. Archiep.", and "23 Maii, 1516, Mag. Robtus Cooper, in musiciis Doctor ad eccl. de Lachyndon cum Capella annexa in Decm. Bucking. ex Coll. Archiep." In a letter dated June 5th, 1525, William Cowper, Dean of Bridgenorth, asked for higher posts for his brother Robert Cowper, saying that the latter was a virtuous man and a good choirman (Letter to Thomas Cromwell, in *Letters and Papers . . . of Henry VIII*, Brewer). This is the last date at which our present information permits us to say he was living. When he died is still unknown.

Cowper did not restrict himself to any one style of composition, and several examples of his music may still be seen, both sacred and secular. The British Museum has work of his in the manuscripts *Roy. App.* 58 ("Petyously Constraynyd am I" by "Doctor Coper", "O gloriosa stella maris"), in *Add.* 31922 ("Alone I leffe", a round written out at length; and a three-part song "I have bene a foster"), and in *Add.* 17802–5 (four settings of the "Gloria in Excelsis"). He is also represented in the manuscript written by John Baldwin (in the possession of H.M. the King; now in the *B.M.*). Wynkyn de Worde printed "In Youth" and "So great unkyndnes", in three parts (1530); while "Alone I live" was made accessible in 1896 (*Plain-Song and Medieval Music Soc.*).

CRANE (William): An interesting figure in the history of early sixteenth century music in England. None of his works have been traced, and we can form no opinion as to his musical talents. But there can be no doubt that he was a great favourite of the King,—not perhaps so much because of his excellence as a singer and Master of the Choristers, as on account of the pleasure he gave his Sovereign in the frequent pageants and plays he devised or in the preparation of which he played a part. A consideration of his career is of value to-day merely as an example of the life led in those early days by the gentlemen of the Chapel Royal. William Crane certainly does appear to have improved the quality of the Chapel,—both in point of numbers and in efficiency,—and as one of the earliest workers in the field of musical drama he has his importance. As a gentleman of the Chapel Royal we meet with Crane first in a list of musicians receiving mourning liveries for the funeral of Henry VII (1509; *L.C.R.*). At the Coronation of Henry VIII, he is again mentioned. In an Exchequer account dated October 21st, 1509, a warrant is entered granting to William Crane a gown " of black Chambelet, *etc.*" On November 14th, 1510, he played in some Court revels, and in a similar connection he is mentioned again in February of the following year, when he took part in the celebrated pageant, " The Goldyn Arber in the Archyard of Plesyr ". On February 22nd, 1510-11, the infant Prince Henry died, and Crane's name is included in a list of gentlemen present at the funeral. Another Exchequer account (December 19th, 1511) allows to " William Crane, one of the gentlemen of our Chapell " a tawny chamlet gown. Playing in the masks and pageants was a recognized duty of the gentlemen of the Chapel during the reign of Henry VIII, and we find many references to such performances in addition to those already mentioned. Thus, in 1514, he played (and probably sang) in the so-called masque, " The Triumph of Love and Beauty ", the accounts of the official scribe naming even the materials in his costume. He is mentioned in a list of gentlemen in 1520, so possibly he was also present on the " Field of the Cloth of Gold ".

The exact date of his appointment as Master of the Children of the Chapel Royal is not to be fixed with certainty, but it must lie between 1523 (when Cornyshe resigned the post) and 1526 when we find him officially designated a " Magister Puerorum Capellae Dom. Regis " (*Exchequer Receipts*, 18 Hy. VIII). This manuscript shows also that his salary was now 40*l.* per annum. Only a few more references to his activities in the Chapel remain. In 1529 he was paid " VI*l.* xiij*s.* iiij*d.* in rewarde " for another of his musico-dramatic performances, and two years later he received

3*l.* 6*s.* 8*d.* for his expenses in fetching children for the Chapel, who were probably "pressed" into the service.

From many of the official documents it appears that either Crane was a great favourite of the King who threw several side appointments in his way and licensed him to indulge in many commercial transactions to his own advantage, or else his duties in the Chapel permitted him sufficient leisure for that purpose ; though I should imagine the former to have been the more likely. A Grant of June 3rd, 1509, states that Crane was to be, during pleasure, water-bailiff of the town and port of Dartmouth, but in November, 1510, he surrendered the patent, receiving for it ten marks a year from the Receiver - General of the Duchy of Cornwall. The State Papers (August 18th, 1511) grant to "William Crane, gentleman of the Chapel, and Thomas Cremour, of London, draper . . . in survivorship . . . a tenement or garden lately built upon, *etc.*" A year later (October 6th, 1512) he and Hugh Clopton, a London merchant, were licensed "to export 600 sack of wool . . .

through and beyond the Straits of Marrok, paying for all Customs and dues, only 4 marks per sack at the end of 5 years after shipment". His business must have involved huge sums of money, for on two occasions at this period we hear of loans to him of such colossal amounts as 1,000*l.*, but for what purpose this money was granted is not clear. At other times he received large sums of money for cables and ships' repairs. There can be no doubt that these entries refer to the musician, for in the Exchequer account No. 47 (December 31st, 1513) he is described as "William Crane, one of the gentlemen of the King's Chapel, Master of the works of his new ship at Wolwiche", and the account was for the repair and rigging of the King's "ship *The Carryke*, at Wolwich". There are other warrants of a similar nature (*Nos.* 49, 53; Brewer, *Letters and Papers . . . of Hen. VIII*, in the *P.R.O.*, *etc.*). On February 21st, 1514, he was made "Controller, during pleasure, of the tonnage and poundage of the petty custom in the port of London". Several other licenses to export various commodities were granted him, and he muſt have become a very prosperous man. Importing, exporting, and the repairing of ships went on merrily until the middle of the century. On November 26th, 1531, he is described as *Armiger*, and in June, 1532, he won 7*l*. 2*s*. 6*d*. " of the King at archery ". And dating from the same period are entries referring to payments for Chapel services. In 1531 too he was granted property in the City. In January, 1540, he ſtill performed before the King, but he muſt have been a fairly old man by then, though his payments as Maſter of the Children went on until 1545. At about that time Richard Bowyer or Bower, became Maſter, and we can only suppose that Crane was unable to continue. Dr. W. H. Grattan Flood (*Mus. Times* article and in *Early Tudor Composers*) gives the information that Crane made his will on July 6th, 1545, and that it was proved on April 6th, 1546. He therefore died at some time between these two dates.

That Crane was married is proved by the mention of his wife in one of the grants alluded to above, and that he had a daughter is clear from a letter written by the Archbishop of York to her future husband. It is possible that Crane composed some of the music for the many pageants and plays produced, but, as already mentioned, no trace of any composition of his has been discovered. He was probably far too busy with archery conteſts againſt the King, with collecting Cuſtoms dues, and with exporting double beer, to have had time to compose much music.

CRANFIELD (William): *see* CRANFORD (William).

CRANFORD (William): A composer of moderate attainments who was fairly popular early in the seventeenth century. The only information we have bearing upon his life is to the effect that he was a singer in the choir of St. Paul's Cathedral; and even this, coming from Anthony Wood, may not be dependable. But he was sufficiently eſteemed to have had work of his included in Ravenscroft's Psalter of 1622 and in Hilton's *Catch that Catch Can*. Much more of his music remained in manuscript. The British Museum has two anthems in *Add.*

30478–9, one of which is repeated in *Add.* 11784. *Add.* 31421 includes the hymn-tune " Ely " by " Cranfield " (probably the scribe's error). Catches by him are also contained in the British Museum collection. A verse-anthem *à* 6, an Elegy on the death of Henry, Prince of Wales, *à* 6, a six-part madrigal (Bass-part missing in each case), a five-part " In Nomine " for instruments and an Almaine *à* 3, are preserved in the Christ Church (Oxford) library. Sacred music of his is also contained in manuscripts at Peterhouse and Durham.

CRANFORTHE (William): *see* CRANFORD (William).

CREIGHTON (Robert): Professor of Greek at Cambridge, Fellow of Trinity College, M.A., and Canon of Wells Cathedral. He is remembered to-day chiefly as a composer of ecclesiastical music, which, though not remarkably original or distinguished by any outstanding talent, became very popular and is still occasionally to be heard. His Service in E-flat has a certain dignity of its own,—but his average work remains that of the clever amateur he was. Born *ca.* 1639, he obtained the degree of Master of Arts in 1662, was Canon and Precentor at Wells from 1674, and died at the age of 94 on February 17th, 1733–4. His best-known works are the Service already mentioned and the four-part anthem " I will arise " (both printed by Boyce). These two compositions, together with a " Sanctus " and a Service in B-flat, are in the library of Christ Church (Oxford) in manuscript. British Museum manuscripts *Harl.* 7338–9 contain another service (in C) and the anthem " Praise the Lord ". He is also represented in *Add.* 31821, 29291 (fragments of E-flat service), and 33239 (copied from *Harl.* 7339). Messrs. Novello have printed three of Creighton's anthems.

CREYGHTON (Robert): *see* CREIGHTON (Robert).

CROSS (Thomas): An engraver who kept a music-shop first in the Holborn district and later in Clerkenwell (London) in the latter part of the seventeenth century and beginning of the eighteenth. He is chiefly noticeable for his fine music-engraving, and for the circumstance that he was the first to issue single songs (sheet-music). His first traceable work is in Purcell's *Sonnata's of Three Parts* (1683), and thence onward he was very active until 1732. His father, Thomas Cross, senior, was also an engraver who occasionally did music in addition to his more usual ornamental and portrait work. The earlier and better work of Thomas Cross, junior, was beautifully engraved on copper; but later, when cheaper production was called for, he appears to have substituted pewter. There is no evidence that he ever produced his music by any other process than engraving, for when John Walsh, who used punches, commenced competing with him, he warned his customers against the new " nonsensical puncht " work.

CUTTING (Francis *or* Thomas): A very celebrated lutenist of the late sixteenth and early seventeenth centuries. It is not clear which Christian name he bore, but the confusion probably arose through a slip of the pen made by Anna of Denmark. The first time we meet him is as a contributor to William Barley's *New Booke of Tabliture* " for the lute (1596). At the beginning of the seventeenth century he appears to have been in the employ of Arabella Stuart, for the Queen (Anna of Denmark) wrote to her that Christian IV was anxious to have Cutting's services: " . . . the King off denmarks gentleman haith ensisted with us, for the licensing your seruant Thomas Cottings to depart from you but not without your permission to our brothers seruice " (March 9th, 1607). Prince Henry added his influence to the princess's request: " The queenes majesty hath commaunded me to signifie to your ladyship that shee would have Cutting your ladyship's seruant to send to the King of Denmark because he desyred the queen that shee would send him one that could play upon the lute ". The lutenist could not have been away very long, for in 1612 his name appears in a list of musicians receiving an allowance for mourning livery for the funeral of Prince Henry of Wales. Beyond this we know nothing of his biography. Since John Dowland was dismissed the Danish service in 1606, the request for Cutting in the early part of 1607 was in all probability made to secure a successor for that famous player.

K

Examples of his music may be seen in manuscripts at the British Museum: *Eg.* 2046 (Jane Pickering's Lute Book, 1616), in which he is named "Frauncis Cuttinge", and *Add.* 31392. In the latter manuscript he is described as "Maſter Cuttinge", and is repre- sented by an Almaine, a Pavane, a Galliard, and a version of "Greensleeves" for the lute. His work may also be examined in the Oxford Music School collection. For the Arabella Stuart correspondence I am indebted to Mr. W. Barclay Squire.

D

DAMAN *or* DAMON (William): A court musician to Queen Elizabeth who achieved fame with a Psalter appearing in 1579. He was undoubtedly a foreigner, Mr. G. E. P. Arkwright in the Chriſt Church Catalogue saying that he was born at Liège and came to England *ca.* 1561–5. In 1581 we find his name among those of half - a - dozen foreign musicians in a liſt given in *Harl.* 1644 (*B.M.*) referring to a Chriſtmas gift of 20*s.* to each of them. The Household accounts of 1590–92 (*Add.* 22924, *B.M.*) ſtill name him, but in Hardy's *Syllabus* he is given as ''deceased'' in 1593 (*Annalen*). His *Psalmes of David in English Meter with notes of foure partes set unto them* (1579, John Day) was probably never intended for the general public, but was written "for John Bull, citizen and goldsmith of London". Edward Hake, in the Preface, says that the tunes were "by peece meale gotten and gathered together from the fertile soyle of his honeſt friend Guilielmo Damon". Bull colleĉted these and had them printed without the composer's pleasure concerning them being consulted. The non-success of the work caused Damon to reconſtruĉt the settings and the new version appeared in 1591 under the title: "The former booke of the Musicke of M. William Damon . . . conteining all the tunes of David's Psalmes . . . moſt excellently by him composed into four parts. In which sett the Tenor singeth the Church tune. Published for the recreation of such as delight in Musicke: by W. Swayne, Gent." (Eaſt),—the composer being probably dead before the date of publication. The "Second Booke" of the same work contained the tunes but "differing from the former in respeĉt that the higheſt part singeth the Church tune". The Chriſt Church (Oxford) library has an anthem, three motets, and some inſtrumental pieces by Damon, all wanting some of the parts. The British Museum has manuscripts containing a specimen of his sacred music as well as compositions for the lute. He is represented in John Baldwin's manuscript, and in *XX*

Konincklijche Fantasien op 3 Fiolen (A m ſt e r d a m, 1648). His " Miserere " (a moſt expressive piece of work) has been printed by Mr. G. E. P. Arkwright in No. XXI of the *Old English Edition.*

DAMASCENE (Alexander). An alto singer, member of the court music, and popular composer of the late seventeenth century. Probably of Italian origin, he was born in France, and on account of his Proteſtantism was forced to leave the country of his birth and came to England, where he obtained letters patent making of him an Englishman by domicile (*Pat. Rolls, Ch. II, July 22nd,* 1682). On July 18th, 1689, a warrant was issued to admit him as " Composer in his Majeſty's private musick in ordinary ", and on the same date he was " appointed to the vocall Musick " (*L.C.R., Vols.* 486–7). A year later he joined the Chapel Royal, the Check Book recording: " 1690. Mr. Alex. Damascene was sworn Gentleman of their Majesties' Chapel Royal extraordinary the 6th day of December ". He was not appointed " in ordinary " until 1695: " Mr. Damascene was sworn in a full place

of Gentleman upon the death of Mr. Henry Purcell, December 10th, 1695 " (*Ch. Bk. C.R.*). The same source of information announced Damascene's death on July 14th, 1719. His will, which he made on May 16th, 1715, was proved on July 27th, 1719.

Moſt of Damascene's printed music consiſts of secular songs, and specimens may be seen in many of the contemporary publications. *Choice Ayres and Songs* (1676, *etc.*), *The Theater of Music* (*Books I-III*, 1685; *Book IV*, 1687), *Vinculum Societatis* (1687, *etc.*), *Comes Amoris* (1687, *etc.*), *The Banquet of Musick* (1688, *etc.*), and the *Gentleman's Journal* (two in 1692, and one each in 1693 and 1694), all contain songs of his. A Trio for ſtrings, — " John Guise's March "—is in *Add. MS.* 22099 (*B.M.*).

DAMON (William):   *see* DAMAN, William.

DANIEL (John):   *see* DANYEL (John).

DANYEL (John):   A luteniſt, singer, and composer who flourished in the firſt quarter of the seventeenth century. Of his early life we know nothing, and we do not meet with him before

1604, when he obtained the Oxford degree of *Mus. Bac.*, being described as of Christ Church, Oxford. In 1606 his only known printed work appeared : *Songs for the Lute, Viol, and Voice*, etc. The book contains, chiefly, songs for a single voice to the lute and gamba. It is thus evident that the cult of the solo-song with instrumental accompaniment was followed by a large number of early English composers, once Jones, Rosseter, and Campion had made a beginning. In 1612 Danyel is named among the " musicians " receiving mourning livery for the funeral of Prince Henry of Wales, which makes it clear that he was then in the royal service. In 1625 his name still occurs in the lists (*L.C.R.*). The Calendar of State Papers gives him under date December 22nd, 1625, as a " musician for the Lute and voice ", and exempts him from paying the subsidies voted to the king by Parliament. Henry Davey (*History of English Music*, 1921) says that Danyel had a warrant to educate children for the drama in 1613 (renewed in 1618), an occupation like that of Robert Jones and

Philip Rosseter. Manuscript examples of Danyel's compositions may be seen in the Music School, Oxford, and in the British Museum (*Add.* 24665, " Yf I could shutt the gates ", and " Drop not, myne eyes "—both from the 1606 publication).

DAVY (Richard): A talented composer of the fifteenth century concerning whom very little is known. He was organist of Magdalen College (Oxford) from 1490 to 1492, as well as singer and instructor of the choristers there. His chief works were a *Passio Domini* (specimen given in the *Oxford History of Music*, Vol. *II*), and other sacred music in the Eton College manuscript (*No.* 178 ; a full account of which was given by Mr. W. Barclay Squire in *Archaeologia*, *Vol. LVI*). The Fayrfax Book (*B.M.*, *Add. 5465*) contains some three-part secular vocal music, and *Harl.* 1709 the medius part only of a motet of his. Single parts of further church music are in St. John's College and University libraries at Cambridge. His name was sometimes spelled Davys.

DAVYS (Richard): *see* DAVY (Richard).

DAY (John): An early music

printer who issued some very important works in the sixteenth century. He was born at Dunwich in Suffolk in 1522, was Master of the Stationers' Company in 1582, and died two years later (July 23rd). He printed many well-known works of general interest. Of his musical productions the most interesting was "*The whole Psalter*, translated into English metre, which contayneth an hundred and fifty Psalmes. Imprinted at London by John Daye, dwelling over Aldersgate beneath S. Martyn's" (1567 or 1568). To this work Tallis contributed nine tunes, but only a few copies were issued and the general publication of the book was not proceeded with. Far better known was "*The Whole booke of Psalmes*, collected into Englysh Meter, by T. Sternhold and I. Hopkins, and others, conferred with the Ebrue, with apt notes to singe them withal . . . Imprinted at London by John Day . . . 1562", and several other editions. In 1563 he published "*The Whole Psalmes* in foure partes, which may be song to al musicall instrumentes, set forth for the encrease of

vertue, and abolishyng of other vayne and triflyng ballades". Day also published Whythorne's "Songes" in 1571 and Daman's "Psalmes of David" in 1579.

DAY (Thomas): A private musician to King Charles I, Master of the choristers at Westminster, and of the Children of the Chapel Royal. We meet with him first in an entry in the Cheque-Book of the Chapel Royal: "1615, John Miners died the second day of July, and Thomas Day was sworne in his place the last of September followinge". On January 30th, 1623, a "Grant, in reversion" was made to him of the office of Master of the singing boys in the King's Chapel for life" (*Annalen*). In 1625 he is given as "Master of the choristers" of Westminster. In 1626 (May 25th) he was given "one singing boy" to keep and teach, and for this service was paid 20*l*. per annum (*L.C.R.*). His total salary in that year amounted to 64*l*. a year (*Cal. S.P.*). The following year a second boy was entrusted to him for tuition, he to receive 20*l*. per annum "beyond the like sum formerly granted for keeping another boy" (*L.C.R.*). In that year (June 1st) his son Daniel was buried in the Cloisters of the Abbey (Rimbault in *Notes and Queries*, *Ser. III, Vol. X*, p. 182). On June 30th, 1628, he is given as a gentleman of the Chapel. At Christmas, 1628, he was rewarded with 100*s*. in the capacity of "musician" (private music of the King), and many similar entries follow in the State Papers. In the list of those "appointed to wayte on his Majesty in his Scottish journey, 1633", Thomas Day's name is found among the "Contratenors" (*L. C. R.*). In 1636 he became Master of the Children of the Chapel Royall (*Ch. Bk. C.R.*). On December 15th, 1637, we find his name (together with that of Nicholas Lanier) associated with a petition of gut-string makers who complained of the swindling prevalent in their calling. By 1640 his salary had risen to 128*l*. per annum, and the fact that he was active in the secular music-making of the King, is proved by his inclusion among the musicians "for lutes, violls, and Voices" in 1641. The Civil War ended his official

career. Rimbault says he died in 1654, and at the Restoration Henry Cooke received 24*l*. per annum "for breeding a boy for vocall musick which T. D. lately enjoyed" (*L.C.R.*). In another of his posts he was succeeded by Alphonso Marsh.

DEARING (Richard): *see* DEERING (Richard).

DEERING (Richard): An important and talented musician who flourished during the first quarter of the seventeenth century. He has not been treated with anything like the respect he merits, and the majority of historians,—with Mr. W. Barclay Squire (*Dic. Nat. Biog.*) as a shining exception, —are content to accept the evidence given by Anthony Wood (*Athenae* and *Fasti Oxon.*) in writing Deering's biography. But before going into the established facts connected with Deering's career, it will be as well,—for the purpose of collation,—to see what Wood wrote, and thus discover how far the different accounts of the composer's life are based upon the words of the Oxford gossip. "On the 26th of April", says Wood, "Richard Deering did as a member of Christ

Church, supplicate for the Degree of Batchelor of Music, and had his desire, as it seems, granted (tho' not registred) because in matters of his composition, which were soon after by him made extant, he entitles himself *Batchelor of Music*. This person, who was born of, and descended from, a right Antient Family of his name, living in Kent, was bred up in Italy, where he obtained the name of a most admirable musician. After his Return he practised his Faculty for some time in England, where, his name being highly cried up, became, after many entreaties, Organist to the English Nuns living in the Monastery of the *blessed Virgin Mary* at *Brussels*. At length, after the marriage of King Charles I, he was made organist to his Royal Consort *Henrietta Maria*, with whom he continued 'till she was forced to leave England by the Presbyterian outrages in the time of the Grand Rebellion ". Let us see how far this biography is borne out by the facts.

Richard Deering was truly " descended from a right antient family ", — but illegitimately. Manuscript *Add. 5534* (*B.M.*) gives his pedigree. The branch of the " truly respectable Family of Dering of the County of Kent " from which the descent of Richard is to be traced was the one headed by one William Dering of Petworth, in Co. Sussex, Esqre., and his wife Elianor Dyke. This William Dering was " the third and younger son of Richard Dering " of Kent, the family (Fitz Dering) being traced back to the reign of Henry III. The composer was the son of Henry Deering of Liss, near Petworth, by the Lady Elizabeth Grey (Hasted, *Kentish Pedigrees*), and of whom the manuscript says: " Henry Dering died single, but had issue by Elizabeth, sister of Henry, Earl of Kent, Richard Dering, organist to Q. Mary, he dyed 1630 ". The date of his death as given in this manuscript does not bear out Wood's statement that Deering was still living at the time of the Great Rebellion, and we shall see that the Hasted MS. is most likely to be correct.

There is nothing surprising in the fact that an illegitimate son was sent abroad at the earliest opportunity, and the musically - inclined and Catholic child could have been sent to no more suitable a destination than Italy. It is not clear with whom he studied, but in view of the fact that some of his works make use of a figured bass, it is highly probable that he acquired his musicianship in the school of one of the early Italian users of the Basso Continuo. The date of his return to England is uncertain. In 1610 he supplicated for the degree of *Mus. Bac.*, and although there is no proof of such a degree having been conferred, there is no reason to think that it was withheld. His faith may have had more to do with his next move than had the cordial invitations he received from the English nuns at Brussels ; he would certainly have found more peace of mind out of England ;— nor was he the only Romanist musician of the period who found it more convenient to travel on the Continent. At any rate, we find him, in 1617, in Brussels ; for the title-pages of works published in 1617 and 1618 say: " Venerabilium Monalium Anglicarum Bruxellae, in Monasterio B.V.M. degentium Organista ".

The marriage of Charles I with Henrietta Maria, and the growing sympathy with Catholicism at Court, brought him home again in 1625 to fill the position of Court organist to the newly-made Queen; probably taking up his duties on the arrival of the consort from France. Besides this we find him in the King's service, for a paper granting certain concessions to a number of musicians, dated December 22nd, 1625, contains Deering's name under the heading " Musicians for the lute and voices ". On June 13th and 22nd, 1626, he is mentioned as receiving his livery allowance (*L.C.R.*). On July 11th, 1626, a list of annual salaries was issued " guaranteeing " to Richard Deering the sum of 40*l.* (*Annalen*). In 1628 he is again twice mentioned in the Lord Chamberlain's Records. The appearance of his name in these records under post-Restoration dates does not mean that he had only just then died. It merely signifies that the musicians mentioned as having been appointed in his place were to occupy the position he held before the execution of Charles I. In any case, Deering's will sets all possible doubt at rest. This document was proved in 1630 (*Ref.* 34, *Scroope,* Somerset House) by Edward Bold, " nearest blood relation of Richard Deering, deceased ". The following extracts from this interesting will may appeal to musicians: " To my aunt Bold I giue a piece of plate of 25 ounces; to Mr. Fonthill 5 pounds to buy a Lute or what ells; to Mr. Nicholas Lanier a piece of plate of 15 ounces, to Mrs. Drue (? Drew) my Virginalls; and to Mr. Drue all my Musicke Books; John Lanier, 3 pounds ". To the King Deering left 40*l.* or 50*l.*, and to the Queen 90*l.* The date of the proving of this will should prove conclusively enough that he died not later than 1630, in which year, too, his place in the royal music was taken by Giles Tomkins. Information given by Burney and Hawkins as to activity on Deering's part at dates later than 1630, is obviously incorrect, and was doubtlessly obtained from a remark of Wood's.

Richard Deering's reputation during his lifetime was a high one,—but being a Catholic and publishing his works abroad he would certainly have been better known on the Continent than in his native country. But the serious musicians of England knew of him and his work; and in spite of what Burney calls " the sober, innocent, psalmodic, dry and uninteresting " nature of Deering's music, he was well liked by his contemporaries. Peacham (1622) ranked him with Morley, Dowland, Wilbye, Kirbie, Bateson, *etc.,* and if we appraise him at something between the enthusiastic finding of Peacham and the biassed opinion of Burney, we should probably not be doing Deering an injustice. Cromwell was fond of Deering's work, and John Hingston with two of his boys would very frequently sing the Romanist's Latin motets to the intensely music-loving Puritan Protector. Mace (1676) said that " the best we did ever esteem were those things which were most solemn and divine; some of which, for their eminency I will name, viz. Mr. Deering's *Gloria Patri* and other of his Latin Songs ".

The press of Phalèse, which produced so many interesting musical publications, seems to have had the monopoly of all Deering's compositions that appeared during his lifetime. The first work of which we find any mention is the volume of *Cantiones Sacrae Sex* (some say *quinque*) *vocum, cum basso continuo ad organum,* supposed by many to have been published in 1597. Surrounding this work is a nebula of doubt and speculation. Mr. W. Barclay Squire states plainly that "his first published work appeared . . . in 1597"; Eitner says that "the work of 1597 is inherited by one book from another like the sea-serpent". Whether this work actually did appear in 1597, or whether it was confounded with one of the later publications, cannot, of course, be decided now; and the unearthing of a copy would be the only way of settling the question. But if this book exists, or ever existed and if the date given is correct, it was undoubtedly the first,—by an English writer, at any rate,—to contain a Basso Continuo. Of Deering's next published work there can be no doubt, for it exists in at least two tangible examples. This is *Cantiones Sacrae quinque vocum cum Basso Continuo ad Organum*" (1617). It consists of six part-books and contains eighteen motets. In the following year another collection of Deering's appeared, called *Cantica Sacra ad Melodiam Madrigalium elaborata senis vocibus cum B.c.* (seven part-books containing twenty-one pieces). In 1619 appeared: *Cantiones Sacrae quinque vocum cum B.c.* In 1620 the contemporary publication of Deering's works stopped after the issue of two books of Canzonets. The first was *Canzonette a quattro voci, con il Basso Continuo* (1620; five part-books), and the other was the work concerning which Professor Dr. Milchsack of the Ducal library of Wolfenbüttel, gave me much information. According to this courteous gentleman, the title-page reads : " Di Richardo Diringo Inglese, Canzonette a Tre Voci con il Basso Continuo. In Anversa appresso Petro Phalesio al Re Dauid. M.D.CXX ". He further said that the book has twenty numbered pages, of which p. 9 was missed in the pagination. The dedication is dated " Di Brusselles a di 2 Aprile, 1620 ". The Wolfenbüttel library possesses the complete set of four part-books.

A reprint of the 1617 set of *Cantiones Sacrae* was published in 1634. In 1662 John Playford issued a collection of pieces chosen from the long list of Deering's sacred compositions: *Cantica Sacra ad Duas et Tres Voces composita, cum Basso Continuo ad organum, Authore Ricardo Deringo, Regiae Majestatis quondam Organista.* It contains fourteen Cantica for two voices and ten for three. The year 1674 saw the publication by Playford of another selection of sacred compositions by various authors, of which some were supposed to have been from Deering's pen. Even Playford himself had his doubts, for he said they were " much of Mr. Deering's way, yet by some believed not to be his ". The full title reads : " Cantica Sacra: containing Hymns and Anthems for two voices to the organ, both Latine and English. Composed by Mr. Richard Dering, Dr. Christopher Gibbons, Dr. Benjamin Rogers, Mr. Matthew Locke, and others ".

Of modern reprints of Deering's writings I know of about a dozen sacred compositions edited by the late Sir Frederick Bridge, including " Jesu, Dulcis Memoria ", an anthem for five voices (1617), " O Vos Omnes ", a motet for six voices (1618), " Factum est Silentium " (*Id.*), " Jesu, dulcedo cordium " (*à 5;* 1617), and " Vox in Rama " (1617), all five published by Bosworth and Co., Ltd. The " Humorous Fancy ", so popular at the period, also attracted Deering, and he left a couple of sets of " Cryes " for voices and instruments. Sir Frederick Bridge published the " London Cryes " (Novello and Co.), and I am scoring the " Country Cryes " for future publication.

A very large number of manuscripts containing compositions by Deering are to be found scattered among several collections. The British Museum contains a particularly rich assembly of handwritings that include pieces, — instrumental as well as vocal, — by Richard Deering. *Add.* 18936–9 contains that interesting and quaint composition, — the " Countrye Crye of V. vo: God give you good Morowe Sir Rees ap Thomas ap William ap Johnes, 3 a clock and a faire Morninge ". *Add.* 29372–7 (Thomas Myriell's Tristitiae Remedium, 1616) contains the anthem " And the King was moved ", *à 5,* the "Countrye Cryes" repeated, and the common street cries commencing "What doe ye lack", à 5. *Add.* 29366–8 includes five Fancies for five instruments, only three of the parts being preserved. In *Add.* 29427 we find the "Country Cryes" and the anthem already mentioned, once more copied (Altus part only). *Add.* 17786–91 contains the six parts of two instrumental "Phantasias". *Add.* 31423 (in John Jenkins's handwriting) includes two Pavanes by Deering. The bass part of an "Almain in *C fa ut*" is preserved in *Add.* 36993. Further specimens of his work are contained in *Add.* 18940–44 (a Pavane for three viols with basso continuo for the harpsichord), *Add.* 11608 (two Cantica à 2, and Gloria Patri, à 3), *Add.* 30478–9 (an anthem for Easter), *Add.* 30382 (another copy of Gloria Patri à 4), *Add.* 17792–6 (Fantasias), and *Eg.* 2013. Manuscript motets, madrigals, canzonets, and Fancies are also to be found in the collections at the Royal College of Music (London), Christ Church (Oxford; Deering's Alma Mater), the Music School (Oxford), and Peterhouse (Cambridge).

DE MILLAN (Milan): *see* LUPO FAMILY.
DENOWS (Richard): A musician in the service of Henry VIII. He is entered in the king's "Household Book" (*Add.* 21481; *B.M.*) in 1509. In the June of that year his salary was 16*d.* per day, and in July he received 40*s.* for the month. In an order to John Heron, the king commanded the payment of 16*d.* a day to Denows "from 1 July instant" (from Greenwich, 18 July, 1 *Hen. VIII*), in which order he is designated "minstrel". Early in 1514 he is still named in the book of payments, but after December of that year his name disappears. Nothing further is known of him.
DERING (Richard): *see* DEERING (Richard).
DIRINGUS (Ricardus): *see* DEERING (Richard).
DOLAND (John): *see* DOWLAND (John).
DOUGLAS (Patrick): A sixteenth century composer of whose biography nothing is known. In a Christ Church (Oxford) manuscript he is described as a "Priste, Scotte borne", and this is all I have been able to discover relating to him. In the manuscript just alluded to are to

be seen two five-part motets, "In Convertendo" with a second part, "Converto Domine" (wanting the Tenor part), and "Ubi eſt Abel" (*Id.*). The laſt-named was printed in the *Musical Antiquary* for Oƈtober, 1910. *Add.* 22597 (*B.M.* late sixteenth century) contains a tenor part of an inſtrumental arrangement of "In Convertendo", and *Add.* 31390 includes both parts of this motet arranged for five viols in parts, signed "Duglas".

DOWLAND (John): One of the moſt celebrated of the luteniſts and among the moſt genial of the composers for the voice aƈtive at the end of the sixteenth century and during the firſt quarter of the seventeenth. For moſt of the biographical details conneƈted with him we are dependent upon Fuller (*Worthies of England*), the prefaces to Dowland's own works, and a letter which he wrote from Nuremberg (November 10th, 1595) to Sir Robert Cecil (*Marquis of Salisbury's Papers, Vol. V*). While the firſt source says that Dowland was born at Weſtminſter, one of his dedications is addressed to "John Forſter . . . of Dublin, Ireland", who is alluded to as "my loving countryman". There was also a ſtudent at Trinity College, Dublin, named John Dowland, and some authorities are now content to identify him with the composer. The coincidence would certainly be ſtriking. At the same time it may not be very easy to reconcile certain dates in his ſtory with the one at which he was supposed to have been in Dublin. Speaking for myself, I do not think this queſtion is conclusively settled. The date of his birth is discoverable from his own references. Speaking of Hans Gerle's publication of 1533 he says that he "was borne but thirty yeares after", which would place his birth in 1563. Again, in the preface to the *Pilgrimes Solace* (1612) he confesses to being "now entered into the fiftieth yeare of mine age",— *i.e.* he was forty-nine years old; this once more gives 1563 as his birth-year. In the light of this, therefore, the year usually given— 1562—is clearly wrong. Little is known of his youth. We meet with him firſt in the service of Sir Henry Cobham, accompanying this ambassador to Paris in 1579. In 1583 Cobham was recalled and Dowland returned to England. He became a Bachelor of Music (Oxford) in 1588. Soon after this he seems to have been endeavouring to obtain a court appointment. When John Johnson died he applied for the vacant post, but was not successful; on account (as he says in the letter of 1595, from which all quotations in inverted commas have been taken) of " my religion . . . whereupon . . . I desired to get beyond the seas ". He found this conclusion the easier to arrive at since he had already been invited to Germany by the Duke of Brunswick. This music-loving prince received him with marked respect, gave him " a rich chain of gold, 23*l.* in money, with velvet and satin and gold lace for apparell ", together with a promise to give him "as much as any prince in the world " if he would enter the ducal service. Dowland, however, was not to be tempted; and leaving the duke went to the Landgrave of Hessen who also extended to him a cordial welcome, and who " sent a ring into England to my wife, valued at 20*l.*, and gave me a great standing cup with cover gilt, full of dollars ",

and great offers for his service. But Dowland, having a " great desire to see Italy ", the Landgrave was no more successful than the Duke had been. His reluctance to stay permanently in Germany was due to the reason that took him to Italy,—he wished to study with Luca Marenzio. He accordingly went to Venice and thence to Florence where he " played before the Duke and got great favours ". There also he came into contact with certain English recusants who promised him a large Papal pension if he would agree to serve Rome. Very little of their conversation sufficed to frighten him, for the thought of becoming a servant of " the greatest enemy of my Prince, country", wife, children, and friends " made him confess that he had never " heard any Mass in England ". It is likely that his object in writing all this to Cecil was to make known at Court that his mind did not tend Romewards, and he may have hoped that such an avowal of Protestantism would secure for him an invitation to return. It will be noticed that Dowland speaks of a wife and children. It is not known when, or whom he married, but that event probably took place soon after his return from Paris. Leaving the company of the recusants he " wept heartily to see my fortune so hard that I should become servant " of the Pope. The result of his weeping was to cause the abandonment of the journey to Rome and Marenzio, and a return by way of Venice and Bologna to Germany. At Nuremberg he made the acquaintance of Johann Cellario, in whose autograph album (facing page 138) he wrote the subjeÆ for a *fuga* and signed it: " Io. Dolandi Lachrima; his owne hand ". It is not dated. The album is now in the British Museum.

In 1598 John Dowland was engaged as lutenist to Christian IV, king of Denmark, and received for his services the then very large sum of five hundred dollars a year. This already great wage was further augmented by occasional gifts, and his autographed receipt for a gratuity of six hundred dollars (1599) is kept in the State Archives at Copenhagen. In 1601 the king presented him with his royal portrait and decorated him. Having been thus signally

honoured, Dowland was sent to England to purchase three hundred dollars' worth of musical instruments for the king.

For the next two or three years Dowland's movements are somewhat uncertain; in the Preface to his third book of songs (1603) he intimates that he is still abroad. But in 1605 we find him in London again, for in that year he was present at the publication of his famous *Lachrymae*. We learn from the foreword to this work that he was compelled to winter in England owing to the storms that raged on the North Sea rendering his return to Denmark impossible at that time of the year. But the question must remain open whether he really much relished the idea of returning to Denmark and continuing his service at Copenhagen. The Danish State Papers contain entries that show him to have fallen into disfavour there. Perhaps his temperament was beginning to revolt against a too long sojourn in one place, or perhaps he was becoming spoiled ; Eitner uses the suggestive words " Anstössiger Lebenswandel " — objectionable mode of living. Whatever the cause may have been, the fact remains that on February 24th, 1606, in the absence of the king from the court, Dowland was dismissed. Voltaire wrote: " On doit des égards aux vivants; on ne doit aux morts que la vérité ".

Consequently in 1606 we find Dowland living in Fetter Lane, London, In the Preface to the *Pilgrimes Solace* (1612) he calls himself lutenist to Lord Walden, but we do not know how long he had been in that service. At any rate, Dowland felt that he was much happier in English service than in any other, for he adds that he had " been long obscured from your sight, because I received a kingly entertainment in a forraine climate, which could not attaine to any (though never so meane) place at home ". Nevertheless, it was an open secret that the lutenist had not got his deserts in England, for Peacham in the same year wrote:—

"So since (old frend) thy yeares have made thee white, And thou for others hath consum'd thy Spring,

How few regard thee, whome thou didst delight, And farre, and neere, came once to hear thee sing." (*Minerva Britanna.*)

The court appointment which Dowland had so long desired came in the autumn of 1612, for on October 28th of that year he was admitted as " musician for the lutes " at a salary of 1s. 8d. per day, plus the usual allowance of 16l. 2s. 6d. for livery (*Audit Office Accounts*; v. Cal. S.P.). The State Papers mention him two or three times more, — he is described as " Doctor " Dowland in 1623, though I have traced no entry referring to a Doctorate having been conferred upon him at any of the Universities, —and in 1626 he is given as " deceased ". The accounts mention payments made to him for the quarter ending at Christmas, 1625, and for " 26 daies in parte of other Lady Day quarter 1626 ". So that he must have died towards the end of January, 1625–6. His son Robert, who succeeded him in the post, was paid at Michaelmas, 1626, from " the death of his said father ".

The reputation that John Dowland enjoyed was very

L

high. Apart from the favour in which he was held by foreign princes, his musical contemporaries and successors had only good to say of him. Poets praised him in such terms as these:

"Dowland to thee is deare,
    whose heavenly touch
Upon the Lute doeth
    ravishe humaine sense."
(*Richard Barnfield.*)

Anthony Wood said of him that he was "the rareſt musician that the age did behold", and as late as 1676 Thomas Mace (*Musick's Monument*) makes the lute say: "Despair I do: Old Dowland he is Dead". As a writer of vocal music he ſtill merits recognition, and Nagel is right when he says: " . . . this beautiful art of the Elizabethan era, which reaches its climax in the ſtriſtly noble works of William Byrd, and in the sweet ſtrain of John Dowland" (*Annalen*).

The printed works of John Dowland, in chronological order, are: Contributions to Eſte's *Psalms* (1592); some lute pieces in Barley's *New Book of Tableture* (1596; probably pirated, for in the *Firſt Book of Songs* Dowland says that some lute pieces of his had already been pub-lished, "but without my knowledge, false, and un-perfeſt); his own *Firſt Booke of Songes or Ayres of foure Partes with Tableture for the Lute* (1597) a work that enjoyed great popularity, having been re-issued in 1600, 1606, 1608, 1613, and 1844 (the laſt time by the *Musical Antiquarian Society*); some verses in Giles Farnaby's *Canzonets* (1598); a com-plimentary sonnet in Richard Alison's *Psalmes*; *The Second Booke of Songes or Ayres* (1600; dedicated to Lucy Countess of Bedford, and dated from Elsinore, June 1ſt); a specimen in Rude's *Flores Musicae* (1600) and another signed "J.D." is also probably his; *Third and Laſt Booke of Songs or Aires* (1603); contributions by "Johannes Dolandi Anglus" in J. B. Besard's *Thesaurus Harmonicus* (1603); *Lachrymae: or seven Teares figured in Seaven passionate Pavans . . . set forth for the Lutes, Viols, or Violins in five parts* (1605, dedicated to Anna of Denmark), a work that became popular enough to be mentioned in Middle-ton's comedy, *No Wit like a Woman's*: "No; thou playeſt Dowland's 'Lach-ryma' to thy maſter"; pieces in Füllsack's *Ausserlesene Paduanen* (1607-9); the translation of Andreas Ornithoparcus's *Micrologus* into English, "written in my house in Fetter Lane, this 10th of Aprill, 1609", and dedicated to Robert, Earl of Salisbury,—a treatise on "the art of Singing digeſted into Foure Bookes" by "John Dowland, Luteniſt, Luteplayer, and Bachelor of Musicke in both Universities"; three dances for viols in T. Simpson's *Opusculum* (1610); a "Fantaisie", some Pavanes, and "Practical Hints on Lute-Playing" in Robert Dowland's *Varietie of Lute-Lessons* (1610),—a work which also contains certain Pavanes "sent to my father ... by Maurice, Landgrave of Hessen, in Honour of John Dowland, the English Orpheus"; eight pieces in Van Den Hove's *Delitiae Musicae* (1612); *A Pilgrimes Solace* (1612), the laſt work which was in its entirety from the pen of the "English Orpheus", and which consiſted of three, four, and five-part compositions for voice, lutes, or viols ; work in Leighton's *Teares or Lamentacions*, *etc.* (1614); contributions to Fuhrmann's *Teſtudo Gallo-Germanica* (1615); a piece

in Besard's *Novus Partus* (1617); and five dances for viols in Simpson's *Taffel-Consort* (1621). This, I believe, completes the liſt of contemporary publications. Some of John Dowland's vocal music has been reissued by Novello and Co. and various other publishers, selected from the three books of songs and *The Pilgrimes Solace*.

Manuscripts containing work by this writer are preserved at Cambridge, Dublin, and the British Museum.

DOWLAND (Robert): A celebrated luteniſt, active during the firſt half of the seventeenth century. The date of his birth is not known; but since his two works were published in 1610, he muſt have been born about 1585, a date which would fit in very well with the theory that his father, John Dowland, married shortly after his return from Paris in 1583. From the dedication to his *Varietie of Lute-Lessons* it is clear that Sir Thomas Mounson was responsible for some share in the expenses of his education, for he says that he inscribes the book to that knight . . . . in gratefull remembrance of your bountie to me, in part of my education, whilst my father was absent from England ". His skill, as he says in the same dedication, " . . . is hereditarie unto mee, my Father being a *Lutenist* and well-knowne amongst you here in England, as in most parts of Christendome beside ". Similarly the dedication of his *Musicall Banquet* to Sir Robert Sydney (Lord Governor of Vlissingen) shows that this knight was Dowland's godfather: " The duty I owe unto your Lordship for two great respects; the one in regard (your Lordship undertaking for mee) I was made a member of the Church of Christ, and withall received from you my name;—the other the love that you beare to all excellency and good learning . . . may it please your Honour therefore to accept these my first labours ". From this it appears that the *Musicall Banquet* was written first, though the *Varietie of Lute-Lessons* may have been printed first, as he mentions the " collected Lute-Lessons which I lately set foorth ". Both works bear the date 1610 on their title-pages.

After the publication of these two books we hear nothing of him for sixteen years. But in 1626 his service at court commenced. British Museum manuscript *Add.* 5750 contains the following order: " Charles R. . . . Whereas wee have appointed Robert Dowland to be one of our Musicians in ordinary for the consort in the place of his father Doctor Dowland deceased, and are pleased to allow him for his wages twenty pence by the day, and for his livery sixteen pounds two shillings and sixpence by the year; We doe hereby will and command you out of our treasure from time to time remayning in your custody, to pay or cause to be paid to the said Robert Dowland or his assigns the said wages . . . from the day of the death of his said father for and during his naturall life, at the four usual termes or feastes . . . Given under our Signett at the palace of Westminster the six and twentieth day of April in the second yere of our Raigne ". Being thus secured, Robert married in the October of the same year, having obtained a licence on the eleventh of that month (Chester: *Marriage Licences*), his bride being one Jane Smalley. His name appears in a list under the heading:

"For the lute and voices" in 1628 (*L.C.R.*, July 15th). He muſt have died in or before 1641, for under date December 1ſt, 1641, we read: "Warrant for the swearing of Mr. John Mercure a musician to his Majeſty for the lutes and voices in ordinary, in the place of Robert Dowland, deceased" (*L.C.R.*). At the Reſtoration his poſt in the private music was occupied by William Howes (*Id.*).

The title-pages of his two chief works read as follows: "Varietie of Lute-Lessons: viz. *Fantasies*, *Pauins*, *Galliards*, *Almaines*, *Corantoes*, and *Volts*: selećted out of the beſt approved Authors, as well beyond the seas as of our owne Country"; and "A Musicall Banquet Furnished with a Varietie of delicious Ayres, collećted out of the beſt Authors in English, French, Spanish, and Italian". The former contains Besard's observations on lute-playing and "a short Treatise thereunto appertayning by John Dowland, Bac. Mus."; seven Fantasies and seven each of the danceforms named in the title by various composers. "Sir Thomas Mounson, his Pavin" and a Galliard to match, are by Robert Dowland himself; for the reſt his work was mainly editorial. In the latter publication are to be found songs with lute accompaniment by Anthony Holborne, John Dowland, Daniel Batchelor, *etc.*, and a complimentary verse by Henry Peacham. G. L. Fuhrmann's *Teſtudo Gallo-Germanica* (1615; *p* 112) contains a *Galliardo* by Robert Dowland.

DRAGHI (Giovanni Battiſta): An Italian musician who was ać̆tive in England in the second half of the seventeenth century, and who became thoroughly naturalized here both in his personal life and his ſtyle of composition. The firſt reference to him in this country is to be found in the *Diary* of Samuel Pepys, where under date February 12th, 1666–7, we read: "With my Lord Brouncker, by coach to his house, there to hear some Italian musique: and here we met . . . the Italian Signor Baptiſta, who hath proposed a play in Italian for the Opera . . . and here he did sing one of the ać̆ts. He himself is the poet as well as the musician; which is very much, and did sing the whole from the words without any musique prickt, and played all along upon a harpsichord moſt admirably, and the composition moſt excellent ... He pretends not to voice, though it be good, but not excellent ". Indeed, Draghi was moſt celebrated as a performer on the keyboard inſtruments and became organiſt in the private chapel of Queen Catherine, consort of King Charles II (1677), in which poſt he came into contact with Matthew Lock (*q.v.*). His salary in the year 1677–8 was 150*l.* per annum (*Add.* 15897; *B.M. v. also Annalen*, *p. 52, footnote*). In 1684 he was given a " bounty " of 50*l.* out of the " Secret Service Monies " (*v. Camden Soc. Publications*). It is doubtful if he remained in England when the queen left the country, though several authorities ſtate that he was ſtill here early in the eighteenth century.

Draghi's moſt important compositions were for the harpsichord, and while in England he composed *Six Select Suites of Lessons for the harpischord in six severall keys* (Preludes, Allemandes, Courantes, Sarabandes, Ariettes, Menuets, and Jigs). In 1685 a couple of songs written by him for Nahum Tate's " Duke or no Duke "

were published. In 1687 he produced a setting of Dryden's Ode for St. Cecilia's Day, " From Harmony, *etc.*". In addition to these, several isolated compositions were printed contemporaneously. He contributed some incidental music to Shadwell's *Psyche*, the reſt of the music being by Lock. The St. Cecilia Ode may be seen in manuscript in *Add.* 33287 (*B.M.*), while earlier music of his (written before he adopted the English manner) is contained in *Harl.* 1272 and *Add.* 24889 (*Id.*). If his ſtay in England did not extend beyond the date of the queen's departure (and moſt of the evidence proves that it did not), he had nothing to do with the composition of music for D'Urfey's *Wonders in the Sun* (1706), which has often been attributed to him.

DUGLAS (Patrick): *see* DOUGLAS (Patrick).

DUNSTABLE (John): The moſt important figure in the hiſtory of English music, inasmuch as he was the firſt musician to leave examples of his talents from which his ſtatus could be gauged. Of his biography we know absolutely nothing beyond the date of his death; but we can form a good idea of the high reputation he enjoyed among his contemporaries from their allusions to him. After the great mass of legend and fanciful imaginings that have collected round him have been cleared away, little enough is left. But that little shows us without any suspicion of doubt that Dunstable was the greatest musician of the first half of the fifteenth century, and that he lived and worked early enough to have been the model for, and perhaps also in some cases the teacher of, the great French and Netherlandish composers of his era. Without going so far as to agree with the writers who claim Dunstable as the " inventor " of composition,— for the art and science of harmony is hardly, on the face of it, a subject to be " invented ",—we cannot do other than maintain that he was actually the first musician to carry the development of the art to a point at which it was—even is to-day—tolerable to sensitive ears. He certainly used devices that have persisted to the present-day, and he as certainly had the courage to waive some of the canons that until his time had lain on music as an incubus. He undoubtedly studied euphony and valued it at a higher rate than he did the adherence to all the monkish practices that made a good deal of the older music more pleasant to read than to hear. A certain amount of freedom being thus countenanced, nothing stood in the way of further progress in the direction of independence of parts and a truer appreciation of the sense of the words to which the music was set. For these reasons Dunstable merits the high praise he received from many authorities; and if we cannot say that counterpoint was invented in England, we can at least claim that the very first great musician worthy of the title was a native of this country.

When and where Dunstable was born we do not know, and nothing can be gained by adding to the store of suppositions and speculations that has already been collected. But one thing seems certain, and that is,—judging by the fact that the majority of his works are to be found in foreign manuscripts, and the circumstance that the only contemporary writers to mention him were foreigners,—he must have spent the greater part of his active life abroad. There is no reason for assuming that between the date of the rota " Sumer is y-cumen in " (first half of the thirteenth century), and that of Dunstable's works, two arid centuries totally devoid of music intervened. The times were not ideal for the preservation of music, but sufficient traces of the art are discernible to show that musicians capable of writing such things as that remarkable rota did not suddenly die out, and that two hundred years later a new school did not as suddenly spring up, fully-grown, out of the desert. Dunstable was not the only English musician before the middle of the fifteenth century, though he certainly was the greatest; and if he was not in active practice the head of the English school of the time, he at least set an example which was copied all over the Continent of Europe while his native successors remained lagging behind. Only thus can be explained the circumstance that while, in Dunstable's lifetime, the Netherlanders were learning from the Englishmen, that Englishman's countrymen were learning from the foreigners

scarcely a single generation later.

The first allusion to Dunstable, and the only one written during his lifetime, occurs in a French poem, *Le Champion des Dames*, by Martin Le Franc (*ca.* 1437–40). We may assume therefore that before 1440 he was already famous in Paris, since the poet says that the French musicians of note followed the example of the English, and particularly of Dunstable:—

" Et ont pris de la contenance
   Angloise, et ensuivy Dunstable."

More important on account of the eminence of the writer are the references to the Englishman by Joannes de Tinctoris, and though already frequently quoted, we cannot afford to omit to notice the paragraph in the *Proportionale*: " Quo fit ut hac tempestate facultas nostrae musices tam mirabile susceperit incrementum quod ars nova esse videatur, cuius, ut ita dicam, novae artis fons et origo, apud Anglicos quorum caput Dunstaple exstitit, fuisse perhibetur, et huic contemporanei fuerunt in Gallia Dufay et Binchois quibus immediate successerunt moderni Okeghem, Busnois, Regis et Caron, omnium quos audiverim in compositione praestantissimi" (printed by Coussemaker, *Scriptores*, *IV*, 154). Dunstable is also mentioned in two more theoretical works of Tinctoris: *Complexus effectum Musices* and *Liber de Arte Contrapuncti*. The internal evidence of Dufay's work (to mention only one) suggests that he had been under the direct influence of Dunstable; and if this were so, then the Englishman assumes a still greater importance, — for through Dufay John Dunstable was indeed a "fons et origo" of the music that followed until the abandonment of the mensural system. John Hothby (Ottobi) mentions "Dunstable, Anglicus ille", as well as Dufay and Okeghem in a manner that suggests the Englishman having been considered famous enough to be mentioned in any company (*Dialogue on Counterpoint*; Coussemaker, *Scriptores*, *III*, *XXXI*). Gaforius also quotes Dunstable in his *Practica Musicae* (1496), giving a musical example composed by the Englishman. This

does not exhaust the list of fifteenth century works that make mention of Dunstable,—but nowhere is there anything from which even a scrap of biographical material could be extracted. And so it comes about that we find no more to satisfy our curiosity than the date of his death, which is December 24th, 1453 ("pridie Natale (?) Sidus transmigrat ad astra"). This information is afforded by an epitaph which Stowe (*Survey*) saw engraved on two "plated stones in the chancel" of St. Stephen's, Walbrook (London), where Dunstable was buried. Another epitaph by Whethamstede of St. Alban's in Weever's *Funeral Monuments* (1631 : from a Cotton Manuscript) was written on "John Dunstable, an astrologian, a mathematician, a musitian, and what not". Since Dunstable was so many-sided, it is more than likely that the astronomical treatise in a Bodleian manuscript (Oxford), bearing a variant of his name, is also his work. Although averse to speculation, I submit that the date given in this treatise (April, 1438) may fix a probable time for Dunstable's return to England. But too much importance should not be attached to so unprovable an assertion, since it is not even certain that the " Dunſtaple " of the treatise is to be identified with the musician. So far as I have been able to discover, the firſt English writer to mention Dunſtable was Thomas Morley (1597: *Plaine and Easie Introduction*), and then in no complimentary fashion; the eminent madrigaliſt blaming the fifteenth century writer for a fault (the dividing of the syllables of a word by reſts) which was of very frequent occurrence when Dunſtable wrote. After this interval of a century and a half, another two centuries had almoſt run their course before Dunſtable was again named in an English hiſtory. It is true that Ravenscroft may have been correct when he alluded to a treatise by Dunſtable (in his *Briefe Discourse*, 1614), but some English hiſtorians have doubted his accuracy, and suggeſt that Tunſted's work was meant. Though such a treatise by Dunſtable is not now known to exiſt, there is no reason for assuming that none ever exiſted,—especially as Gaforius appears to have seen some such work.

In considering the work of John Dunſtable it is easy to forget his period and attach too little importance to his achievements. Perhaps Dr. Riemann has given in as few words as any the chief reasons for honouring this fifteenth-century composer: " A careful examination of the music belonging to the period from the fourteenth century to the fifteenth, will give the surprising result that Dunſtable transferred the artiſtic ſtyle of song-writing with inſtrumental accompaniment (which arose in Florence after 1300) . . . to the music of the Church, and thus became the creator of paraphrased church-song (Hymns, Motets, Anthems, *etc.*). He treated mass-movements in similar manner. In this field Dufay and Binchois followed closely in his footſteps . . ." Three main sources have supplied the examples of Dunſtable's music known to us. The choir books from Trent Cathedral (now in the possession of the Miniſtry of Education in Vienna) were discovered by Dr. F. X. Haberl, and are being issued in the series. *Denkmäler der Tonkunſt in Oeſterreich*. They contain music by Dunſtable and other

English composers, and are of the greatest value to the historian of the period. Some of the music contained is amazing in its excellence, considering its date. In Modena (*Bibl. Estense, Cod. VI, H.* 15) there are no fewer than thirty-one compositions by Dunstable, the whole set having been scored by Mr. W. Barclay Squire and deposited in the British Museum (*Add.* 36490). The third collection (Bologna, *Liceo Musicale, Cod.* 37) contains a *Credo, Regina Celi* (*sic*), *Sub tuam protectionem,* and *Quam pulchra es,* which have been reproduced in photographic facsimile in *Early English Harmony* (H. E. Wooldridge, 1897). Various versions of some of the works are to be found and in the case of the secular *Puisque m'amour,* and especially in that of *O Rosa bella,* they have been the subject of much literature. The last-named composition, a truly remarkable three-part vocal piece, was first discovered in a Vatican manuscript, and later in another version at Dijon. The Trent manuscripts contain three masses based on this melody, the only copy of which bearing Dunstable's name being the one at Rome.

Other collections possessing music by this composer are the *Liceo Communale* and the University Library (Bologna), and the Old Hall manuscript (College of St. Edmund's, near Ware); while manuscripts in the British Museum (*Lans.* 462, *Add.* 31922 and *Add.* 10336,—the last containing a musical puzzle of Dunstable's), among others, have specimens of his work. An excellent thematic catalogue of practically all the known works of this composer was given in the *Sammelbände* of the *Internationale Musik-Gesellschaft* (*II,* 1). *Crux Fidelis,* from the Modena manuscript has been printed in Volume II of the *Oxford History of Music,* and *Grove* (*Vol. I,* 1912 *ed.*) gives *Quam pulchra es,* from the Bologna *Codex* 37.

DUNSTAPLE (John): *see* DUNSTABLE (John).

D'URFEY (Thomas): A popular writer of plays and song-texts who also sang and dabbled in composition. Born at Exeter soon after the middle of the seventeenth century, he was descended on his father's side from a Huguenot family which had escaped persecution by flight to England. It is to be regretted that a good deal of D'Urfey's dramatic work was marked with that obscenity so common at the period; a circumstance which caused it to be neglected when the stage was purified shortly afterwards. Many of his lyrics were set by the most celebrated musicians of his day, — among others Henry Purcell, John Blow, Draghi, *etc.* His musical composition was confined to songs which he often performed himself, and as a singer he was much in request at court. But he was not able to take advantage of his prosperity, and the last ten years of his life were passed in very straitened circumstances. He died on February 26th, 1723, and lies buried at St. James's Church (Piccadilly, London). His claims as a composer rest on very uncertain foundations, and it is not known how far the few musical compositions issued under his name were his own unaided work.

DYGON (John): A composer of some note who flourished early in the sixteenth century. He was one of the priors of St. Augustine's Abbey (St. Austin's), Canterbury (Hawkins); but there are so many men connected with that foundation all bearing the same name that nothing can be stated with any degree of certainty concerning his life. At the dissolution of the monasteries most of these clerics changed their names and further difficulties are encountered in attempting to identify the composer. No good object can be served by speculation. He is known to-day by a three-part motet (*Ad lapidis positionem*) of clever workmanship in Baldwin's manuscript (printed in Hawkins's *History*). The only fact relating to this composer is that he became a Bachelor of Music at Oxford in 1512, the *Fasti Oxonienses* describing him as a Benedictine monk.

E

EAGLES (Henry, John, Solomon, *and* Thomas): *see* ECCLES.

EAST (Michael): A madrigalist of the early seventeenth century whose work was rather more popular than profound. He always avoided monotony, and though his music achieved some success with the early Stuart amateurs, it was not at the expense of art. His sacred works, as well as his instrumental compositions, are sound enough, but show no really outstanding merit. His fame rests more upon such cheerful and insouciant things as " How merrily we live " than upon any work of depth or magnitude. Almost nothing is known of his life. In 1606 he appears to have been resident at Ely House, Holborn (London), but whether as a private musician to Lady Hatton, as some suggest, is not to be decided with certainty, though it is probable. In the same year he became a Bachelor of Music at Cambridge. Before 1618 he was appointed " Master of the Choristers " at Lichfield Cathedral; but exactly when he entered that position is not clear, nor do we know how long he held it. A publication of his dated 1638, shows that he was still at Lichfield as organist, and after this date we lose sight of him.

Michael East wrote and published a large amount of vocal music, most of which—after the fashion of the Elizabethans — he endeavoured to make suitable for instruments also. His first work to appear in print was the madrigal written for the *Triumphes of Oriana* (1601)— " Hence stars, you dazel but the sight ". This piece was delivered too late for any possible classification, and it was printed on the reverse of the dedication before No. 1. A printer's note states that " This song being sent too late, and all my other printed, I plast it before the rest rather than to leave it out ". The first book entirely from his own pen to be issued was *Madrigales to 3, 4, and 5 parts apt for Viols and voices,* etc. (1604; name spelled Michaell Este). This book has been reprinted by Dr. E. H. Fellowes as Volume XXIX of the *English Madrigal School.* " The Second Set of Madrigales to

3, 4, and 5 parts: Apt for Viols and voices, *etc.*" appeared in 1606 (*Vol. XXX* of the *English Madrigal School*, also containing the Oriana Madrigal). In this set his name is spelled Eſt. The next work was "*The Third Set of Bookes* wherein are Paſtorals, Anthemes, Neopolitanes, Fancies, and Madrigales, to 5 and 6 parts. Apt both for Viols and Voyces" (1610; name spelled Eaſte), dedicated to the "Rt. Worshipfull Mr. Hy. Wilughby . . . his singular good maſter". This set is reprinted in Dr. Fellowes's Volume XXXI. "*The Fourth Set of Bookes;* wherein are Anthemes for Versus and Chorus, Madrigales, and Songs of other kindes. To 4, 5, and 6 Parts: Apt for Viols and Voyces, *etc.*" appeared in 1619 (which may be the date of a reprint, since the fifth set is dated 1618). The title-page of the laſt-mentioned work reads: "*The Fift Set of Bookes,* wherein are Songs full of spirit and delight, so composed in 3 Parts, that they are as apt for Vyols as Voyces". In 1624 appeared "*The Sixt Set of Bookes* wherein, are Anthemes for Versus and

Chorus, of 5 and 6 parts; Apt for Violls and Voyces". This book is dedicated to John Williams, Bishop of Lincoln, out of gratitude for an annuity granted by him to the composer. Eaſt's laſt published work was "*The Seventh Set of Bookes,* wherein are Duos for two Base-Viols . . . also Fancies of 3 Parts for two treble viols, and a base Violl : So made, as they muſt be plaid and not sung. Laſtly ayerie Fancies of 4 Parts, that may be as well sung as plaid, *etc.*" (1638). This laſt set was republished by Playford at about the middle of the century. Beyond the modern reprints already mentioned, the Musical Antiquarian Society issued some anthems with ſtring accompaniments in 1845, until then unpublished. Manuscript music by Eaſt is preserved in the Chriſt Church (Oxford) library,—an incomplete six-part anthem, the organ part of a five-part anthem, and some five-part Fancies. The anthems were edited by Rimbault and published by the Musical Antiquarian Society. The British Museum possesses a larger amount of manuscript music by Eaſt: *Add.* 29366–8,

29427, 29372–7, 17792–6, and 30478–9, all including anthems by him.

EAST (Thomas): A printer who flourished during the second half of the sixteenth century, and who issued practically all the important musical works of the period. Very little is known of his life, and all we possess by way of biographical material has to be gleaned from his title-pages and the Registers of the Stationers' Company. He is first mentioned officially in 1565, when, on December 6th, he was created a Freeman of his Company. It is therefore highly probable that he was not born much later than 1530–35. He held the licence to print music from William Byrd (q.v.), Thomas Morley, and William Barley, in succession; and such well-known works as William Byrd's *Psalmes, Sonets, and Songs, etc.*, of 1587, *The Whole Booke of Psalmes* of 1592, Young's *Musica Transalpina*, Morley's *Triumphes of Oriana* (1603), and about thirty more, appeared. He was held in high esteem as a printer, and must have been in affluent circumstances. In 1604 he was compelled to present a piece of plate to the Stationers' Com-

pany in order to be exempt from holding an office for which he had either no leisure or no inclination. The date of his death is not to be fixed with certainty, but evidently is to be placed before 1609, for on January 17th Thomas Snodham (who was made a Freeman of the Company in 1602) " entered for his copyes with the consent of Mistress East . . . these bookes followinge which were Master Thomas Eastes copyes " (*v.* Arber, *Stationers' Registers*). The printer's widow survived him by a good many years, and when she died in 1631 willed 20*l.* for plate to her late husband's Company.

ECCLES (Henry) (*also* EAGLES): A son of Solomon Eccles I, and an able violinist. *Grove* and the *Dictionary of National Biography* both state that he was in court service from 1694; but the Lord Chamberlain's Records give his name as early as 1689, when (July 17), he was appointed to the private music of the king (*L.C.R.*, *Vol.* 486, *etc.*). At St. Andrew of that year his name appears in a list of musicians receiving the usual livery allowance of 16*l.* 2*s.* 6*d.* (*Id.*, *Vol.* 467). He accompanied King William on the latter's journey to Holland in 1690–1. In 1694 his salary is given as 40*l.* per annum. He eventually left England and joined the French king's Band of Violins. His works include *Premier livre de Sonates a Violon seul et la Basse* (Paris, 1720), and *Second Livre de Sonates a Violon, etc* . . . *avec Deux Sonates pour la Flûte Traversière* (Paris, 1723). Mr. Alfred Moffat edited one of his sonatas (D-Minor) for violin and pianoforte (1906). ECCLES (John) (*also* EAGLES) : The eldest son of Solomon Eccles I, and a very popular composer for the stage during the last two decades of the seventeenth century, and the early part of the eighteenth. He was a pupil of his father, and this circumstance would point to his having been born not later than 1650; for we cannot suppose that the fanatical Quaker would have permitted his son to take up music as a profession, much less be his teacher, had John arrived at an age for training later than 1660. His contributions to many of the seventeenth century plays became very popular, marked as they were by ease, vigour, and a certain charm of a roughish kind. His material was generally well-suited to the purpose for which it was to be used, but his method of handling that material was not of the best, and on this account his work cannot compare with the best of its kind. Still, it must not be forgotten that musicians writing for the stage towards the end of the seventeenth century were required to produce work of a standard set up by Henry Purcell if they wished to be ranked with the best of their time. That John Eccles was talented there can be no doubt; but that he was an outstanding genius is not to be claimed. Purcell must have considered him a musician worthy of attention or we should not find the two musicians collaborating as they did in the third part of *Don Quixote*. The first music written by him for use in a play was composed in 1681, and thence onwards he produced a tremendous amount of work of this nature. Besides this activity he was connected with the royal music for a great many years. Already in the masque of 1674 we find the name " Mr. Eagles " (*L.C.R.*, *Vol.* 745), as that of a violinist, but whether John or Henry Eccles is meant is not quite clear. On June 22nd, 1694, John Eccles was appointed a musician at court, in the place of Thomas Tollet (*L.C.R., Vol.* 183), but an entry dated March 28th, 1695, shows that he was not yet salaried: "Mr. John Eccles, musician in ordinary without fee, to come in ordinary with fee next after Mr. Thomas Tollett upon the firſt vacancy of any of the twenty-four musicians, and then to enjoy all salaries" (*Id., Vol.* 186). He had not long to wait, for on September 2nd of the following year he was appointed on the decease of Mr. Tollett. In 1697 his salary was 40*l.* per annum, and on June 30th, 1700, he succeeded Dr. Staggins as Maſter of the King's Musick at a salary of 200*l.* a year. On March 21ſt, 1699, a competition was advertised in the *London Gazette* to secure the beſt setting of Congreve's "Judgment of Paris". John Eccles entered and secured the second prize, John Weldon taking the firſt. His duties as Maſter of the Music included the setting of the various odes in honour of royal birthdays and other occasions, and in 1701 he wrote the St. Cecilia ode (words by Congreve).

It will serve no useful purpose to recite the names of all the plays for which John Eccles wrote songs, for in many cases his work amounted only to one or two pieces. The moſt popular of the works by him or containing music by him were: *The Spanish Friar* (1681), *The Lancashire Witches* and *The Chances* (1682), *Juſtice Busy, The Richmond Heiress* (1693) *Don Quixote* (*Part* 3, in collaboration with Henry Purcell, 1694), *Love for Love* (1695), *The Loves of Mars and Venus* (in collaboration with Godfrey Finger (1696), *Macbeth* (1696), *The Provoked Wife, The Sham Doċtor* (1697), *Europe's Revels* (1697), *Rinaldo* (1699), *The Fate of Capua, The Way of the World, The Mad Lover, The Novelty,* and *Semele.* This does not exhauſt the liſt of plays in which he is represented. Many isolated numbers were published from time to time, and in 1704 and 1710 colleċtions of his songs were published. He is further represented in the miscellaneous colleċtions of vocal and inſtrumental music of

M

the day, as well as in various manuscripts. He died on January 12th, 1735, at Kingston-on-Thames.

ECCLES (Solomon) (I) (*also* EAGLES): An able teacher and performer on the virginal and viols who flourished in the seventeenth century. He was descended from, and the ancestor of, a number of musicians; and there can be little doubt that he would have left a far greater impression upon English music had religious fanaticism not deranged his mind. Born in the second decade of the seventeenth century, Solomon Eccles was probably trained by his father, and during the Commonwealth he was reckoned with the best teachers of the time. He had, before the Restoration, been a member of various sects and had experimented with many shades of religious belief. The culmination of his mania came when, in 1660, he joined the Society of Friends and cut himself off from the "vanities" of his world for ever. The statement that he subsequently returned to music as a profession is not founded on fact; and the error is doubtless due to his having been confused with Solomon Eccles II, who was one of his sons or perhaps some other relative. Solomon I became a shoemaker in 1660, this being, as he thought, the least "vain" of all callings. Since the Quakers of the seventeenth century did not countenance music, he sold all his music and instruments. But a little reflection brought him to the conclusion that he was placing the soul of the purchaser in jeopardy, and forthwith bought them back again. To prevent the prince of darkness working any evil by means of his books and instruments he destroyed them all by fire on Tower Hill. From this moment he was probably no longer accountable for his actions. To show his contempt for the authorized form of worship, he attempted to repair shoes in city churches, for which he was arrested and imprisoned, but subsequently released. In 1665, during the plague, he paraded Smithfield in a state of nudity with a dish of burning sulphur on his head, warning the people to depart from their evil ways lest they be visited with the punishment of Sodom and Gomorrah. Loiterers whipped "him grievously on his naked back but that could not allay his fervent zeal " (Sewel, *History of the Society of Friends*). He was again arreſted and committed to Bridewell. For preaching againſt the ſtate religion and various other eccentricities he was periodically incarcerated. In 1671 he went to the Colonies with George Fox, but continued to get into trouble with the authorities. He died on February 11th, 1683, and was buried in Spitalfields. The writer of the *History of the Society of Friends* knew Solomon I personally, and described him as a very zealous man, pious though fanatical.

In 1667 Solomon Eccles published "*A Musick Lector :* or the Art of Musick .... Discoursed of by way of Dialogue between three men of several Judgments: The one a Musician, ... The other a Baptiſt, . . . The other a Quaker ". In this work he follows the usual line of argument as to the legitimacy of the practice of music. He muſt at that time have been quite convinced of his own sincerity, for he gave up a good living, having earned as much as 200*l.* per annum as a teacher,—a sum equal to that earned by the Maſter

of the King's Music. Whether he composed any music is very doubtful, and probably all the compositions bearing his name were the work of Solomon II (*q.v.*). ECCLES (Solomon) (II) (*also* EAGLES). A composer and court musician active during the second half of the seventeenth century and the beginning of the eighteenth. Possibly a son of Solomon I (*q.v.*), he was appointed as musician in ordinary to King James II on October 10th, 1685, and an allowance of 3*s.* a day for his "riding charges" was made to him on November 12th of the same year for " attending the King and Queen on their progress at Windsor and Hampton Court " (*L.C.R., Vol.* 751), His salary in 1689 is given as 30*l.* a year (*Id., Bundle* 21), and on July 17th, 1689, he was appointed to the private music of the king. He accompanied the king on his journey to Holland in 1691. In 1693–4 (March 9th) he appears to have got into financial difficulties, for under that date the Lord Chamberlain's Records contain a " petition of Dr. Fisher Littleton againſt Solomon Eccles, Musitian, disbursed and lent, 400*l.*"

Both parties were summoned to appear before the Lord Chamberlain. In 1694 his salary was 40*l.* per annum (Chamberlayne, *Magnae Britanniae Notitia*). He was still in the royal service at the opening of the eighteenth century, and I have not been able to trace when he died.

The British Museum has string trios by Solomon Eccles, but it is not certain to which of the two men of this name they are to be attributed. Solomon II most probably wrote the little pieces in the *Division Violin* of 1685 (second edition), and those in the *Division Flute* (Walsh). He is also to be identified with the " Solomon Egle " who wrote the tunes for the play *Venice Praeserved, or a Plot discovered* (*B.M. Add.* 29283–5).

EDWARDES (Richard): A celebrated poet, playwright, composer, and Master of the Children of the Chapel Royal, who flourished in the sixteenth century. He is, at the present time, best known by the madrigal " In going to my naked bed ", a composition which has been attributed to him so persistently, and with so little opposition, that there seems to be no need to question the justice of the ascription. There is no reason for thinking that Edwardes could not have written it, and in the absence of other claims to the piece, we may assign it to him. The words were certainly written by Edwardes. The music to this madrigal is typical of the period and full of feeling. The play written by him for the entertainment of the court, and for which he probably wrote also the music, was a very early example of its kind, for, as Rimbault remarks, " the actors are also singers " (*Damon and Pythias*, 1565). Richard Edwardes was a Somersetshire man, and was born in 1523. We find him at Corpus Christi College, Oxford, in 1540, whence he graduated Master of Arts in 1547. He followed Richard Bower as Master of the Children of the Chapel Royal in 1563, and as the holder of that post, devised many of the dramatic and musical interludes for the diversion of the court. Besides the play already named, Edwardes wrote another produced before the Queen at Christ Church, Oxford, on September 3rd, 1566. In 1565 he received 53*s.* 4*d.* for presenting a play at Lincoln's Inn, — a sum which was probably intended to be a reward for the choristers who took part, as well as remuneration for Edwardes. The poet and musician had been made a member of the Inn in the previous year. He died on October 31st, 1566, only a few weeks after his play had been produced at Oxford. *Add.* 30513 (Mulliner's Manuscript, *B.M.*) contains the much-debated " In going to my naked bed ", and also " O the Syllye man " which bears the name " Edwardes ", the former composition being also contained in *Add.* 36526A. " Awake ye wofull weights " (*sic*) is present in *Add.* 15117, and is one of the songs from *Damon and Pythias*. The words of " In going to my naked bed " are given in Edwardes's poetical publication *A Paradyce of Dainty Devices*. He is represented by one composition in Day's *Psalter*.

ELLIS (William): A well-known and popular figure in the musical world at Oxford where, during the Commonwealth, he held music-meetings at which some of the most celebrated of contemporary artists performed. By these means he helped to keep the professional in touch with his public. The date of his birth is not known. He qualified for the degree of *Mus. Bac.* in 1639. His appointments were all to organists' posts, — first at Eton College, and afterwards at St. John's College, Oxford. The date of his engagement at the latter is uncertain, but he held the post until the Civil War broke up the Chapels and their music-making. At the Restoration he was most likely re-appointed to his organ at St. John's College, but proofs of this are wanting. Mr. J. E. West, who has dealt very carefully with the organists of the period in his useful *Cathedral Organists* (Novello and Co.) can only say that Ellis " is supposed " to have been re-appointed. He died at Oxford in 1674, and is buried there. The Christ Church (Oxford) library has the organ parts of " Holy, holy " and of " O Lord our Goverour " (anthem *à* 4); the bass part of three Almains, one Courant, one Saraband, and a composition labelled " Michaelmas Day "; and thirteen pieces for the harpsichord. The Catalogue of this collection suggests that the same manuscript (No. 1236) contains other, unsigned, compositions by

Ellis. *Add.* 29386 (*B.M.*) contains the Catch " My Lady and her Maid ", which is repeated in *Add.* 31462 (*Id.*). The only printed works of his that I have been able to trace are three compositions in Hilton's *Catch that Catch Can* (1658).

EMERIE (John): *see* AMERY (John).

ESTE (John) (*also* ESTO): A popular violiſt and singer of the seventeenth century, who, during the Commonwealth enjoyed a considerable reputation as a teacher (*v.* Playford, *Musical Banquet*). Nothing is known of his life, though Henry Davey (*Hiſtory of English Music*, 1921), without giving his authorities, says that he had been a barber. There is nothing surprising in a seventeenth-century barber being musical (*v. Dic. Old Engl. Mus.*, *s.v.* " Cittern "). Examples of John Eſte's work,—short dance tunes,—may be seen in *Musick's Recreation on the Viol, Lyra-Way* (1669), which contains fourteen pieces (Almains, Sarabandes, Corants, a Jig, and Ayres). The edition of 1682 contains ten pieces by him.

ESTE (Michael): *see* EAST (Michael).

ESTO (John): *see* ESTE (John).

ESTRANGE (Roger L'): *see* L'ESTRANGE (Roger).

ESTWICK (Sampson): A clergyman who deserves remembrance on account of one or two works that served the musical art. Born about the middle of the seventeenth century, he passed through the University of Oxford, obtaining the degrees of B.A. in 1677, M.A. in 1680, and B.D. in 1692. He became a Minor Prebend of St. Paul's Cathedral, London, in the latter year, and was given the control of the choir six years later. His subsequent appointments were all of a clerical nature. He appears to have continued to sing in the Cathedral service until well advanced in years, Hawkins saying that " when little short of ninety years of age " he preserved " his faculties and even his voice, which was a deep bass, till the laſt ". He died on February 16th, 1738–9.

He is remembered chiefly as the author of the sermon preached at Chriſt Church, Oxford, on St. Cecilia's Day, 1696, the subjeĉt being, " The Usefulness of Church Musick ". This sermon was afterwards published. A couple of vocal compositions with instrumental accompaniment (in score) are preserved in the library of Christ Church (Oxford), and a song, —" An Amorous Sigh ",— is contained in *Add.* 33234 (*B.M.*).

EVESEED (Henry) (*also* OVESEED): A Gentleman of the Chapel Royal who deserves mention merely on account of two or three famous names that must be alluded to and because a slight account of this notorious character helps to illustrate the disciplinary measures taken to secure decorum in the Chapel Royal in early Stuart days. He is first mentioned in the Cheque-Book of the Chapel Royal in 1585, when he succeeded Thomas Tallis. In 1603 he is among the Gentlemen of the Chapel who received a mourning livery for the funeral of Queen Elizabeth (*L.C.R.*, *Vol.* 554). In 1612 he is mentioned in the same connection when Prince Henry of Wales was buried (*Id.*, *Vol.* 555). In September, 1620, the Subdean and Gentlemen of the Chapel petitioned the Dean to remove Eveseed from his post. They charged him with " beinge infected with a fowle

disease . . . to the great offence of all . . .''; he " . . . very much abused himselfe through drunkennesse . . .''; with being " drunke many daies together, so that he was alwaies fightinge with his fellowes . . . to the great disquiett of the officers of the Greencloth "; that he rose from his bed naked and ran through a glass window; that he spoiled a dish of pottage " which Mr. Harrison and others wer eatinge of "; and, crowning offence, that on " St Peter's Day last, did violently and sodenly without cause runne uppon Mr. Gibbons, took him up and threw him downe uppon a standard wherby he receaved such hurt that he is not yett recovered of the same, and with all he tore his band from his neck to his prejudice and disgrace ". As a minor crime it was noted that Eveseed said the Subdean " sate in chapter as the Knave of clubbs ". The Dean read the petition in chapter at Hampton Court on September 29th, 1620, and it pleased him to suspend Eveseed until the feast of All Saints. The culprit pleaded guilty, condemned his weakness, and promised to reform himself. He was ordered to " submit himself to the Gentlemen offended ". He omitted to do so, whereupon the Dean " pronounced his place to be utterly voyd " (March 3rd, 1620–21; *Ch. Bk. C.R.*). It will be noted that in the article on William Heather the Cheque-Book entry alludes to Eveseed's death in 1614–15. It is obvious that if he died in 1614 he could not have been guilty of the offences named in 1620, and *vice versa*. Many of the Cheque-Book entries were made after the event, and one of these two dates is wrong.

EVESHAM (Walter de): *see* ODINGTON (Walter).

F

FAIRFAX (Robert): *see* FAYRFAX (Robert).

FARDING (Thomas), FAREDYNGE (Thomas): *see* FARTHING (Thomas).

FARMER (John) (I.): A celebrated madrigalist and able organist at the turn of the sixteenth century. His versatility was considerable, and he wrote a contrapuntal treatise as well as some excellent four-part settings of the Psalms. On a title-page of 1599 he calls himself a "Practicioner in the Art of Musique" and it is quite likely that he taught composition. His madrigals are noticeable for the remarkably fine sense of rhythm they exhibit, and he seems to have aimed at such results, for in the work of 1599 he says that he has so linked ". . . music to number, as each to give to other their true effect, which is to make delight".

The dates of his birth and death are unknown; but since he wrote a theoretical treatise in 1591, we may suppose that he was not born later than 1560; and as he contributed to the *Triumphes of Oriana* it is clear that he lived at least until 1601 (probably until 1603? when the *Orianas* were published). He lived in London until 1595 when he left for Dublin. In 1591 (when his treatise was issued) he was a resident in the City of London, for that pamphlet was "to be sould in Broad Streets neere the Royal Exchange at the Author's house". The Chapter Acts of Christ Church Cathedral (Dublin) provide the next source of information. It is entered that on February 16th, 1595, "Mr. John Farmer shall have as Master of the Children and organist for this yeare fifteene pounds current money of England". On August 10th, 1596, he was sworn Vicar-Choral in the place of Robert Jordan, resigned. Less than a year later Farmer appears to have left Ireland without leave, for on July 18th, 1597 "it is ordered that if Mr. John Fermer doe not return by the first of August, 1597 . . . his place to bee voyd in this Church for departing the land without licence". He left for London in 1599 and at the end of that year his post as vicar-choral was declared vacant.

His firſt published work was the treatise already alluded to: "Divers and sundry waies of two parts in one, to the number of fortie, upon one playn Song . . . Performed and published by John Farmer, in favoure of such as loue Musicke, with the ready way to Perfeƈt knowledge" (Thomas Eſte, 1591; a copy in the Bodleian Library, Oxford). In 1592 Eſte's *Whole Booke of Psalmes* appeared and John Farmer contributed largely to it, the greateſt number of the four-part settings being by him. His moſt important work appeared in 1599: *The Firſt Set of English Madrigals to Foure Voyces* (William Barley), dedicated to the Earl of Oxford, who is described by the composer as his "very good Lord and Maſter"; which may indicate that Farmer was in the employ of this peer. The work contains sixteen four-part madrigals and one in eight parts, the whole set having been reprinted by Dr. Fellowes in Volume VIII of the *English Madrigal School* (1914). Although we cannot claim for John Farmer that he was the equal of the beſt contributors to the *Triumphes of Oriana*, his six-part madrigal in that colleƈtion,—"Fair Nymph I heard one telling",—is ſtill an excellent piece of work. It was reprinted by Dr. Fellowes in the volume already mentioned, while Hawkins gave one of the four-part madrigals (1599). A few manuscripts contain music by John Farmer. Chriſt Church, Oxford, has "Looke up sad Soule" (four-part) and an adaptation of one of the 1599 madrigals. In the British Museum (*Add.* 29996) there is a complete score of the sixteen four-part madrigals of 1599. He is also represented in the Oxford Music School colleƈtion and in the Fitzwilliam Museum, Cambridge.

II. Another musician of the same name is mentioned in the Lord Chamberlain's Records, firſt as a "page of the Chapel (Royal) whose voice is changed and is gone from the Chapel" (*L.C.R.*, January 8th, 1668–9), and again as one of the violins who assiſted in the masque of 1674. It is not certain whether these entries refer to the same individual. At all events this seventeenth-century John Farmer does not appear to have been a man of any outſtanding importance.

FARMER (Thomas): A violinist who flourished during the second half of the seventeenth century. He must have been a performer of great skill, for he was nominated to succeed no less an instrumentalist than John Banister in the private music of the king. According to Anthony Wood's manuscript notes (Bodleian library), Farmer was one of the Waits of London, and it was probably while in that company that he acquired his art. The waits were a far more highly trained body of instrumentalists than is generally supposed, and more than one celebrated musician rose from their ranks (*cf.* article " Waits " in *Dic. Old Engl. Mus.*). He obtained the Bachelor's degree at Cambridge in 1684. The date of his death is not to be determined with absolute certainty, but it must lie somewhere between 1690, when he published a book, and 1695, when Henry Purcell died. That he died before Purcell is clear from the fact that the latter wrote an elegy on the death of the violinist (*Orpheus Britannicus*). The rest of the biographical material available is to be gleaned from the Lord Chamberlain's Records. On November 4th, 1671, he received his expenses for attending the king at Windsor; on November 9th, 1674, he was paid 5s. a day for " ryding charges " in accompanying his majesty to Newmarket; in the same year he was among the violinists who performed in the celebrated masque. On September 4th, 1675, he was admitted as violinist in ordinary, in the place of John Strong, deceased; his " wages and fees ", as given in the entry for May 24th, 1676, being 46l. 12s. 8d. yearly. On March 5th, 1677–8, he was paid 12l. " for a new treble violin bought by him for his Majesty's service ". A warrant was issued in 1679 (November 6th) admitting " Thomas Farmer as musician in ordinary to his Majesty with fee, for the private musick, in the place of John Bannister, deceased ". This entry is crossed out and a warrant follows appointing Banister's son to the post; so it is possible that Farmer did not receive this additional post. In 1685 (August 31st) Thomas Farmer, entered in the list of Counter-tenors, was sworn into the service of James II. The entry of

November 12th, 1685, mentions him again as a violinist. Many similar references to this musician occur in the records, but after 1687 his name disappears.

Thomas Farmer's written music is chiefly secular vocal, instrumental, and dramatic work of the lighter type. His contributions to the popular collections of the time included vocal compositions to the second edition of. Playford's *Choice Ayres, etc.* (1675), *The Theater of Musick* (1685, Bk. I, three songs; Bk. II, one song; 1687, Bk. IV, five pieces), D'Urfey's *Choice New Songs* of 1684; his third collection of *New Songs*, 1685; *Apollo's Banquet* (Violin music), and other similar collections. His own publications were: *A Consort of Musick in four Parts* (thirty-three lessons commencing with an "Overture") in 1686; and *A Second Consort of Musick in four Parts* (eleven lessons commencing with a "Ground") in 1690. In the earlier of these two consorts he speaks of his own success in performing the music contained, and adds that he wrote the work " to justifie what our Age dares attempt . . ." Stage music written by Thomas Farmer included tunes for the *Princess of Cleve* (the parts in the British Museum: *Add.* 29283–5, dated 1682), and, according to Rimbault, compositions for Nath. Lee's *Constantine the Great* (1684). *Add.* 24889 and 31429 (*B.M.*) also contain specimens of his work. The Music School collection and the Christ Church library (Oxford) possess further compositions,—the latter having the violin parts only of some half-dozen airs.

FARNABY (Giles) : An important writer of virginal music and canzonets who flourished towards the end of the sixteenth century. If his keyboard music is any indication of his own skill as a performer on the instrument, he must have been the possessor of a very considerable technique. His work for the virginal was of a very virtuosic order, and in point of digital technics it was little behind that of the most famous composers of this class of music. His vocal music, too, deserves close attention, and a study of his work is necessary fully to understand the direction of the musical art in England at the end of the sixteenth century.

Of his life very little is known. Many small pieces of evidence would point to his being of Cornish descent. He lived in London in 1589 (information given by Mr. W. Barclay Squire from the Churchwarden's accounts of St. Helen's, Bishopgate), and in 1592 (July 7th) he obtained the degree of *Mus. Bac.* at the University of Oxford (from Christ Church). In supplicating for this degree he stated that he had studied music for twelve years (*i.e.* since 1580), so that his birth might be placed somewhere near 1565. The entries in the St. Helen's (Bishopgate) registers show that he was married there at the end of March, 1587, and another entry tells us that a son of his was baptized in the following year (St. Mary-le-Bow).

His best-known work was the "*Canzonets to Foure Voyces, with a Song of Eight parts.* Compiled by Giles Farnaby, Bachilar of Musicke*", which appeared in 1598. It was dedicated to the "right worshipful Master Ferdinando Heaburn, Groome of her Majesty's Privie Chamber", and in the address to Ferdinand, the composer says, "I make bold to intrude these sillie works as the first fruits of my labor . . ." The book was reprinted under the editorship of Dr. E. H. Fellowes (*Vol. XX* of the *English Madrigal School*, 1922). Oliphant reprinted one number (" My lady's coloured cheeks ") with different words (" A nosegay of Spring flowers "), in 1847, and a couple of Farnaby's Canzonets were issued by Mr. W. Barclay Squire in 1888 and 1889. One of the pieces in the book was arranged by Farnaby himself for the virginal, and is included in the *Fitzwilliam Virginal Book*, where a total of 52 compositions and arrangements for that instrument may be seen. Professor Granville Bantock issued *Quodling's Delight*, (1909), an album of selected pieces (1912), and a suite of seven pieces (1914), all arranged for the pianoforte. Nine of the settings in East's *Whole Book of Psalms* (1592) are by Giles Farnaby, and *Add.* 29427 and *Add.* 31421, in the British Museum, contain work by him.

FARNABY (Richard): A composer of virginal music

who flourished early in the seventeenth century. Nothing is known of his life except that he was a son of Giles Farnaby (*q.v.*), one of his compositions in the *Fitzwilliam Virginal Book* (" Nobodye's Gigge ") having the note attached: " Richard Farnaby, sonne to Giles Farnaby ". The Fitzwilliam volume contains four pieces by this composer.

FARRANT (Daniel): The name of a musician (or two musicians,—the one a performer on the viols and the other on the violin) dating from the firſt half of the seventeenth century; and although there were several musicians of the same surname, it is not possible certainly to conneɗ Daniel Farrant with any one of them. The firſt appearance of the name is in the State Papers (*Dom. Ser. reg. James I*): " Warrant to pay Daniel Farrant, one of the king's musicians for the violins, 46*l.* per annum " (November, 1607). There are no means of ascertaining how long he had been in that service, and it is quite possible that the Daniel Farrant of this entry was the father of the Daniel Farrant we meet with in the Lord Chamberlain's Records

for 1619 onwards. This is the only explanation I can advance for the gap of twelve years that occurs. But there is nothing to prevent these entries all referring to the same man, for only a normal lifetime of aɗivity separates 1607 from the Commonwealth, when the name disappears. On June 23rd, 1619, we read that a warrant was issued " for allowance of a yearly livery to Daniell Farrant, appointed a Viall, in the place of Thomas Browne, deceased " (*L.C.R.*). The wording of this entry seems to suggeſt a fresh appointment, and that it does not refer to a man who was already in service. In 1621 and 1624 there are further orders respeɗting livery. In 1625 his name appears in " The Consorte " at the funeral of the king and on December 22nd of the same year he is one of the musicians exempted from paying the subsidies voted to the king by Parliament (*S.P.*). In 1628 the Lord Chamberlain's Records give " Danyell Farraunt " undèr the head " For the lutes and voices ", a caption that covered moſt of the musicians in the old consort (the violins being given in a separate liſt). It appears that this Farrant played the viol and not the violin. At Michaelmas, 1631, he is distinctly described as " un de lez Violls "; and similarly, but in English, at Michaelmas, 1632. The last entry giving his name before the Commonwealth, once more includes it among the " Lutes, Violls, and Voices ".

At the re-establishment of the royal music after the Restoration, we read: " 1660, June 16. Musitians of the Private Musick. William Gregory in the place of Daniel Farrant, private, a Viol " (*L.C.R.*), so that Farrant must have died during the Interregnum. Indeed, the warrant admitting Gregory into Farrant's place (*L.C.R.*, September 13th, 1660) described the latter as " deceased ".

Yet in spite of the paucity of references to him, Daniel Farrant is an interesting figure. He is credited with having been one of the first to use the viol " Lyra-way " (*v. Dic. Old Engl. Mus.*), and in *Musick's Recreation on the Viol, Lyra-way* (1669) Playford says: " This way of playing on the viol, is but of late invention, in imitation of the Old English Lute or Bandore . . . The first Authors

of Inventing and Setting Lessons this way to the *Viol*, was Mr. *Daniel Farunt*, Mr. *Alphonso Ferabosco*, and Mr. *John Coperario* ". Playford already describes this method of writing and playing in *Musick's Recreation on the Lyra-Viol* (1652). This celebrated music publisher says further (1661): " Daniel Farunt . . . was a person of much ingenuity for his several rare inventions of instruments, as the Polyphant and the Stump, which were strung with wire ". Judging his information by the date of the work giving it, no doubts need be entertained; but in his *Introduction to the Skill of Musick*, Playford says that Queen Elizabeth " did often recreate her self on an excellent Instrument called the Polyphant ". Now, if the Daniel Farrant under consideration invented that instrument, he must have been a very old man when he died before the Restoration of Charles II, and Elizabeth must have been a very old woman when she performed upon it. Supposing Playford's assignment of the Polyphant to Daniel Farrant to be correct, I submit that the instrument was invented by the Farrant mentioned in the

State Papers, entry of 1607, and that he was the father of a later Daniel. It is most probable that all the information given by several authorities on manuscripts containing organ-music, *etc.*, by Daniel Farrant, is erroneous. Similarly the suggestion, often made,—that Daniel Farrant was a son of Richard Farrant can hardly be treated seriously. Until we know when the two men were born, nothing definite can be said on this point. Taking chronological possibilities into consideration, the first Daniel could have been the son or nephew of Richard, assuming that there were two Daniels. I think there is much to support the theory that the State Papers refer to two distinct men of the same name in the entries occurring between 1607 and 1661;—not the least of the proofs being that the first Daniel is spoken of as a violinist, and the second as a viol,—a distinction very clearly marked in the early seventeenth century.

FARRANT (John): An organist who flourished during the second half of the sixteenth century. A certain amount of difficulty presents itself when an attempt is made to follow the chronology of his activity. Organists bearing this name were at work in at least five different churches, and the dates in one or two cases overlap. It is possible that more than one musician of that name existed contemporaneously; at the same time it is not impossible that all the references apply to the same man, who would in that case have been of rather a restless disposition. A John Farrant was organist at Ely from 1566 to 1572; but we also find the name in connection with Bristol in 1570–1. This may argue the existence of two John Farrants. In 1592–3 we meet him (or one of them) at Hereford, and from 1598 to 1602 a John Farrant was organist at Salisbury. Christ Church, Newgate Street, London, also had an organist of that name near the end of the century and it is impossible with the data at our disposal, to decide how many John Farrants there were, and if only one, how he fitted his various appointments to agree with the written records.

The Christ Church (Oxford) library possesses a *Kyrie* and *Creed* by " Mr.

Farrant of Salisbury " (organ part), and the same part of a *Te Deum* which Ouseley published as Richard Farrant's. If " O Lord Allmighty, thou God of Israell ", a full anthem in Tudway's collection (*B.M. Harl.* 7340) is by John Farrant, he must have lived a long while after the last date given in the Salisbury records, since Tudway states that he " lived in King Charles the First's time ". The *Service in D* (manuscripts at Ely and Peterhouse, Cambridge) would have been written—judging from the style—by the earlier of the two Farrants, if there were two. This one would in all probability have been the organist at Ely; but which of the other appointments he also held, cannot be determined (*v. also* J. E. West, *Cathedral Organists, ed.* 1921; and Havergal, *Fasti Herefordensis*).

FARRANT (Richard): A distinguished writer of sacred music who flourished during the second half of the sixteenth century, and who may be taken as one of the representative church musicians of the Tudor period. The little music he has left is of excellent quality, noteworthy more often for its simple charm and deep tenderness than for any other feature. His part-writing, as may be expected of so excellent a contrapuntist, is very fine, though, of course, he cannot escape the false relations so common at that period. A certain amount of care must be exercised when considering music bearing his name, for compositions which have for centuries passed as his may possibly have to be attributed to others. In some cases the question must remain open. An example in point is the truly beautiful anthem " Lord, for Thy tender Mercies' sake ", which in some manuscripts is attributed to John Hilton I, and in others to Richard Farrant. Several modern authorities reject both ascriptions and suggest Tye as the composer of the anthem. But, all things considered, I see no reason why Richard Farrant should not have written it. The *Service in G-Minor*, similarly, may be the work of someone else,— possibly of another Farrant,— and in this composition the style of the writing may make the doubt more justified.

The date of Richard Farrant's birth is a matter

N

for conjecture. The earliest reference to him is the one in *Stowe MS. 571* (*B.M.*; *fol. 36b*), where he is given as a Gentleman of the Chapel Royal in 1552. He could thus have been born hardly later than 1530. He probably remained in the Chapel until he was transferred to Windsor (St. George's Chapel) in 1564 to become Master of the Children there. That he was one of the organists at Windsor is not certain. The entry in the Cheque-Book of the Chapel Royal reads: " 1564. Tho. Sampson was sworne gentleman in Richard Farrant's roome the 24th of Aprill ". For the keep and instruction of the choristers he received 81*l.* 6*s.* 8*d.* and while at Windsor he lived in the building known as the " Old Commons ". He remained there little over five years, returning to London in 1569 to take the place of Thomas Causton, deceased: " 1569. Mr. Causton died the 28th October, and Richard Farrant was sworne in his place the 5th of November, *Ao.* 120. from Windsor " (*Ch. Bk. C.R.*). The date of his death is also open to doubt. The Cheque-Book contains two entries, one in 1580 and another in 1581, both stating that Farrant died on the 30th November. Which of the two dates is wrong cannot be determined. Boyce, Rimbault, and Hawkins, probably deriving their information from a common source, give 1585 as the date of Farrant's death. Like all the other Tudor Masters of the Choristers, Farrant provided many of the entertainments given at court, and many entries in the State Papers refer to payments for this kind of work. Probably the little secular music he wrote was composed for such interludes.

Examples of his work may be seen in manuscripts at the British Museum (*Harl.* 7337, 7338, 7340; *Add.* 17820; *Add.* 17840; *Add.* 17786-91; *Add.* 29289; *Add.* 17784; *Add.* 30478-9; *Add.* 30087; some of these containing duplicated compositions). The organ music in *Add.* 30513 is not certainly by Richard Farrant, though the possibility remains that the signature — " Farrante " — may refer to Richard. Christ Church (Oxford) library has an organ-part of a *Benedicite*, and the Royal College of Music possesses incomplete works. Richard Farrant is represented in Barnard's book of 1641, and music by him is contained in the collection of Boyce. The *Service in G-Minor* has been published by Novello, edited by John E. West; *Te Deum, Benedictus, Magnificat,* and *Nunc Dimittis,* by the Church Music Society; the debatable " Lord, for thy tender Mercies' Sake " exists in no fewer than a dozen different editions; " Call to Remembrance " appeared in the *Musical Times* for 1845, and in an edition by Hullah; and in Tonic Solfa (Novello); " Hide not Thy Face " was edited by Mr. J. E. West for Novello in 1903, by the same editor for Bayley and Fergusson in 1909, and issued in Tonic Solfa in 1903 (Novello). This does not exhaust the list of old and new editions of Farrant's works, but several, in addition to those named, are easily obtainable from the various publishers.

FARTHING (Thomas) : An early sixteenth-century composer who was in the royal service as a Gentleman of the king's Chapel in the second decade of the century. He is first to be met with in the Lord Chamberlain's Records under date February 27th, 1510– 11, when he received a mourning livery for the funeral of Prince Henry, the infant son of Henry VIII, who died on February 22nd aged seven weeks. Among his contemporaries in the Chapel were such famous men as Fayrfax, Cornyshe, and Crane. In July, 1511, he was made a grant of ten marks a year "in consideration of his services to the Countess of Richmond " (Brewer, *Letters and Papers of Henry VIII*), and in the Exchequer Accounts for October 16th of the same year there is a warrant for the delivery to him of chamlet gowns, *etc.* (*Id.*). Similarly on April 16th, 1512, " Thomas Fardyng, gentleman of our most honourable Chapel ", received black velvet for coats, *etc.* (*Id.*). In 1513 he surrendered a corrody which he held in the monastery of Ramsey in favour of one John Porth (May 9th, 5 *Hen. VIII*). A couple more of entries referring to the delivery of materials for liveries complete the tale of what we know of Farthing. The last official date of a document relating to him, so far discoverable, is October 3rd, 1514. Specimens of his music may be seen in the British Museum (*Add.* 31922): Rounds written out at length, "Aboffe oll thynge", "Hey now" (without words), and "In May, that lusty sesone", and three madrigal-like compositions entitled, "The Thowght within my Brest", "With sorrowful syghte", and "I loue trewly".

FAYRFAX (Robert): One of the most outstanding figures in the history of early sixteenth-century English music, Robert Fayrfax stood at the head of the reactionary school of composers who broke away from the traditions of the Low Countries. His work, taking his date into consideration, is markedly impressive and dignified, and he possessed a gift of scoring that produced some exceedingly fine and massive effects. His melodic line is typical of his period, of course ; but much of what may appear to be arid and aimless to-day is amply atoned for by the wonderful nobility and the rich sonority of his harmony. He came at a time when music in England had been marking time for some years. John Dunstable had been long dead, and the feeble imitators of his generation were gone the same way. After an interval of apparent silence, we suddenly come across a school of musicians with Robert Fayrfax at its head, which proved itself capable of producing works of extraordinary merit. Writers from Francis Meres (*Palladis Tamia*, 1598) to myself (*Musical News*, January 20th to February 10th, 1917) and Mr. S. Royle Shore (*Musical Times*, August, 1920), have spoken of his work and the place it should occupy in the minds of the musical historian; indeed, the subject has been so thoroughly discussed that there will be no need to go over the ground again. But it should be remembered that the music of this early period can only be judged by actual performance of the works. Forming their opinions upon the work of Robert Fayrfax from the written score,— and then not always examining his best examples,—many writers have come to unjust conclusions.

The exact date of Fayrfax's birth is not known ; but considering later circumstances it must have fallen in the second half of the fifteenth century (*ca.* 1465–70), and most authorities (from Bishop Tanner onwards) give Bayford in Hertfordshire as his native place. The first official mention of him is in 1497 when we learn from the *Calendar of Patent Rolls* that he was a Gentleman of the Chapel Royal and that the grant of a chapel was made him: "December 6, 1497. Westm.: Grant to Robert Fayrfax, one of the Gentlemen of the King's Chapel, of the free chapel in the Castle of Snodehill, in the diocese of Hereford, void by the death of Master Richard Jaqueson". He held this for only eleven months, for on November 16th, 1498, we read: "Grant to Robert Couper of the free chapel within Snodhille Castle . . . void by the surrender of Robert Fayrefax . . . resigned" (*Cat. Pat. Rolls*, 1916). At the end of the fifteenth century Fayrfax became organist at St. Albans Abbey. He must certainly have excelled in the organist's art to have been selected for this appointment, for the organ at St. Alban's (presented by Abbot John Wheathampstead in 1438) was held to be the finest

in the kingdom. In 1502 Fayrfax obtained his doctorate, being licenced to proceed in these words: " 1501–2. Item. Conceditur magistro Fayerfax erudito in musica quod post gradum bacallariatus, sua erudicione possit stare pro forma ad incipiendum in musica " (*Cambridge Grace Book, Gamma, p.* 2*b*). In 1511 he incorporated at Oxford, and in that year says that he had possessed a doctor's degree for seven years. His exercise was the five-part " O quam glorifica " which may still be seen in the splendid choirbook in Lambeth Palace (*Cod.* 1). In 1503–4 (February 23rd) we have evidence of his having been in the Chapel Royal, for in that year he received a livery for the funeral of Queen Elizabeth, the wife of Henry VII (*L.C.R., Vol. 550, fol. 68d*). In the list of " Gentilmen of the King's Chapell " the name of " Robert Fairfaux " comes ninth. When Henry VIII came to the throne Fayrfax was first on the list of Gentlemen (*L.C.R., Vol.* 424). The *Letters and Papers, Foreign and Domestic, of the Reign of Henry VIII*, edited by J. S. Brewer (1862), gives a transcription of an interesting document

(*No.* 207): "For Robert Fayrefax, gentleman of the Chapell. To have an annuity of 9*l.* 2*s.* 6*d.* part payable out of the farm of Colemere, Hants., by the prior of South-wyke, and part out of the issues of Co. Hants". It is dated "I. Hen. VIII, 22 June; delivered Westminster 26 June" (1509). In the following year he had two boys to train and keep: "Dr. Fayrfax, for board of William Alderton, child of the King's Chapel, 12*d.* per week, 37 weeks, and for Arth. Lovekyn, 54 weeks; besides 46*s.* 8*d.* for their learning" (*King's Bk. of Payments,* P.R.O.). A year later Fayrfax received 7*l.* 17*s.* 4*d.* " for the diet and learning for a whole year of . . . our Scholars ". In 1510–11 " Mr. Dr. Farefax " received a livery for the funeral of the infant Prince Henry. *Add. MS.* 18826 (*B.M.*) mentions a warrant to the Great Ward-robe " for a riding gown for Dr. Fairefax ". In 1513 (March) Fayrfax surrendered a Corrody in the monastery of Stanley, when it was granted to John Fyssher, another gentleman of the Chapel Royal (*Document* 3773, Brewer's *Papers of Henry VIII*; original in the

P. R. O.). In November, 1513, the annuity of 9*l.* 2*s.* 6*d.* was shared by Robert Bythesee and Robert Fayrfax " in survivorship ". Document 169 (Brewer) repeats this in 1515. In 1514 Fayrfax became one of the Poor Knights of Windsor: " For Robert Fairfax . . . To be one of the Knights of the King's Alms in the College of St. Mary and St. George, in Windsor Castle, with 12*d.* a day for life. Delivered Knoll, 10 September, 6 Hen. VIII " (*P.R.O. Document* 5397, Brewer). For any special work done Fayrfax was suitably rewarded. At New Year the king and his musicians usually exchanged presents, and any music com-posed for the occasion would be well paid for. Thus on New Year's Day, 1516, " Dr. Fairfax, for a book, 13*l.* 6*s.* 8*d.* (*King's Bk. of Payments*); January, 1517 (the king being at Greenwich) " for a book of Anthems, 20*l.*"; January, 1518, " for a pricksonge book, 20*l.*"; January, 1519, " for a balet boke limned, 20*l.*" (*Id.*). These sums are far too large for them to be looked upon as payments for the mere copy-ing of the music, as many writers suppose; the reward was quite sufficient for the composition of the music itself. Are we to suppose that after being paid 5 3*s*. 4*d*. for teaching two boys for a whole year, he would receive such amounts as 13*l*. 6*s*. 8*d*. and (several times) 20*l*. for the merely mechanical labour of copying music,—even though it were " limned ? "

In 1520, Fayrfax accompanied his king to the historic Field of the Cloth of Gold, still occupying the first position in the list of Gentlemen of the Chapel Royal. This is practically all that we know of his life. He died on October 24th, 1521, letters of administration being granted to his widow on November 14th. He was interred in the Abbey of St. Alban's, and, according to *Add. 5465 (B.M.)*, " iacet sepultus in ecclesia Monastinalis sci. Albani . . ." An account of the slab which covered the grave was given in the *Home Counties Magazine* (1899) by William Page, and in 1643 John Philpot, Somerset Herald, gave the foot-inscription as: " Pray for the soules of Master Robert Fairfax, Doctor of Music, and Agnes his wife, the which Robert deceased the xxiiii day of October the year of our Lord God MVXXI on whose soules Jeshu have Mercy Amen ".

The works of Robert Fayrfax exist chiefly in manuscript, and until comparatively recently hardly any had been correctly printed. The only sixteenth-century book to include a printed version of any of his work was *Wynkyn de Worde's Song Book* of 1530 (*Triplex* and *Bassus* parts in *B.M.*), " Ut re my fa sol la " in four parts, and " My hartes lust " in three parts, being contained. Burney (*History*) and John Stafford Smith (*Collection of English Songs*, 1779) printed a few specimens of his music, and Hawkins gave an extract from a motet. " Who shall court my fair ladye ", for three voices, is included by Rimbault in his *Ancient Vocal Music of England* (*No.* 10, 1847). Recent issues of Fayrfax's compositions include a *Magnificat* (with additions by the editor, Mr. S. Royle Shore,—an unwarrantable liberty) published by Novello, and another *Magnificat* (by the same editor, who added a *Nunc Dimittis* by William Mundy). A list of manuscripts containing work by Fayrfax is given in my article on this musician (*Musical News*, February 10th, 1917.)

FERRABOSCO FAMILY: A large and influential Italian family of musicians, at least five members of which became celebrated in England. At its head stood Domenico Maria Ferrabosco, who was Master of the Chapel at S. Petronio in Bologna, and, in 1546, at the Basilica Vaticana at Rome, besides being a singer in the Papal Chapel between 1550 and 1555. He published a volume of madrigals in 1542 besides several isolated madrigals and motets in the different collections of his time. He was born on February 14th, 1513, and died in February, 1574. The first member of the family to come to England was his son Alfonso, who in this book will be called Alfonso I. The son of the latter was already English by birth, and became one of the most celebrated musicians at the time in England,—especially from the dramatic point of view. He is referred to below as Alfonso II. Two sons of the last-named,—Alfonso III and Henry,—also held important positions in English musical circles, and the fifth member of the family to become a noteworthy musician,—John, was most probably a brother of the last two. The difficulty of isolating the various members of the family,—especially those bearing the same Christian name,—is very great, and a case in point will be seen below in the article on John Ferrabosco.

FERRABOSCO (Alfonso) (I): The son of Domenico Maria Ferrabosco was born at Bologna and came to England before 1562; for in letters written to various statesmen of Queen Elizabeth in 1564 he speaks of his long service with the queen. He appears to have left Italy without the consent of the authorities, and he says that in consequence his property had been confiscated. There are records of a good deal of petitioning for pensions, *etc.*, and he was the subject of much jealousy and intriguing. A foreign musician in England had been murdered at about this time, and Ferrabosco was accused of the crime. Further correspondence and petitions followed, some documents protesting his innocence and others begging for an audience with the queen. At length her majesty received him, the various doubts and suspicions removed, and the musician was secured in a pension of 100*l.* per annum (March 26th, 1569). After giving a promise to return he left for Italy to put his affairs there in order. On the journey further troubles overtook him, and he was robbed by a servant; but on arrival at Bologna he repeated his promise to return to England. More than a year elapsed before he obtained from the Pope the necessary licence to travel. That he returned is clear from the fact that he participated in the masque of 1572. But six years later he broke the promise he made in writing to the queen (*viz.* that he would remain in her service all his life), and left the country. On the title-page of his publication of 1587 he is designated " gentil uomo dell' Altezza di Savoia ". The work was dated from Venice, September 4th, 1587. A year after the issue of this book he died at Turin. During his absence from England he left his two children to be cared for by one Gomer van Osterwyck, a member of the Chapel Royal, who was still a creditor of Alphonso I for their maintenance when the latter died. The reputation enjoyed by

this Ferrabosco was a very high one; Peacham (*Compleat Gentleman*, 1622) said that: " Alphonso Ferabosco the father . . . for iudgement and depth of skill (as also his sonne yet liuing) was inferior unto none: What he did was most elaborate and profound, and pleasing enough in Aire, though Master Thomas Morley censureth him otherwise ". What the last phrase means is not quite clear; for Morley really praised him (*Introd. to the Skill of Musick*). Alfonso I was an intimate friend of William Byrd, and the two musicians frequently pitted their skill against one another in friendly rivalry (*v.* Byrd, William). His chief printed works were two volumes of five-part madrigals published at Venice in 1587, a copy of the second book under the title *Il secondo libro de Madrigali a Cinque, etc.* . . . is in the British Museum. Several madrigals of his were contained in *Musica Transalpina* (1588–97) and a couple of lute pieces are included in Robert Dowland's *Varietie of Lute-Lessons* (1610). There he is clearly named " the most artificiall and famous Alfonso Ferrabosco of Bologna ", but in many cases, especially in manuscripts, it requires close study in order to decide which Alfonso is meant. A tremendous amount of music undoubtedly by him is preserved in manuscripts kept in most of the more important collections. Mr. G. E. P. Arkwright (*Old English Edition*) has re-issued nine madrigals from the 1588 *Musica Transalpina* in No. XI, and another five in No. XII. FERRABOSCO (Alfonso) (II) Son of the foregoing, probably born before his father went to Italy in 1578. In a list of annuities paid by Queen Elizabeth in 1594 his name appears against a payment of 26*l*. 13*s*. 4*d*. (Nagel, *Annalen*), and since a similar sum was paid him two years earlier, it is possible that this money was paid for his musical education. At the funeral of Elizabeth his name appears under the heading " Lutes and Others " as " Alphonso Forobosco " (*L.C.R., Vol.* 554). At Michaelmas, 1604, he was paid 50*l*. as his annual salary, for services as one of the " Violins " (probably treble or tenor viol; *v. Dict. Old Engl. Mus. s.v.* " Viols "). Wood said he became excellent " at the Lyra Viol, and was one of the first that

set lessons Lyraway to the viol "; certainly he shared with Daniel Farrant and Coperario the honour of being one of the first to write music in this way for the Gamba. But his chief work lay in the masque. He wrote the music for Ben Johnson's *Volpone* (1605), *The Masque of Blackness* (1605), the masque performed at Lord Haddington's marriage (*The Hue and Cry after Cupid*; 1608), *The Masque of Beauty* (1608), *The masque of Queens* (1609), and others. He was a friend of the poet's, and in the published account of *Hymenaei* (1605–6) Jonson pays the composer some high compliments. At Christmas, 1610, he supplied music for the masque *Love freed from Ignorance and Folly*, and in the accounts for the expenses of the production he is entered as having received 20*l*. " for making the Songs ". Shortly before this activity in masque-composing, he was appointed music-master to Prince Henry of Wales; and when the latter died in 1612 his services were retained for Prince Charles (afterwards Charles I). At the accession of this prince in 1625 Alfonso II is entered as a musician in the " Chamber of K.

Charles " (*L.C.R.*, *Vol.* 557). In July, 1626, he became " composer of music to the king " at a salary of 40*l.* per annum in the place of Coperario, deceased " (*Annalen*). On March 15th, 1628, he was succeeded by Thomas Tomkins (*Annalen*) —so he mu&t have died shortly before this date (*v.* Ferrabosco, Henry),—and was buried at Greenwich. Besides the masques Alfonso II published a book of *Ayres* (dedicated to his pupil Prince Henry) as his " Fir&t fruits " in 1609, and in the same year *Lessons for* 1, 2, *and* 3 *Viols, etc.* The latter book uses the viol tuned Lyraway. It contains verses by Ben Jonson, " To my excellent Friend Alfonso Ferabosco " in which he gives good advice to all who publish works for public criticism. This Alphonso contributed three numbers to Leighton's *Teares or Lamentacions* (1614). Rimbault (1847) reissued " Shall I seek to ease my grief " (from the 1609 set of *Ayres*) in his *Ancient Vocal Music of England* (*No.* 6). Care mu&t be exercised when ascribing compositions to any of the Alfonsos; for in some colle&tions Alfonso II is called

" the younger " when named with his father, and " the elder " when he is mentioned in relation to his son. FERRABOSCO (Alfonso) (III): Son of the above. Of his early years we know nothing, and he does not appear in the official accounts until after his father's death; —and if he does, he is not to be di&tinguished from the second Alfonso. In 1628 (March 28th) he was allowed the pension of 50*l.* per annum enjoyed by his father while the latter was in&tru&tor to Prince Henry (*Annalen*, quoting the *Cal. S.P.*). He appears to have played a wind-in&trument besides the viol or (possibly) the violin, for in an " order concerning the waiting of the musicians for the Wind In&truments ", he is mentioned (*L.C.R.*, *Vol.* 738; May 6th, 1630). In 1631 he is described as a " musician violin " (*Id.*, *Volume* 49). The Lord Chamberlain's entry for March 4th, 1632–3, shows that he played cornet, for on that date Andrea Lanier was paid 20*l.* 10*s.* for six cornets and a set of books for six musicians, among whom is Alfonso Ferrabosco (*L.C.R.*, *Vol.* 738). The fa&t that he played two in&truments

accounts for his receiving two liveries. In 1640 his salary is given as 50*l.* per annum (*Annalen*, quoting a document in the *P.R.O.*). His name appears in the Lord Chamberlain's Records until 1641, and he was presumably in the royal service until the Civil War ended the music-making at Court. His death must have occurred during the interregnum, for in 1660, when the royal band was got together again, we find William Child appointed " in Forobosco's place, Alphonso's, composer of wind musick " (*L.C.R.*, *Vol.* 477), and John Hingston " for a Viol, in place of Alphonso Forobosco " on June 23rd (*Id.*). The date given for his death in the *Dictionary of National Biography* (1661) is most probably too late. The fact that he is entered as " deceased " in the post-Restoration accounts simply proves that he died some time during the Commonwealth.

The singer Mrs. Ferrabosco, mentioned by Pepys in 1664 was evidently a daughter-in-law of Alfonso III;—the entry cannot refer to his widow for she would have been too old by then to have sung " most admirably ". Moreover, the diarist says that he was glad to hear that she was proposed as a gentlewoman for his wife, " . . . but I hear she is too gallant for me, and I am not sorry that I misse her ".

FERRABOSCO (Henry): Another son of Alfonso II, who shared his father's posts with his brother Alfonso III. We meet with him as a musician to the king before his father's death (*L.C.R.*, *Vol.* 148, November 8th, 1625) when he received a livery allowance. On November 28th of the same year he is described as " one of the musician flutes ". On March 29th, 1627, he was sworn in as a " musician in ordinary . . . for the voices and wind instruments in the place of his father Alfonso Ferabosco, deceased ". To the last entry from the Lord Chamberlain's Records there is appended the note (alluding to Alfonso III and Henry): " Their father enjoyed four places, viz. a musician's place in general, a composer's place, a Violl's place and an instructor's place to the Prince in the art of musique. The benefit of all which places did descend unto his sonnes by his Majesty's special grant " (*Vol.* 738). Henry was probably a good singer, for in

1631 he is especially mentioned as a "musician for le voices". Since he served a "double place", he, like his brother, drew two liveries, and a receipt signed by him for 32*l.* 5*s.* in 1632–3 is preserved (*Vol.* 179, *L.C.R.*), the allowance for each livery being 16*l.* 2*s.* 6*d.* The entry for March 4th, 1632–3, which provides a cornet for his brother Alfonso, also mentions him. In 1640 his salary, according to a document in the Public Record Office, was 80*l.* per annum (probably 40*l.* for each of his two places). Henry Ferrabosco is mentioned in the State records until 1641, when court music in London came to a temporary standstill. In the Civil War he followed the king to Oxford. Later during the Interregnum he was mentioned by Playford as a well-known teacher of singing and viol-playing in London. At the Restoration his place was occupied by Thomas Bates ("for a Violl") and by Matthew Lock as composer, a place "late enjoyed by Henry Ferabosco, deceased". From this it is clear that he died, as his brother did, during the Commonwealth.

FERRABOSCO (John):

Most probably a younger son of Alfonso II and brother of the two foregoing musicians. If this supposition is correct (and the dates do not disprove it), he was the John Ferrabosco baptized at Greenwich on October 9th, 1626 (about a year before his father died). But on January 15th, 1630–1 we meet with a John Ferrabosco in the Lord Chamberlain's Records as a "musician for the windy instruments", when the child just mentioned would have been four years old. It is thus clear that the entries mentioning "John Ferrabosco" in these records cannot refer to the son of Alfonso II. There must have been another John Ferrabosco, probably an uncle of the child baptized in 1626. It will thus be useless to follow these entries until they end at the Rebellion. John, the son of Alfonso II was appointed organist of Ely Cathedral in 1662, when he would have been thirty-six years old,— which would be an age that could reconcile the dates of his birth and appointment. He became a doctor of music at Cambridge in 1671 by royal letters patent of Charles II, and died in 1682 (buried October 15th). His salary at Ely was 30*l.* per annum, augmented by a further 6*l.* paid for " holding the office of cook, which was doubtless a sinecure " (Dr. A. W. Wilson, *Organs and Organists of Ely Cathedral*). John Ferrabosco composed a good deal of church music which is preserved in manuscript at Ely (fourteen services,— one scored by Tudway,—and eleven anthems), and a set of dance-forms for the harpsichord is in the Christ Church (Oxford) library.

FERTHING (Thomas): *see* FARTHING (Thomas).

FILIPPI (Petrus): *see* PHILIPS (Peter).

FINCH (The Hon. Edward): A clergyman who composed a few specimens of ecclesiastical music which, to judge by the inclusion of a couple of them in Tudway's collection, were in frequent use. The fifth son of the first Earl of Nottingham, Edward Finch, was born in 1664, his biography being that of the average churchman. He obtained his M.A. degree in 1679, and was elected a Fellow of Christ's College, Cambridge. He was a Member of Parliament for the University of Cambridge in 1689–90 and in 1700 became a deacon. His ecclesiastical appointments included those of prebendary of York and, in 1710, of Canterbury. He died on February 14th, 1738. The examples of his work mentioned above are to be seen in *Harl.* 7342 (*B.M.*),—a *Te Deum, à* 5, and a full anthem, " Grant we beseech Thee, merciful Lord ". The Euing library (Glasgow) possesses " A Grammar of Thorough Bass " by him (MS.).

FINGER (Godfrey) (Gottfried): A native of Olmütz who came to England in 1685 and contributed a good deal of dramatic music to the English stage, collaborating at times with John Eccles and Daniel Purcell. That he was Master of James II's Chapel, as is often stated, is open to doubt. Two references in the Lord Chamberlain's Records give him merely as an instrumentalist in the Chapel. He is supposed to have left England, after 1701, in disgust at receiving only the fourth prize in a competition to set Congreve's *Judgment of Paris*. He was undoubtedly the most accomplished musician among the competitors, North saying that he returned to Germany because he " thought he was to compose musick for men and not for boys " (*Memoires of Musick*). In 1702 he became a chamber-musician to Queen Sophie Charlotte in Berlin. His work in England included a great quantity of incidental music for stage-plays, solos for the violin, flute, and organ, instrumental duets, trios, and quartets, and a large number of songs. He composed the Ode for St. Cecilia's Day in 1693, the first performance of which was advertised in the *London Gazette* for February 1st to take place on the fifth of the month at York-Buildings (*v.* also Rimbault's notes to the Musical Antiquarian Society's edition of North's *Memoires of Musick*).

FLOYD (John): *see* LLOYD (John).

FLUDD (Robert): A physician and philosopher of some importance whose voluminous writings on philosophical questions gained for him a European reputation. His interest to musicians lies only in his authorship of two treatises in *Utriusque cosmi maioris minoris metaphysica, Physica atque technica historia, etc.*, which contain, among many other things, information on musical physics. The whole work was published at Oppenheim between 1617 and 1624. He was the son of a State official under Queen Elizabeth, — one Thomas Fludd, or Flud,—and was born in Kent in 1574. He was educated at St. John's College, Oxford, and abroad, and during this period he obtained the degrees of M.A. and M.D. and became a Fellow of the College of Physicians. He died in London on September 8th, 1637, and lies buried in his native Bearsted, Kent.

FLUYD (John): *see* LLOYD (John).

FORD (Thomas): A chamber-musician in the royal service, and composer of vocal and instrumental music. He belonged to the class of performer-composers whose depth of feeling and contrapuntal skill were not sufficiently great to secure for them a position in the very front rank of contemporary writers. Ford, however, wrote some very charming little things, — graceful and melodious, — and his music undoubtedly reflects one aspect of his period. His *Book of Ayres* appeared at a date when almost every composer made essays in accompanied song writing, though Ford also wrote some very attractive madrigals. Pro-bably some of his best work still remains unpublished. Less known, though quite good, is some sacred music of his.

The date of Ford's birth is not known, though that usually assigned to this occurrence, — ca. 1580, — cannot be far out. He appears to have been a musician to Prince Henry of Wales, for in the list of those who had been employed in his service, and who attended his funeral in 1612, we find the name of " Mr. Ford " (*L.C.R., Vol. 555*). Dr. Birch's *Life of Prince Henry* gives Ford's salary in 1611 as having been 30*l.* per annum. After 1612 we lose sight of him, and do not find his name in the official records until 1625 when Thomas " Fourd " appears in a list of musicians in " the Chamber of King Charles " (*L.C.R., Vol. 557*). The Calendar of State Papers, under date July 11th, 1626, gives his salary as 120*l.* all told (*Annalen*), while Rymer's *Foedera* gives information that makes his salary 80*l.*,—" 40*l.* for the place he formerly held, and 40*l.* in that which John Ballard deceased held ". On July 15th, 1628, he is entered under the head " For

the lutes and voices " (*L.C.R., Vol.* 738). Thence onwards, until the Civil War, his name is frequently mentioned in connection with the allowance of his livery of 16*l.* 2*s.* 6*d.* per annum. He died in 1648 and was buried at St. Margaret's, Westminster. At the Restoration Charles Coleman and Henry Lawes shared his posts.

The only work published by Thomas Ford was: "*Musicke of Sundrie Kindes Set forth in two Bookes.* The First Whereof are Aries for 4 Voices to the lute, orpharion, or Basse-Viol . . . The Second are Pauens, Galiards, Almaines, Toies, Iigges, Thumpes, and such like, for two Basse-Viols;— Liera-way, *etc.*, 1607 " (for the forms mentioned in this title see *Dic. Old Engl. Mus.*). The work contains ten Ayres (including the popular " Since first I saw your face ") and eighteen of the dance-forms named in the title. He is twice represented in Leigh-ton's *Teares, etc.* (1614), and Hilton's *Catch that Catch Can* (1652 and 1658) contains various Canons by him. Isolated pieces by Ford have been reprinted fairly fre-quently. The anthem " Let God arise " was published by the Musical Antiquarian Society in 1845 (Rimbault). The British Museum and the library of Chriſt Church (Oxford) have manuscripts containing music by him;—the former having chiefly Canons and Ayres from the printed collection; and the latter anthems, madrigals, ayres, etc., some of them incomplete. Novello and Co. have issued "Come Phyllis, come unto these bowers", "Now I see thy looks were feigned", "Since firſt I saw your face", and "There is a ladie sweet and kind" (all four-part). Clifford's collection of anthem-texts (1663) includes the words of "Look, Shepherds, look".

FOREST: A composer belonging to the period graced by Dunſtable and Power. Nothing is known of his biography though, in view of the faét that he is represented in manuscripts at Modena and Trent, he may—like others of his generation— have spent moſt of his life abroad. Two compositions by him are contained in the Old Hall manuscript (St. Edmund's College, near Ware, Herts.). *Add.* 36490 (*B.M.*), transcribed by Mr. Barclay Squire, contains the opening phrases of four com-

positions by Foreſt,—"Alma Redemptoris", "Tota pulcra eſt", "Ave regina celorum", and "Gaude, mater".

FORNSETE (John of): A learned monk of Reading Abbey who flourished in the firſt half of the thirteenth century and who was keeper of the Cartulary. His importance to the musical hiſtorian lies in the circumſtance that to him is generally ascribed the venerable rota, "Sumer is icumen in" (*ca.* 1226). That the round is in his handwriting seems to be clearly enough eſtablished; but that he aétually composed it is more open to doubt. There is certainly nothing to prevent him having done so and the work has never been claimed by, or attributed to, anyone else. That he was alive in 1238 is proved by an entry of his in the Cartulary; and that he died before the end of 1239 is shown by an entry written by his successor: "Ora, Wulſtane, pro noſtro fratre, Johanne de Fornsete". If John of Fornsete did nothing more than transcribe the round into the manuscript now known as *Harl.* 978 (*B.M.*), he deserves the gratitude of all Englishmen for having preserved a composition which

o

gives to England the honour of having produced a work in the early thirteenth century which is remarkable in its part-writing, and which argues the high state of English music at this very early period. The rota, together with an excellent summing up of all the evidence deducible from the manuscript, is contained in W. S. Rockstro's article in the 1914 edition of *Grove* (*Vol. IV*, pp. 747–754).

FOX (William): An organist of Ely Cathedral who is known to us, as far as I have been able to discover, only as the composer of a full anthem (4-part),—" Teach me Thy way, O Lord " — given in *Harl.* 7338 (*B.M.*), and published, first in 1847 (in the series *The Parish Choir*), and, edited by John E. West, by Novello in 1906. Of his biography only the last seven years are known ; he was organist at Ely from 1572 until his death in 1579. His salary at Ely was 13*l*. 6*s*. 8*d*. per annum (*Chapter Accounts*; Willis, *Survey*).

G

GALLANDUS (Joannes) :
see GARLAND (John).
GAMBLE (John): A seventeenth century violinist and performer on the cornet who composed a good deal of third-rate music which in spite of its mediocrity became very popular with its author's contemporaries. Not very much is known of his life, and of the little we know most is based upon the none too trustworthy evidence of Anthony Wood. According to this Oxford gossip, Gamble is supposed to have played in, and to have composed for, the king's theatre. Wood speaks of having had him as a guest at Oxford in 1658. At the Restoration we find him active at court. In 1660 he was appointed to the wind-music in the royal band " in the place of William Lanier " (*L.C.R.*). In the following, year his instrument is specifically stated to have been the cornet, and he played it in the Chapel Royal also (*v. Dic. Old Engl. Mus. s.v.* " Cornet "). In a petition it is said that he lost all his possessions in the great fire; but he appears to have been financially embarrassed before this calamity overtook the metropolis, for on June 2nd, 1666, there is an account in the Lord Chamberlain's Records of the sum of 2*l.* lent him. After the fire he borrowed another 5*l.* (October 20th). However, his pecuniary position need not have been caused by the fire alone, for three years' livery money was owing to him by 1666. In the same year he is also included in the lists of violinists, thus showing that he occupied what was then known as a " double place ". In 1666–7 he was forced to petition for the payment of some of his salary, since this was already over four years in arrears. His wage as a cornettist was 46*l.* 10*s.* 10*d.* (*L.C.R.*). In the masque of 1674 he played with the violins. By 1685 the treasury owed Gamble 112*l.* 17*s.* 6*d.*, a sum which James II ordered to be paid out of the " new imposition on tobacco and sugar " (*L.C.R.*). Whether he received the money before he died in 1687 is not known.

His best-known work was *Ayres and Dialogues, To be Sung to the Theorbo-Lute or Base-Viol*, published in 1656, and a second book of *Ayres and Dialogues* for from one to three voices, followed three years later. The earlier of these works contains a portrait of the composer. *Harl.* 6947 (*B.M.*) contains a collection of poems set by Gamble, but giving only the melodies without accompaniments. *Add.* 32339 (*B.M.*) has the same set of songs with " basses ". He wrote a commonplace-book which passed out of Dr. Rimbault's possession to go to America. This is a distinct loss to English workers, because the volume contains music by the two Lawes, Dr. Wilson, *etc.* Gamble made his will in 1680, and bequeathed his music and 20*l.* of the money owing to him from the State coffers to his grandson and namesake. The residue of his estate went to his wife, and all other relatives were disinherited.

GARLAND (John) (*or* John de GARLANDIA). An eminent writer of theoretical treatises on music who flourished early in the thirteenth century. A good deal of confusion exists regarding his chronology, and it was probably the circumstance of Pits and Bale placing him in the eleventh century, that caused him to be identified with another Jean de Garlandia of that century. All the evidence at our disposal, however, points to the writer on music to have been the author of the interesting manuscript *De triumphis Ecclesiae* (*B.M.*). In this work Garland calls England his mother and France his nurse. Indeed, practically all the information we possess concerning his life is to be derived from the manuscript mentioned. The date of his birth is somewhat uncertain; but he studied in Paris under Alain de Lille (L'Isle), and the fact that Alain died in 1202 would make certain that Garland could not have been born in 1190 as Coussemaker says. His birth is therefore to be placed rather some ten years earlier. Before going to Paris he had been a pupil of John of London at Oxford. Attempts to fix upon his birthplace are speculative. He was a man of wide culture, and, as was usual with the learned in the middle ages, he was an alchemist, a grammarian, and theologian as well as a musician. In Paris he settled down to teach in the " Clos de Garlande " (later Rue Gallande). He was connected with the founding of the

University of Toulouse, but eventually returned to Paris. Since *De triumphis Ecclesiae* was completed in 1252 we may suppose that he died after that date. He enjoyed a great reputation, and his works are quoted by Hanboys, Handlo, and other theoreticians of the fourteenth and fifteenth centuries.

His works are of great importance on account of their date. He evidently wrote before Franco of Paris was active, for the latter removed the older method of reading ligatures by which Garland was still influenced. It is highly probable that *De Musica Mensurabile Positio* (manuscript in the Vatican; printed by Coussemaker, *Vol.* I) is to be attributed to Garland, for Jerome of Moravia, who flourished near enough to the Englishman's period of activity to have known, considered him the author. Coussemaker's version of this manuscript is contained in his *Scriptorum, etc.* (*Vol.* I, 97, *Ed.* 1864). If this work is by Garland, he can also claim *Tractatus de Cantu Plano* which he mentions. A manuscript entitled *Optima Introductio in Contrapunctum pro rudibus* is attributed to

Garland in two manuscripts (one at Pisa and one at Einsiedeln), and is printed by Coussemaker (III, 12) beginning " Volentibus introduce in arte contrapunctus, id est notam contra notam ". This treatise is fairly advanced for its period, for he objects to consecutive fifths and allows thirds and sixths. A manuscript at St. Die (Public Library), entitled *Introductio Musicae Planae et etiam Musicae Mensurabilis,* bears his name. Coussemaker has it in Volume I, 157, " codice Sancti Deodati extraximus." Martin Gerbert printed a couple of short incomplete acoustical treatises, — *De fistulis* and *De notis*—from a Viennese manuscript. It should, however, be remembered that although the probability is very great that the same John Garland, born in England, wrote all these works, they cannot all be claimed for him with absolute certainty. The *Optima Introductio,* for example, may be almost too late to have been written by a man who was a professor in the earliest decades of the thirteenth century.

GARLANDIA (John de): *see* GARLAND (John).

GERWAYS: A musician

belonging to the generation of Dunstable and Power. Nothing is known of his life, and only one composition by him is known to me,—in the Old Hall Manuscript (St. Edmund's College, near Ware, Herts.).

GIBBONS (Christopher): A well-known organist and virginalist of the transitional period, perhaps more highly esteemed by his contemporaries as an executant artist than as a composer. Nevertheless, though so completely eclipsed by the amazing genius of his father, Christopher Gibbons still merits some recognition to-day, and a few of his compositions might well be resuscitated at the present time.

Born in August, 1615, (baptized August 22nd), Christopher Gibbons was the second son of Orlando Gibbons (*q.v.*). He received his earliest training at the Chapel Royal, while his father was organist there, and continued—after the death of Orlando—in the choir of Exeter Cathedral, where his uncle Edward Gibbons was organist. His first appointment as an organist was at Winchester Cathedral (1638) and he held that post until the Civil War put a stop to the Cathedral music. In 1644 "when the dean and prebends fled, he accompanied them, and served in one of the garrisons" (*v.* Rimbault, *Notes and Queries, Ser.* III, *Vol.* X, *p.* 182). During the Commonwealth he practised as a teacher of organ and virginal playing (Playford, *Musical Banquet,* 1651), and in 1654 (July 12th) John Evelyn heard him play at Oxford: ". . . we walked to Magdalen College . . . and there was still the double organ, which abominations (as now esteemed) were almost universally demolished. Mr. Gibbons, that famous musican, giving us a taste of his skill and talents on that instrument". At the performance of *The Siege of Rhodes* (Davenant, 1656) he played in the orchestra. At the Restoration the royal musical establishment was made up anew, and Christopher Gibbons immediately secured important posts. On November 17th, 1660, a warrant was issued "to admit Christopher Gibbons, musician upon the Virginalls, in the place of Thomas Warwick, deceased, with the yearly salary of 86*l.* to be paid quarterly" (*L.C.R.*).

Another entry of 1660 reads: " Mr. Gybbons approved of by the King at Baynards Castle ; and an organ to be made for him ". The appointment was to Westminster Abbey. How far Wood's statement that Christopher Gibbons was a " grand debauchee " and " would often sleep at Morning Prayer when he was to play the organ ", is correct, we cannot decide to-day. But the fact remains that, either because of, or in spite of, this questionable mode of life, he was a great favourite of the king's, and it was due to a royal command that the University of Oxford conferred upon the organist the degree of Doctor of Music " by Royal letters " in 1664. His exercise for this degree was, according to Wood (*Fasti Oxonienses*), performed at St. Mary's Church " with very great honour to himself and his faculty ". Exactly what happened to the new doctor after this is not quite clear. After the great fire of London Albertus Bryne (or Bryan), who had been organist at Whitehall, went to Westminster Abbey. In 1667–8 (January 7th) we read that Christopher Preston was " appointed musician in

ordinary to his Majesty for the Virginalls and private musique without fee in the place of Dr. Christopher Gibbons, to come in ordinary with fee after the decease of the said Dr. Gibbons, and then to enjoy the same place " (*L.C.R.*). Yet in the lists of salaries paid to performers in the private music of the king in 1668 and 1669, we find that the name of Gibbons still appears, and that his wage was 40*l*. per annum (*Id.*). In 1668 his name appears among the " musitians that doe service in the Chappell Royall, whose selleryes are paid in the Treasury of His Majesty's Chamber " (*Id.*). In 1676 we are given notice of his death: " Dr. Christopher Gibbons, organist of his Majesty's Chapel Royal, departed this life the 20th day of October, 1676 " (*Ch. Bk. C.R.*), and on October 25th, Christopher Preston was admitted " to play upon the virginalls in the place of Dr. Gibbons, deceased " (*L.C.R.*). He was buried in the Cloisters of Westminster Abbey. According to Rimbault (in the *Notes and Queries* article mentioned above) Christopher Gibbons married a daughter of Dr.

Robert Kercher, Prebend of Winchester.

His compositions were of a varying nature; sacred music, instrumental, and at least one attempt at writing for the stage. Anthems and fancies for strings are preserved in the British Museum, the Royal College of Music, Ely Cathedral, and elsewhere. An anthem of his was transcribed for use in the Chapel Royal (*L.C.R.*, August 1st, 1676), and Playford included some of his work in *Cantica Sacra* (1674). It was probably his experience as a performer in the orchestras during the Commonwealth that prompted him to make an essay in masque-music. In 1653 he collaborated with Matthew Lock in the writing of the music to Shirley's *Masque of Cupid and Death*, performed on March 26th in Leicester Fields before the Ambassador from Portugal. This composition was typical of the work that was produced at the culmination of the period of transition—if such a phrase is permissible—and the Masque itself was one of the most elaborate of the English productions of this class. *Add.* 17799–17800 (*B.M.*) contains the music of the Masque; Volume I has a transcript by Lock made for the representation of 1659, and Volume II gives a later copy and a modern arrangement of the first scene for wind and strings. Mr. J. E. West has issued an organ piece of Christopher Gibbons's (1907). A portrait of the composer hangs in the Music School, Oxford.

GIBBONS (Edward): The eldest son of William Gibbons, that wait of Cambridge, who became famous through the celebrity of his three sons—Edward, Ellis, and Orlando. The first we hear of Edward is the conferring of the Oxford *Mus. Bac.* degree upon him in 1592. He incorporated from Cambridge, but when he obtained the degree there is not known. In the same year he was appointed organist and instructor of the choir-boys of King's College, Cambridge, holding the post until 1599, when Thomas Hammond, the previous organist, returned. The college account-books for this period mention Gibbons as the recipient of 4*l.* a year as salary, in addition to 11*s.* 8*d.* per quarter for his work as Master of the Choristers. On leaving King's College, he appears to have gone to Bristol, where he served as organist at the Cathedral, choirmaster, and priest-vicar, —having probably first taken holy orders. At the same time it is a peculiar circumstance that the books of Bristol Cathedral do not mention him; and it is possible that Boyce (who is apparently responsible in the first place for the information regarding the Bristol appointments) may have made a mistake. At all events, he was doing duty as organist and " custos of ye college of Priests Vicars " at Exeter in 1611. He appears to have remained at Exeter until the arrival of the Republican forces. The story that he incurred the dislike of the Parliamentarian powers because he advanced 1,000*l.* to Charles I comes from Walker's *Sufferings of the Clergy*, which also contains the information that Gibbons was ejected from his house though over eighty years of age. How far this information is based on fact we cannot say with any degree of certainty to-day, but confiscation was commonly the result of Royalist tendencies in those days. He died probably during the Commonwealth, and would then have been

very near the age just mentioned. Examples of his work may be seen in the British Museum manuscript *Harl.* 7340 (Tudway's collection; verse-anthem, " How hath the City sate solitary," for two voices with two instrumental parts), in the *In Nomine* collection at the Oxford Music School, and at Ely Cathedral. In the Christ Church library (Oxford) is " Awake and arise " (*à* 3) and Commandments and Creed to William Mundy's Short Service. Mr. J. E. West edited an organ-prelude in 1906. Among Edward Gibbons's pupils at Exeter are to be counted his nephew Christopher Gibbons and Matthew Lock.

GIBBONS (Ellis): The second son of William Gibbons, the wait of Cambridge, and thus the elder brother of the far greater Orlando Gibbons. Very little is known of him except that before the publication of the *Triumphes of Oriana* he was organist of Salisbury Cathedral. This information seems to rest upon the authority of Anthony Wood and there is no corroborative evidence in the official documents of Salisbury Cathedral. This may possibly be accounted for by the loss of the Chapter Acts covering the years when he would have been active there. Judging by the ages of his elder brother, Edward, and his younger brother, Orlando, his birth must be dated between *ca.* 1572 and 1582. The date of his death is similarly uncertain, and the only scrap of material left to work upon is the fact that his connection with Salisbury was severed round about 1610. If he died at that date he must have been very young; but in view of the circumstance that the only known compositions from his pen are two madrigals (one five-part and one six-part) in the *Triumphes of Oriana*, this may have been the case. With the exception of the editor, Thomas Morley, he was the only composer who was twice represented in the original edition of that famous collection. These two madrigals are available in two modern reprints,—those of L. Benson (1895, *etc.*) and Dr. E. H. Fellowes (*The English Madrigal School, Vol.* XXXII).

GIBBONS (Orlando): A composer of great talent and versatility who commands a place by the side of William Byrd and Henry Purcell as one of England's three greatest musicians. The clearest reflection of his genius can best be seen in the spontaneous nature of his characterization; in the fitness of his music to the purpose for which it was written; in the artistic restraint everywhere exhibited; and in the sheer beauty of his thoughts and the manner in which he expressed them. Inferior to none but Byrd in his sacred music, Gibbons avoids invidious comparison by the differing nature of his work in this domain. He did not follow, as Byrd did, the traditions of the Roman church, and he was in some sort the actual founder of true Anglican music of the highest type. There is a magnificence, a dignity, and a nobility about his ecclesiastical work that place it above all criticism ; and it is gratifying to note that he, at least, of the English musicians of the late Tudor period, is well-known to-day through many modern editions of his works and by frequent performance in our Cathedrals. Remembering the church atmosphere in which he was trained, it is not surprising to find that his secular vocal music is marked by seriousness of thought, rather than by the lightness and gaiety of such a madrigalist as, say, Morley. But his madrigals show a distinctly modern tendency in their harmony, and in them it may be said that Gibbons finally leaves the ancient modal system behind him. In his Fancies for strings he allows his ecclesiastical austerity to influence him perhaps a little too much. But these works were very early for compositions written expressly for instrumental use (*i.e.* not being adaptations from vocal music), and if they lack the brightness and lightness of the fancy-writers' work of the later Stuart period, they also avoid the deterioration in quality of the latter. From the purely musical point of view,— ignoring the showy technical demands of virtuose instrumentalists, — Gibbons's fancies stand as the finest examples of this class of composition. He also supplied music for the keyboard instruments, and even experimented with the vocal fancy of the popular type,— a setting of the *Cries of London* for four voices and instruments. The glory of Orlando Gibbons lies in the

circumstance that he could adapt his mood to whatever he had in hand, and, choosing his own subjects and method of treatment, he was successful in everything he did. There are very few musicians in the whole history of the art of whom as much could be said with justice.

Orlando Gibbons came of a very musical family. He was the youngest of the three sons (he also had several sisters) of William Gibbons, a wait of Cambridge, and was born in 1583. The waits in that era were musicians of good training (*v. Dic. Old Engl. Mus., s.v.* " Waits ") and there can be little doubt that Orlando received his first instruction from his father. At the age of thirteen he became a chorister at King's College, Cambridge, where his elder brother Edward was organist and master of the choir-boys. His father's tuition was supplemented by that of this brother, and it is easy to see how this early experience of church-music helped to mould a mind that was naturally of a meditative and contemplative order. He was only eighteen years of age when he received small - sums for composing or arranging music "in festo Dominae Reginae" (college accounts for 1601, *etc.*) and for other occasions. In 1603 he left Cambridge for London and entered the Chapel Royal, for on May 19th of that year his name appears as a witness to the signing of a document (*Ch. Bk. C.R.*). In 1604 he became organist of the Chapel: "Arthur Cock died the 26th of Januarie, and Orlando Gibbons sworne in his roome the 21st of Marche followinge" (*Id.*). In 1606 he obtained the bachelorship at Cambridge, the *Grace-Book* (*E., p.* 73) containing the entry: "Conceditur Orlando Gibbons regius organista ut studium septem annorum in musica sufficiat ei ad intrandum in eadem, sic tamen ut canticum componat cantandum, hora et loco per vice cancellarium designandis coram universitate in die comitiorum et ut presentetur per magistrum regentum in habitu bacchalauri in artibus". He appears, after this date, to have devoted himself seriously to the study of the virginal and to the composition of music for that instrument; the wonderful quality of some of the work in *Parthenia* shows that he

was a master of the instrument and later we find that he was a private virginalist to the king (1619; *Audit Office Accounts*). In 1612 he was mentioned among the musicians receiving mourning livery for the funeral of Prince Henry of Wales. In this year, too, his *First Sett of Madrigals* appeared, and in the dedication to Sir Christopher Hatton, Gibbons says that "they were most of them composed in your owne house, and doe therefore properly belong to you". The organist must have been on very friendly terms to have composed in Hatton's house, and there can be no doubt that this knight patronized Gibbons in a very practical way. In 1615 the duties of organist at the Chapel Royal were shared by Gibbons and Edmund Hooper, and on November 2nd an arrangement was made between the two as to the division of work (*Ch. Bk. C.R.*). The two men are named as organists at the funeral of Queen Anna, Consort of James I, in 1618 (*L.C.R.*). In May, 1622, he was accorded the degree of Doctor of Music at Oxford when William Heather also obtained it. The occasion was the founding of the history professorship by Camden. Though Heather was a member of the Chapel Royal he does not appear to have possessed sufficient creative talent to write an exercise for the degree. That Gibbons wrote " O Clap your Hands " for the founder of the future Oxford professorship in music is clear: The late Dr. Cummings's copy of this composition bears the note: " Dr. Heather's Commencement Song, compos'd by Dr. Orlando Gibbons ". In 1623 he was living in the Woolstaple (where Bridge Street, Westminster, now stands), and in the overseer's books of St. Margaret's, Westminster, there is an entry as to his rating (Rimbault, in *Notes and Queries, Ser.* III, *Vol.* X, *p.* 182). In the same year he became organist of Westminster Abbey. In the *Life of Archbishop Williams* there is an account of his performance on the Abbey organ. The occasion was the visit to the Abbey of the French Ambassadors who were charged with the arrangements for the forthcoming marriage of Prince Charles with Henrietta Maria: " The Embassadors, with the nobles and Gentle-

men in their Company, were brought in at the North Gate of the Abbey, which was stuck with Flambeaux everywhere, that the Strangers might cast their eyes upon the stateliness of the Church. At the Door of the Quire the Lord Keeper besought their Lordships to go in and take their seats there for a while. At their entrance the organ was touched by the best Finger of that age, Mr. Orlando Gibbons." The late Sir Frederick Bridge discovered in the Muniment room of the Abbey a quaint letter of Gibbons's (probably the only letter of his extant) addressed to the Treasurer and referring to a payment to the organ-blower: " Mr. Ireland: I know this bill to be very reasonable for I have already cut him off ten shillings therfore I pray despathe him, for he hath delt honestly with ye church soe shall I rest yr. servant, Orlando Gibbons ". In 1625 he was commanded to Canterbury in connection with the reception of Henrietta Maria, and while there he died. Thanks to the discovery by Mr. W. Barclay Squire of a letter and medical certificate, it appears that Gibbons did not die of small-pox as is generally supposed, but that his illness was at first "lethargicall" leading to convulsions; afterwards "he grew apoplecticall and so died". The date of his death is given in the Cheque-Book of the Chapel Royal with all necessary details : " Mr. Orlando Gibbons, died the 5th of June, being then Whit-Sunday, at Canterbury, wher the Kinge was then to receave Queene Mary who was then to com out of Fraunce, and Thomas Warwick was sworne in his place organist the first daie of July followinge . . ." Gibbons was married to Elizabeth, *née* Patten of Westminster, and she survived him by little more than a year. Of his seven children only one— Christopher — became a famous musician. A portrait of Orlando Gibbons is in the Music School, Oxford, and a bust was dedicated to his memory by his widow in Canterbury Cathedral, where he was buried. A replica of this bust in black marble was unveiled at Westminster Abbey in 1907 and placed there by the generosity of Mr. Crews, Master of the Worshipful Company of Musicians.

Not very much of Orlando Gibbons's music was published during his lifetime. The celebrated three-part *Fancies for Viols* should be mentioned first because their date is not to be determined with certainty. The *Fantasies* must have appeared after 1606 since the composer is described as " Bachelor of Music ", and before Edward Wray—to whom they are dedicated—left his position at Court in 1622. They were reprinted both at home and abroad, and the Musical Antiquarian Society published a score edition of them in 1843. In 1611 Gibbons was associated with Bull and Byrd in the writing of "*Parthenia*: or the Mayden-head of the First Musick that ever was printed for the Virginals " (reprinted several times). Gibbons's share consisted of two Galliards, a Fantasia, a Pavane, a Prelude, and " The Queen's Command ". The justly-famed set of madrigals followed in 1612, under the misleading title: *The First Sett of Madrigals and Mottets of five parts, apt for viols or voyces*—misleading because it contains no motets. These madrigals,—including the serene " Silver Swan ", which has reached, in the modern mind, the highest point of celebrity on the gramophone record, — rank immediately after the best of Gibbons's sacred music in their sheer beauty and poetic conception. They were reprinted by the Musical Antiquarian Society in 1841 and by Dr. E. H. Fellowes in 1914 (*Vol. V, English Madrigal School*). Some of the madrigals have been issued separately under various editorships, six of them by Novello and Co. To Sir William Leighton's *Teares, etc.* (1614) he contributed two hymns, and to Withers's *Hymns and Songs of the Church* (1623) sixteen, —wholly or partly reprinted several times.

Music of his printed after his death includes "The Silver Swan" in Playford's *Musical Companion* (1672), two Services, Preces, and Anthems in Barnard's collection (1641) and Ouseley's reprint of 1873, and a fair selection in Boyce's work. Most easily accessible at the present day are the specimens published by Novello and Co., and the catalogue of this firm contains the names of a very representative collection of Gibbons's sacred works.

They have also published— under the editorship of Sir Frederick Bridge—*The Cryes of London* (manuscript in the *R.C.M.*; and in *B.M., Add.* 29372–7, together with other compositions of a similar nature). I have it from Sir Frederick that he scored this vocal fancy from the British Museum manuscript (Thomas Myriell's collection of 1616), and the date of this manuscript fixes the latest possible date for its composition. The article in *Grove* (*Vol. II, p. 168, Ed.* 1913) contains what was a complete list of Gibbons's published works up to the date of that edition; a few numbers have been added since,—notably some by Novello, and Dr. Fellowes's issue of the madrigals.

Very little of Gibbons's work remains unpublished. In *Benjamin Cosyn's Virginal Book* (belonging to his Majesty the King) there are twenty-five pieces, among which is a virginal arrangement of "Mr. Gibbons' Service". In the Christ Church (Oxford) library there is a large amount of his music, —most of it already printed, —*MS.* 21 in that collection being mainly in his autograph. The *Fitzwilliam*

Virginal Book Pavane and Fantasia have, of course, been reprinted in the Breitkopf and Haertel edition of that celebrated manuscript. It is interesting to note in passing that the splendid concluding "Amen" which was sung at the Coronation of King Edward VII and of King George V (now known as the "Abbey Amen") was extracted by Sir Frederick Bridge from an anthem "made for the King's being in Scotland" (James I). Many of the compositions alluded to in this article have been copied and recopied into a great many manuscript collections in various libraries, but no useful purpose would be served by a recital of their names and catalogue numbers.

GILES (John): A gentleman of the Chapel Royal who flourished early in the sixteenth century. It is possible that he is to be identified with the "Master Giles, Luter", who is frequently mentioned at the same period. John Giles is named in the list of gentlemen of the chapel who assisted at the funeral of Prince Henry,—the son of Henry VIII,—in 1511. This is the only place where I have found the Christian name used; but it is probable that the "Mr. Gyles" in the entry dating from April, 1515,—"To Mr. Cornisshe, for Mr. Gyles who played on the organs in the chapel, 6*l*. 13*s*. 4*d*." (*King's Book of Payments*),— is the same man. The other "Mr. Giles"— supposing him not identical with the Giles just mentioned—is always given as a "luter" or "minstrel of the Chamber". He is entered in the *Household Book* in July, 1509, as receiving 40*s*., and in *Eg.* 2604 (*B.M.*) is again mentioned (1526). Belonging to the same period is a trumpeter also named Giles or Gyles, who should not be confused with the lutenist and (or) gentleman of the Chapel Royal.

GILES (Nathaniel): A celebrated organist, choirmaster, and composer of sacred music. The date of his birth is not known, but in view of the circumstance that he obtained the degree of *Mus. Bac.* in 1585, it would appear that *ca.* 1560 was the period at which this event took place. His tombstone (1633) gives the information that he was seventy-five years of age at his death, placing his birth in 1558; but none of the dates on this tombstone are dependable. It seems clear that he was descended from a family belonging to Worcestershire, and that he was born in that county. The statement generally made that he was a chorister at Magdalen College, Oxford, in 1559, cannot be proved; nor is it likely to be correct. According to Anthony Wood, he was " noted as well for his religious life and conversation (a rarity in musicians) as for excellence in his faculty ". In 1581 he became organist at Worcester Cathedral, a post he held until 1585. In the latter year he graduated at Oxford and became Master of the Choristers at St. George's Chapel, Windsor (J. E. West, *Cathedral Organists*, Ed. 1921). The useful volume just mentioned gives the contents of a deed dated October 1st, 1595, which nominates Nathaniel Gyles as a clerk in the chapel, and one of the organists and instructor of the ten boys. For fulfilling these duties he received 8*l*. 6*s*. 8*d*. per annum in addition to free lodgings. One of the conditions of the appointment was that Giles should fill all vacancies in the ranks of the choristers within three months of their creation, being permitted to " press "

boys into the service should need arise. Further, he was to teach the choristers singing and composition, and train such as were suitable in instrumental music (*cf. MS. Ashmole* 1125,33). In 1597 he succeeded Hunnis in the Chapel Royal: " 1597. William Hunnis died the 6th of June, instructor of the children; and Nathaniel Giles sworne gentleman and Master of the Children in his place, the 9th of the same, from Windsor " (*Ch. Bk. C.R.*). Another entry in the old Cheque-Book under date June 9th, 1597, informs us that Giles was appointed in compliance with the Lord Chamberlain's orders and that he was " before extraordinary ". In 1603 a list of " fees granted to sondry persons in the several offices and places " includes Giles's name against the payment of an annual salary of 40*l*. (*Cotton MS.*, *Tib. B*. III, *fol.* 248; quoted in *Annalen*). In the same year he received an allowance of mourning livery for the funeral of Queen Elizabeth (*L.C.R.*, *Vol.* 554). In 1607 he supplicated for the degree of Doctor of Music, and his request was granted conditionally. He was expected to compose an eight-part choral work, and since he did not do this the degree was not conferred (C. F. Abdy Williams, *Degree in Music*). In the year that Giles supplicated the famous banquet was given by the Merchant Taylors' Company in honour of the king. For this funâ€ion Giles " together with divers singing men and children of the said Chappel, did sing melodious songs at the said dynner " (July 16th, 1607). The next day the popular Maâ€ter of the Children was honoured by admission into the Company's livery. Writing a poem " in approbation " of Ravenscroft's *Brief Discourse* in 1614, Giles signed himself: " Bachelar of Musicke, Maiâ€ter of the Children of his Maieâ€ties Chappels, of Household, and Windsor ". It was not until July 5th, 1622, that the degree of Doâ€or was conferred upon him. The old condition was waived and Giles was invited to " dispute " with Dr. Heather on three topics: " Whether discords were to be allowed in music; whether any artificial inâ€ruments can so fully and truly express music as the natural voice; whether the praâ€ice be the more useful part of music or the theory ". The disputation probably never took place, for the very good reason that Dr. Heather was far too ignorant of the technics of music to maintain it. At all events, Giles received the degree. An intereâ€ing document of Auguâ€ 26th, 1626, is quoted by Rimbault in the introduâ€ion to the *Cheque-Book of the Chapel Royal (Camden Soc.)* referring to the powers veâ€ed in the Maâ€ter of the Children for " pressing " choriâ€ers into the service. In this commission " to take up well-singing boys " there is the following condition : " . . . Provided always and we â€raightly charge and command, that none of the said Choriâ€ers or children of the Chapell, soe to be taken by force of this commission, shalbe used or imployed as Comedians, or Stage players, Interludes, comedies, or Tragedies; for that it is not fitt or desent that such as should sing the praises of God Almighty should be trained or imployed in such lascivious and prophane exercises ". Until Giles was well advanced in years, he and Dr. Child shared the organiâ€'s duties; but later on it appears that the latter did all the work alone.

And when Giles died it was decided that Child should fill both organists' posts and that he should "in future enjoy the stipend of both" (Dean and Chapter of St. George's, Windsor, April 4th, 1634). Nathaniel Giles died on January 24th, 1633–4, and was buried at Windsor on February 2nd.

Examples of Giles's music may be seen in Leighton's *Teares*, etc., of 1614, in Barnard's collection of 1641, in manuscripts at Christ Church, Oxford, the Fitzwilliam Museum, Cambridge, in Baldwin's manuscript (royal property, now in *B.M.*), and in the British Museum manuscripts *Add.* 17792–6, 30478–9, 17784, 17820, 31418, 30085–7, *Royal App.* 63, and *Harl.* 7337 and 7339 (Tudway), etc. These compositions are in various forms and include Services, Anthems, and a couple of secular songs. An exceedingly clever piece of work is Giles's "Lesson of Descant of thirtie eighte Proportions of sundrie kindes" on a plain-song, and shows that he possessed all the academic learning of his age. It is printed in Hawkins's *History*.

GILES (Thomas): There were undoubtedly two musicians bearing this name, —father and son,—and Mr. West is most probably correct in saying that Thomas Giles was the father of Dr. Nathaniel Giles (*q.v.*), and Henry Davey (after Rimbault) right in giving him as a brother of the same. The elder Thomas was organist of St. Paul's Cathedral between 1582 and 1590 (West, *Cathedral Organists*), and the younger known only as the writer of a song in the "Maske in Honour of Lord Hayes and his bride", performed at Whitehall in 1607. The masque (book by Campion) contained five songs,— two by Thomas Campion, two by Lupo, and one ("Triumph now with joy and mirth") by Thomas Giles. Mr. G. E. P. Arkwright has edited this music as *No.* 1 of the *Old English Edition*.

GILLES (Nathaniel): *see* GILES (Nathaniel).

GODBID (Anne) : *see* GODBID (William).

GODBID (William): A well-known printer who was active in the seventeenth century, and who issued a large number of musical publications. He printed for John Playford, senior, for twenty years, and was noted for his type-printing of music. He died probably *ca.* 1678, when his widow (the " A[nne] G " of some of the title-pages) continued the business with John Playford II as partner. On the death of Anne, Playford, *junior*, worked alone.

GOLDING (John) : *see* GOLDWIN (John).

GOLDWIN (John): Organiſt of St. George's Chapel, Windsor, and composer of some excellent sacred music. Living as he did at the end of the seventeenth century he enjoyed many advantages. He was not too far from the influence of the beſt pre-Reſtoration composers, was able to profit by the works of Henry Purcell, and had such a good teacher as Dr. William Child. Remembering his period, it is not surprising that his writing should exhibit a certain variety and unevenness of quality. When he worked on the solid contrapuntal methods of the generation which preceded him, his music is exceedingly intereſting and worthy of ſtudy and revival. He was not sufficiently great a genius to show any fine individual ſtyle, and here and there the influence of his contemporaries is easily discernible. This is moſt noticeable when he writes in a declamatory ſtyle; and then it will not be difficult to see the sway that Purcell held over the lesser man. Taken all together, the old methods and the new are curiously blended in John Goldwin, and on this account he is well worthy of close attention.

Born round about 1670, Goldwin was known to have been in the choir of St. George's Chapel, Windsor, in 1690, for in that year his name appears in the official records dealing with property assessment. He had been a pupil of Dr. Child and in 1697 (April 12th) became organiſt at the Chapel in succession to his teacher. In 1703 the Maſtership of the Choriſters was added to his duties. His death occurred on November 7th, 1719.

His works include a Service (in F) which was printed by Arnold (Cathedral Music), several anthems (some printed by Boyce and Page) besides a little inſtrumental music. A good deal of his work is ſtill in manuscript. The British Museum has several examples: Tudway's collection (*Harl.* 7341) has " O Lord God of Hoſts " and " Hear me, O God ", and (*Harl.* 7342) " Ascribe unto ye Lord ", " Thy way, O God, is holy ", " O praise God in his holiness ", " I will sing unto ye Lord ", and " O be joyfull in God ". In *Add.* 17819 there are two anthems, in *Add.* 37072 is another, and in *Add.* 17784, one more. *Add.* 31120 contains Vincent Novello's organ arrangements, published in 1831. The " Whole Service in F, with Jubilate instead of Benedictus, and including the Sanctus " is in *Harl.* 7341 (Tudway), and *Add.* 6324, contains settings of the Sanctus, including the one in F from Goldwin's Service. The Christ Church (Oxford) library possesses a very large collection of Goldwin's work in manuscript, and he is also represented in the collections at the Fitzwilliam Museum (four anthems) and Ely Cathedral. The only modern reprint of anything of Goldwin's is " I have set God always before me " (anthem for six voices), published by Messrs. Novello with Vincent Novello's organ part.

GOODGROOME (John). Lutenist, Violinist, Singer, and Composer, and probably more to be esteemed as a practical musician than as a writer. Born in the second quarter of the seventeenth century, at Windsor, he received his earliest musical training as a chorister. He was probably ready to launch forth as an independent musician when the Civil War intervened and robbed him even of his Chapel post at Windsor. In common with most of the royal musicians, Goodgroome taught singing and viol-playing during the Commonwealth. At the Restoration he was given Thomas Purcell's place among the musicians " For lutes and voyces, theorboes, and Virginalls " (*L.C.R., Vol.* 482). At the same time he was appointed " Composer for the Violins ", — Henry Purcell, senior, having been first suggested for this post. (*L.C.R., Vol.* 479),—and a gentleman of the Chapel Royal. On August 20, 1664, Goodgroome was made a member of " the private musick for the lutes, voyall, and voyces in the place of Henry Purcell " (*Id.*). The salary attached to this post was 40*l.* per annum (*Id., Vol.* 742). After this appointment Goodgroome's name occurs very frequently in the State Papers, chiefly in connection with accounts for livery allowance, often much in arrears. In 1671 (November 4th) he was paid his travelling expenses while attending with the Gentlemen of the Chapel at Windsor, and three years later (1674), in a " list of the gentleman of the Chappell that are to wayte and constantly attend his Majesty's service at Windsor during his residence there ", we find his name among those of the " Counter Tenners " (*L.C.R., Vol.* 745). James II, coming to the throne, made a valiant attempt to pay off the arrears accumulated under his predecessor, and from an account prepared on February 25th, 1685–6, we learn that to John Goodgroome was due livery allowance for the years 1664–7, 1670, and 1676 to 1684, amounting to some 225*l.* 15*s.* This amount was ordered to be paid on September 21st, 1686, out of the tobacco and sugar imposition (*L.C.R.*). In 1694 Chamberlayne (*Magnae Britanniae Notitia*) places Goodgroome's salary as Gentleman of the Chapel Royal at 73*l.* per annum. This musician was active until 1704, when an entry in the Cheque-Book of the Chapel Royal tells us that " Mr. Goodgroome . . . departed this life June 27th, 1704 ". The " Goodgroome " mentioned by Pepys on December 17th, 1666, may have been the musician here treated, unless Theodore Goodgroome be meant (*cf.* Pepys, *Diary,* July 1st, 1661). This Theodore, who was Pepys's singing-master, may have been related to John.

The compositions of John Goodgroome are chiefly slight songs of a popular character, and examples of them may be seen in several of the Playfords' publications, —four representative pieces being contained in the *Musical Companion* of 1672 (" Ayre ", " The Jovial Beggar,—a Glee ", and " Brightest, since your pitying eyes ", *à* 2, and " Will Cloris cast her sunbright eye " *à* 3). The last-named song is strongly reminiscent of one under the same title attributed to Simon Ives in *Add.* 11608 (*B.M.*).

GOODSON (Richard): A well-known figure in the musical life of Oxford, in the second half of the seventeenth century. Born in 1655, he found his first musical employment as a chorister at St. Paul's Cathedral. In 1682 he became *Choragus* or superintendent of the music-students' practice (becoming later Professor of Music at the University), and his degree of *Mus. Bac.* was probably also obtained in the same year. At the same time he was appointed organist of New College, Oxford. In 1691 he became organist of Christ Church, giving up the New College appointment in 1694. He died on January 13th, 1718, and was buried in Christ Church Cathedral. He is remembered with gratitude for having considerably enriched the Christ Church library with his own collection. Besides the examples of his work preserved at Oxford, there are specimens at the British Museum; *Add.* 22099 has a three-part Catch (in score), " Sit nemo morosus " (" Let none be incivil "), and a harpsichord piece, " I come to ye waters ", in the same manuscript, may also be his, though, being signed merely " Goodson ", can possibly be by his son, also named Richard. *Add.* 30493 and 33965 contain catalogues of the Oxford Music School collection by Richard, junior, copied " from the Riting of my Father's ". The son succeeded the father as organist of Christ Church in 1718, dying in 1741.

GOSTLING (John): A celebrated seventeenth-century singer possessing a bass voice of exceptional range and power. So famous was he that Henry Purcell wrote special music for him which enabled his unusual compass to be employed. He was born at about the middle of the century, and was a native of Kent, receiving his education at Rochester School and St. John's, Cambridge. A letter written by Thomas Purcell is extant which states that Gostling was there (February 8th, 1678–9) engaged on work which would secure his appointment in London. The Cheque-Book of the Chapel Royal contains the entry: " Mr. John Gostling, sworn gentleman of his Majesty's Chapel extraordinary the 25th of February, 1678 ", and a few days later: " William Tucker dying in whose place was admitted in ordinary Mr. John Gostling, a base from Canterbury, Master of Arts ". The mention of this degree forces us to the conclusion that the student of the same name, who became a Master of Arts from St. John's College in 1672, must be identified with the singer. In 1684–5 (January 27th) he received 36*l.* 18*s.* for his " rydeing charges and other expenses in his attending upon his Majesty at Windsor in 1683 and 1684 for 123 days at the rate of 6*s.* by the day " (*L.C.R.*). On the accession of James II he was appointed to the king's private music as a " base " (*Id.* 1685, August 31st), and on September 10th, the certificate of appointment was issued (*Id.*). In 1689 (July 19th) he secured a post in " the vocall musick " (*Id.*), and the same day was confirmed as a private musician at the court of William and Mary. A letter of his written on July 19th, 1691, gives him as " of the parish of St. Gregory by St. Paul's, London " (*Id., Vol.* 199). In 1694 his salary as gentleman of the Chapel Royal was 73*l.* per annum (Chamberlayne). In 1696–7 (March 23rd), he was given John Harding's place in the king's " private musick for the voice " (*L.C.R.*). In 1697 a warrant was issued awarding him 120*l.* in respect of livery-money due to him for the years 1689 to 1696 (at 16*l.* 2*s.* 6*d.* per annum). In addition to his Chapel post Gostling held various clerical appointments, such as minor

canon of Canterbury, vicar of Littlebourne, sub-dean of St. Paul's, and prebendary of Lincoln. He was also one of the king's chaplains. He died in 1733 (July 17th).

GRABU (Louis): A French violinist and composer who exercised considerable influence upon the tendency of the more popular forms of composition in England, and who helped Charles II to spread the Gallic methods in music. According to Rimbault, Grabu was an " obscure musician of very mean abilities, who came to this country with Charles II at the Restoration "; and there is no reason for disagreeing with this opinion. Grabu does not appear to have been distinguished by any extraordinary talent, either in performance or in his compositions; but he was French, and that was a sufficiently good passport into the graces of him whom Rimbault calls " the wretched Charles ". Pepys did not think very highly of the Frenchman's talent, but was forced to admit that " the instrumental musick he had brought by practice to play very just ". Pelham Humfrey's verdict on Grabu was that " he underſtands nothing, nor can play on any inſtrument, and so cannot compose" (Pepys, *Diary*, November 15th, 1667). Nevertheless, Charles II thought well enough of him to make him Maſter of the royal music.

We meet with him firſt at the Reſtoration when his name appears in the Lord Chamberlain's Records in place of that of Nicholas Lanier. He is mentioned again in a liſt dated November 12th, 1663; but in both of these cases his name was added at a later date, and we cannot be certain when he actually entered the royal service. But on March 31ſt, 1665, he was "appointed composer in his Majeſty's musique" (*L.C.R., Vol.* 479). On November 24th, 1666, his admission to the poſt of Maſter was entered as follows: "Warrant to admit and swear Louis Grabu Maſter of the English Chamber musick in ordinary to his Majeſty, in the place of Nicholas Lanier, deceased, to inspect and governe the same, with the accuſtomed allowances and powers as Mr. Lanier formerly enjoyed" (*L.C.R., Vol.* 742). In 1666 (December 24th) he was advanced over the head of a better man (*v.* John Baniſter I), and under the date quoted we read the order "that Mr. Banniſter and the 24 Violins appointed to practise with him and all his Majeſty's private musick doe, from tyme to tyme, obey the directions of Louis Grabu, maſter of the private musick . . ." (*L.C.R., Vol.* 742). His salary is given in 1666–7 (February 27th) as 200*l*. per annum,—a colossal wage in those days. According to *Eg.* 2159 (*B.M.*) he was given two boys to inſtruct in music (February 21ſt, 1668–9), and a couple of months later he was paid the very large sum of 165*l*. 9*s*. 6*d*. "for fayre writing severall dances, aires, and other musick, *etc.*" (*L.C.R., Vol.* 743). When Charles was firmly asked to effect some retrenchment in his expenditure, he found he could not do without his twenty-four violins, and Grabu was ordered to continue as before, "any order of retrenchment to the contrary notwithſtanding." On March 11th, 1671–2, he received a further 117*l*. 4*s*. 6*d*. for writing music. His court appointment appears to have been brought to an end in or before 1674, for at St.

Andrew of that year there is written against his name " Vacatur. Mr. Staggins in his place " (*L.C.R.*, *Vol.* 463). After this date he was connected with some stage-productions, and it was probably for such a performance that twelve musicians from the court band were ordered " to attend to practise Mons. Grabu's musick " in 1676–7 (January 17th). By May 5th, 1677, he seems to have fallen on evil days, for he petitioned the king to the effect that he had " lately fallen under very grievous misfortune,—the greatest of which hath been His Majesty's willingness to receive another person into his place during pleasure. Your Majesty was, nevertheless, graciously pleased a few days since to declare that the petitioner should receive the growing benefitt thereof until the arrears due to the petitioner should be paid to him, which he accordingly humbly presents in the paper annexed, which arrears being paid to the petitioner for the keeping him from arrests and the providing some subsistence for his distressed family, your petitioner shall, though with much griefe, retire from being a meniall servant to your Majesty ".

The cheery Charles referred the account to the Lord Chamberlain and asked for a report. The reply of Lord Arlington ran to the effect that there was due to Grabu a tremendous sum : " Out of your Majesty's Exchequer, the sum of 450*l.*; out of the office of the Treasury Chamber 145*l.* 4*s.* 6*d.*; and out of the Great Wardrobe 32*l.* 5*s.* And I find his condition to be very poor and miserable, all which I humbly submit to Your Majesty's wisdom " (*L.C.R.*, *Vol.* 746). The last time that Grabu's name appears on a document in the Lord Chamberlain's department was in a memorandum that he received " all his arrears as master to his late Majesty, although not actually in his Majesty's service at the time of his decease " (*L.C. Papers, Bundle* 20, December 8th, 1687). " At the time of his decease " refers to the king and not to Grabu. The exact date of his death is not known. Riemann says he was in London until 1694. He was certainly still composing in 1690.

In 1674 Grabu wrote the opera *Ariadne*, which was produced at Drury Lane. In 1685 he composed the music

to Dryden's *Albion and Albanius*, played for six nights from June 6th, but proved a failure. According to some reports, the fiasco was due to the rebellion of 1685, but the real reason will be more likely to have been the mean quality of the music. Grabu's reward was a flood of satire; and in the seventeenth century this could be very biting. A specimen verse of the century will illuſtrate what an unsuccessful author had to expeꜩ:
" Each aꜩor on the ſtage his luck bewailing,
Finds that his loss is infallibly true;
Smith, Nokes, and Leigh in a feverish railing,
Curse Poet, Painter, and Monsieur Grabu."
In 1690 he wrote the inſtrumental music used in *The Maid's Tragedy* by Beaumont and Fletcher. He is also represented by slighter works in contemporary publications such as the *Theater of Music* (1685), Greeting's *Pleasant Companion* of 1682 (four short pieces of the dance-type), and "A Levet to the Artillery and set to an excellent minuet of Monsieur Grabu's " (Playford, 1684).
GRABUT (Louis): *see* GRABU (Louis).

GRAFTON (Richard): A celebrated printer of the sixteenth century, who was responsible for a few of the firſt publications containing music for the English service. At the inſtigation of Cromwell, he went to Paris with associates to print an English Bible. The Inquisition, however, interfered and Grafton returned to England hurriedly. In 1539 he and another, Edward Whitchurch, were granted a patent to print the Bible in English (Henry VIII), and several editions,—also some including the Psalter—followed. Cranmer's " Exhortacion unto praier . . . also a Letanie with sufferages to be said or songe . . ." also came from his press in 1544, and six years later he issued Merbecke's " noted " Book of Common Prayer. Grafton did a good deal of general printing, and also some literary work. He died, presumably, in 1571 or 1572, though both dates muſt be queried.
GREAVES (Thomas): A composer whose reputation reſts upon a single work, and of whose life we are in entire ignorance. The only faꜩ we have concerning him is that he was luteniſt to Sir

Henry Pierrepoint at the latter's seat in Nottinghamshire, and to whom his music was dedicated. The British Museum has a copy of his collection of vocal compositions: "Songes of Sundrie Kindes: first, Aires to be sung to the Lute, and Base Violl. Next, Songes of Sadnesse for the Viols and Voyce. Lastly Madrigalles, for five voyces, *etc.*" (1604). Of the first class of song there are nine examples, and of the second and third six each. Three of his madrigals have been reprinted: " Come away sweet love " (in 1843 and 1857; in *The Choir*, 1865; and edited by Mr. W. Barclay Squire, in 1910); " Lady, the melting crystal of your eye " (in 1843 and 1859); and " Sweet Nymphs that trip along " (in 1843 and 1859 with a pianoforte accompaniment [!] by G. W. Budd; and in 1908, edited by L. Benson).

GREBUS (Louis):   *see* GRABU (Louis).

GREETING (Edward):   *see* GREETING (Thomas).

GREETING (Thomas): A celebrated performer on the instruments of the fipple-flute family and teacher of the flageolet, active in the second half of the seventeenth century. In 1662 (December 15th) he was appointed musician in ordinary in the king's private music, but without fee (*L.C.R.*). In 1670 (May 6th) his name is included in a list of musicians detailed " to attend in the Chappell " (*Id.*). He served a " double place " in the royal band, for on October 7th, 1673, he was paid 12*l.* for a violin supplied (*Id.*), and on February 7th, 1673–4, he was admitted as " musician in ordinary to his Majesty for the Violin without fee, to come in ordinary with fee, on the death or other avoydance of William Saunders " (*Id.*). On March 6th, 1673–4 an order was issued to " prepare a bill containing a grant unto Thomas Greeting of the office of musician in ordinary for the Violin and also for the Sackbutt in ordinary in his Majesty's Chapel Royal, . . . with the fee of 2*s.* 4*d.* a day, 16*l.* 2*s.* 6*d.* for his livery to commence the Annunciation now next coming, 1673 " (*Id.*). In 1677 he appears as a musician to Lady Anne in the household of the Duke of York (*Add.* 18958, *B.M.*; *Annalen*). He performed in the famous masque at court given in 1674, and in 1682 (July 5th) he is given as "deceased" with John Crouch in his place as violinist (*L.C.R.*). The accounts of the money spent on the Secret Service (published by the *Camden Soc.*) contain the entries: "To Joyce, Widdo. of Thomas Greeting, dec'ed, one of the musitians to K. Charles the Second, bounty, 10*l.* (April 3rd, 1688)", and "To Joyce Greeting, wido. of Thomas Greeting on 40*li.* per annum bounty, for half a year ended at Midsumer last, 20*l.* (October 2nd, 1688)". Several entries in the *Diary* of Samuel Pepys refer to this musician. On February 28th, 1666–7, Pepys wrote: "Up, and then comes to me one Drumbleby with a flageolet, made to suit with my former, and brings me one Greeting a master to teach my wife. I agree by the whole with him to teach her to take out any lesson by herself for 4*l.*" The diarist was so pleased with his wife's progress that "I am resolved for the encouragement of the man to learn myself a little for a month or so" (May 8th, 1667). On July 12th, 1667, we read: "Comes Greeting, and begun a new month with

him, and now learn to set anything from notes upon the flageolet, but, Lord! to see how like a fool he goes about to give me directions would make a man mad",—which is truly Pepysian. At the end of August in the same year he "reckoned with him for his teaching of my wife and me . . . to this day, and so paid him for having as much as he can teach us". On August 13th, 1668, Greeting came and played flageolet duets by Lock with Pepys, "and this day my wife begins again to learn of him. . . ." According to entries in the *Diary*, it appears that Greeting played in dance-bands (*cf.* Pepys, February 2nd, 1668–9).

Greeting's written music was confined to lessons for the flageolet. In 1680 (Hawkins says 1675) he published *The Pleasant Companion: or New Lessons and Instructions for the Flagelet* (further editions in 1682 and later). The music in this book is written in a special tablature suitable for wind-instruments with finger-holes (*v. Dic. Old Engl. Mus. s.v.* "Dot-way"). Pepys mentions that on April 16th, 1668, he bought "Greeting's book" for one shilling, but

I have not been able to trace any publication of his bearing so early a date.

An Edward Greeting is mentioned in the Lord Chamberlain's Records as a Counter Tenor, and he may have been a son of Thomas. In 1685 (August 31st) he was sworn in as private musician to the king, "... his father drowned at sea" (*L.C.R.*).

GREGORY (Henry): *see* GREGORY (William).

GREGORY (William): A flautist and violist of the Stuart era, and composer of music in the popular style. We meet with him first as a performer on the "windy instruments" in 1625, when he is given in a list of musicians attending the funeral of James I (*L.C.R., Vol.* 557). On February 2nd, 1626, he was appointed to the court band of Charles I, in the place of James Harding, deceased, at a salary of 1s. 8d. per diem, plus 16l. 2s. 6d. for livery (*Add.* 12512, *B.M.* and cited in *Annalen*). In 1630 he was ordered to "wait on play nights instead of Mr. Jeronimo Bassano, who is the ancientest musician the king hath" (*L.C.R., Vol.* 738). During the Commonwealth he supported himself by teaching (*v.* Playford, *Musical Banquet*), and in 1656–7 he was one of the five musicians who unsuccessfully petitioned the "Committee of the Councel for Advancement of Musicke" to found a music-college so that the art of the country should not be utterly lost (*P.R.O. Dom. Ch. II, Vol.* 153, *v.* also *Annalen, p.* 48). At the Restoration he obtained the post of violist in the king's "private Musick". On August 26th, 1662, he was allowed 60l. per annum for teaching two boys in flute and cornet playing, a duty formerly fulfilled by Andrew Lanier (*v.* also *L.C.R.*, September 13th, 1662, *Vol.* 814).

On August 20th, 1663, he died, and his will was proved on September 15th (*Annalen, p.* 55). On September 16th a warrant was issued admitting "Henry Gregory musician in ordinary for the wind instruments in the place of his father William Gregory, deceased", with the same salary (*L.C.R., Vol.* 741). In the face of the evidence provided by this appointment and by the will there can be no doubt that William Gregory died in 1663. Yet we find a William Gregory named in the State Papers until 1684 at least; and we can only assume that here was another case of the scandalous method of book-keeping in vogue, or that there was another William Gregory, possibly related to his namesake, active at court. When William Gregory died in 1663 a goodly sum was owing him from the Treasury, and his will directs that it be paid to his widow Mary, his two daughters, the wife of his son Henry, and a grand-daughter. To Henry he left the residue of his estate. This Henry Gregory was a musician for the wind instruments appointed on March 13th, 1661–2 " in ordinary without fee, to be assistant with his father, William Gregory, and after the decease of the said William Gregory, to come in ordinary with fee " (*L.C.R.*, *Vol.* 741). As in the case of William, we find Henry's name in the official records until almost the end of the century ; and since it is applied to a violinist as well as to a flautist, it is possible that here again there may have been two of the same name. At the same time one Henry Gregory can have filled both posts, especially as his

" debenter fee " amounted to 10*s.* which would cover two places.

Examples of William Gregory's work, consisting chiefly of short Ayres and dance-forms, may be seen in several of the contemporary publications; and in British Museum manuscripts (*Add.* 14399 in Lock's handwriting; *Add.* 29386, a Glee; *Add.* 29397, a Song; and *Add.* 31430, dance forms). His signature is in *Harl.* 1911 (*B.M.*; Minutes of the Cor-poration of Music).

GWINETH *or* GWIN-NETH (John): *see* GWYN-NETH (John).

GWYNNETH (John). A musician and writer of polemical and anti-Protestant tracts who flourished at the middle of the sixteenth cen-tury. The son of poor Welsh parents he was assisted in his studies by some " ecclesiastical Mecaenas " (Wood), and sent as an exhibitioner to Oxford. The first piece of authentic in-formation concerning him is his supplication for the degree of *Mus. Doc.* at Oxford. In 1531 (December 9th), he petitioned that since he had already written the Responses for an entire year, three five-part masses, five four-part masses, antiphonic works, hymns, and other church music, he might be allowed to proceed without writing the customary exercise. After charging him 20*d*. for expenses, the University honoured him with the degree. Practically all this material comes, in the first place, from Anthony Wood's quotations from the Oxford University Registers (Wood, *Fasti Oxonienses*). He was presented to a Welsh church in 1543 but was not permitted by the Bishop to officiate until, after much litigation, Gwynneth was upheld at the court of the Star Chamber. He could not have held this cure for long since on September 19th of the same year he left Wales and came to London where he occupied the rectory of St. Peter's in Westcheap for about three years. He gave up the living in November, 1556. The dates of his birth and death are unknown.

Although he wrote and printed a number of tracts on matters of religion, the only published piece out of all the music he is supposed to have composed, is the four-part song, " My love mournyth ", included in *Wynkyn de Worde's Song-Book* of 1530 (two parts in the *B.M.*). G Y L E S (J o h n *and* Nathaniel): *see* GILES.

H

HABYNGTON (Henry): *see* ABINGDON (Henry).

HALL (Henry): An organist and composer of church music who enjoyed a considerable reputation in his day. The son of a captain in the army, he was born at Windsor soon after the middle of the seventeenth century. He commenced his musical career in the Chapel Royal under Henry Cooke. He became a lay-vicar, and in 1674 was appointed as organist at Exeter Cathedral. Five years later he became a vicar-choral, and in 1688 transferred his activities as organist to Hereford Cathedral. He died at Hereford on March 30th, 1707, and lies interred among the vicars-choral in the cloisters there. Hall was a very serious musician and did much to maintain a high standard in the music wherever he was active; he had some gifts as a poet and was accounted an excellent organist. Examples of his work may be seen in the British Museum: *Harl.* 7242 (Anthems), *Add.* 17840 (*Id.*), *Add.* 17784 (*Id.*), *Harl.* 7340 (Morning and Evening Service in E-flat), *Add.* 31444–5 (Anthem), *Add.* 30931 (Anthems), *Add.* 33234 (Song), *Add.* 31453 (Songs). The *Theater of Music* (*Bk. II*, 1685) contains " A Dialogue betwixt Oliver Cromwell and Charon ", by Hall. It has been suggested that the lighter works bearing Hall's name were from the pen of his son (also Henry); but in view of the fact that the *Theater of Music* was published in 1685, there can be no doubt that this dialogue at any rate, was the work of the father.

HALL (William): A violinist of some repute whose name appears in the lists of royal musicians from 1671 until his death in 1700. The *Dictionary of National Biography* gives him as the son of Henry Hall (*q.v.*), but since he was in the royal orchestra in 1671 and published music in 1673, this cannot be correct. He performed in the famous masque of 1674, and his salary as violinist in ordinary is frequently given as having been 40*l.* per annum. In 1680 he was appointed to the private music of the king (*L.C.R.*) in the place of John Young,

Q

deceased. In 1685 he was confirmed in his appointments by James II, and thence onwards is often mentioned in the Lord Chamberlain's Records. The entry of June 3rd, 1700, gives him as " deceased ". Lock's *Melothesia* (1673) contains a piece by William Hall, and a cantata (" Awake fair Goddess ") and a song (" These two full houres ") in *Add.* 22100 (*B.M.*), are also most likely by him.

HAMBOYS (John):   *see* HANBOYS (John).

HAMPTON (John): Organist of Worcester Cathedral from 1484 to 1522. Little is known of him beyond the fact that he received 20*s.* as a reward for " making of Balades " when Henry VII visited Worcester in 1495. His salary as organist amounted to 3*l.* 13*s.* 4*d.* per annum, payable quarterly, plus a gift of fourteen loaves and fourteen measures of ale (*v.* also J. E. West, *Cathedral Organists*, and Sir Ivor Atkins's work on the Worcester organists). The only known composition by John Hampton is a " Salve Regina " in the Eton College manuscript.

HANBOYS (John) (*also* HAMBOYS). An eminent writer of theoretical treatises who enjoyed a European reputation in the fifteenth century. Our only source of information is Bale (*Scriptorum Catalogus*, 1559, *p.* 617) or Pits (1619), and Holinshed (*Chronicles*) who followed the latter. The first-named authority is responsible for the statement that Hanboys enjoyed a good education, which in view of his writings was a fairly safe thing to say. Further that he was made a Doctor of Music " communi suffragio ", —no University being named. Bale continues that Hanboys was the most celebrated personage of his period and that he flourished in the reign of Edward IV. The treatise upon which his fame rests is entitled: " Super musicam continuam et discretam " (*B.M. Add.* 8866; printed by de Coussemaker in his *Scriptorum Med. Aev. Ed.* 1863, I. 403), ending with the words, " Summa Magistri Johannis Hanboys Doctoris musicae reverendi ", whence probably the Doctor of Music story originates. It is a full commentary on the writings of Franco of Cologne and Franco of Paris, besides containing much original material. The same manuscript contains another treatise which has been attributed to Hanboys ("Quatuor principalia totius artis musicae", dated 1351), but which Burney ascribes to Tunsted. Coussemaker in his introduction thinks Burney likely to be right, though the question is still open to doubt. At any rate, "Quatuor Principalia" is too early a work to have been written by Hanboys. Tanner, on this point (*Bibl. Britt. etc.*) is wholly untrustworthy, since he places "Quatuor Principalia" later, in order to give it to Hanboys, thus treating the date given by the scribe responsible for the manuscript as erroneous. Bale attributed more works to Hanboys, but no copies of them have come to light. The value of Hanboys' "Super musicam continuam, *etc.*" lies in the information it affords on the subjects of mensurable music and the manner in which the rules of the late fourteenth and early fifteenth centuries were applied.

HANDLO (Robert) *de*: A writer on theoretical music who flourished in the fourteenth century. Next to nothing is known of his life. He was most probably con-nected with the family of that name resident near Ton-bridge (Kent), obviously taking the name from the manor of Hanlo,—later Hadlow. The only known work by this author is *Regulae cum maximis magistri Franconis, cum additionibus aliorum musicorum*, dated 1326. The tract deals with notation and is in effect a commentary upon the rules of Franco of Paris,—not of Franco of Cologne as Coussemaker has taken pains to point out: "Non in Franconem Colon . . . sed in Franconem Parisiensis commentatur Robertus". Hawkins, Forkel, Burney, *etc.*, fall into the error mentioned. The manuscript was in the Cot-tonian library as *Tiberius B. ix*, until it was destroyed by fire in 1731. Fortunately Dr. Pepusch had previously made a copy of it, which is now in the British Museum as *Add. 4909*. Each paragraph of the treatise is headed by the name of the musician re-sponsible for the statement contained; an arrangement that has caused many writers to suppose the work to have been in dialogue-form. Coussemaker printed it in his *Scriptorum (Vol. I, 383)*.

Among the authorities quoted in the " Regulae " of de Handlo is John Garland (*q.v.*).

HARDING (James) : A flautiſt of the late sixteenth and early seventeenth centuries whose reputation travelled as far afield as Germany, for he is represented in Füllsack's *Auserlesene Paduanen und Galliarden* (1607). He appears in the State Papers as James Harden or Hardyn in 1581, when he received the usual New Year's gift of 20*s.* given to the regular musicians in the royal service (*Harl.* 1644, *B.M.*). Later on his name is given as Harding. He probably died in 1626, for on February 2nd, William Gregory was appointed in his place. *Add.* 30485 (*B.M.*) contains a Fancy arranged for the virginal by " Mr. Jeams Harden " and signed at the end " James Hardinge ". *Add.* 30826–8 has a Galliard by him.

HARDING (John): A member of the Chapel Royal, and, during the Commonwealth, a noted teacher for " Voyce or Viol " (Playford, *Musical Banquet*). He was appointed to the Chapel at Lady Day, 1638, and remained in that service until his death in 1684. The date of his birth is not known, but in 1671 the Cheque-Book of the Chapel Royal describes him as a " Gentleman of thirty years' ſtanding ",— which does not agree with the ſtatement that he entered in 1638. Except for information on the payment of salary and of livery money, and the reimbursement of expenses incurred when on journeys made with the Chapel when attending the king away from London nothing further is known of his life. At the Reſtoration he was appointed to the private music of Charles II, and reinſtated in his poſt at the Chapel. He may have been a son of James Harding (*q.v. sup.*).

HART (James): A bass-vocaliſt and popular composer of the late seventeenth century. His reputation among his contemporaries muſt have been a fairly high one, for we find him collaborating with such men as John Baniſter I and Pelham Humfrey. He was born at York near the middle of the century, and began his musical career as a singer in the Minſter there. Little is known of his early life. In 1670 Mr. Edmund Slater dying, " was sworne

Mr. James Hart the seventh day of November, 1670, a base from Yorke" into the service of the Chapel Royal (*Ch. Bk. C.R.*). He is frequently mentioned in the State Papers in connection with his office. In 1678 (April 15th) an order was made for the payment to him of 30*l.* yearly for the maintenance of a child of the Chapel "whose voyce is changed and is gon from the Chapel" (*L.C.R.*, *Vol.* 747). Chamberlayne, in *Magnae Britanniae notitia* (for 1682), says that James Hart was among the "most eminent of England in their Profession". In 1694 the same source gives his salary at the Chapel as 73*l.* per annum, besides which he was also a lay-vicar of Westminster Abbey. He died on May 8th, 1718 (*Ch. Bk. C.R.*).

Examples of his music, chiefly slight vocal numbers, can be seen in *The Theater of Music* (1685, four pieces; *Bk. III*, three pieces; 1687, *Bk. IV*, three pieces). "Where could coy Aminta run", given anonymously in Book V of Playford's *Choice Ayres and Songs* (1684), is also by Hart, a manuscript copy of it being in the Christ Church library (Oxford). A

song of his was published in the *Gentleman's Journal* for August, 1692 (*pp.* 30–32), and he collaborated with Banister and Humfrey in the songs for *The Tempest* (1675). Manuscript music by James Hart is contained in the British Museum collection: *Add.* 19759, *Add.* 22100, *Add.* 29396, *Add.* 29397, *Add.* 31453, and *Add.* 33234. The "Mr. Hart" mentioned twice in the Lord Chamberlain's Record in connection with the masque of 1674 was probably also James.

HAWKINS (James): Organist and composer of church music. A native of Cambridge, he commenced his long association with music as a chorister at St. John's College (Cambridge). In 1682–3 he became organist at Ely Cathedral and deserves the thanks of all students of ecclesiastical music for having made copies of a tremendous number of compositions of that class and presented them to the Cathedral. Among this mass of music are (*Vol.* 7) seventeen Services and seventy-five Anthems from his own pen. The Cambridge degree of *Mus. Bac.* was conferred upon him in 1719. He died on October 18th,

1729, and was buried in Ely Cathedral, his epitaph ſtating that he was "forty-six years organiſt of this Church", that he was "eminent in his Profession", that he was "regular in the discharge of his duties", and "cheerful and friendly in his Deportment". The inscription adds that he was in his sixty-seventh year when he died; the date of his birth is therefore to be fixed at 1663.

Besides the music at Ely there are examples of his work in the British Museum (*Add.* 31444–5, *Harl.* 7341–2, *Add.* 30932, and *Add.* 33568,— Services and Anthems). Hawkins came into contaſt with Tudway when the latter was compiling his set of manuscript volumes (*B.M.*, *Harl.* 7337–42) and there is some correspondence relating to Tallis's forty-part composition which was then in the possession of "honeſt James Hawkins" (*Harl.* 3782). Hawkins's son (also James) was organiſt of Peterborough Cathedral, but falls outside the scope of this volume.

HAYWOOD (John):   *see* HEYWOOD (John).

HEATHER (William): A Gentleman of the Chapel Royal who secured celebrity by founding the Oxford music-professorship. He does not seem to have been very deeply learned in theoretical music, and even the exercise required as a matter of form when he received the (probably honorary) degree of *Mus. Doc.*, was written by Orlando Gibbons. Heather, —if the faſt that he desired sixty-four poor men to receive sixty-four mourning gowns at his funeral be taken to prove that he was sixty-four years of age when he made his will (1627),—was born in 1563 at Harmondsworth in Middlesex. Exaſtly when he became a choriſter at Weſtminſter Abbey is not known, but in the liſt of "singing-men of Weſtminſter" who attended the funeral of Queen Elizabeth, his name appears (1603). He succeeded the notorious Henry Eveseed as Gentleman of the Chapel Royal in 1615: "Henry Eveseed died the 18th of November, and William Heather from Weſtminſter was sworne in his place the 27th of March followinge" (*Ch. Bk. C.R.*, see also article on Henry Eveseed for a discrepancy in the dates). William Camden, at that time maſter of Weſtminſter

School, exercised a great influence on Heather, and the
two men were on the moſt
intimate terms of friendship.
Camden had reason to be
grateful to the Gentleman of
the Chapel, for the latter had
nursed him through various
illnesses, and it was in
Heather's house at Chisle-
hurſt that Camden died
(1623). When Camden en-
dowed a chair for hiſtory
at Oxford, Heather bore the
deeds to the Chancellor of
the University (1622). On
this occasion the degrees of
Bachelor and Doĉtor of Music
were conferred upon him. A
letter from Vice-Chancellor
Piers to Camden mentions
the gift of gloves to Heather
and his wife as a graceful
aĉt of courtesy. The late
Dr. W. H. Cummings was
the owner of a manuscript
containing a copy of "O
Clap your hands" inscribed:
"Dr. Heather's Commence-
ment Song, composed by Dr.
Orlando Gibbons". The
"disputation" arranged between Heather and Dr. Giles
(July 5th, 1622) did not
take place (v. also Nathaniel
Giles). Camden provided the
funds for the hiſtory leĉture-
ship by transferring to the
University the income from
a certain eſtate (producing

400l. per annum) on con-
dition that Heather, his heirs,
and executors, should enjoy
the profits for ninety-nine
years, his friend paying the
professor 140l. a year.

By a deed dated February
2nd, 1626–7, Heather
founded the Oxford music
professorship and endowed
it, according to the terms of
his will, with 17l. 6s. 8d.
of which 13l. 6s. 8d. was to
be the salary of the professor,
while the remainder was to
be paid to the reader of a
theoretical leĉture. The professor was required to impart
a minimum of one music-
lesson a week, and was
expeĉted to keep the inſtruments in good order and
repair. Heather presented a
harpsichord, a set of viols,
and a supply of printed and
manuscript music. The firſt
holder of the professorial
appointment was Richard
Nicholson, Bac. Mus.,
organiſt of Magdalen, and
John Allibond was the firſt
reader of the leĉture. The
latter had no successor, and
his duties were handed over
to another. The professor
soon became known as the
Choragus, and his duties consiſted in superintending a
weekly music praĉtice. The
later hiſtory of the professor-

ship does not concern us here.

Heather died in July, 1627, and was buried on August 1st in Westminster Abbey. His portrait in doctor's robes hangs in the Music School, Oxford.

HENRY VI, KING *of* ENGLAND : The earliest of England's really musical sovereigns, the sixth Henry, produced some compositions quite up to the standard of his time. They were distinguished by originality and fine sonorous effect. A " Gloria " and a " Sanctus " by him are contained in the Old Hall manuscript (at Old Hall, near Ware, Hertfordshire), and are given as by " Roy Henry "; the date of the manuscript deciding which Henry is referred to. The " Sanctus " is printed in the *Oxford History of Music*, II, 151, 2), and the composition is also contained in " Gloria in Excelsis " (" Sanctus " and " Benedictus "), *à* 3, published in Berlin (1901) in the Appendix of Mr. Barclay Squire's *Notes on an undescribed Collection of English Fifteenth - Century Music*. There will be no need to give the life of the king, for all that is necessary

to know of it will have been taught in the schoolroom. For purposes of reference it may be well to remember that Henry VI was born in 1421 (Windsor), ascended the throne with a regent in 1422, was deposed in 1461, and died in the Tower of London (most probably murdered) in May, 1471.

HENRY VIII, KING *of* ENGLAND: The influence exercised by this music-loving sovereign on the cultivation of music in England was incomparably greater than the importance of his own compositions. Judged as an amateur, his writings command a certain amount of respect, and would merit detailed description and criticism. But in a work dealing with the best of England's professional musicians, his interest is merely historical. Early in his life he devoted as much of his leisure as possible to composition, and produced several harmless and elementary things,—pleasant enough, some of them, but in no way outstanding either in originality or workmanship. But he set an excellent example to society in the enthusiastic way in which he encouraged music and musicians. Personally, Henry was endowed with many gifts. Besides being an excellent linguist, he could play well on the keyboard instruments and lute, and, like most educated men of the Tudor era, could sing at sight. The standard of the music performed at court and in chapel was, according to the reports sent home by the Venetian embassy, very high. He gathered together a splendid set of musicians, native and foreign, and collected a magnificent array of instruments (v. Harl. 1419A, B ; B.M.).

From Hall's *Chronicles* we learn that Henry composed two complete Masses which were sung in the Chapel Royal, and a motet of his is contained in a volume in the Royal library. *Add.* 31922 at the British Museum contains a large number of Henry's songs and other compositions; they are invariably headed, "The Kinge H. VIII", and his "Pastyme with good Companye" and "Grene growith ye Holy" seem to have achieved a certain popularity. No doubt the rank of the composer had a good deal to do with this. Since I wrote my account of Henry VIII as a musician in the *Monthly Musical*

Record (February, 1913), I have had the opportunity of examining these royal compositions more carefully, and have had to reverse many of the complimentary remarks I made. " O Lord, the Maker of all Thing ", popularly given to Henry, and so ascribed in the Christ Church (Oxford) manuscript *No.* 16, is possibly by John Shepherd and probably by one of the two Mundys. The Novello reprint (edited by Sir Walter Parratt) gives Henry as the composer. A couple of the secular songs were printed by H. E. Wooldridge, M.A., in his edition of Chappell's *Old English Popular Music,* 1893). Several songs have been printed separately, but it is not at all certain that Henry composed all that was attributed to him by his editors. " Passetyme with goode cumpany " is also contained in *Add.* 5665 (*B.M.*). John Stafford Smith (*Musica Antiqua,* 1812) printed a Pavane and Galliard by the king from a manuscript in the same national collection.

HEPTINSTALL (John): A music-printer active in London during the last decade of the seventeenth century and the first of the eighteenth. He was responsible for some improvements in the art of music-printing, such as the " tied note " (grouping tailed notes with movable types) and introducing the round-headed note in place of the diamond (lozenge) shape. Heptinſtall issued a number of important works,—notably several by Purcell, some Psalters, *etc.*

HEYTHER (William): *see* HEATHER (William).

HEYWOOD (John): A virginaliſt and composer of interludes aſtive during the Tudor regime. According to Nagel (*Annalen*) he appears in 1520 as a singer. In 1525–6 he is given in *Eg.* 2604 (*B.M.* Payments from the Household Book of Henry VIII) as a player on the virginals. *Ar.* 97 gives his salary in 1538 as 50*s.* a quarter. In 1552 he appears in *Stowe* 571 (*fol.* 27*b*) as a " Plaier on the Virginalles " to Mary Tudor. The laſt English reference to him is to be found in 1553, when a gratuity of 30*s.* was made to him by the Princess Elizabeth (Rimbault). On the accession of Elizabeth he left England on religious grounds, and spent the remainder of his days in Mechlin. The only traceable musical composition by Hey-wood is in a British Museum manuscript (*Add.* 4900),— " What heart can think or tongue express ", a song with lute-accompaniment in tablature. His dexterity in writing interludes and his lively wit made him a great favourite of Henry the Eighth, and Sir Thomas More direſted the attention of Princess Mary to the talents of the musician. Rimbault, quoting Pattenham, says that he was especially patronized by Mary rather " for his mirth and quickness of conceit, than good learning that was in him ".

HILTON (John, I): An organiſt and composer of madrigals and sacred music dating from the latter part of the sixteenth century and the firſt decade of the seventeenth. With two or three exceptions he has been badly confused with another John Hilton in the usual books of reference (unfortunately including the *Diſtionary of National Biography*, in which even the mention of the *Mus. Bac.* degree in 1601 [*Triumphes of Oriana*] and another clear conferring of the same degree in 1626, did not make the writer suspicious). The elder Hilton is no doubt the member of the Lincoln Cathedral choir mentioned in the Chapter Records there (1584). Mr. G. E. P. Arkwright draws attention to some interesting and illuminating references to Hilton while he was at Lincoln. Thus on January 21st, 1593, he was paid 30s. for his share in the preparation of two comedies to be performed by the choristers; and on leaving Lincoln he was permitted to do as he wished with his house, in recognition of his conscientious service. He was second organist of the Cathedral before he left to take up the position of organist at Trinity College, Cambridge, in 1594 (January 26th). His successor at Cambridge was active in 1612, so that shortly before this date, John Hilton must have died.

His printed works consist of " Fair Oriana, Beauty's Queen " (five-part, *Triumphes of Oriana*, 1601; copy in score, without words, in the Christ Church, Oxford, library), and a couple of four-part madrigals printed by Oliphant in 1835. The manuscripts bearing the name of John Hilton present a certain amount of difficulty; for it is not always easy to attribute each composition to the right Hilton. " Lord for thy tender Mercies' sake " is undoubtedly to be attributed to the elder Hilton, as it was written before the two Hiltons became confused and later editors took it away from both and gave it to Farrant. The anthem, " Call to Remembrance ", in the Bodleian part-books, is labelled " John Hilton, *senior* ". The two anthems mentioned above may be seen in the British Museum (*Add.* 30478–9 and *Harl.* 7340). Several other compositions are preserved in the same collection, but only a careful examination of the internal evidence can decide which are to be attributed with any degree of certainty to John Hilton the Elder.

HILTON (John, II): An organist and composer of popular music who flourished in the first half of the seventeenth century. Most probably a son of John Hilton I, he was born, on the evidence of his portrait in the Oxford Music School, in 1599. This date may very well be correct, for in 1626 he graduated Bachelor of Music at Cambridge (from Trinity College where the elder Hilton was organist). He has been considered a pupil of Dr. William Heather on the strength of one sentence in his dedication to the *Ayres, or Fa-las,* in which he says that the work was but "a Drop that I received from you the Fountaine". Exactly how far this was the case we cannot be certain ; but it is well-known that Heather's knowledge of music was not very great. Mr. G. E. P. Arkwright, in the 1913 *Grove,* suggests that Heather may have been Hilton's patron, which is rather more likely. In 1628 Hilton removed to London on his appointment as Parish Clerk and organist of St. Margaret's, Westminster. He died in 1657, his burial being registered in the books of St. Margaret's under date 21st March, 1656–7. Wood's assertion that Hilton was interred in the " Great Cloysters at Westminster " is thus most probably erroneous. But another piece of information given by the Oxford historian may be true. He says that as at that time " the singing at burials being silenced, as Popish, the Fraternity of Musitians who intended to sing him to his grave, sang the anthem in the House over the corps before it went to the Church, and kept time on his coffin " (manuscript notes in the Bodleian library, Oxford).

Hilton's work is mostly of a lighter character, though he also wrote a little sacred music; but he is best remembered by his " Fa-Las ", which still adhere to the earlier style, and by his Canons, rounds, and catches. In 1627 he published *Ayres or Fa La's for Three Voyces,* etc. The pieces contained in this work still reflect a little of the madrigalian atmosphere, but though charming and neat, cannot be compared with the work of the earlier writers in this style. The work was reprinted by the Musical Antiquarian Society. On the death of William Lawes Hilton wrote an elegy which was published in the *Choice Psalms* of the brothers Lawes in 1648. In 1652 he issued his collection of catches, *etc.,* by various writers including himself, under the title: *Catch that Catch can, or a Choice Collection of Catches, Rounds and Canons for three or four Voyces.* A second edition " corrected and enlarged " appeared from the Playford press in 1658, and another edition followed in 1663. Subsequent issues of the work bore the title *Musical Companion*. Some of the catches were published separately in the eighteenth century. Specimens of Hilton's work, both sacred and secular, may be seen in manuscripts preserved in various collections, but some caution must be exercised in accepting compositions merely headed " Hilton " as the undoubted work of the younger bearer of the name.

HINGESTON (John): *see* HINGSTON (John).

HINGSTON (John): A celebrated organist and teacher of the keyboard instruments whose period of activity extended from the middle of the seventeenth century to 1683. The date of his birth is not known, but it must have fallen very early in the century, for Orlando Gibbons, who was his teacher, died in 1625. We hear little of him (except that he served in the musical establishment of Charles I) until the publication of John Playford's *Banquet of Music* (1651) when he is described as an excellent teacher of the organ and virginal. He became a great favourite of Cromwell's, and taught the Protector's daughters. When the organ from Magdalen College (Oxford) was re-erected at Hampton Court, Hingston became Cromwell's state organist, receiving 100*l*. per annum as " pension ". Cromwell's love for music is well-known, and he often listened to his organist accompanying a couple of boys in the performance, curiously enough, of old Catholic sacred music, Richard Deering being a particular favourite (Wood, *MS. Notes*). The story of Cromwell's surprise visit to Hingston's house in St. James's Park may be seen in the article on Roger L'Estrange in this volume. In 1656 Hingston and other musicians petitioned the " Comittee of the Council for Advancement of Musicke" for the founding of a college of music in order to raise the standard of the art in this country. This appeal was unsuccessful.

At the Restoration of the House of Stuart, Hingston went back to the royal service. On June 23rd, 1660, he was appointed " for a Viol, in the place of Alphonso Ferrobosco " (*sc.* Ferrabosco), and on July 2nd of the same year he was engaged as " tuner and repairer of organs, virginalls, and wind instruments, in the place of

Arthur Norgate" (*L.C.R.*). On January 24th, 1660–1, a warrant was issued granting to Hingston the livery allowance " such as Alphonso Ferrabosco . . . formerly held and enjoyed " (*Id.*). Large sums of money were paid to him from time to time, representing his salary and expenses in connection with repairs to the instruments under his care. In 1662 he directed the enlarging of the organ-loft at Whitehall, and the erection of an organ in the Banquetting house. A salary of 60*l.* per annum is mentioned in an entry for 1668, but this referred only to Hingston's post as tuner and repairer of the organs. As private musician he received 50*l.* It is not known with what regularity his salary was paid; but it is highly probable that Hingston, in common with most of the other Stuart musicians, suffered considerably under the erratic financial methods obtaining at the court of Charles II. His livery allowance was frequently in arrears, and we often find him petitioning for payment. On June 10th, 1673, Henry Purcell is mentioned as Hingston's assistant and destined successor (*L.C.R.*). Exactly how it happened is not clear, but in 1676 the repairer of the organs fell into debt to Bernard Smith, and the Lord Chamberlain's Records contain the entry: " June 15th. Whereas Bernard Smyth hath petitioned for leave to take his course at law against John Hingston for debt due, order that John Hingston give an appearance at the Common law " (*L.C.R.*), but with what result is not known. In December, 1683, he is given as " deceased ", Henry Purcell taking his place as " organ maker " and Robert Carr as " Violl ". Hingston was buried at St. Margaret's Church, Westminster, on December 17th, 1683.

He is frequently credited with having been the teacher of John Blow, but of this there is no positive proof. He was a member of the " Corporacion of Musick ", and his signature may be seen in the Minutes of the meetings (*Harl.* 1911, *B.M.*). Not much of his music has been preserved. The British Museum has a few manuscript examples: *Add.* 31436, a collection of fancies, *etc.*, for three bass-viols, contains fantasias and various dance-forms besides other compositions for three ſtringed inſtruments with harpsichord bass. In the Chriſt Church library (Oxford) there is an organ " Voluntarie " by him, while in the Music School collection (Oxford) are his beſt compositions,—a set of six-part fancies for ſtrings. A portrait of John Hingſton hangs in the laſt-named locality.

HINKSON (John): *see* HINGSTON (John).

HOLBORNE (Anthony): A composer, and presumably a luteniſt, active at the end of the sixteenth century. Very little is known of his life beyond what can be gathered from the title-pages and dedications of his published works. He muſt have been on terms of personal friendship with such musicians as Giles Farnaby, John Dowland, and Morley, for to the solo *Canzonets* (1598) issued by the firſt he wrote some verses in Latin, for the Plain Introduction of the laſt he composed some English lines, while Dowland inscribed a song to the " moſt famous Anthony Holborne ". His firſt publication was "*The Cittharn Schoole.* Hereunto are added sixe Short

Aers Neapolitanlike to three Voyces without the Inſtrument; done by his brother William Holborne. 1597 ". The only other known work of Anthony Holborne's was " *Pauans, Galliards, Almains,* and other short Aeirs both graue and light to fiue parts, for Viols, Violins, or other Musicall Winde Inſtruments " (1599). So far as I know only one copy of each of these works is known to exiſt: of the former at the Royal College of Music and of the latter in the British Museum. The cithren book was dedicated to " Thomas, Lord Burgh, baron Gainsburgh " and was published to counter certain pirated issues of the "sixe short Aers ". The set of five part-books containing the " Pavans, *etc.*" was inscribed to " Sir Richard Champernown ", and in this work Holborne is described as " gentleman and servant to her moſt excellent majeſty ". Robert Dowland included in his *Varietie of Lute Lessons* (1610) a Pavane " composed by the moſt famous and perfect artiſt, Anthonie Holborne, Gentleman Usher to the moſt sacred Elizabeth, late Queene of England ". Another piece by him,—a song with lute accompaniment,—is contained in Robert Dowland's *Musical Banquet* of the same year. He is further represented in Füllsack's *Auserlesene Paduanen und Galliarden* (Hamburg; 1607–9) and a Pavane of his is included in Joachim van den Hove's *Delitiae Musicae* (Antwerp, 1612) among the works of the best musicians of the time. In Jane Pickering's manuscript lute-book (*B.M.* 1616; *Eg.* 2046) there is "The Countiss of Pembruth (Pembroke) fineralle", while a Pavane in lute-tablature is to be found in *Add.* 31392 (*B.M.*).

HOLBORNE (William): Brother of Anthony Holborne; but except for the appearance of his name on the title-page of Anthony's publication of 1597, nothing is known of him.

HOLDER (William) : An eminent divine who possessed musical talents and theoretical knowledge of a high order. Born in Nottinghamshire in 1616, he occupied various rectories at different times, besides being prebend of Ely. In 1643 he obtained the Oxford M.A. degree and in 1660 he became a Doctor of Divinity. In 1662 the Royal Society created him a Fellow, probably in recognition of his researches in the science of Speech (a treatise on which,—*The Elements of Speech*,—he published in 1669). In 1672 he became a Canon of St. Paul's Cathedral, and two years later Sub-Dean of the Chapel Royal: "1674. Dr. William Holder was sworne Subdeane of his Majesty's Chapel Royal the second day of September, 1674. Be it remembered that Dr. William Holder was sworne Subdeane by the Lord Chamberlaine, at the speciall request of the Deane, who was then absent at the Bath " (*Ch. Bk. C.R.*). He resigned the post at the Chapel Royal " before Christmas of the yeare of our Lord, 1689 ". Dr. Holder married Susanna, daughter of Christopher Wren (Dean of Windsor), and sister of the famous architect who came much under the influence and training of his clerical and musical brother-in-law. Holder died on January 24th, 1697–8, and lies buried in St. Paul's Cathedral.

The most interesting work that came from the pen of this learned and exacting clergyman was his *Treatise of the Natural Grounds and Princi-*

ples of Harmony (1694), an excellent work, prepared for the use of the members of the Chapel Royal. It was re-issued in 1731 (" To which is added: Rules for Playing a Thorow-Bass, *etc.* Also directions for Tuning an Harpsichord or Spinnet. By the late Mr. Godfrey Keller. Revised and Corrected "). Specimens of Holder's compositions may be seen in the British Museum: *Harl.* 7338 (Anthem and Service in C) and *Harl.* 7339 (five-part Verse Anthem). *Sloane* 1388 contains a letter to Holder on the subject of his treatise and *Add.* 4921 gives extracts from the Philosophical Transactions of the Royal Society, including some from Holder's work of 1694.

HOLE (William): The first in England to engrave music on copper, who will go down in history as the engraver of " Parthenia, or the Maydenhead of the First Musicke that ever was printed for the Virginalls " (*v.* William Byrd, Bull, and Orlando Gibbons). The date of this work is not given on the title-page, but is undoubtedly 1611. Other important works engraved by him were the *Prime Musiche Nuove* of Angelo Notari (an Italian in the English court-

service) in 1613, and Orlando Gibbons's set of nine " Fantasies of Three Parts . . . cut in copper, the like not heretofore extant ". In view of the last claim, it is possible that the date of this publication was earlier than that of *Parthenia*.

HOLMES (John): A celebrated organist and composer of madrigals and sacred music. Of his earliest years nothing is known beyond the fact that he was organist of Winchester Cathedral, at the end of the sixteenth century. In 1602 he became organist at Salisbury where he succeeded Ellis Gibbons. He held this post until 1610, and produced from the ranks of his pupils such famous organists as Edward Lowe and Adrian Batten. His death is recorded on March 25th, 1638.

That he was highly esteemed by his contemporaries is proved by the circumstance that he contributed to the *Triumphes of Oriana* (1601) the five-part madrigal " Thus Bonny-boots the birthday celebrated " (reproduced by Novello). A *Magnificat and Nunc Dimittis* has also been published by Novello. His works still in manuscript are more

R

numerous. At Christ Church (Oxford) there are the organ parts of a *Magnificat* and of a Verse Anthem (" O Lord of whome I do depend "), a " Pavane " for instruments (three-part), and a virginal " Fantazia ". The Royal College of Music possesses another anthem. Adrian Batten copied a large number of Holmes's sacred compositions (St. Michael's College, Tenbury), the manuscript organ-book containing the note: " All these songs of Mr. John Holmes were prict from his own pricking in the year 1635 by Adrian Batten, . . . who some time was his scholler ". The British Museum has works by him in *Add.* 17786–91 and *Add.* 30932.

His son Thomas was sworn a Gentleman of the Chapel Royal on September 17th, 1633, but he has left us nothing of great importance, the bulk of his work belonging to the popular Catch category,—Hilton's *Catch that Catch can* (1658) containing specimens of his composition. He wrote some anthems, the words of two being included in *Harl.* 6346 (*B.M.*).

HOLMES (Thomas): *see* HOLMES (John).

HOOPER (Edmund): An organist and composer of the second half of the sixteenth century and the first two decades of the seventeenth, active at the Chapel Royal and Westminster Abbey. His sacred compositions, though not voluminous, are worthy of serious consideration, his " O thou God Almighty " and one or two other works being distinctly above the average for the period. Born at Halberton in Devonshire, soon after the middle of the sixteenth century, his movements are uncertain until we meet with him in the choir at Westminster Abbey *ca.* 1581 or 1582. In 1588 he became organist at the Abbey, his patent dating from December 3rd, 1588. On March 1st, 1603 (*Ch. Bk. C.R.*) he was " sworne . . . in Mr. Randoll's roome " as organist of the Chapel Royal, sharing the duties there from 1604 onwards with Orlando Gibbons. Under date November 2nd, 1615, the Cheque-Book contains an entry showing the arrangement made by Gibbons and Hooper for the division of the work. In 1606 (May 9th) he was given the organist's post at the Abbey also, deriving further income by copying choir-books and adjusting the organ. He held his Abbey and Chapel Royal posts until his death in 1621, the Cheque-Book announcing that " Edmund Hooper organist, died the 14th daye of July, and Thomas Tompkins, organist of Worcester, was sworne in his place the second daye of August followinge ". He lies interred in the Abbey Cloisters. Hooper was twice married, his eldest son James and his grandson William both being musicians,—the former a " singing man " of Westminster, and the latter he who took Pepys " in among the quire " of the Abbey where the diarist " sang with them in their service " on December 29th, 1661.

Comparatively little of Edmund Hooper's music has been printed. Settings by him may be seen in East's *Whole Booke of Psalms* (1592) and two numbers in Sir William Leighton's *Teares, etc.* (1614) are from his pen (" Alas that I offended ever ", four-part, and " Wellspring of Bounty ", five-part). Barnard's collection of 1641 contains anthems by him, one of them (" Teach me thy way, O Lord ") having been reprinted by Novello and Co. under the editorship of Mr. J. E. West. Examples of his works, including some of the pieces already mentioned, may be seen in manuscript at the British Museum: *Add.* 17784, 17792–6, 17820, 29289, 29372–7, 30087, 30478–9, 31405, 31418, 31443, and 37072; *Harl.* 7337 and 7340; *Royal App.* 63. A few specimens of his composition are contained in manuscripts at the Royal College of Music (London), Ely Cathedral, and Peter-house (Cambridge).

HOOPER (James), HOOPER (William): *see* HOOPER (Edmund).

HOTHBY (John) (*also* OCTOBI, OTTEBY, *and* OTTOBI): A famous fifteenth-century writer of theoretical treatises who enjoyed a great reputation during his lifetime, and whose works are of great importance to the student of medieval music. Henry Davey and Riemann say that he lectured at Oxford and graduated there, but neither gives any authority in support of the statement. Cousse-maker says that " consedit Florentiae *ca. ann.* 1440 ", and that he had visited Spain, France, and Germany. He joined the Carmelites at

Ferrara, and lived there for a number of years. The most important period of his life, however, was spent in Lucca whither he went in 1467. At the monastery of S. Martin in that city he taught grammar, mathematics, and music; and when he left was given a very laudatory reference. In March, 1486, he was called home by the king (Henry VII),—for what purpose is not known, but he died in London the following year (it is said on November 6th, 1487). His death must have occurred somewhere about this date, for ten days later the news reached Lucca. There are a few sacred and secular works (nine in all) original, now lost, but of which Padre Martini made a copy. He is known to have had a pupil named Frater Matthaeus, for in the national library at Paris there is a manuscript (*Fonds lat.* 7369) written by him, which includes a poem in Hothby's high praise, saying that " A Gange ad Gades par tibi nullus erat ".

His best-known work is probably *Calliopea legale* (*Nat. Libr.*, Florence; St. Mark's, Venice; *cf. also B.M. MS. Add.* 36986). This treatise, written in Italian, was repro-duced by Coussemaker in his *Histoire de l'harmonie, etc.*). The treatise *Proportiones secundum Joannem Otteby, magistrum in musica,* beginning " Quid est Proportio ", is contained in British Museum manuscript *Add.* 10336, while another copy is at Lambeth Palace. *Tractatus quarundam regularum artis musicae* is preserved at Florence (*Palatino MS.*), and in the British Museum. *Regulae super Proportionem* is in the *Bibl. Nat.* of Paris, in the *Liceo Comm.* of Bologna, and at St. Mark's, Venice. Coussemaker has printed it (*Scriptorum, Vol.* III, 328, *ed.* 1863–76); it begins " Omnis numerus habet tot partes . . ." *De Cantu Figurato* is extant in a manuscript at Bologna (*Liceo Comm.*), once in Ferrara. This also was printed by Coussemaker (*Script., Vol.* III, p. 330). *Regulae super Contrapunctum* is likewise present at Bologna, and another copy is at Florence. Coussemaker included it in Volume III (*No. XXVII*) of his work. *Ars Musica* (Florence), *Dialogus de Arte Musica* (*Ib.*), *Manus per genus diatonicum declarata* (Bologna) and *Regulae de monochordo manuali* (*Ib.*) must be added to the list of works by Hothby. Three little tracts were published in *Caecelia* for 1874 (*No. 5*) in translated form (information from Mr. W. Barclay Squire). A letter in Italian replying polemically to a censurer is preserved in the National Library at Florence, and another copy is at Bologna (*Liceo communale*).

HOWES (William): In considering the seventeenth-century musician bearing this name we have the option of looking upon him as a very versatile man or of coming to the conclusion—which appears to me to be more justified—that there were two men of the same name, one a member of the Chapel Royal and the other a member of the king's band as performer on the wind instruments and the violin. Henry Davey told me that he had evidence of Howes having been a wait of Worcester who later became a canon at Windsor. There can be no doubt that a William Howes was a musician enjoying a high reputation, for he was among those signing the petition of February 19th, 1657, asking Cromwell to found a College of Music. He was sworne in as a Gentle-

man of "his Majesty's Chappell Royall" in troublous times, his appointment dating from November 25th, 1643 (*L.C.R.*). So far we are probably dealing with one man. But at the Restoration we find a William Howes appointed to the private music of the king as a violinist "in the place of Robert Dowland" at 40*l*. 12*s*. 8*d*. per annum (*L.C.R.*, June 20th), as a Treble Lute "in the place of John Mercuer" (*sc.* Mercure; *Id.*), and to another post "in the place of John Hickson" (*sc.* Hingston ?) at a salary of 1*s*. 8*d*. per day plus livery-allowance (*Id.*, November 9th, 1660). On July 4th, 1661, a William Howes was to receive 5*s*. a day for his "extraordinary charges" in attending the king at Windsor as violinist (*Id.*), this being one of many similar entries. He was good enough a violinist to be included in John Banister's select band on July 10th, 1665 (*Id.*). At the same time we find entries (such as that of December 10th, 1663) in which he is described as a Gentleman of the Chapel Royal. It is doubtful whether the same man is meant, for such a multiplicity of engagements would be more than any one musician could manage even in the days of multiple poſts. In 1674 the entries commence to be ſtill more puzzling, for in that year we find a William Howes, *senior*, and a William Howes, *junior*, mentioned. Whether an attempt had at laſt been made to diſtinguish two men of the same name, or whether a son of the elder William Howes had entered the royal service, cannot be determined. It is not until we come to the announcement of his death that we are forced to incline to the belief that the William Howes, *senior*, who was the orcheſtral player and the William Howes who was a gentleman of the Chapel Royal, were one and the same man. The Lord Chamberlain's Records (May 3rd, 1676) contain an entry giving him as " deceased ", his place being filled (for the wind inſtruments) by Edmund Flower. The Cheque-Book of the Chapel Royal also enters: " 1676. Mr. William Howes gentleman of his Majeſty's Chapel Royal departed this life the 21ſt of Aprill, 1676, in whos place was sworne Mr. Alphonso Marsh, junior . . ." A William Howes is repre-

sented in Hilton's *Catch that Catch can*.

HUDSON (George): A seventeenth-century singer, luteniſt, violiniſt, and composer of light popular music and incidental tunes for the ſtage. He was sworn in as musician to the king " for the lutes and voices extraordinary " on January 18th, 1641–2 (his appointment to date from December 3rd, 1641; *L.C.R.*, *Vol.* 740). In 1641 there was no poſt vacant and Hudson was to wait his turn, being second on the waiting liſt for an appointment as musician " in ordinary ". The Civil War probably prevented him achieving that position until the Reſtoration. During the Commonwealth he spent his time composing and teaching; and in Playford's *Musical Banquet* (1651) he is mentioned as one of the eminent London teachers for " Voyce or Viol ". He took a share in the writing of the entr'aċte music to Davenant's epochmaking *Siege of Rhodes* (1656). He was also in the service of Cromwell, for in a petition to the Proteċtor, dated February 19th, 1657, he is described as a " Gentleman of His Highness's musique ". At the Reſtoration he was appointed "a violin in the private musick", at a salary of 42*l.* 12*s.* 10*d.* per annum. In November, 1660, he was engaged as composer to the king at 200*l.* per annum. He must have occupied a high position in the court music of that era, for on May 31st, 1661, he was given authority to superintend the practice of the band and to report negligence (*L.C.R.*, *Vol.* 741). On July 10th, 1665, he was appointed one of John Banister's band of violins, formed of the best players selected to provide a set of violinists comparable with the French king's "24 Violons du Roi". His salary as composer is given in 1668–9 as 42*l.* 10*s.* 10*d.* (*L.C.R.*), while on January 9th, 1668–9, he is said to have received 200*l.* for that service (*Id.*, *Vol.* 482). No explanation is forthcoming for this discrepancy; and it is hardly likely that there would have been two composers of the same name active at the same time. In *Eg.* 2159 (*B.M.*) his name is bracketed with that of Matthew Lock as composer (1669). On January 10th, 1671–2, Thomas Purcell and Pelham Humfrey were "appointed composers in ordinary to his

Majesty for the violin without fee, and assistant to George Hudson, and upon the death or other avoydance, to come in ordinary with fee" (*L.C.R.*, *Vol.* 773). Hudson died before the end of the year, for under date December 10th, 1672, the Lord Chamberlain's Records contain his verbal will (*L.C.R.*, *Vol.* 198). In 1674–5 his executors were to be paid 64*l.* 10*s.*, being four years' arrears of Hudson's livery-allowance, owing for the years 1665–7 and 1670. George Hudson was a member of the Corporation of Music, and in the Minutes of the meetings (1672) his signature is written (*B.M. Harl.* 1911).

His compositions, judging by what has been preserved, were not ambitious in magnitude nor in any way distinguished. *Musick's Recreation on the Viol, Lyraway* (1669) contains ten airs and dance-forms, and *Court Ayres* (1655), seven pieces of a similar nature. *Add.* 15118 (*B.M.*) has a suite of three dance-forms for a viol. In the Christ Church (Oxford) library are preserved five sets of short pieces, two for treble and bass and three for two trebles and bass, with a thorough-bass part in each case.

HUDSON (Richard): One of the violinists in John Banister's celebrated band for court service, and keeper of the king's instruments. Whether he was any relation to George Hudson (*q.v.*) is not clear. At the Restoration Richard Hudson was appointed a violin in the private music of the king, and at the same time " keeper of the Lutes and Violls ", his salary as violinist being 46*l*. 12*s*. 8*d*. per annum (*L.C.R., Vols.* 741 *and* 180). On April 15th, 1663, he was ordered to have the king's arms " cut in mother of pearl and inlayed in the finger-boards of the several instruments . . . to the end they be not changed . . . " (*L.C.R., Vol.* 741). In 1668 (March 27th) he is entered in the records as " deceased " with Thomas Fitz in his place, and it is to be presumed that he died shortly before that date. Beyond several entries in the State Papers similar to the above, only one more fact is known in connection with his work;—during the Commonwealth he was one of the five musicians who approached the " Committee of the Council for Advance-

ment of Musicke " with the proposal that a College of Music be founded (1656). Nothing came of the suggestion.

HUME (Tobias): An amateur gambist and composer of vocal and instrumental music of some worth. He was by profession a soldier and served as a mercenary in Sweden. In the dedication to one of his works he says that " My life hath been a soldier, and my idleness addicted to music ", while in another he writes : " My Profession beeing, as my education hath beene, Armes, the onely effeminate part of mee, hath beene Musicke; which in me hath beene alwaies Generous because never mercenarie ". He rose to be a captain, and although before he died he called himself " Colonel ", this flight must be attributed to the fanciful wandering of a diseased mind. His music is not without character, and in his instrumental work he makes attempts at a realism that would in later times be considered " programmatic ". At the end of 1629 he joined the brotherhood of the Charterhouse. While there his mind weakened, and in 1642 he issued a bombastic petition offering to do naval and military wonders. He died insane on April 16th, 1645.

His first published work was: "*The First Part of Ayres, French, Polish*, and others together, some in Tabliture, and some in Pricke-song: With Pauins, Galliards, and Almaines for the Viole de Gambo alone, and other musicall Conceites, for two Base Viols . . . and for two Leero-Viols . . . and some songs, *etc.* . . . . also an Invention for two to play upon one Viole" (1605). Two years later he published: "*Captain Humes Poeticall Musicke*. Principally made for two Basse-Viols, yet so contrived, that it may be plaied 8. severall waies upon sundry Instruments with much facilitie" (John Windet, 1607). The British Museum copy of this work was the one presented to Queen Anna (consort of James I), the back of the title-page bearing the following note in the composer's handwriting: "I doe in all humylitie beseech yr. Ma: that you woulde bee pleased to heare this Musick by mee ; hauinge excellent Instruments to performe itt ". The first piece is headed: "A new Musicke made for the Queenes most excellent Majestie, and my New-Yeeres gift to her Highnes ". About half-way through the book there is a sub-title, "Graue Musickes for three Bass-Viols with the Voice " followed by "The Hunting Song ", a "descriptive " piece illustrative of a stag-hunt. He seems to have been in difficult circumstances at the time of publication, for he begs in his dedication that the Queen should not "esteeme my songs unmusicall, because my Fortune is out of tune ", and adds that she was the "onely and last refuge of my long expecting hopes. . . ." British Museum manuscript *Add.* 15117 contains his "Faine would I chainge that note " (from the *First Part of Ayres*, 1605).

HUMFREY (Pelham): A talented composer of great individuality and importance, whose early death prevented him from fully developing his undoubted genius. One of the Restoration school of musicians, he necessarily came under the influence of the composers who catered for the tastes of Charles II. A declamatory style and a certain " theatrical vein " pervades to a greater or lesser degree the work of all the writers of this period. But it cannot be said that Humfrey employed these methods in anything but an artistic manner. Boyce goes so far as to say that he was the first of our ecclesiastical composers who had " the least idea of musical pathos in the expression of the words ", — which is, of course, hyperbolous. All his work is marked by directness of purpose, originality of treatment, and a certain melodic charm. There can be no doubt that he played a great part in founding a style that persisted until Purcell had given it a status of its own. In measuring the quality of Humfrey's genius we must never forget that he died at the age of twenty-seven, and that for a youth of such short experience his writing stands out as that of a highly gifted natural talent. Certainly he allowed human feelings to have more to say than the hard and fast rules of the earlier and more academic musicians. Hullah stated his achievements very concisely when he wrote that Pelham Humfrey, " like his master . . . formed his style, though at second hand, on that of Carissimi, and on his return home was the means of making his artistic brethren acquainted with a number of effects, many of them beautiful and all new, and a system of composition differing, in plan and detail, from that of the great English masters of the second period as widely as the ' Lyrical Ballads ' of Wordsworth differ from the ' Pastorals ' of Pope ". He also adds that he saw in Lully's works many " passages and turns of expression which I had heretofore believed to be the invention of Purcell ", and says that Humfrey's " connection with Lully explains everything ". The young Englishman was, as Riemann says, " one of the most important of the older English composers; and he was in effect a transitional composer who grafted on a good native foundation certain foreign characteristics that were being asked for by the English world of art. We cannot dream of comparing his work with that of Gibbons, say, neither in greatness of conception nor in continuity of style. But what he lacked in these particulars he made up for in a rhythmic and lyrical manner of writing that clearly exhibits the germs of the homophony that was coming.

Pelham Humfrey was born in 1647 and may have been related to Col. John Humfrey, one of Cromwell's adherents; at any rate,—if Anthony Wood is to be believed,—a pupil of that noted amateur musician. At the age of thirteen he appears in the lists of singers of the Chapel Royal (*L.C.R.*, 1660, *Vol.* 482) where he is entered under the heading " For Lutes and Voyces, theorboes and virginals ". He thus becomes one of the first set of Children of the Chapel Royal formed by Captain Henry Cooke at the Restoration. In another list he is given as a " member of the private musick ". He began to write very early, for in an entry of 1660 (with later additions) he is named jointly with Thomas Purcell as " composer ". This information, of course, may have been inserted at a later date; but much later it could not have been, for Clifford's *Divine Services and Anthems (second edition*, 1664) already contains the words of five anthems by " Pelham Humfrey one of the Children of His Majesties Chappel ". The celebrated " Club-

Anthem ", written in collaboration with two of his young colleagues in the Chapel—Turner and Blow, —also belongs to this very early period in his career. His talents were evidently recognized at court, for in 1664, at the age of seventeen, he was sent abroad for the purpose of further study. The expenses of his stay on the Continent were paid out of the Secret Service monies and amounted to 450*l.* " . . . to defray the charge of his journey into France and Italy " (200*l.* in 1664, 100*l.* in 1665, and 150*l.* in 1666). His absence from England could not have extended to more than three years, for on March 10th, 1665–6, he was appointed " musician for the lute in the place of Nicholas Lanier, deceased " (*L.C.R.*). On May 20th, 1666, the warrant admitting him to this post was issued, giving his salary as " 40*l.* yearly, with 16*l.* 2*s.* 6*d.* as livery, to commence the Annunciation last past ". In the same year he re-entered the Chapel Royal : " 1666. Mr. Thomas Hazard, one of the Gentlemen of his Majesties Chappell Royall, departed this life the 23 of January, 1666, in whose place was admitted Mr. Pelham Humfrey the next day following, and sworne the 26th day of October, 1667" (*Ch. Bk. C.R.*). On November 24th, 1666, his name is bracketed with those of Thomas Purcell and Matthew Lock for the composer's post (*L.C.R.*). He was probably appointed to his posts during his absence abroad, and the date of his return must have been shortly before his swearing-in at the Chapel Royal. This supposition is borne out by Pepys, who entered into his *Diary*: " November 1, 1667, . . . and so I came to Chapel . . . and heard a fine Anthem, made by Pelham (who is come over) in France, of which there was great expectation, and indeed is a very good piece of musique, but still I cannot call the Anthem anything but instrumental musique with the voice, for nothing is made of the words at all ". On the 15th of the same month the genial diarist wrote: " Thence I away home, . . . and there find . . . Mr. Caesar and little Pelham Humphreys, lately returned from France, and is an absolute Monsieur, as full of form and confidence, and

vanity, and disparages everything and everybody's skill but his own. The truth is, everybody says he is very able, but to hear how he laughs at all the King's musick here, as Blagrave and others . . ."; a very illuminating piece of information, which, if not based on prejudice, is at least a proof of Humfrey's youth. But Pepys confessed that he was biassed against the young composer on account of " his vanity ". The day following the music at the diarist's house, Pepys again heard work by Humfrey at Whitehall " before the King . . . I got into the theatre-room, and there heard both the vocall and instrumental musick, where the little fellow stood keeping time; but for my part, I see no great matter, but quite the contrary in both sorts of musique. The composition I believe is very good, but no more of delightfulness to the eare or understanding but what is very ordinary ". It should not be forgotten that there were many music - lovers in England at the Restoration period, who did not take kindly either to Charles's tastes in music, or to the importation of foreign methods, especially "the French fantastical light way", as Evelyn called it.

Although we have seen the name of Pelham Humfrey bracketed with those of Thomas Purcell and Lock as "composer" in 1666, we meet with the following in the Lord Chamberlain's Records for January 10th, 1671–2: "Thomas Purcell and Pelham Humphreys, gentlemen, appointed composers in ordinary to his Majesty for the violins without fee, and assistant to George Hudson, and upon the death or other avoydance, to come in ordinary with fee". In 1672 he was elected a warden of the "Corporacion for regulating the art and science of Musick", and towards the middle of that year more work was given him. A few days before the death of Captain Henry Cooke he was expected to check the practice of the violins in the band (*L.C.R.*, July 2nd, 1672). On July 15th, 1672, a warrant was issued "to swear and admit Pelham Humfrey in the place and quality of Master of the Children of his Majesty's Chapel Royal and composer in his Majesty's private musick for voyces

in ordinary, in the place of Henry Cooke deceased" (*L.C.R.*),—this being two days after Cooke's death. The Cheque-Book also notes the appointment of Humfrey in Cooke's place as Master of the Children. Being thus secured materially, Humfrey married, but all we know of his wife is that she was of remarkable beauty (*v.* John Stafford Smith's *Musica Antiqua*, 1812, *notes*, p. 10). Humfrey's salary at about this period was 200*l.* per annum (North, *Memoires of Musick*, ed. Rimbault, *note*, p. 98).

In addition to his duties at the Chapel Royal, and as composer, Humfrey was also given children to train in the art of music, and many entries in the State Papers refer to payments for this class of work. One specimen must suffice: "1673. May 2nd. Warrant to pay to Pelham Humfrey 58*l.* 19*s.* for the Children's learneing on the lute, violin, and theorbo, for fire, and strings for the musick room in the Chapel, for ruled paper and penns and inke, and for strings for the lutes, theorboes, and for other service by him done for half a year . . .", a detailed account following (*L.C.R.*).

At the end of the entry is the note: " In this warrant was nothing for fetching children from several Cathedrals, as is sometymes ". On July 24th, 1673, it was arranged that 24*l*. yearly be paid for his teaching and boarding of each of two boys " for his Majesty's private musique for voyces " (*L. C. R.*), that he receive Henry Cooke's salary of 40*l*. as musician for the " lute and voyce ", and that he be paid 20*l*. annually for strings,— " in all the sum of 108*l*. during his natural life ". The addition of all the monies derived from his several posts must have afforded him a comfortable income,—if promptly paid. By the autumn of that year it is evident that Humfrey found himself with too much to do, for on September 29th he entered into an agreement with John Lilly, by which the latter taught four of the children in the master's stead, receiving a proportionate share of the salary (*L.C.R.*).

Humfrey's death was recorded in the Cheque-Book of the Chapel Royal in these terms: " 1674. Mr. Pelham Humfrey one of the Gentlemen of his Majesty's Chapel Royal, and Master of the Children, departed this life at Windsor the 14th day of July, 1674, in whose place as Master of the Children came Mr. John Blow ". In his will, witnessed by Blow, Humfrey appointed his widow Catherine his " executrix and mistress " of all his goods. John Blow benefitted to the extent of 20*s*. for a ring. The will was made on April 23rd in the year of the testator's death. Pelham Humfrey was buried on July 17th, in the cloisters of Westminster Abbey. An epitaph stating the date of his death was no longer legible in the eighteenth century, but is given by Keepe (*Monumenta Westm.*).

The music by Humfrey that was published during the seventeenth century consisted mainly of short songs, and examples are to be seen in many of the collections of the period. In 1670 Humfrey collaborated with John Banister in the music to the Dryden and Davenant version of the *Tempest*, Humfrey's work being the song " Where the bee sucks ". It may be mentioned in passing that Humfrey also wrote " Where-ever I am" for Dryden's *Conquest of Granada* (1672). A large number of songs of differing types are contained in Playford's publications between 1673 and 1688. The celebrated song " I pass all my hours " (the words by Charles II) appeared in *Choice Ayres, Songs, and Dialogues, etc.* (1675). *The Pleasant Companion* (1682), *The Theater of Music* (1685), and *Harmonia Sacra* (1688), all contain examples of Humfrey's smaller pieces, but none are of sufficient importance to merit more detailed notice.

In the eighteenth century, " I pass all my hours" appeared again separately in 1700 and 1705, and three sacred vocal pieces are included in Book II of *Harmonia Sacra* (1714) together with a " Dialogue " written in collaboration with Blow. Boyce (*Cathedral Music*) printed three anthems for three voices and four for four voices, and from these a better idea of Humfrey's treatment of this class of music can be gained. Hawkins once more reproduced " I pass all my hours " (*History*).

Of more modern editions of Humfrey's music,

examples appeared in the *Cathedral Magazine* (*Vol.* II), and J. T. Field's *Music for the Church*; two anthems (" O Give Thanks unto the Lord " and " Hear, O Heavens ") were issued by Novello; the *Octavo Organ Book* (Vincent Edition) contains a Largo by Humfrey; Hullah gives a couple of anthems; and Professor Granville Bantock included " I pass all my hours " (with the original parts unaltered) and " O, The Sad Day " in his *Hundred Songs of England*. John Stafford Smith printed five songs by Humfrey (including " Wherever I am ") in his *Musica Antiqua*.

A tremendous quantity of Humfrey's music remains in manuscript. The British Museum has a great many handwritings containing work by him, *Harl.* 7338 and 7339 being particularly rich in examples of his sacred music. This is the collection made by Dr. Tudway, and includes the famous " Club-Anthem " together with a note by the compiler which is not borne out by history. Tudway thought that this anthem was written to celebrate a victory over the Dutch,—but the assertion does not bear close examination. The anthem was in all probability written as a little exercise by three friends. Further manuscripts giving work by Humfrey are: *Add.* 33287 (containing a birthday ode to the king, and a New Year's Ode), 30931–2, 31444, 31445, 31459, 29396, ("O The Sad Day", printed by Professor Bantock), 17784, 33235, 17820 ("Like as the Hart" and "Lord, teach us to number our days"), 29481, 35040, 34609 ("The Grand Chant"), 29968, 34203, 19759, 33239 (Evening Service in E-minor; and anthems from *Harl.* 7338–9), 33289, and 17840. Six anthems and a Service by Humfrey were transcribed into the books of the Chapel Royal (*L.C.R.*, August 1st, 1676). The library of Christ Church, Oxford, possesses manuscripts containing the Service in E-Minor (organ-part), anthems, and songs,— some of them copied from Playford's publications and Boyce's collection. The manuscripts in the Fitz-william Museum (Cambridge) provide a number of sacred compositions, some of them duplicated (30 *G.* 10, in the handwriting of Dr. Blow; 23 *H.* 13; 30 *G.* 24; and 32 *F.* 23). Further

examples of his work are preserved in manuscripts at Ely, Windsor, Salisbury, Christ Church, Oxford, and the Royal College of Music (London).

Pelham Humfrey led a busy but all too short life. At court his duties were many and exacting; he conducted, taught singing and three or four instruments, prevented the musicians from shirking their duties and practice, composed a great deal of music for various occasions, and played the lute and sang "tenner" himself. In addition he had to see that the Children of the Chapel were well cared for, clothed, and fed; and when one of them happened to be "sick of the small-pox" it also fell to him to nurse the invalid (*L.C.R.*, September 29th, 1673). He brought a lighter though more dramatic touch to the composition of sacred music, and introduced the instrumental symphonies which so pleased Charles II. Among his pupils is to be counted Henry Purcell, —and through the teachings of Humfrey the methods of Lully were made to influence the greatest of English dramatic composers.

HUMPHREY, HUMPHREYS (Pelham): see HUMFREY (Pelham). HUNNIS (William): A poet and musician of the sixteenth century, and for thirty years Master of the Children of the Chapel Royal. From the dedication to his *Abridgement, or Briefe Meditation on certaine of the Psalmes in English Metre* (1550) we gather that he was at that time in the service of the Right Hon. Sir William Harberde ; but according to *Stowe* 571 (*fol. 36b, B.M.*) he was in the Chapel Royal in 1552 (Edward VI). Being a Protestant of conspiratorial disposition he got into trouble during the reign of Mary Tudor. In 1555 he was among the dozen chosen to murder the Queen, but the attempt—if one were made— was unsuccessful. In 1556 he made another essay in treason against the State. He was asked to assist in robbing the treasury,—a course made easy by his friendship with Sir Nicholas Brigham, guardian of the royal treasure, —the object being to place Elizabeth on the throne with the money thus obtained. In this connection Froude (*History*) gives his name as Heneage. The date of this plot fits in badly with the fact that in March, 1555, he was arrested, tried, and cast into the Tower. It is possible that he was released before the accession of Elizabeth, since in 1557, he was admitted into the Company of the Grocers. This being so, he could well have taken part in the treasury breaking attempt. Once Elizabeth was on the throne he was safe, and in the first year of the reign he was appointed as a Gentleman of the Chapel Royal. In 1559 (June) Hunnis married Margaret Brigham, the widow of his friend. The union lasted only until the autumn of the same year, when Margaret died. As was common with Tudor Gentlemen of the Chapel Royal, Hunnis enjoyed certain posts which augmented his income. Thus in 1562 he was made keeper of the orchards and garden at Greenwich, with an accompanying salary of 12*d.* per day and further additions in kind. In 1566 he followed Richard Edwardes as Master of the Children (*Ch. Bk. C.R.*), and as such assisted at the entertainments given in honour of Elizabeth at Kenilworth, and at other similar performances. Whether he wrote the music to these interludes is not certain; but it is quite likely that he wrote the words at leaſt. In 1583 he petitioned for an increase of salary, saying that he could not keep an usher, a man-servant for the boys, and a woman to keep them clean on 6*d*. a day and per head with " 40*l*. a year for apparel and all expenses ". He further complained that no allowance was made for extraordinary expenses. What came of this petition is not known. William Hunnis " died the 6th June (1597), Maſter of the Children, and Nathaniell Giles sworne gentleman and Maſter of the Children in his place " (*Ch. Bk. C.R.*). Some lines written on the flyleaf of Sir Thomas More's works, and attributed to Hunnis, give the information that he appointed no executors in order to avoid ſtrife, and " because the goodes that I shall leave wyll not pay all I owe ".

Hunnis's chief works are *Certayne Psalmes chosen out of the Psalter of David and drawen furth into English meter* (1549); *A Hyve full of Hunnye, Contayning the firſt Book of Moses, called Genesis, turned into English Meter* (1578); " *Seuen Sobs of a Sorrowfull soule for Sinne*: Comprehending those seven Psalmes of David commonlie called Poenitentiall, *etc.*" (with music ; editions appearing in 1583, 1587, 1615); and others. He contributed to *The Paradyse of Daynty Devises* (1576), and several other publications.

HUNT (Arabella): A celebrated singer who enjoyed a high reputation during the laſt third of the seventeenth century. Praĉtically all that intereſts the musical reader concerning her career is to be found in Hawkins's *Hiſtory*, where a good account of her court-life under Queen Mary and Queen Anne (whom she taught singing when Princess) may be seen. Her voice was supposed to have resembled the piping of the bullfinch, and the poets and epigrammiſts of the day wrote in praise of her. She was also accounted an excellent luteniſt. John Blow and Henry Purcell, like the court and society, fell beneath her spell and both composed vocal numbers expressly for her use. Congreve's ode " On Mrs. Arabella Hunt's Singing " ſtands as one of the fineſt of his shorter poems.

HUNT (Thomas): A com-
poser whose chief claim to
distinction lies in the fact
that he was a contributor to
the *Triumphes of Oriana*
(1601). His work in that
collection was "Hark, did
ye ever hear so sweet a
singing?" (six-part). He is
described as a Bachelor of
Music, but no official record
of the degree having been
conferred is traceable. An
anthem of his belongs to the
Royal College of Music (London), and the words only of
an anthem are given in *Harl.*
6346 (*B.M.*). Of his life
nothing has so far been discovered.

HYGONS (Richard): A
fifteenth-century organist and
composer of ecclesiastical
music. From about 1487
until two years before his
death in 1509, he was organist
at Wells, where his efforts
must have been appreciated;
for the Dean and Chapter were
so pleased with him that they
gave him,—"for his diligent
labour and good service,"—
26s. 8d. a year over and
above his annual pension, the
money to come from "the
proceeds of a vacant stall".
Mr. J. E. West (*Cathedral
Organists*) says that Hygons
studied under Abyngdon, but
quotes no authority. From
the Chapter Acts of Wells,
it is clear that Hygons was
instructor of the children, for
he agreed to pay Richard
Bramston (*q.v.*) 40s. per
annum to take this duty off
his hands. Hygons is represented in the Eton College
manuscript by a "Salve
Regina".

I

INGLOTT (William): A celebrated organist and Master of the Children, the whole of whose activity appears to have been consecrated to the service of Norwich Cathedral. Born in 1554, he commenced his musical career as a chorister, becoming organist in 1608. As Master of the Children he succeeded his father in 1579. He died in 1621 at the age of sixty-seven, and was buried according to the memorial in the Cathedral, on the " last day of December ". He lies interred in Norwich Cathedral, and the epitaph alluded to informs us that,

" For Descant most, for Voluntary all
He passed on Organ, Song, and Virgainall."

The only music of his that I have been able to find is in the *Fitzwilliam Virginal Book*, — " A Galliard Ground " and " The Leaues bee greene " (*pp.* 375 and 381 of the printed edition prepared by Messrs. W. Barclay Squire and J. A. Fuller-Maitland

IVES (Simon): A vicar-choral of St. Paul's Cathedral, and composer of popular music, who flourished in the middle third of the seventeenth century. He was born at Ware (Hertfordshire) in July, 1600 (baptized on the 20th of the month), but nothing is known of the first thirty years of his life. In 1633 he must have been enjoying a high reputation among his contemporaries for in that year he collaborated with no less a musician than William Lawes in the composing of Shirley's masque *The Triumph of Peace*, which was performed by the Gentlemen of the Inns of Court, and for which he received the large sum of 100*l*. When the Civil War put a stop to his activities at the Cathedral, he supported himself by teaching singing. Nothing further is known of him except that in 1661 he returned to St. Paul's as a minor prebendary, and that he died in the City of London on July 1st, 1662.

Examples of his printed music may be seen in Lawes' *Choice Psalmes* (1648; an Elegy to the memory of his friend William Lawes, reprinted in Smith's *Musica Antiqua*, 1812); in *Court Ayres* (1655); in *Catch that*

Catch can (1658; three pieces à 3); in *Musick's Delight on the Cithren* (1666; two pieces); in *Musick's Recreation on the Viol, Lyra-way* (1669; eleven pieces); in the 1682 edition of the same (nine pieces); in the *Musical Companion* (1672; four pieces); and in Playford's *Select Ayres and Dialogues* (*Book* II). A Catch for three voices, " Come honeſt friends ", was reprinted in the *Lady's Magazine* for Auguſt, 1784, and a Glee à 3, "Now we're met, let's merry be ", was published in 1780(?). In the Chriſt Church (Oxford) library are preserved in manuscript the catch " Boy go down ", and " Sad clouds of grief " (elegy on the death of William Auſtin of Lincoln's Inn), besides several inſtrumental pieces including a *Fancy*, two *In Nomines*, and some dance-forms. The British Museum has a good deal of his music in *MSS. Add.* 17792–6, *Add.* 18940– 4, *Add.* 31423, *Add.* 31424, *etc.* (the laſt-named in the handwriting of John Jenkins).

Ives had a son, also named Simon, who contributed a piece to *Musick's Recreation on the Viol, Lyra-way*. He ſtudied at Cambridge, but nothing further is known of him.

J

JACKSON (John): An organist active at Wells Cathedral in the second half of the seventeenth century. It is almost certain that he is to be identified with the John Jackson, who was teacher of the choristers at Ely, for a single quarter in 1669. He became a vicar-choral and organist at Wells in 1674, and is mentioned in the Cathedral records until 1688. He died probably during 1689, for his widow Dorothy was granted the administration of his estate in December. A couple of anthems of his were printed by Playford in Deering's *Cantica Sacra* (1674), and these (with a piece in the *Theater of Music, Bk.* IV, 1687), as far as I can discover, are the only specimens of his work that have been printed. In manuscript there are an anthem ("The Lord said unto my Lord") in *Harl.* 7338 (*B.M.*); the words and melody only of another anthem (one of those in *Cantica Sacra*) in *Add.* 29396 (*B.M.*); a Service at Wells Cathedral; and the organ-part of eight anthems and some chants in the Royal College of Music (London).

A few incomplete parts of other compositions are in the books at Wells.

JEFFREYS (Christopher): *see* JEFFREYS (George).

JEFFREYS (George) (*also* JEFFRIES): A voluminous composer of sacred music who flourished at the middle of the seventeenth century. His son Christopher was a personal friend of Anthony Wood, and thus the information given by the latter may be accepted in this case without fear. According to the Oxford gossip's manuscript *Lives of the Musicians* (*Bodl.*), Jeffreys was a descendant of Matthew Jeffries, an Elizabethan church musician. George was organist to Charles I when the king was at Oxford in 1643, and five years later became steward of the Hatton estate in Northamptonshire. In the British Museum (Hatton-Finch Correspondence) are a number of letters written by Jeffreys to his employer on matters connected with the property in his charge. He died not later than 1685.

George Jeffreys left a huge quantity of sacred music of no outstanding merit, the

British Museum and the collection at the Royal College of Music (London) containing manuscripts with over a hundred compositions,—most of them in autograph. Further examples are preserved in the Christ Church library (Oxford). He wrote Latin motets as well as English anthems.

His son Christopher gained a scholarship at Westminster School and went to Christ Church (Oxford) in 1659. In 1663 he became a Bachelor of Arts and three years later Master. Wood says he was a good organist and virginalist, but he does not appear to have practised as a professional musician.

JEFFREYS (Matthew): A Bachelor of Music (Oxford) of 1593–4 and vicar-choral of Wells Cathedral. Thomas Myriell's collection (*B.M. Add.* 29372–7) contains three sacred compositions by him, and further specimens of his work are included in *Add.* 17792–6 and *Add.* 30478–9.

JEFFRIES (Christopher, George, Matthew): *see* JEFFREYS.

JENKINS (John): A very popular seventeenth-century composer, chiefly of bass-viol music, and an excellent performer on that instrument.

His work appealed principally on account of its suitability to the instrument for which it was written, and because it was attractive rather than academic. According to Roger North he was "a person of much easier temper than any of his faculty, he was neither conceited nor morose, but much a gentleman and had a very good sort of wit, which served him in his address and conversation, wherein he did not please less than in his compositions". Yet, in spite of the "horse-loads" of music that Jenkins is said to have composed, practically nothing of his is known to-day, except a little three-part round "A Boat, a Boat, Haste to the Ferry". Even when North wrote the *Memoires of Musick*, Jenkins had already declined from the great favour in which he had been held a little earlier, so that the writer of the *Memoires* was constrained to say: "For nothing is more fashion than musick . . . and the grand custome of all is to effect novelty, and to goe from one thing to another and despise the former . . ." Still, during his long lifetime, he supplied most of the instrumental music in use, also writing some very pleasant vocal pieces. In his writing we see very well the evolution of that essentially English form of composition,—the *Fancy*, —and the *In Nomine* theme can be followed in almost all of them sandwiched between the other parts weaving their elaborate web above and below it. Thus Jenkins's work becomes quite important historically (*see also Dic. Old Engl. Mus. s.v.* " Fancy " *and* " In Nomine "). Taken altogether, Jenkins, with his often excellent work and occasionally careless, hurried writing, forms instrumentally a connecting link between the Elizabethans and the Stuarts.

John Jenkins was born at Maidstone, Kent, in 1592, and although we do not know under whom he studied it is evident from his work that he must have acquired the principles of his art from one of the more orthodox of the Elizabethans. We must expect a considerable variation in his style when we remember that his life extended from the reign of Elizabeth to that of Charles II. He was very skilful on both Lute and Bass-Viol, and on the latter instrument (in the handling known as Lyra-way) he became a virtuoso.

He performed before Charles I, who was himself a good gambist, and very much pleased that monarch by doing " wonders on an inconsiderable instrument ". Yet when he was engaged as a court musician it was as lutenist. He lived on terms of great friendship with such men as Christopher Sympson, Stefkins, William Lawes, and others, and his readiness to appreciate the talents of others provided another reason for his popularity.

During the unsettled times of the Civil War the court organizations were disbanded, and Jenkins, in common with the other Royal musicians, was forced to seek a means of livelihood elsewhere. He does not appear to have suffered many deprivations during this period, for he was made very welcome wherever he went, and as Roger North says, " in most of his friends' houses there was a chamber called by his name ", and he was always " courted to stay ". His first patron was one Dering or Deerham, a landed gentleman of Norfolk, and it was through his influence that Jenkins was later admitted to the houses of the other county worthies. Thus he was entertained by Sir Hamon L'Estrange, and taught the son of the house,—the celebrated Roger L'Estrange. The dates relating to Jenkins's movements at this period of his life are very uncertain. He probably stayed with Sir Hamon until the death of the patron in 1654, but what happened between this date and 1660, when he entered the service of Lord North at Kirtling, is not to be determined. Here he appears to have spent about six happy and musically active years, teaching Montague and Roger North for one pound a quarter. Roger North became the famous writer of the *Memoires of Musick*, a work that affords the best account of Jenkins's life, and in it he says, " I never heard that he articled with any gentleman where he resided, but accepted what they gave him ". Soon after the Restoration Jenkins was once more appointed to the royal music, the Lord Chamberlain's Records containing the entry, " June 16th, 1660. Mr. Jenkins for the lute . . ." At St. Andrew, 1660, the payment of 16*l*. 2*s*. 6*d*. for livery is ordered. In another list dated 1660 Jenkins is entered as a player on the

theorbo, while on December 31st, his salary was fixed at 40*l*. per annum. On July 16th, 1661, a warrant was issued for the payment of 20*l*. to Jenkins for a year's supply of strings. A large number of entries referring to this royal appointment are to be seen in the State Papers until 1678. But although Jenkins was allowed to keep his court place until his death, it is evident that his health did not permit him to attend to his court duties during the last few years of his life ; so much we may learn from North's *Memoires*. Jenkins spent the closing years of his life at Kimberley in Norfolk as the guest of Sir Philip Wodehouse, and died on October 27th, 1678. He must have been superseded a little earlier than this, for we read in the Lord Chamberlain's Records under date September 27th, 1678 : " Order for the allowance of a yearly livery to John Mosse in the place of John Jenkins ". In the parish register of Kimberley is to be read: " John Jenkins, Esq., was buried October 29th, 1678 ", and on the chancel floor of the church there is a slab in which the following is incised :

"Under this Stone Rare Jenkins lie,
The Mafter of the Musick Art;
Whom from ye earth the God on High,
Call'd unto Him to bear his Part;
Aged eighty-six, October twenty-seven,
In anno seventy-eight he went to Heaven."

And under this ftone lies the musician whom Anthony Wood called "the little man with the great soul".

It will be impossible to mention all Jenkins's works, for even Roger North said he could not "give an account of his compositions, they were so many that he himself outlived the knowledge of them". Examples of his writing that were printed can be seen in Henry and William Lawes's *Choice Psalms*, 1648 (*Part* II, "An Elegiack Dialogue on the sad losse of his much-efteemed Friend, Mr. William Lawes"); in Edward Benlowe's ("Benevolus") *Theophila*, "several parts thereof set to fit Aires by Mr. John Jenkins"; and in John Hilton's *Catch that Catch Can* (1652 and 1658) is to be found the only piece by which Jenkins is remembered to-day, the round "A Boat, A Boat, Hafte to the Ferry". The same work contains also "Come pretty Maidens," for three voices, and in its later form (as the *Musical Companion*, 1667 and 1672), "See, See the bright light shine" and "When fair Aurora" (both in two parts). Playford's *Musick's Recreation on the Lyra-Viol* (1652) contains eight pieces for that inftrument, while in the edition of 1669 there are some pieces not in the earlier issue. Several short dance-forms are to be seen in Playford's *Court Ayres*. In Playford's *Musick's Hand-Made* (1663) we find the "Mitter Rant", a very popular composition at the time. This does not by any means exhauft the lift of works containing specimens of Jenkins's works, but enough have been named to make it possible for those interefted in the man to see examples of his art. Goovaerts, in his *Hiftoire et Bibliographie de la Typographie musicale dans les Pays-Bas*, gives, "J. Jenkins. Engels Speel-Threfoor van CC. de nieuwfte Allemanden, Couranten, Sarabanden, Ayres, *etc.* gefteld door elf de konftighfte Violiften deser tydt in England voor Bass en Viool, en ander Speel gereetschap, mede LXVII spelſtucken als Allemanden, Couranten, *etc.* voor twee Violes en Bass, als mede een Bassus continuus ad placidum. Amſterdam. 1664 ". This would appear to have been a very intereſting collection of English Viol music if it ever had exiſtence; but unfortunately I have never been able to trace a copy. I include the Goovaerts entry in the hope that it may meet the eye of the fortunate possessor of an example of the book. Similar myſtery overshadows the *Twelve Sonatas for Two Violins and Bass*, which, according to Hawkins, were the " firſt essay towards the introduction of the Sonata into England ". Many authorities mentioned the work, but no one has yet seen a copy; and I am firmly of opinion that this work never exiſted in print and that the origin of the ſtory lay in the manuscript set of sonatas in the Bodleian library. The only writer I have found with the courage to confess his ignorance respecting these sonatas was Henry Davey (*Hiſt. of Engl. Mus.*) who says: " I have been unable to verify

Hawkins's ſtatement (copied by all other writers), *etc.*" Later reprints of a few of Jenkins's pieces are in John Stafford Smith's *Musica Antiqua* (1812),—" Sute in D-sol-re ", from *New Lessons for Viols or Violins*, 1678, " Lady Katherine Audley's Bells " and the " Mitter Rant ". Hullah's *Hiſtory of the Transitional Period* contains a Fancy, and Burney and Busby both give the " Five-Bell Consort ". The music of the round " A Boat, A Boat ", was issued by F. Lancelott (Standard Edition), but the words differ from the original. Concerning the " Five-Bell Consort " or " Lady Catherine Audley's Bells " it may be intereſting to note that Burney, Busby, and all who copied them, suppose that this " conceit " owed its origin to a book published in 1668,—*Tintinalogia, or the Art of Ringing*; but unfortunately for the theory, this and many similar pieces called " Bells " or " La Cloche" appeared before the book was printed.

It will be impossible to give more than the location and numbers of the manuscripts containing work by Jenkins, for in this form there are literally " horseloads ". In the British Museum there are *Add.* 15118, *Add.* 17792–6, *Add.* 18940–4, *Add.* 27550, *Add.* 29290, *Add.* 29369, *Add.* 30487, *Add.* 31423 (*Autograph* ; containing many dance-forms by different composers and copied by Jenkins, besides some work of his own), *Add.* 31424 (*Autograph*), *Add.* 31426 (*Id.*), *Add.* 31428 (containing twenty-one Fancies by Jenkins), *Add.* 30488–90 (containing the same Fancies as the last manuscript, differently arranged; *No.* 12 is dated 18 Dec., 1661, *No.* 13, 2 Jan., 1666, and *No.* 21, 27th January, 1666), *Add.* 31430 (containing what the catalogue says are " evidently the ' Twelve Sonatas ' . . . published by him in 1660 "; the handwriting appears to be that of John Playford, and possible mention by him of these pieces may have been the origin of the rumour referred to above), *Add.* 31431, *Add.* 31432, *Add.* 36993, and many others. Examples of work by Jenkins are preserved also in manuscripts in the collections of the Music School and Christ Church (Oxford), the latter library containing a large amount of instrumental music for various combinations, and some sacred music; the Royal College of Music (London); and the Municipal Library of Hamburg. The majority of these manuscripts are, of course, only copies from the originals of Jenkins, and instrumentalists desirous of scoring any of these works would do well to consult an autograph where possible, for copyists were not always as careful as they might have been.

JEWETT *or* JEWITT (Randall *or* Randolph): A seventeenth-century organist and composer of ecclesiastical music. Born apparently at Chester at the beginning of the century, he was a chorister there,—if he is to be identified with " Randle Juet ",—between 1612 and 1615. Hawkins, without proving his statements with documentary evidence, says that Jewett was a *Mus. Bac.* of Dublin, that he was a pupil of Orlando Gibbons, and that he " acquired great esteem for his skill ". His first appointment as organist was to Christ Church Cathedral, Dublin, in 1631. He held that post until 1639, when his place was occupied by Benjamin Rogers. Two years later Rogers left and Jewett resumed his work at the Cathedral for another year or thereabouts. Simultaneously he was organist at St. Patrick's Cathedral, Dublin (1631–42). In 1643–4 he was organist at Chester Cathedral; but exactly how long he stayed is not known, since the records dealing with the two decades from 1644 onwards have been lost. He probably left Chester as soon as the first Civil War ended, for we find him as a vicar-choral at Dublin in 1646. The exact date of his arrival in London is not to be determined; but in 1660 he became almoner of St. Paul's Cathedral (London), and in the following year a minor canon. In 1666 he migrated to Winchester, where he held the important posts of organist and instructor of the choir, besides being a lay-vicar. Jewett died at Winchester on July 3rd, 1675, at the age of seventy-two, and was buried in the Cathedral.

An example of his work may be examined in Tudway's collection (*B.M. Harl.* 7339; "I heard a voice from Heav'n", described in the manuscript as by "Mr. Jewett of Exeter"). The

words of four more anthems are contained in Clifford's work. He also wrote an Evening Service, but of all his compositions the only one now known complete in all its parts is the anthem in the Harleian MS. mentioned above.

JOHNSON (Edward): A madrigalist of some note who, from the fact that he is mentioned by Francis Meres (*Palladis Tamia*, 1598) and contributed to Este's *Whole Booke of Psalmes* (1592) and to the *Triumphes of Oriana* (1601), must have been considered by his contemporaries as one of the foremost musicians of his day. His *Oriana* contribution ("Come blessed byrd", à 6) does not compel us to think less of him; and though his work in Este's Psalter is of not nearly so high a standard,— nor even in keeping with the best traditions of the true Tudors,—his art, taken as a whole, certainly secures for him a worthy place in the history of purely English music.

I see no reason for disagreeing with Mr. G. E. P. Arkwright's suggestion in *Grove* (1913) that Edward Johnson was possibly employed to contribute some of the music for the entertainment of Queen Elizabeth on her visit to Lord Hertford at Elvethum (September, 1591), and this would be the first dated piece of information connected with him (*v. Grove*, 1913, II, 537; *B.M. Add.* 30480–4; and Nichol's *Progresses of Q. Elizabeth*). His degree of *Mus. Bac.* dates from 1594 (Cambridge), and in his supplication he mentions that he has practised music for many years. From the documents at Hengrave Hall it appears that Johnson was employed in the household of Sir Thomas Kytson, contemporaneously with Wilbye, and that on the death of Sir Thomas the two musicians were not on the best of terms.

Besides contributing to the two famous works already mentioned, Edward Johnson has three pieces,—one, " Thomson's Medley " by himself, and a Pavane and Galliard of his " sett by Will. Byrd ",—in the *Fitzwilliam Virginal Book*. A three-part madrigal (two sections) is in manuscript in the Royal College of Music. His fame spread abroad, for he is represented by instrumental music in Füllsack's *Auserlesene Paduanen und Galliarden*

(1607–9) and in Thomas Simpson's *Taffel-Consort* (1621). It is not to be decided with certainty whether music signed simply " Johnson " in some of the old manuscripts (*e.g. B.M. Add.* 30485 and *Eg.* 2046) is to be attributed to Edward Johnson or to the more celebrated lutenist of the same surname.

JOHNSON (John): A celebrated lutenist of the Elizabethan era. The date of his birth is not known, nor is there any evidence to show when he entered the Queen's service. In 1581 he received 1*l.* as a New Year's Gift (*Harl.* 1644; *B.M.*), in 1586 he is named as one of the Queen's " musicians " (*Harl.* 1641), and in 1593–4 he is still included in the list of royal musicians (*Annalen*, quoting from *Harl.* 1642). He must have died between 1594 and 1595, for in the latter year his widow, Alice, received a lease of a manor house in Dorset in appreciation of John Johnson's services (*Cal. S.P.*, January 25th, 1595). His place was not filled until 1599 when his successor, Edward Collard, was appointed (*Cal. S.P.*). He may have been in the service of Sir Thomas Kytson of Hengrave, a supposition which is strengthened by the circumstance that Sir George Carey, to whom his son Robert was articled, was married to Kytson's grand-daughter. Rimbault confuses John Johnson with more than one other Johnson.

JOHNSON (Robert) (I): A Scottish priest who, to escape a charge of heresy, fled to England. He flourished in the first half of the sixteenth century, and probably lived at Windsor. John Baldwin, when writing his manuscript volume in the royal collection, speaks of Johnson as " of Windsor ", and in a manuscript in the Christ Church library (Oxford) he is described as a " peticanon of Windsore ". He is a figure of some importance,—certainly the most important composer that Scotland had produced. He is often referred to as having been chaplain to Anne Boleyn, but apart from John Stafford Smith's remarks, there appears to be no proof of this. In dealing with Johnson's music the greatest care must be exercised. So many musicians bearing the name were active at or near the period under consideration, that it is by no means easy to decide with certainty whether manuscript pieces headed '' Johnson '', or even " Robert Johnson ", are the works of this man or not. Of the compositions known to be his the following are the more important: Three compositions in Day's *Certaine Notes* (1560), and the same publisher's *Morning and Evening Prayer* (1565); " Ave Domini Filia " (*MS. in R.C.M.*); " Ave Dei Patris filia " (*MS.* in *B.M. Add. 5059, and in the Bodleian, Oxford*); " Domine in Virtute " (*MS. B.M. Add. 33933; St. Michael's College, Tenbury ; and Christ Church and Bodleian, Oxford*); " Sabbatum Maria " (*Christ Church, Oxford; printed by Burney, History*); " Laudes Deo " (*Buckingham Palace, now B.M.; and Christ Church, Oxford*), besides compositions in the British Museum in *Add.* 29240, *Add.* 30480–4, *Add.* 17802–5, and *Harl.* 4900. Secular songs are to be seen in *Add.* 30480–4, *Add.* 30513, and *Harl.* 7578. " Defyled is my name " (alleged to be the complaint of Anne Boleyn) was printed by Hawkins. Some instrumental compositions are also to be attributed to this Robert Johnson.

JOHNSON (Robert) (II): A celebrated composer and lutenist of the early seventeenth century. It will be well to notice that much confusion exists in the writings of the earlier historians, and those who copied them, on the subject of this musician. It was probably Rimbault who first confounded this Robert Johnson with Edward Johnson (*q.v.*) and the writer of the article on him in the *Dictionary of National Biography* still falls into the same error. Robert Johnson II was a son of the Elizabethan lutenist John Johnson, and all that is known of his youth is that he was apprenticed to Sir George Carey as a servant in 1596, the master engaging to be responsible for the youth's musical education, etc. (*v.* Mr. W. Barclay Squire's article in *Musical Times* for February, 1897). Eight years later he entered the royal service as lutenist, and according to a list printed by Hawkins, served in a like capacity in the establishment of Prince Henry in 1611. At the funeral of James I he is mentioned with the rest of the consort (*L.C.R., Vol.* 557). His salary in 1626 was 40*l.* per annum, with an additional

20*l.* for strings. In 1628 he petitioned for the post rendered vacant by the death of Thomas Lupo (*Annalen*). He died before November 26th, 1633, for on that date the famous player Duvall was appointed to one of the posts held by Robert Johnson, " deceased ", and Lewis Evans to another (*L.C.R., Vol.* 738). Johnson enjoyed a very high reputation and was much in request as a composer for the stage and as a performer. Mace (*Musick's Monument*, 1676) makes the lute say: " Despair I do; old Dowland he is dead; Robert Johnson too ; Two famous men ".

Specimens of his work may be seen in Leighton's *Teares or Lamentacions* (1614), in Playford's *Select Musical Ayres and Dialogues* (editions of 1652 and 1659; " As I walkt forth "), in Hilton's *Catch that Catch Can* (1652), and other mid-seventeenth century publications. " As I walkt forth " was reprinted by Rimbault as No. 7 of his *Ancient Vocal Music of England*. His fame spread abroad, and he is represented in Brade's *Newe Ausserlesene Branden*, etc. (1617), and in Simpson's *Taffel Consort* (1621: Eitner, *Quellen-*

Lexicon). J. Wilson printed examples of Johnson's music for ſtage use in his *Cheerful Ayres and Ballads* (1660), and Rimbault attributes to Johnson a composition in Middleton's *Witch* (*Ancient Vocal Music of England*, No. 1). Johnson also set songs used in plays by Beaumont and Fletcher. Manuscripts containing music by Robert Johnson II are preserved in the British Museum (*Royal App.* 63; *Add.* 11608; *Add.* 29396; *Add.* 29289; *Add.* 15117; *Add.* 31418; and others). He is also represented in the library of Chriſt Church, Oxford. The *Fitzwilliam Virginal Book* contains a Pavane by Robert Johnson arranged for the virginal by Giles Farnaby, and three Almains, one of them "set" by the same virginaliſt.

JONES (Robert) (I). A composer of sacred and secular vocal music who flourished round about 1530. Nothing is known of his life, and the only works I have been able to trace are a Mass (*Spes Noſtra*) and a *Magnificat* in the Peterhouse (Cambridge) Part-Books, and a three-part song, — "Who shall haue my fayr lady",— in Wynkyn de Worde's song-book of 1530 (*Triplex*

and *Bassus* parts in *B.M.*). *Add.* 34191, also in the British Museum, contains the bass-part of a work by Robert "Jonys", who may be identified with this Jones. This musician muſt not be confused with the Elizabethan luteniſt of the same name (*v. inf.*).

JONES (Robert) (II): One of the moſt celebrated of the Elizabethan luteniſts and vocal composers. He was one of the very firſt to write the true solo song with inſtrumental accompaniment, and although not to be compared with the beſt of his contemporaries on the score of dignity and harmonic ingenuity, he merits an important place in the hiſtory of English music. His *Second Book of Ayres* (1601) ranks with the work of Rosseter and Campian as the earlieſt example of solo-song writing. In this book Jones asserts that there had "not been anie extant of this fashion",—and, indeed, if Jones or Rosseter and Campian claim priority, there can be a difference of only a few weeks between the dates at which the two works were published; at any rate, not far enough apart for one to have copied the other. Even

T

the innovator Caccini, though he may have sung his monodic compositions before the end of the sixteenth century, was a year later than the three Englishmen mentioned above in the publication of his *Nuove Musiche* (1602).

Of Robert Jones's biography very little has come to light; but that little is all well-authenticated. We meet with him first in 1597 when he graduated as a Bachelor of Music at Oxford (April 29th, from St. Edmund Hall). He is given under that date as having studied music for sixteen years (Clark; *Registers, Univ. of Oxford*), and from this information some guess may be made at the date of his birth,—which may well have been *ca.* 1570. Beyond the publication of his works, only two more pieces of information remain,—both connected with the stage. The first was the granting of a licence in 1610 to Robert Jones, Rosseter, and others, to instruct children for the Queen's revels ; the other was a patent dated 13 *James I* (1615) empowering Jones and three associates to build on the ground occupied by his house at Blackfriars (near Puddle Wharf) a playhouse for the performances of these children. Why objection should have been raised to the project when the building was almost complete is not clear; all we know is that the Lord Mayor and Aldermen of London obtained the royal order to render the edifice unfit for its intended use within three days. The date of Jones's death is unknown.

His earliest publication was *The First Booke of Songes and Ayres of four parts* with a lute accompaniment in tablature (1600). The next work was *The Second Booke of Songs and Ayres*, " set out to the Lute, the Base Violl, the Playne way, or the Base by tablature after the leero fashion " (*i.e.* " lyra-way ", *q.v.* in *Dic. Old Engl. Mus.*), published in 1601. In the same year he contributed to the *Triumphes of Oriana* the six-part madrigal " Fair Oriana, seeming to wink at folly ". The vogue enjoyed by the madrigal at that period was probably responsible for his next work; he certainly possessed no talent for this class of composition comparable with that of many of his contemporaries. This work was *The First Set of Madrigals* " of 3, 4, 5, 6, 7, 8, parts, for Viols and Voices, or for Voices alone, or as you please " (1607). In the following year he issued *Ultimum Vale*, " or the Third Book of Ayres of 1, 2, and 4 Voyces ", of which the Royal College of Music (London) owns what seems to be the only known example. A year later he produced *A Musicall Dreame, Or the Fourth Booke of Ayres* (1609), containing numbers for two voices, lute, and gamba; four voices, lute, and bass-viol; and " one voyce alone, or to the lute, the Base Viole, or to both if you please ". In 1610 appeared *The Muses Gardin for Delights, or the Fift Booke of Ayres only for the Lute, the Base Vyoll and Voyce*. Mr. W. Barclay Squire published a beautiful numbered edition of the words only in 1901, giving a reproduction of the original title-page, and adding a biographical notice of the composer. In that essay Mr. Barclay Squire denies the persistent legend that Jones was a poet and wrote the words of his songs, pointing out that the composer more than once alludes to the " ditties " having been written by others, and showing that the style of the poems varies so much that

they could not have come from any one pen. The *Gardin for Delights* appears to have been the last of his own publications. Sir William Leighton's *Teares or Lamentacions* of 1614 contains three pieces by Jones, and these would be the last of his compositions to be printed during his life-time.

Modern reprints of Jones's music include: " Farewell deare love since thou wilt needs be gone " (mentioned by Shakespeare in *Twelfth Night*) from the *First Booke of Ayres* (1600), and " My love bound me with a Kisse that I should no longer stay " (from the *Second Booke of Songes and Ayres*, 1601), in John Stafford Smith's *Musica Antiqua* (1812); two songs from *Ultimum Vale* (1608) in Rimbault's *Ancient Vocal Music of England*; the *Oriana* madrigal in L. Benson's and Dr. E. H. Fellowes' editions; " Sweet Kate " (from *A Musicall Dreame*) edited by A. Somervell in 1897, and " Though your Strangeness " (from the same) in C. K. Scott's edition of 1905.

In manuscript one or two sacred compositions remain, the British Museum *Royal App.* 63, and a manuscript in the Christ Church library (Oxford), containing ecclesiastical music of his. The latter collection also possesses in manuscript four songs copied from the *Second Booke of Songes and Ayres* (1601).

JONŸS (Robert): *see* JONES (Robert).

K

KINDERSLEY (Robert): A musician "for the lute and voice" and also a bass-violist in the service of Charles I. We meet with him as a royal musician first in the Lord Chamberlain's Records, under date July 15th, 1628; on April 12th, 1631, he is entered as a player on the bass-viol; and on March 28th, 1633 (*L.C.R.*) we hear of the appointment of "Robert Tomkins, a musician for the consort, in the place of Robert Kyndersley, deceased". He is twice represented in Leighton's *Teares and Lamentacions* (1614), Nos. 14 and 52 being from his pen.

KING (Robert): A member of the private music of Charles II, having been appointed on February 6th, 1679-80 "with fee, in the place of John Bannister, deceased" (*L.C.R.*). He served in a similar capacity in the establishments of James II, William and Mary, and Anne. In 1684-5 (January 26th) he was among the musicians ordered to practise for a ball "which is to be before his Majesty" at the Theatre Royal (*Id.*). In 1689 he was appointed "Composer in ordinary" (*Id.*). He became a Bachelor of Music at Cambridge in 1696. Riemann states that he instituted with Johann Wolfgang Franck some public concerts in London between 1690 and 1693, basing his information on a *Musical Antiquary* article by Mr. W. Barclay Squire (*v.* Riemann, *Lexicon, Ed.* 1922, *p.* 378).

King's works were chiefly of a popular nature, and examples may be seen in *The Theater of Music* (*Bk. I*, 1685, four pieces; *Bk. II*, 1685, five pieces; *Bk. III*, 1685, three pieces; *Bk. IV*, 1687, one piece), and in the second book of *Harmonia Sacra* (1693; "A Divine Hymn" for two voices). He contributed songs to Crowne's *Sir Courtly Nice*, wrote a St. Cecilia Ode (1690), and is represented in many other contemporary publications. A set of twenty-four of his songs appeared in one book (Walsh). It is not known when he died,—but it was certainly after 1711.

KING (William): A composer of sacred and secular vocal music and organist who flourished in the second half of the seventeenth century.

Born at Winchester (where
his father, George King, was
organist) in 1624, he became
a clerk of Magdalen College
(Oxford) in 1648. He
graduated in Arts in the
following year. During the
Civil War he was one of the
eminent circle of musicians
who collected at Oxford. He
became organist of New
College (Oxford) in 1663,
and held that post until his
death in 1680 (Novem-
ber 17th). His works in-
clude a Service in B-flat,
by which he is best known,
the Litany from which has
been published by Novello
under the editorship of John
B. Lott, *B.Mus.* The same
publishing firm has also
issued (edited by John E.
West) the anthem "The Lord
is King" (four voices and
chorus). A volume of William
King's secular songs was published at Oxford in 1668,
the book containing some
very interesting work.
KINNERSLEY (Robert):
see KINDERSLEY (Robert).
KIRBYE (George): A
talented composer of
madrigals and sacred music
who flourished towards the
end of the Elizabethan era.
His work, although not
voluminous, is excellent in
workmanship, and, in his best

examples, marked by real
dignity, and other enduring
qualities. Like most of the
Elizabethan madrigalists
Kirbye was given to harmonic
experimenting, frequently
using, as Byrd did, the major
and minor third on one root;
a practice that was, as Mr.
Arkwright suggests in his
admirable edition of the
madrigals, not successful.
That excellent editor gives
an interesting account of this
and other "licences" which
Kirbye sanctioned; but even
if we cannot see beauty in
all the dissonances which he
produces by forcing passages
in contrary motion and so
forth, it does at least show
him to have possessed a progressive spirit and a good
deal of healthy imagination.
After all, the fault was caused
by one of the virtues of the
whole school of English madrigalists,—the ardent desire
to portray the mood of the
poetry in the music which was
set to it. At the same time
there are compositions of
sheer beauty among Kirbye's
works, and sometimes he
attains to really great heights.
On the whole his work lacks
the spontaneous gaiety of
Morley, but his melancholy
is often very impressive.
It is not known when

George Kirbye was born, but assuming that he was about twenty-seven years of age when he contributed to Este's Psalter, he muſt have been born somewhere near 1565. This date would make him sixty-nine years old at his death, which is not an unreasonable age. It is in Este's publication that we meet with his name for the firſt time, and he moſt certainly muſt have enjoyed a considerable reputation by then, for he was one of the two chief contributors. After the appearance of this Psalter we hear no more of him for five years. In 1597 he issued the set of madrigals upon which his fame reſts to-day: *The Firſt Set of English Madrigalls to 4, 5, and 6 voyces*, " Made and newly published by George Kirbye ". The book contains twenty-four numbers which the composer describes, with that modeſty to which we become accuſtomed after reading a few Elizabethan dedications, as the firſt fruits of his " poore knowledge in Musicke ". As a matter of faƈt his knowledge in music was very great indeed. The dedication to the daughters of " Syr Robert Jermin . . . my very good maiſter " gives us one of the few pieces of information that we possess concerning Kirbye's life. In addressing the young ladies he says that the madrigals " . . . for your delight and contentments were firſt by me compiled ". There can be little doubt, then, that he was employed in the Jermyn household at Rushbrooke Hall, near Bury St. Edmunds. The set of madrigals was reprinted by Mr. Arkwright in *Parts* III–V of his *Old English Edition* (1891) and by Dr. Fellowes in *Vol.* XXIV of *The English Madrigal School.* The only other printed work of Kirbye's is the six-part madrigal in the *Triumphes of Oriana* (1601), —" Bright Phoebus greetes moſt cleerely ". Kirbye's music appears to have been firſt set to words beginning " With Angells face and brightnesse ", and copies of the colleƈtion are known giving one or other of these poems. The music is the same in both cases, and no reason for the change can be discovered, unless it be because another contributor to the *Triumphes* had already used the other text. William Hawes's (1814) and L. Benson's (1907) editions of the madrigal begin with

" Bright Phoebus ", as does the Bodleian library example of the original. The British Museum copy gives the other text (v. also Dr. E. H. Fellowes, *The English Madrigal Composers*).

Only two more pieces of information remain. The first is an entry relating to the burial of Kirbye's wife, Anne, at St. Mary's, Bury St. Edmunds (June 11th, 1626), and the second the evidence of his death in his will. Mr. G. E. P. Arkwright gives this document in *Part* V of the *Old English Edition*, and from it we learn that Kirbye made it on March 10th, 1633. He bequeathed " to Agnes Seaman his servant and kinswoman to his late wife deceased, all that messuage and tenement wherein he dwells .. situate in Whiting Street, in Burie St. Edmond . . ." No children are mentioned; but to his brother Walter and to his sister Alice he left 10*l*. each. The will was proved on October 7th, 1634,—the musician having been buried at St. Mary's the previous day (*Bury Wills, Liber Colman*, 1631–5, *fol.* 368). I am indebted to Mr. Arkwright for this information,—and, indeed, practically all we know of Kirbye's life is the result of that gentleman's researches.

Some little sacred and secular music in manuscript (most of it incomplete,—the rest being adaptations from printed pieces) is preserved in the British Museum and the Royal College of Music (London), and in the Christ Church and Bodleian libraries (Oxford). In addition to the modern reprints already mentioned there are " An abridgement of the . . . Psalmes . . . With Tunes by . . . Mr. Kirby, *etc.*" (1777), an anthem ("O Jesu, look", from *Add.* 29372, *B.M.*) published by H. Froude for the Church Music Society (1911), and the latter again in the *Old English Edition* (*Part* XXI).

KNIGHT (Thomas) (*also* KNIGHTE *and* KNYGHTE): An organist of Salisbury Cathedral described in the records of 1530–40 as a " lusor ad organa ". British Museum manuscripts *Add.* 17802–5 contain Masses or parts of Masses in four parts, and among them some work by one Knight, as well as two motets,—" Ex Mortuis jam non moritur " and " Sancta Maria virgo ", by

" Knyght ". Taking into consideration the fact that the manuscripts date from the second half of the sixteenth century, these compositions can very well be attributed to the organist of Salisbury. There is no further evidence to justify the ascription except that they have been claimed for no other Knight.

L

LANIER FAMILY: A large family of musicians settling in England shortly after the middle of the sixteenth century. The first member domiciled in England was John Lanier I (*q.v.*) who owned property in Crutched Friars, London, and who, in documents relating to it, was described as a Frenchman from Rouen. The earliest members of the family probably did come to England from France; but the possibility is not excluded that they had some admixture of Italian blood in their veins. The greatest difficulties present themselves when an attempt is made to decide the exact relationship of the various scions of the family, and only in a few cases is their descent known. Nicholas Lanier I was not the father of Nicholas II,— more probably his uncle. Nicholas II was the son of John Lanier II. Nicholas I was the father of John (possibly the third), Alphonso (granted 20*d.* a day as "musician in the place of William Damans, deceased" on March 23rd, 1593 ; mentioned as a performer on the recorder in 1603 with a salary of 46*l.* 10*s.* 6*d.*; and entered as "deceased" on November 23rd, 1613), Innocent (mentioned as a flautist in the State Papers in 1593–4, 1603, and 1625), Jerome (*q.v.*), Clement (*q.v.*), and Andrea (*q.v.*). In addition to these six sons, Nicholas I had four daughters. Much intermarrying among the members of the family makes it still more difficult to identify some of them. A William Lanier, son of Jerome Lanier, is mentioned in a Public Record Office account of 1635 (quoted in *Annalen*), his salary being given as 46*l.* per annum. In 1640 (July 6th and 7th) a warrant was issued to swear him in as musician "for the wind instruments in the room of John Adson, deceased"; also a patent to grant him a fee of 1*s.* 8*d.* per diem and 16*l.* 2*s.* 6*d.* yearly as a livery-allowance (*L.C.R., Vol.* 739). At the Restoration his posts were held by John Gamble and John Singleton. In this work Jerome and Jeremy Lanier have been treated as identical, but Mr. J. A. Fuller-Maitland, in the 1913 *Grove*, need not be incorrect when he says that Jeremy was the son of Jerome, and thus a brother of the William juſt mentioned. Henry Lanier is mentioned as a musician for the flutes in 1629, in succession to Nicholas Guy; but in 1633 John Adson already took his place. The Lord Chamberlain's Records contain a petition of " Jone " Lanier, the widow of Henry, asking that her child be given to Andrea Lanier for training. The petition was successful. (*See also* LANIER, Andrea, Clement, Jerome John, Nicholas I *and* II, *and* Thomas).

LANIER (Alphonso): *see* LANIER FAMILY.

LANIER (Andrea): The son of Nicholas Lanier I and, like his father, was a flautiſt in the royal band. We meet with him firſt in 1603 when he was entered in a British Museum manuscript (*Cotton MS. Tib. B. III, f.* 248), and his salary given as 17*l.* 9*s.* 2*d.* This manuscript was written after Elizabeth's death; but since the grants contained were made by the queen, we may suppose that Andrea was already aĉtive during her reign. In 1612 his name is entered in conneĉtion with his appoint-

ment for life (*Cal. S.P.*). On September 20th, 1618, he inherited his father's place (*v.* Lanier, Nicholas I). He was entruſted with the musical education of two boys, and on June 6th, 1626, a warrant was issued for the payment of 59*l.* 13*s.* 4*d.* for the summer and winter liveries of two boys committed to his care as pupils in playing the " flutes and cornetts " (*L.C.R., Vols.* 148–150). Such entries occur frequently in these records. In 1628–9 (January 10th) he received 23*l.* for " four setts of musique books at 5*l.* a sett, and 3*l.* more for two Italian musique cards to compose upon at 30*s.* each " (*L.C.R., Vol.* 738). In 1639–40 he was given two members of his own family to train, the order being contained in the Lord Chamberlain's Records (*Vol.* 739) under date January 12th: " Whereas Andrea Lanier . . . hath long since received Order from his Majeſty for the trayning and breeding up of two boyes or youthes in the quality of musique . . . because the two boyes he lately had . . are, because enabled, preferred to his Majeſty's service, these are to certify that in their room I have appointed two others to be bred by him in musique, namely William L a n i e r a n d T h o m a s Lanier ". Entries referring to Andrea Lanier appear right up to the time of the Rebellion. Whether he was ſtill alive at the Reſtoration when he was appointed " musician upon the flute in ordinary " with two boys to train (July 13th, 1660, L.C.R., Vol. 180), is not certain; but at St. Andrew of that year Thomas Lanier, as " executor to Andrea Lanier, deceased ", signed a receipt for money owing to the late musician (Id., Vol. 460). He muſt have been a very old man in 1660, for it should be remembered that he was already in the royal service in 1603. He probably died during the Commonwealth (See also LANIER FAMILY).

LANIER (Clement): A player on the recorder who was aĉtive at court at the turn of the sixteenth century. In 1604 he appears as a sackbuttiſt with a salary of 20l. per annum. Whether he is to be identified with the Clement Lanier whose name is entered in the Lord Chamberlain's Records from 1625 onwards, and who is given as a " musician for the

recorders " in 1628, is not to be determined. But it was not unusual for musicians at that period to serve " double places ", and play more than one inſtrument. From an entry dated March 4th, 1632–3, it would appear that he also performed on the cornet (L.C.R., Vol. 738). In 1637 (December 22nd) he was one of the wind-inſtrumentaliſts ordered to wait " in the Chapel and at his Majeſty's table . . . at the principall feaſts " (Id., Vol. 739). His salary in 1640 was 46l. per annum (Annalen). He occupied this poſt until the Civil War disbanded the royal orcheſtra, and in 1651 (February 19th), he was promised by the Republican Government that his arrears of salary would be paid. On July 28th of the following year his wife Hannah received 10l. on account. At the Reſtoration William Child was appointed in his place (L.C.R., Vol. 479), Lanier being noted as " deceased " (see also LANIER FAMILY)

LANIER (H e n r y), LANIER (Innocent): see LANIER FAMILY.
LANIER (Jeremy): see L A N I E R (Jerome) and LANIER FAMILY.

LANIER (Jerome or Jeremy): This member of the family appears as a musician for the "hoboys and sackbuts" to the king in 1603, when his name is included in the list of musicians receiving mourning livery for the funeral of Queen Elizabeth (*L.C.R.*, *Vol.* 554). His salary is given in a list at the Public Record Office (*Annalen*) as 70*l.* per annum; but beyond these, and similar entries in the State Papers, nothing further is known of him. He is still mentioned in 1641, and on August 1st, 1652, he visited John Evelyn, who describes him as "old Jerome Lanier"; but at the Restoration his place was filled by Humphrey Madge (*L.C.R.*, *Vol.* 741). *See also* LANIER FAMILY.

LANIER (John): Three members of this family of naturalized musicians, named John, are known to us. The first appears to have been the founder of the English branch of the Laniers. He came from Rouen, owned property in London, and died in 1572. In what relationship, exactly, the other members of the family stood to him is not always clear.

The second John Lanier appears on April 14th, 1564, as a musician for the sackbut (*L.C.R.*, *Vol.* 811), and is mentioned intermittently until 1605.

The third bearer of the same Christian name is met with first in 1625 as a "musician" (*L.C.R.*, *Vol.* 557). It will be impossible to identify John Lanier III with John Lanier II, for the former was active until the Commonwealth. Moreover, this last John is given under the heading "For the lutes and voices" and not as a flautist or player on the sackbut. On July 10th, 1634, he received 15*l.* "for a new lute bought by him" (*L.C.R.*, *Vol.* 739). His salary in 1640 was "guaranteed" 40*l.* per annum (*P.R.O.* quoted in *Annalen*). He appears for the last time in an entry of 1641 giving the musicians "for lutes, violls, and voices" (*L.C.R.*, *Vol.* 476). At the Restoration Edward Colman was appointed "in the place of John Lanier for a voyce" (*Id.*, November 9th, 1660).

It was probably John Lanier II who married the daughter of Marc Anthony Galliardo (or Galliardello) in the Church of the Trinity, Minories (London), in 1585, and who was the father of

Nicholas Lanier II (*see also* LANIER FAMILY).

LANIER (Nicholas) (I): A flautist engaged at the court of Queen Elizabeth. His name appears in the State Papers as early as 1565 (*Annalen*) and a warrant for his livery-allowance is entered in the Lord Chamberlain's Records under date April 30th, 1566. In 1581 he received the usual New Year's gift from the Queen (*B.M. Harl.* 1644). In 1593 a list of all the court-musicians with their salaries is given and from it we learn that the flute-players received 18*l.* 5*s.* each. In the accounts ending at Michaelmas, 1615, Nicholas Lanier, "one of the flutes" is still mentioned (*L.C.R., Vol.* 47), but he evidently died in or before 1618, when his son Andrew Lanier was "appointed musician for the flute, in the place of his father Nicholas Lanier deceased" (*Id., Vol.* 812). *See also* LANIER FAMILY.

LANIER (Nicholas) (II): Master of the King's Music and dramatic composer. He was by far the most important of the large family of musicians of that name, and did much towards preparing the way in England for the declamatory style of composition. He was the son of John Lanier II (*q.v.*). Born in September, 1588, and baptized on the 10th of the month in the church of the Trinity, Minories (London), he became one of the most popular musicians of the early and middle seventeenth century. An enormous number of entries in the State Papers refer to the bearer of the name, and in some of the early references a Nicholas Lanier is also given as " singer ". It is, of course, not unlikely that the same man is meant in each case. In 1625 (June 6th) a warrant was issued for the delivery of a livery to Lanier as " luter to the king "; this being the first entry relating to him in the Lord Chamberlain's Records (*Vol.* 148, *etc.*). On June 22nd, 1626, he is named as Master of the Music (*L.C.R., Vol.* 813), and on July 11th, 1626, he was guaranteed an annual salary of 200*l.* (*Cal. S.P.*). At St. Andrew, 1630, he was paid his livery allowance as Master, and also " paid to him more as luter, a livery " (*L.C.R., Vol.* 799), which disposes of any doubt as to whether the Master and the lutenist were to be identified.

In 1636 he became the first Marshal of the Corporation of Music, founded by Royal Charter in that year. There is the evidence of passports among the State Papers that he travelled on the Continent during the Commonwealth. Immediately after the Restoration of the House of Stuart he appears again as lutenist and Master of the Music, and held these posts until February, 1665–6, when he died. An entry in the register at Greenwich dated February 24th says: "Mr. Nicholas Laniere buried away". On March 10th Pelham Humfrey received his post as lutenist and on November 24th, Louis Grabu was appointed to that of Master of the Music (L.C.R., Vol. 478, 9). According to an entry in the Lord Chamberlain's Records (Vol. 181) probate of his will was granted to his widow, Elizabeth, on March 24th. This is followed by a certificate of Thomas Plume, vicar of Greenwich, also giving the date of Lanier's burial as February 24th.

Nicholas Lanier II was considered an authority on all questions of art, and Charles I made much use of his talents in forming the fine collection of paintings which he brought together. On June 13th, 1626, he was sent to Italy with 2000l. in his pocket for the purpose of purchasing pictures. He was later given a post as Keeper of the King's miniatures, and for many of the masques to which he supplied all or part of the music, he also painted or designed the scenery. During the Commonwealth the collection of pictures which he had helped to form was sold by auction, and the members of the Lanier family made large purchases. Nicholas II bought his own half-length portrait by Vandyck. A portrait of Lanier,—self-painted,—hangs in the Oxford Music School.

The fame of this musician and artist rests upon his achievements in the realms of stage-music. In 1613 he collaborated with Campian and Coperario in the masque written in honour of the marriage of the Earl of Somerset, and produced in 1614. One of the songs by Lanier is included in John Stafford Smith's *Musica Antiqua* (1812; the song,—"Bring away this Sacred Tree",—is given erroneously by Smith as occurring in

Luminalia, which is mentioned below). The composition which has caused him to be remembered more than any other, was the music he wrote for the masque performed at the residence of Lord Hay on February 22nd, 1617. This was Ben Jonson's masque *Lovers made men*, and in it Lanier is said to have introduced for the first time into England, the *Stilo recitativo* from Italy. This style of writing, which became so popular during the Interregnum, was certainly not so named before 1617, but many passages may be found in the works of earlier composers, which foreshadow the coming vogue. In the same year Lanier wrote the music to Ben Jonson's court-masque *The Vision of Delight*, and in 1637 he composed the masque *Luminalia, or the Festival of Light*, in the performance of which the Queen and the ladies of the court took part. Specimens of his music may be seen in Playford's *Select Ayres and Dialogues* (1652, 1653, 1659), in the *Musical Companion* (1667 and 1672), in the *Treasury of Musick* (1669), and in *Choice Songs and Ayres*, fourth book (1685). He wrote the New Year's odes for 1663 and 1665 and composed an elegy on the death of Charles I. "The Lily," a song, was published in Paris in 1912. He is well represented in the British Museum manuscripts, and examples of his skill are contained in *Add*. 11608, *Add*. 29396, *Eg*. 2013, *Add*. 22100, and *Add*. 31460. A Cantata entitled, *Hero and Leander*, is in Add. 14399 and *Add*. 33236. Further work of Lanier's is in the libraries of Christ Church and the Music School (Oxford), and the Fitzwilliam Museum, Cambridge. LANIER (Thomas): A court musician from 1660 onwards. He was a pupil of Andrea Lanier (*q.v.*) and commenced his training in 1639–40. The Civil War doubtlessly prevented his immediate appointment, and it was not until the Restoration that he was admitted as "musician upon the flutes and cornets, or some other part amongst the lutes and voice in ordinary, in the place of Andrea Lanier, deceased, with the allowance of 1*s*. 8*d*. per diem, 7*l*. 11*s*. 8*d*. yearly for boardwages, and 29*l*. 9*s*. 2*d*. yearly for apparrell; also one other 1*s*. 8*d*. per diem, and

16*l*. 2*s*. 6*d*. yearly for his livery " (*L.C.R.*, Vol. 741, November 15th, 1660). On December 13th, 1661, he petitioned for three places promised him and his father in 1643, before the latter was imprisoned (*Annalen*). Following this petition he received the places of a flautiſt and a violiniſt. He also ſtated that he had been educated by Nicholas Lanier. In 1662 he is described as Andrea Lanier's son (*L.C.R.*, *Vol. 56, Michaelmas*, 1662), and was paid for the " keeping and teaching of two boys ". This payment was probably made to him as Andrea's executor. A great many entries refer to petitions presented to the Lord Chamberlain, complaining that Thomas Lanier was in the petitioners' debt; but these are to some extent to be explained by the number of entries that mention Lanier's allowances to be in arrears. Stuart musicians were frequently reduced to the necessity of making assignments of their salary in advance to creditors, on account of the irregularity of their receipts from the treasury. In 1663 he appears among the " lutes and voices "; in 1666 among the violins; in 1668 among the wind-inſtrument players. There are no means of determining whether all these entries refer to the same musician, or to two men, perhaps cousins, of the same name. In 1677 Thomas Lanier refers to Mrs. Joyce Lanier as his mother. James II made some attempt to clear up the chaotic ſtate of the court finances, and set about paying the arrears in his musicians' livery-allowances. In 1685–6 there was owing to Thomas Lanier livery-money for the years 1660 to 1667 and from 1678 to 1684—no trivial matter in those days, for the debt amounted to 170*l*. 10*s*. On September 21ſt, 1686, the sum was ordered to be paid to him out of the proceeds of the tobacco and sugar imposition. After this date Thomas Lanier disappears from the Lord Chamberlain's Records. It is not known when he died (*see also* LANIER FAMILY).

LANIER (William): *see* LANIER FAMILY.

LAWES (Henry): A son of Thomas Lawes, of Salisbury, and younger brother of William Lawes. Devoting himself almost entirely to the production of secular vocal music, he followed the traditions of his age and became a writer of very popular declamatory music. As a pupil of Coperario he had the Italian methods in common with his contemporaries, but in him the instinct for true prosodial values was far more marked. At the same time Milton was allowing his friendship to gain the ascendency over justice when he assigns to Henry Lawes the honour of having been the first to teach " our English musick how to span Words with just note and accent, not to scan, With Midas' Ears, committing short and long "— for the Elizabethans already paid the closest attention to this point, although perhaps not bringing out the dramatic force of the words with such unnecessary obviousness as did the Stuart writers. Still, the reputation he enjoyed among his contemporaries was very high, and his colleagues and the foremost poets of the day vied with each other in the singing of his praises. Certainly he invariably chose the best poetry for setting. His friendship with Milton probably had very far-reaching results for both men, and it is more than probable that Henry Lawes had a good deal to do with the acquisition by the poet of the great musical knowledge that distinguished him. Nevertheless, although the music of Henry Lawes sometimes rises to great dramatic heights, and almost always possesses great lyric charm, a good deal of his writing is plainly made to order, and is neither finished in style nor balanced in form. His songs undoubtedly set a fashion that was followed later by greater men, and the solo-song with orchestral accompaniment owes much to the influence of Henry Lawes. He broke away almost completely from the contrapuntal methods of his immediate predecessors, and although he makes tentative essays in the olden style in the little sacred music he has left, his tastes lay all in the direction of the secular, which was a direct reflection of the art of his period.

Born at the end of 1595, he was baptized on New Year's Day, 1595–6, at Dinton in Wiltshire. We do not meet with him in any official documents until the Cheque-Book of the Chapel Royal gives the entry: " 1625(6). John Cooke died the 12th of September, and Henry Lawes was sworne in his place the firſt of Januarie followinge, piſtoler '' (epiſtler). On November 3rd, of the same year he was sworn in as a gentleman on the death of Francis Wiborowe. On January 6th, 1630–1, he appears in the Lord Chamberlain's Records on his appointment as " a musician for the voices in the place of Robert Marsh " (*L.C.R.*, *Vol.* 738), and on February 28th he was allowed a " patent of 20*l.* per annum " as " musician for the lutes and voices in ordinary ", with the usual 16*l.* 2*s.* 6*d.* for livery (*Id.*). In 1640 his salary as royal musician was ſtill 20*l.* During the Commonwealth he devoted himself to teaching (*v.* Playford's *Musical Banquet*), and to the composition of dramatic music. He moved in good circles and among his pupils he numbered the daughters of the Earl of Bridgewater, the dedication of the firſt book of *Ayres and Dialogues* (1653) being addressed to the " Right Honorable, The two moſt excellent siſters, Alice Countesse of Carbery, and Mary Lady Herbert of Cherbury . . . moſt of them being composed when I was employed by your ever Honour'd Parents to attend your Ladyshipp's Education in Musick ". He appears to have suffered much financial loss through the Civil War, but refused to cheapen his art in order to increase his income. In the Preface to his second book of *Ayres and Dialogues* he says: " As for myself, although I have loſt my Fortunes with my Maſter (of ever blessed memory) I am not so low to bow for a subsistence to the follies of this Age. . . ." To the Interregnum period belongs also a letter written by Lawes to the Receiver-General in 1647 (preserved in the British Museum in *Harl.* 1911). This document provides us with a specimen of his signature, and begs that " such moneys as is allowed unto me in your liſt (whyther it be Twenty nobles, more or less) " be paid " unto my friend Mr. Wilks Fichet ". The money appears to have been paid, for Mr. Fitchet's receipt is written on the back of Lawes's letter (*v. also Add.* 33965, *B.M.*).

After the Reſtoration, Henry Lawes was made composer " in the private musick for the lutes and voices in

Mr. Thomas Ford's place " (*L.C.R.*, *Vol.* 477, June 16th, 1660). On April 20th, 1661, he was sworn in as a musician for the lutes and voices in the place of Robert Marsh (*Id., Vol.* 181). At this time Henry Lawes lived in the Almonry at Westminster, where the Purcell family were also probably living (information given me by the late Sir Frederick Bridge). Lawes died in 1662, his death being announced in the Cheque-Book of the Chapel Royal in the following terms: " 1662. Mr. Henry Lawes one of the Gentlemen of his Majesties Chappell Royal and Clerke of the Check, died October 21st and in his place was sworne as Gentleman Dr. John Wilson . . ." Dr. Charles Colman was appointed to his post as composer, John Clements received his place in the private music, and as composer for the violins Thomas Purcell was sworn in on November 16th, 1662 " in place of Henry Lawes ". He was buried in the Cloisters of Westminster Abbey, but there is to be found no trace of his grave. A portrait hangs in the Music School, Oxford.

Specimens of the music of Henry Lawes are easily accessible. In 1637 he issued " A Paraphrase upon the Psalmes of David. By G. S. (George Sandys) set to new Tunes for private Devotion, *etc.*", the British Museum possessing copies of the editions of 1648 and 1676. This was followed in 1648 by the volume of three-part Psalmes in which he collaborated with his brother William. The first thirty compositions in the volume are by Henry, followed by " A Pastorall *Elegie* to the memory of my deare brother William Lawes " and other elegies upon the death of the elder brother (*v.* William Lawes) by Dr. Wilson, John Cobb, Simon Ives, *etc.* In 1653 appeared *Ayres and Dialogues for One, Two, and Three Voyces . . . The First Booke.* The second book followed in 1655, and the third in 1658. In the prefaces to these three works Lawes says much that throws a good deal of light on the conceits and foibles of the age, and these introductions are of some historical value, —they are certainly very entertaining. One of the songs from the first book was reprinted by Rimbault as No. 5 of the *Ancient Vocal*

Music of England series. Work by Henry Lawes is contained in Playford's *Seleƈt Musical Ayres and Dialogues* (1652, 1653, 1659), in *Catch that Catch Can* (1658; five Canons), and in its later edition—*The Musical Companion* (1672; twenty compositions).

Of Henry Lawes's dramatic music the beƒt-known is certainly that which he wrote for Milton's *Comus*. It is quite likely that the masque was written by Milton at the suggeƒtion of Lawes who was at the time of its conception employed by the Earl of Bridgewater. The arrival of the Earl at Ludlow Caƒtle as Lord President of Wales was the occasion of its performance, and Lawes's pupil Lady Alice, and her two brothers took part in it. Lawes was responsible for the publication of *Comus* in 1637 (Humphrey Robinson), but the music which he wrote for it did not appear in his lifetime. Rimbault says that he discovered the five songs now known in the British Museum (presumably *Add.* 11518) and printed them as No. 8 of his *Ancient Vocal Music of England*. Sir Frederick Bridge edited the music for

Messrs. Novello and Co. from the autograph copy in the possession of the Rev. Dr. Cooper Smith. In the performance of 1634, Henry Lawes himself played the part of "The attendant Spirit afterwards in the habit of Thyrsis". He wrote music for several other ƒtage produƈtions, such as the firƒt and fifth "entries" of Davenant's *Siege of Rhodes*, *The Firƒt Day's Entertainment* (1656), *The Rival Friends* (in *Add.* 10338, *B.M.*), *The Masque of Vices* (*Id.*), Carew's *Coelum Britannicum* (1633–4), and *The Royal Slave* (Cartwright, 1636). The writing of the *Comus* music, and Lawes's share in the *Siege of Rhodes*, juƒtify Sir Frederick Bridge's remark that "the composer of the music to the laƒt important masque" also helped "in what was apparently the firƒt English opera". For the Coronation of Charles II he composed the anthem "Zadok the Prieƒt". Manuscripts containing music by this writer are fairly numerous,—the British Museum possessing over a dozen. In addition to the manuscripts already alluded to, works by Henry Lawes may be seen in *Add.*

30273, *Add.* 11608, *Add.* 31434, *Add.* 29396, *Add.* 32343, *Add.* 4388, *Add.* 14399, *Add.* 31813, *Add.* 29386, *Add.* 34071, *Add.* 31806, *Harl.* 7549, *Eg.* 2013, *etc.*, examples of anthems, canons, carols, choruses, motets, being included besides the music mentioned. LAWES (William): A prolific and popular composer of secular music who flourished in the first half of the seventeenth century. In his instrumental works he is typical of his period; rather ingenious than imaginative, thinking more of clever workmanship than of original treatment. Nevertheless, some of his songs are quite charming and dainty specimens of their class. In the instrumental fancy he adhered to the methods made popular by the writers of John Jenkins's type, although his work cannot be said to be so eminently suited to the instruments written for as was that of the older composer mentioned. In his own day, however, he seems to have enjoyed a high reputation; his brother Henry wrote of him: "Besides his Fancies of 3, 4, 5, 6 parts, to the Viols and Organ, he hath made above thirty severall sorts of Musick for

Voices, and Instruments: Neither was there any Instrument then in use, but he compos'd to it so aptly as if he had only studied itt",— which was perhaps dictated by fraternal admiration. Though his talents lay chiefly in the direction of secular music, he composed some anthems and other short pieces to sacred texts.

William Lawes was the elder son of Thomas Lawes, and was born at Dinton or Salisbury (Wiltshire) before the end of the sixteenth century. He was a chorister at Chichester Cathedral until 1602, when he left for London. Since he was a gentleman of the Chapel Royal by 1602–3, he must have been twenty years of age at least in that year, a supposition which would place the date of his birth round about 1582–3. The Cheque-Book of the Chapel Royal records his admission in these terms: "1602. William Lawes (from Chichester) was sworne the 1st of Januarie in Tho: Sharpes place". In the metropolis he enjoyed the patronage of the Earl of Hertford, who procured for him the tuition of Coperario. He is mentioned in the

Cheque-Book of the Chapel Royal in 1603 and 1604 as a witness to certain documents, and in the latter year participated in the general increase of salaries. According to the Cheque-Book he "resigned this place the 5th of Maye unto Ezechiell Waad who was sworn into the same that very daie" (1611); but on October 1st of the same year he appears to have been re-admitted "without paie, a parte of whose othe was not to sue to be in ordinarie paye, unlesse he be first lawfully called therunto by the Deane, Subdeane, and major parte of the Company" (*Ch. Bk. C.R.*). On April 30th, 1635, he was sworn in as a musician to the king " in ordinary for the lutes and voices " (*L.C.R., Vol.* 739), his salary being fixed on May 14th, at 40*l.* with the usual livery-allowance. The outbreak of the rebellion found him a staunch Royalist, and in spite of his already advanced age he joined the Royal forces. His reputation at Court caused his commander to create him a Commissary; but in spite of the comparative safety of the appointment, he appears to have courted danger to an extent sufficient to bring about his death at the siege of Chester in 1645, having been struck by a random shot. The king felt his loss deeply enough to wear mourning for his patriotic musician (Hawkins.)

Comparatively little of William Lawes's music was printed. In 1648 he shared with his brother Henry the task of writing : " *Choice Psalmes Put into Musick. For Three Voices.* The most of which may properly enough be sung by any three, with a Thorough base . . . Compos'd by Henry and William Lawes, Brothers; and servants to His Majestie. With divers *Elegies,* set in Musick by sev'rall Friends, upon the death of William Lawes. And at the end of the Thorough Base are added nine *Canons* of 3 and 4 *Voices,* made by William Lawes ". He is represented in *Select Musicall Ayres and Dialogues* (John Playford, 1653 and 1659; seven pieces,—one in the edition of 1652 not included in 1653), in *Catch that Catch Can* (1658; twenty pieces), in the *Musical Companion* (1672), in *Musick's Hand-maide* (1663 ; four pieces), in *Musick's Delight on the Cithren* (1666; three pieces), and in *Court Ayres*

(1655; fifty-three two-part pieces, mainly dance-forms). In 1633 he collaborated with Simon Ives (*q.v.*) in the composition of the music to Shirley's masque *The Triumphes of Peace*, receiving as his share the large sum of 100*l*. Two years later he set the music for Davenant's masque *The Triumph of the Prince D'Amour* (Music School library in the Bodleian, Oxford). He is represented in reprints by Boyce and in the *Lady's Magazine* for May, 1794. A vast amount of his music, besides the two masques mentioned, remains in manuscript. The British Museum has some autographs of his (*e.g. Add.* 31432 and *Add.* 17798), and another manuscript (*Add.* 31431) is notable on account of the " Royal Consort " which it contains. This set of short suites for three Viols, or other combination, is representative of his ordinary instrumental writing. Other manuscripts in the National collection containing work by William Lawes are: *Add.* 10445, *Add.* 11608, *Add.* 18940–4, *Add.* 29290–1, *Add.* 29386, *Add.* 29396–7, *Add.* 29410, *Add.* 30273, *Add.* 30826–8, *Add.* 31429, *Add.* 31433, *Add.* 31462–3,

Add. 31813, *Add.* 35043, and *Eg.* 2013. The Christ Church and the Bodleian libraries also contain manuscript music of his.

LEIGHTON (Sir William): A poet and composer of the early seventeenth century, who is remembered chiefly through his collection of vocal compositions with and without instrumental accompaniment. Born in Shropshire about the middle of the sixteenth century, he first appeared in print in Allison's *Psalmes* (1599) to which he contributed some verses. In 1603 he published : *Vertue Triumphant, or a lively description of the foure Vertues Cardinall.* This was a poetical work in praise of James I. He must have been in contact with the court for some years, for at that time he was a Gentleman Pensioner of the king. The publication of " Vertue Triumphant " probably occasioned his elevation to knighthood. In 1608 Sir William Harmon prosecuted him for debt (according to one of Leighton's dedications, without ground); in 1610 he was outlawed and later imprisoned. It was during his incarceration that he compiled the first version of his best-known work in

1613. In 1614 this book appeared with music under the title *The Teares or Lamentacions of a Sorrowful Soule. Composed with Musicall Ayres and Songs, both for Voyces and divers Instruments,* etc. The settings of these metrical Psalms and hymns were from the pens of such men as Byrd, Bull, Gibbons, D o w l a n d, C o p e r a r i o, Weelkes, Wilbye, John Milton the Elder, and others. Eight of the compositions were by Leighton himself. The book is an interesting specimen of that class of publication printed with the parts facing various ways so that the requisite number of singers or players could perform from a single copy. It is not known when he died. No other music of his is known. In the British Museum the manuscript *Royal App.* 63 contains the *cantus* part of the *Teares* with an accompaniment for the treble viol and lute, while *Add.* 31418 contains a copy of the vocal score.

L E N T O N (J o h n): A violinist, flautist, writer of instruction-books for the violin, and composer of music for the stage, who flourished towards the end of the seventeenth century

and the beginning of the eighteenth. It is not known when or where he was born, and the earliest date of his activity discoverable is 1681, when, on August 2nd he was appointed a " musician for the violin " in the royal band (*L.C.R., Vol.* 480). On August 31st, 1685, he was sworn in as a singer in " his Majesty's private musick " as a counter-tenor (*Id., Jas. II*). On November 10th of the same year he entered the Chapel Royal as a Gentleman Extraordinary (*Ch. Bk. C.R.*) and he attended the king on his trip to Holland (1691). In 1694 his salary is given as 40*l.* per annum (Chamberlayne, *Notitiae Brit.*). He probably received a further 40*l.* a year as instrumentalist (*cf. L.C.R., Vols.* 487, *pp.* 23–26, *and* 488, *pp.* 30–34). The date of his death is not known, but probably is to be placed in the second decade of the eighteenth century, during which he falls out of the state records.

The work by which Lenton is perhaps best-known is his *Gentleman's Diversion, or the Violin Explained* (1694). This, according to the little that can be gathered concerning the work, was a very elementary treatise, obviously intended, as the title suggests, for the amateur. Its upward limit does not exceed the first C on the E-string, no change of position is called for, and none is mentioned. In this respect the book did not go, technically, so far as some other works on the subject already published ; which is surprising when we remember that he must have come in contact with such able and advanced violinists as John Banister II. Lenton, it is possible, intended to write only an elementary work, and Hawkins takes too much for granted when he asserts that because Lenton makes no mention of shifting, and because his compass extends no higher than C, it proves the "comparatively small degree of proficiency to which masters of the instrument were at that period arrived ". A second edition appeared in 1702 as *The Useful Instructor for the Violin*, with an appendix, but without the tunes contained in the first edition. In 1694 he published, in association with Thomas Tollet, *A Consort of Musick in Three Parts*. The popular publications of the day contain a few short compositions by him; two are to be seen in *The Theater of Music* (1685), and he is represented in D'Urfey's *A Third Collection of New Songs* (1685), and in *Apollo's Banquet* (*Ed.* 1693). He "corrected" *Vol.* IV of *Wit and Mirth*: *or Pills to Purge Melancholy, second edition* (1707; the British Museum catalogue giving the date 1709 also). The *Pleasant Companion* contained Catches of Lenton's as late as 1720, and Playford's *Dancing Master* (second volume, 1713) was revised and edited by him. The music written by Lenton for the stage includes incidental pieces and overtures to *Venice Preserved* (1682; some parts of which are present in manuscript in *R.C.M.*), *The Ambitious Step-Mother* (1700; tragedy by N. Rowe; first violin and bass parts, 1702 (?) in *B.M.*), *Tamburlain* (1702), *The Royall Captive* (1702 ?), *The Fair Penitent* (1703), *Liberty Asserted* (1704), *Abra Muley* (1704), and *The Gamester* (1708). John Playford published separately "A new song set to Music by Mr. John Lenton" (1685). In manuscript at the British Museum are the flute or violin part of " Mr. Lenton's Tunes played before ye King at his Returne" (*Add.* 35043), Overture and eight tunes from *The Moor of Venice* for string quartet and other arrangements (*Add.* 24889), a tune for the violin or flute (*Add.* 17853), a "Dialogue between Venus, Adonis, and a Messenger" (*Eg.* 2013), *etc.*

L'ESTRANGE (Roger): An interesting and important figure in the musical world of the seventeenth century, who though an amateur in the art, is encountered so often in the musical publications of the period that he cannot be omitted from such a work as this. Born on December 17th, 1616, at Hunstanton (Norfolk), he showed remarkable aptitude for music at a very early age. He studied with the celebrated John Jenkins, who was then domiciled in the house of his pupil's father, Sir Hamon L'Estrange. His political career need not detain us here, but it must be remembered that he was a staunch Royalist and that he followed his king into exile. He was a fierce pamphleteer and on questions of Church and State his quarrels often brought troubles on his head. Macaulay held the view that L'Estrange was "ferocious and ignoble"; Pepys (*Diary*, December 17th, 1664), on the other hand, thought: "He is a man of fine conversation, I think, but I am sure most courtly and full of compliments", and Evelyn (*Diary*, May 7th, 1685), says he was "a person of excellent parts, abating some affectations". His house was the centre of an active musical life, and he was one of the founders of Britton's musical club. Ned Ward (a great friend of Britton's) said the club was "confirmed by Sir Roger-le-Strange, many years before his Knighthood, who was a very musical gentleman, and had a tolerable Perfection on the Bass Viol". Roger returned to England during the Commonwealth (1653), and his political enemies lost no time in accusing him of seeking Cromwell's favour by means of his skill in music. This attack he countered in his pamphlet of 1662 (*Truth and Loyalty Vindicated*) where he says: "Mr. Edward Bagshaw will have it that I frequently solicited a private conference with Oliver, and that I often brought my fiddle under my Cloak to facilitate my entry. Surely this Edward Bagshaw has been pastor to a Gravesend boat; he has a vein so right; a Fiddle under my Cloak? Truly my Fiddle is a Bass Viol, and that's somewhat a troublesome instrument under a cloak . . . Concerning the story of the Fiddle, this, I suppose, might be the Rise of it. Being in St. *James* his *Parke*, I heard an *Organ* Touched in a little Low Room of one Mr. Hinckson's. I went in, and found a Private Company of some five or six Persons. They desired me to take up a Viole, and bear a *Part*. I did so; and *That*, a Part too, not much to advance the Reputation of my cunning. By and By (without the least colour of a *Design* or *Expectation*) in comes *Cromwell*; He found us Playing, and (as I remember) so he left us ". It was nothing unusual for a gentleman in the seventeenth century to be asked to " bear a part " in a consort, for everyone of culture was expected to be in a position to do so. But the circumstances attending the visit of the Protector to this particular music-making gave L'Estrange the nickname of " Roger the Fiddler ". The " Hinckson " mentioned was John Hingston, at one time Cromwell's organist, and later private musician and

" Keeper of the Organs " to Charles II.

Roger L'Estrange subsequently became Licenser of the Press during the reigns of Charles II and James II, and some of his introductory letters to the musical publications of the day make very interesting reading. He died on December 11th, 1704, aged 89, and was interred in St. Giles Church. He was a close friend of Christopher Simpson and Matthew Lock, and the latter dedicated his *Melothesia* to " the ever Honour'd Roger L'estrange".

LICHFILD (Henry): A madrigalist of the Elizabethan era who published a volume of five-part madrigals in 1613. He is not to be classed with his greater contemporaries; but this is due not so much to the inferiority of his work, as to the great heights some of the others attained. His part-writing is interesting and neat, and several of his vocal pieces are quite worthy of performance to-day. Of Lichfild's life we know absolutely nothing, except that he was- a member of Lady Cheney's household at Toddington, Bedfordshire. He probably played some instrument and possibly sang; alternatively, or in addition, he may have taught music. But this is merely supposition. The date of his birth is unknown, and of his death we can only be certain that it had not taken place when his patroness made her will, for she bequeathed him 20*l.* She died in 1614. Lichfild's book of twenty madrigals appeared in 1613 under the title *The First Set of Madrigals of 5 Parts: apt both for Viols and Voyces.* Some of his pieces have been republished by Mr. W. Barclay Squire (Laudy and Co., and Breitkopf and Haertel), and by C. K. Scott. Dr. E. H. Fellowes issued the complete set as *Vol.* XVII of *The English Madrigal School* (1922).

LISLEY (John): A madrigalist of the late sixteenth century, of whom absolutely nothing is known. The only work of his that has been preserved is the six-part madrigal contributed to the *Triumphes of Oriana* (1601)—" Faire Cytharea presents her doves".

LLOYD (John): A gentleman of the Chapel Royal during the reign of Henry VIII. Born at Caerleon (Monmouthshire) about 1485, we meet with him first in a warrant of October 21st, *1 Hen. VIII* (1509), when he was allowed a gown of " black chambelet " as a gentleman of the chapel. In 1511 his name appears with the rest of the chapel at the funeral of Prince Henry as " John Lloilld ". In some of the State paper entries his name is spelled Floyd, or Fluyd (*e.g.* April 16th, 1512, *etc.*). In March, 1512, he was granted a corrody in " the monastery of St. Austen (Bristol) " which was one of the several signs of royal favour of a similar nature. In another document of April, 1512, he is given as " Johannis Lloid, de Capella Regis ". In the Public Record Office there is a letter from the Bishop of Winchester to Cardinal Wolsey, dealing with the " unruly " doings of the canons of St. Augustine's, Bristol, ". . . one Lloyd of the King's Chapel is the chief author of this mischief." All the entries quoted are contained in Brewer's *Letters and Papers of Henry VIII.* Lloyd accompanied the King, with the rest of the Chapel, to the celebrated Field of the Cloth of Gold in 1520, and he afterwards made a pilgrimage to Jerusalem. He died on April 3rd, 1523, and was interred in the Church of the

Savoy under the name of Johannis Floyd and with the character of "Virtutis et religionis cultor". He is generally credited with a degree, but C. F. Abdy Williams (*Degrees in Music*) was not able to trace any record of it. Probably a remark in *Add.* 31922 (*B.M.*), —"Flude . . . in armonia graduat",—was the origin of the supposition. This manuscript contains a three-part round, "Deem the best of every doubt", by him.

LOCK (Matthew) (*also* LOCKE): A popular composer of the Restoration period, though by training and temperament he leaned rather to the older order. He associated with the best musicians of his period, and was held in the highest esteem by his contemporaries. All his work is marked by an obvious desire to do his best,—often in a style that did not suit him. Thus his sacred music, though good, lacks that spontaneity which his dramatic work exhibits. Finally, realizing the direction of his talents, he "conformed at last to the modes of his time, and fell into the theatrical way, and composed to the semi-operas divers pieces of vocal and instrumental entertainment, with very good success and then gave way to the divine Purcell and others " (North, *Memoires of Musick*). North's designation " semi-opera " is perhaps the best that could be devised to name Lock's dramatic work, savouring as it did of the older masque, and looking forward to the true Opera. His music generally, as North says, " had a robust vein, and many of his compositions went about ". He was proud of his vocation and jealous of the rights that belong to talent, the latter often dragging him into violent polemics. Born at Exeter not later than 1630, Lock was a chorister at the Cathedral there and a pupil of William Wake (for whom the *Little Consort* was written), and of Edward Gibbons. The date given for his birth is arrived at by the fact that on the old organ screen of the Cathedral is scratched " Matthew Lock, 1638 ", and again " M. L. 1641 ". Such a prank would emanate from a boy of eight to eleven years of age; but in view of certain other dates, he may have been two or three years older. The first piece of dated information that we possess concerning him after his schoolboy days, is his visit to Flanders when he was about eighteen or twenty years of age. The object of that visit is not known, but while there he copied a volume of music, chiefly foreign, and added the heading " A Collection of Songs made when I was in the Lowe Countries, 1648 ". This manuscript once belonged to Dr. Rimbault, but is now in the British Museum as *Add.* 31437. In 1653 he wrote, in collaboration with Christopher Gibbons (*q.v.*), his first important dramatic music. This was the masque *Cupid and Death* (Shirley), an autograph copy of the music being in the British Museum (*Add.* 17799). Another date given for the production of the masque is 1659, but this may refer to another performance (*v. also* Christopher Gibbons). In 1656 he issued his *Little Consort of Three Parts: Containing Pavans, Ayres, Corants, Sarabands, for Viols or Violins. In 2 several Varieties*, and in the same year shared with Henry Lawes, Coleman, Cooke, and Hudson the writing of the music for Davenant's *Siege of Rhodes*, being responsible for the fourth act. In this production Lock took an active part, sustaining the rôle of the Admiral, and having among his stage-companions Henry Purcell the Elder. It was about three years after this that we meet with Lock in the *Diary* of Samuel Pepys. Under date February 21st, 1659–60 we read: " . . . to Westminster Hall . . . Here I met with Mr. Lock and Purcell (the elder), Master of the Musique, and went with them to the coffee-house, into a room next the water, by ourselves, where we spent an hour or two . . . Here we had . . . a canon for eight voices which Mr. Lock had lately made on these words: ' Domine Salvum fac Regem ' ", — thus foreshadowing the return of the Stuarts to the throne of England.

On June 16th, 1660, Matthew Lock was appointed " composer in the private musick " of the king, " in the place of John Coperario " (*L.C.R., Vol.* 477). On November 9th his salary is given as 40*l.* per annum (*Id.*). A " new place " was also created for him as " composer for the violins " (*Id., Vol.* 479). In connection with the Coronation of Charles II

Lock composed the wind-music performed during the royal progress to Whitehall from the Tower of London (April 22nd, 1661, *v.* Ogilby, *Relation of his Majesty's Entertainment, etc.*), but those writers who say that he received his appointments in the private music as a reward for this service are incorrect; it has been seen that these appointments date from 1660. The Stuart methods of payment were notorious, and Lock's receipts soon began to be irregular, livery-money fell into arrears, and he evidently incurred debts. In 1664 the Lord Chamberlain's Records mention the payment of 8*l.* 10*s.* to one Margaret Pothero for seventeen weeks' lodging for Lock and his servants at 10*s.* a week; it thus seems unlikely that the composer was married at that period, as some authorities suggest. In 1664, too, he is referred to in the Minutes of the Corporation of Music (*Harl.* 1911, *B.M.*), and to the same period belongs his music to Stapylton's *The Stepmother* (Rimbault says that it was performed at the close of 1663). An innovation which he attempted in 1666 (April 1st) raised objections

among the choristers who spitefully ruined the performance. The novelty consisted of a different setting for each repetition of the Kyrie between the Commandments. Pepys refers to the incident under date September 2nd, 1667: "Spent all the afternoon . . . singing of Locke's Responses to the Ten Commandments, which he hath set very finely, and was a good time since sung before the King and spoiled in the performance, which occasioned his printing them for his vindication, and are excellent good". Lock's "Vindication" was certainly thorough-going, for his pen was acrid when he was annoyed. The publication mentioned by Pepys was Lock's *Modern Church Musick, Pre-Accus'd, Censur'd, and Obstructed in its Performance before His Majesty, Aprill 1, 1666. Vindicated by the Author, etc.* (a copy is in the British Museum).

The exact date at which he became organist in the Catholic Chapel of the Queen is not clear, nor do we know how he reconciled the religion of the Chapel Royal with that of the Somerset House Chapel. The State Papers show that he still retained his court appointment, even while employed in the Queen's chapel. Roger North says that " he was organist at Somerset House Chappell as long as he lived, but the Italian masters, that served there, did not approve of his manner of play, but must be attended by more polite hands; and one while one Sabinico (*sc.* Giovanni Sebenico) and afterwards Sig. Baptista Draghi, used the great organ and Lock (who must not be turned out of his place, nor the execution) had a small chamber organ by, on which he performed with them the same services". It is hardly to be expected that Lock enjoyed the state of affairs, but he does not appear to have rebelled. Possibly his religious sympathies tended towards Rome, and he may have welcomed the opportunity of working in any capacity in such a chapel. At that period Lock lived in the Strand, and on July 19th, 1669, is described as " of St. Martin's in the Fields " (*L.C.R.*, *Vol.* 195).

In 1670, or perhaps a little earlier, he wrote the instrumental music for the Dryden-Davenant version of *The Tempest*, and probably it was this play,—to sing in which certain members of the Chapel Royal had permission to absent themselves from Windsor,—that is mentioned in the Lord Chamberlain's Records under date May 16th, 1674. The music to *Macbeth* has been the subject of long debate, and it can hardly be stated with absolute certainty even now that this music was written by Lock. It is my opinion that there may have been two versions of the music, one by Lock and the other by someone more technically advanced. In such case the version edited by Boyce (1770 ?) as " The Original Songs, Airs, and Choruses which were introduced in the Tragedy of Macbeth in Score . . ." was not Lock's. Rimbault may be partially correct when he says that this version was composed by Richard Leveridge and first performed in 1704 or a little later, and that Lock's *Macbeth* music " composed in the reign of Charles II is entirely different " (*Introduction to the Musical Antiquarian Society's edition of Purcell's Bonduca*). Leveridge only wrote fresh music to the second act, and he scarcely merits consideration in this connection. The remaining

x

possibility is that Purcell wrote the well-known music. There certainly is a manuscript version of it in Purcell's handwriting. But if Purcell wrote the music in time for performance in 1672, he could have been only fourteen years of age when he did so. This is hardly probable, though by no means impossible. All sources of information have been searched in vain for conclusive proof, and the matter remains as open to doubt as ever it was. It was Downes, the prompter of the Dorset Gardens Theatre, who first named Lock as the composer of this music, and his evidence is by no means trustworthy. At the same time, he may on this occasion have been right. In 1673 Lock wrote the necessary music to Shadwell's *Psyche*, the entr'actes being by G. B. Draghi. Lock evidently considered his performance in connection with Shadwell's text as a true opera; but in reality the work exhibits a closer family likeness to the masque of ten to fifteen years earlier. This music, together with that of *The Tempest* was published in 1675 under the title: *The English Opera, etc.* It cannot be said that Lock's claim to be the originator of English opera is made good, and nothing really deserving of the name appeared until Purcell had produced it. 1673 also saw the publication of *Melothesia : or Certain General Rules for Playing upon a Continued Bass. With a Choice Collection of Lessons for the Harpsichord or Organ of all sorts . . .*", which appears to be the first work produced in England containing rules for playing from a figured bass;—at least the first work to survive. William Penny is supposed to have written on the subject before 1670, but no copies of his book are known to exist. Lock's *Melothesia* was dedicated to Roger L'Estrange (*q.v.*). 1673 was a very busy year for the composer, for in it he also conducted his spirited defence of the traditional system of notation against the innovations suggested by Thomas Salmon (*q.v.*). Beyond references to him in the Lord Chamberlain's Records there is nothing of importance to add, and in August, 1677, Lock died. On May 22nd, 1677, he was authorized to act in the absence of Nicholas Staggins, the Master of the Musick (*L.C.R., Vol.* 746), and on September 10th of that year he is given as "deceased" with Henry Purcell "composer in ordinary . . . for the violin to his Majesty" in his place (*Id.*, *Vol.* 480). Purcell contributed an Elegy "on the Death of his Worthy Friend, Mr. Matthew Locke" to Book II of *Choice Ayres and Dialogues*. Lock did not attain to any great age, being only about forty-seven years old at his death; but his influence was undoubtedly great in the domain of stage-music, and although we know that Henry Purcell obtained most of his inspiration from other sources, there can be little doubt that "his Worthy Friend, Mr. Locke" had something to do with the development of the younger man's theatrical style. Portraits of Lock are contained in *Add.* 33965 and *Add.* 17801 (*B.M.*), the latter engraved from the portrait in the Music School, Oxford.

Lesser compositions of Lock's are contained in *Musick's Hand-Maide* (1663 and 1678), *Musick's Delight on the Cithren* (1666), *The Musical Companion* (1672), Greeting's *Pleasant Companion* (1682), Book IV of *The Theater of Music* (1687), *Harmonia Sacra* (1688), and many other publications of the period. Boyce included an anthem of Lock's in his collection of Cathedral Music, and Rimbault edited five pieces (*Ancient Vocal Music of England*, Nos. 16–18, 22 *and* 24). Novello and Co. have issued three anthems by him (two edited by Mr. J. E. West, and one by H. W. Hunt). A tremendous amount of sacred and secular music remains in manuscript, the chief collections possessing specimens being the British Museum (Canons, Duets, an Ode, a Masque, Part-Songs, Solo-Songs, Bass-Viol Duets, an Organ Solo, Harpsichord Solos, String Duets and Trios, extracts from *Melothesia*, Motets, Anthems, and a Service,— some autograph), Christ Church library, Oxford (Sacred Vocal and Instrumental), the Fitzwilliam Museum, Cambridge (a volume in Purcell's handwriting), Ely Cathedral, King's College, Cambridge, and the Royal College of Music, London.

LOOSEMORE (George) : Like his father Henry Loosemore (*q.v.*) George was an organist and composer of sacred music. He commenced his career as a chorister at

King's College (Cambridge) while his father was there, and obtained his post as organist at Trinity College (Cambridge) at the Restoration and the resumption of the Cathedral services. When his father resumed work at Cambridge, George may have taken his place in the North establishment at Kirtling. At the same time, it is a significant feature that Roger North, who gives so good an account of John Jenkins in his *Memoires of Musick*, should make no mention of Loosemore. It is not known when the organist died, but since he was succeeded at Trinity College in 1682, we may suppose this to have been the date of his death, or, at least, retirement. He became a Doctor of Music in 1665 (Cambridge). Tudway's collection (*Harl.* 7339, *B.M.*) contains his full anthem, " Glory be to God on high ". He is also represented in the Ely Cathedral organ-books.

LOOSEMORE (Henry): An organist and composer of ecclesiastical music who began his long association with the music of Cambridge as a chorister. Since he was organist of King's College in 1627, he could have been born not much after the opening of the century ; and at the organ of that College he remained active until the year of his death (1670). He became a *Mus. Bac.* of Cambridge in 1640. During the Commonwealth he resorted to the teaching of music, and was one of the masters to whom the North children of Kirtling owed their high musical culture. At the Restoration he resumed his work at King's College, lending his own organ until a new one was built. The *Dictionary of National Biography*, Henry Davey's *History* and other authoritative works suggest that Loosemore went abroad and died in a priory across the seas. This information seems to come from Anthony Wood, and is not likely to be correct. The King's College accounts show that he was in Cambridgeshire during the whole period lying between 1627 and 1670. His works include Services, Litanies (two printed by Jebb), Anthems, *etc.*, and a little instrumental music. Examples may be seen in the collections at Ely Cathedral, Peterhouse (Cambridge), and the British Museum. *Add.* 34800 *A, B, and C*, contain a composition for three viols and organ by this composer. One of the litanies in Jebb's collection has been reprinted by Novello and Co. (edited by J. B. Lott).

LOWE (Edward): An organist and writer of sacred music who enjoyed a considerable reputation during his lifetime. A native of Salisbury, he must have been born early in the seventeenth century, inasmuch as he was a chorister at Salisbury in the days of John Holmes, and organist of Christ Church, Oxford, in 1629–30. From this date onwards for fifty-two years he held the post, and after the Restoration added to it another of a like nature (with Dr. Child and Christopher Gibbons) in the Chapel Royal. In addition, he occupied the chair of music at the Oxford University (*Choragus*) in Dr. Wilson's place (*Life and Times of Anthony Wood*). Lowe played an important part in the musical life of Oxford during the Commonwealth, and was one of those who kept high the artistic standard of the concerts given in the houses of enthusiastic musicians. He died on July 11th, 1682, and lies interred in Christ Church Cathedral,

Oxford, Henry Purcell being sworn into his place as Chapel Royal organist.

Lowe's best-known work was a book the title-page of which describes its contents and purpose: "*A Short Direction for the Performance of Cathedrall Service.* Published for the Information of such Persons, as are Ignorant of it, and shall be call'd to officiate in Cathedralls, or Collegiate Churches, where it hath formerly been in use. By E. L. Oxford. 1661". Three years later he issued *A Review of some Short Directions . . with many usefull additions according to the Common Prayer Book, as it is now established.* Not much of his music has survived. A verse-anthem, " O Give thanks unto ye Lord," is contained in Tudway's collection (*Harl.* 7339 *B.M.*), and a second one, " When the Lord turned ", is in the Royal College of Music (in an example of Barnard's *Church Music*). Ely Cathedral possesses odd parts of further work of Lowe's. *Add.* 29396 (*B.M.*) includes a song to which he added a part. The major portion of this manuscript is in Lowe's handwriting, and it is possible that other (anonymous) compositions contained in it may be by him.

Lowe married Alice Peyton of Doddington, near Ely, in 1631, and had two daughters and seven sons, his second wife presenting him with another daughter.

LUDFORD (Nicholas): A composer of sacred music of some distinction who flourished early in the sixteenth century. Absolutely nothing is known of his life, and the only date we can fix with any degree of certainty is 1536 as the latest for some of his compositions. This is determined by the fact that the manuscript *Roy. App.* 45–48 (*B.M.*), which contains Masses by him,—one for each day of the week,—bears on the covers the arms of Katherine of Aragon (died 1536), the wife of Henry VIII. It is possible that Ludford held some appointment at the court of that Queen, but no proof is forthcoming. He is known to us only by his work, and such as is left is well worthy of revival; indeed, Sir Richard R. Terry has had music by Ludford performed at Westminster Cathedral.

In addition to the seven masses, offertoria, sequences, *etc.*, in the manuscript already alluded to, Ludford is represented in British Museum manuscripts *Harl.* 1709 (Motets: "Salue Regina, pudica mater", *fol.* 9; "Salue Regina, mater misericordie", *fol.* 49*b*; medius part only), and *Add.* 30520 (two mutilated leaves from an ancient choir-book, containing two out of the four parts of a *Benedictus* and an *Agnus Dei* by Ludford). Among the Gonville and Caius College manuscripts (Cambridge) are preserved four masses and other sacred compositions by him, and in the Peterhouse part-books he is also represented.

LUPO FAMILY: A family of Italian musicians who settled in England and became an important factor in the musical life at court for over a century. The "Lupus Italus" of the Peterhouse manuscripts may have been the first member of the family to come to England; but the earliest real information we possess refers to Ambrose Lupo. All doubts as to whether entries relating to "Ambrose", "Ambrosio", and "Ambrose de Milan" (with many variations in spelling) are to be taken as applying to Ambrose Lupo are cleared up by *Harl.*

1641 (*B.M.*) where "Ambrose de Millane alias Lupo " is mentioned in 1586. This being the case, we may suppose that this musician arrived in England (or at any rate, was already active here), early in 1540 (*temp. Henry VIII*), for among the new appointments entered in May of that year, we find that Ambrose da Milano was admitted as " Viall ". He was permanently engaged on November 3rd of the same year. In 1559 he is given as Lupso and in 1570 his salary is mentioned in a Public Record Office account as having been 20*d.* per day with the customary 16*l.* 2*s.* 6*d.* for livery. In 1578–9 he received a New Year's gift from Queen Elizabeth. At New Year, 1587, Ambrose presented the Queen with two vessels of " sweet water ",—whatever that may have been. According to Hardy's *Syllabus*, Ambrose Lupo died early in 1594, and was succeeded at Lady Day by William Warren. The *Dictionary of National Biography* gives the date of his death as 1596, and refers the reader to the Hatfield manuscripts, *Part* IV, 19).

In 1563 (November 26th) we meet with Joseph Lupo for the first time, when a warrant was issued for six liveries (*L.C.R., Vol.* 811). In 1586 he is included among the violins (*Harl.* 1641, *B.M.*), and in the accounts for 1594 he is again mentioned. Three years later he also received a New Year gift from the Queen, and in 1602 he is mentioned in the same connection. In 1603 he attended Elizabeth's funeral. In the following year we meet with him for the last time in the State Papers, and the date of his death is not to be determined with certainty. A madrigal by him,— " Dueil, double Dueil ",— is contained in the British Museum manuscript *Royal App.* 57, and in 1594 he wrote some verses for John Mundy's *Songs and Psalms.*

Peter or Pietro Lupo found his first employment with the Earl of Leicester (*Dic. Nat. Biog.*), but in 1570 we find him among Queen Elizabeth's " Violins " with the salary of 20*d.* per diem and the usual livery-allowance. He also received the New Year's gifts mentioned above (in 1581, 20*s.*, 1587, 1602, and 1605), and after the last date vanished from the records.

Horatio Lupo was engaged for life as a violinist on February 6th, 1612, and in 1625 he was still mentioned (*L.C.R., Vol.* 557). Nothing more is known of him.

The most important members of the family were two men named Thomas. They are both frequently mentioned in the State Papers, and it is almost impossible to separate them. Thomas I is found in 1593 as a violinist, and is mentioned in 1597 as the recipient of a New Year's gift. In 1605 Thomas *senior* and Thomas *junior* are named in the same document, and all doubt as to the existence of two musicians of the same name,—for a time contemporaneous, — must vanish. Indeed, it is possible,—and very probable, —that there were actually *three* Thomases active at the same time. Of the two named together in 1605, one is given as the son of Pietro Lupo and the other as son of Joseph Lupo (*Annalen*). No attempt will be made to identify any one of these musicians with the subject of any particular entry, for such an attempt would be sheer waste of time. One of the few things we know of these three Thomases is that one of them (probably Joseph's son) died in 1627 or 1628, for in May of the latter year Robert Johnson petitioned for the vacant post. The second Thomas died before May 19th, 1637, for on that date, Lydia Lupo, widow of Thomas Lupo, petitioned for her late husband's arrears of salary. The same document states that Theophilus Lupo was their son (*Cal. S.P.*). The three Thomases were probably a pair of cousins and their uncle. The youngest of these three evidently died during the Commonwealth, for at the Restoration his successor was appointed,— "Philip Beckett in the place of Thomas Lupo" (*L.C.R., Vol.* 741).

Several compositions in various manuscripts are headed with the name of Thomas Lupo; but, except with very great reservations it will be impossible to apportion them justly among the two or three bearers of the name. It might be assumed, again conjecturally, that the sacred compositions may have been the work of the son of Joseph Lupo, while the viol and other instrumental music may have to be ascribed to the son of Pietro.

As before, no attempt can here be made to separate the compositions. Not much of the music under consideration has been printed. Two numbers by Thomas Lupo appear in Leighton's *Teares or Lamentacions* of 1614, and works by the same are contained in *XX Koninck-lycke Fantasien* for three gambas (Amſterdam, 1648). In 1607 one of them collaborated with Thomas Giles in writing the songs for the Campion masque in honour of Lord Hay's wedding. This song,—" Shows and nightly Revels ",—has been reprinted by Mr. G. E. P. Arkwright, in his *Old English Edition* (*Pt.* I, 1889). British Museum manuscripts with work by one or other of the Thomases are: *Add.* 29427 (Anthems, *ca.* 1616), *Add.* 29372–7 (Myriell's collection, 1616), *Add.* 17792–6, *Eg.* 995 (after 1604), and *Roy. App.* 63 (being a copy of Leighton's *Teares, etc.*). A few compositions are in the library of Chriſt Church, Oxford, and the " Lupus " of the Elizabeth Rogers Virginal Book is moſt likely also one of these musicians.

It is possible that some rough classification might be attempted to differentiate between the two later Thomases by taking one to have been a luteniſt and singer, and the other a violiniſt. But the difficulty is that so many references merely give the name of the musician and omit to mention the employment.

The son of one of the Thomases (either Joseph's or Peter's grandson), Theophilus, was appointed as one of the King's " musicians in ordinary in the place of his father Thomas Lupo, deceased ", with " the sum of 40*l.* yearly as wages . . . with 16*l.* 2*s.* 6*d.* yearly as livery " (*L.C.R., Vol.* 738). In 1631 he played " contratenor " in the band of violins (*Id.*). His name occurs frequently in these records until 1641, after which the Rebellion disbanded the royal orcheſtras. He muſt have died during the Interregnum, for after the Reſtoration he was entered as " deceased " and Humphrey Madge was appointed to fill his poſts (*L.C.R., Vol.* 479).

There can be no doubt that the earlier members of this family exercised considerable influence upon the English performers,— especially on the bowed inſtruments,—and on this account they have been included in this volume. The later branches of the family are, of course, to be considered as Englishmen. Before the seventeenth century had half run its course the English players on the viols had little to learn from abroad. On this point, and regarding the use of the word " violin " in connection with the earliest Lupos, see the article on " viols " in my *Dictionary of Old English Music*.

LUPO (Ambrose, Horatio, Joseph, Peter (Pietro), Theophilus, Thomas): *see* LUPO FAMILY.

LUPPO, LUPSO: *see* LUPO FAMILY.

M

MACE (Thomas): A lutenist, teacher of lute-playing and the author of a book which is a valuable commentary upon the musical methods of its time. The date of his birth can only be arrived at approximately. The portrait prefixed to his work of 1676 bears the legend that the author was sixty-three years of age. But there is nothing to show that the picture was drawn and engraved in the year of publication, and he may have been born in 1612 or even earlier. The statement that Mace died in 1709 at the age of ninety (thus placing his birth in 1619) can scarcely be accepted, since the portrait printed in 1676 with the inscription " aet. suae 63 " is more likely to be correct. He spent the earlier years of his life at Cambridge, and sang in the choir of Trinity College. Round about 1636 he married a lady from Yorkshire, for in *Musick's Monument* he gives a composition entitled " The Author's Mistress ", inspired by thoughts of his fiancée, and " made forty years ago ", while he was at Cambridge and she at York. Mace's story of this piece provides a pleasant word-picture of the musician's home-life: " After I was married and had brought My Wife Home, to Cambridge; It so fell out, that one Rainy morning, I stay'd within; and in My Chamber, My Wife and I, were all alone; she intent upon Her needle-works, and I Playing upon my Lute, at the Table by Her; she sat very still and Quiet, Listening to all I Play'd, without a Word a Long Time, till at Last, I hapned to Play this Lesson: which, so soon as I had once played, she earnestly desired me to Play it again; For, said She, that shall be called, My Lesson . . . and most of my Scholars since, call It, Mrs. Mace, to This Day ". During the Civil War he appears to have gone to York, for he was in that city when it was besieged by the revolutionary forces. He evidently was an excellent teacher of practical music, but was prevented from becoming a great executant by a couple of physical disabilities. He had had his arms broken, and although the injury healed successfully, he was never after able to aspire to the technic required at that time. In addition to this he gradually loſt his hearing as he advanced in age, and finally experienced great difficulty in making the pursuit of music provide him with a sufficient suſtenance. He appears to have fallen into great ſtraits towards the end of his life, and a British Museum manuscript contains an advertisement offering his inſtruments and music for sale.

The work by which he is remembered was published in 1676 under the title: *"Musick's Monument*; or a Remembrancer of the beſt Practical Musick, Both Divine and Civil, that has ever been known, to have been in the World. Part I shows the necessity for singing the Psalms well, in Parochial Churches, or not to sing at all; Directing how They may be Well sung, Certainly; by Two several Ways, or means . . . also showing that Cathedral Musick may be much improved, and Refined. Part II Treats of the Noble Lute, (the Beſt of Inſtruments) now made easie; and all. Its occult lock'd-up Secrets Plainly laid open, never before

Discovered; whereby It is now become so Familiarly easie, as any inſtrument of worth, known in the world; . . . Part III. In the Third Part, The Generous Viol, in Its righteſt use, is Treated upon; with some curious observations, never before Handled, concerning it, and Musick in general ". The inſtructions were sound and practical, and Mace's son John, and John Immyns, to mention only two, learnt to play the lute from this book alone. The " Epiſtle Dedicatory " shows him to have been a devout and sincere man. The dedication reads : " To Thee One-only-Oneness, I Direct my Weak Desires, and works, *etc.* . . . I am not of that Catholick Belief (I mean the Roman's Faith) who seek relief (at th' second Hand) from Saints ; . . . Thou know'ſt, O Searcher of All Hearts how I, With Right Downright-Sincere Sincerity, Have longed long, to do some little Good ". Moſt of the Prefaces, Introductions, and Epiſtles are in verse, and Mace answers objectors by saying that they are good verses, and, moreover, " . . . 'Tis for my Recreation, Thus I do ". The book contains a picture of " The Dyphone:

a Double-Lute, The Lute of fifty strings. Invented by myself and made with my own hands, 1672 ". It shows a lute with a tremendous body, a neck at each end, and a duplicate set of strings. He evolved this instrument to give him a lute of greater tone-volume and power, to combat his growing deafness. He was wont to place his teeth at the edge of the belly of the instrument and thus hear what he played by direct vibration. The increase of tone obtained with this instrument came largely from the sympathetic vibration of the second set of strings. In 1675 he wrote a non-musical pamphlet entitled: "Profit, conveniency, and pleasure, to the Whole Nation. Being a short rational Discourse, lately presented to His Majesty, concerning the Highways of England, etc." *Add.* 11581 (*B.M.*) contains extracts from *Musick's Monument* in the handwriting of Dr. Charles Burney. The date of Mace's death is not to be fixed with certainty.

MARBECK (MAR-BECKE) (John) (*also* MER-BECKE): A celebrated organist and composer of sacred music of the sixteenth century. His fame is based chiefly upon a Mass and his *Booke of Common Praier noted* (1550). It may seem curious that the man who wrote the latter, and narrowly escaped the stake for heresy, should have written a mass; and the only explanation is that he must have composed the latter in his early years,—at any rate before he attached himself so ardently to the cause of the Reformation. But whatever the explanation for the mass, and whatever its period, the fact remains that it secures for him a place among the good Tudor musicians. The work is too uneven and disconnected to give him the right to claim equality with the best men of the period; but the total effect is one of breadth and dignity, added to occasional exquisite tenderness.

Born early in the sixteenth century, Marbeck is first to be met with as a lay clerk of St. George's, Windsor. In 1541, he became organist there. According to the dedication to Edward VI of Marbeck's *Concordance* (1550), he said that he had been "brought up in your highnes college at Wyndsore in study of musike and plaiyng on organs, wherin I consumed vainly the greatest part of my life ". The word "vainly" says much in explanation of the fact that after the year in which the *Booke of Common Praier noted* appeared, he devoted himself almost exclusively to the writing of books against the Roman cult. He was much influenced by Calvin's doctrines, and in 1542–3 when search was being made at Windsor for heretical literature, a good deal of damaging evidence was discovered at Marbeck's lodgings. Among other writings the manuscript of a *Concordance* of the Bible in the vernacular brought about his immediate arrest and he was conveyed to London. After having been examined by Bishop Gardiner he was censured for having dared to attempt to replace Latin with English, and on July 26th, 1544, was sent back to Windsor for trial. After one disagreement among the jurymen, he was eventually found guilty and condemned. Others who were tried with him were executed on the following day, but Marbeck, on account of the favour shown him by Gardiner and others, received a royal pardon. His musical talents are supposed to have

secured this release for him. After this sharp lesson, he was content to keep his religious opinions to himself until it was safe to express them aloud. In 1550 the *Booke of Common Praier noted* appeared, — an adaptation based upon the early Plain Chant and suited to the requirements of the Prayer-Book of Edward VI. In the same year the degree of Doctor of Music was conferred upon him by the Oxford University. He was still active as organist at Windsor during the early years of Elizabeth's reign, but it is not known when he retired from the post. The date given for his death is *ca.* 1585. His religious writings do not concern us here. Foxe, in the second English edition of the *Actes and Monuments*, says that Marbeck was still living in 1583.

The *Booke of Common Praier noted* was reprinted in facsimile in 1844 ; in 1845 by Rimbault, in 1857 by Jebb, and various sections of it have been issued separately by several publishers. The mass, " Per Arma Justitiae ", is preserved in six part-books in the Forrest-Heyther collection at

Oxford, and parts of it (" Et in terra Pax ", " Pleni sunt coeli " and " Benedictus " are in Dr. Burney's handwriting in *Add.* 11586 (*B.M.*), apparently copied from the Oxford manuscripts. A motet by Marbeck, " Domine Jesu Christi "—is in Sadler's Part-Books (Bodleian, Oxford) and another composition (" Ave dei Matris ") is in the Peterhouse collection (Cambridge). He is represented in Hawkins's *History* by a three-part anthem.

MARSH (Alphonso) (I): Like his father Robert Marsh (*q.v.*), Alphonso the Elder was a lutenist and singer in the royal service. He was most probably born in January, 1627 (he was baptized at St. Margaret's, Westminster, on the 28th of the month), and beyond this we know nothing of his early life. In 1647–8 (February 8th), when in his twenty-first year, he married Mary Cheston in the church where he was baptized. At the performances of Davenant's *Siege of Rhodes* in 1656 he sang the part of Pirrhus (Bass). From that moment we lose sight of him until the Restoration of the House of Stuart when he was appointed to the " Private

music in ordinary in the place of Thomas Day for a voyce ", at a salary of 40*l.* per annum. He was also a Gentleman of the Chapel Royal and in 1671 (May 20th) the Cheque-Book mentions him as an authority on the customs of the Chapel. In 1674 he sang and played the theorbo in the famous masque at court. In the account of payments (May 27th, 1675) made to musicians playing in this masque at Whitehall, " Mr. Marsh, senior ", is mentioned as having given " extraordinary attendance " on the " Harpsicalls and Lute " (*L.C.R., Vol.* 745). He died in 1681, the Cheque-Book containing the entry: " Mr. Alfonso Marsh, senior. . . . departed this life the 9th day of Aprill, 1681 ". In the private music of the king he was succeeded by John Abell (*L.C.R., Vol.* 480). His will was proved by his second wife, Rebecca Marsh, and by it he bequeathed one-third of the money due to him from the treasury to his son by his first marriage, and two-thirds to his widow.

Specimens of his popular vocal music may be seen in the publications of 1669–76, and one song of his,—" Sure 'twas a dreame ",—from *Select Ayres and Dialogues* (1669) was copied into *Harl.* 7549 (*B.M.*). His signature is contained in *Harl.* 1911 (Minutes of the "Corporacion for regulating the Art and Science of Musick ").

MARSH (Alphonso) (II): The son of Alphonso I by his first marriage, Alphonso II came to the notice of the court when he sang in the Whitehall masque of 1674. He is entered under the heading "Vocall Musick" as "Mr. Marsh, junior" (*L.C.R., Vol.* 745). He was appointed to the Chapel Royal in 1676: "Mr. William Howes . . . departed this life the 21st of Aprill, 1676, in whos place was sworne Mr. Alphonso Marsh, junior, the 25 of the same month, being S. Markes Day, 1676 " (*Ch. Bk. C.R.*). He was admitted to the private music of the court (William and Mary) on July 20th, 1689 (*L.C.R., Vol.* 486), and died in 1692, the Cheque Book of the Chapel Royal recording: "Mr. Alphonso Marsh departed this life the 5 day of Aprill, 1692 ". He was buried four days later in the Cloisters of Westminster Abbey.

His compositions, like those of his father, were of a popular type, and examples are contained in the *Theater of Musick* (*Bk.* IV, 1687, one song), in the *Banquet of Musick* (1688, *etc.*, two songs), and in *Choice Ayres* (1673, *etc.*, four songs).

MARSH (Robert): Singer and lutenist, and member of Charles the First's musical establishment from 1625 to 1630–1. Beyond his court activities nothing is known of him, and but for the fact that he was the founder of a musical family he would hardly merit remembrance to-day. We see his name first in a list of royal musicians attending the funeral of James I, which would point to his having already been in the service of that king. The Calendar of State Papers, quoting from the official lists, gives 20*l*. per annum as his salary. The Lord Chamberlain's Records, under date January 6th, 1630–1, mentions his death, which must therefore have occurred at the end of 1630 or in the first five days of 1630–1: "Warrant to swear Mr. Henry Lawes a musician for the voices in place of Robert Marsh deceased ".

MARSON (George): One of the contributors to the

Triumphes of Oriana (1601) where he is described as *Mus. Bac.* and the composer of some anthems and services. Until quite recently nothing more was known of him. The publication of Davey's *History of English Music (Ed.* 1921), however, brought to public notice the fact that Marson was organist at Canterbury Cathedral, married there in 1599 and was buried in February, 1631–2. The Oriana madrigal, " The Nymphs and Shepherds dance Lavolto's ", has been reprinted by L. Benson and later by Dr. Fellowes.

MASON (George): An organist of Trinity College, Cambridge (from 1612) who is remembered to-day through his having, in collaboration with one John Earsden, provided a set of short compositions for the King's entertainment while James I was visiting the Earl of Cumberland. These slight pieces were published in 1618 with the title, " The Ayres that were sung and played at Brougham Castle in Westmerland, in the King's entertainment . . . Given by the Rt. Hon. the Earle of Cumberland and his right noble sonne the Lord Clifford ".

Add. 30826–8 (*B.M.*) contains eight Pavanes in five parts for viols (Cantus, Altus, and Tenor parts alone preserved). Davey thinks that Mason may have been the Earl of Cumberland's lutenist; but there appears to be no justification for such a supposition.

MATTEIS (Nicola): An Italian violinist who came to England about 1672 (certainly before 1674), and whose playing and teaching exercised a great influence upon the art of violin-playing in this country towards the end of the seventeenth century. There can be no doubt that he was an excellent musician and his printed music is remarkably rich in markings to indicate phrasing,—a point generally left entirely to the discretion of the performer in those days. Roger North, who was contemporary with the violinist, and obviously had heard him play, gives what is doubtlessly the best and most authoritative account of Matteis's character and powers. In his *Memoires of Musick* he says that Matteis's " manner was singular, but in one respect excelled all that had bin knowne before in England, which was the

Y

Arcata (bowing). His ſtac- catos, tremolos, divisions, and indeed his whole manner was surprising, and every ſtroke of his was a mouthfull ". His work, as may be expected, is eminently suited to his inſtrument, and exhibits an originality and a brightness quite equal to the beſt pro- duced at the period. North considered him second only to Corelli. John Evelyn heard him on November 19th, 1674, and wrote in his *Diary*: " I heard that ſtupendous violin, Signor Nicholao . . . whom I never heard mortal man exceed on that inſtrument. He had a ſtroke so sweet, and made it speak like the voice of a man, and, when he pleased, like a concert of several inſtru- ments . . . nothing approached the violin in Nicholao's hand. He played such ravishing things as aſtonished us all." North gives an excellent account of Matteis's life in England: " When he came over firſt he was very poor, but not so poor as proud, which was the reason that kept him back, so that he had no acquaintance for a long time, but a merchant or two who patronized him. And he valuing himself at an excessive rate, squeezed considerable

sums out of them. By degrees he became more taken notice of; he was heard play at court, but his manner did not take, and he behaved himself faſtously; no person muſt whisper while he played, which sort of attention had not bin the fashion at Court. . . . . In short, he was so outrageous in his demands, especially for his high pieces solos, that very few would come up to him and he con- tinued low and obscure a long time. And he had continued so but for two or three vertuosos; who were Dr. Walgrave . . . Sir Roger Leſtrange . . . and Mr. Bridgman the under-secretary . . . They got him into their acquaint- ance and courting him in his owne way by discours, shewing him the temper of the English . . . They brought him by degrees into such good temper as made him eſteemed and sought after, and having got many scollars, though at moderate rates his purs filled apace, which con- firmed his conversion, and he continued tractable as long as he lived ". After an unprofit- able trip to Paris, Matteis returned to London where " he fell into such credit and imployment that he took a great hous, and after the mode of his country lived luxuriously, which brought diseases upon him of which he dyed. He left a son Nicholas, whom he taught upon the violin from his cradle; and I have seen the boy in coats play to his father's Guittarre ". It may be mentioned in passing that Matteis also played and wrote for the Guitar.

He published a good deal of violin music in England, chiefly short airs and dance-forms such as Allemandes, Sarabandes, Courantes, and Gigues. A list of his works is given in Rimbault's notes to the Musical Antiquarian Society's edition of North's *Memoires of Musick*. Matteis also wrote some vocal music, notably *A Collection of New Songs . . . made purposely for the use of his Scholars*, a copy of which was in Rimbault's possession. He wrote the St. Cecilia Ode for 1695, and a performance of it was advertised in the *London Gazette* for January 4th, 1696. Two years later another "Consort of vocal and instrumental music" of his was performed in York-Buildings, and advertised in the *Gazette* (May 30th, 1698). Mention must also be made of Matteis's "*False*

Consonances of Musick, or Instructions for the playing a true Base upon the Guitarre, with choice examples and cleare Directions, *etc.*" A song of his,—" When ere I gaze in Sylvia's face ",— was printed in the *Gentleman's Journal* for February, 1691–2 (*pp.* 33, 34). In the British Museum manuscripts are an organ solo, trios, and quartets by Matteis, as well as violin and harpsichord duets by his son.

MAYNARD (John): A lutenist and composer of vocal and instrumental music in the first half of the seventeenth century. Beyond what the dedication to his publication of 1611 tells us, we know nothing of his life. From the inscription just mentioned we gather that his " ever honoured lady and mistris " was Lady Joan Thynne of " Cause " (Caux) Castle (Shropshire), and that " this poore play-worke of mine had its prime originall and birthwright in your own house, when by nearer seruice I was obliged yours . . . ." He was also lutenist, and probably teacher of that instrument at St. Julian's School (Herts). On the authority of Anthony Wood (*Manu-*

script *Lives of Musicians*), Maynard was among the firſt to write for the gamba lyra-way. This is not unlikely; his date will fall within the period at which the earlieſt examples of this usage appeared (Tobias Hume, 1605; Ferrabosco, 1609). The work by which he is known to us at the present-day is: "*The XII Wonders of the World.* Set and Composed for the Violl de Gambo, the Lute and the Voyce to sing the Verse, all three jointly, and none severall: also Lessons for the Lute and Base Violl to play alone, *etc.*" (1611). This title sufficiently describes the contents of the work. The words of the twelve songs were designed to define the charaĉters of twelve different persons,—the Bachelor, the County Gentleman, the Courtier, the Divine, the Lawyer, the Maid, the Married man, the Merchant, the Physician, the Soldier, the Wife, and the Widow,—and were the work of Sir John Davies. Wood (*Athenae Oxon.* III, 892) quotes "the Courtier" and "the Deuine". On the title-page of the book there is a Canon in eight parts ("Oh, follow me, Tom"; given in score in *Add.* 34071

B.M.). *Add.* 10444 (*Id.*) contains an Almain by Maynard, and an organ piece of his is in the Royal College of Music (London).

MELL (Davis) (*also* Davies *or* David): One of the small number of really excellent English violiniſts who flourished in the seventeenth century, Anthony Wood (*Diary of his Life*) saying that he "was accounted hithertoo the beſt for the violin in England, . . . but after Baltzar came unto England, and shew'd his moſt wonderful parts on that inſtrument, Mell was not so admired, yet he played sweeter, was a well-bred gentleman, and not given to excessive drinking as Baltzar was ". Born at Wilton, near Salisbury, on November 15th, 1604, Davis Mell was the son of a man in the service of the third Earl of Pembroke. He was originally a clockmaker, but at the age of twenty-one we already find him mentioned in the Lord Chamberlain's Records as one of the "musicians for Violins" (account of the funeral of James I, 1625, *L.C.R., Vol.* 557). On January 22nd, 1628–9, he was granted twenty marks for a treble violin which he supplied for use in the royal music (*Id.*, *Vol.* 738). In April, 1633, he was paid for providing music-books " for the violins " (*Id.*). On March 6th, 1635–6, further similar payments were made to him. During the Commonwealth he shared the fortunes and misfortunes of most of the royal musicians, and supported himself by teaching (*v.* Playford's *Musical Banquet*). He must have taken an active part in the musical schemes of the times, for his name appears with those of others in a petition to the " Committee of the Councel for Advancement of Musicke " (1656) suggesting that a college of music be founded (*Annalen*). The petition was unsuccessful. On August 1st, 1652, Mell visited the diarist John Evelyn who called him a " rare musician " (*Diary*). Wood heard the violinist when the latter visited Oxford in March, 1657–8, writing that " the company did look upon Mr. Mell to have a prodigious hand on the violin, and they thought that no person, as all in London did, could goe beyond him. . . . (He) played farr sweeter than Baltzar, yet Baltzar's hand was more quick ". In

the petition to Cromwell Mell styles himself " Gentleman of His Highness' Musique " and on the death of the Protector, the violinist followed in the funeral procession. At the Restoration Mell was reappointed to his old place, was given the posts of private musician to the king, a place in " the broken Consort ", and, jointly with George Hudson, the direction of the band of violins (*v.* *L.C.R.*, *Vol.* 741, *under date May* 31st, 1661). His salary in 1660 (November 9th) was given as 110*l.* per annum (*Id.*, *Vol.* 741). On August 30th, 1662, Mell is entered as " deceased ", with William Yowckney in his place as violinist (*Id.*, *Vol.* 741), but Nagel (*Annalen*) speaks of a warrant issued as early as May 3rd, of that year, granting one of Mell's places to John Banister I. The Lord Chamberlain's Records mention the admission of Banister into the place of " Daniel " Mell on March 20th, 1662–3. The Christian name is obviously a clerical error, and Mell's death is thus to be placed early in 1663. Some of his livery allowance was owing when he died, and in 1667 the money due for the year 1661 was still owing to his executors (*L.C. Papers, Bundle* 23).

Short compositions by Mell are to be seen in *Court Ayres* (1655) and in the *Division Violin* (1685). He is also represented in *Courtly Masquing Ayres* (1662; a copy in the library of the *R.C.M.*). *Add.* 15118 contains two Preludes, two Corants, a Saraband, and an Almain by him (*B.M.*).

A Thomas Mell is frequently mentioned in the State Papers as a musician for the wind-instruments between 1625 and 1666, and a Leonard Mell is also given as a "Tenor Violin"; but they do not appear to have left any compositions behind them. It is not known if they were related to Davis Mell.

MELL (Leonard, Thomas): *see* MELL (Davis).

MERBECKE (John):   *see* MARBECK (John).

M I L T O N (John): The father of the poet, judging from those examples of his work that have come down to us, was a most accomplished musician. Whether he was trained with the object of embracing music as a profession is much open to doubt ; but there is nothing remarkable in the son of a yeoman in comfortable cir-

cumstances at that period receiving a good education in this art. John Aubrey,— antiquarian, inveterate gossip, and friend of the poet, —may not be the most trustworthy of historians, but it is possible that this information concerning the Miltons is in the main correct, for he had in the poet a ready source of knowledge. From him we learn that John Milton, senior, was connected with Christ Church, Oxford, and it is possible that his predilection for sacred music was bred while singing in the choir there, though no means of verifying this are available.

Born about 1563 in Oxfordshire, John Milton was "cast out" by his father (Richard) for abjuring the Catholic faith. This must have been before 1595. He came to London, was bound apprentice to a member of the Scriveners' Company in 1595, and before the century closed was a freeman of that Company, becoming Master thirty-four years later (though he did not serve in that capacity). He lived in Bread Street, in the City, where all his children were born, and where his poetical son grew up in an atmosphere of music, meeting under the scrivener's roof the best-known musicians of the day. Masson (*Life of Milton*) advances the suggestion that the elder Milton practised music professionally when he came to London,—but we must not forget that his scrivenership would have left him little time for such a pursuit. It is likely that he managed to draw some income from both callings, since he became quite well-to-do. After living successively at Horton (Bucks.) and Reading he died at his son's house in the Barbican (London, E.C.) in March, 1646–7. He is buried at St. Giles's, Cripplegate.

Although we cannot pretend to see in John Milton a musician of the first rank, he is far from being negligible. His music is generally characterized by a certain lack of ease; but " O had I wings " (in Leighton's *Teares and Lamentacions*, 1614), and " Fayre Orian in the morne " (*The Triumphes of Oriana*, 1601) are particularly good, and deserving of present use. What the son thought of the father's musicianship is clear from that exceedingly fine Latin sonnet, " Ad Patrem ":
" Nunc tibi quid mirum, si me genuisse poetam

Contigerit, charo si tam prope sanguine juncti
Cognates artes, studiumque affine sequamur:
Ipse volens Phoebus se dispertire duobus,
Altera dona mihi, dedit altera dona parenti,
Dividuumque Deum genitorque puerque tenemus."
Milton's grandson, Edward Phillips,—obtaining his knowledge from his poetical uncle,—tells us that the scrivener " compos'd an *In nomine* of Forty Parts: for which he was rewarded with a Gold medal and Chain by a Polish Prince to whom he presented it ". John Aubrey's version makes of the composition (supposing him to be alluding to the same work) " a song of four-score parts for the Lantgrave of Hesse, for wch. highnesse sent a medall of gold o.a.n.p." (or a noble present). Speculation on this point would be useless.

The traceable works of John Milton include the six-part contribution to *The Triumphes of Oriana* already alluded to. To Sir William Leighton's *Teares, etc.*, he sent, in the first series (" Consort Songs ") one piece accompanied by a lute-part in tablature; and among the five-part compositions " for voyces ", Nos. 4, 15, and 20 in good style are from his pen. For Thomas Ravenscroft's *Whole Booke of Psalmes* (1621) Milton harmonized two tunes, one of them, — " York " — in two versions. Both this tune and " Norwich " are still used. Sir Frederick Bridge informed me that these tunes were not the inventions of Milton, but that he was responsible only for the harmony; " York " tune, said Sir Frederick, was already printed in Edinburgh, in 1615. Thomas Myriell's interesting manuscript, " Tristitiae Remedium " (1616; *B.M. Add.* 29372–7) contains five compositions by Milton (two five-part and three six-part), while the Christ Church (Oxford) collection includes a four-part sacred work and some instrumental fancies. Six anthems have been reprinted under the editorship of Mr. G. E. P. Arkwright (*Old English Edition*).

MORLEY (Thomas): One of the leading musicians of the Elizabethan era, whose fame is based upon his achievements as a madrigalist. Deriving encouragement from the beginnings made by his teacher, William Byrd, he developed the madrigal to a pitch of excellence which entitles him to be regarded as the head of the school of composers who were contemporaneous with him, and as an example to be followed by his successors. Leaning more to the secular branch of vocal music, Morley may be said to have reached a point similar to that attained by Byrd in sacred music. Like his teacher he was very versatile; and although his madrigals, canzonets, and ballets show him at his best, some of his sacred and instrumental music is not by any means negligible. His secular vocal music still surprises us in its modernity; and it may stand as an example of what can be achieved by a musician of imagination and talent, with forms that were then not yet quite free from the influence of the ancient modes. Temperamentally Morley was a composer who could write such peaceful, and at times pathetic, music as occurs in the Burial Service in G; and who could, when the visions of cloistered serenity and heaven's eternity had faded from his mind, compose his care-free madrigals and ballets with all the enthusiasm of a musical Epicurian. It is difficult for us to realize that the writer of the *Plaine and Easie Introduction* and the composer of some of the melodies contained in his publications,—so popular in character and so tuneful that at least two of them have been considered as traditional, —should be one and the same person. There are not many musicians of whom it may be said,—as it can of Morley,—that his workmanship is as near perfection as human ingenuity can make it. In addition to the two classes of vocal music already alluded to, Morley was also very successful as a writer for the keyboard instruments, and his string-music, though written at an age when vocal influence on instrumental music was still very strong, is up to, and even above, the standard that prevailed for some years after his death. With his master, Byrd, he shares the distinction of having been one of the first to write music for stage-lyrics, although the sweet and intimate " It was a lover and his lass " (which can undoubtedly be given to Morley) was vastly different in character from Byrd's " Preces Deo

fundamus " (to Legge's *Richardus III*). The late Sir Frederick Bridge, who saw one of the few authentic copies in existence, made a transcript of it that is faithful to the original text. He looked upon the lyric with great reverence, and once told me that he thought it " an uncanny thing that we should be able to hear a song the words of which were written by Shakespeare, and the music by a composer contemporaneous with him; the two men living near each other in London, being assessed for the income-tax together, and appealing against it at the same time ". Again like his teacher, Morley enjoyed a high reputation during his lifetime. Francis Meres names him in *Palladis Tamia* (1598), while Thomas Weelkes wrote a very fine *Lament* (six-part) on the death of his " dearest friend " Thomas Morley. Ravenscroft, about eleven years after Morley's death, wrote of him as " the Sun in the Firmament of our Art " who first gave light in our understanding with his precepts ". One more piece of contemporary evidence of Morley's reputation, generally attri-

buted to Drayton, is worth
quoting :
" Such was old Orpheus'
    cunning,
That senseless things drew
    near him
And herds of beasts to
    hear him.
The stock, the stone, the ox,
    the ass came running.
Morley! but this en-
    chanting
To thee, to be the music
    god, is wanting;
And yet thou needst not
    fear him.
Draw thou the shepherds
    still, and bonny lasses,
And envy him not stocks,
    stones, oxen, asses."
If the information given
in a manuscript preserved in
the Bodleian library (Sadler's
part-books,—" Domine non
est ") is correct, Morley was
born in 1557, for he is given
as being aged nineteen in
1576. On his own showing
he was a pupil of William
Byrd, but beyond this nothing
more is known of his early
life. The first piece of
authentic information we have
of him relates to his graduating as Bachelor of Music
at Oxford in 1588. At
about this time he is supposed
to have been organist of
St. Giles', Cripplegate, in
the City of London. This
supposition is based upon the
entry in a register of that
church which alludes to
" Thomas ye sonne of Thomas
Morley, Organist ". But it
cannot be said to prove that
Thomas, senior, was organist
of St. Giles'. To this period,
also, belongs the granting
of the printing licence
(previously held by Byrd and
Tallis) for twenty-one years
from 1588, his chief assigns
being Este and William
Barley ; the latter, indeed,
securing the monopoly on
Morley's death. That he
was organist of St. Paul's
Cathedral is certain, for in
an account of an entertainment given in Queen Elizabeth's honour (1591) he is
described as " organist of
Paules church ". Moreover,
the State Papers contain a
document (also 1591) sent
from the Low Countries,
in which it is said that there
was " one Morley that playeth
on the organes in poules ".
Exactly when he was
appointed to this post is
not to be decided with certainty. From the same paper
it appears that Morley
dabbled in religious politics
and that he was at one moment
a " good Catholicke " and
at another an apprehender
of the same. His connection

with the Cathedral terminated in 1592 when he was elected a member of the Chapel Royal. The Cheque-Book of that institution contains the entry : " 1592. Tho. Morley sworne 24th of July in Mr. Grene's roome " ; and on November 18th of the same year : " The same day also was sworne . . . . Mr. Morleye from the Epistler's place to the Gospeller's place and waiges". Of his marriage we know nothing beyond the fact that his wife's name was Susan. The Assessment Rolls for 1598 and 1600 (the former, printed by Hunter in 1845, being famous on account of its also containing Shakespeare's name) show that Morley was at that time living in the parish of St. Helens, Bishops-gate, and that both he and Shakespeare were assessed at 5*l.* The title-page of Carlton's *Madrigals* (1601) still shows that Morley was living in " little Saint Hellen's ". The registers of that parish record the baptism of his daughter Frances (August 19th, 1596) and her burial on February 9th, 1598–9. The baptismal entries referring to two more children appear : that of his son Christopher on

June 26th, 1599, and of his daughter Anne on July 28th, 1600. Towards the end of the sixteenth century Morley suffered considerably through indifferent health and mentions it in the preface to his *Plaine and Easie Introduction* (1597), adding, indeed, that he found the time to write that treatise by reason of " the solitarie life which I lead (being compelled to keep at home)". By the second year of the new century he was compelled (probably on account of his failing health) to leave the Chapel Royal. The Cheque-Book records on October 7th, 1602, that " George Woodson (from Winsore) was sworne . . . . in Thomas Morleyes room ". He could not have lived more than a year after his retirement, for on October 25th, 1603, his widow, Margaret Morley, was allowed to administer his possessions. All the dates fit in so well with the known circumstances of Morley's biography that we must suppose that this alludes to the musician under consideration. Accepting this we must similarly assume that Margaret was his second wife, for the mother of the children baptized in 1599 and 1600 was named Susan. Born in 1557 and dying in 1603, Morley was only forty-six years of age at his death. Taking into consideration Morley's comparatively short life and the calls made upon his time by his official appointments, he left a good deal of written music. His printed work, in chronological order, appeared as follows : 1593, *Canzonets, or Little Short Songs to Three Voyces* (containing twenty canzonets, each signed " Tho. Morley "; Cantus, Altus and Bassus) ; it was reprinted in 1606 and 1631 (also by Dr. Fellowes in *Vol.* I of the *English Madrigal School*) ; two German editions, translated by J. von Steinbach, appeared in 1612 and 1624 (Riemann). 1594, *Madrigalls to Foure Voyces* (twenty numbers ; twenty-two in the second edition, 1600) ; reprinted by Dr. Fellowes in *Vol.* II of the *English Madrigal School.* 1595, *The First Booke of Ballets to Five Voyces* ; second edition 1600 ; in score, edited by E. J. Rimbault in 1842 and by Dr. Fellowes in *Vol.* IV of the *English Madrigal School*; an Italian translation, London, 1595 ; an edition with German text by V. Haussmann, 1609 (Riemann).

1595, *The first Booke of Canzonets to Two Voyces* (twenty-one pieces, canzonets and instrumental fancies ; Dr. Fellowes, *Vol.* I) ; a second edition appeared in 1619. *Canzonets or litle Short Aers to fiue and sixe voices* was issued in 1597 (with lute accompaniment), containing twenty-one examples of Morley's finest work in this category ; it was reprinted by Dr. Fellowes in *Vol.* III of his series. In the same year he edited a selection of Italian *Canzonets, or Little Short Songs to foure voyces,* two of them being by Morley himself ; these are given by Dr. Fellowes in his *Vol.* II. We can see that the composer's failing health did not prevent him from doing editorial and literary work— for in addition to the two works just mentioned, he issued his celebrated *Plaine and Easie Introduction to Practical Musicke, set down in forme of a dialogue . . . ,* the first part teaching to sing, the second dealing with Descant, and the third treating of " Composition in Parts ". As a charming act of gratitude Morley dedicated this work " To the most excellent Musician Master William Birde ", hoping that it would show his "thankful mind : and the entire love and unfained affection" he had for his teacher. In all humility he says : "Accept . . . of this booke, . . . that you may exercise your deepe skill in censuring of what shall be amisse, as also to defend what is in it truly spoken, as that which somtime proceeded from your selfe". The instruction given was quite sound and perfectly adequate for the period. It was, indeed, the first book of the kind to appear in England, and it enjoyed great popularity, many writers referring to this work, when they mention no other by Morley. It is especially valuable to-day from an historical point of view, since it shows how far the older rules of mensurable music still applied. Here also is the source of that much-quoted story concerning the man who, when asked to sing or play in consort, had to confess he could not ; the confession occasioning wonder as to where he had been brought up. The work was re-issued in 1608, and again (with a supplement of compositions) in 1771. Riemann says that the *Introduction* was translated into

German by J. Kaspar Trost under the title *Musica Practica* ; but there is no evidence of its having been printed. The translation is preserved at Wolfenbüttel. In 1598 Morley edited and issued a second collection of Italian music—*Madrigalls to Five Voyces*. In 1599 an important work, in the historical aspect, appeared. This was Morley's edition of "*First Booke of Consort Lessons* . . . . for Sixe Instruments to play together, *viz.* the Treble Lute, the Pandora, the Citterne, the Bass-Viall, the Flute, and the Treble Violl". These pieces were "made by divers exquisite Authors", and show the tendency towards pure instrumental music which developed so rapidly during the next two reigns. Hitherto by far the greater part of the instrumentalist's repertoire was taken from the vocal books; and although Morley's collection shows vocal influence very strongly, it serves the historian as a milestone in the study of string music. The book reappeared, with additions, in 1611. The "*First Book of Aires*, or little Short Songs to sing and play to the lute with the Bass-Viol" appeared in 1600 and contained the popular "It was a lover and his lass". This song has been reprinted by Chappell (*Popular Music of the Olden Time*). In 1601, shortly before he left the Chapel Royal, Morley issued what was perhaps the most celebrated collection of madrigals of the period,—*The Triumphes of Oriana to Five and Sixe Voyces*. The best-known writers of secular vocal music contributed and the editor included two madrigals of his own, — "Arise, Awake," and "Hard by a Crystal fountain", reprinted by Dr. Fellowes in *Vol.* III of the *English Madrigal School*. Surprise has often been expressed that William Byrd did not add a specimen of his work to the collection, —especially as his pupil was responsible for the editing. Perhaps Byrd could not reconcile it with his conscience to write music in praise of Elizabeth (in whose honour the volume was issued), though he could accept monopolies and grants and Chapel Royal service at her hands. On the other hand, it is likely that both Byrd and Morley were conscious of the fact that, great as the former was in ecclesiastical writing, he could

not hope to equal the best of the contributors to the *Triumphes* with his madrigals. The book was issued in score in 1814 (W. Hawes).

To the *Whole Booke of Psalmes, etc.* (printed by William Barley in 1604) Morley contributed four excellent settings; but the work was not produced in good style and from the point of view of those who used it, many shortcomings rendered it much inferior to the earlier Psalters. In 1610 a Pavane "Composed by the excellent musition Thomas Morley, Bac. Mus., and organist in the Chappell of the most sacred Elizabeth, late Queene of England" appeared in Robert Dowland's *Varietie of Lute Lessons*. In Ravenscroft's Psalter of 1621 a new version by Morley of the first psalm was added, and Barnard's collection of church music (1641) included a verse anthem, an evening service (five-part) and a morning and evening service by him. "Now is the month of Maying" (two-part) appeared in the *Musical Companion* of 1672. The eighteenth century honoured Morley in only one publication, the burial service in Boyce's work of 1760. Later issues of Morley's music include the virginal music in the *Fitzwilliam Virginal Book* (*Ed.* J. A. Fuller-Maitland and W. Barclay Squire), a motet for four voices,—" Nolo Mortem Peccatoris ",—edited by W. Barclay Squire (Novello), and a *Magnificat* and *Nunc dimittis*, edited by Francis Burgess and Royle Shore (*Id.*).

Some manuscript music by Morley is preserved in various libraries,—notably in *Harl.* 7337–42 (Tudway) and Thomas Myriell's collection (*B.M.*); service music (some in Barnard), a couple of madrigals (from the 1594 book, with new words), and Canzonets *à* 3, from the published set, in the Christ Church library (Oxford); in Sadler's Part-Books (Bodleian), in a Peterhouse (Cambridge) manuscript, in the Royal College of Music, eight pieces in the *Fitzwilliam Virginal Book* (Cambridge), and keyboard music in Will. Forster's Virginal-Book.

MOSS (John) (*also* MOSSE): The successor of John Jenkins in the private music of the king, appointed in 1678. Very little is known of him, and his reputation was rather that of a writer of popular tunes than of profound works. He is represented by seventeen short dance-forms in *Musick's Recreation on the Viol, Lyra-way* (1669), by a Jig in *Musick's Hand-maide* (1663), by three pieces in *Melothesia* (1673), and compositions of a like slight nature.

MUDD (John), *see* MUDD (Thomas).

MUDD (Thomas); A composer of ecclesiastical music belonging to the second half of the sixteenth century, and mentioned by Francis Meres in *Palladis Tamia* (1598) as one of England's most famous musicians. A certain amount of confusion exists, in which this sixteenth-century Mudd has become confounded with his seventeenth-century namesake who was an organist at Lincoln with a sad reputation for drunkenness. In addition, a John Mudd occurs in some manuscripts, and it cannot be determined if there actually were three musicians of this name or only two. Possibly John Mudd might be identified with the Lincoln Mudd. The Thomas Mudd of the sixteenth century appears to have studied at St. Paul's School and subsequently at Cambridge

(Meres gives him as a Fellow of Pembroke Hall). Music that may with comparative safety be attributed to this Thomas Mudd is preserved in the British Museum : *Add.* 30478–9, *Add.* 31459, and *Harl.* 7340 (Sacred); *Add.* 18940–4 and *Add.* 31390 (Instrumental); in the Peterhouse collection (two anthems); at Ely (a Service and four Anthems); at Lichfield; and at Hereford.

MUNDAY (John William), see MUNDY (John *and* William).

MUNDY (John): An Elizabethan and early Stuart madrigalist whose works are distinguished by originality and artistic treatment. Like that of his father, William Mundy, his work was not consistently of the same high quality; but the best examples of his art are worthy of attention and revival. He was much esteemed as an organist and virginalist, and it was probably his instrumental practice that turned his thoughts towards secular composition. He received his musical training from his father. The date of his birth is not known, but since he became a Bachelor of Music (Oxford) in 1586 we may suppose that he was born at about the time when his father entered the Chapel Royal, or perhaps three or four years earlier. His appointment as organist at St. George's, Windsor, would date from the period of his admission to the bachelorship. Anthony Wood (and subsequently Hawkins) says he had been organist at Eton College. He proceeded Doctor of Music in 1624, Wood saying that he was " in high esteem for his great knowledge in the theoretical and practical part of music " (*Fasti Oxon.*). His exercise for this degree was a song in five or six parts (*Oxford Univ. Registers*). He died at Windsor on June 29th, 1630, and was buried in the Cloisters there.

John Mundy's most important work was published in 1594 : *Songs and Psalmes composed into 3, 4 and 5 parts, for the use and delight of all such as either loue or learn Musicke* (Este copy in *B.M.*). One madrigal contributed to the *Triumphes of Oriana* (1601) completes the short tale of the music published during his lifetime. Burney gives examples of his work, but has some very harsh things to say of them. The Oriana madrigal was reprinted by L. Benson, and a sacred composition by C. K. Scott (*Euterpe*). The British Museum has several manuscripts containing work by John Mundy, but care must be exercised in the case of compositions not expressly designated by his Christian name (*v.* Mundy, William). Some incomplete works are at Christ Church, Oxford, as well as a copy of the Oriana madrigal in score (without the words). He is also represented in the Oxford Music School collection of *In Nomines.* Perhaps the most interesting of Mundy's manuscript music is contained in the five pieces in the *Fitzwilliam Virginal-Book* (printed by J. A. Fuller Maitland and W. Barclay Squire). Included is a version of the popular " Goe from my window", and a Fantasia which is an early attempt at "storm" music of the " programme " type,—sections being headed " Faire Wether ", " Lightning ", " Thunder ", and " A Cleare Day ". The standard of virginal-technique is very high, and we can see in these pieces a justification for the reputation that Mundy enjoyed as a virginalist.

MUNDY (William): A composer, chiefly of church music, who was active during the second half of the sixteenth century. Although not capable of bearing comparison with the greatest musicians of his time, he has left some compositions of real worth and great beauty. In the majority of his works he shows himself to be the possessor of great talent, but his writing is very unequal. Nevertheless, his best is to be ranked with the works of all but the greatest of the Tudor writers. We know of him first as a vicar-choral of St. Paul's Cathedral whence he was appointed to the Chapel Royal. His admission is entered under date 1563: " Mr. Walker was slaine the 27th of November, and William Munday was sworne in his place the 21st of February from Poules " (*Ch. Bk. C.R.*). Nothing more is known of him except that in 1591 the Cheque-Book states : " Anthony Anderson sworne the 12th of October in Mr. Mundaies roome "—but whether the latter was dead or had merely resigned is not to be decided.

Very little of William Mundy's music has been printed. Barnard's collection of 1641 contains a Service (four, five, and six-part) and four Anthems, one of them,

z

—" O Lord, the Maker of all Thing ",—having been given to a variety of composers including John Sheppard and King Henry VIII; personally, I should think it most likely to be Mundy's. Boyce prints it as the work of Henry VIII. Beyond one or two small sacred compositions that have been printed in more recent years, nothing else has been published. Manuscripts containing music by William Mundy are preserved in the British Museum (*Add.* 17802–5, *Add.* 29289, *Add.* 31390, *Harl.* 7578); Christ Church, Oxford (fifteen motets wanting the tenor-part; one of them complete in another manuscript); Music School, Oxford; Fitzwilliam Museum, Cambridge; Lambeth Palace; Royal College of Music, London; and elsewhere. It is not always possible to decide with certainty whether a composition signed " Munday " or " Mr. Mundy " is by William Mundy or by his son John ; and there are still a few manuscripts not mentioned above which may contain further examples of William Mundy's work. In spite of his appointment to the Chapel Royal under Elizabeth, there is abundant evidence in his compositions that William Mundy remained,—as Byrd did,— a Roman Catholic at heart.

N

NELHAM (Edmund): A Gentleman of the Chapel Royal (previously in the choir of Weſtminſter Abbey), and a composer of the canons and catches so popular in the seventeenth century. Nothing is known of his early life, and the firſt official mention of him is in the Cheque-Book of the Chapel Royal: " 1617. Jo. Greene was dismissed . . for his ill behaviour, and for marrying of two wives and Edmund Nelham was sworne in his place the 5th November following ", and also: " 1617. Edmund Nellam (sic) (Deacon), a basse of the Churche of Weſtminſter, was sworne . . . the 6th of November ". Hilton's Catch that Catch Can (1658) contains thirteen catches signed by Nelham, and possibly some of the anonymous specimens are also by him. The Musical Companion (1672) gives four examples of his work, and in manuscript there are catches, sacred and secular canons, and similar light compositions in Add. 29291, Add. 29386, Add. 30273, Add. 31441, Add. 31462, and Add. 31463 (B.M.).

NEWARD (William), see NEWARK (William).

NEWARK (William): A musician already aᶜtive during the reign of Edward IV and who was Maſter of the Choriſters in the Chapel Royal in that of Henry VII. We meet with him firſt as the recipient of the grant of a corrody in the Monaſtery of St. Mary, Thetford (Cal. of Patent Rolls, November 28th, 1480), the grant dating from the previous year. In 1484 he received the rent arising from a royal manor in Surrey amounting to 20l. a year (Pat. Rolls, April 6th, 1485). In 1493 Newark was made Maſter of the Children, being the next musician of diſtinᶜtion, after Gilbert Baneſtre, to hold that poſt. Baneſtre died in 1487, and between that date and 1493 one of the king's chaplains held the position. Newark is mentioned a few times in the Royal Household Accounts, as, for example, in 1493 when he received 1l. for composing a song for New Year's Day. On February 23rd, 1503–4, we find his name among the " Gentilmen of the King's Chapell " in the liſt of musicians receiving mourning livery for the funeral of

Queen Elizabeth (consort of Henry VII). His name again appears in a similar connecton at the funeral of the king (*L.C.R.*, *Vol.* 424). After the coronation of Henry VIII he was confirmed in his position at the Chapel Royal in the following terms: "William Newark, gentleman of the Chapel in the Household. To be Maſter of the ten boys of the Chapel during pleasure. Greenwich, May 23rd. *I. Hen. VIII* (Brewer, *Letters and Papers of Henry VIII*). But he survived this renewed appointment only a few months, for on November 12th of the same year we read in a paper of *I. Hen.* 8 : "William Brown, miniſter of the Chapel. Grant of the Corrody in the Monaſtery of Glouceſter lately held by William Newark, deceased". He muſt have died between November 5th, when he made his will (*Rocheſter, Bk. VI*) and November 12th; and he was interred at Greenwich. His will was proved on the 13th of the following month.

Very little of his music remains. The Fayrfax manuscript (*B.M. Add.* 5465) contains seven compositions by him : "The farther I go ",

"What causyth me wofull thoughtis ", "So fer I trow ", and "O my desyre " (two-part), and "But why am I so abusyd " (second part, "I wote not where "), "Yowre Counturfetyng" (second part, "Hit were to grete pite "), and "Thus Musyng " (three-part). *Add.* 11583 contains copies of three of these, and *Add.* 11585 a copy of another. The only modern edition of any of his works is "Thus musing ", scored by H. B. Briggs and edited by Mr. C. F. Abdy Williams (Novello, 1893).

NEWERK (William), *see* NEWARK (William).

NICHOLAO *see* MATTEIS (Nicola).

NICHOLSON (Richard), *see* NICOLSON (Richard).

NICOLA, *see* MATTEIS (Nicola).

NICOLSON (Richard): Organiſt, madrigaliſt, and firſt Oxford professor of music. We do not hear of him before his appointment as organiſt of Magdalen College, Oxford, and Maſter of the choir there in January, 1595–6. A month later he became a Bachelor of Music. In 1626 William Heather founded the Oxford Professorship of Music and Nicolson was the firſt occupant of that poſt (Choragus). He retained the organiſtship of Magdalen until his death in 1639.

His compositions are not numerous. In 1601 he contributed "Sing Shepherds all" (a good example of the madrigal in five parts) to the *Triumphes of Oriana*, and a few more compositions of the canzonet-type are to be seen in manuscript. *Add.* 17786–91 and *Add.* 17797 contain sacred and secular compositions by Nicolson, and some canzonets (one of them duplicated in the British Museum) at Carlisle.

NORCOMBE (Daniel): A good deal of doubt exiſts concerning this musician, and there is a possibility of there having been two men of the same name aɛtive, for a time, contemporaneously. We hear of a Daniel Norcome, born at Windsor in 1576, who was a lay-clerk at St. George's Chapel, as his father John had been before him. According to Fétis who has his information from the Belgian Royal Archives, this Norcombe or Norcome was exiled on account of his Roman tendencies in 1602, became an inſtrumentaliſt of some sort in the Chapel of the Archduke-Governor of the Low Countries, and was ſtill there in 1647. On the other hand, Dr. Fellowes (*English Madrigal Composers*) says he muſt have died before 1626 since in that year the chapel regiſters of Windsor mention the burial of his widow. It muſt be evident that either this entry refers to a Norcombe different from the individual who was at Brussels, or that the dates in the Belgian document are wrong. I incline to the theory that there were two Norcombes. The matter becomes ſtill more complicated when we learn that Henry Davey discovered a Daniel Norcombe who was engaged, at a salary of 350 dollars a year, in the service of the Danish court between 1599 and 1601 after which he fled (for what reason is not clear) through Germany, Hungary, and Italy. Mr. Davey says that this Norcombe turned Romaniſt and joined the court music at Brussels. Now, if he was in the Danish service between 1599 and 1601, he could not have been banished from England in 1602, for he would then have been on his way to Italy. These considerations help to ſtrengthen the theory that there were two musicians bearing the name. But they appear to have become so hopelessly mixed that we can hardly expect to separate the evidence and follow the chronology of each.

One madrigal by Daniel Norcombe is included in the *Triumphes of Oriana* (1601), —" With Angel's face and brightness ",—a copy in score (without the words) being in the Christ Church library (Oxford). If there were two Daniel Norcombes, it is not to be decided whether this madrigal should be attributed to the lay-clerk of Windsor, or to the instrumentalist who was at Brussels. The individual who was at the Danish court in 1599 would hardly be a likely claimant to the composition of 1601. But would the work of a Romanist exiled on account of his religion, according to Fétis in 1602, be included in a volume issued in honour of Queen Elizabeth ? The question is full of difficulty and cannot be settled until more information is forthcoming.

NORCOME (Daniel) *see* NORCOMBE (Daniel).

NORRIS (William): A composer of ecclesiastical music who was active during the last decade of the seventeenth century. His name is first met with in a paper preserved in the Public Record Office (*L.C. Papers, Bundle* 11) in which a warrant is contained " to provide clothing for William Norris, late child of the Chappell whose voice is changed". He later became a chorister at Lincoln and rose to be Master of the Choristers there (1690). This appointment was for one trial year, his permanent engagement dating from 1691. Work of his in the British Museum includes a solo anthem and a Morning Service in G Minor (*Harl.* 7340; on one page of which he is described as " Vicar Choiral of the Cathedrall Church at Lincoln ", and on another as " one of ye choir and Master of ye Children " in the same place). Anthems by him are also contained in *Add.* 30932, *Add.* 31444–5, *Add.* 17840, and *Add.* 37072. He is similarly represented in the part-books at Lincoln. An ode for St. Cecilia's Day bearing his name was sung in 1702 (the manuscript of which was in private hands early in the last century, but is now lost sight of) ; but whether it was written earlier cannot be determined. His name appears in the Lincoln records no later than 1700, though some authorities say that he lived until 1710. NORTH (Francis) (*First Baron* Guilford): A celebrated amateur musician of the seventeenth century who exhibits the plane of excellence arrived at by the Society of the period. Born at Kirtling (Cambs.) in 1637, he took up the study of law to augment the scanty family income, and rose to be Chief Justice and Lord Keeper of the Great Seal. At the age of forty he published *A Philosophical Essay on Musick* which was one of the earliest treatises on musical acoustics. It is true, as Burney says, that " some of the philosophy of this essay has been found to be false, and the rest has been more clearly illustrated and explained " ; but for the time at which it was written it was a work worthy of great praise. His brother Roger's *Life of the Lord Keeper* allows us to obtain many glimpses of the lawyer's musical activity. He was a good performer on the Bass-Viol (lyraway), and " was in town a noted member of musick-meetings ". After marriage he dwelt in Chancery Lane and entertained a large circle of artistic friends which included the most celebrated musicians of the time (*see also* NORTH, Roger).

NORTH (Hon. Roger): A seventeenth-century amateur who secured a place for himself in the musical history of England by writing the *Memoires of Musick*. This work, slight as it is, incomplete and one-sided though it be, is of great value. The section dealing with the author's own times, particularly, is of great importance to the student of that period, for it contains information out of North's own personal experiences which fills in many gaps in our histories of Stuart music. He brought a legally-trained mind to bear upon his subject, and his criticism is generally remarkable for unbiassed judgment and clear perception of causes and effects. At the same time, North was essentially a child of his era, and a conservative pupil of conservative teachers.

Roger North was the youngest son of Dudley, fourth Lord North, and was born in Suffolk on September 3rd, 1653. He was brought up in the study of law, and as a protégé of his favourite brother, Francis, he achieved a certain distinction in legal circles. There will be no need to enlarge upon his activities in this field in a work of this nature, but it should be recorded that Roger North and Sir Charles Porter were " the only two honest lawyers I have met with " (Clarendon). The whole family was a musical one. Roger's brother Francis, when he was Lord Keeper, still practised the bass-viol assiduously. It is not to be determined with certainty as to who was responsible for the musical training of these brothers, but there is no doubt that John Jenkins had a good deal to do with it. He taught music to Roger and Montague North, and was paid at the rate of one pound a quarter. Jenkins's financial matters were treated by him in a very care-free manner, and doubtlessly he added the comforts he enjoyed in such houses to the comparatively small pecuniary remuneration he received. North, in the *Memoires of Musick* says that " I never heard that he articled with any gentleman where he resided but accepted what they gave him ".

The *Memoires of Musick*, by Roger North, are best known to us from Rimbault's edition, prepared in 1846. The original manuscript is a quarto containing two hundred and sixty-five pages, of which a hundred and eighty-five contain a treatise entitled *The Musicall Grammarian*. The manuscript was in the possession of the family for over a hundred years, after which George Townsend Smith, organist of Lynn, obtained possession of it from the dealer into whose hands it had come. Smith offered the manuscript to the Musical Antiquarian Society for publication. The " Memoires " were first brought to the notice of the public by Dr. Burney, who saw the manuscript while it belonged to the Rev. Dr. North, Prebend of Windsor, and who quoted from it at great length in his *History of Music*. The *Musicall Grammarian* has just been printed, and another autograph of it is in the British Museum as *Add.* 32533. " The *Memoires of Musick*, being some Historico-Critticall Collections of that Subject " (1728), covers a vast amount of ground. From the modes of Ancient Greece and the music of Biblical times, he passes through the period in which the art " proceeded from bad to worse till it sunk in the Gothic warrs ". These early pages are, of course, full of error and impoverished by omissions. But when he deals with the practices of his own times and those immediately preceding them,—a period of which he was informed by the knowledge imparted to him by his teachers, older friends, and his own experience,—he treads on safer ground ; and when he does so, his work becomes more useful to us. His pages dealing with the music of James I and Charles I are full of interesting material. It may be as well to remember that Rimbault's notes are by no means of uniform value,—several glaring errors laying the rest of his information under suspicion. A new annotated edition of the North " Memoires " would not come amiss just now, while interest in our early music is reviving, and its study would be found to be entertaining as well as instructive. The last few years of his life were not so fully treated ; he confesses that he had not kept himself in touch with the most recent developments, " being so many years an alien to the faculty, and at present a

deprivado ". He died at Rougham (Norfolk) on March 1st, 1733–4. The organ by Father Smith which he installed in the Rougham music-gallery was removed to Dereham Church.

The mere existence of the " Memoires ", taken with or without the knowledge that Roger North found time in his busy professional and social life to devote to the study of practical and theoretical music and its literature, is in itself eloquent testimony in favour of the assertion that the influence of the Elizabethan age was still making itself felt, though now only among the more serious-minded and conservative of the musicians, amateur and professional. Every word that we can glean from North's period is of value to us, for he lived during a period of transition ; one that saw the culmination of instrumental performance and composition, the highest flights of Viol and Lute technics, the rise of the declamatory style in vocal music, the evolution of the dramatic and the programmatic in the musical art, the descent of the opera from its parents the Masque and the " semi-opera ", and the glories of the Purcellian era. He lived through the last age during which the music of this country could be said to be truly English in spirit and character, although in his later years foreign, and especially French, influences in vocal music and Italian in instrumental music, were making themselves felt. They were eventful years in the history of English music through which Roger North passed ; he was born during the Commonwealth, before the influence of men like Orlando Gibbons and William Byrd had quite faded away, and lived until the very year in which the partnership between Heidegger and Handel was dissolved.

NURCOME (Daniel), *see* NORCOMBE (Daniel).

O

OCTOBI (Joannes), *see* HOTHBY (John).

ODINGTON (Walter de) (*also* WALTER *of* EVESHAM): An eminent mathematician and writer on musical theory. If his name is to be derived from Oddington in Glouceſtershire, we are to suppose that he was a native of that county. His alternative name came from the circumſtance that he was a Benedictine monk at Evesham Abbey. He is not to be confused with an Archbishop of Canterbury who was deposed by the Pope (Walter of Eynsham), for many authorities identify the two. The monk of Canterbury, however, lived much earlier than Odington. Since the latter is known to have written a Calendar for 1301 we may place his birth between 1260 and 1280. The only other authenticated dates are 1316, when his name was included among the mathematicians then active, and 1330, when he was ſtill in residence at Merton College, Oxford.

Manuscripts containing works by him on non-musical subjects are preserved at Oxford and Cambridge. The only surviving treatise on music in his *De Speculatione Musice*, with a Proemium beginning : " Plura quamqua de musice speculatione, *etc.*," and with Part I commencing : " Quoniam de musica presens, *etc.*" This work is highly important and gives a very full account of the ſtate of music in the thirteenth and very early fourteenth centuries, covering a great deal of ground and dealing with inſtruments, metre, plain-chant, measured music, composition, and, above all, rhythm. He had very advanced ideas, and an important feature in his harmonic scheme was the ranking of major and minor thirds among the consonant intervals. The treatise is present at Cambridge (Corpus Chriſti Collection), Burney printed generous extracts, and de Coussemaker issued the whole work in 1864 (*Script. I.* 182). No better proof is needed to show the ſtate of musical academics in England in the thirteenth and fourteenth centuries than the exiſtence of the works of Garland (*q.v.*), Walter de Odington, and Tunſted (*q.v.*).

OKEOVER (John) (*also* OKER): An organist and composer of sacred and secular music, especially noteworthy on account of the originality of his instrumental Fancies which are above the average for the period. Details of his early life are wanting, and we do not encounter him until he enters Wells Cathedral as vicar-choral and organist in 1619–20 (according to Wood, on February 16th). In 1633 he obtained the degree of *Mus. Bac.* at Oxford, and seven years later left Wells Cathedral to become organist at Gloucester. He stayed there until the Civil War stopped the Cathedral services and returned to Wells after the Restoration in 1660.

The exact date of his death is not known, but he was succeeded in his post in 1664, and references to him in the Wells records cease in 1663.

Specimens of his music may be seen in *Add.* 17786–9 and 17791 (B.M.; two Pavans and half-a-dozen Fancies for five viols), and in *Add.* 17792–6 (" Fantasia " for five viols). There is evidence of his having also written some anthems.

OKER (John), *see* OKEOVER (John).

OLDRIG (Henry), *see* ALDRICH (Henry).

OTTEBY *or* OTTOBI, *see* HOTHBY (John).

OVESEED (Henry), *see* EVESEED (Henry).

P

PAISIBLE (James) (*also* PEASABLE): A popular composer of instrumental and vocal music for the stage, active at the end of the seventeenth century. Of his early life we know next to nothing, Fétis saying that he came to England from France in 1680. The first official mention of Paisible is found in the LordChamberlain's Records under date August 31st, 1685, when " James Peasable " was sworn in as a " Counter tenor " in the private music of James II. He is named several times in the lists of musicians receiving payment for attendance on the King and Queen at Windsor. In one of these entries he is included among the " Instruments ", and in another (March 25th, 1689) his salary is given as 80*l.* per annum. His name in contained in State Papers until 1719. His work in England, outside of his royal service, consisted chiefly in providing the music for entertainments arranged for the edification of members of French Society resident in London. The Duchesse de Mazarin was a particular patroness of his, and with Monsieur de St.

Evremond he devised several concerts and other forms of musical entertainment. Before the end of the century he was writing for the public stage, and early in the eighteenth century he supplied the music to very many of the set dances invented by the celebrated Mr. Isaac (several examples being preserved in the British Museum). Paisible made his will in January, 1720–21, and died during the summer of 1721.

A large quantity of music by this writer is easily accessible in the national and other collections, including, in printed form, pieces for flutes, violin, and oboe (published at Amsterdam), sonatas for two flutes (*Id.*), some short dance-forms in Playford's *Apollo's Banquet* (1690), incidental music to *King Edward III* (1691), to *Oroonoko* and to *The Spanish Wives* (1696), *etc.* Several examples of his music to Isaac's dances were printed by Walsh. British Museum manuscripts containing work by James Paisible are as follows : *Add.* 17853, *Add.* 19759, *Add.* 24889, *Add.* 29397, *Add.* 30839, *Add.* 31429, and *Add.* 35043.

PARSLEY (Osbert) (*also* PERSLEY): A composer of Church music belonging to the sixteenth century. Hardly anything is known of his life except that he was instructor of the choristers at Norwich Cathedral for half a century, and that he died there in 1585. The British Museum has a few of his compositions in manuscript. *Add.* 34726 contains his " Conserva me, Domine " (a lute accompaniment arranged for this work in *Add.* 29246–7, together with the same to " Multiplicati Domino " and " Benedicam Domino "). *Add.* 30480–3 includes a Benedictus beginning " Blessed be ye Lord . . for he hath, *etc.*" *Add.* 31390 has an arrangement of his " Spease Noster " (*sic*) for five viols, and *Add.* 32377 a five-part *In Nomine.* *Add.* 30480–4 contains the five parts of " Perslis Clocke ". He is represented also in the *In Nomine* collection of the Oxford Music School.

PARSONS (John): A seventeenth-century organist and Master of the Children at Westminster Abbey. His skill as a performer was above the average if the epitaph on Parsons (in Camden's *Remaines*) is to be credited :

" Death passing by and hearing Parsons play,
Stood much amazed at his depth of skill.
And said, ' This artist must with me away '."

We meet with him first as parish clerk and organist at St. Margaret's, Westminster, in 1616. Five years later, when Edmund Hooper died, Parsons was appointed organist at the Abbey, having also the supervision and training of the choristers (December 7th, 1621). His salary there was 16*l.* per annum with an additional 36*l.* 13*s.* 4*d.* for teaching and keeping the children. He held these posts for little more than eighteen months, dying near the end of July, 1623. He was buried on August 3rd in the cloisters of the Abbey. He is represented in the R.C.M. manuscripts.

John Parsons is generally believed to have been the son of Robert Parsons ; but this is by no means certain. It is rather improbable that we should meet him being appointed to such a post as that of organist at St. Margaret's so late. For even if he were born immediately before his father's death (1570) he would have been

forty-six years of age at his
firſt appointment. Nothing
is to be discovered concerning
John Parsons before 1616,—
i.e. only seven years before
his death.

PARSONS (Robert) (*also*
PERSONS): A Gentleman
of the Chapel Royal and
composer of some very fine
sacred music. Active as he
was during the early part of
the Elizabethan era, he
ſtands out a little below the
beſt writers of his time. His
part-writing is always ingenious and his conſtant
endeavours to produce
original effects of harmony
made his music exceedingly
intereſting. He was born
at Exeter and is mentioned
in Laud's visitation of that
Cathedral as a vicar-choral.
Anthony Wood was probably
responsible in the firſt place
for the legend that Parsons
was organiſt to King James I.
Dr. Rogers, from whom Wood
had received the information,
had evidently muddled
Robert with John Parsons
(*q.v.*). Very little is known
of his biography. In *1563*
he joined the Chapel Royal,
the Cheque-Book containing
the entry : " Merton died
the 22nd of September, and
Roberte Parsons sworne in
his place the 17th of October,

Anno Quinto ". He held the
poſt for only five or six years,.
having met with an accidental
death in 1569, the illuſtrious
William Byrd being his successor: " Robert Parsons was
drowned at Newark upon
Trent the 25th of January
and William Bird sworne
Gentleman in his place at
firſt the 22nd of February
following " (*Ch. Bk. C.R.*).

Not much of Parsons music
has been printed. In
Barnard's collection of 1641
(*Selected Church Music*) there
are a complete service (" A
Morning, Communion and
Evening Service ") in four,
five, six, and seven parts,
and a Full Anthem *à* 6
(" Deliver me from mine
enemies "). Low's *Direc-
tions* (1664) contains Parson's
Burial Service. Burney
printed a secular piece (the
five-part madrigal " Enforced
by love and feare "). An
" Ave Maria " *à 5* was issued
under the editorship of Sir
Richard R. Terry in 1907.
An essay on " Early Elizabethan Stage Music " in the
Musical Antiquary for October,
1909, contains a song (" Pan-
dolfo ") in score by Robert
Parsons. Much of Parsons'
music remains in manuscript.
The British Museum has
work of his in *MSS. Harl.*

7339 (Tudway's collection; the anthem printed by Barnard), *Add.* 29289 (a *Magnificat*), *Add.* 11586 (Burney's copies of " Ave Maria ", " Te Fili ", and an *In Nomine à* 5, from the Christ Church MSS. Oxford), besides settings of *In Nomines* (a favourite form of composition with Parsons), madrigals, motets, and arrangements, in *Add.* 22597, *Add.* 29246, *Add.* 31390, *Add.* 30380–4, and *Add.* 17786. He is also represented in the libraries of Christ Church and the Music School, Oxford, the Royal College of Music in London, the Fitzwilliam Museum at Cambridge and the collections in the Cathedrals at Durham, Ely, and Gloucester. It should be borne in mind that some of the compositions alluded to are merely headed " Parsons " and that we have no means of ascertaining whether they were all the work of Robert.

Another Robert Parsons was a vicar-choral at Exeter in 1634, but how near was the relationship between them cannot be determined. A William Parsons contributed to Day's Psalter of 1563, and the organ part of a composition by him is in the library of Christ Church, Oxford. Whether the Christian name was a slip of the scribe or not is doubtful. But it should be noted that there are hymns and motets in British Museum manuscripts by a William Parsons also.

PARSONS (William), *see* PARSONS (Robert).

PASHE (William) (*also* PASCHE, PASSHE, PASCE) : A composer of sacred music who flourished at the end of the fifteenth century and the beginning of the sixteenth. Nothing certain is known of his life, and in spite of the determined researches of a few workers, none of the discovered information can be made to apply to him with provable accuracy. Dr. W. H. Grattan Flood found the Will of a William Pasche, made on May 17th, 1525, asking that the testator be buried in the chancel of St. Margaret's, Friday Street, London. This Will was proved on July 12th, 1525. There is, of course, nothing to disprove Dr. Flood's theory that this William Pasche was the composer ; but until further research reveals something that will connect the testator with the composer of the music we know, the evidence of the

Will must be accepted with caution. Dr. Flood says that this Pashe was a Gentleman in the chapel of Anne, Duchess of Exeter, but gives no reasons for so thinking. The *Dictionary of National Biography* mentions the Pashe of the will alluded to above, and also names another William Pasch who was in holy orders in 1561,—obviously too late for him to have been the composer. The writer of the music bearing this name cannot very well be dated later than the very beginning of the sixteenth century, or even earlier. Morley includes "Mr. Pashe" in his list of early Tudor "Practicioners" in music.

In the Peterhouse part-books there are a "Sancta Maria" and a "Magnificat" by Pashe, the motet being a fine example of early Tudor music. It appears that there were once two Magnificats at Peterhouse. He is also represented in manuscripts at Caius College and the University Library, Cambridge. His greatest work is the Mass "Christus Resurgens", a score of which is at Caius College (a single part in the University Library and another at St. John's College, Cambridge). Com-

positions headed "W.P." may be by Pashe (where the style of the work is in keeping with the period at which he worked), and a motet so labelled is contained in *Add.* 5665 (*B.M.*).

PATRICK (Nathaniel): An organist and composer of sacred and secular vocal music who flourished in the second half of the sixteenth century. He has some very fine church music to his credit and it is a thousand pities that no example of his book of songs, hymns, and madrigals has come to light. Very little is known of his biography, and that little is to be gleaned from the registers and account-books of Worcester Cathedral, where he was organist from 1590 to 1594 or 1595. The last salary paid to him was entered at Michaelmas, 1594, and in March 1594–5 he died, being buried on the 23rd of the month. He had been married exactly eighteen months when he died ; and between his wedding day (September 23rd, 1593) and the date of his death in 1594–5 he had also buried his child Francis. His Will was proved in May, 1595, and may be seen (*Worcester Wills, Vol.* VII, *fol.* 83) reprinted in Sir Ivor Atkins' interesting book on the Worcester organists and Masters of the Choristers.

The only work of Patrick's that was printed appeared a little over two years after his death. The announcement of this publication in the registers of the Stationers' Company is all the evidence we have of the book's existence, for no examples of it are known to exist. It was entered under date October 22nd, 1597, as "Songs of Sundrye Natures whereof some are Divine, some are Madrigalles, and the rest Psalmes and Hymns in Latin . . . by Nathaniel Patrick, some tyme Master of the Children of the Cathedral Church of Worcester and organist of the same". These compositions were for five or six voices, one being for eight. His "Whole Service in G Minor" is contained in *Harl.* 7337 (*B.M.*), Arnold's collection, and in the part-books at Worcester. Mr. J. E. West edited it (transposed to A) for Messrs. Novello and Co. This service is to be found attributed to Richard Patrick (*q.v.*), but there is no doubt that it was the work of the earlier musician. Further examples of Patrick's writing may be seen in the British Museum : *Add.* 17786–91 (the madrigal " Send foorth thy sighes ", in six parts), and *Add.* 18936–9 (" Sacred Pan ", in four parts). *Add.* 31120 contains Vincent Novello's organ arrangements, one of which is from a composition of Patrick's. This was published in 1831 in the series " Cathedral Voluntaries ".

The Richard Patrick to whom the service of Nathaniel Patrick was formerly ascribed, is not to be confused with the latter. Richard was a lay-vicar of Westminster Abbey in the first quarter of the seventeenth century. In the account of the funeral of James I (1625), the name of Richard Patrick is to be found among those of the " Singing men of Westminster " (*L.C.R., Vol. 557*). Deprived of the honour of having written Nathaniel's service in G Minor, Richard Patrick falls to an unimportant position in the history of early English music.

PATRICK (Richard), *see* PATRICK (Nathaniel).

PEACHAM (Henry): This celebrated early seventeenth-century writer is better known as the author of the *Compleat Gentleman* (1622),—a work which is often quoted by the musical historians of the present day,—than as a practical musician. Indeed, only one composition of his is known, — the madrigal "Awake softly with singing Oriana sleeping" for four voices in parts, written (in the same hand as the rest of the manuscript) at the end of Peacham's *Basilikon*, etc. (*Harl.* 6855; *B.M.*). In music the author was a pupil of the celebrated Italian madrigalist, Orazio Vecchi.

PEARSON (Martin), *see* PEERSON (Martin).

PEASABLE (James), *see* PAISIBLE (James).

PEERSON (Martin): A madrigalist and Master of the Choristers of St. Paul's Cathedral, who flourished in the first half of the seventeenth century. Exactly when he was born is not known, but since his *Mus. Bac.* degree (Oxford) dates from 1613, it would not appear likely at first glance that he was born much earlier than 1590, or later than 1595. Degrees were taken at an early age in the seventeenth century, it is true ; but we shall see later that he must have been born considerably earlier. Anthony Wood writes that Peerson was born, "as is seems", at Ely; and taking into consideration the fact that in his Will he left 100*l.* to purchase an annuity capable of producing a sufficient income to provide from eight to twelve poor people of Dunnington with two-penny loaves, it might also "seem" to us that the musician came from the neighbourhood of March (*v.* *Will* registered *P.P.C.*, *Grey*, *fol.* 9). We do not know with certainty when Peerson became the Master of the Choristers at St. Paul's ; he may have been connected with the Cathedral soon after he graduated at Oxford. At all events he was there in 1633, for an entry of that date is in the State Papers (Charles I *Dom. Ser., Vol.* 236, *Document No.* 17), referring to the demolition of houses around the Cathedral: "April 15, 1633. Report on the composition to be paid to Mr. Pearson, Master of the Singing boys of St. Pauls whose houses are being demolished. The writers have arranged with Mr. Partridge for his interest in another house, part of the college, large enough for Mr. Pearson and his boys, for 240*l.*, subject to a rent of 12*l.* Pray order the Chamberlain of London to pay the 240*l.*" He died after Christmas,

1650, or early in the New Year, 1650–51. What he did between the date at which the Commonwealth orders prevented the Cathedral music being performed and that of his death is not clear ; but he seems to have died possessed of considerable means, for besides the bequeſt already mentioned he left property in the West Central diſtrict of London and at Walthamſtow (now a North-Eaſtern suburb). He was buried in the Chapel of St. Faith (under St. Paul's Cathedral).

The earlieſt piece of music he wrote to which a date may be attached was the song, " See, Oh, See who here is come a-maying ", sung when the King and Queen attended the May-day revels at Highgate in 1604. Now, if this was the setting that was used in that year, we have the alternative of believing that Peerson was between nine and fourteen years of age when he composed it, or that his birth muſt be placed earlier than 1590, or the setting used in 1604 ascribed to someone else. This song is the laſt number in his publication of 1620 : " Private Musicke, or the Firſt Booke of Ayres and Dialogues. Contayning Songs of 4, 5 and 6 parts . . . for Voyces and Viols. And for want of Viols, they may be performed to either the Virginall or Lute . . . All made and composed according to the rules of Art ". Out of this book the part-song, " Upon my Lap my Soveraigne sits ", has been republished by L. Benson (Novello, 1897). His other work appeared ten years later : " Mottects or Graue Chamber Musique. Containing Songs of fiue parts of seuerall sorts, some ful, and some Verse and Chorus. But all fit for Voyces and Vials, with an Organ Part ; . . . also, a Mourning Song of Sixe parts for the Death of the late . . . Sir Fulke Grevil . . ." (1630). This Fulke Greville (Firſt Lord Brooke) died in 1628, and was an early patron of Peerson's. All the lyrics in the laſt-named publication came from his pen. Peerson's writing is a curious connecting link between the ſtyles of two periods ; moſt of his music could be sung to an accompaniment, or used in the manner of the unaccompanied madrigal. But there can be no doubt that this writing belongs to the accompanied-song category rather than to that of the pure madrigal. The organ part of this book of 1630 exhibits one of the earliest English uses of a figured bass. He contributed three sacred songs to Leighton's *Teares*, *etc.* (1614). In manuscript there are several Fancies, dance-forms, part-songs, and anthems ; and examples may be seen in the British Museum (*Add.* 29372–7, *Add.* 17786–91, *Add.* 29427, *Add.* 29366–8, *Add.* 30478–9, *Add.* 28864, *Add.* 31420, *Add.* 31421, and *Roy. App.* 63 ;—the music in the first set of manuscripts having been written before 1616), in the Christ Church, Oxford, library (an incomplete Verse Anthem, a five-part Fantasy short of the Alto and Bass parts, and four six-part Fantasies), and elsewhere. Clifford's *Divine Anthems* gives the words of two anthems by Peerson. To Ravenscroft's *Briefe Discourse* he contributed some laudatory remarks (1614), and in the *Fitzwilliam Virginal Book* are to be seen four pieces by him.

PERSLEY (Osbert), *see* PARSLEY (Osbert).

PERSONS, *see* PARSONS.

PHILIPPES (Peter),

PHILIPPI (Pietro), *see* PHILIPS (Peter).

PHILIPS (Peter): A composer and organist who lived between *ca.* 1580 and *ca.* 1640, and who spent the greater part of his active life abroad. He was in very high repute during his lifetime, and as far as we are able to judge, it is probable that he was considered a greater organist than conposer. Henri Hymans, describing the set of Flemish pictures (" The Five Senses ") in the Prado Museum at Madrid, says of the artist, Breughel de Velours, " The conscientiousness of the artist can be judged by the fact that on the open book of music on the instrument, one can discern the words . . . ' di Pietro Phillippi Inglese, Organista, *etc.*' . . . Thus we see that Peter Philips, English ecclesiastic, was organist to the Archduke and Arch-duchess, and composer of madrigals, at the moment when Breughel was painter to their Highnesses, a title which he shared with Rubens " (*Gazette des Beaux-Arts*, *Per.* 3, *Vol.* XI, *pp.* 188-190, Paris 1894). Philips must have been enjoying a great continental reputation at that time to have been selected by the artist. Having spent so much—perhaps all—of his life in the Low Countries, we might expect to find much information concerning Philips in the records of his adopted country. But this is by no means the case. One or two entries in certain municipal accounts, added to the information afforded by the title-pages to his printed works, are all the documentary materials we possess for his biography. E. van der Straeten, when writing his *History of Music in the Netherlands*, hunted through practically all the sources of information ; and it would be poor gleaning after him.

The date and place of Philips's birth are alike unknown. That he was English we are sure, for in most of his published works he calls himself " Inglese " or " Anglus ". That his birth must have occurred about 1560 we can suppose on the strength of the earliest dated work of his known to us. We know nothing of his early years and cannot say with any degree of certainty who was responsible for his training. He may have been related to one of Cornyshe's boys, Robert Philips, and the Phelyppes represented in the Fayrfax

Book may have been some connection of his. But we cannot afford to accept as facts what are at best only suggestions. The *Fitzwilliam Virginal Book* contains a Pavane which was " the first one Philips made ". There should be no reason for doubting this scrap of information. The Pavane is dated 1580. It is comparatively elementary in form and workmanship, and would seem to have been an early endeavour. It is thus a by no means extravagant proposition to fix the date of its composer's birth not more than twenty years earlier. An interesting note that throws some light upon Philip's early years is that written by Mr. G. E. P. Arkwright in the *Musical Antiquary* (April 1913, *p.* 187). There, in the Will of Sebastian Westcote (April 3rd, 1582), we read that " to Peter Phillippes likewise remaining with me 5*l.* 13*s.* 4*d.*" was bequeathed. I do not think that Mr. Arkwright is going too far when he says that " we may infer that he had been brought up as one of the St. Paul's boys and that he was living with Westcote at the Almonry House as an old boy (pupil or assistant perhaps) at the time of Westcote's death in April, 1582 . . ." The date, viewed together with that of the Pavane of 1580, seems a possible one. Moreover, no other Peter Philips is traceable at this period, and I think we can accept the suggestion put forward. From this moment, however, until 1590 the biographer is faced by a blank. It is not known when Philips left England. Mr. W. Barclay Squire (*Grove*) disposes of the story given by Eitner who supposes that because the Berlin Royal Library (now State Library) *MS.* 191 contains a " Pavana Dolorosa . . Composta in Prigione del P.P. *ca.* 1594 ", Philips was in England at the time. This Pavane is dated 1593 in the *Fitzwilliam Virginal Book*, and was most likely the work of Tregian, whose abbreviated signature " Tre . ." it bears. Philips probably merely arranged the Berlin version. There is more evidence to prove that he was already in Antwerp before the end of 1590, for a collection of madrigals which he edited,—*Melodia Olympica*,— has a dedication dated from that city on December 1st, 1590, the year of publication being 1591. This, says Paul

Bergmanns (lecture on " L'Organiste des Archiducs Albert et Isabelle : Peter Philips ", October 12th, 1902, printed 1903) is the first certain trace of the arrival of Philips in the Netherlands. The religious changes of that period made of the Low Countries a more congenial centre of activity for Catholic musicians than did England. Fétis tells us that in 1595 Philips journeyed to Italy and lived for some months in Rome. This, of course, is not out of the range of possibility ; but Fétis does not quote his authorities for the statement and it has hitherto not been proved true. Certain it is that in 1596 Philips was resident in Antwerp, for his first book of madrigals (*à* 6) was published there in that year and contains a dedication dated January 8th, 1596. The title-page of this work merely gives his name without stating that he had any official position. But on the title-page of the book of eight-part madrigals, published in 1598, he is described as organist to the Archduke Albert. This would appear, then, to have been his first important appointment. The second book of madrigals

(1603) describes him as organiſt to the Archduke Albert and Arch-duchess Isabella. The work is dedicated to the vice-regal couple and is dated Antwerp, November 10th, 1603. He seems to have enjoyed great favours at that court (*v.* E. van der Straeten, *La Musique aux Pays-Bas, etc.*, 1882, VI 506). Exactly when Philips entered holy orders is not clear ; but according to the *Regiſtres journaux de Lettres Patentes de l'Audience*, 1608–18 (*Archives Gén. du Royaume*; *Reg.* 844, *fol.* 60 *verso*) it is evident that on March 9th, 1610, Philips was appointed a canon in the collegiate church of Saint-Vincent at Soignies. But, as will appear later, he retained his position as organiſt at Brussels. In 1611 Philips, occupying so important a poſt, was summoned, in company of some of his colleagues, to Malines, there to examine the new organs placed in the church of St. Rombaut. It is highly probable, from the accounts of payments in the municipal archives, that he took part in the Eaſter service of that year. The accounts for 1611 contain : " Betaelt voer vi ſtadſtoepen renschen wijn gepresenteert aen heer Peeter

Philippus organiſt ende ander van de Capelle van Syne Hoochheyt, ten respeéte zoo van de visitatie der nieuwe orghele doen ſtellen in Ste Rombauts Kercke als andere dienſten by deselve gedaen ter vereeringe van de goddelycken dienſt ter processiedaghe van Paesschen 1611 . . . xxiiii *livres* xv *sous* " (*Comptes Communaux de Malines*, 1610–11, *fol.* 165, *verso*) Thus it is clear that the " six ſtoups of Rhine wine presented to Philips and others of His Highness's Chapel " was as much in recognition of their work " in the honouring of the divine service for the procession-day of Eaſter " as it was for their visit to the new organ. At the end of the same year we read of Philips being back in Brusselſ officiating at the funeral of the Archduchess Maria of Auſtria on December 12th and 13th, 1611. The firſt publication to follow the appointment at Soignies was the *Cantiones Sacrae à 5* (1612) the title-page of which placed the " reverend " prefix of " R.D." before the composer's name and describes him as Canon of Soignies. The work was written at Brussels. It is clear that he fulfilled both offices simultaneously. On January 5th, 1621, Philips exchanged the canonry of Soignies for a perpetual chaplainship in the church of Saint-Germain at Tirlemont (*Arch. Gén. Reg.* 942 *ff.*, 60–61). We cannot always accept the statements on the title-pages of his publication as conclusive proof of his having occupied the posts named there in the years of these works' publication. The publishers can easily have printed a list of past and present positions on them in order to give the whole a more imposing appearance. Thus, on the title-page to the second edition of the *Deliciae* (1622) Philips is still called "Canon of Soignies"; in the Litanies of 1623 he is called "Canon of Bethune"; and on the title-page of the *Paradisus* (1628) he is again entitled "Canon of Soignies". Van der Straeten (1882, *p.* 506) says he was the first organist of Bethune; while the title-page of the Litanies says he was Canon of Bethune and organist to the Archduke. The 1613 edition of the eight-part *Cantiones Sacrae* gives him as Canon of Soignies, while the 1625 edition says he was Canon

of Bethune. At any rate, he was still living in Brussels in 1628, for he dates the dedication of the *Paradisus Sacris* from that city on March 31st, 1628.

The date of Philips's death is not certain. In 1628 he published the first part of the *Paradisus Sacris*, and in 1633 the second and third parts appeared. This seems to have been the last work published during the lifetime of the composer. The third part was reprinted in 1641, but as it was edited by Phalèse, it can hardly be taken as evidence that Philips was then still living. It is therefore between 1633 and 1641 that we must place the date of his death. A portrait of Peter Philips appeared in *Pompa Funebris . . . principis Alberti Pii . . .* (1623) where he is pictured at the head of the "Chapellains de la Chapelle de la Court" and labelled "Pierre Philippe Organiste".

The work of Peter Philips is well worthy of resurrection in spite of a certain tediousness. But to counteract this monotony of style he has some fine, clear, and strong music to show : he sounds self-reliant and his ecclesiastical writing is convincing and real. His madrigals, as Peacham (1622) remarked, are in " the Italian veine ". His later work, as Mr. Barclay Squire points out, was much influenced by the school of the Netherlanders ; and this need occasion no surprise, for there is every reason to believe that Philips and Sweelinck were on intimate terms of friendship.

Philips published a fair amount of music, but all his printed works are rare ;— in many cases only one or two copies being known to exist. His first venture was not with a work entirely from his own pen. In 1591 he edited and published *Melodia Olympica*, a collection of madrigals by the best-known Italian and Flemish musicians, including four numbers of his own. The work was re-printed in 1594 and 1611. The first book issued , by Philips containing work exclusively from his own pen was *Il Primo Libro de Madrigali a Sei Voci*, in 1596 (twenty-one madrigals in six part-books). Some writers say that the book was re-printed in 1603, an error which was doubtless caused by the confusing of the first book of six-part madrigals with the second. The first book was re-issued in 1604. The next published work, in chronological order, was *Di Pietro Phillipi Inglese . . . Madrigali a otto voci . . ."* (1598 ; twenty-one eight-part madrigals). It appears to have been reprinted in 1599,—at any rate, some examples bear this date. A second edition appeared in 1615. The second set of six-part madrigals were published in 1603 (twenty-four madrigals ; some copies dated 1604). A second edition followed in 1615. In 1612 Philips's best-known work appeared : *Cantiones Sacrae. Pro Praecipuis Festis Totius Anni et Communi Sanctorum Quinis Vocibus*. When Eitner wrote the *Quellen-Lexicon* the British Museum possessed only the Altus, Tenor, and Bassus parts of this work, but the missing parts have since been supplied. The Museum Basso Continuo may belong to an otherwise unknown edition, since it is dated 1617. This may be a misprint, of course, but there are one or two trifling points on which the title-page of this part differs from those of the other parts. The eight-part motets followed : *Cantiones Sacrae octonis vocibus auctore R. D. Pietro Philippi,*

Anglo . . . 1613 (*chez* Phalèse). Of this work also the British Museum has the entire set of eight part-books. A second edition appeared in 1625. The year 1613 also saw the publication of *Gemmulae Sacrae Binis et Ternis Vocibus Cum Basso Continuo ad Organum* . . , a set of part-books containing thirty-nine motets. A second edition appeared in 1621, the Royal College of Music possessing three of the parts, the British Museum having two of the same parts. Two and three-part compositions also occupied Philips's next publication : *Deliciae Sacrae binis et ternis vocibus, Cum B.C. ad Organum* (1616). It is dedicated to Albert and Isabella and contains forty-one numbers,—twenty-one *binis* and twenty *ternis vocibus.* Another edition was issued in 1622, of which the British Museum has a Cantus part. Some question has been raised as to the authenticity of *Les Rossignols Spirituels*, and Eitner calls it the " doubtful work ". But I think there is no reason for doubting that to the texts of the Jesuit Guillaume Marci, Philips adapted well-known melodies which he harmonized. The book was published by Jean

Vervliet in Valenciennes, and bears the title : *Les Rossignols Spirituels. Liguez en Duo. Dont les meilleurs accords, nommement les Bas, releuent du Seigneur Pierre Philippes Organiste de leurs Altezes Serenissimes.* The first edition appeared in 1616, the " privilege " being signed by de Groot on December 23rd, 1615. The work contains sixty-nine two-part and two four-part hymns. This little duodecimo volume is exceedingly interesting, as it gives us some knowledge of the airs popular at the commencement of the seventeenth century. From this book the carol " Le Bel Ange du Ciel de vertu supernelle " was extracted and arranged for a mixed choir by F. A. Gevaert for performance at the Brussels Royal Conservatoire on February 4th, 1883. It was repeated in the month following on the occasion of the visit of the Prince of Wales, later King Edward VII. The first edition is represented by a copy in the British Museum, an example in which the pagination is much muddled. The second edition, " Regaillardis au Primevere de l'an 1621 ", is also in the British Museum. A third edition appeared in

1631 without Philips's name, and a fourth was published at Cologne in 1647. The next work to appear was : *Litaniae beatae Mariae virginis in ecclesia Loretana cani solitae,* 4, 5, 6, 8 *et* 9 *vocibus, cum B.C. ad Organum* (1623). The work consists of twelve Litanies of Loretto, and a second edition appeared in 1630. The last work to have been published during its author's lifetime was the *Paradisus sacris cantionibus consitus, Una, duabus, et tribus vocibus decantandis. Cum Basso-Generali ad Organum* (First Part, 1628). A copy of this interesting book is in the possession of H.M. the King, and is at present in the British Museum. In 1633 the Second Part of *Paradisus Sacris* appeared, and the Third Part followed later in the same year. A new impression of the Third Part was issued in 1641. It was long thought that Philips composed no masses, but the finding of the catalogue of music in the library of King John IV of Portugal showed that that monarch possessed a volume of " Missas y Salmos . . . a 8 and 9 . . . Obras Postumas ". No copy of these masses is now known to exist, and King John's example was almost certainly destroyed in the great earthquake of 1755.

Peter Philips contributed to many contemporary collections, and work by him may be seen in : *Madrigali a otto voci* (published at Antwerp by Phalèse in 1596), *Paradiso musicale di Madrigali et Canzoni a cinque* (*Id.*), Thomas Morley's *Madrigals to fiue voyces* (1598 ; containing " The Nightingale ", followed by the second part, " O False Deceit ", by Philips), Morley's *First Booke of Consort Lessons* (1599 ; containing " Philips Pavin " from the *Fitzwilliam Virginal Book* and the Galliard thereto), *Ghirlanda di Madrigali a sei voci* (1601, Phalèse), Willem Swart van Arnhem's *Den Lust-Hof der Nieuwe Musycke* (1603 ; an arrangement of the 1580 Pavane to a Dutch text " Wy engelen goet "), H. L. de Haesten's *Nervi d'Orfeo* (Leyden ; 1605), Michel Herrerius's *Hortulus Musicalis* (Munich, 1606–9), Füllsack's *Ausserlesener Paduanen und Galliarden* (Hamburg, 1607–9), Thomas Robinson's *New Citharen Lessons* (1609 ; the 1580 Pavane again, this time in tablature), the *Promptuarium Musicum* of Abraham Schadeus (Strassburg, 1611–

17), *Les Raisons des Forces Mouvantes* by Salomon de Caus (Frankfort-on-Main, 1615 ; "65 mesures du madrigal ' Che fera fed' al cielo', d'Alessandro Strigio. Mis en Tablature par Pierre Filippe ". The complete arrangement is in the *Fitz-william Virginal Book*), *In-stitution Harmonique* by de Caus (1615 ; some examples of Counterpoint), Thomas Simpson's *Taffel-Consort* (1621 ; an " Aria " *à* 4) ; *Amoenitatum Musicalium Hor-tulus, etc.* (Leipzig, 1622), Donfrid's *Promptuarium Musi-cum* (Strassburg, 1622–7 ; two motets), and Andrea Pevernage's *Laudes Vesper-tinae, etc.*, (1629 ; two " Noels ",—one *à* 4 and one *à* 5). Philips included two compositions by this Pever-nage in his *Melodia Olympica* of 1591.

Modern reprints of Philips's works include examples in Hawkins's *His-tory*, in A. H. Jewell's *Madri-gal and Motett Book* (1856), in A. G. Ritters' *Geschichte des Orgelspiels* (1884), in the Breitkopf and Haertel edition of the *Fitzwilliam Virginal Book* (edited by J. A. Fuller Maitland and W. Barclay Squire), in Sir Richard R. Terry's *Downside Motets*, and

in C. T. Gatty's *Arundel Hymns*. In addition, Mr. W. Barclay Squire has edited madrigals and motets.

Manuscript copies of music by Philips are preserved in the British Museum (*Add.* 30816–9, *Add.* 29366–8, *Add.* 18936–9, *Add.* 29372–7, *Add.* 31442, and *Add.* 14398, —the contents of which, as far as concerns Peter Philips, were given in my article in *Musical Opinion* for January, 1922), and a good many are in the library of Christ Church, Oxford. A list of foreign manuscripts containing work by Philips is given in the article just referred to.

In examining English manuscripts containing work by " Philips " it will be necessary to exercise care. The music of Philip van Wilder is frequently desig-nated by the Christian name only, and this has led to a good deal of confusion. But Philip van Wilder was active so much earlier than Philips that there should be no great difficulty in separating the work of the two men. In the Christ Church (Oxford) Manuscript No. 979–83 there is an " Aspice Domine " by " Mr. Phillips of the King's Privi–Chamber ", which makes it clear that Peter is not meant ; and this composition is also present in the British Museum (*Add.* 31390). It is likewise probable that the Philip van Wilder who was guardian of Henry the Eighth's musical instruments was only one of several musicians of that name (*v.* Philip van Wilder.

PHILLIPS (Arthur): An organist and Oxford Choragus. Born in 1605, he came of a Winchester family and devoted himself to the study of academic and ecclesiastical music. At the age of seventeen, he became a clerk of New College, Oxford, and sixteen years later (December, 1638) we meet with him as organist at Bristol Cathedral. This post he held for less than a year, for in 1639 he was appointed organist of Magdalen College, Oxford, succeeding Nicolson as Choragus in the same year. In 1640 he obtained the degree of *Mus. Bac.* It is generally supposed that Arthur Phillips was of the Anglican church and that during the Commonwealth he became a Romanist and left England to serve Queen Henrietta Maria in France. If, as Anthony Wood says, Phillips had been related to Peter Philips, he would not have needed conversion.

He ended his days on March 27th, 1695, as steward to a Romanist in Sussex—one Caryll.

He is credited with the composition of the music for " The Requiem, or Liberty of an Imprisoned Royalist ", " The Resurrection ", *etc.*,— but the only work of his that I have been able to trace is a " Ground " (with variations) in *Add.* 29996 (*B.M.*). This composition, however, is ascribed to " T. Tomkins " in the index prefixed to the manuscript.

PIERSON (Martin), *see* PEERSON (Martin).

PILKINGTON (Francis): A lutenist and madrigalist of the late sixteenth and early seventeenth centuries who enjoyed a great reputation in his lifetime. But his work appears to have made its appeal more by reason of its brightness and simplicity than by any great emotional qualities. Burney thought his music almost devoid of originality ; but the findings of this historian have been so frequently reversed by the opinion of later periods that much importance cannot be attached to his criticism. The present-day revival of the Elizabethan art-forms has taught us to look for virtues different from those that made a composition seem good to Dr. Burney, and to us Pilkington's work appeals with a new force. He is full of grace for one thing, and his writing is almost always neat and finished. The date of his birth is not known. We meet with him first in 1595 when the University of Oxford conferred upon him the degree of *Mus. Bac.*, and since the grace-book states that he had studied music for sixteen years, he must have been born round about 1562–65. Much later than this we cannot place his birth, because in 1624 he calls his Muse "aged". We find no further dated information concerning him until 1602 when he appears on the Treasury Books of Chester Cathedral as a "Chanter" or singing man. At about this time he was patronised by the Earl of Derby, for in the introduction to his publication of 1605 he says that he must confess himself "many waies obliged" to his Lordship's family, adding that his father and brother had also "received many Graces" of the Earl's father and that he had also reason to be grateful to the Earl's brother. Pilkington took holy orders, became a minor canon, and was ordained by the Bishop of Chester in 1614, as is clear from an entry in the Holy Trinity Church register of baptisms referring to "the first child he baptized" (December 23rd, 1614). He was a Precentor in 1623, and died in 1638.

Pilkington's first published work appeared in 1605 : *The First Booke of Songs or Ayres of four parts : with Tableture for the Lute or Orpherion, with the Violl de Gamba, etc.*,—the gamba being employed only in the last number, a Pavane for Lute and Bass Viol. Several of the pieces in this book have been reprinted by Oliphant, Hullah, and John Stafford Smith, and the whole set of twenty-two compositions has appeared in Nos. XVIII, XIX, and XX of Mr. G. E. P. Arkwright's *Old English Edition.* His next work appeared in 1613 : *The First Set of Madrigals and Pastorals of 3, 4 and 5 Parts, etc.* The dedication is dated September 25th, 1612 "From my mansion in the Monastery, Chester ". Dr. Fellowes, who issued the set as Vol. XXV of his *English Madrigal School,* gives its date as 1614. It is possible that some copies may be so dated, but the British Museum example bears the date 1613 on its title-page. An Oriana madrigal—not included in the 1601 edition of the collection—was also written by Pilkington ("When Oriana walked to take the air"), but it was undoubtedly written after the death of Elizabeth, for the laſt line of the poem reads : "In Heaven lives fair Oriana". This madrigal contains some very fine passages. To Leighton's *Teares*, *etc.* (1614) he contributed two numbers, one *à* 4, and one *à* 5. The *Second Set of Madrigals and Paſtorals of* 3, 4, 5, *and* 6 *Parts : Apt for Violls and Voyces*, *etc.*, appeared in 1624, and was republished by Dr. Fellowes (*Vol.* XXVI of the *English Madrigal School*, omitting the inſtrumental pieces). In the Altus part there is "A Pavin made for the Orpharion, by the Right Honorable William, Earle of Darbie, and by him consented to be in my Bookes placed" (*B.M.* copy).

There is not much manuscript music of his in exiſtence. The British Museum has by "Fra: Pilkington, Bache. of Musick" two unnamed pieces in lute tablature, two Pavans, and "Goe from my wyndowe",

all for the lute (*Add.* 31392). He is also represented in the University Library, Cambridge.

PLAYFORD (Henry): A son of John Playford I and his business successor in 1684 on the retirement of the father. He was born on May 5th, 1657, Henry Lawes being his godfather. In the earlier ſtages of his publishing career Henry Playford was associated with Richard Carr, a son of John Carr, with whom John Playford had had business connexions ; but he subsequently became independent of partners and continued his business alone. Chief among his publications were Purcell's Sonatas and his St. Cecilia composition for 1697, the miscellaneous collexion *Orpheus Britannicus* (1698, *etc.*), *Amphion Anglicus* (1700), and others ; besides new editions of his father's issues. Henry Playford did not enjoy the freedom from competition that his father had, and at the end of the seventeenth century he inſtituted concerts in a coffee-house, followed by a similar venture at Oxford in 1701. He then added pictures and prints to his ſtock-in-trade, and gradually allowed his competitors—notably

Walsh—to oust him from the trade. The year of his death, like that of his father, is not to be fixed with certainty—various dates between 1706 and 1710 being given. According to the *Dictionary of National Biography* his Will was proved in 1721. I have been able to trace no compositions by Henry Playford. PLAYFORD (John) (I): The most important music publisher in England during the seventeenth century, composer of short pieces of no great value, and author of a theoretical work which was the standard book for almost a century. Descended from a Norfolk family, John Playford was born in 1623. The first we hear of him is that he was active as a bookseller in the metropolis in 1648. Before the middle of the century his interest in publishing was a general one ; but with the issue of *The English Dancing-Master* (1651) — a fine collection of traditional tunes which Playford thus helped to preserve for us— he was attracted to the publication of music. From this date he seems to have published nothing but music, and, indeed, he enjoyed what was really a monopoly, for the music-books which did not pass through his hands did not together number a score. In 1653 he became clerk to the Temple Church and had his place of business " near the Church door " as his title-pages say. He retained these business premises even when he transferred his home to Islington (where his wife had a boarding school for girls). When his wife died (1679) John returned to town, and lived in Arundel Street. In a publication of 1684 Playford took leave of his friends and customers, and forced by increasing age and ill-health, he retired from the business in favour of his son Henry. The date of his death is not to be fixed with certainty. It took place after November 5th, 1686, when he made his Will. But this Will remained unsigned, and was proved in 1694 after the handwriting had been identified and claimed to be his on oath. The range of possible dates for his death thus lies between November, 1686, and 1694, with the probability of the former year being the correct one. Henry Purcell expressed the sentiments of most of the London musicians when he set an elegy of Nahum Tate's

B b

on Playford's demise. The genial publisher muſt have been a man of fine charaéter and kindly disposition. He was intimate with the Pur-cells, the Lawes, Hilton, Pepys, and, indeed, prac-tically all the famous musicians and amateurs of the time. Among them he earned for himself the title of " honeſt John Playford ". Several portraits of him are known, painted at different times, and given in certain of his publications.

John Playford does not appear to have done his own printing and different printers at various times did this work for him. Moſt of his publications were impressions from movable type, the few remaining being from en-graved copper-plates. The more important of his publi-cations were *The English Dancing-Maſter* (issued at the end of 1650, though dated 1651), *Court Ayres*, *Courtly Masquing Ayres*, *Musick's Delight on the Cithren*, Hilton's *Catch that Catch Can* (later editions as the *Musical Companion*), *Seleét Musicall Ayres and Dialogues*, and similar colleétions of short songs, rounds, catches, canons, etc., *Musick's Recreation on the Viol, Lyra-way, The Whole*

Book of Psalms, Cantica Sacra, Choice Ayres and Dialogues, The Division Violin, and many more, several of them passing through many editions. Moſt intereſting was Playford's own little *Introduétion to the Skill of Musick* which enjoyed a tremendous vogue and out-lived a score of editions (between 1654 and 1730). It deals with the basic prin-ciples of theoretical music, playing on the viols and singing, and the art of com-position. In some editions extra essays were included, such as inſtructions in singing after the Italian manner, the order of performing the Cathe-dral Service, and so on. The seétion on Descant was changed as the older writers fell from favour and a more up-to-date essay was demanded. Thus Campion supplied this part of the work (later annotated by Chriſto-pher Simpson). In 1683 Campion's pamphlet was removed and one by an anonymous writer inserted. Later the name of Henry Purcell appeared on the title-page of this seétion. I am the fortunate possessor of two copies of this work,— one of the Seventh Edition (1674) with the Campion-Simpson *Descant*, and one of the Thirteenth Edition (1697) with *The Art of Composing in Parts* by Purcell.

As a composer of music John Playford was modeſt. Work of his is included in *Seleƈt Ayres and Dialogues* (1659), *Musick's Delight on the Cithren* (1666), *Catch that Catch Can* (1667), *Musical Companion* (1672, 1673), *Cantica Sacra* (1674), and other books. "Comely Swain", a very popular song from the *Musical Companion* (1672, *p.* 117, *à* 3) was reprinted in *The Harmonicon* (VI, 120). The same song (called "a *fa-la* or ballet") is in *Add.* 31441 (*B.M.*). Three more vocal numbers (two *à* 3 and one *à* 4) are contained in *Add.* 31806 (*Ib.*). Further examples of his work, in the form of inſtrumental arrangements of songs and hymns, are also included in manuscripts preserved in the same national colleƈtion.

PLAYFORD (John) (II): A music-publisher of the seventeenth century. The son of Matthew Playford, reƈtor of Stanmore Magna, he was born in 1655 and was a nephew of John Playford I. It is highly probable that he served the celebrated London printer and publisher William Godbid (who printed some of his uncle's publications), and subsequently entered into partnership with Godbid's widow. On the death of Anne Godbid, Playford continued to work the business alone, printing for a time the music published by his cousin Henry Playford. John II died in 1685 (*v.* also Frank Kidson, *British Music Publishers*, the most authoritative work on music-publishing in England).

PORTER (Walter). A Gentleman of the Chapel Royal and composer of some intereſting sets of vocal pieces, madrigals in charaƈter, but written to inſtrumental accompaniments in a manner that renders them distinƈt from the true madrigals. Tradition has it, on unknown authority, that Portman was a pupil of Monteverde ; but whether this was the case or not, the suspicion remains that he was influenced by some Italian maſter. So many features in his compositions point to Italian models, that it is difficult to imagine him to have been free from such influence. A habit of his,— that of writing reiterated notes on a single syllable,—was a typical Monteverdian trait, and Dr. E. H. Fellowes (*English Madrigal School*) quotes examples of this idio-syncrasy. According to Wood he was a son of Henry Porter (*Mus. Bac.* from Christ Church, Oxford, 1600) ; but we know nothing regard-ing his early years. In 1616 Walter Porter " by warrant from the reverend Father in God, James Lord Bishopp of Winton and Deane of his Majestes Chappell, was sworn Gentleman of his Majestes said Chappell in ordinarie, without paye, for the next place that shall happen to be and shall fall voyd by the deathe of any tenor that now is in ordinarie in the said Chappell, and tooke and re-ceived his oathe to that effect the fifth daie of Januarie the yeare abovesaid, and paid for his oathe five poundes and other duties ". He had not long to wait for a dead man's shoes ;—" Peter Wright died the 27th daye of Januarie (1617) ; and Walter Porter was sworne in his place the first daie of Februarie followinge " (both citations from the *Ch. Bk. C. R.*). In 1639 he became Master of the Choristers at Westminster Abbey. He lost the Chapel Royal and Westminster posts during the Civil War, and on November 30th, 1659, he was buried at St. Mary's, Westminster.

Porter's first published work appears to have been : *Madrigales and Ayres of two, three, foure, and fiue Voyces, with the continued Base, with Toccatos, Sinfonias, and Ritor-nellos to them. After the manner of Consort Musique. To be performed with the Harpes-chord, Lutes, Theorbos, Base Violl, two Violins or two Viols. Published by Walter Porter, one of the Gentlemen of his Majesty's Chappell.* 1632. This title has been copied from the example in the British Museum, the work being of excessive rarity. He says that he has " exprest in the part of the Harpsechord, the maior and minor sixses by Flats and Sharpes, the figures I haue put over the head of euery Note as neere as I could. I haue made the singing Base also a thorow Base, in which you are not to sing but where there are words or this signe :||: of repetition ". In this work he also uses the terms *forte, tace, etc.* A volume of *Ayres and Madrigals* appeared in 1639, but it may possibly have been a reprint of the 1632 set—no copy of the later publication being known to exist. In 1657 he published :

Mottets of Two Voyces for Treble or Tenor and Bass. With the continued Bass or Score : To be performed to an Organ, Harpspycon, Lute or Base-Viol, etc., a very imperfect example being in the British Museum. Playford is supposed to have printed more of Porter's music later on, but I have not been able to see copies for the purpose of deciding whether they were original works or merely reprints of older publications. It is possible that some of this music, though advertised by Playford, may never have been issued. That Porter composed anthems is proved by *Harl.* 6346 (*B.M.*) which contains the words of such compositions by him.

PORTMAN (Richard): An organist and writer of ecclesiastical music who flourished in the first half of the seventeenth century. Enjoying the instruction of Orlando Gibbons he occupied his teacher's post as organist of Westminster Abbey from 1633 onwards, Thomas Day having held the position for seven years between the two. Portman became a Gentleman of the Chapel Royal in 1638 in succession to John Tomkins who died on September 27th in that year. According to

Rimbault (*Notes and Queries,* X. 182) Portman had been in France in the company of Dr. Williams, Dean of Westminster, before this appointment. During the Commonwealth he supported himself, —as so many of the Court and Cathedral musicians did, —by teaching pupils on the keyboard instruments (Playford, *Musical Banquet*). He died during the Interregnum.

A Whole Service in G, preceded by the Venite by " Mr. Portman, Servt. to Charles ye I and organist of Westminster " is contained in *Harl.* 7337 (Tudway MS. *B.M.*) and another British Museum manuscript, —*Add.* 30478-9,—includes three anthems by him, while *Harl.* 6346 gives the words only of another among " The Anthems used in the King's Chapel ". Further examples of his sacred music are contained in the choir-books preserved in other libraries.

POWER (Lionel): An eminent English theoretician and writer of ecclesiastical music belongng to the fifteenth century, but, as with the majority of his contemporaries, next to nothing is known of his life. Judging from the circumstance that examples of his work are to be found in many foreign manuscripts we may suppose that part, at least, of his life was spent abroad. The reputation he enjoyed in England can be gauged to some extent by the fact that one English manuscript (that at Old Hall) contains over a score of compositions by him. Like his contemporaries Power is noticeable chiefly for the cleverness and skill with which he approached his subject and less on account of the emotional appeal of his music. But his melodic line is a noble one and he may with justice be looked upon as the forerunner of the greater men who flourished in later Tudor times. As a theorist he was a progressive and once and for all sanctioned the unconditional use of thirds and sixths as consonant intervals, while denying the legitimacy of consecutive fifths and octaves. It can scarcely be realised at the present day how great an innovation the prohibition of consecutive fifths must have been in those far-off days when the most frequent method of harmonisation was in fourths and fifths (*v.* also articles " Quatrible " and " Quinible" in *Dic. Old Engl. Mus.*). The period of his activity is variously placed, but I am inclined to give, roughly, 1450 as the central point of his career. Earlier than this he could easily have been active, but scarcely later. He is mentioned by the name of " leonel " by Hothby (Coussemaker mis-spells the name), and the fact that this high authority speaks of Power in the same breath with Dufay and Dunstable will demonstrate the regard in which he was held. His name is to be found in a variety of forms, such as : Lyonel, Leonel, Leonello, Polbero, Powero, *etc.* The speculations of some writers on the subject of this musician are to be accepted with caution ; many are of a very fantastic nature, some even identifying him with Dunstable.

The theoretical treatise by which Power is best known is contained in *Lans.* 763 (*B.M.*) a volume of tracts on the musical methods of the times which Tallis presumably found at Waltham Abbey and removed at the Dissolution. It was later in the hands of Thomas Morley. Power's share of the work is entitled : "Tretis . . . upon ye Gamme . . . for hem yat wilbe syngers, or makers, or techers ", and it has been printed by Hawkins (*History*) and Riemann. The manuscript at Old Hall, near Ware (Herts) contains twenty-one compositions by Power in three and four parts, the majority of them being sections of Masses. *Lans.* 462 (*B.M.*), the tenor part of a Sarum Gradual, includes a " Kyrie for Saturday " by " Lyonel ", the same manuscript containing work by Dunstable. The Bodleian Library (Oxford, *Selden, B.*26) possesses a four-part " Ave Regina". *Add.* 36490 (*B.M.*), Mr. W. Barclay Squire's transcription of much contemporary music, gives the first few notes of some compositions by Power, useful for the purpose of identification. Many Continental collections preserve work by this Englishman, specimens having been copied into the Trent choir-books (now at Vienna), a set of part-books containing eleven compositions by him ; into the Modena *Codex VI. H.*15 (*Bibl. Estense*), eight compositions ; into the Bologna *Codex* 37 (*Liceo Musicale*), three works, with a fourth in the Bologna University MS. No. 2216. One " Ave Regina," from the Old Hall manuscript has been printed by the *Internationale Musik-Gesellschaft* (1901), the " Ave Regina " in the Oxford manuscript was issued by Stainer (same year), and three of the Trent compositions have been published in the first volume of the *Trienter Codices* (1900). One of the latter is identical with the Oxford manuscript, from which the example printed in *Vol.* II of the *Oxford History of Music* was taken.

PRESTON (Christopher): An organist and virginalist active during the second half of the seventeenth century. He was " appointed musician in ordinary to his Majesty for the Virginalls and private musique without fee in the place of Dr. Christopher Gibbons, to come in ordinary with fee after the decease of the said Dr. Gibbons, and then to enjoy the same place " (*L.C.R., January* 7th, 1667–8). In an entry dating from January 20th, his salary is given as " 46*l.* per annum and 40*l.* per annum ",—one fee probably as virginal-player and the other for his work in the private music. He must have died before January 1st, 1689–90, for on that date his widow " Mary Preston of York . . . " appointed " Mr. Allan Chambers, her true and lawful attorney" (*L.C.R.*, *Vol.* 199). The only music of his composition that I have been able to find consists of five short pieces in Matthew Lock's *Melothesia* (1673).

PURCELL (Daniel): The youngest of the three sons of Henry Purcell I. The date of his birth is not known with certainty, but since his brother Henry II was born in 1658 and his father died in 1664, Daniel must have first seen the light of day between 1659 and the last-mentioned date. 1660 is the earliest that can be accepted in view of subsequent events. The sources of his musical knowledge are equally speculative; his father died certainly too early to have had anything to do with his training. There remain his brother Henry and his uncle Thomas, and it was most probably from these that he received his first instruction in the art. He enjoyed a considerable reputation as a composer,—particularly of dramatic music,—and though in the presence of his brother's genius his own must appear dwarfed, he is by no means a negligible musician.

The earliest reference to Daniel Purcell is to be found in the Lord Chamberlain's Records (*Vol.* 747), where an order is noted for the payment of 3*s.* a day to a number of Children of the Chapel for attending at Windsor in 1678. Since the designation " Child of the Chapel " was used only until the voice broke, it is obvious that Daniel Purcell could not have been born before 1660. It is impossible to say how long he had been in the Chapel Royal, and thus the influence of John Blow upon him cannot be gauged. We learn nothing more of his activities until 1688 when he was appointed as organist to Magdalen College, Oxford. His stay there lasted only until 1695 when he resigned the position. There can be little doubt that the illness of his celebrated brother was the prime cause for Daniel's return to London, for we find him in 1695 adding music to, and completing, works upon which Henry had been engaged when the state of his health compelled him to relinquish his tasks. The music to a scene in the fifth act of *Pausanias* (1695–6 ; MS. at St. Michael's College, Tenbury) was one such example, and the masque in the fifth act of *The Indian Queen* another (MS. *Add.* 31449 and *Add.* 31453 ; 1696 ; *B.M.*). The first composition of Daniel's to which we can assign a date was the music to the Ode for St. Cecilia's Day, 1693, performed while he was still at Oxford. Some of his sacred music,—influenced by his post at the College,— may possibly be even earlier. A year after his return to London he supplied the music necessary to *Ibrahim XII* by Mary Pix. Then followed a number of plays in rapid succession, all containing music by Daniel Purcell,— among them being *Brutus of Alba* (by Powell and Verbrugghen ; the music printed in 1696, the play produced in the following year). In 1697 he joined forces with Jeremiah Clarke (*q.v.*) and together the two men wrote a good deal of music, vocal and instrumental, for the contemporary stage. Thus appeared *The New World in the Moon* (Settle, 1697), *Cynthia and Endymion* (D'Urfey, 1697), *Phaeton* (Gildon, 1698), and many others. In 1698 he set Bishop's Ode to St. Cecilia for the London celebration of that year (*v.* advertise-

ment in the *London Gazette* for December 29th, 1698), and composed an Ode in honour of Princess Anne's birthday (autograph score in the British Museum). In collaboration with Jeremiah Clarke and Leveridge he wrote music for *The Island Princess* (Motteux, 1699), and in the same year set Addison's Cecilia Ode for the Oxford celebration. On March 21st, 1699–1700 a competition for composers was announced in the *London Gazette*, Congreve's *Judgment of Paris* being the text to be set. Daniel Purcell entered and secured the third prize, the first and second going respectively to John Weldon and John Eccles. Later in the year he scored his best success with *The Grove, or Love's Paradise* (Oldmixon), produced at Drury Lane ; and from this moment he enjoyed an unchallenged reputation as a writer for the stage. Contributions followed to *The Unhappy Penitent* (Catherine Trotter, 1701), *The Inconstant* (Farquhar, 1702), *Orlando Furioso* (for the opening of the Haymarket Theatre in 1704–5), and a great many others. In 1707 he wrote another St. Cecilia Ode for Oxford. Apart from this activity he organised concerts at which his own and other music was performed,—one such function being advertised in the *London Gazette* for March 31st, 1712 : " On Wednesday the third of April, at Stationers' Hall, Mr. Daniel Purcell, brother of the memorable Mr. Henry Purcell, will exhibit an entertainment of vocal and instrumental musick, entirely new, and all parts to be performed with the greatest excellence ". In 1713 he returned to the organ and obtained the post at St. Andrew's Church, Holborn, in the City of London, working there until his death in 1717. On December 12th the post was declared vacant in the *Daily Courant* and Henry's son, Edward Purcell, was named as a candidate " in the room of his uncle, deceased ". The organist's post took Daniel back to sacred music once more, and in 1718 his *Psalms set full for the Organ or Harpsichord* appeared.

A huge number of Daniel Purcell's more popular compositions were published early in the eighteenth century, and it will be impossible and unnecessary to detail them here. " Single Songs in the *Opera* of *Brutus of Alba* " were issued by Playford in 1697 ; and the composer is represented in *Harmonia Sacra* (*Book II*, 1693), *Deliciae Musicae* (1696 ; containing the additional music to *The Indian Queen*), and other collections. The British Museum and the Royal College of Music, to name only two libraries, possess a great amount of his vocal music, besides sonatas and movements for the violin and flute with figured bass.

The British Museum is particularly rich in manuscripts containing work by Daniel Purcell, many of them in his autograph. *Add.* 30934 contains the Ode " Again the Welcome Morn ",— " Upon ye Birth Day of . . . Princess Ann of Denmark, February 6th, 1699–1700 ", the Cecilia Ode " Begin and strike the harmonious lyre ", and the Ode in honour of " King William's return from Flanders " (1697). Specimens of his vocal music for the stage may be seen in *Add.* 15318 (*The Island Princess*), *Add.* 22099 (fragments from *The Triumph of Virtue*, *The Judgment of Paris*, and *The Tender Husband*), *Add.* 29378 (" The Mask in ' Ye Pilgrim ' "), *Add.* 29398 (*The

Judgment of Paris), *Add.* 31405 (a song), *Add.* 31453 ("Last Act" by Daniel Purcell to Henry Purcell's *Indian Queen*), *Add.* 31461 (Songs ; one from *Ibrahim XII*), *Add.* 33351 (Song "Cease, ye Rovers", from *The Island Princess*), *Add.* 35043 ("A Symphony for 'Alexander ye Great'", and an item from *The Taming of the Shrew*), and *Add.* 37027 (possibly by Daniel Purcell). Examples of his sacred music are contained in *Add.* 17841 (autograph anthems), *Add.* 30932 (the catalogue ascribes one anthem in this manuscript to Daniel Purcell,—no Christian name is given,—while several others are signed Henry Purcell), *Add.* 31445 (anthem) and *Add.* 31461 (anthems). Music for violin and bass-viol to the harpsichord is contained in *Add.* 31466 and a piece for the harpsichord in *Add.* 17853. Novello and Co. have published a *Magnificat* and *Nunc Dimittis* in E Minor, edited by Stainer. PURCELL (Edward): The youngest son of Henry Purcell II and the only one to grow to manhood. Born in 1689 (baptised in Westminster Abbey, September 6th) he was a very young child when his father died

in 1695. He received a good education under the supervision of his mother, who died when Edward was sixteen years of age. She left no written testament, but in a verbal will she directed that her late husband's requests be carried out ; namely, that his musical library, instruments, various articles of plate, *etc.*, be handed to Edward. The latter specialised in organ-playing and secured his first appointment at St. Clement's, Eastcheap, in the City of London. In 1717, when his uncle Daniel (*v. sup.*) died, Edward was a candidate for the vacant post of organist at St Andrew's, Holborn, but was not successful. He took over the organ at St. Margaret's, Westminster, soon after the middle of the year 1726. His life was quite uneventful, and he died on July 1st, 1740. PURCELL (Henry) (I): A Gentleman of the Chapel Royal, Master of the Westminster Choristers, and a composer of very moderate attainments, whose fame to-day,—in spite of the popularity he enjoyed during his lifetime,—rests upon his having fathered the greater Henry. The parents of great men,—be they insignificant as in the case of Brahms, or comparatively important as in the case of Mozart,—always deserve a place in a work which gives an account of their sons ; for in each of the three cases the celebrated son has been influenced by the less famous parent.

The ancestry of the Purcells has given rise to very much speculation ; but although the most persistent and indefatigable of research workers have devoted their energies to the quest after the forbears of this musical family, no satisfactory solution of the mystery has yet been arrived at. An old-established family of the name was settled in Shropshire (their arms are reproduced in the younger Purcell's three-part *Sonatas* of 1683) ; the name was very common in Ireland ; and a slight variation of it (Pourcel) not infrequent in France. But with none of these families can that of the musician be connected with absolute certainty. The French ancestry was propounded by one Dr. C. Purcell-Taylor (who claims to be a descendant of the musician) in the *Radio Times* for September 4th, 1925,—but no documentary evidence in support of the

theory was cited. I have endeavoured to get into touch with Dr. Purcell-Taylor, but have so far failed. The Irish theory is more likely to bear close examination successfully. Dr. W. H. Grattan-Flood has followed clues given in the Irish State Papers of the time of Elizabeth and the results of his researches are given in faint outline in a note appended to the late Sir Frederick Bridge's *Twelve Good Musicians*. The same book also gives some interesting notes on the claim of Shropshire. Should Purcell's descent from the Irish family be proved, it would be unfair in me to rob Dr. Grattan-Flood of the fruits of his labours ; but it may perhaps be mentioned that the Irish Purcells were closely related to members of the Peerage,—a circumstance not disproved by the culture and education displayed by the musicians of the family. The name of Purcell is given more than once in the will of John Fyssher (1547), a Gentleman of the early Tudor Chapels Royal. In this document there are bequests to a John Pursell, a Nicholas Pursell, a George Pursell, and a Thomas Purshell. Again no definite conclusions can be arrived at, and the nearest we can approach to the truth is to suppose that all these English and Irish Purcells (and perhaps the French branch also) were in some way related. It may be remarked in passing (for the disturbance of those who seek the ancestry of a musician in the idioms of his music) that the musical idiosyncrasies of a composer, —and especially those of a great composer,—need not prove to be a clue to his descent.

Our first meeting with Henry Purcell the Elder takes place in 1656, when he participated actively in the production of Davenant's *Siege of Rhodes*. He was in all probability quite a young man at the time, a circumstance which may account for the absence of earlier proofs of his professional existence. Pepys speaks of meeting " Pursell, Master of the Musique ", on February 21st, 1659–60 ; but whether Henry Purcell I or his brother Thomas (*q.v.*) be meant, is not clear. Nor can we be certain as to what the diarist meant by the term " Master of the Musique " at that date. Sir Frederick Bridge, while

organist of Westminster Abbey, had ample opportunities for examining the local records ; and he unearthed a few interesting facts. He told me that there could be little doubt but that the elder Purcell resided in the " Almonry " where the Westminster singing-men were accommodated. The Westminster Palace Hotel now occupies the site. The first official mention of the elder Henry is made in the Lord Chamberlain's Records, where it is shown that he was appointed in the place of Angelo Notari as composer for the violins. Sir Frederick Bridge discovered a book in the Westminster library in which the appointment of Henry Purcell to some post in the Abbey is recorded with the information that the book itself was accepted in lieu of his fee of 5*s.* payable on such appointments. This may refer to his Mastership of the Choristers at the Abbey. At the coronation of Charles II he was among the Chapel Royal choristers. At the Restoration also he was made music-copyist to the Abbey, —at that time considered a post of some distinction. His office as a private musician to the king included the exercise of his voice and lute, and for the latter services his salary was 40*l.* per annum (*L.C.R., Vol.* 741). The Cheque-Book of the Chapel Royal records his death as having taken place on August 11th, 1664, his successors being John Goodgroome and Thomas Richardson (the one for the private music and the other in the Chapel Royal).

Of the children of Henry Purcell, the eldest, Edward (1653–1717) lived the life of a distinguished soldier and with the rank of Lieutenant-Colonel took part in the capture of Gibraltar and of Barcelona. The second and third sons were the musicians Henry and Daniel (*q.v.*).

Only the slightest evidences of the elder Purcell's skill as a composer survive. A three-part song, " Sweet Tyranness " (which has also been attributed to his son Henry,—though probably without sufficient reason) was printed in Playford's *Musical Companion* of 1667, *etc.*, and the same composition, headed " Glee ", is contained in *Add.* 29386.

PURCELL (Henry) (II): In estimating the value and importance of musical compositions it is very necessary to take into consideration the period at which their creators worked. The standards set up for the musicians who came after Beethoven cannot be employed for a man who died when Bach was only ten years old. But although the idioms of different periods may vary, and though the technical and mechanical means at the disposal of composers are always changing, the eternal truths of art and aesthetics remain unaltered throughout the ages. Which means that while Henry Purcell was looked upon by his contemporaries as the culmination of a long development and the greatest composer this country had ever seen, his work can still give pleasure to-day by reason of its sheer beauty, its spontaneity, and its constant fulfilling of the requirements of good taste. It is true that the music of Purcell, like that of all but two or three of the elect, bears a date upon almost every note of it ; the musical language of Purcell is that of the late seventeenth century. But is *Paradise Lost* a less admirable poem because its English is that of the Stuarts ? Apart from his genius Henry Purcell was very fortunate ; as

Schumann said of Brahms, —" at his cradle Graces and heroes mounted guard " ; he was the son of a musical father and the nephew of a musical uncle ; he was given the opportunity of early study in an environment that facilitated the rapid development of his talents ; he came after Tallis, Tye, Byrd, Gibbons, and Morley had left him their work to serve as his models ; he allowed himself to be influenced by the best of foreign art and methods just sufficiently to denationalise, to a slight extent, his utterance. But lucky as he was in regard to all these outside aids, Henry Purcell had other helpers within. His imagination was vivid and his characterisation just and balanced ; his heart was ever allowed to speak its generous message, unchecked —though gently curbed— by the mind. His youthful memories were peopled by men who had held hands with the Elizabethans and men who had witnessed the dramatic developments in France and Italy ; he was sufficiently a child of his own era to have fallen a victim to the lure of over-ornamentation and over-indulgence in variation, and at the same time original enough to write harmonies as daring and as effective as those of the Leipzig Cantor. He could sound prophetic to his contemporaries and yet he retained a curious liking for the false relation admired, or at least tolerated, by the Elizabethans. His thematic material often seems to have been drawn from the past and his treatment of it from the future ; occasionally the reverse seems to have been the case. He was a product of a period of transition and ably did he work at stabilising all these wavering features, at moulding a form that had for half a century been seething in the melting-pot. There will be little need to dwell in detail upon the excellencies of Purcell's work ; it suffices to note that by reason of his charm of method, his originality of harmonic treatment, his vigorous and dignified thematic material, his ready imagination, his very versatility,—he must occupy the foremost place in the history of English music. His industry covered every inch of ground in the field of music ; and into each of the forms he touched he infused new life. He beautified them all with the gorgeous raiment he beſtowed upon them and made once more the name of an English musician resound over the Continent of Europe. The opinion of his contemporaries on Purcell's work was as high as our own. Tudway knew him from the Chapel Royal days and said that he " had a moſt commendable ambition of exceeding every one of his time, and he succeeded in it without contradiĉtion, there being none in England, nor anywhere else that I know of, that could come in competition with him for compositions of all kinds ". But in his heart of hearts, was Purcell a typically English composer ? Scarcely. It is true that in some few compositions,— such as the fine song, " Come if you dare ",—his *spirit* is essentially not only English but British ; but for the reſt he was far less influenced by his Tudor forerunners than he was by his Italian models. Taken unawares his heart often spoke English ; following premeditation he went beyond the seas. This is no fantasy ; it was his intention to do so. In the dedication to *Dioclesian* he says: " Musick is but in its nonage ; a forward child, which gives hope of what it may be hereafter in England, when the maſters of it shall find more encouragement. 'Tis now learning Italian, which is its beſt maſter, and a little of the French air to give it somewhat more of gayety and fashion. Thus, being further from the sun, we are of later growth than our neighbour countries, and muſt be content to shake off our barbarity by degrees. The present age seems already disposed to be refined, *etc.*" —which shows thatherealised the shortcomings of the poſt-Reſtoration music and, incidentally, also proves that his musical hiſtory was a little muddled. Certainly Purcell looked abroad for his methods, thereby merely following the fashion created at the Reſtoration, and treading in the footſteps of his teacher Pelham Humfrey. For this reason Purcell does not exhibit the truly English charaĉteriſtics of the art as do, say, Byrd and Gibbons, and Morley. It was by combining the virtues of both schools of thought that he secured for himself the position he held and holds. In Canon, Fugue, and all the contrapuntal devices of his time he was the direct follower of his Tudor forbears ; but in his dramatic development John Cooper, Pelham Humfrey, and Lully played a greater rôle than did the writers of purely English training. Henry Purcell, at the culminating point in a period of transition, is himself a connecting link between the Morleys, the Campions, the Jenkinses, the Simpsons, and the Lawes on the one hand, and the solitary George Frederick Handel on the other. Knowing the Continental musicians as we do, we must come to the conclusion that Handel owed a good deal to Purcell ; and there is no doubt that Purcell had fully developed the manner that foreshadowed the great musician of Halle long before the latter was born. This aspect of Purcell's work (his relation to Handel) was clearly not illuminated by France or Italy, and unless he knew of the work of the early seventeenth-century Germans, he must have possessed genius even greater than we suspect. Harmonically Tallis seems to be, not one century, but five in the rear ; contrapuntally, Handel only appears to be one day in advance. Unfortunately the English successors of Purcell and Handel chose to model themselves on the latter rather than on the former, and the eighteenth-century English musicians branded themselves as the imitators of an imitator rather than as followers of one who showed real development. As it is, Henry Purcell II remains as the last of the great Englishmen who knew how to adapt and assimilate outside influences and produce from them something characteristic and something enduring. What wonder then, that Arcangelo Corelli should decide to make the long journey to England in order to look upon the great Purcell ; what wonder, too, that he should turn back after reaching Calais, when he heard of Purcell's death.

The sacred music of Henry Purcell, though it is generally very fine indeed, and often comparable with the greatest achievements in this field,— does not show the consistently high standard of his dramatic work. We seem to feel rather than know that he is not so much in his own element ; we see glimmerings of the footlights here and there ; we hear rhythms that suggest Terpsichore rather than the altar ; we have a

c c

suspicion that Purcell was not the devout man that Byrd was, and therefore conclude that Purcell's sacred music does not express his religious feelings as Byrd's did. Yet some of his church compositions are so magnificent and of such tremendous emotional effect that we are carried away in ecstasy. How can we account for it unless we seek the reason in the workmanship and in the intensely dramatic nature that was enclosed in Henry Purcell's young body. Perhaps we can say with justice, then, that Purcell's sacred music is impressive, noble, and dramatically great ; but not imbued with the pure devotional spirit of the earlier writers. After all, if Purcell's music for the church has its effect by influencing the hearer from the outside, as it were, instead of calling it from out of the listener's heart, it was not so much a shortcoming of the composer's own as it was a true reflection of the spirit of the age. Do we not frequently see some of his finest anthems disfigured, as Rimbault says, "by fiddling symphonies invented only to tickle the ears of the wretched Charles." These instrumental interludes are now often omitted, and though there may be a slight gain from the devotional point of view, their absence is to be deplored from the historical viewpoint. One has to agree with Dr. Walker in his condemnation of the modern editors when they "with scandalous lack of historical conscientiousness, which their sense of ecclesiastical fitness cannot outweigh, reduce to minute fractions of the originals " these *ritornelli*. But, in spite of this slight falling-off in the quality of Purcell's average sacred compositions, it remains on the highest plane ; for it only exhibits shortcomings when compared with his own best work. It was when writing for the stage that Purcell developed his greatest powers and reached his greatest heights ; heights not attained by any other composer of his own age and no English composer of any age. *Dido and Aeneas* is the only composition from his pen that can be given the name of Opera in the modern sense of the word ; but whether we examine this work or those other magnificent examples of incidental music to dramas, we see the same fine characterisation, the same

consistent attention to atmosphere, the same originality
and inspiration, the same
individuality which is Purcell
himself. In his instrumental
music also he takes a place
far ahead of that occupied
by any of his countrymen.
He had not the properly
organised orchestra to work
with as we know it to-day,—
not even as Mozart knew it ;
yet his effects, produced by
strings, hautboys, flutes, bas-
soons, and trumpets, are very
fine and dramatically equal
to the tasks imposed upon
them. His compositions for
the stringed instruments,—
especially for the violin,—
were undoubtedly influenced
by the Italian school of
writers. But to what better
school could he go ? Corelli
as composer and Nicola
Matteis as executant were
quite sufficient to discover
for him the capabilities of
the instrument, and he was
not slow in availing himself
of the lessons he learned.
His harpsichord music is
marked by freshness and
vigour, and is clearly the
expression of his own in-
dividual feelings ; but being
powerfully influenced by Continental models (which, in
this particular branch, he
need not have been), his

music for the keyboard instruments is not so typically
in his own style as is his
work for the stage.
The most remarkable
feature of all Purcell's music
is the very slight variation
in the quality of all his
works. It is true that his
working life was not a very
long one ; but it is nevertheless significant that between
the first of his successful
compositions and the last
there is not that great difference in excellence noticeable
in the works of every other
composer. Purcell reached
the highest point in his
development very early in
his career,—and stayed there
until, at only half the age
allowed by the Psalmist, he
laid aside his pen for ever.
Henry Purcell the Younger
was the second son of Henry
Purcell I, and was born (in
spite of the legend that
designates a house in St.
Ann's Lane, Old Pye Street,
Westminster, as his birthplace) in the " Great
Almonry " where his parents
lived until the death of his
father. The exact date of
his birth cannot be fixed
with certainty, for the only
information we have on this
point is such as is given by
his tombstone, which states

that he died in his thirty-seventh year. The earliest date for his birth, therefore, is November 21st, 1658, and the latest November 20th, 1659. His baptism does not appear to have been registered. Sir Frederick Bridge once told me that he had had investigations made, but without result. He came to the conclusion that the child was baptised in the Abbey. Similarly the name of the elder Purcell is not given in the rate-books of the parish, which helps to prove that he was still living in the Almonry (which is within the precincts of the Abbey) when his second son was born. The father could have had very little to do with the early musical education of his son, for he died in 1664 when the boy would have been between five and six years of age. The child was adopted by his uncle Thomas Purcell (*q.v.*) and it was from the latter that he received his first musical instruction. In the same year Thomas secured his nephew's admission to the Chapel Royal, where he came under the influence of Captain Henry Cooke (*q.v.*). For the next eight years (*i.e.* until Cooke was succeeded by Pelham Humfrey in 1672)

Purcell was instructed by the first master of the children to be appointed after the Restoration. Here, then, were sown the first seeds of later blossoms, and here we see how, influenced by Cooke's own tastes, the future Purcell was moulded, — church musician by virtue of his post, dramatic composer by inclination. The children of the Chapel Royal were taught to compose very early, and Henry Purcell was no exception. In 1670 (*æt.* 11–12) he wrote " The Address of the Children of the Chapel Royal to the King and their Master, Captain Cooke, on his Majesties Birthday. A.D. 1670, composed by Master Purcell, one of the children of the said Chapel ". In the Fitzwilliam Museum (Cambridge) there is a volume of anthems in Purcell's autograph, dated 1673. This book contains eleven anthems of his own composition which must have been written before his fifteenth year. The song " Sweet Tyranness ", in the *Musical Companion* of 1667, has frequently been attributed to the boy, who would then have been between eight and nine years of age. Precocious he certainly was and the composition of this song need not have been an impossible thing for him. But all circumstances considered, it will perhaps be more reasonable to ascribe the piece to his father. The manuscript of the " Address of the Children ", which was known to Rimbault and Cummings, was in the handwriting of Pelham Humfrey, and the two were probably good friends before Humfrey followed Cooke as Master of the Children in 1672. For two years Purcell received the tuition of Lully at second-hand, and when Humfrey died in 1674, the fifteen-year-old boy became a pupil of John Blow, who was Master of the Children from 1674 onwards.

While dealing with this period of Purcell's life, it will perhaps be as well to allude to the music to *Macbeth*, so often attributed to him. This was produced in 1672 when Purcell was not more than fourteen years of age. It seems, leaving all supposition out of the question, that the only thing to connect Purcell with this composition is the fact that Dr. Cummings had a manuscript of it in the youthful handwriting of the boy. But it was no uncommon thing for composers to make copies of other men's work, and this may be one of these cases (*v.* article on Matthew Lock).

In 1673 Purcell's voice broke and other employment was found for him to prevent him going too far from the court service. Thus on June 10th, 1673, a warrant was issued " to admit Henry Purcell in the place of keeper, maker, mender, repayrer, and tuner of the regalls, organs, virginalls, flutes, and recorders, and all other kinds of wind instruments whatsoever, in ordinary, without fee, to his Majesty and assistant to John Hingston, and upon the death or other avoydance of the latter, to come in ordinary with fee " (*L.C.R., Vol.* 744). On December 17th we read in the same volume of the records : " Warrant to provide outfit of clothing for Henry Purcell, late child of his Majesty's Chappell Royall whose voice is changed, and gon from the Chappell " and " Warrant to pay Henry Purcell . . . the sum of 30*l.* by the year to commence Michaelmas last past " (1673). In the following January there is an entry relating to " fine Holland for Henry Purcell . . . going off"; in February a bill for handkerchiefs for the same, and at Michaelmas an order for a "felt hat for Henry Purcell, a boy leaving the Chapel Royal". These entries provide details which prove the general assumption that the boys of the chapel were well looked after to be a just one. In 1676 he was appointed as music-copyist to Westminster Abbey, a post previously held by his father,—and it was probably this appointment that caused Hawkins and Burney to say that he became organist of the Abbey at this period. At this stage also the biographers of Purcell generally commence to make mention of his compositions for the stage ; but it would appear that the time for that had not yet arrived. It is true that *Sophonisba* was first produced in 1676, but it is highly doubtful if the music Purcell wrote for it was used for the first performance. All that remains, a song to the verses "Beneath the Poplar's Shadow", was most likely written for a revival of the play,—either in 1685 or 1693 (this song, as "A Mad Song", is printed in *Orpheus Britannicus, Bk. II*).

But the "Elegy" on the "death of his worthy friend", Matthew Lock, he certainly wrote in 1677 (given in *Choice Ayres, Bk. II* 1679, with other work of his).

On September 10th, 1677, Purcell was appointed composer in ordinary "with fee for the violin in the place of Matthew Lock, deceased" (*L.C.R., Vol.* 480). Dr. Cummings, in his *Life of Henry Purcell*, prints an interesting letter from Lock to the younger man, in which he says that he expected some musicians in the evening and asks Purcell to bring with him the anthem he had recently composed. His compositions, indeed, were now occupying more and more of his time, so that in 1678 he was compelled to resign the post of copyist to the Abbey. To this period belongs the first performance of *Timon of Athens* (Shadwell's alteration of Shakespeare's play, 1677–8), but the music which Purcell wrote for the masque contained in it most probably dates from the time of a revival (1694). The music is to be seen in manuscript in *Add.* 5337, *Add.* 35043, and *Add.* 31447 ; the score being printed by the Purcell Society (*Vol.* II).

In 1680 John Blow resigned his poſt as organiſt at Weſtminſter Abbey in order to make way for Purcell. No reason for this change has been discovered, and we can be generous enough to assume that the teacher gave the pupil an opportunity of exercising his skill in this direction. There can be no doubt that this work at the Abbey muſt have had some influence upon the music he produced at the period under consideration. His employment as " Composer for the Violin to the King " muſt also have given him plenty of occupation. To this year (1680) muſt be ascribed the set of Fantasias in *Add.* 30930 (autograph), some of which are dated (June and Auguſt, 1680). The year is also important from the point of view of Purcell's dramatic music, for it was probably in 1680 that the firſt of his work to be used on the ſtage was written. This was the music he supplied for the production in 1680 of Nat. Lee's *Theodosius,* Downes (*Roscius Anglicanus,* 1708) ſtating that this was " the firſt he e'er compos'd for the ſtage ". In the same year he wrote the overture and the act-tunes for

D'Urfey's *Virtuous Wife* (the two songs in it *not* by Purcell). His music for this play is contained in *Add.* 35043. The British Museum manuscript catalogue gives 1680 as the date of an ode (" A Song to Welcome home his Majeſty from Windsor ") contained in *Add.* 22100.

The great event for Purcell in 1681 was his marriage, and in the same year he composed the " Welcome Song ", —" Swifter Isis, swifter flow" (*Add.* 33287). A song for Tate's version of *King Richard the Second* and some music for D'Urfey's *Sir Barnaby Whigg,* also belong to 1681. On his marriage he muſt have removed to Great St. Ann's Lane, for in 1682 his name appears in the Rate-Books of the parish as that of a householder there. In that year also he was elected organiſt to the Chapel Royal in succession to Edward Lowe (*q.v.*). Other joys and sorrows came to Purcell in 1682. In Auguſt his foſter-father and uncle, Thomas Purcell, who referred to his nephew as " my sonne Henry ", died. Shortly after this event Henry Purcell's firſt child, John Baptiſta, was born, only to live a few months. The compositions of this eventful year include a "Welcome Song" performed before James, Duke of York,— "What, what shall be done on behalf of the man" (*Add.* 33287) and some music written for the feaſt in connection with the election of Sir William Pritchard as Lord Mayor of London. The entr'acte music for a revival of Beaumont and Fletcher's *Double Marriage* may belong to 1682 or possibly a little later.

In 1683 were written the odes "From hardy climes" (on the occasion of the marriage of Prince George of Denmark with Anne, daughter of James, Duke of York ; *Add.* 33237 and *Add.* 33287), "Welcome to all the pleasures" (for the St. Cecilia celebration of that year, printed by Playford in 1684 ; *Add.* 33287, and autograph organ-part in *Add.* 33240), and "Laudate Ceciliam" for some Roman chapel celebration of the same year. 1683 was a very important year also from the viewpoint of the hiſtorian of English music for the ſtringed inſtruments. Purcell having made the usual concession to the paſt in trying his hand in the Fancy form (*v. sup.* 1680), now went to Italy for a model and produced in 1683 his twelve *Sonnata's of III Parts* for two violins and violoncello, with a Continuo for harpsichord or organ. The work was issued from his house in St. Ann's Lane and was dedicated to the King. One of the four part-books gives a portrait of the composer *aetatis suae* 24. In the preface he ſtates plainly that he has imitated the Italian method in writing for these inſtruments. Certainly between the Fancies of 1680 (which take one back to the ſtyle of the pre-Commonwealth writers) and the Sonatas of 1683 there is a very great difference of ſtyle and outlook,—and the later set exhibits an enormous advance, both technically and musically.

On December 17th, 1683, we read in the Lord Chamberlain's Records of the appointment of Henry Purcell "to be Organ maker and keeper, *etc.*, in the place of Mr. Hingſton, deceased ", and in the entry of February 16th, 1683–4 we are told that he was given authority to purchase all the necessary materials and engage the labour required, for the repairing and building of organs, etc., in the king's name and " at reasonable and lawfull prices " (L.C.R., Vol. 749). In 1684 he shared with Blow the task of demonstrating the virtues of the organ built by Father Smith in the Temple Church (v. article on John Blow).

The year 1685 was another fruitful one from the musical point of view. For the coronation of James II, Purcell, by virtue of the authority vested in him by the order alluded to a little earlier, had an organ erected at Westminster Abbey (and subsequently removed). For this work he received 34l. 12s. from the Secret Service Money (v. Camden Society's Publ.). At the coronation service he sang in the choir, and had the satisfaction of assisting in the performance of two of his own anthems (" I was glad " and " My heart is inditing ", — the latter written expressly for the service). The ode " Why, why are all the Muses mute " belongs to the same year (Add. 33287). On August 31st, 1685, he was sworn in as musician in ordinary for the harpsichord to the new king (L.C.R.). The Theater of Music, edited by Purcell and Blow in 1685, contains a number of vocal pieces by the former. Whether Purcell wrote the music used in Charles Davenant's Circe or not, is still an unsolved problem. Downes credited John Banister I (q.v.) with its production, while some manuscripts give Purcell's name. In favour of Banister's claim we might depend upon Downes's statement ; but in Purcell's favour is the style of some of the music which is decidedly reminiscent of the greater man. Possibly the two shared the work ; and an alternative suggestion is that Banister may have supplied the whole of the music (or, at least, part of it) for the first production of the tragedy in 1677 while Purcell may have been more largely drawn upon for some revival, ca. 1685 (v. also Add. 31447). In 1686 Purcell composed the ode " Ye tuneful muses " at the performance of which John Abell and William Turner sang the solos (v. Add. 33287), and to the same year (or, possibly, to that of a later revival) may belong the music written for Dryden's Tyrannick Love. At this period Purcell removed to Bowling Alley East, and from the mantelpieces and banisters of this house the late Sir Frederick Bridge had his cupboards made at his dwelling in the Littlington Tower of Weſtminſter Abbey. In 1686 Purcell's second child, Thomas, died, and in the following year the third son, Henry, was born, only to die after a few months. The music of 1687 includes the royal birthday ode " Sound the trumpet, beat the drum " (solos by John Abell, Alphonso Marsh, junior, William Turner, etc., Add. 31447 ; Chaconne and bass air, "While Caesar like ye morning ſtar " in Add. 31813), the " Elegy " written on the death of John Playford, and eleven pieces contained in Book IV of the *Theater of Music.*

In 1688 Purcell's fourth child, a daughter named Frances, was born, and she was the firſt of his children to survive childhood, living until 1724. In 1688 Purcell contributed a dozen sacred songs and hymns to *Harmonia Sacra,* and, in the same year, D'Urfey's *A Fool's Preferment* appeared. The venture was not successful, although Purcell supplied eight pieces of music for the performance ; but possibly the political troubles that were brewing had something to do with

this. The anthem " Blessed are they that fear the Lord " also belongs to this year.

On July 22nd, 1689, Purcell was appointed to the private music of William and Mary. At the coronation of these sovereigns the Abbey organiſt was like to have incurred serious displeasure. It appears that Purcell allowed visitors to witness the ceremony from the organ-loft. For this accommodation he probably received a goodly sum. The Dean and Chapter did not look favourably upon this, and demanded the money received. Purcell demurred, and was threatened with dismissal. He evidently paid over the money eventually, for there is a receipt in the Treasurer's accounts : " Received of Mr. Purcell (his poundage and other charges being dedućted) 78*l.* 4*s.* 6*d.*" In the same year Purcell's son Edward was born (*v.* Edward Purcell). To 1689 also is to be ascribed the ode to the Prince of Denmark, " Celesial music " (*Add.* 33237), performed " at Mr. Maidwell's, a schoolmaſter, on the 5th of Auguſt, 1689", the words by one of his scholars. In this or the following year was written the fine ode " Of old when

Heroes " (The Yorkshire Feaſt Song) ; it is given in *Add.* 31447, *Add.* 33237, *Add.* 31455 (incomplete), and *Add.* 31451 (such parts as are not contained in *Orpheus Britannicus*). In 1689 also Purcell " revised and corrected " *Musick's Hand-maid,* and supplied to it a number of harpsichord pieces. The queſtion as to when the opera *Dido and Aeneas* was written is another knotty one. The dates generally given for its production lie between 1680 and 1690, but as far as sensible and reason-able argument can decide the queſtion, it muſt be placed nearer the latter date than the former. The whole matter has been gone into in a thoroughly scholarly manner by Mr. W. Barclay Squire in his *Purcell's Dramatic Music (Sammelbände der Internationale Musik-Gesell-schaft)* and to this work the reader is referred. According to the line of argument followed, the date of the opera would be somewhere between 1688 and the summer of 1690. Certainly it is worthy of Purcell's later years. It is a true opera in that there is no spoken dialogue ; everything being set to music. The chorus

" With drooping wings " and Dido's " When I am laid in earth " are two numbers that will always endear Purcell to the hearts of those who can appreciate real beauty in music. Unfortunately the libretto is quite unworthy of the music.

The year 1690 was another important one from the point of view of those intereſted in Purcell's dramatic music. *Dioclesian, or the Phrophetess* (Betterton's adaptation of Beaumont and Fletcher's work) was performed in the summer of 1690 and con-tained some of Purcell's fineſt incidental music, particularly in the masque which forms so great a part of Act V. Downes said that the music "gratify'd the expectations of Court and City ; and got the author great reputation ". The music was printed in the following year, the copies being corrected in Purcell's own handwriting. The late Sir Frederick Bridge possessed one of these books and greatly prized it. " What shall I do to show how much I love her ", for this work, and " Let ye soldiers rejoyce", are contained in *Add.* 35043. *Amphitryon* was produced in the autumn of 1690 and published with the " musick of the songs compos'd by Mr. Henry Purcell" in the same year. Dryden, who adapted the work from Plautus and Molière, thought that in it Purcell showed that we had at last "found an Englishman equal with the best abroad". Other works appearing in 1690 and containing music by Purcell were : *The Massacre of Paris* (two versions of a short song, " Thy Genius lo ! "), *Distressed Innocence* (overture and entr'actes), *Sir Anthony Love* (Overture and Dialogue, two songs and variations on a ground ; present in a manuscript at St. Michael's College Tenbury), and the *Knight of Malta* (a Catch ; printed 1691). The ode, " Arise, my Muse " (for the queen's birthday) also belongs to 1690, and is contained in *Add.* 31447. Playford's *Apollo's Banquet* appearing in 1690 (*Edit.* 6) gives three pieces by Purcell.

The most important work of 1691, and containing what is perhaps the greatest of Purcell's dramatic music, was *King Arthur* (Dryden). The complete score was lost ; but by piecing together the isolated numbers found in various manuscripts, it is thought that practically the whole of the music has been recovered. The musical sections in this case do not form an integral part of the plot and the work cannot be called an opera ; —but there can be no doubt that it vastly increases the dramatic effect of the whole. It is impossible to do justice to the excellent work that Purcell has put into *King Arthur* in the space at our disposal here ; it must suffice merely to name such sections as the " Frost Scene ", the scene of the sacrifice, the song and chorus " Come if you dare ", and the beautiful song " Fairest Isle ". In *King Arthur* Purcell keeps up a uniformly high standard throughout. A Dialogue from this work is in *Add.* 33236 and other parts of the music are to be found in *Add.* 5333 and *Add.* 31447. In the same year he supplied five songs to Southern's comedy *The Wife's Excuse*, and some instrumental music to *The Gordian Knot Untied*. A song by Purcell was probably used in *The Indian Emperor* (1691). " Welcome, glorious morn ", a birthday ode to the queen, also dates from 1691, and is a particularly fine piece of work.

The great achievement of

1692 was the *Fairy Queen*, produced in the Spring. Downes says that it was "excellently performed : chiefly the instrumentall and vocal part compos'd by the said Mr. Purcell . . . but the expences in setting it out being so great, the company got very little by it ". The score of this fine music was lost for two centuries. On October 13th, 1700, the *London Gazette* contained the following advertisement : "The score of the Musick for the Fairy Queen set by the late Mr. Henry Purcell, and belonging to the patentees of the Theatre Royal in Covent Garden, London, being lost by his death ; Whosoever brings the said Score, or a copy thereof to Mr. Zachary Baggs, Treasurer of the said Theatre, shall have 20 Guineas Reward ". The discovery of the manuscript in the library of the Royal Academy of Music (1901) was a romantic event of great importance, and the story is told by Mr. W. Barclay Squire in *Musical Times* for January, 1920. The full score was published by the Purcell Society and the pianoforte score by Novello. What more can one say of the

Fairy Queen than was said by Dr. Ernest Walker who supposed that if a Purcell-lover were compelled to part with all his music except one single work, he would cling to the *Fairy Queen*.

For a revival of *Oedipus* (Dryden and Lee), probably that of 1692, Purcell wrote a good deal of intensely dramatic music (parts of it in *Add.* 31447, and *Add.* 31452). The music written for *The Libertine* (Shadwell) was probably written for the revival of 1692, and includes the ever-popular "Nymphs and Shepherds" and the chorus "In these delightful pleasant Groves" (both in *Add.* 31405 ; *v.* also *Add.* 31447). One can only agree with Mr. Barclay Squire that this music could not have been written for the first (1676) performance of the play. Other plays of 1692 for which Purcell composed music were : *Cleomenes*, *Henry II* (song given in *Comes Amoris, Bk. IV*, *Regulus*, *The Marriage-Hater Matched*, and *Aureng-Zebe* (for the revival of 1692, possibly, 1694). The Cecilia ode which is perhaps Purcell's finest achievement in this class of composition was that produced in 1692,—"Hail bright Cecilia" (*Add.* 31447 and *Add.* 31448). In the same year he wrote "Love's Goddess, *etc.*", for the queen's birthday (*Add.* 31447).

According to the Westminster Rate-Books Purcell appears to have removed to Marsham Street in time to pay the rates for 1693. The dramatic works for which he supplied music during this year included: *The Maid's Last Prayer* (two songs in a concert-scene and a third on *p.* 52 of the printed version), *The Female Vertuosos*, *Epsom Wells*, *The Richmond Heiress* (*v. Add.* 35043), *The Double Dealer* (overture, entr'actes, and a song), *Rule a Wife and have a Wife* (a revival), and *The Old Bachelor* (overture, entr'actes, and songs ; *v. Add.* 35043),— for some of them only a song or two. The queen's birthday ode for the year was "Celebrate this Festival", an ambitious work for five solo voices and four-part chorus (*Add.* 17835, *Add.* 33237, *Add.* 31447, and an arrangement for a single voice in *Add.* 22099). The second book of *Harmonia Sacra* also dates from 1693 and contains five sacred compositions by Purcell.

In 1694 Purcell made an excursion in a new direction. The section in Playford's *Introduction to the Skill of Musick* dealing with the art of composing in parts had become antiquated (*v.* articles on Campion, Christopher Simpson, and John Playford I) and Purcell set about supplying a more up-to-date treatise. This was his *Art of Descant* in the edition of 1694 and later reprints. I possess a copy of the thirteenth edition (1697) of the *Introduction*, including the Purcell contribution. To the same year belongs the magnificent *Te Deum* and *Jubilate* written for the St. Cecilia celebrations of that year. It was published by Mrs. Purcell in 1697, mutilated by Boyce, and re-issued from the original score by Sir Frederick Bridge (Novello). The dramatic work of the year included songs in *Don Quixote* (Parts I and II), the celebrated "Genius of England", sung by Mrs. Cibber (*née* Catherine Shore, *q.v.*) to the trumpet obbligato of her brother, being contained in *Add.* 35043 (the same manuscript also giving a Dialogue from that play). He wrote a song for the 1694 revival of *Love Triumphant* (Dryden), two for *The Fatal Marriage* (one of them given in *Add.* 35043), a Dialogue for *The Canterbury Guests* (printed in Hudgebutt's *Thesaurus Musicus* in 1695), and an overture, entr'actes, and a song for *The Married Beau.* Early in the year he wrote the ode for the foundation - commemoration celebrations of Trinity Hall, Dublin, — " Hail, great Parent " (*v. Add.* 31447, " Perform'd att Christ Church in Dublin ", January 9th, 1693–4).

The last year of Purcell's activity was close-packed with dramatic work. *Bonduca* (an adaptation of Beaumont and Fletcher's work) was supplied with the necessary music by Purcell, and the whole has been printed by the Musical Antiquarian Society. Parts of it are to be found in *Add.* 35043, *Add.* 31405, *Add.* 31452, *Add.* 31453, and *Add.* 31447). *The Indian Queen,* including such well-known music as " Ye twice ten hundred Deities ", and " I attempt from Love's sickness to fly ", is preserved (partly in Purcell's autograph) in *Add.* 31449 (*v.* also *Add.* 31453, *Add.* 31447, and *Add.* 35043). For *Oroonoko* Purcell wrote the Dialogue " Celemene, pray tell me ", a number which appears to have

been inserted into the *Conquest of Granada* at a revival of the latter. Further plays to use examples of his music were: *The Rival Sisters* (*v. Add.* 35043 ; the R.C.M. possesses a first violin part and the figured bass of a good deal more of the music, there attributed to Purcell), *The Mock Marriage, Abdelazer* (a revival ; *v. Add.* 35043), *Part III* of D'Urfey's *Don Quixote* (produced after Purcell's death), *The Tempest* (an adaptation which Mr. Barclay Squire places in 1695 ; only one song of which can with certainty be given to Purcell), *Pausanias,* and *The Spanish Friar* (Purcell's music probably dating from the 1695 revival). The anthem " Blessed is the man " and a March for trumpets were written for the funeral of Queen Mary (March 5th, 1695). The fine ode for the Duke of Gloucester's birthday, " Who can from joy refraine " (*v. Add.* 30934) is also dated 1695.

On November 21st, 1695, Henry Purcell died, aged thirty-seven. Into the unauthenticated story that he met his death by having been locked out of doors by his wife on a cold night, we need not go. Had this been true, we should hardly expect to find the dying man call her his " Loving wife " in the will which he made the day before he died. His death was in all probability caused by the consumptive tendency which explains the early death of so many members of his family. Officially his death was announced in the Cheque-Book of the Chapel Royal : " 1695. Mr. Henry Purcell, Organist in his Majesty's Chapel Royal departed this life the 21 day of November, 1695 " ; on November 26th he was buried below his old organ in Westminster Abbey.

By his will Purcell left all his property to his wife, who lived until 1706. In addition to the five children already mentioned, there was a sixth, a girl named Mary Peters, who probably arrived at no great age. Dr. Cummings, in his *Life of Purcell*, goes carefully into the question of the composer's character and habits, and refutes many cruel libels that gossip had directed against this simple and clean-living man.

After Purcell's death a number of works by him were published. The more important were *Ten Sonatas in Four Parts* (1697), *Lessons*

for the Harpsichord (1696), *Ayres for the Theatre* (1697), containing a large number of pieces from the dramatic works, and *Orpheus Britannicus* (1698, 1702).

It is almost impossible to catalogue all the works of Henry Purcell, for many of them are his only by tradition and some must still be hidden in various collections. The British Museum catalogues of printed and manuscript music give as full a list as can be expected until someone has the courage and the leisure to search all the libraries where work of his may be housed. Mr. Fuller Maitland gives a good list in *Grove* (*Ed.* 1913). Portraits of Henry Purcell are in the National Portrait Gallery (London), a fine drawing by Kneller, which belonged to the late Mr. Alfred Littleton, engravings prefixed to some of his published works, and others. The Kneller portrait was published in a pamphlet issued for the bicentenary celebrations in 1895 (Novello ; *v.* also *Musical Times* for September, 1920, for three unpublished portraits of Henry Purcell).

PURCELL (Thomas): A brother of Henry Purcell the Elder who exercised far more influence upon the younger Henry that did the latter's father. Dying when the gifted son was but six years of age, Henry I left the boy's upbringing in the hands of Thomas ; and if for no other reason, the child's uncle deserves a proud position in any work of this kind. But apart from this, Thomas was also a very popular musician in his day, and served his king as Master of the Royal Music, as well as in several other capacities. We find Thomas Purcell's name in 1660 in a list of musicians of the Chapel Royal (*L.C.R., Vol.* 482). In the following year he was appointed, like his brother Henry, as copyist to Westminster Abbey and also as a lay-vicar. In 1662 he was given a post " for lute, voyall, and voyce " left vacant by the decease of Henry Lawes, the king " for this service and attendance " being " pleased to allow him the wages and livery of six and thirty pounds, two shillings, and six pence by the year during his life " (Royal warrant of November 29th, 1662). In lists issued in 1666 (November 24th) and in 1668–9 we find the names of Thomas Purcell, Pelham

Humfrey, and Matthew Lock bracketed as composers to the court. Whether this post was distinct from that of " Composer for the violins " is not clear, but we must suppose that it was, otherwise we could find no reason for a warrant of 1672 : " Whereas we have been pleased to take into our service as Composer in ordinary for the violins, Thomas Purcell and Pelham Humphreys, Gentlemen, in the room of George Hudson, deceased, and for their entertainments in consideration of services done, and to be done, unto us, we have given and granted and by these presents do . . . give and grant . . . for their wages and fee, the sum of fifty-two pounds fifteen shillings and tenpence, by the year during their natural lives, and the life of the longer liver of them, the first payment to commence from the feast of St. Michael the Archangel 1672 " (Warrant dated August 8th). In the same year Thomas Purcell was elected " Marshall of the Corporacion of Musique " (*Harl.* 1911), and in February, 1672–3, he is mentioned in the Lord Chamberlain's Papers as " Groom of the Robes " (40*l.* a year), which shows him to have been very popular at court and among the members of the company of professional musicians. In 1673 the fee paid to the " Composers for the violins " was 200*l.* per annum, and this sum was enjoyed jointly by Purcell and Humfrey, and then by the " longest liver of them " (*L.C.R., Vol.* 744). On March 9th, 1673–4, he was given the place in the " Private Musick " rendered vacant by the death of John Wilson,—which gave him a further 20*l.* a year (*Id.*). The entry for April 14th, 1674, gives the names of the Gentlemen who were to attend upon the king at Windsor, and among them we find Thomas Purcell given as a " Tenner " (*Id., Vol.* 745). Unless some of these posts were merely honorary, Thomas must have lived a very busy life as singer, violinist, lutenist, Gentleman of the Chapel, Groom of the Robes, and Master of the Musick. In 1681 he signed a document, which his wife Frances witnessed, empowering their son Matthew to act as his lawful attorney. The death of Thomas Purcell was announced in the Cheque Book of the Chapel Royal as having taken place on

" the last day of July, 1682 ", and two days later he was buried in the Cloisters of Westminster Abbey. He thus lived long enough to see his nephew and pupil Henry II appointed organist at the Chapel Royal and to witness the fruition of his labours.

The only music by Thomas Purcell known to exist is confined to two or three chants (among them a Funeral or Burial chant that became well-known). These specimens of his work may be seen in *Add.* 9073 (Vincent Novello's transcriptions from a Westminster Abbey organ-book), *Add.* 17784, and *Add.* 29968, all in the British Museum.

PYGOTT (Richard): Master of Cardinal Wolsey's Chapel and later a Gentleman of the Chapel Royal. He was also a composer of considerable daring for his period and used dissonances then disallowed. We meet with him first in the letter written by Pace to Wolsey on March 29th, 1518, on the subject of a Chapel-boy sent to the king by the cardinal (*v.* article on William Cornyshe) in which the writer speaks of Cornyshe's praise of the boy and of his extolling " Mr.

Pygote for the teaching of him ". In the lists of Gentlemen assisting at the coronation of Edward VI and at the funeral of Henry VIII we find Pygott's name. Of his music only one piece has been printed : in Wynkyn de Worde's song-book of 1530 (specimen in the *B.M.* containing Triplex and Bassus parts only). In manuscript there are the motet " Salve, Regina, mater misericordie " (Medius ; *Harl.* 1709), the motet " Grande Pastore ", and part of a mass, " Veni, sancte spiritus " (Tenor part ; *Add.* 34191), a carol in four parts (*Add.* 31922), and three compositions in the Peterhouse part-books.

R

RAMSEY (Robert): Very little is known of this organist and church composer. From the Cambridge *Grace Book* (E., *p.* 243) we learn that he supplicated for the degree of *Mus. Bac.* in 1616, having studied the art for seven years. The degree was promised on the condition that he compose a "Canticum" to be sung at the Church of St. Mary "coram Universitate". We meet with him as organist of Trinity College (Cambridge) in 1628, becoming Master of the Choristers two or three years later. During the troublous times of 1644 we lose sight of him. Most of his music is to sacred texts. A "Whole Service in F, with *Jubilate* instead of *Benedictus* ", is contained in Tudway's collection (*Harl.* 7340). Other British Museum manuscripts preserving work by Ramsey are : *Add.* 29289 (*Te Deum*), *Add.* 29427 (Anthem, Altus Part, "When David"), *Add.* 29366–8 (an Anthem and three Madrigals), *Add.* 11608 (an Anthem, "A Dialogue betweene Saul, the witch of Endor, and Samuel's Ghost,—In Guiltie Night ", also in *Add.* 29396 ; and a song of an elegiac character, probably written after the death of Prince Henry,— "What Teares, deare Prince ") and *Add.* 17786–91 (a Madrigal, "Wilt thou, unkind, now leave me ", six-part). He is also represented in manuscripts at Ely Cathedral, St. Peter's, Cambridge, the Bodleian, Oxford (which has his "Commencement Song "), and, in autograph, in the Euing library, Glasgow.

RANDALL (William): An organist and composer of sacred music who flourished in the latter part of the sixteenth century. Meres (*Palladis Tamia*) counts him among the "excellent musicians " of the day, but his work is in no way comparable with that of the giants of the period. Nevertheless, he has one or two quite interesting compositions to his credit, and he is representative of the lesser creative artists of his era. He came from Exeter, where he served as a choir-boy. He entered the Chapel Royal in London in 1584, and is given in the Cheque-Book as organist in 1592. The date of his death is not to be determined with certainty;

but Edmund Hooper was sworn "in Mr. Randoll's roome" in 1603.

He is best known by an anthem " Give sentence with me " (*Add.* 17792-6, *B.M.*) and an *In Nomine* at Oxford (Music School). *Harl.* 6346 (*B.M.*) contains the words of two more anthems, but the music to them has not come to light. This William Randall should not be confused with later musicians bearing the same name.

RAVENSCROFT (John): A popular violinist active at the Goodman's Fields Theatre in the East-End of London, enjoying a great reputation as a writer of dances, notably Hornpipes. Biographical details are wanting, but the dates of his compositions would place the period of his greatest vogue from about 1685 to 1740. He died between the latter date and the middle of the century. An interesting collection of Sonatas for two violins and violone (or archlute) and basso continuo, was published by Mascardi at Rome in 1695 (reprinted by Roger at Amsterdam). Specimens of his dances may be seen in Hawkins's *History*. A song, " Foolish Woman fly men's charms " by John

Ravenscroft was published in London, *ca.* 1725.

RAVENSCROFT(Thomas): An industrious editor, arranger, and writer of music belonging to widely different categories, who, though having nothing of a really outstanding nature to his credit, still occupies an important place in the history of English music in the early seventeenth century. His *Psalter*, his *Brief Discourse*, and his sets of rounds and catches, exhibit an amazing versatility, and he was a useful man in his own age if he was not exactly a brilliant one. He appears to have been something of a prodigy, for he was very young indeed when his earliest works were issued. In the *Brief Discourse* (1614) his age is given as twenty-two, and his extreme youth is alluded to. If this information can be trusted, he must have been born in 1592 or 1593, and was consequently only fourteen or fifteen years of age when he became a Bachelor of Music at Cambridge in 1607. Dr. E. H. Fellowes (*English Madrigal Composers*) suggests that " the Latin epigram which refers to his age probably belongs to an earlier date, although printed in the 1614 edition ",—a supposition that would place the date of his birth earlier. There is certainly sufficient in Ravenscroft's age at the publication of such a work to arouse suspicion ; but such precocity is not unknown, and there is really no valid reason for thinking that he was older than twenty-two when the *Brief Discourse* appeared. Moreover, a marginal note in that work states quite plainly : " Ad annos 14 creatus eſt Baccalaureus facultatis Musicae in Academ. Cantabrig."

Of Ravenscroft's life we know comparatively little. He was trained in the choir of St. Paul's Cathedral at the time Edward Pearce (Piers or Peers) was Maſter, and the only other faɛt conneɛted with his biography is that he was an inſtruɛtor in music at Chriſt's Hospital from 1618 to 1622.

The firſt work to contain music by Ravenscroft was *Pammelia : Musicke's Miscellanie : or Mixed Varietie of pleasant Roundelays and delightful Catches of 3, 4, 5, 6, 7, 8, 9, 10 parts in one*, which he edited in 1609, some of the contents being of his own composition. The book was the firſt of the kind to appear in England, and its editor evidently intended it to make a popular appeal, for he added to the title : " None so ordinary as musicall, none so musicall, as not to all very pleasing and acceptable ". A second edition appeared in 1618, one " round or catch for eleven voices " (" Sing we now merrily ") was printed by J. Stafford Smith in *Musica Antiqua* (1812), and some specimens were given by Burney (*Hiſtory*). In the same year (1609) a second book of similar Catches and Canons appeared under Ravenscroft's editorship : *Deuteromelia : Or the second part of Musick's Melodie, or Melodius Musicke of Pleasant Roundelaies, K. H. Mirth or Freeman's Songs and Such delightfull Catches. Qui canere poteſt canat. Catch that Catch Can*. This set included such well-known ditties as " Three Blind Mice " and " Hold thy peace, thou Knave " (used by Shakespeare in *Twelfth Night*). Exaɛtly what is meant by " K. H. Mirth " is not quite clear ; but it probably refers to some music club or tavern where catch-singers foregathered. In 1611 he issued *Melismata. Musicall Phansies. Fitting the*

Court, Citie, and Country Humours. To 3, 4 *and* 5 *Voyces.* To this title he appended a quaint recommendation : " To all delightful except the spiteful ; to none offensive except to the Pensive ", which was surely jingling enough to satisfy any taſte. According to an account given in the *Musical Worid* for Auguſt 27th, 1840 (*II, p.* 139), a great collection of old music was found buried encased in ſtrong-boxes, and included was another work of Ravenscroft's : *Musalia, or Pleasant Diversions in Rime, several varieties of catches, roundels, canons, etc.,* dated 1613.

The work which Ravenscroft evidently intended to be his moſt important publication appeared in 1614 : *A Briefe Discourse of the true (but neglected) use of Charaɛ̌'ring the Degrees by their Perfeɛ̌ion, Imperfection, and Diminution in Measurable Musicke. Againſt the Common Praɛ̌ice and Cuſtome of these Times.* It was an unsuccessful attempt to revive the obsolescent syſtem of Mensurable Music (*see this in Dic. O. E. Mus.*), faſt disappearing even from the minds of musicians, and for praɛ̌ical purposes already obsolete. A few four-part madrigal-like compositions were included by way of illuſtration, written by Ravenscroft, Edward Pearce, his old maſter at St. Paul's, and the madrigaliſt John Bennet. His other great publication was : " *The Whole Booke of Psalmes* : with The Hymnes Evangelicall, and *Songs* Sprituall. Composed into 4 parts by sundry Authors, with such seuerall Tunes as haue beene, *and are usually sung in England,* Scotland, *Wales,* Germany, Italy, France, and the Netherlands : Neuer as yet before in one volume published. Also : A brief Abſtraɛ̌ of the Prayse, Efficacie, and Vertue of the Psalmes, etc." 1621. This title-page was copied from the fine example in the library of the late Mr. A. H. Littleton. To this work Ravenscroft himself contributed half-a-hundred of the four-part settings. A second edition appeared in 1633.

Four anthems by Ravenscroft are to be seen in the library of Chriſt Church, Oxford (*à* 5, wanting the bass), of which three are verse-anthems and the other " full ". The British Museum has a treatise in *Add.* 19758 which contains a good deal of the matter used in the *Brief Discourse*. It is not known when Ravenscroft died ; the date generally accepted lies between 1630 and 1635.

READING: A considerable amount of uncertainty must exist in connection with musicians bearing this name, five at least rejoicing in the Christian name John. As far as has been possible these men have been separated in the following articles, but it cannot be determined with absolute accuracy whether the works of the Readings have all been assigned to their true authors. Briefly we are confronted with a John Reading whom we shall call John Reading I, and who was organist at Winchester ; a John Reading II, who was organist at Chichester ; a John Reading III, who was born in 1677 and died in 1764 ; a John Reading IV, who was a vocalist at Drury Lane Theatre at the end of the seventeenth century, and whose chief claim to remembrance to-day appears to be the circumstance that he was fined 20 Marks for riotous behaviour at a tavern in 1695; a John Reading V, who was a Prebendary of Canterbury Cathedral and who delivered a sermon on Church Music in 1663 ; besides a Balthazar, or Valentine, Reading, who was a singer in the Chapel Royal between 1685 and 1689. Only the first three interest us in this work, but it will be difficult to make quite sure of our ground even when dealing with no more than three.

READING (John) (I): Of all the John Readings this one is perhaps the best known, owing probably to his connection with Winchester College. The Cathedral accounts of Lincoln give us the only information we possess of his early years, and from them we learn that on October 10th, 1667, he was made a Junior Vicar-Choral and on November 28th a Poor Vicar. On June 7th, 1670, he was appointed Master of the Choristers. At that time the Dutchman Hecht was organist at Lincoln and Reading was forced to look elsewhere for such a post. His opportunity came when Randall Jewett died, and in 1675 Reading was engaged as organist to Winchester Cathedral. In 1681 he changed the scene of his activities to Winchester College, Daniel Roseingrave succeeding him at the Cathedral in the following year. While John Reading was at the College, the salary of the organist was increased from a purely nominal 5*l.* a year to the living wage of 50*l.* per annum. He died in 1692 and was followed in his College post by Jeremiah Clarke.

There is every reason to believe that the celebrated Winchester School-song, *Dulce Domum*, was the work of this John Reading. It has appeared in a large number of editions and in various arrangements. Two or three of the printed versions are much earlier than the manuscript containing the melody at the British Museum (*Add.* 31813). The Latin Graces used annually at election times at the College were also from his pen, and of these, likewise, several printed versions have appeared. Some doubt must exist as to the authorship of the " Hymn on the Nativity ", *Adeste fideles,—* printed by almost every publisher of sacred music ; but I am inclined to give it to John Reading I. Further compositions which may be the work of this Reading are mentioned below in the article on the second of that ilk.

READING (John) (II): Of the second John Reading hardly anything is known. He was organist at Chichester Cathedral from 1674 until 1720, when, presumably, he died. It is not known whether he was related to any of his namesakes. Occasional specimens of Church music bearing this name crop up in manuscripts, but it is not possible to decide which of the first two Readings has the right to them. The third Reading hardly complicates this question, for his style would be a whole generation ahead of that of the other two. For convenience, the following works are mentioned here, belonging as they obviously do, to one of the first two Readings ; but we cannot determine which of the two was responsible for these slight compositions : Three pieces in the *Theater of Music* (*Bk.* IV, 1687), and specimens in the *Division Violin* (1685, Edition 2) and the *Pleasant Musical Companion* (1701).

READING (John) (III): Except for about five years spent at Lincoln, John Reading III passed all his active life in London. Born in 1677, he was educated musically in the Chapel Royal, coming under the tutorage of

John Blow. He left the Chapel before 1699, for in that year a belated order was issued to the following effect: " Warrant, upon certificate of Dr. John Blow, Master of his Majesty's Musick, for the allowance of a suit of clothing to John Reading, late Child of the Chappell, whose voice is changed, and is therefore removed from the service of the Chappell. Also for the sum of 20*l.* to be paid to him, being the usual allowance " (*L.C.R.*, *Vol.* 756, 826). It is quite likely that he had already left that service before 1696, when he obtained employment as organist at Dulwich College —a post which he held until 1698. It is possible that he served for another two years in the same capacity and place, between 1700 and 1702. The Lincoln books give us the next information. On November 21st, 1702, he became a Junior Vicar at Lincoln Cathedral, advancing to be Master of the Choristers within eleven months (October 5th, 1703). A year later he had further confidence placed in him, for he was retained to teach singing to the choristers. In 1707 he returned to the metropolis, becoming organist of St. John-

at-Hackney (now North-East London) in 1708, and later of St. Dunstan's-in-the-West and of two City Churches. He lived until the autumn of 1764.

In composition he was a self-avowed admirer of the Italian style and published, early in the eighteenth century a *Book of New Songs, after the Italian manner, with Symphonies and a Thorough Bass fitted to the Harpsichord.* A volume of anthems by him was issued at about the same time. Several authorities give him the credit for writing *Adeste fideles* ; but this is doubtful (*v. also* John Reading I).

REDFORD (John): An eminent organist and composer of instrumental and vocal music who flourished during the first half of the sixteenth century. Certain examples of his keyboard music are exceedingly fine and may rank with the very best productions of the period; and if the anthem " Rejoice in the Lord " be indeed by him, his vocal music may be placed on at least as high a plane. There is certainly nothing in the last-mentioned composition to prevent us attributing it to John Redford. Hawkins appears to be responsible for the ascription of the anthem to this composer, and when he wrote it is possible that there was some evidence in support of the theory. It would be interesting to discover when and from whom the anthem received the English words that are always associated with it, for every other composition by Redford that I have seen bears a Latin superscription. As was the custom of the time Redford was also responsible for many of the court entertainments, and there is sufficient evidence left to prove that he wrote the words of two plays, and probably also the music used in them.

John Redford was probably connected with St. Paul's Cathedral throughout his active life. He certainly was a Vicar-Choral there in 1534, before he became organist and almoner (*v. also* J. E. West, *Cathedral Organists*, 1921). According to Thomas Tusser's autobiographical poem Redford was instructor of the boys also. The author of *Five Hundred Points of Husbandry* says :
" But mark the chance, myself to 'vance,
By friendship's lot to Paules
I got,

So found I grace a certain space
Still to remain.
With Redford there, the like no where,
For cunning such, and virtue much,
By whom some part of Musicke art
So did I gain."
It is not known how long Redford retained the organist's post at St. Paul's ; but since Sebastian Westcott is known to have filled that position shortly after the middle of the century, Redford either died or resigned before 1550.

The majority of his works consist of arrangements of sacred compositions for the organ ; but they are so well adapted to the instrument that we must look upon Redford as one of the very foremost instrumental composers of his day. The collection made by Thomas Mulliner (*B.M. Add.* 30513) contains no fewer than twenty-three such pieces. Whether the Latin titles they bear were those of the tunes used, and whether the original compositions were by Redford or not, I am not in a position to say. In the absence of all mention of a composer, it seems highly probably that the arrangements were based upon the organist's own works. The pieces bear such headings as : " Eterne Rex Alltissime ", " O Lux (on the fabourden) ", " O Lux (with a meane) ", " Exultet celum laudibus ", " Christe, Qui Lux," *etc.* The doubtful anthem mentioned above,— " Rejoice in the Lord ",—is also to be found in this manuscript ; and it was probably this circumstance (that it was discovered in the company of so many compositions by Redford) that caused Hawkins to look upon the St. Paul's organist as its author. Mr. G. E. P. Arkwright thinks Tye the composer, and Henry Davey advanced the claims of Causton, his style " being perhaps nearest ". Personally, I see nothing in the composition that would make Redford's claim ridiculous. It was probably its very excellence that caused so many writers to seek a different and better-known composer for the anthem ; but judging by his other work I should say that " Rejoice in the Lord " is just what one would expect a vocal work of Redford's to be, supposing him to have been in his best form when he wrote it. *Add.* 29996 (part of which is in Redford's handwriting) also contains some very fine keyboard music, and all the unnamed pieces in the series are most likely by him. A motet by Redford,—*Christus Resurgens,*—is in *Add.* 17802–5. *Add.* 15233 is extremely interesting since it contains, besides organ pieces (most probably autograph), poems by Redford and the words of *The Play of Wyt and Science.* This is a morality in which such virtues and vices as Reason, Instruction, Wit, Honest Recreation, Idleness, Ignorance, Experience, *etc.,* are the characters. There is some evidence of three songs having been written for this interlude,—" Gyve place, giue place to honest recreation ", "Exceedyng mesure with paynes continuall ", and " Welcum, myne owne ". At the end of the libretto is the direction : " Heere cumith in fowre wyth Violes and syng ' remembreance ', and at the last quere all make curtsye and so goe forth synging ". The same manuscript contains a page of another play of a similar nature, at the end of which is also to be found the direction : " Here the syng, Hey nony nonye, and so go forth syngyng ". These plays were undoubtedly written, —as were those of Cornyshe and Crane,—for court entertainments. The firſt seven folios of the manuscript are missing. *Royal App.* 31–35 contain motets with the manuscript colophon " finis qd. Maſter Redford ", but it is very doubtful whether these are of his composition. A second specimen of Redford's vocal music is preserved in the library of Chriſt Church, Oxford (" Veſtri precinĉti ", *à* 6, wanting the tenor book), besides a " Voluntary " for the organ and other organ-arrangements. Modern issues of his works are singularly few in number. Mr. John E. Weſt published (Novello, 1906) the " Glorificamus " for the organ, and the debatable anthem " Rejoice in the Lord " has been printed by Hawkins, *The Choir*, and Novello and Co.

RICHARDSON (Vaughan): Organiſt and composer of ecclesiaſtical music. The date of his birth is unknown ; but in view of the faĉts that he was already in 1678 aĉtive as a child of the Chapel Royal and that in 1688 his voice broke, we may assume that he was born about 1670. The firſt piece of information is given in the Lord Chamber-lain's Records (*Vol.* 747) and the second in Volume 752 under date June 17–18, 1688, " Order to deliver 20*l.* for one year and a suit of plain clothes, to Vaughan Richardson, late child of his Majeſty's Chapell Royall, whose voyce is changed and is gon from the Chappell ". At the Chapel he came under the tutorage of John Blow. From 1686 to 1688 he was engaged temporarily as organiſt of Worceſter Cathedral, and in 1693 he took up his poſt at Wincheſter which he held for the remaining thirty-six years of his life. He died at Wincheſter in 1729.

Not much of Vaughan Richardson's music has been preserved, but some of it is diſtinĉtly high in quality. *Harl.* 7342 contains his Evening Service in C (" Composed on ye Peace, 1713 ") and Harl. 7341 the full anthem, " O Lord God of my Salvation " (the latter being repeated in *Add.* 31821). *Add.* 31120 contains Vincent Novello's organ transcriptions, and among them is an example based on one of Richardson's anthems. To celebrate the Peace of Ryswick (1697) he wrote " An Entertainment of New Musick ", and for the Winchester St. Cecilia celebrations of 1703 (and possibly also for those of an earlier year) he composed appropriate music. The most characteristic among his pieces have been printed: A collection of songs " for One, Two, and Three voices, accompany'd with Instruments ", appeared in 1701 ; and " O how amiable " was printed by Page (*Harmonia Sacra*), Novello (*Musical Times*, 1856), R. Cocks and Co. (*Collection of Cathedral Services, etc., No.* 31 ; 1859) and, in a Tonic Sol-fa version, by Novello.

ROBINSON (Thomas): An important lutenist and teacher of music who flourished at the end of the sixteenth century and the commencement of the seventeenth. Of his life we know nothing beyond what may be gathered from the prefaces to his publications. In 1603 he issued " *The Schoole of Musicke* : Wherein is taught the perfect method of True Fingering of the Lute, Pandora, Orpharion, and Viol de Gamba with most infallible generall rules, both easie and delightfull. Also, a method how you may be your owne instructor for Prick-song, by the help of your Lute, without any other teacher : with lessons of all sorts, for your further and better instruction ". The work is dedicated to James I, and in the address to the king, Robinson says : " . . . and yet I can say for my selfe, that once I was thought (in Denmarke at Elsanure) the fittest to instruct your Majesties Queene, our most gracious Ladie and Mistress ", from which it may be assumed that this musician, like John Dowland, was at one time active at the Danish court. For this, however, we have no other proof than the dedication just alluded to. The book is in the form of a dialogue between " A Knight (who hath children to be taught) and Timotheus, that should Teach them ", and contains rules for the management of the lute and gamba, and some hints for the study of singing. The work, in addition, gives a number of pieces for practice in tablature. Six years later Robinson published " *New Citharen Lessons*. With perfect Tunings of the same, from Foure course of strings to Fourteene course, even to trie the sharpest teeth of Envie, with Lessons of all sorts, and Methodicall Inŝtruĉtions for all Professors and Praĉtitioners of the Citharen, 1609 ". On the title-page of this work the author calls himself " Student in all the seven liberall sciences ". Like the other work, this also is in the form of a dialogue between maŝter and " scholler ". Many of Robinson's remarks are whimsical, such as " The Fifth rule : Note, that you do not ŝtrive with any ŝtoppe, but do it with ease, for painefull playing, causeth many odde anticke faces ",—a hint that might be remembered to-day. From the dedication to Sir William Cecil, " son and heir to the Earl of Salisbury ", we learn one or two faĉts when Robinson speaks of " your Grandfather's bountifull . . . kindnesse towards my Father, who was (untill his dying day) his true and obedient servant. Dutie bindeth me, for that I was my selfe sometimes servant unto the Right Hon. Thomas Earle of Exceŝter, your Honours Uncle, and alwaies have taŝted of the Comfortable liberalitie, of your Honours Father . . ." Nothing further is known of Thomas Robinson, and no other examples of his music have come to light.

ROGERS (Benjamin): A very popular seventeenth-century organiŝt and composer of music of every kind, Benjamin Rogers was looked upon by his contemporaries as one of the beŝt inŝtrumental composers of his day. But in the course of time his secular works were forgotten, and in later years he was, and is, remembered chiefly as a writer of ecclesiaŝtical music. It was probably owing to the circumŝtances that some of his Fancies were presented to the Archduke Leopold when the latter visited England in 1653, and that the ardently musical divine, Nath. Ingelo, took examples of Rogers's work to Sweden when he attended the English embassy to Scandinavia, that he attained to so high a European reputation. His inŝtrumental music, which dates for the moŝt part from the pre-Reŝtoration period, belongs to the older school of composition which had its inspiration from the later Elizabethans and earlier Stuart writers ; and it follows the lead of no one so much as of John Jenkins. His later, ecclesiaŝtical, music ŝtill shows him to have been under the influence of the older men and, wanting their genius, he produced some rather monotonous though thoroughly dignified work. The best of his music is distinctly above the average for his period, while his least interesting compositions are not nearly so badly marred by faulty writing as are those of many of his contemporaries.

Benjamin Rogers was born at Windsor in 1614 (before June 2nd, when he was baptised) and was the son of Peter Rogers, a lay-clerk at St. George's Chapel. He commenced his musical training in the choir of that Chapel under Nathaniel Giles, becoming a lay-clerk like his father. His first appointment as organist was to the Cathedral of Christ Church, Dublin, in 1639. He held the post for two years,—until the Irish Rebellion of 1641,—when he returned to England. He rejoined the choir at Windsor and remained there until the discontinuance of the services in 1644. Following the example of most of the musicians of his time, he subsisted by teaching the organ and virginal during the Commonwealth. He was in Cromwell's good graces, and besides granting him a pension, the Protector issued a mandate (May 28th, 1658) ordering the University of Cambridge to confer upon him the degree of *Mus. Bac.* At the Guildhall banquet given in the king's honour upon his return to England, a "Hymnus Eucharisticus" was sung, Rogers setting a text of Dr. Ingelo's. It is interesting to note that both Rogers and Ingelo managed to keep on good terms with both the republican and royalist governments. At about the same time he was re-instated as lay-clerk of St. George's, Windsor, and held some post (probably that of organist) at Eton College from about 1661 to, presumably, 1664, when he became organist and instructor of the choristers of Magdalen College, Oxford. In the latter appointment he enjoyed a salary of 60l. a year and free lodgings,—a fee higher than that paid to any previous organist. In 1669 he proceeded Doctor of Music at Oxford. In his old age he developed a somewhat crotchety if not eccentric character. He would speak loudly while presiding at the organ, persist in playing "Canterbury Tune" instead of the Services that the choir were "willing and able to sing", and otherwise annoy everyone connected with the chapel. For this behaviour he was dismissed with a pension equal to half his salary in 1685–6, and in spite of his desire to be re-inſtated in 1687, he remained in retirement until his death in 1698 at the age of eighty-four. He was buried at St. Peter-le-Bailey on June 21ſt. He was married and left a widow who survived him by a few months.

Examples of Rogers's sacred music may be seen in British Museum manuscripts : *Harl.* 7338 (Morning service), *Add.* 30831–4 (three vocal parts and organ score of two Evening Services and one Whole Service ; seven anthems), *Add.* 31404 (organ part of Service in D), *Add.* 30932 (six anthems in score), *Add.* 29481 (two anthems), *Add.* 29430 (Service in D), and *Add.* 31120 (Vincent Novello's transcription of an anthem for the organ). *Add.* 29386 and 31806 contain the Glee "Bring quickly to me Homer's lyre ". Four services and three anthems by Rogers were transcribed into the Chapel Royal books in 1676. Other manuscripts containing work by him are preserved at Oxford (Bodleian, Magdalen, New College, and Chriſt Church), at Gloucester, at Ely, and elsewhere. A " Hymnus Euchariſticus " (different from the one composed in 1660) is sung annually early in the morning of May Day on the summit of Magdalen tower, and the firſt verse is used daily as a Grace in the college.

A good deal of Rogers's music has been printed. *Court Ayres* of 1655 contains thirty-six short dance-tunes ; some inſtrumental music is to be found in *Courtly Masquing Ayres* (1662), and *Musick's Handmaid* (1663) ; and six anthems appeared in *Cantica Sacra* (1674). Glees of his composition may be seen in the *Musical Companion* (1672 and 1673). More modern reprints include work issued by Boyce, Page, Ouseley, Rimbault, Hullah, Goss and Turle, Cope, and J. E. Weſt.

ROGERS (John): A celebrated lutaniſt of the seventeenth century who enjoyed a great reputation in London as a virtuoso on his inſtrument. The firſt official mention of him was made in 1660 (*L.C.R., Vol.* 477 ; June 16th) when he was appointed as lutaniſt to Charles II, " in the place of James Gaultier ", a performer of international fame. In the same year he is given as being also " in the place of Henry Brockwell ", so we may assume that he was keeper of the king's instruments too. His salary as private lutenist to the king was 100*l*. per annum (*L.C.R.*, Nov. 9th, 1660). According to the Lord Chamberlain's Record he was also a violinist. His death is generally placed in *ca.* 1663, but his signature is to be seen in the Minutes of the Corporation of Music for 1672 (*Harl.* 1911), and in the same manuscript a reference to his death is made under date 1675. His successor in the Royal service was appointed on October 23rd, 1676 (*L.C.R.*). He probably died in 1675, for Thomas Mace (*Musick's Monument*, published in 1676 but written earlier) mentions him as the lute's greatest friend: " . . . but he grows old now ; has not long to stay ".

ROSEINGRAVE (Daniel): An organist and writer of ecclesiastical music who flourished during the second half of the seventeenth century and the first quarter of the eighteenth. The exact date of his birth is not known, but in view of the fact that he was organist at Gloucester in 1679 he must have been born about half-way through the Commonwealth régime. He commenced his connection with music in the Chapel Royal, obtaining his earliest training there. He held his Gloucester post until 1681, receiving a similar one at Winchester Cathedral in the following year. He remained at Winchester for ten years. His activities were then transferred to Salisbury, where he was elected as Cathedral organist in 1692. Six years later he asked for leave of absence in order to seek a new post in Dublin. He overstayed his leave and his post at Salisbury was filled ; but this did not concern him much, for in 1698 he was given the position of organist at Christ Church Cathedral, Dublin, and also at St. Patrick's Cathedral in the same city. Some authorities state that he resigned his St. Patrick's post in 1719 to his son Ralph. But as a fact, Ralph became Vicar-Choral in 1719 and did not succeed his father until the latter's death in 1727, having acted as assistant organist for one year prior to that event. Daniel held both of the Dublin posts until he died. He was a man of excitable temperament and frequently got into trouble on account of his readiness to enter into quarrels. He insulted a colleague at St. Patrick's, fought with him at a tavern, was called before the Dean and Chapter, and was fined and compelled to apologise publicly. At Christ Church also he was found guilty of assault and again fined. He married a clergyman's daughter and left a number of children, of whom two sons, Ralph and Thomas, b e c a m e w e l l - k n o w n musicians. Ralph, as we have seen, succeeded his father in his two Dublin posts, while Thomas was organist of St. George's, Hanover Square, London. The Roseingrave of whom Burney has so many flattering things to say, was Thomas. Both Thomas and Ralph come too late for detailed treatment in this work.

Very little of Daniel Roseingrave's music survives. *Add.* 29481 contains one part only of an anthem, " Haste Thee, O God, to deliver me " (for eight voices,—four Decani and four Cantoris) ; this anthem is also preserved in the Bodleian, Oxford. Another

anthem can be seen in the collection at Christ Church, Oxford. While at Dublin he was paid 3*l.* for writing three Services, but they have not been discovered. Four more anthems of his are in private ownership.

ROSEINGRAVE (Ralph), ROSEINGRAVE (Thomas), *see* ROSEINGRAVE (Daniel).

ROSINGRAVE, *see* ROSE-INGRAVE.

ROSSETER (Philip): A celebrated lutenist and popular composer of Ayres and instrumental music who belongs to the first quarter of the seventeenth century. His work is quite characteristic of its period, especially so far as concerns the instrumentally accompanied solo-song. The date of his birth is not known, and we do not meet with him until the publication of his first work : " *A Booke of Ayres*, Set foorth to be sung to the Lute, Orpherian, and Base Violl . . . to be sold at his house in Fleetstreete neere to the Grayhound . . . 1601 ". To this work he contributed twenty-one songs, while his life-long friend Thomas Campion supplied an equal number. The words of the whole set of forty-two songs were by Campion. The music is undoubtedly the fruit of a new period ;—an epoch influenced by the *Nuove Musiche* of the Italians. Rosseter and Campion share with Robert Jones (*q.v.*) the honour of being the firſt to publish solo-songs with independent inſtrumental accompaniment. Of this book Mr. C. K. Scott has edited, and Breitkopf and Haertel have published, eight songs (*Euterpe*). The next piece of dated information is an entry in the State Papers referring to Rosseter's salary as 20*l.* per annum with an allowance of 16*l.* 2*s.* 6*d.* for livery (November 8th, 1604 ; *v. Annalen*). In 1609 he edited: " *Lessons for Consort* : Made by Sundry excellent Authors, and Set to Sixe seuerall inſtruments : Namely, the Treble Lute, Treble Violl, Base Violl, Bandora, Citterne, and the Flute ". Of this work an example of the Cittern part

only is in the Royal College of Music. This seems to have been the laſt work he published before he devoted himself to ſtage business.

From January 1609–10 onwards, Rosseter was associated with Robert Jones, Philip Kingman, and Ralph Reeve, in the inſtruction of children for the Queen's Revels, and also in the patent granted these four men in 1615, authorising them to erect a new playhouse at Blackfriars, a project that ended so disappointingly (*v.* Robert Jones). Rosseter died on May 5th, 1623, his verbal will having been proved by his widow on May 21ſt. He was buried at St. Dunſtan's-in-the-Weſt on May 7th. Besides the two works mentioned above, the only other compositions by Rosseter known to me are a Pavane and a Galliard in Jane Pickering's Lute-Book of 1616 (*Eg.* 2046).

S

SALMON (Thomas): A clergyman whose interest in music lay in the direction of simplifying the notation then is use and in studying the Greek scale-systems and the phenomena connected with what is now called Equal Temperament. He was born at Hackney (now a metropolitan borough) on June 24th, 1648, and was educated at Trinity College, Oxford. After obtaining the degree of Master of Arts he became rector of Mepsal (Meppershall, *co.* Bedford) where he died and was buried (August 16th, 1706). The *Dictionary of National Biography* gives a full account of his non-musical writings.

The work which drew Salmon into the arena of bitter controversy was his "*An Essay to the Advancement of Musick* by casting away the Perplexity of Different Cliffs. And uniting all sorts of Musick . . . in one Universal Character" (1672 ; Preface by John Birchensha, *q.v.*). His curiously prophetic idea was to remove all the ancient apparatus of multitudinous clefs, tablatures, gamut,—indeed, the entire hexachord system,—and to substitute for them the present system of octaves (in which he was forestalled by William Bathe, *q.v.*). The different pitches were to be designated on the three staves he proposed using by the letters B (Bass), M (Mean), and T (Treble), each of them one octave apart. The lowest line of each stave was to carry the note G (as in the older system ; *v. D.O.E.M., s.v.* Gamut). The simplicity of such a system should have been apparent to all, for, as Salmon claimed, a student who could read one octave could read the others with equal ease. The pitch of any note was immediately recognisable by the clef-letter, and the movement from one series to the other was as easy as it is to perform a passage 8*va.* and then *loco.* But simple and praiseworthy though the idea was, the traditionalists, probably fearing for the safety of their teaching-connections, attacked the essay with fury. Notable in this frog-and-mouse war was Matthew Lock, whom Salmon had at one time approached with the object of taking lessons in composition. Lock, not having

" Contriv'd any method that way " sent the student to Simpson's *Compendium*. It is a pity that Lock had not the courage to defend what he must surely have recognised as a distinct advance in music. But, aided and abetted by Playford, who probably also had commercial considerations in mind, he fell upon Salmon's booklet with *Observations upon a Late Book, entitled An Essay to the Advancement of Musicke*, etc. (1672). Addressed from his " lodging near the Savoy ", on April 11th, the pamphlet attacks Salmon and his work with a frenzy worthy of a different cause. Vituperation and scurrility are more apparent than logical reasoning, and Lock's essay probably pleased only those in whose interests it was to deride the prophet. The worthy rector, having spent years in profound mathematical study, could not allow such a piece of literature to pass unnoticed, and in the same year he replied with *A Vindication of an Essay to the Advancement of Musick from Mr. Matthew Lock's Observations*, etc. (1672), a far more dignified and reasoned piece of work than was Lock's, and far more convincing. To the essay was subjoined a letter from " your friend and servant, N.E.,—Norwich, May 28th, 1672 ", in support of the rector's case. " N.E." has not been identified. But Lock's stock of language was by no means exhausted, and in 1673 he countered Salmon's stroke with *The Present State of Musick vindicated against the Exceptions and New Way of attaining Musick lately Published by Thomas Salmon*, etc. To this was added " Duellum Musicum " by John Phillips, " Gent.", together with a " letter from John Playford to Mr. Thomas Salmon by way of Confutation of his essay ". The John Phillips mentioned was a nephew of John Milton and the writer of a book of rank obscenity besides having been the poet's biographer. How far Salmon was himself responsible for the vicious attacks made upon him, cannot be decided at this distance of time ; but the opposition of Lock was probably called forth in the first place by the rector's careless suggestion that the teachers of the time would not welcome a system that had as its object the shortening of the time necessary to musical study. Perhaps Locke the Royalist disliked personally the man who had married Katherine, the daughter of the regicide Serjeant John Bradshaw. In 1688 Salmon reappeared in print with a work called *A Proposal to perform Music in Perfect and Mathematical Proportions*, dealing with the problems of temperament, — but it attracted no great attention. In 1705 he lectured the Royal Society at Gresham College on " Just Intonation " and had illustrations played by Frederick and Christian Stefkins who used viols with separate frets for each string. The experiment shows that Salmon must have expended a good deal of thought upon the question of temperament, but, although the employment of separate frets for each string brought the player nearer to just intonation, the latter could not be really attained in all keys until the frets had been entirely swept away. The *Philosophical Transactions* (No. 302 ; August, 1705) of the Society contained " The Theory of Musick reduced to Arithmetical and Geometrical Proportions by the Reverend Mr. Tho. Salmon ", and in it reference is made to the Gresham College experiments. On December 4th, 1705, Salmon wrote Sir Hans Sloane expressing gratitude for the printing of the paper, and writing something on the Greek enharmonic system (*Sloane*, 4040). On Jan. 8th, 1705–6 he wrote again asking Sloane to " find mee out some Patron who may espouse this cause " (*Id.*). Much of what Salmon proposed has since been adopted and a great deal of his speculative material is still subject to speculation. Had he lived a few years longer he might have died a happy man instead of a disappointed one, —for he passed away a little over half a year after asking Sloane for a patron.

SALTER (Humphrey): The editor (and composer of parts) of a work for the Recorder. Nothing is known of him except that on the title-page of his book he is designated as " Gentleman ". It is therefore possible that he was an amateur musician ; but his collection of tunes for the instrument in question is of sufficient historical importance to give him a place in this volume. The work, which was issued in 1683, is entitled: *The Genteel Companion ; being exact Directions for the Recorder with a Collection of the Best and Newest Tunes and Grounds Extant . . Composed and Gathered by Humphrey Salter.*

SAMPSON (Richard): A cleric of the early sixteenth century who has left a couple of motets to show that he was the possessor of musical talent well above the average. Although apparently influenced by contemporary Continental work, these examples are interesting as specimens of the class of music produced very early in the century. The vellum manuscript containing the motets (" Quam pulcra es amica " and " Psalite, felices protecti culmine rose purpuree " [*sic*]) is preserved in the British Museum as *Royal* 11 *E.XI* and dates, according to various authorities, from between 1516 and 1520. " Quam Pulchra es " is printed in *Volume* II of the *Oxford History of Music.* It will suffice for the purposes of this work to note that he enjoyed successively (and sometimes concurrently) the honour of being Dean of St. Stephen's, Westminster, Canon of St. Paul's, Dean of the same, Bishop of Chichester, Coventry, and Lichfield. He had, in the meantime, been imprisoned for a short time on account of his sympathy with the Roman service. He had also been Dean of the Chapel Royal between 1523 and 1540. He died at an advanced age in 1554. Readers desirous of following Sampson through his various clerical appointments are referred to Dr. W. H. Grattan-Flood's book on the *Early Tudor Composers.*

SAVILE (Jeremiah) (Jeremy): A writer of light music who flourished at the middle of the seventeenth century. Practically nothing is known of his life. John Playford (*Musical Banquet*) says that Savile was one of the celebrated London teachers of singing and viol-playing during the Commonwealth. His chief claim to remembrance to-day lies in his having written the popular " Here's a Health unto his Majesty ". This song (*à* 3) is to be found in the *Musical Companion* of 1672, together with three more numbers by Savile. He is represented also in the *Select Musical Ayres and Dialogues* of 1653 and 1659. The pieces contained in these publications, numbering only four songs all told, are present in British

Museum manuscripts *Add.* 31415 (" The Waits "), *Add.* 31806 (*Id.*), *Add.* 31812 (*Id.*), *Add.* 34126 (Catch : " Had she not care enough "), and *Add.* 30273 (*Id.*). " Here's a Health unto his Majesty " has appeared in a large number of modern reprints between 1842 and 1915, and " The Waits " has been issued by H. W. Dean (1810), *Musical Times* (1849), Cassell (1867), *etc.*

SERES (William): A music-printer of the Tudor era responsible for the issue of several important works,— notably Psalters. His activity is to be dated round about the middle of the sixteenth century, and he was in partnership with John Day (*q.v.*). He rose in his guild to be Master of the Stationers' Company and worked at the sign of the " Hedge Hogg " in Aldersgate Street, London.

SHAW, *see* SHORE.

SHEPHERD (John): A celebrated composer of sacred music who flourished at the middle of the sixteenth century. The date of his birth is not known, but judging from the statement that in 1554 he had been a student of music for twenty years, we can accept the date usually given,—1520–1525,

—as being near enough. Commencing to compose at the middle of the century, Shepherd would fall between the two periods,—too late to be classed with the pre-Reformation composers and too early to compare with the best of the true Elizabethans. His work partakes, to some extent, of the characteristics of both eras, and, though excellent in many ways, cannot be compared with the best of either. His boyhood was spent as a chorister at St. Paul's Cathedral in Thomas Mulliner's day. In 1542 he became Master of the Choristers and organist at Magdalen College (Oxford), but held the post only until 1543. In 1545 he returned to Magdalen and remained there in the same capacity until 1547 when he received 8*l.* as yearly remuneration as instructor of the choristers. In that year he resigned the post, but his connection with the college was not entirely severed. In 1548 he received 5*s.* for twelve music-books (*Dic. Nat. Biog.*), and from 1549 to 1551 he was Fellow of the College. In Mulliner's manuscript (*B.M.*) and in MS. 979-83 (Christ Church library, Oxford) he is given as " of the Chapel ", but the compiler of the Chriſt Church catalogue says that Shepherd's appointment to such a poſt is " not recorded elsewhere ". But in *Stowe* 571 a liſt of the Chapel Royal in 1552 gives his name (*fol.* 36*b*). In 1554 he supplicated for the degree of *Mus. Doc.* (it is not known whether he ever took the Bachelor's degree), and ſtated that he had been a ſtudent of music for twenty years. His grace was granted (W. F. Abdy Williams, *Degrees in Music*), but he is never subsequently given the title in any of the records. He is mentioned again in the books of Magdalen College in 1555, when he was censured for using unnecessary brutality in dragging a boy " in vinculis " from Malmesbury, probably as a " pressed " choriſter. The date of his death is not known.

Not very much of Shepherd's music has been printed. Barnard's colleċtion of 1641 contains a couple of specimens, John Day's *Certayne Notes, etc.* (1560) has an anthem, and he is represented in Day's publication of 1565. Burney printed the motet " Esurientes ", and Hawkins gives a short

example of Shepherd's work. The anthem " Haſte Thee, O God " has been issued by Novello under the editorship of Mr. John E. Weſt ; but this, as many other compositions bearing the name " Shepherd ", may possibly be by another John Shepherd or a Thomas Shepherd. The authorship of many works in manuscript is thus similarly open to doubt.

The more considerable compositions of John Shepherd ſtill remain in manuscript. The British Museum contains a large amount of music by him, including four Masses (one of them based upon the popular tune " Weſtern Wind "), parts of masses, anthems, and motets. The majority of Shepherd's pieces are to Latin texts, but a few specimens of Anglican service music are included among his works. Some inſtrumental arrangements are also preserved in the British Museum. Further examples of his work are contained in the Royal Colleċtion, in the Chriſt Church (Oxford) library, the Royal College of Music, Durham Cathedral, *etc.* " O Lord, the Maker of all Thing ", attributed to Shepherd, had also been ascribed to one of the Mundys and to King Henry VIII ; it is moſt probably by William Mundy. " I give you a new Commandment ", persiſtently given to Shepherd is undoubtedly by Tallis.

The John Shepherd who was sworn in as a Gentleman of the Chapel Royal on December 1ſt, 1606 (*C.B.C.R.*) was of the next generation and may have been a son of the above. It is probably to him that many doubtful compositions bearing the name " Shepherd " but obviously written in a later ſtyle are to be ascribed. Works superscribed "Thomas Shepherd " may be by one of the Johns, and the Chriſtian name conceivably an error on the part of the transcriber.

SHEPHERD (Thomas), *see* SHEPHERD (John).

SHEPPARD (J o h n), SHEPPERD (John), *see* SHEPHERD (John).

SHERYNGHAM: A composer of diſtinɗion who flourished early in the sixteenth century, and probably as early as the latter part of the fifteenth. Nothing whatever is known of his life, and his reputation reſts upon a composition of six seɗions contained in the Fayrfax

manuscript (*Add.* 5465): " Gentill Jhesu ", " Uppon the cross nailid ", " My blody wowndes ", *etc.* (signed " Sheryngam "), and one, " My wofull hart ", in *Add.* 11583. The latter was printed by Burney (*Hiſtory*, II) and may be accepted as a typical composition of the period.

SHORE (Catherine): A well-known vocaliſt of the late seventeenth century. A daughter of the trumpeter Matthias Shore (*q.v.*), she was able to form influential conneɗions at court and was brought under the influence of Henry Purcell who taught her singing and harpsichord-playing. In 1693 she married Colley Cibber and subsequently became famous as a singer in the Purcellian music-dramas. Her interpretation of a song in *Don Quixote* (*Part III* ; " The Genius of England ") to the trumpet obbligato of her brother John Shore (*q.v.*) was recorded as an especially fine achievement.

SHORE (John): One of the moſt famous trumpeters of all times, John Shore was a son of Matthias Shore (*q.v.*) and brother of William and Catherine (*q.v.*). He was appointed as trumpeter in ordinary to the king on March 30th, 1688, and followed his brother William as Sergeant Trumpeter. His skill attracted the attention of Henry Purcell, who wrote many showy accompaniments for him. Examples of such song-accompaniments are contained in *Orpheus Britannicus*. His performance at the St. Cecilia celebration of 1691 was especially mentioned in the *Gentleman's Journal* for the following January. A good deal of gossip has been retailed concerning this musician, but none of the information conveyed is trustworthy or important. He has frequently been confused with another John Shore who was a lutenist (*v. inf.*), *Grove* being among the works giving the error.

The second John Shore,— it is not known whether he was related to the above bearer of the name or not,— was appointed on March 29th, 1695, as a "musician in ordinary without fee, to come in ordinary with fee" at the first vacancy, there being two before him on the waiting list. His active life, therefore, falls chronologically outside the scope of the present volume. He received 40*l.* per annum as one of the "Instrumental Musick" and later added a similar amount to his income by an appointment as lutenist.

SHORE (Matthias): A celebrated trumpeter of the Stuart era and father of William, John, and Catherine Shore. He was appointed trumpeter in 1681–2 (January 5th), and in 1687 (October 5th) he was advanced to the coveted post of Sergeant Trumpeter ("Sergeant of the trumpeters, drummers, and fifes in ordinary to his Majesty"). As Sergeant he had the right to collect a fee of 12*d.* per day from every player on the trumpet, drum, or fife at public performances, or, as an alternative, to issue annual licences at 20*s.* He (as also his son William) was prompt in the collection of these sums, which he gave to the magistrates for the benefit of paupers. His salary, in 1697, is given as 100*l.* per annum plus his livery. His death must have occurred before May 21st, 1700, for on that date his son William was appointed Sergeant Trumpeter in his place (*L.C.R.*).

SHORE (William): A trumpeter appointed to the service of Charles II in 1679

(June 27th). He was a son of the famous Matthias Shore (*q.v.*) and in 1691 he attended King William on his journey to Holland. In Flanders he was attached to the " firﬅ troop of Horse-Guards " and during this " laﬅ campaigne in Flanders " was robbed of his trumpet and livery (*L.C.R.*, January 27th and March 22nd, 1693–4). A new silver inﬅrument weighing thirty-six ounces one pennyweight, was supplied to him on March 2nd of the same year. His receipt is contained in the Lord Chamberlain's Records (*Vol.* 440). In 1697 he was one of the four trumpeters who accompanied the king's " Ambassadors and Plenipotentiaries for the Treaty of Peace ", and in 1700 he succeeded his father as Sergeant Trumpeter. An entry of January 23rd, 1682–3 (*L.C.R.*) names William Shore as " Sergeant Trumpeter ", but this was either a clerical error or the record of some temporary appointment or work as deputy. After this date he is not again referred to as Sergeant Trumpeter until 1700. He died in 1707. A song of his entitled " Prince Eugene's March into Italy " (" Ye words by a Person of Quality ") was published *ca.* 1700.

SHORT (Peter): A Tudor music-printer who published a number of highly important works which are of the utmoﬅ intereﬅ to the musical hiﬅorian. Working in London (at the sign of the " Star " in Bread Street Hill), he issued Anthony Holborne's *Cittharn Schoole*, Dowland's *Firﬅ Booke of Songes*, Morley's *Canzonets*, the same writer's *Plaine and Easie Introduﬄion*, and the *Seven Sobs of a Sorrowfull Soule*, *etc.* (all in 1597) ; Farnaby's *Canzonets* in 1598 and Cavendish's *Ayres* a year later.

SHOW *or* SHOWER, *see* SHORE.

SIMPSON (Chriﬅopher): One of the moﬅ eminent of the violiﬅs of the seventeenth century, Chriﬅopher Simpson deserves a far more honoured place in the hiﬅory of English music than is generally accorded him. His works dealing with his own particular inﬅrument are so excellent, his outlook so honeﬅ and charaﬄeriﬅically British, and his virtuosity tempered by refined aeﬅhetics so amazing, that he merits more than the passing mention he usually receives in works of reference. Born during the first decade of the seventeenth century, Christopher Simpson was the last of the really great players on the bass-viol. His genealogy can be traced in *Harl. 5800, fol.* 21, to a Christopher Simpson, " descended from that name and familie originally in Nottinghamshire ". This was the gambist's great-grandfather. His grandfather, George, " of Richmond in Yorkshire ", married Elizabeth, daughter of a Mr. White of the same county. His father, also Christopher, was the son of this marriage and is described in the manuscript as " of Westonby in ye County of York." Christopher, senior, married Dorothy, daughter of William Pearson, " of Rostall in ye County of Yorke ", and their eldest son was our musician, " of Hunt house in the Wapentake [1] of Pickering in the County of Yorke ".

We are in ignorance of the biographical facts relating to the first half of Simpson's life. His teachers and his means of livelihood are alike unknown to us. It can be

[1] A "Wapentake" in Yorkshire was a division as a "Ward" or a "Hundred" was in other parts (Anglo-Saxon *Waepen-getaec*, a weapon-taking).

imagined that the son of a yeoman who was a Catholic Royalist would have lost all he possessed during the Civil War ; and it is quite conceivable that he should turn to music as a profession. So much can be read between the lines of the dedication of his *Division Viol* (*Second Edition*, 1665) in which he addresses Sir Robert Bolles : " This Treatise, upon the first Publication, was dedicated to your late Father, and not without good reason . . . First, as he was a most eminent Patron of Musick and Musitions, Secondly, as he was not only a lover of Musick, but also a great Performer in it. Thirdly, as the said Treatise had its Conception, Birth, and Accomplishment under his Roof, in your minority. Lastly, as he was my peculiar Patron, affording me a cheerful maintenance, when the iniquity of the times had reduced me (with many others in that common calamity) to a condition of needing it ". While in the house of Sir Robert Bolles his task was to instruct John,—younger son of the family,—and Sir John St. Barbe, in music; and it was primarily for the use of these pupils that Simpson wrote the works that made his name. This part of his musically active life was passed at the Bolles seat in Scampton (Lincolnshire), and when the head of the family died, Simpson stayed on with his successor. There are only two more pieces of evidence dealing with Simpson's biography. One is the information that he accompanied his pupil to Rome in 1661, and the other his witnessing of Sir Robert Bolles's will in 1663, a document which directs that a legacy of five pounds be paid to Simpson. He must have been fairly well to do by then, for he bought the farm of Hunt House which he settled by deed upon his nephew Christopher. The fact that he left his property, his music, and "whatsoever is of that concernment", to his nephew, would seem to point to the fact that he died a bachelor.

Whether Simpson died at Scampton or in London is not to be determined with certainty. On the evidence of his will this event must have taken place between May 5th and July 29th, 1669, but authorities are at variance on this point. Musgrave's *Obituary* gives 1666 ; Riemann has *ca.*

1677 ; and Wood (*Diary*) enters May 29th, 1669 : " Mr. Simpson, the musitian, a composer, died this month at Sir John or Sir William Bolls " ; a later addition of Wood's says, " Sure he was living after this " ; and still later he adds " True ". The *Dictionary of National Biography* gives the date of the will, and this, I think, we can accept.

The reputation enjoyed by Simpson was very great. Thomas Mace (*Musick's Monument*, 1676) mentions him with John Jenkins and William Lawes, and says : " The Three Famous Men, although Two of Them be laid asleep (or as we say, Dead ;) yet by their most singular and Rare Works They Live ". Later Mace says that he would have treated of the Bass-Viol at greater length " had it not been already so Exactly done " by Simpson. Sir Roger L'Estrange said of him : " The esteem I ever had for Mr. Simpson's Person, and Morals, has not engag'd me in any sort of Partiality for his Works ; but I am yet glad of any occasion wherein I may fairly speak a manifest Truth to his Advantage ; and at the same time, do a Justice to the Dead, and a Service to the Living ". Indeed, Simpson's moral character seems to have been as greatly admired as were his writings. During the celebrated Lock-Salmon controversy the former said, " He abuses Mr. Christopher Simpson, a Person whose memory is precious among good and knowing Men, for his exemplary life and excellent skill " ; to which Salmon replied : " Simpson . . . whom indeed I greatly honour, for that double accomplishment of his *exemplary life*, as well as *excellent skill* ; and know nothing more necessary than to commend the former to my *Observer's* imitation " (the " observer " being Matthew Lock ; *v.* Thomas Salmon).

Simpson lived in an age when the bass-viol was the most popular instrument in England, and his skill must have been very great to enable him to stand pre-eminent among his contemporaries. In the art of playing " Divisions " extempore and in that of writing in the Fancy form he was an accepted authority (*v. Dic. O. E. Mus.*, *pp.* 78, 79).

His published works in chronological order are as follows : In John Playford's *Court Ayres* (1655) there are eight short pieces by him. In the earlier editions of Playford's *Introduction to the Skill of Musick*, the " Art of Discant ", by Dr. Campion, was supplied with annotations by Simpson. These were but minor tasks compared with the excellent *Division Violist* and the *Compendium*. The *Division-Violist* : *or An Introduction To the Playing upon a Ground : Divided into Two Parts*. " The First Directing the Hand, with Other Preparative Instructions, the Second, Laying open the *manner* of Playing *Ex-tempore*, or Composing *Divisions* to a Ground. To which are Added some *Divisions* made upon *Grounds* for the Practice of Learners . . . 1659 ". This issue contains a fine portrait of the composer. Dr. Charles Colman called this work an " excellent Treatise ", while John Jenkins thought that " Simpson's great Work will teach the World to Play ". L'Estrange was of opinion that it was " the Best, as the only Treatise I find extant upon this argument ". These compliments can be accepted as honestly meant, for John

Jenkins and Roger L'Estrange were probably the two best seventeenth-century authorities on the bass-viol,—the one as a professional and the other as an amateur. A second edition appeared in 1665 or 1667 with a Latin translation added, the title beginning : *Chelys Minuritionum artificio exornata*, etc. L'Estrange, in a letter of recommendation, says of this issue that, " whoever has this Book by him, has one of the best Teachers in the World at his Elbow ". A third edition was published in 1712.

The first edition of the *Compendium* was issued in 1665 with the title : " The Principles of Practical Musick delivered in a Compendious, Easie, and New Method : For the Instruction of Beginners, either in Singing or Playing upon Instruments. To which are added, Some Short and Easie Ayres Designed for Learners . . . 1665 ". The work is dedicated to Sir John St. Barbe, Bart., " . . . part of it being framed for your particular Instruction ". The second, much enlarged, edition appeared in 1667 entitled *A Compendium of Practical Musick in Five Parts*, etc. This book is dedicated to " the truly Noble, Magnanimous, and Illustrious Prince, William Cavendish, Duke . . of Newcastle ", under whom he possibly served in the Royal interests during the Civil War. Roger L'Estrange said the *Compendium* was the " clearest, the most Useful, and Regular Method of Introduction to Musick that is yet Extant. And Herein I do but joyn in a Testimony with greater Judges. This enough said on the Behalf of a Book that carries in it self its own Recommendation ". Even Henry Purcell thought very highly of Christopher Simpson " Whose *Compendium* I admire as the most Ingenious Book I e'er met with upon this Subject ". But Purcell thought Simpson's " Rule in Three Parts for *Counterpoint* is too strict, and destructive to good air, which ought to be preferr'd before such nice Rules " (Purcell's *Art of Descant* in Playford's *Introduction, edition* 13). Nine editions of the *Compendium* appeared between 1665 and the end of the eighteenth century.

Playford's other publications contain isolated pieces by Simpson, and a good deal

F f

of excellent music (principally for the viols) is preserved in manuscript in the British Museum. A complete list of his known works in manuscript is given in an article of mine which appeared in *Musical News* for February 12th, 1916.

Christopher Simpson was an honest, straightforward, and cleanliving man, and his music is a reflection of his mentality : sane, direct, fresh and virile. It was his opinion " that if a man had made any discovery, by which an art or science might be learnt with less expence of Time and Travail, he was obliged in common Duty, to communicate the knowledge thereof to others ".

SIMPSON (Thomas): An English gambist who achieved a great name as a performer and composer on the Continent during the first quarter of the seventeenth century. His importance lies in the circumstance that he was one of the small band of famous English musicians who maintained the reputation of our music on the Continent of Europe and who transplanted many of the purely English technical features across the seas. Very little is known of his life, and that little we have to glean from his publications. He appears first as violist at the court of the Elector Palatine before 1610. Between 1617 and 1621 he acted in a similar capacity in the household of the Count of Holstein-Schaumburg. For a short time during this latter period he was at the Court of Denmark, playing in the royal orchestra ; but although the appointment is recorded, no date is given.

The first of his dated works was *Opusculum Neuwer Pauanen, Galliarden, Couranten, und Volten . . .* for several instruments, in five parts, but best suited to the viols (Frankfort, 1610). This book contains twenty-four pieces by Simpson, while the remaining six numbers are by John Dowland, John Farmer, and Thomas Tomkins. Copies are preserved in the Berlin State Library (Bass part), the Municipal Library of Hamburg, and in the Germanic Museum at Nuremburg (Eitner, *Quellen-Lexicon*). In 1617 was published his *Opus newer Paduanen, Galliarden, Intraden, Canzonen, Ricercaren, Fantasien, Balletten, Allmanden, Couranten, Volten unnd Passamezen, auff aller-*

hand Instrumenten, in five parts (Hamburg, 1617) The work, containing twenty-two pieces, is present in the Berlin library (two parts) in the Cassel library, in the Municipal library of Hamburg, and in the Ducal library at Wolfenbüttel. This edition of 1617 contains an appreciative poem in Latin by Michael Praetorius dated 1614, which may argue an edition printed in that year. The first edition, as far as we know, appeared in 1611, —this having been recorded by some authorities as a different work. Perhaps his best-known work was the *Taffel Consort . . . von allerhand Newen Lustigen Musicalischen Sachen mit 4 Stimmen neben einem General Bass . . .* (Hamburg, 1621) The book contains fifty pieces by a number of celebrated composers, among whom are John Dowland, Peter Philips, Alfonso Ferrabosco, Robert and Edward Johnson, *etc.* Seven of the pieces are by Simpson. The bass-part is in the British Museum, while the Wolfenbüttel library has the set wanting the bass. A Pavane of Simpson's was printed in a collection issued by Hagius in 1617, and another example was con-

tained in Oberndorfer's *Allegrezza* (1620). Two numbers from the 1617 *Opus Newer Paduanen, etc.*, were reprinted by Riemann (*Reigen und Tänze aus Kaiser Matthias Zeit*, 1897).

SMEGERGILL (*also* SMERGERGILL) (William): A composer of light popular music who flourished at the middle of the seventeenth century. Nothing is known of his life. A couple of " Pastoral Dialogues " for " two voices to sing to an instrument " and another two " short ayres or songs for three voices " are contained in Playford's *Select Musical Ayres and Dialogues* (1653) ; while " If any live that fain would prove ", not included in this edition, is present in that of 1652. " Welcom, Brother to this Arbour " is in the *Musical Companion* (1672). What his real name was is not known with certainty ; in the work of 1653 abovementioned, he is given as " Mr. William Smegergill alias Caesar ". He should not be confused with Dr. Julius Caesar who was an amateur composer of catches. SMITH (Edward): Like his father, William Smith, Edward was organist at Durham Cathedral from 1609 until 1611, when he died. These two years constitute the only period of his life of which we have any knowledge. Three verse-anthems of his,—one of them written on the occasion of the discovery of the " Gunpowder Treason ",—are contained in *Add.* 30478–9 (two tenor parts), and other church music by him is in the Durham Cathedral choirbooks.

SMITH (Robert): A musician who flourished during the second half of the seventeenth century. His active career, as far as we know it, was a very short one, and this may account for the circumstance that the undoubted promise he showed in some anthems contained in Clifford's collection did not come to proper fruition. We meet with his name first in the Lord Chamberlain's Records when, on June 20th, 1673, he was " admitted a musician in ordinary ". An entry in the same records dated August 3rd, 1674, shows that he succeeded Pelham Humfrey in the royal service. The entry of November 22nd, 1675, announces Richard Hart as the successor of Robert Smith, " deceased."

Hart's salary was to commence from September 29th, 1675, and we may assume that Smith died shortly before that date. Besides the anthems alluded to above (the words in Clifford's book), Smith contributed three short pieces to *Melothesia* (1673), and, posthumously, two to Greeting's *Pleasant Companion* (1682) and one to the *Division Violin* (1685). Further specimens of his lighter work are contained in *Add.* 17853, *Add.* 29396, and *Add.* 29397.

SMITH (William): An organist and composer of ecclesiastical music who flourished late in the sixteenth century. Robert Masterman was organist at Durham Cathedral until 1594, and since he was succeeded by Smith, we should assume that the latter's appointment dates from that year. But the Cathedral records show a payment made to him in 1589, and he must consequently have been active there in some other capacity before his engagement as organist. He was followed by William Browne in 1599. Examples of his composition are to be seen in *Add.* 30478–9 (two tenor parts) and in the Durham Cathedral library.

SMYTH, *see* SMITH.

SNODHAM (Thomas): A music-printer who worked in London early in the seventeenth century. He married the daughter of the celebrated printer Thomas Eaſt or Eſte (*q.v.*), and in 1609 with the consent of his mother-in-law, took over Eaſt's ſtock-in-trade. He continued the business in a highly successful manner and was responsible for the appearance of Maynard's *Twelve Wonders of the World* and Byrd's *Psalms, Songs, etc.* (both in 1611), Tailour's *Hymns* (1615), and many other important books. He did not negleƈt the works issued by his father-in-law, and published some of the latter's ventures in new editions.

SNOW (Moses): A singer and composer of songs who was aƈtive towards the end of the seventeenth century. On July 11th, 1689, he was appointed to the private music of the king, and also to the " vocall musick " (*L.C.R.*) ; in the same year (December 17th) he was sworn in as a Gentleman of the Chapel Royal, " extraordinary into the firſt vacancy that shall fall " (*C.B.C.R.*). On April 8th, 1692, he was admitted " in ordinary in the place of Mr. Alphonso Marsh " (*Id.*), and on September 22nd, 1694, he was sworn " into one ful place of a Gentleman of the Chapel Royal " (*Id.*). His salary in 1694 is given as 73*l.* per annum. The end of his aƈtivity was announced officially in 1702 : " Mr. Moses Snow, one of the Gentlemen of the Queen's Chapell, departed this life the 20th of December, 1702" (*Id.*).

Work of his may be seen in the *Theater of Musick* (1685 ; " What cruel Pains " ; *Bk.* III, 1685, " Ah, cruel Beauty " ; *Bk.* IV, 1687, containing four pieces by him), and in *Musick's Hand-Maide* (*Part* 2, 1689). The song in the British Museum manuscript *Add.* 29397, and the melody in *Add.* 35043 are also probably by Moses Snow, though only signed " Snow ".

STAGGINS (Isaac), *see* STAGGINS (Nicholas).

STAGGINS (Nicholas): An inſtrumentaliſt and Maſter of the Royal Music who flourished during the second half of the seventeenth century. Intereſting and important, like many of his contemporaries, more on account of the sidelights which a consideration of his activities shed upon the life of the court musicians of the day, than for any great merit of his own, Nicholas Staggins owed most of his success to royal favour. He commenced his career, as far as official documents prove, soon after the Restoration, when he was appointed as one of the violins in the royal orchestra. His way at court was probably made easier by his father, Isaac Staggins, who played the tenor hautboy in the same service. Nicholas's first post was in all probability " extraordinary without fee ", for in an entry in the Lord Chamberlain's Records dated December 21st, 1671, we read : " Nicholas Staggins appointed musician in ordinary . . . for the violin in the place of William Young, deceased, with wages of 20*d.* by the day and 16*l.* 2*s.* 6*d.* a year for livery, to commence Michaelmas, 1670 " (*L.C.R.*). The arrears of salary due to the unfortunate William Young at his death were to be paid half to Staggins and half to the executors of the deceased gentleman, " until the arrears are fully paid " (*L.C.R.*). This means that for some time Staggins was on half-pay. To compensate him for this,

he was given a place in the orchestra among the flutes (" double places " being quite common in the Stuart bands). For the work connected with this post he received (or was owed) the same amount as was due to him as violinist. In 1674 he was created Master of His Majesty's violins (*L.C.R.*), in the place of Louis Grabu, and in the same year he performed with the others in the Masque that made so great a stir at court. Of this work we shall have occasion to speak again. On January 29th, 1674–5 he was admitted as " Master of the English Chamber Musick " and was empowered " to inspect and govern the same with the accustomed allowances of Mr. Grabu, and to enjoy all privileges belonging thereto as Mr. Grabu or Mr. Lanier or any other formerly enjoyed ",— the salary attached to the post being the then large one of 200*l.* per annum. In addition he often received extra sums for supplying instruments and in 1675–6 he was paid 93*l.* 2*s.* " for faire writing and pricking several sorts of musick, and for paper, penns, and inke, and for the writers' and Prickers' dyes and chamber rent " (*L.C.R.*,

Vol. 745). A command issued on February 18th, 1678–9, is too interesting to omit : "Order directed to Mr. Nicholas Staggins, Master of his Majesty's Musick, that his Majesty's four and twenty violins should attend his Majesty every night that a play is acted at court"(*L.C.R.*). In 1682 the king secured the degree of *Mus. Doc.* for his protégé, the usual exercise being waived. This unusual procedure gave rise to a certain amount of gossip and ill-will and two years later Staggins resolved to end this state of affairs by offering to compose a test-piece. The performance of this work at Cambridge satisfied the malcontents and gave Staggins yet another post : "Dr. Nicholas Staggins . . being desirous to perform his exercise upon the first public opportunity, for the said degree, has quitted himself so much to the satisfaction of the whole University this Commencement, that by a Solemn vote they have constituted and appointed him to be a public professor of music there" (*London Gazette*, *No.* 1945 ; Grace dated July 2nd, 1684). He was the first to occupy that chair at Cambridge.

On March 25th, 1685, Staggins was confirmed in his post as Master of the King's Music by James II, and at about the same time the king set about paying up some of the arrears in the musicians' salaries. On September 21st, 1686, Staggins was paid no less than 193*l.* 13*s.* of the amount due to him, the money being produced by the taxes on tobacco and sugar (*L.C.R.*, *Vol.* 805). He was living at that period in "Little Chelsey (Chelsea) in the parish of Kensington" (*Id.*, *Vol.* 199). On November 9th, 1686, he received 19*l.* 11*s.* 6*d.* for writing and scoring a composition for the coronation of James II (*Id.*, *Vol.* 751). On July 24th, 1689, Staggins was re-appointed as Master of the Music to William and Mary (*Id.*, *Vol.* 753). In 1691 he accompanied the king to Holland, and on August 17th, 1692, he was paid 52*l.* 2*s.* 6*d.* for "fair writing and pricking of compositions for the Coronation Day and the Queen's Birthday" (*Id.*, *Vol.* 755). In 1692, 1693, and 1694 there are entries relating to similar Birthday Odes. It is sad to have to record that on March 23rd, 1695–6,

Mr. Anthony Nurse, brewer, had to petition the Lord Chamberlain for the payment of 120*l.* for " beare and ale " supplied to Dr. Staggins. The Lord Chamberlain had all parties before him, but with what result is not known. Staggins retained all his posts until he died on June 13th, 1700 (at Windsor). Several authorities give the date of Staggins's death as 1705, but the Lord Chamberlain's Records state plainly that on June 30th, 1700, John Eccles was " appointed Master of the Musick, in the room of Dr. Staggins, deceased " (*L.C.R., Vol.* 488).

Not much of Staggins's music is now traceable, and that little is of no great value. He seems to have pleased his contemporaries with the music he wrote for the masque of 1674,—John Crowne's *Calisto, or the Chaste Nymph,*—for the librettist in the preface to the printed version says that " Mr. Staggins not only delighted us with his excellent composition, but with the hopes of seeing in a very short time a master of music in England equal to any France or Italy have produced ". A few examples of his work are preserved in the British Museum :

Add. 19759 (songs, " From Celia's bright eyes ", " The pleasures of love ", " Since all our Griefs ", " Hide, thou Charming creature " ; and the unaccompanied duet, " While others on downy nests "); *Add.* 29283–5 (string trio arrangement of one piece without title) ; *Add.* 29396 (" How unhappy a Lover am I ", from Dryden's *Conquest of Granada, Pt.* II ; this and other songs were printed in *Choice Songs and Ayres,* 1673); and *Add.* 29371 (the tune of " Staggins Jigg ").

STEFKINS (Christian), (Christopher), (Diedrich), (Frederick), (Theodore William), *see* STEFKINS (Theodore).

STEFKINS (Theodore): A teacher of bass-viol playing and performer on the stringed instruments, who came to England from the Continent. His name appears in official accounts from the Restoration until 1674, but the dates of his birth and death are unknown. He must have enjoyed a great reputation and was reverenced by the acknowledged heads of his profession. John Jenkins (*q.v.*) was a particular friend of his, and Roger North in the *Musicall Grammarian (Add.* 32533) relates how he was in the habit of being sent by his master, Jenkins, to carry some new composition of the latter's to Stefkins as a present. North goes on to say that Jenkins esteemed the foreigner very highly. Salmon (*Essay to the Advancement of Musick*, 1672) speaks of Stefkins as of a great artist. In 1661 the Lord Chamberlain's Records mention the payment to Stefkins of 10*l.* " to buy and provide one basse Violl for his Majesty's service ". The entry of November 29th, 1662, probably gives the date of his appointment : " Warrant to admit Theodore Stefkins musician in ordinary for the Violl, with the wages of 1*s.* 8*d.* per day and 16*l.* 2*s.* 6*d.* yearly for livery to commence from St. John Baptist, 1660 " (*L.C.R.*, *Vol.* 741). In 1663 and again in 1670–71, he received 12*l.* from the Treasury for a Lyra-Viol. In 1674 he is given as one of the instrumentalists who played in the great masque of that year. This is the last piece of dated documentary evidence relating to him.

A Theodore William Stefkins is mentioned as a violist in some of the entries, but it is not clear in what relationship he stood to Theodore Stefkins. A brother of Theodore's had been employed at the English Court as violist before the Commonwealth. This was Diedrich Stefkins, who succeeded Maurice Webster, deceased, on April 6th, 1636. Theodore's two sons, Frederick and Christian, were also active in the royal band. A Christopher Stefkins is also frequently mentioned in lists of royal musicians,—but it is uncertain whether he was not identical with Christian. I have not been able to see any compositions by a member of this family. The importance of Theodore Stefkins would seem to be,—apart from his activity as a teacher, —in the influence he probably exercised over the English school of violists, especially since he was so highly esteemed by Jenkins.

STEIFKINS, STEPHKINS, *see* STEFKINS.

STEVENSON (Robert): An organist and composer of ecclesiastical music. Very little is known of his life and the dates which limit his activities can only be given approximately. He was appointed organist of Chester Cathedral in succession to Robert White in 1570, and held the post until 1599, when

Thomas Bateson followed him. In his successful supplication for the degree of *Mus. Bac.* at Oxford in 1583 he stated that he had been a student of music for thirty-three years, so that the date of his birth must be placed somewhere before 1540. He was granted the degree in 1587 and in 1596 he proceeded to the Doctorate. *Add.* 18936–9 contain four parts of a composition beginning " Miserere " (obviously an exercise in counterpoint, for six voices with the Plainsong in the tenor part), and an anthem by him is preserved in the Peterhouse collection (Cambridge).

STONARD (William): An organist and writer of ecclesiastical music who flourished during the first quarter of the seventeenth century. Nothing is known of his early life and training, and the first piece of dependable information that we encounter concerning him is the record of his having become a Bachelor of Music at Oxford in 1608. He was appointed organist at Christ Church Cathedral, Oxford, in the same year, and held the post until he died in 1629–30. Some authorities state that Stonard held the Doctorate in Music, but there is no documentary evidence in support of the assumption.

A *Magnificat* and a *Nunc Dimittis* of his are preserved in the Christ Church (Oxford) collection. *Harl.* 7337 (Tudway's manuscript) contains an " Evening Service in C (five voices)" with an obviously erroneous date attached to it. This Evening Service was printed by the Motet Society. Further British Museum manuscripts containing work of Stonard's are *Add.* 17797 (two anthems *à* 5) and *Add.* 30478–9. The Music School collection at Oxford also has examples of his composition. A Catch (" Ding, ding, ding, dong bell ") signed " Stonard " or " Stoner " was very popular and is to be seen in a number of British Museum manuscripts. He is twice represented in *Catch that Catch Can* (1658).

STONER (William), *see* STONARD (William).

STOURTON (William), *see* STURTON (William).

STROGERS (Nicholas): A composer of sacred and instrumental music belonging to the early seventeenth century. Beyond the fact that he was an organist we know nothing whatever of his life. Since he is represented in Barnard's collection of 1641 he must have died before that date, since only the work of deceased composers was included. *Add.* 30085 contains a " Whole Service of four Partes " (D-Minor in score), *Add.* 29289 (*ca.* 1629) the altus part of an anthem and a Service, *Add.* 17784 the bass part of the Service in D, and *Add.* 17853 the tenor part of a *Benedictus.* Examples of his instrumental music may be found in Jane Pickering's Lute-Book (*Eg.* 2046 ; 1616, A Galliard), in *Benjamin Cosyn's Virginal-Book* (an arrangement of the Morning and Evening Service in D), in the *Fitzwilliam Virginal-Book* (a Fantasia), and in the Oxford Music School manuscripts (*In Nomines*). A Pavane for the Cittern from a manuscript in the Cambridge University library was printed under the editorship of E. W. Naylor in 1908. Further specimens of his composition are preserved in the libraries of Christ Church (Oxford), Peterhouse (Cambridge), and Ely Cathedral.

STURTON (William): A singer and composer who flourished at the opening of the sixteenth century. His name is included in a list of " Gentilmen of the King's Chapell " in 1503–4 when he assisted at the funeral of Queen Elizabeth, consort of Henry VII. He continued in the same post at the coronation of Henry VIII, and in 1510–11 received his mourning livery for the funeral of Price Henry. This is the last official information we possess concerning him. Specimens of his work may be seen in Lambeth manuscript *No.* 1 (" Ave Maria ") and in the Eton College manuscript (two hymns).

SYMPSON (Christopher), *see* SIMPSON (Christopher).

T

TAILOUR (Robert). The composer of a dozen tunes in five parts to which some fifty Psalms could be sung to an instrumental accompaniment. Almost nothing is known of his life. The late Dr. Cummings told me that he had found the name of Robert Tailour in the Royal service in 1618, but his source has unfortunately escaped me. The work by which Tailour is now known is : " *Sacred Hymns* : consisting of Fifti Select Psalms of David and others, Paraphrastically turned into English verse. And by Robert Tailour, set to be sung in Five parts, as also to the Viole, and Lute or Orph-arion. Published for the use of such as delight in the exercise of Music in hir original honour " (London : Thomas Snodham, " by the assignment of the Company of Stationers ", 1615). The tunes are written for Treble, Mean, Counter-tenor, Tenor, and Bass, in separate parts (not all on one pair of pages as was generally the case, two copies at least being necessary for performance). The *Dictionary of National Biography* suggests that the paraphrases were the work of Robert Tailour, the author of the comedy, *The Hog hath lost his Pearle* ; but this is incorrect, and in any case Robert Tailour the musician and his namesake the dramatist are not to be identified.

TALLIS (Thomas): Undoubtedly the greatest musician in sixteenth-century England, and one of the greatest in all Europe. From whichever point of view his work is regarded, it is always interesting, always instructive, and always beautiful. As is natural in the work of a musician who attained to a great age, there are differences to be discerned in the compositions belonging to the various periods of his life ; —but the main point of difference lies in the circumstance that some of his works are even more beautiful than the others. Whether he made light of the most difficult problems in counterpoint or wrote in the simplest methods of the Reformed service, he exhibits a mastery and an ease that can only come from great genius, perfect taste, and technical perfection. His versatility was as great as his genius, and in styles of widely differing characteristics he remains worthy of respect for his performances in each. Known for so long as the " Father of English Cathedral Music ", there will be little need to dwell upon the importance of Thomas Tallis in the history of English music ; but from his achievements in the simplest of his Anglican anthems to the stupendous workmanship of his unequalled forty-part motet (*Spem in alium non habui*, for eight five-part choirs), and from the nobility and dignity of utterance in one class of composition to the tender language in another, Tallis stands as one of the very greatest glories in the story of this nation's music. The changing state of the divine service in the different reigns during which he was active, accounts to a certain extent for the great variation that is to be noticed in the treatment of many of his compositions. But these differences, so far from detracting from his work, actually enhance it, in so far that he has written music which can appeal to every taste, and from which every music-student and music-lover can derive profit and pleasure. How far the Tudor musicians had developed their technics is perhaps as well shown in the forty-part composition already alluded to, as anywhere else ; and in this really difficult form of polyphonic music England was well in advance of every other European country. The fact that Thomas Tallis could write for the most extreme form of the Reformed church-service and also shine as did no one else of his own period in the complicated horizontal weaving of his Latin compositions, must remain as the most imperishable monument to his memory. Whenever and wherever pure beauty of melody and form is prized, then and there will the music of Tallis be heard ; in it every Englishman may take the same pride as he feels in the achievements of Caedmon, Chaucer, Henry the Fifth, Shakespeare, Newton, and Lister ; and from it perhaps our younger generation of musicians may still gain inspiration and guidance, and give back to this country the musical crown that is our rightful heritage, and which was light-heartedly exchanged for a mess of seventeenth-century French pottage. Great as were the writings of William Byrd and others, what works appeared in this country before the genius of Henry Purcell awakened England to a short Indian summer of renown that could compare with the " Lamentation " quoted by Dr. Walker (*History of English Music*), the examples printed by Hawkins and Burney, or the popular *O Sacrum Convivium* (" I call and I cry ") of Thomas Tallis ? Great as Henry Purcell undoubtedly was, there were certain aspects in which Tallis was even greater.

Very little is known of the early life of this musician. Taking into consideration some of the authenticated dates, we may assume that he was born about 1510,— probably not later than 1512 or 1513. He is supposed to have been a chorister at St. Paul's Cathedral or the Chapel Royal, but no proofs are available. He may have been noticed by the youthful and music-loving king, and Henry's frequent visits to Waltham may account for Tallis's appointment as organist to the Abbey there. Exactly when he took up his duties is not known ;

but it certainly was some years before 1540, when the dissolution of the monasteries robbed him of the post. When he left Waltham he was paid 20*s.* as wages and 20*s.* " in reward " (*v.* Dr. Cummings in *Musical Times*, November, 1876). How soon after this he entered the Chapel Royal as a Gentleman is not clear ; but certainly before 1546–7, for he is mentioned in the Lord Chamberlain's Records as receiving his livery for the funeral of Henry VIII and another for the Coronation of Edward VI. In 1552 Tallis married, and according to the epitaph preserved in Strype's edition of Stow's *Survey*, he lived with his wife Joan " in love full three and thirty years ". He is named in a list of the Gentlemen of Mary Tudor's chapel, and in 1557 he received from that queen a twenty-one years' lease (with Thomas Bower) of the manor of Minster (Thanet). This grant was the only sign of royal favour shown him throughout nearly forty years of service, as he remarks in a petition addressed to Queen Elizabeth. In 1575–6 (January 21st) the queen granted to Tallis, in association with William Byrd, the monopoly for publishing music for a term of twenty-one years. Two years later the two musicians petitioned Elizabeth for the lease of lands to compensate them for the losses incurred in the working of the monopoly and as a recompense for their long service. In this document Tallis says he is "now aged, having served the Queen and her ancestors almost forty years". Property to the value of 30*l.* was thereupon leased to them without fine" (*v. also* William Byrd). The Cheque-Book of the Chapel Royal is the authority for the statement : "Thomas Tallis died the 23rd of November, 1585, and Henry Eveseed sworne in his place the last of the same. Childe there ". The last two words have generally been accepted as evidence that Tallis was in the Chapel as a boy ; but nothing else appears to support the supposition, and the words can as easily refer to Eveseed, of inglorious memory. Tallis was buried at Greenwich in the parish church, and until that edifice was rebuilt early in the eighteenth century, a brass plate was to be seen containing the epitaph. This has already been alluded to,

and can be read in full in Strype's edition of Stow's *Survey.* It says that he excelled in "honest vertuous lyff" and that he served four sovereigns "with grete prayse" ; further, "he married was, though children had he none." A portrait supposed to represent Tallis was prepared for Nicholas Haym's *History of Music.* This work never appeared, but reproductions of the portrait have been preserved. It was given in *Musical Times* for December, 1915, together with a facsimile of Tallis's signature (from the manuscript volume of treatises in the British Museum, *Lans.* 763, once at Waltham Abbey). His will was proved by his old friend and, as some think, pupil, William Byrd, on November 29th ; and among other bequests Tallis left 40*s.* for the benefit of the poor of Greenwich, his widow to distribute six loaves every Friday. To his old colleagues of the Chapel Royal he left 3*l.* 6*s.* 8*d.* for a feast. He willed his interest in the music-printing monopoly to his godson Thomas Byrd (*q.v.*), after William Byrd ; for it would have reverted automatically to the latter on Tallis's death.

Thomas Tallis has left a tremendous amount of music, most of which still remains to be printed. In 1575 he wrote and published jointly with Byrd, as the first product of their monopoly, the *Cantiones Sacrae*. Some of Tallis's contributions to this work have been reprinted by various editors, four of them having been supplied with English words. He is represented in John Day's *Morning and Evening Prayer,* *etc.* (1565), in Archbishop Parker's *Psalter* (1567–8), and in Barnard's collection of 1641. Later reprints of examples of Tallis's music are to be seen among the works of Boyce, Burney, Hawkins, Rimbault, Jebb, Arnold, Crotch, J. S. Smith, Bishop, Burns, Warren, Rochlitz, Dr. Sir Richard R. Terry, and Dr. Mann, and in the series of the Motet Society and the *Parish Choir*. There will be no need to catalogue these works in greater detail, for an excellent list is given in *Grove* (*ed.* 1914 ; V. 12, 13) and various publishers' catalogues (*e.g.* Novello, Curwen, *etc.*) will give sufficient information as to more recent reprints. A good deal of Tallis's work can be seen in manuscripts preserved in the British Museum, Christ Church and Bodleian libraries (Oxford), the Royal College of Music, Ely Cathedral, Peterhouse (Cambridge), *etc.* Arrangements of sacred compositions for the virginal are contained in *Benjamin Cosyn's Virginal-Book* and the *Fitzwilliam Virginal-Book*, while organ music by Tallis is in the British Museum and Christ Church (Oxford). The catalogues of both these collections are sufficiently full and informative to render further details unnecessary.

TAVERNER (John): A highly important composer of the mid-sixteenth century who has left some remarkably interesting work of great beauty and worth. In the popular mind Tallis and Tye superseded him, for they were technically in advance, while Taverner leaned rather towards the older school and has more in common with Fayrfax. The date of his birth is not known and the first that we learn of him is the statement in Foxe's *Acts and Monuments* (*Book of Martyrs*) to the effect that he was called to be Informator of the choristers in the Chapel of Wolsey's college (Cardinal College, now Christ Church), *ca.* 1525. Correspondence shows that he was at first reluctant to leave " his living at Tattershall and the prospect of a good marriage which he would lose by removal " (letter from the Bishop of Lincoln to Wolsey). But after some argument Taverner was persuaded to accept the Oxford appointment, and arrived there at the end of 1526. He appears to have been a native of Boston, Lincolnshire, and Foxe, who was also from that place, would probably be correct on this point. The famous martyrologist also gives him as organist ; and although there is no mention of this in the official appointment, there can be no doubt that he, like most of the contemporary " Masters of Song " played that instrument. In 1528 he was in danger of persecution for heresy. " He was playing at Evensong on February 21st, 1528, when the Cardinal's Commissary arrived to inquire into the orthodoxy of the College " (*Introduction* to the Christ Church Catalogue of MS. Music, quoting Foxe, *ed.* 1641, II, 523). Taverner was suspected " and imprisoned in a deep cave under-ground " (Foxe). But

his offence appears to have been trivial, amounting only to concealing " Mr. Clarke's books and being privy to the letter sent to him by Garret after his flight " (Letter to Wolsey from Dean Higden). The cardinal thought it unnecessary to press the charge against Taverner since " he was but a musician ". This " but a musician " was probably only a sop to Wolsey's conscience, and he forgave Taverner because he was desirous of retaining the services of so excellent a musician for his very fine chapel. According to the cardinal's *Statutes,* Taverner received 10*l.* per annum in addition to four yards of cloth at 3*s.* 4*d.* per yard for a livery, and 1*s.* 8*d.* a week for his commons, the total equalling 15*l.* a year. This was a very high salary in those days, and was next in magnitude to that received by the Sub-dean. In 1538 and 1539 he had dealings with Thomas Cromwell in connection with the suppression of four friaries (Gardner, *Letters and Papers of Henry VIII's reign*), and after 1540 we lose sight of him. He was probably dead when Foxe wrote his *Acts and Monuments* (*i.e.* before

1563). He was most probably buried in his native place, for in the Christ Church (Oxford) manuscripts Nos. 981 and 983 there is a note saying of Taverner that he was "of Cardinall Wolsayes Chappell who died at bostone and there lieth . . Homo memorabilis ".

The work by which Taverner is best known to-day is his mass based on the popular song " Western Wind, why dost thou blow?", being one of three famous musicians to compose masses on this melody (v. John Shepherd and Christopher Tye). It was issued, with alterations, under the editorship of Mr. H. B. Collins in 1917. A great deal of his music is preserved among the British Museum manuscripts. *Add.* 17802–5 contains the mass " Western Wind ", besides other compositions (four Alleluias, *etc.*). He wrote other masses,— of which " Gloria tibi Trinitas ", " The Plain-song mass *Corona Spinea* ", and " O Michael ", are the best known, and extracts from which are contained in *Add.* 18936–9, *Add.* 11586–7 (Burney's specimens), and *Add.* 29246. An *In Nomine* (one of the earliest examples

of the kind,— if not the earliest) is in Mulliner's manuscript *Add.* 30513, and also in Baldwin's manuscript in the Royal collection (now *B.M.*). Motets, anthems, Alleluias, *etc.*, are to be found in *Add.* 31390, *Add.* 15166 ("In Trouble and Adversity"), *Add.* 30480–4 (" O Geve thankes unto ye Lord "), *Add.* 34191, *Add.* 34049, *Add.* 18936–9, *Add.* 15059, *Add.* 4900, and *Harl.* 1709. In the library of the Royal College of Music there are also extracts from a mass and several motets. In the Peterhouse Part-books (Cambridge) are masses, motets, and a *Magnificat.* He is also represented in the manuscripts at St. John's College and in the University library (Cambridge). At Christ Church (Oxford) are the mass " Gloria tibi Trinitas ", a *Te Deum*, and ten other sacred works, besides " Quemadmodum " *à* 6, and an *In Nomine* for instrumental use. " Western Wind " and four motets are contained in Sadler's Part-books (*Bodl.*) and in the Forrest-Heyther manuscripts (Music School, Oxford) are the Plainsong mass mentioned above, " Corona Spinea " and " O Michael ".

The only contemporaneous printed work to contain music by Taverner was Wynkyn de Worde's *Song-book* (1530): " The bella " (four-part), " My harte my mynde " (three-part), and " Loue wyll I " (three-part). An excellent liſt of his manuscript works is given by Mr. G. E. P. Arkwright in the 1914 *Grove* (*Vol.* V., 31), while further particulars may be gleaned from the catalogues of the collections mentioned above.

This John Taverner is not to be confused with another of the same name who became Gresham Professor in 1610 and who later entered Holy Orders (*v. Sloane MS.* 2329, for copies of some of his lectures).

TAVERNER (Rev. John), *see* TAVERNER (John).

TAYLOR (John): A royal musician and composer of popular music who flourished in the firſt half of the seventeenth century. He was the son of Robert Taylor (a " musician for Lutes and Voices " in the royal service from 1625 to 1637) and succeeded his father as a musician " for the Violles and Voices " on October 3rd, 1637. An entry of 1641 in the Lord Chamberlain's Records shows that he was a lutenist also (*L.C.R., Vol.* 476). During the Commonwealth John Taylor resigned or died, for at the Reſtoration his poſts were filled by others. Examples of his work may be seen in Lawes's *Choice Psalms* of 1648 (An " Elegy to the memory of his Friend and Fellow Mr. William Lawes "), in Playford's *Selecı Musicall Ayres and Dialogues* of 1653 (a song to the Theorbo or Bass-Viol), in *Court Ayres* (1655 ; an Ayre and a Saraband), and in the *Musical Companion* of 1672 (" Lay that sullen Garland by thee ", two-part). The laſt-named song is contained in *Add.* 29396.

TAYLOR (Silas): Antiquarian, Civil servant, and composer of trivial music, who was typical of the amateur musician of the seventeenth century. Born at Harley, near Much Wenlock in Shropshire, on July 16th, 1624, he was educated at Shrewsbury, Weſtminſter, and New Inn Hall, Oxford (at the beginning of 1641). On the outbreak of the Civil War he left Oxford to join the forces of Cromwell and rose to be a captain in that army (he was given as Captain Silas Taylor in the contemporary collections of music). It was probably Taylor's friendship with John Playford, Henry Purcell the Elder, and Matthew Lock, that gave him the standing he enjoyed, and it is more than probable that his intimacy with the last caused sacred music of his own to reach performance in the chapel of Catherine of Braganza (*v.* Matthew Lock). " He hath composed many things, and I have heard anthems of his sung before his Majestie in his chapell, and the King told him he liked them," says Aubrey (*Lives of Eminent Men*). Pepys often mentions Captain Silas Taylor : on February 21st, 1659–60 ; November 7th, 1663 (when he received a piece of plate from the Captain for a favour expected) ; November 4th, 1664 ; and May 7th, 1669 (when Taylor brought Pepys a play he had written). According to the genial diarist, Taylor " understands musique very well and composes bravely ", but an anthem which he heard performed in the Chapel Royal was a " dull, old-fashioned thing . . . that nobody could understand ".

It seems that Silas Taylor at one time used the *alias* of Domville. Anthony Wood informs us that he did so, though the *Dictionary of National Biography* says that Taylor does not appear ever to have used it. At the same time *Add.* 4910,—" A Collection of Rules in Musicke from the most knowing Masters in that Science ",— bears the legend, " Collected by mee, Silas Domville, *alias* Taylor ". He died in 1678.

Two Ayres, two Corants, and two Sarabands by " Captain Silas Taylor " are contained in *Court Ayres* (1655), and " Anacreon's Ode" by him (*à* 2) is included in the *Musical Companion* of 1672. A piece without a title by " Taylor ",—most probably Silas,—was copied by John Jenkins into *Add.* 31423 (Treble and Bass parts only of a four-part composition). THEINRED: A musical theorist who lived in the last quarter of the fourteenth century. The only work of his that is known to us is dated 1371 and is entitled *De legitimis ordinibus Pentachordorum et Tetrachordorum* (*Bodl.*). All that is known of his life is that he became a monk of the Benedictine brotherhood and eventually was raised to be their Precentor at the monastery of Dover. The treatise in question is in three parts, or books, and deals with intervals and type-scales. It is addressed to Alured (of Canterbury), a circumstance that has caused many superficial observers to give Theinred the Christian name of Alured (the Rev. Sir F. A. Gore-Ouseley, in the English edition of Naumann's *History*, calls him Aelred, while Moreri christens him David). Boston of Bury in mis-quoting the title of the treatise gave Bale the excuse for supposing that Theinred wrote two treatises. Pits followed him in the error, and both give the theorist an excellent character,—probably from the imagination of the first. The manuscript is interesting in that it gives some insight into the modes of the period. Coussemaker promised to include it in his *Scriptores*, but did not do so.

THORNE (John) (" of York "): A composer of ecclesiastical music who enjoyed a considerable reputation during the second half of the sixteenth century. Only three examples of his work have been preserved, but they suffice to place him among the foremost musicians of his day. A motet of his in the Baldwin manuscript exhibits some fine characteristics such as really live part-writing, clever imitation, and, above all, dignity. Although perhaps not on a level with the best of his English contemporaries, Morley was still sufficiently influenced by tradition to place him in the same category with Tallis and Redford (*Introduction to Practicall Musick*, 1597).

Practically nothing is known of his life. He was in some way connected with York Minster, but in what capacity is not known ;—his work might suggest that he was an organist. The only dated information we have concerning him is provided by his tombstone (in the Minster), which contained the following inscription :

" Here lyeth Thorne, musician
 most perfect in his art,
In Logick's Lore who did
 excell ; all vice who set
 apart :
Whose Life and conversation did all men's love allure,
And now doth reign above the skies in joys most firm and pure.
Who dyed December 7th, 1573."

He is best known by the three-part motet " Stella Coeli

454]   [Tomkins

extirpavit" in Baldwin's manuscript (the property of His Majesty the King ; at present *B.M.*), printed by Hawkins. *Add.* 29996, an interesting manuscript in the hand of John Redford (*q.v.*) contains an organ arrangement of " Exultabunt Sancti ". A third specimen of his work is to be seen in the *In Nomine* collection at the Oxford Music School.

Thorne claimed consideration also as a logician and poet, and *Add.* 15233 contains metrical work of his (printed by the Shakespeare Society). Edwards's *Paradyse of Daintie Devyces* (1576) included two of Thorne's poems.

TOMKINS (G i l e s) (I) : Organist successively of King's College, Cambridge, and of Salisbury Cathedral. He was a son of Thomas Tomkins I (of Gloucester Cathedral), and brother of John Tomkins and half-brother of Thomas Tomkins II. The date of his birth is not known, but could not have been earlier than 1587 (*cf.* Tomkins, John). The first authentic information we possess concerning his activities is to the effect that he became organist of King's College in 1624 ; thus

succeeding his brother John after an interval of a couple of years, during which one Matthew Barton held the post (*v.* West, *Cathedral Organists*, Ed. 1921). Giles Tomkins himself was only organist there for two years (until 1626), his salary having been the same as that of his brother John. What he did between 1626 and 1629 is not clear. There is evidence of his having had a post at Salisbury Cathedral in the latter year, but his appointment as organist dates from 1631. In 1630 he was appointed " musician for the Virginalls with the voices in ordinary, in the place of Richard Deering, deceased ", at a salary of 40*l.* a year. On June 30th of the same year he received his livery as a royal musician. Apparently the date of his appointment as virginalist in 1630 clashes with that of the Salisbury appointment of 1631 ; and were there not evidence to the contrary we might be justified in supposing that there were two contemporary bearers of the same name, which would not be a very far-fetched theory when dealing with so large a family of musicians. But Laud in 1634 was told

that Giles Tomkins was sometimes called from Salisbury
to the Chapel at court, and
that the choristers were consequently left without guidance. It would thus appear
that Giles was actually employed at Salisbury and that
his post in London did not
call for his continual presence.
His name is included in a
list dated November 3rd,
1635, giving the salaries of
the court-musicians (*P.R.O.*,
S.P., *Dom. Ser.* Charles I).
Another list in the same place,
dated 1640, gives the salary
of " Egid. Thompkins " as
40*l.* per annum. After the
Restoration he received back
both of his posts. He is
frequently mentioned in the
State Papers, and by 1665–6,
seven years' livery allowance
was owing him. In 1667
he already appears to have
ceased active participation in
the court music, for the outstanding livery account was
now owing to his " assignee";
indeed, Giles Tomkins would
have been nearly eighty years
of age at that time. Before
St. Andrew, 1668, he was
dead (*L.C.R.*). Distinguished
men succeeded him in both
his posts. At Salisbury he was
followed by Michael Wise,
and at court by John Blow
(" 1668–9, January 15th,

Appointment of John Blow
in the place of Giles Tomkins
as one of His Majesty's
musicians for the Virginalls";
L.C.R., Vol. 482).

So far as I have been able
to discover Giles Tomkins
left no music ; but that he
composed anthems is proved
by the presence of words in
Harl. 6346 which he had set
to music.

TOMKINS (Giles) (II): A
son of Giles Tomkins I of
whom very little is known.
He was born at Salisbury
in 1633, while his father was
organist there, and became
the successor of his uncle
Thomas as organist of Worcester Cathedral after the
Restoration of the House of
Stuart and the resumption
of a choral service (1661).
He was dismissed on April
26th, 1662, for absenting
himself from duty.

TOMKINS (John): A
celebrated organist of the
first part of the seventeenth
century. He was the eldest
son of Thomas Tomkins I,
by his second wife, and thus
a half-brother to Thomas
Tomkins II (*q.v.*). In the
book of songs (1622) by the
latter there is prefixed a
complimentary poem by John
Tomkins addressed " To my
brother the Author ". John's

epitaph gave his age in 1638 as fifty-two ; he was thus born in 1586. Of his early life we know nothing until we learn that he was organist of King's College, Cambridge, in 1606. His salary there was 10*l.* per annum, plus 11*s.* 8*d.* per quarter as instructor of the choristers. His salary as organist was later raised to 58*s.* 4*d.* per quarter (*v.* West, *Cathedral Organists*). It is not to be decided with absolute certainty how long he held the post at Cambridge, for in the official entries of wages paid he disappeared in 1619. His name is included in other documents relating to members of the College until 1621, and it is possible that he served as organist at King's College until the latter date. In the meantime he had obtained the degree of *Mus. Bac.* in 1608. After he left Cambridge he became organist of St. Paul's Cathedral. His colleagues there at that time were Adrian Batten (also organist) and Martin Peerson as Master of the Choristers. In 1625 he was appointed to the Chapel Royal : " Memorandum, that Mr. John Tomkins, organist of St. Paule, London, was sworne extraordinarie gentle-

man of his Majesty's Chapel for the next place of organist there, or the place of Anth. Kirkly, which of them shall first fall voyde " ; and the following year : " 1626, Frauncis Wiborowe, died at Ely the 28th of October, and John Tomkins organist of St. Paule was sworne in his place the 3rd of November following. Episteler." (*C.B.C.R.*). In 1628 he is entered in the Lord Chamberlain's Records as a Gentleman of the Chapel, and in 1633 he is mentioned again, sharing the organist's post when the King went to Scotland with Giles Tomkins (*q.v.*). He died in 1638 (September 27th) and was interred in St. Paul's Cathedral. His epitaph, which was originally in the old cathedral, read : " Johannes Tomkins, musicae Baccalaureus, organista sui temporis celeberrimus, postquam capellae regali per annos duodecim, huic autem Ecclesiae per novem decem sedulo inserviisset ad coelestem Chorum migravit Septembris 27, Anno Dom. 1638. Aetatis suae 52. Cujus desiderium moerens uxor hoc testatur marmore " ; it was reprinted by Hawkins in his *History*. William Lawes composed

" An Elegie on the death of his very worthy Friend and Fellow-servant, Mr. John Tomkins, organist of his Majesties Chappell Royall ", and printed it in the book of Psalms published in 1648 by the brothers Lawes.

A few examples of John Tomkins's music are preserved in manuscript. *Add.* 29372–5, in Barnard's collection, and the words of anthems (*Harl.* 6346) remain to show that he composed in that form.

Another John Tomkins is known to have been organist of Worcester Cathedral in 1590, and he was most likely a brother of Thomas Tomkins and thus an uncle of his namesake treated above.

TOMKINS (Robert): A chamber-musician of the first half of the seventeenth century who was active at court. He was probably a member of Thomas Tomkins's family. On March 24th, 1633–4, he was sworn in as " musician in ordinary for the Consort, in the place of Robert Kyndersly, deceased " with the salary of 1*s.* 8*d.* a day and the usual livery allowance of 16*l.* 2*s.* 6*d.* a year (*L.C.R.*, *Vol.* 738). His salary is again given in 1635 in MS. 301 (*P.R.O.* quoted in *Annalen*). The same source gives 46*l.* per annum as his pay in 1640. In the following year we find his name in a list of musicians under the heading " For Lutes, Violls and Voices " (*L.C.R.*, *Vol.* 476). At the outbreak of the Great Rebellion he lost his post and presumably died during the Commonwealth, for in 1660 we read of the appointment of " Henry Hawes in the broken consort in the place of Robert Tomkins, formerly belonging to Robert Kinnersley, for a violl " (*L.C.R.*). *Harl.* 6346 contains the words of anthems and in it Robert Tomkins is represented, showing that he composed music for the church. None of it has survived.

TOMKINS (Thomas I): A Precentor of Gloucester Cathedral who flourished in the second half of the sixteenth century, and whose chief claim to recognition lies in the circumstance that he was the founder of a large family of able musicians. He has been credited with the composition bearing his name in the *Triumphes of Oriana*, but the likelihood is much greater that this was the work of his son Thomas, organist at the Chapel Royal and at Worcester Cathedral.

The family appears to have come originally from Cornwall and a pedigree in the College of Arms (1634) traces the Tomkinses back to a series of Ralphs who belonged to Lostwithiel in that county. Thomas Tomkins, senior, was the son of the last of these Ralphs, and he is said to have disposed of his property in Cornwall in order to enter the Church. Both Thomas senior and Thomas junior appear in the entries in the St. David's Cathedral books (*v. also* Thomas II). In 1571 the former must have committed some petty fault for which he was reprimanded, the occurrence being noted in the Chapter books. The same source supplies the information that in 1577 he was Master of the Choristers and organist. He was at that time in rather straightened circumstances, for he petitioned for a higher salary. His son Thomas was then a chorister, and in order to find the means of increasing the salary of the older man, the Archbishop's agents appointed the chorister to a Vicar's stall, so that he might " enjoy all profits . . . belonging to the same stall . . . to the end that his poor

Father . . . may thereby . . . be relieved " (April 29th, 1577). Now, it does not follow that Thomas junior was the distinguished composer and organist of Worcester. The Precentor had two sons, both bearing the Christian name of Thomas. Strange as this may appear to-day, it was not at all an uncommon occurrence late in the sixteenth century for a man to name more than one son after himself. The Thomas who was a chorister and who was promoted to the vicar's stall appears to have been the elder of the two similarly-named brethren. In 1586 this Thomas was sent down from the Cathedral for some offence, and to dispose of him, we can look upon the Thomas Tomkins who was killed in the *Revenge* in 1593 as the expelled vicar-choral. The composer of the *Oriana* madrigal was thus the younger of the two Thomases (*q.v. inf.* ; *v. also* Dr. E. H. Fellowes in *Vol.* XVIII of the *English Madrigal School*, and Sir Ivor Atkins, *The early occupants of the office of Organist, etc.*, 1918, printed for the Worcester Historical Society).

TOMKINS (Thomas) (II): A prominent composer whose

most important work dates from the first quarter of the seventeenth century. His vocal writing, if not comparable with the best products of the madrigalian school, is correct and original, exhibits a refreshing happiness, and proves the composer to have been the possessor of a really servicable technique. His contribution to the *Triumphes of Oriana* (1601), although a long way from being among the most masterly of the madrigals in the set, nevertheless shows that he was held in high esteem by his contemporaries. The younger of the two brothers named Thomas, he was the son of Thomas Tomkins, Precentor of Gloucester (*v.* Thomas Tomkins I), and was born not later than 1575 since he was organist at Worcester in 1596 (*v. Treasurer's accounts*). From the dedication of his *Book of Songs* to the Earl of Pembroke in 1622 it is clear that he was born in Pembrokeshire, for he says : " I first breathed, and beheld the sunne, in that county to which your Lordship gives the greatest lustre, taking the Title of your Earledome from it ". In addition to this dedication each of the songs is inscribed to some person whom the composer evidently desired to honour. The fact that No. 14 is dedicated " To my Ancient and much reverenced Master, William Byrd " probably proves that he was Byrd's pupil, and thus possibly a chorister in the Chapel Royal. In 1607 he obtained the Oxford degree of *Mus. Bac.*, graduating from Magdalen College. The chronology of his activity at Worcester and Magdalen College is not very clear. In 1613–14 he was at Worcester, for he was connected with the building of organs in the Cathedral ; but not later than June 29th, 1620, he was in London at the Chapel Royal, for on that date his name appears as a witness to a document. The Cheque-Book of the Chapel Royal contains an entry proving his appointment in the following year : " 1621, Edmund Hooper, Organist, died the 14th daye of July, and Thomas Tompkins, organist of Worcester, was sworne in his place the 2nd daye of August followinge." In 1622 was published the work by which he is best known : *Songs of 3, 4, 5 and 6 parts.* A Cheque-Book entry of 1625 shows that he was paid "XL*s*. for composing of many songes again&t the coronacion of Kinge Charles", and in the same year the Lord Chamberlain's Records give him as organi&t of the Chapel (*Vol. 557*). In June, 1628, his name again appears as a member of the Chapel Royal (*L.C.R., Vol.* 738), while on March 15th of the same year he was appointed for life as the successor of Alfonso Ferrabosco, deceased (*Cal. of S.P.*). After this date we miss him from the London records, and next find him at Worce&ter again, being once more named in regard to the con&truction of organs in the Cathedral there (1639–40). He lo&t his po&t during the Civil War, and we know no more of him until his death is recorded as having taken place in 1656. He was buried at Martin Hussingtree, not far from Worce&ter.   He was married before the close of the sixteenth century, and his wife, who died before him, was interred in the Cathedral at Worce&ter.   A collection of his sacred music, including five services and nearly one hundred anthems, was published po&thumously in 1668 with the title : *Musica Deo Sacra et Ecclesiae Anglicanae.*

Manuscript specimens of his work are preserved at the British Museum (*Add.* 29372–7, *Add.* 29996, the Tudway MSS., *etc.*), in the Fitzwilliam Museum (a volume in Purcell's autograph), at Magdalen College and Chri&t Church (Oxford), and at Ely Cathedral.   The British Museum collection also contains arrangements of Hymns and Madrigals by him for in&truments, besides autograph organ music and &tring trios and quintets.   The *Fitzwilliam Virginal-Book* contains five pieces by him, the la&t being called "Wor&ter Branles".   Of modern reprints may be mentioned : "Great and Marvellous are Thy works" (edited by John E. We&t), "I heard a Voice from Heaven" (edited by Sir Ivor Atkins), and one or two others issued by the same publishers (Novello and Co.). Dr. E. H. Fellowes re-issued the 1622 *Book of Songs* in 1922 as *Vol.* 18 of the *English Madrigal School,* and included in it Tomkins's *Oriana* contribution : "The Fauns and Satyrs tripping" (five-part). Mr. W. Barclay Squire edited one more of his secular vocal compositions, "See the Shepherd's Queen."

TUCKER (William):   A

cleric responsible for some ecclesiastical music well above the average in quality. He flourished during the second half of the seventeenth century and held the posts of Gentleman of the Chapel Royal and Precentor of Westminster Abbey after the Restoration. An entry in the Lord Chamberlain's Records for 1674 gives his voice as a bass. His death was announced in the Cheque-Book of the Chapel Royal under date February 28th, 1678, and he was buried in the Cloisters of Westminster Abbey.

A " Whole Service in F " by William Tucker is contained in *Add.* 30478 (old Choir-Book of Durham Cathedral) and an " Evening Service in F " is in *Add.* 34203. The rest of his known works are anthems. " O Give Thanks " is in *Add.* 30478–9, *Add.* 31404, *Add.* 17820, *Harl.* 7339 (Tudway's MS.), and printed by Page and Novello and Co. (1854). " I will Magnifie " is contained in *Add.* 30478, *Add.* 34203 (Organ score), *Add.* 31404, and *Harl.* 7339, " Wherewithall shall a yonge man " is included in *Add.* 30478-9, and *Add.* 17820. " Comfort ye, my people " is to be seen in *Add.* 30932

and *Add.* 30478. " This is ye day " is in *Add.* 17784 and *Add.* 30478, the last-named manuscript containing also " My heart is fixed ", " Lord, how long wilt Thou " and " Lord, send us ". All these manuscripts are in the British Museum. *Add.* 36871 has a hymn-tune signed " Tuckers " which may possibly also be his. He is likewise represented in the Ely manuscripts. On August 1st, 1676, an entry was made in the Lord Chamberlain's Records that a Service and eleven anthems by Tucker were transcribed into the books of the Chapel Royal (*L.C.R., Vol.* 745).

TUDWAY (Thomas): An organist and composer of church music belonging to the second half of the seventeenth century and the beginning of the eighteenth. His claim to remembrance is based almost entirely upon the services he rendered to musical historians by collecting the services and anthems contained in *Harl.* 7337–42 ; for as a composer he can hardly be said to have risen far above the commonplace. The date of his birth is not known, but it could not very well have been later than 1646, for he was admitted as a tenor at Windsor in 1664 (April 22nd). And if this date is the latest for his birth, it is also the earliest, for he was a child of the Chapel Royal soon after the Restoration. Two entries in the Lord Chamberlain's Records relating to a Thomas Tedway probably refer to Tudway. The first is dated January 8th, 1668–9, and orders the delivery of certain clothing to Captain Henry Cooke (*q.v.*) for the use of " Thomas Tedway . . . page of the Chappell whose voice is changed and who is gone from the Chappell " (*L.C.R. Papers*). The second, of March 17th in the same year, directs that 30*l.* be paid to Captain Cooke " for keeping Thomas Tedway, one of the Children of his Majesty's Chappell, *etc.*" (*L.C.R., Vol.* 712). There can be little doubt that these entries refer to Tudway. The error in the spelling is trivial when compared with some of the variations in these entries ; no other reference to either Tedway or Tudway is made in the records, and the lateness of date can be explained, as can so many of the Stuart irregularities in the paying and booking of accounts (*cf.* Turner,

William). Warrants were very often issued four or five years after the occasions to which they relate. In 1670 he was appointed organist at King's College, Cambridge, afterwards becoming organist to the church of the University (St. Mary's) and Pembroke Hall. The King's College records give the information that during the first half of 1680 he was Master of the Choristers there. A year later the degree of *Mus. Bac.* was conferred upon him. The death of Nicholas Staggins in 1700 rendered the chair of music at Cambridge University vacant, and in January, 1704–5, Tudway was elected to the Professorship, proceeding to the Doctorate of Music in the same year. On July 28th, 1706, he found himself in serious trouble owing to his unconquerable habit of making play upon words. Witty, though punning, remarks of his were taken to be reflections on the Queen's policy and that of her statesmen, and Tudway was relieved of his degrees and posts. Less than eight months later, however, he publicly withdrew all that he had said and he was returned to his former dignities and honours (March 10th, 1706–7). He died November 23rd, 1726. A portrait hangs in the Oxford Music School.

It was in 1714 that Edward, Lord Harley (later Earl of Oxford) commissioned Tudway to form the collection of sacred music that made him famous. Between that year and 1720 he was busily engaged in scoring the three thousand odd pages that make up the six ponderous tomes. During the progress of this work he formed a close friendship with Harley's librarian (Humphrey Wanley), and the letters that passed between them make interesting reading. As originally planned the work was to comprise three quarto volumes, but it was not long before Tudway realised that six would hardly contain all he wished to include. The payment he received,—thirty guineas per volume,—can scarcely be considered excessive. The set of manuscripts certainly forms a collection of Anglican service music representative of English talent in the sixteenth and seventeenth centuries. The compositions included were copied and scored from the choir-books of Ely, Dur-

ham, Wells, and Exeter Cathedrals, York Minster, Westminster Abbey, Eton College, the Chapel Royal, and Oxford. The sixth volume of the set (*Harl.* 7342) contains an historical sketch by Tudway of the story of music,—and especially of sacred music,—down to his own times. A thematic catalogue in the handwriting of Dr. Burney is preserved in *Add.* 11587 and *Add.* 11589.

Most of Tudway's own compositions are interesting on account of the occasions for which they were written. His exercises for the *Mus. Bac.* degree in 1681 were a setting of Psalm XX to English words and of Psalm II to Latin,—"Quare fremuerunt gentes", performed at St. Mary's, Cambridge, Commencement, 1681 (*Add.* 31444 and *Harl.* 7338). The other anthem for this Act was "The Lord hear thee in ye day of trouble" (verse anthem with five-part chorus and orchestral accompaniment ; *Harl.* 7338). "Is it true that God will dwell with men" (verse anthem for three voices) was "sung to the Queen at the opening of her Chappell at Windsor, July 13th, 1702" (*Harl.* 7341, *Add.* 30932, *Add.*

31459). Tudway, in the first of these three manuscripts, says that the anthem was "designed for ye opening of St. Paul's Church and sung at ye opening of King's College Chappell". "I am the Resurrection" was sung in King's College Chapel at the funeral of Lord Blandford on February 24th, 1703–4 (full anthem ; *Add.* 30932, *Add.* 31444, and *Harl.* 7341). "I will sing unto the Lord" (verse anthem for three voices) was "sung before the Queen after the victory at Blenheim" (August 13th, 1704), and is to be seen in *Harl.* 7341 and *Add.* 30932. "Thou, O Lord, hast heard" was sung before the Queen on her visit to Cambridge in the year of Tudway's doctorate (April 16th, 1705). It was on this occasion that Her Majesty conferred upon him the title of "Composer and Organist Extraordinary". The anthem is contained in *Harl.* 7341, and was printed by Arnold. "Behold, how good and joyful" was written in 1707 "for the Union with Scotland", "O Praise ye Lord" in 1708 for the victory at Oudenarde (July 11th) and "My heart rejoyceth" (with orchestral accompaniment) in

1713 for the Peace of Utrecht (all three in *Harl.* 7342 ; the last of them also in *Add.* 30932). Besides those already mentioned, there are nine more anthems by Tudway in *Harl.* 7341 and 7342, and further work by him can be seen in *Add.* 30932, *Add.* 17841, *Add.* 31444, *Add.* 31445, *Add.* 31459, and *Add.* 37072. For the consecration of Lord Harley's chapel at Wimpole (August 31st, 1721) Tudway composed a Morning Service and Evening Service in B flat (*Harl.* 7341 and *Add.* 36268) besides three verse anthems for the same celebration (*Add.* 36268, which also includes "the Psalm tunes used at Morning and Ev'ning Pray'r"). "Hail, happy Day", an ode in honour of Queen Anne's birthday (for solo voices, chorus and instruments) is preserved in *Add.* 17835. Secular songs by Tudway are contained in *Add.* 29397, and isolated examples in contemporary printed collections. A *Magnificat in A* was printed in the second edition of the second book of the *Voice of Melody* (1750). A two-part song beginning "Now my Freedom's regain'd" was printed and a copy is preserved in the library of the Royal College of Music. TUNSTED (Simon) (*also* TUNSTEDE): A learned theologian, scientist, and musician of the fourteenth century. A member of a Norfolk family (deriving their name from Tunstead in that County), he was born at Norwich ; but little is known of his life. He joined the brotherhood of the Minorite Franciscans at Oxford and eventually became their head. The only musical work attributed to him is *De Quatuor Principalibus Musice*, a very complete account of fourteenth-century music, particularly useful to the musical historian, since it shows, as de Coussemaker remarks, " en quelque sorte la transition entre le XIII siècle et le XIV." The treatise is known from three manuscripts,— two in the Bodleian library, Oxford, and the other in the British Museum (*Add.* 8866) ; and from one of the former Coussemaker had a copy made for his publication (*Scriptores*, *etc.*, *Vol.* IV, 200). The manuscripts are dated 1351 with the closing remark that the work was by Simon Tunsted, Regent of the Minorites at Oxford. On the strength of this colophon the treatise

is claimed for Tunsted ; but there is no real reason for attributing it to anyone else and in the light of our present knowledge of the fourteenth century it might definitely be given to Tunsted. One of the Oxford manuscripts differs from the others in having a short introduction beginning, " Quemadmodum inter triticum et zizania quamdiu herba est, *etc.*", and it was this manuscript that Coussemaker used. But the introduction and an earlier mis-cataloguing led many to believe that this manuscript contained a different work. The references to a treatise by John Dunstable in Ravenscroft's *Briefe Discourse* (1614) come from this manuscript of Tunsted's. He is supposed to have died in the nunnery at Bruisyard (Suffolk) in 1369. TURGES (Edmund): An early sixteenth century composer of ecclesiastical and secular vocal music. Nothing is known of his life. The Fayrfax manuscript (*Add.* 5465) contains the largest number of his compositions. This vellum includes Turges's " Alas, it is I " (*à* 3), " I am he that hath ", " From Stormy Wyndis " (with second part, " O Blessid Lord of Heuyn " ; a third part, and a fourth part in honour of Prince Arthur), and " Enforce your-selfe " (with a second part " Soverayn Lord ",—*i.e.* Henry VII,—and a third part, " God hath gyff you "). The song in honour of Prince Arthur has the date 1501 (apparently in a later hand) beside the name of the com-poser. This was the year in which the prince married Catherine of Arragon ; he died in the following year. *Add.* 11583 has an eighteenth-century copy of " Alas, it is I ". Sacred music by Turges is contained in the Eton College manuscript, in No. 667 of the Gonville and Caius College manuscripts, and in *Add.* 5665. " Enforce yourself " has been issued in score for three voices by Novello and Co. (1893), under the editorship of Dr. C. W. Pearce.

TURNER (William): An excellent singer and composer of moderate endowments active during the last quarter of the seventeenth century and the first quarter of the eighteenth. He was born at Oxford in 1651, his father having been a cook at Pem-broke College. As soon as the Restoration of the monarchy permitted the cathe-dral choirs to officiate once more, Turner became one of the choir-boys at Christ Church, Oxford, coming under the guidance of Edward Lowe (*q.v.*). He could not have remained in that choir for very long for in 1667 (April 3rd) we find his name in the Lord Chamberlain's Records as a chorister at the Chapel Royal : "Warrant to pay Captain Henry Cooke . . . 30*l.* by the year for the keeping of William Turner, one of the children of the Chappell whose voice is changed and gone from the Chappell, to commence 29 September, 1666"(*L.C.R.*, *Vol.* 742). Turner was fortu-nate in his friends : after Lowe, Cooke ; and in the chapel he formed friendships with many boys who became famous, such as Pelham Hum-frey, John Blow, and others. He was associated with Hum-frey and Blow in the com-position of the so-called "Club Anthem ", said by many writers to have been written at a day's notice to celebrate a victory over the Dutch. Unfortunately for the legend, no victory over the Dutch can be discovered at that date. Turner's contribution to the anthem was the bass solo (middle section ; *v.* also article on Pelham

Humfrey). As soon as the period of mutation was over he spent a short time as a chorister at Lincoln Cathedral. In 1669 Turner was sworn in as a Gentleman of the Chapel Royal in the place of Edward Colman, deceased (*C.B.C.R.*), becoming, a little later, a vicar-choral of St. Paul's Cathedral and a lay-vicar at Westminster Abbey. That the popularity he enjoyed at court was very great is proved by the fact that in addition to all the posts he now held, he was admitted " in the place and quality of musician in ordinary in his Majesty's private Musick for lute and Voyce, in the place of Henry Cooke, deceased " (*L.C.R., Vol.* 744). In the Lord Chamberlain's entry for January 26th, 1673–4, we see another example of the financial methods of the Caroline courts : " Warrant to pay to William Turner late child of his Majesty's Chapel Royal whose voice being changed, went from the Chapel, the sum of 30*l.* by the year, by the space of four years, from Michaelmas, 1666, to Michaelmas, 1670, in all 120*l.*" (*L.C.R., Vol.* 744). We can only wonder whether the money was ever paid.

His voice, after it had " changed " became a counter-tenor of excellent quality, judging by the great request in which it stood. In 1674 he was one of the singers in the court-masque of that year, and also at a performance of *The Tempest* at His Royal Highness's Theatre. In 1685 he was the composer of the St. Cecilia ode (words by Nahum Tate), and during the next two years his name appears as a singer (together with John Abell and others) in odes by Blow and Henry Purcell (*v. Add.* 33287). In 1686, too, he received some of his arrears of salary and livery money (amounting to 96*l.* 15*s.*) out of the tobacco and sugar tax (James II). He graduated *Mus. Doc.* at Cambridge in 1696. At about this date he commenced on a series of odes, coronation-anthems, and royal birthday songs, and so greatly did he please his contemporaries that in a Latin poem written in honour of his doctorate, he is described as having no peer but Purcell. Later centuries, however, did not endorse this judgment. William Turner died on January 13th, 1739–40, at Westminster, having survived his wife only four days. This genial and worthy couple had shared life's blessings and the Stuart debts for little short of seventy years, and on January 16th they were buried in the same grave in the Westminster Abbey Cloisters. He left five children, but evidently did not hold them in very great affection, for by his will (dated 1728) he bestowed his entire estate upon his wife with the exception of one shilling to each of his children. This Turner should not be confused with another, and later, William Turner, who wrote instrumental sonatas and a treatise called *Sound Anatomised*.

Dr. William Turner's compositions in manuscript include Services, Anthems, Songs for plays, Duets, Catches, *etc.*, and specimens may be seen in many collections. Tudway's manuscripts (*Harl.* 7339,7341) contain a "Whole Service in A", a Morning and Evening Service, the " Club " anthem, the Cecilia ode for 1697 ("The King shall rejoice "), the coronation anthem for Queen Anne (1702; "The Queen shall rejoice "), and other anthems. Further examples of his work may be found in *Add.* 17820 ("Lord, Thou hast been our refuge " ; also preserved in other manuscripts and printed by Boyce), *Add.* 17784, *Add.* 19759, *Add.* 22099, *Add.* 22100, *Add.* 29386, *Add.* 29397. *Add.* 30932, *Add.* 31405, *Add.* 31443, *Add.* 31445, *Add.* 31463, *Add.* 33234, *Add.* 33239, *Add.* 33287, *Add.* 33289, and *Add.* 34609. In 1676 three of Turner's anthems were transcribed into the books of the Chapel Royal, and anthems of his are to be seen in the libraries of Westminster Abbey and Ely Cathedral. A huge number of songs, rounds, catches, *etc.*, by this composer are contained in a manuscript in the Fitzwilliam Museum (Cambridge). Not much of Turner's music has appeared in print. The *Theater of Music* (1685) contains four vocal numbers (*Book IV*, 1687, has one more), *Harmonia Sacra* (1688) gives one composition, and *Musick's Handmaid* (1689 ; *Part* 2) has an unnamed piece on page 6. The anthem " Lift up your heads " has been printed in Warren's *Chorister's Handbook* and as No. 48 of *The Parish Choir*. It was reissued under the editorship of John E. West (Novello) in 1906. Rimbault's *Cathe-*

dral Chants and Volume I of the *Parish Choir* contain chants by Turner. TYE (Christopher): One of the most important figures in the history of English music, Tye stands as one of the glories of the mid-sixteenth century. Contemporary with Robert Whyte and Tallis, his work is comparable with theirs,—in many respects surpassing it. Indeed, during the period of his greatest maturity he merits a place among the greatest of several European composers, and his mass "Euge Bone" may be considered as a specimen of the earlier Tudor service-music at its best. In such works as this Tye exhibits a grandeur of conception and an excellence of workmanship that give him the high position he holds in English music. His work possesses a melodic charm too often absent from the music of that period, and his chief aim appears to have been an effect of beauty rather than ostentatious virtuosity. At the same time there were very few musicians whose contrapuntal skill and dexterity in part-writing exceeded his. There is much fine work contained in his anthems, too, and his

setting of the first fourteen chapters of the Acts of the Apostles is broad and dignified. He wrote for the older service as well as for the Reformed cult. If we are to believe Anthony Wood,—who does not state the source of his information,—Tye was "a peevish and humorsome man, especially in his later days, and sometimes playing the organ in the Chapel of Queen Elizabeth which contained much music, but little delight to the ear, she would send the verger to tell him that he played out of tune ; whereupon he sent word that her ears were out of tune" (*MS. Notes, Bodleian*). The reputation he enjoyed among his contemporaries was a high one, and in Samuel Rowley's play, *When you see me, You know me* (1605) King Edward VI is made to say :
"Doctor, I thank you and
    commend your cunning.
I oft have heard my Father
    merrily speake,
In your high praise, and thus
    his Highness sayth,
' England one God, one
    truth, one Doctor hath
For Musicks Art and that
    is Doctor Tye '."
It is generally believed that Tye was music-master to

Edward when Prince of Wales, but there is no direct evidence to prove it. In support there is only the information that Bishop Richard Cox was tutor to the Prince and that he may have introduced his friend Tye as music-teacher.

The place and date of Tye's birth are unknown. The most likely theory is that he commenced his musical career as a chorister at King's College, Cambridge, a boy named Tye having been in the choir there in 1511. If this boy was the musician under consideration, he was most probably born about 1500–1502. Wood, for no apparent reason, says that Tye came from the West of England ; but the greater likelihood is that he was a native of Cambridge or one of the adjacent counties, the name having been, as Mr. Arkwright says, not uncommon in the Eastern counties of England. The late Sir Frederick Bridge informed me of a document discovered in the muniment room of Westminster Abbey which contains the name of John Tyes as organist, at 10*l.* a year, in 1399. This may have been an ancestor of Christopher ; at any rate

the list may account for Fuller's statement that Tye was a Westminster man. No doubt can be entertained, however, that Christopher Tye was a lay-clerk at King's College (Cambridge) in the year 1537, for his full name then appears in the college records. Shortly before this date he graduated as Bachelor of Music in the same University, the entry in the Grace-book reading : " 1536, In primis conceditur Cristofero Tye ut studium decem annorum in arte musica cum practica multa in eadem, tum componendo, tum pueros erudiendo, sufficiat ei ad intrandum in eadem, sic ut componat unam missam vel paulo post comitia canendam, vel eo ipso die quo serenissimi principis obseruabitur aduentus, *etc.*" (*Gamma, p.* 156*b*). It is clear from this that Tye must have been an instructor of choristers before 1536. What he did during the next few years is not clear. Some authorities say that he was at the Chapel Royal from 1537, but there is nothing to support such a supposition. It is true that Tye, much later (*Acts of the Apostles*) describes himself as a " Gentleman of the King's Chapel ", but there is no record of his appointment. The celebrated Cheque-Book of the Chapel Royal contains no entries so early, and in the Lord Chamberlain's Records Tye is not mentioned at all. Honorary membership of the Chapel Royal was not unknown ; and Tye by virtue perhaps of his association with Prince Edward, may have obtained the title in this manner. His next appointment is open to no doubt. In 1541 he became Master of the Choristers at 10*l.* per annum in the Cathedral of Ely. He proceeded Doctor of Music in 1545, incorporating at Oxford in 1548. For the Cambridge doctorate he was again required to write a mass as his exercise, and to have it sung before the authorities. In 1553 Tye published that fruit of the Reformation, — " *The Actes of the Apostles*, translated into Englyshe metre, and dedicated to the Kynges most excellent Maiestye, by Christopher Tye, Doctor in Musyke, and one of the Gentylmen of hys Graces moste honourable Chappell, with notes to eche Chapter, to synge and also to play upon the Lute, very necessarye for students after theyr studye,

to fyle theyr wyttes, and also for all Christians that cannot synge, to read the good and godlye storyes of the lyves of Christ hys Apostles ". Two impressions appear to have been published in the same year, one printed by William Seres and the other by Nicolas Hill. The music (four-part) to these fourteen chapters of the *Acts* is infinitely better than the " poetry " Tye wrote, and it is possible that the poverty of the verses was responsible for the comparatively small success of the publication. At all events, it was not continued.

In 1560 Tye took holy orders, his friend Richard Cox having ordained him in that year. In the autumn he became rector of Doddington-cum-March, and, having given up his post at Ely Cathedral, settled in his new quarters in the following Spring. Later two more livings were given him, but they were subsequently sequestrated on account of Tye's negligence in the payment of certain dues. The date of his death must lie between August 27th, 1571 (when he signed a document ; *MS.* at Ely) and March 15th, 1572–3 (when " rectoriam

. . . per naturalem mortem venerabilis viri Chriſtoferi Tye, mus. doᴄt. . . . ibi vacantem ", a successor was appointed).

Tye has left us quite sufficient examples of his skill to enable us to form a correᴄt opinion on his talents, and Mr. Arkwright in his article in the 1914 *Grove* gives a good liſt of the surviving works. His larger compositions include three masses (one in four parts on the popular tune " Weſtern Wind why doſt thou blow ?", one in five parts, and the celebrated *Euge Bone*, à 6). In addition he wrote a large number of anthems (a form of composition which he may be said to have settled), motets, Services, *In Nomines*, and a few works of a secular nature. Examples of his work are to be found in manuscript in the British Museum: (*Harl.* 7337, 7340; *Add.* 5059, *Add.* 11587, *Add.* 15166, *Add.* 17802–3, *Add.* 29289, *Add.* 29246, *Add.* 29372–7, *Add.* 30087, *Add.* 30478–9, *Add.* 30480–4, *Add.* 30513, *Add.* 31226, *Add.* 31415, *Add.* 31443, *etc.*), at Chriſt Church, Oxford (motets and anthems, several of them incomplete), the Music School, Oxford (*In Nomines* and the *Euge Bone* mass in the Forreſt-Heyther colleᴄtion), and Peterhouse, Cambridge (a mass). This does not exhauſt the liſt of Tye's works, but the compositions in the manuscripts named are sufficiently representative. In addition, a fair amount of Tye's music has been printed. Anthems are contained in the collections of Barnard (1641) and Boyce, and further specimens were printed by Hullah, Burney, *etc.* Novello and Co. have issued a number of anthems (moſtly under the editorship of Mr. J. E. Weſt), a specimen adapted by Oliphant from the *Aᴄts of the Apoſtles* (edited by Dr. Walford Davies), and other Latin and English sacred vocal pieces. The same firm has also published the *Euge Bone* mass, and, under the editorship of J. E. Weſt, a *Magnificat* and *Nunc Dimittis*. Mr. G. E. P. Arkwright has also printed the *Euge Bone* mass in *No.* X of *The Old English Edition*.

V

VANWILDER, *see* WILDER.

VAUTOR (Thomas) : A composer of Ayres who flourished in the early seventeenth century, and whose work is distinctly advanced in many respects. Hardly anything is known of his life. From the dedication to his only publication,—to the "Right Honorable the Marquesse of Buckingham",—we gather that he was an "individual appendant of your . . . noble Mothers house and name", —*i.e.* that he was in the service of Anthony Beaumont in Leicestershire. The daughter of this gentleman became the wife of Sir George Villiers, and after her marriage Vautor appears to have continued in her service. The dedication already alluded to also says that some of the contents of the book "were composed in your tender yeares, and in your most worthy Fathers house (from whom, and your most honourable Mother, for many yeares I received part of my meanes and livelyhoode), which hath the rather emboldened mee, with many other more neere respects to intreat your Honour to let them passe under your Gracious favour . . ." The nobleman to whom this work was dedicated, and in whose "tender years" some of it was written, later became the famous Duke of Buckingham. The only other information we possess concerning Vautor, is that he supplicated for the Bachelorship in music at Oxford. He was excused attendance at lectures owing to his non-residence at Oxford, and the degree was conferred upon him on July 4th, 1616, after he had written a hymn of six parts. It should be noted that the grace (as given in Mr. C. F. Abdy Williams's *Musical Degrees*) is to "*John* Vauter", doubtlessly a slip of the pen. Judging by his name it is not improbable that Vautor was of French descent—perhaps the son of a Huguenot.

The only work of his known at present is "*The First Set* : Beeing Songs of diuers Ayres and Natures, of Fiue and Sixe parts : Apt for *Vyols* and *Voyces*. Newly Composed by Thomas Vautor, Batchelor of Musicke, 1619". The British Museum possesses a copy of this excessively rare work in a splendid state of preservation, the bass part being almost new. Three numbers from this book have appeared in later reprints. "Mother, I will have a Husband" was issued in 1905, and "Sweet Suffolk Owle" in 1909,—both in *Euterpe* (edited by Mr. C. K. Scott). "Shepherds and Nymphs" has been published by Breitkopf and Haertel with English and German words (edited by Mr. W. Barclay Squire). Some of Vautor's work really deserves revival. It is undoubtedly influenced by the great English madrigal school, and even if Vautor was only an imitator, he was at least a successful one.

VAUTROLLIER(Thomas): A music-printer of the Elizabethan era who issued some highly interesting and important music-books from his press. A Huguenot of excellent education, Vautrollier came to England before October 2, 1564, when he was admitted a member of the Stationers' Company. He was in all probability employed by some established printer until 1570 when he founded his own press at Blackfriars and published his first book. He then went to Scotland and did some business as a bookseller in Edinburgh while preparing to open a publishing house there. During his absence from London, his wife worked the Blackfriars business. On his return to the metropolis it seems that he offended the Star Chamber with some publication, and he once more left for Edinburgh, where he commenced publishing in 1584. He was at that time patronised by the King (James VI). Two years later he was back in London and still working at the original address, for a dedication of 1587 says that the work was issued from "my poor house in Black ffryers, 9th May, 1587". He died in London before March 4th, 1587–8.

The majority of his books were not concerned with music, but the few which did contain it were important: compositions by Tallis and Byrd (excellently produced) and a couple of Psalters being his best achievements in music-publishing.

W

WALKELEY (Anthony): An organiſt and ecclesiaſtical composer of the late seventeenth century. Born in 1672, he became successively a choir-boy at Wells, and Vicar-Choral. In 1698 or thereabouts he was appointed organiſt to Salisbury Cathedral, dying in 1718 (January 16th). Manuscripts containing sacred music by him are preserved at Ely and in the Royal College of Music (London). The British Museum has a Morning Service in E-flat (*Te Deum* and *Jubilate*) in *Harl.* 7342 (Tudway's *Vol.* VI), the same being repeated in *Add.* 30933.

WANLESS (T h o m a s): Organiſt and writer of sacred music who flourished at the end of the seventeenth century. He was appointed to York Minſter in April, 1691, and became a Bachelor of Music at Cambridge seven years later. The date of his death is not known with certainty, but it muſt be placed before 1722 when Quarles succeeded him. He may have been in failing health from 1715, for in that year a temporary organiſt was engaged. His works include a volume containing the words of the anthems sung at York (1703), and a Litany (which exiſts in a large number of variable copies), printed by Jebb, and reprinted by Novello and Co. (edited by J. B. Lott). In 1702 was issued " The Metre Psalm-Tunes, in Four parts, composed for the use of the Parish-Church of St. Michael's of Belfrey's in York, *etc.*", by Thomas Wanless (copy in the *B.M.*). In manuscript the British Museum has the verse-anthem à 3, " Awake up, my Glory " (*Harl.* 7341 ; Tudway), and another, " I am the Resurrection " (Funeral Service) in *Add.* 17820. In *Harl.* 1911 (Minutes of the " Corporacion of Musique ") there is mention made of a Thomas Wanless,—which may refer to the same man.

WARD (John): A writer of sacred and secular music who flourished in the early part of the seventeenth century. He is an important figure in the hiſtory of English music, although his work is not comparable with that of the beſt of his contemporaries. He is moſt remarkable for his daring harmonic innovations,—the whole of the English madrigal school being more or less distinguished by fearless attempts to break away from the older hampering restrictions. Some of his ecclesiastical music is marked by solidity relieved by many lyrical passages in the best style. He is imaginative and distinctly above the average for his period in the happy manner his music illustrates his text. In his more dramatic moments he decidedly anticipates the methods of the last years of the century more than does anyone among the writers of his own period. His madrigals, and especially those à 6, are exceedingly good, and it is a fortunate thing for the singers of to-day that so excellent an edition of them as that of Dr. E. H. Fellowes is available.

Of Ward's life very little is known. He was in the household of Sir Henry Fanshawe of Ware Park (Hertfordshire), and apparently supplied much of the music made in that exceptionally musical establishment. He witnessed his patron's will and was the recipient of many generous bequests. He died before 1641, since some work of his is printed in Barnard's collection of that year,—no music by living composers being included in it.

The earliest dated work of his was : *The First Set of English Madrigals to* 3, 4, 5 *and* 6 *parts apt both for Viols and Voyces. With a Mourning Song in memory of Prince Henry, etc.* (six part-books, 1613). Prince Henry was a personal friend of Ward's "very good Master Sir Henry Fanshawe, and he possibly came into contact with the composer at Ware Park or at Fanshawe's city house which contained a large number of instruments and a huge collection of music,— sufficient to delight this music-loving prince who died too soon. *The First Set, etc.,* has been reprinted by Dr. Fellowes (*Vol.* XIX, 1922, *English Madrigal School*). To Leighton's *Teares, etc.* (1614) Ward contributed two pieces, and some settings of his are included in Ravenscroft's Psalter of 1621. Barnard's *Selected Church Music* (1641) contains an Evening Service and two verse-anthems of his ; and these would seem to complete the tale of the seventeenth-century publications containing work by Ward. Several modern reprints render examples of his music easily accessible. Novello and Co. have published specimens of his sacred music as well as three of the madrigals, and the Church Music Society has issued the anthem " O let me tread " (1911). " Die not, fond man " (one of Ward's most popular compositions) and " Hope of my Heart ", have been admirably edited by Mr. W. Barclay Squire. In manuscript there are verse-anthems and a madrigal not in the printed set in *Add.* 29372–7, and instrumental Fancies in *Add.* 17786–91. The Christ Church (Oxford) library possesses six Fancies *à* 4, eleven *à* 5, nine *à* 6, and two *In Nomines à* 6. Will. Forster's Virginal-Book (in the possession of his Majesty the King ; now in the *B.M.*) contains nine arrangements for the keyboard instrument.

WARROCK (Thomas), *see* WARWICK (Thomas).

W A R W I C K (Thomas), *also* WARROCK): An organist and composer of anthems active at the end of the sixteenth century and the first forty years of the seventeenth. His first appointment was as organist of Hereford Cathedral in 1586, holding the post until 1589. From this moment

we lose sight of him for thirty-six years and do not meet with him again until 1625, when he was given two posts (one of them that of organist at the Chapel Royal) which were formerly held by Orlando Gibbons ; receiving for one 40*l.* per annum and for the other 46*l.* (*C.B.C.R.* and *Annalen*). In 1628 he is mentioned as a Gentleman of the Chapel (*L.C.R.*, *Vol.* 738) and in 1641 he is " For the Virginall " (*Id.* 476). An interesting entry is that of March 29th, 1630, when " Mr. Thomas Warrick received a check of his whole paye for the moneth of March becawse he presumed to playe verses on the organ at service tyme, being formerly inhibited by the Deane from doinge the same, by reason of his insufficiency for that solemn service " (*C.B.C.R.*). He died during the Commonwealth, for in 1660 we find Christopher Gibbons appointed to his place as virginalist, *etc.*, with the same 86*l.* per annum (*L.C.R.*).

Warwick's anthem, " I lift my hart up to the hils " is given (incomplete) in *Add.* 29366–8, while another, " O God of my salvation " is contained in *Add.* 30478–9. The words only of both are given in *Harl.* 4142. A Pavane and Galliard of his are in the *Fitzwilliam Virginal-Book* (printed under the editorship of W. Barclay Squire and J. A. Fuller Maitland). That he wrote a song of forty parts rests on the authority of Hawkins.

Thomas Warwick came of a good Cumberland family, and his son,—Sir Philip Warwick, —became Treasury Secretary after the Restoration. Anthony Wood's information concerning Thomas Warwick must be accepted with caution, as his statements are not borne out by any documentary evidence.

WATERHOUSE (George): A Gentleman of the Chapel Royal during the reign of Elizabeth, who became celebrated as a writer of Canons on the plainsong *Miserere.* He was sworn in as a Gentleman in July, 1588, coming from Lincoln Cathedral (*C.B.C.R.*). In 1592 he supplicated for the degree of *Mus. Bac.* at Oxford, and in 1595–6 joined his fellow-choristers in their successful petition for an increase of salary (*C.B.C.R.*, January 20th). The same book announces his death as having occurred on February 18th, 1601. The species of com-

position affected by Waterhouse was very popular at the time (*cf. Medulla Musicke* by Byrd and Alfonso Ferrabosco, *s.v.* William Byrd, and the book of Canons in Byrd's autograph in the *B.M.*), and Thomas Morley as his "friend and fellow ", went into rhapsodies over his achievements. In the *Introduction to Practical Musick* (1597) we may read that " Mr. George Waterhouse . . surpassed all who ever laboured in that kind of study ". Perhaps the best that can be said of these things is that they exhibit very great ingenuity and that they may be useful models for students. The University library at Cambridge possesses a manuscript containing canons by Waterhouse, " two parts in one upon [the plainsong *Miserere* 1163 ways," with explanatory matter as to their structure. This volume is one of two bequeathed to the University ; the other is lost.

WEBB (William): A composer of light music who flourished in the first half of the seventeenth century. Nothing is known of his life beyond the facts that he was a Gentleman of the Chapel (a receipt of his, dated 1647, is preserved in *Add.*

33965), a member of the king's "public and private musick" before the Civil War (Playford, *Select Ayres and Dialogues*, 1659), and a celebrated teacher of singing and viol-playing during the interregnum (*Musical Banquet*). He is represented in *Select Musical Ayres and Dialogues* of 1652 and 1659, while the edition of 1653 contains twelve pieces by him (four airs to the theorbo or gamba, and eight for three voices). Hilton's *Catch that Catch can* gives five numbers by Webb, and the *Musical Companion* (1672) still presents two three-part compositions of his.

WEBSTER (Maurice): A singer, lutenist, and violist during the reign of Charles I. His name is first to be encountered in the list of musicians belonging to the "Consort" at the time of the funeral of James I (1625), in whose service he had been. His fellows in the consort were such men as Charles Colman, Robert Johnson, John Dowland, Daniel Farrant, and Nicholas Lanier, and he must have enjoyed a considerable reputation. In 1631 (April 27th) he was to receive 15*l.* for a three-years supply of lute-strings, and in 1635–6 (January 2nd) he is given as "deceased" (*L.C.R.*). He is represented by four pieces of viol music in the *Taffel Consort* (1621) of Thomas Simpson, and also in *Add.* 18940–4 (three pieces for three viols), in *Add.* 31423 (imperfect parts in the hand of John Jenkins; two Pavanes), and in *Add.* 31429 (a piece in C, for three viols).

WEEKES *or* WEEKS, *see* WEELKES.

WEELKES (Thomas): A late Tudor composer who merits a place in the very front rank of native musicians as much on account of his great versatility as for the superlative worth of his work. As a madrigalist he is comparable only with Wilbye, vastly though the music of the two may differ in treatment. The salient feature of Weelkes's secular vocal music is the wholly admirable way in which he expresses the dramatic contents of the poetry. In this particular he is second to none among the Elizabethan madrigalists. His characterisation is well-nigh perfect, and his method of expression is always intensely human and personal. His imagination never failed him, and he is one of the

very few writers who suc-
ceeded in hiding profound
scholarship behind a screen
of natural feeling, which,
perhaps more than anything
else, made of him the popular
composer he undoubtedly was.
In his sacred music he differs
still more from the other
madrigalists, in so far as his
work in this field is really
solid and rich in feeling ;
reminding one more, *mutatis
mutandis*, of the musicians
who had the outlook of a
William Byrd. His church
music is noticeable on account
of the manner in which he
suits his music to the meaning
of the words as much as are
his madrigals remarkable for
the same reason. His Fancies
for strings, too, are marked by
great originality and imagination ; and in the adding of
voice parts to the instrumental
Fancy he was one of the
first to write in this then
popular form.

The date of Weelkes's
birth is not to be fixed with
absolute certainty ; but other
circumstances in his life,—
such as his marriage, the
birth of his children, his
appointments, *etc.*, would
seem to suggest that 1576
would not be very far out.
He is not likely to have been
born earlier than this. Of
his earliest years we know
nothing, and we are equally
ignorant on the subject of
his training. All that we
can gather (from a dedication
to one of his works) is that
in 1598 he was engaged in
the household of " Edward
Darcye, Groome of hir
Majesties Privie Chamber ",
the inscription stating that
that gentleman entertained
in his service " the least pro-
ficient in Musicke, who with
all dutiful observancie
humbly " commended his
" poore labours to your wor-
ships protection ". He is
next to be met with at Winchester College, and he seems
to have remained there as
organist until late in 1602.
He used New College,
Oxford, for the purpose of
taking his degree. His
supplication for the Bachelorship of Music is dated
February 12th, 1601–2, and
he obtained it on July 13th
of the same year. He appears
to have married shortly before
he left Wykeham's College
(Winchester), for during the
major part of his residence
there he lived in the college (*v.*
dedication to " Lord Winsor "
in the work of 1600). His next
appointment was at Chichester
Cathedral, but whether he
was installed there before

or after he took his degree is not known. At all events, he commenced his work at Chichester before the end of 1602. The Subdeanery Registers of that city contain entries which prove him to have been in residence (with his family) in 1603, since his son Thomas was baptized there on June 9th of that year. Three years later (September 17th) " Alles Wilkes, the daughter of Thomas Wilkes, organiste ", was baptized. In 1608 he described himself as " Gentleman of his Majesty's Chapel " as well as organist of Chichester Cathedral (title-page to *Ayeres or Phantastike Spirites, etc.*) but no trace of his name is to be found in the Chapel Royal records. I can offer no explanation for this announcement, nor can I guess at the reason for his possession of the title,— unless he was elected as an honorary member. In 1622 his wife (Elizabeth) died, and was buried on September 7th, Weelkes surviving her by only thirteen months. His will, printed by Mr. G. E. P. Arkwright in *Part XIII* of the *Old English Edition*, fixes the date of his death as November 30th, 1623, and the house of his friend Henry Drinkwater in London (where he appears to have been visiting) as the place. He was buried on December 1st at St. Brides, Fleet Street, London, the entry referring to it having been discovered by Dr. E. H. Fellowes in the parish registers (*v. English Madrigal School, Part IX*). Weelkes's will mentions a second daughter (Katherine) in addition to the two children already alluded to.

The first published work of Thomas Weelkes was issued in 1597, entitled *Madrigals to 3, 4, 5 and 6 voyces, etc.* He described the contents as the " first fruits of my barren ground ", but among the madrigals included are some very fine examples, — " Cease, Sorrows ", in particular, is of remarkable quality and beauty, and this one piece alone would be enough to give Weelkes the right to immortal fame. In 1598 his *Balletts and Madrigals to fiue voyces with one to six voyces*, appeared (second edition in 1608). He was still conscious of his " yeeres unripened " and mentions the fact with unnecessary modesty, for this book, like the preceding one, contains some undoubtedly original work. In

1600 two sets of madrigals appeared, one " of five parts " and one of six. As may be expected Weelkes contributed to the *Triumphes of Oriana* (1601) and his madrigal " As Vesta was from Latmos Hill " is one of the most masterly in the book. In 1608 he issued *Ayeres or Phantastike Spirites for 3 voices, etc.* (William Barley). The pieces contained in this work are truly, for the most part, fantastic, and not up to the standard of the earlier music ; they are altogether slighter. But the book includes his " Remembrance of his friend, Thomas Morley "—" Death hath deprived me of my dearest friend ". I have not been able to find out when and how Weelkes and Morley could have met ; but it is just possible that the former may have come to London for the purpose that entitled him to call himself a member of the Chapel Royal. To Leighton's *Teares, etc.* (1614) he sent two numbers.

The first music to be published after his death was an anthem in Barnard's collection of 1641. The Musical Antiquarian Society reprinted the 1597 set of madrigals and published a couple of anthems. Isolated pieces have been printed from time to time by various editors. Six dignified contributions to the literature of Thomas Weelkes are Dr. Fellowes's edition of the 1597 madrigals, the 1598 Balletts, the five-part madrigals of 1600, the six-part madrigals of 1600, and the work of 1608, in *Volumes* IX–XIII of the *English Madrigal School*, and Mr. Arkwright's issue of the 1598 " Balletts " in *Part* XIII of the *Old English Edition*.

The British Museum possesses a good deal of manuscript music by Weelkes : *Add.* 5054, *Add.* 31418, *Add.* 30087, *Add.* 17786–91, *Add.* 30485, *Add.* 29289 (an Altus part only), *Add.* 29427, *Add.* 29372–7, *Add.* 17792–6, *Add.* 30478–9 ; *Harl.* 4142, *Harl.* 7339 ; *Roy. App.* 63 ; and others, containing work by him,—some of it copied from the published books. The Royal College of Music, the Oxford Music School, and Christ Church collections of manuscripts all possess examples of Weelkes's sacred or secular writing. His " Crie of London " (for voices and instruments) is contained in the British Museum MS. *Add.* 37402–6. Benjamin Cosyn's Virginal Book (property of his Majesty the King ; now in *B.M.*) contains "Weelks Seruice" and "Absollon my sonne" arranged for the virginal. WELDER (Henry, Matthew, Peter, Philip Van), *see* WILDER (Philip Van). WELDON (John): An organist and composer of sacred and secular music. In the latter he rarely rose above the average for his period (end of the seventeenth century and beginning of the eighteenth) ; but in his ecclesiastical compositions he attained to greater heights, and two or three of his anthems exhibit admirable qualities—Burney's judgment notwithstanding. Born at Chichester on January 19th, 1676, he received his first musical instruction from John Walter, organist of Eton College, where Weldon was educated. Later on he enjoyed some lessons from Henry Purcell. His earliest employment was as organist of New College, Oxford, to which he was appointed in 1694 in succession to Richard Goodson. In 1699–1700 (March 21st) the *London Gazette* advertised that "several persons of quality having for the encouragement of musick, advanced 200 Guineas, to be distributed

in four prizes (100, 50, 30, and 20 Guineas) to such masters as shall be adjudged to compose the best . . .", a competition was announced, the text to be set being the *Judgment of Paris* (Congreve). John Weldon entered and secured the first prize. The other successful competitors were John Eccles, Daniel Purcell, and Godfrey Finger (*q.v.*). With the exception of the number, "Let Ambition fire thy mind" (and one other song), Weldon's winning music is lost. The original manuscript appeared at the sale of the Rev. J. Parker's library in 1813 (lot 37). The melody of the section mentioned was adapted by Arne to a duet in *Love in a Village*.

On June 6th, 1701, Weldon was sworn in as a "Gentleman Extraordinary" of the Chapel Royal (*C.B.C.R.*), and a year later he left his post at New College to Simon Child. In 1708 he was sworn in as organist to the Chapel Royal in "Dr. Blow's place" (*Id.*). In 1715 a new post was created at the Chapel for a "second composer", and on August 8th Weldon obtained it. As an organist he was very popular, and he afterwards added the churches of St. Brides, Fleet Street, and St. Martin's-in-the-Fields to the Chapel Royal. His work in the last-named establishment, however, was shared by Maurice Greene from 1727 onwards. John Weldon died on May 7th, 1736, and was interred in the churchyard of St. Paul's, Covent Garden. He was succeeded at the Chapel Royal by William Boyce as composer and by Jonathan Martin as organist.

A fair amount of Weldon's music has been printed,— secular songs published separately early in the eighteenth century, anthems in the collections of Boyce, Arnold, and Page, and instrumental music, chiefly for violins and flutes. Novello and Co. have issued two of his best-known anthems, " In Thee O Lord " and " O Praise God in His holiness ". Hawkins printed a specimen of his work, and a piece appeared in the second edition (*Bk.* I) of *Harmonia Sacra* (1703). There has been a nineteenth-century edition of the *Sanctus* and *Gloria* from Weldon's service-music. His anthems may be seen in British Museum manuscripts : *Add.* 17841, *Add.* 22099, *Add.* 30932, *Add.* 31405, *Add.* 33568, *Add.* 34076, *Add.* 31821, and *Harl.* 7341. Organ parts of anthems are contained in *Add.* 30931. The *Sanctus*, with figured bass, is in *Add.* 6324, and a Single Chant in G minor is contained in *Add.* 31819. The song, " Sleep, downy Sleep ", is to be found in *Add.* 22099. " Let Ambition fire thy mind " (from the 1700 competition-music) in included in *Add.* 31806 (Bass and Thorough-Bass parts in *Add.* 31455), while *Add.* 32099 has " Far from thee be anxious care ", also from the *Judgment of Paris* (1700).

WELDRE (Henry, Matthew, Peter, Philip Van), *see* WILDER (Philip Van).

WHEELER (Paul): An excellent violinist who flourished during the Commonwealth. He was held to be one of the best performers in this country before the arrival of Baltzar (Evelyn, *Diary*, March 4th, 1656). Whether Paul Wheeler was actually his name, or whether it was a corruption from some such Cornish name as Polewheel, Polwhele, or Polewhele, is not clear. He appears as Paulwheel and Powlwheel in the *Division Violin* (*Ed.* 1685).

WHITE (Matthew): A

member of the Chapel Royal and composer of many catches and rounds of the popular order. Very possibly he is not entitled to the important position he has held in the past, for it is exceedingly doubtful whether the anthems and other ecclesiastical compositions attributed to him (probably first by Tudway) were really by him. The works of the far more celebrated Robert Whyte have frequently been ascribed to this Gentleman of the Chapel Royal. He was sworn into his post in 1613 : " Robert Stone of the age of 97 yeares died the second day of July, and Matthew White, Minister, and a Basse (from Welles) was elected and admitted gospeller in his place at the first, the 2nd of November followinge and was sworn the 27th daie of December then next ensuinge " (*C.B.C.R.*), and resigned in September, 1614. In 1629 he took the degrees of Bachelor and Doctor of Music at Oxford. The anthem given to him in Barnard's collection of manuscript music (*R.C.M.*) may possibly be his, but great care must be exercised in the case of most other sacred compositions bearing his name. *Add.* 29386, *Add.* 29291, *Add.* 31462, *Add.* 31463, *Add.* 30273, contain two or three rounds and catches by him in many copies, and the " Mr. White " represented in *Catch that Catch Can* (1658) may also be Matthew. The *Musical Companion* of 1672 includes a couple of compositions, presumably by him. Tudway says that he was organist of Christ Church, Oxford, in 1611, but there is no confirmation of this.

WHITE (Robert), *see* WHYTE (Robert).

WHITE (William): A composer of instrumental and vocal music who flourished early in the seventeenth century. His name is found in a list of " singing men at Westminster " who received an allowance of mourning for the funeral of Queen Elizabeth (*L.C.R.*) Beyond this, nothing is known of him. Specimens of his work may be seen in the British Museum : *Add.* 29372–7 (Thomas Myriell's manuscripts) containing a verse anthem for six voices, " Almighty Lord " and second part, " Bend down " ; also some instrumental work in *Add.* 17792–6. Further examples of his music are preserved at Peterhouse (Cambridge), and the Music School (Oxford). The *Magnificat* in the latter collection, dated 1570, is probably by Robert Whyte (*q.v.*), or by a different William White of an earlier generation.

WHITEHORNE (Thomas) *see* WHYTHORNE (Thomas).

WHYTE (Robert): One of the most important of the Elizabethan composers of ecclesiastical music ; indeed, the only one who can be mentioned in a breath with Tallis and Tye. His work as a rule is distinguished by nobility and dignity, and softened by real charm and adroit handling. There is every reason for supposing that he was Tye's son-in-law, and thus would probably have come more under the influence of the older man, though, in any case, the two musicians would have been in close contact by reason of their Cathedral work. If Whyte took Tye as a model, he availed himself of the work of Tye's best period, and in many respects the music of the younger man compares very favourably with that of the other. Before the sixteenth century closed Whyte was enjoying a very high reputation ; John Baldwin and Thomas Morley ranking him with the best composers of the age. Yet, curiously enough, he was quickly forgotten, and except for an anthem printed by Barnard (1641), nothing of his was made accessible to the general public until Burney (this time laudably free from the bias that so frequently warps his judgment) sang his praises. Ambros becomes enthusiastic in the contemplation of Whyte's " noble thought " and " fine taste " ; while Nagel puts the composer's countrymen to shame by pointing out that it was little short of a national duty to have all of Whyte's compositions printed. There can be no doubt that Robert Whyte deserves consideration side by side with Tye, Tallis, and the best of their Continental contemporaries.

It is not known exactly when Whyte was born ; but since he became a Bachelor of Music in 1560 after having studied the art for ten years, we may suppose that the date of his birth must be somewhere near 1535. His name is found in connection with one Magister White who was paid for work done on the Magdalen College (Oxford) organ, and it is most likely that he was the son of the organ-builder. Again he is mentioned in the account of the Holborn church of St. Andrew's as having received 5l. for the " great organs which his father gave to the church ". It is not clear why Whyte, junior, should have been paid this amount for an instrument which his father gave to the church ; but the entry further connects the two men. The first absolutely authentic document relating to the composer is the entry in the Cambridge Grace-Book (*Delta.*, *p.* 60*b*): " 1560. Conceditur 13 decembris Robto. Wight, ut studium 10 annorum in musica sufficiat ei ad intrandum in eadem, sic tamen ut componat communionem cantandam in ecclesia beate marie coram universitate in die comitiorum sub pena quadraginta solitorum (omnia peregit)." Between the date of his degree and 1562 he became Master of the Choristers at Ely Cathedral, apparently in the place rendered vacant by the retirement of Tye (1561). He certainly became organist at Ely not later than 1562, for in the following year he was paid his annual salary for the preceding year. In 1566 he was succeeded in this post by John Farrant. In 1567 his name is to be found in the Chester records, sharing the organist's salary with Richard Saywell (Sewell). There should be no valid reason for supposing that the " Mr. White " of the Chester entries was other than the Robert Whyte under consideration. As much as is known concerning his activity in Chester is contained in an article by Dr. J. Cox Bridge in the Chester Archaeological Society's *Journal* (*Vol.* 19 ; 1903). In 1570 he entered Westminster Abbey as *Magister Choristorum*, but held the post for only a short time, dying during the great plague at Westminster in 1574 (buried November 11th at St. Margaret's). His wife was Ellen Tye, most probably a daughter of Christopher Tye, and he had by her five daughters : Marjery, baptized at Ely in 1565, Margaret (Westminster, 1570), Elizabeth (1571), Prudence (1573), and Anne. Of these children three died during the plague, only Anne and Marjery surviving. Robert's wife outlived him by a few days. His will, made only two or three days before he died, describes him as " Bacheler of Musicke and Master of the Queristers of the Cathedrall Churche of St. Peter in the Cittie of Westminster ", and in it he expresses the desire to be buried at St. Margaret's, near to his children's graves. His father, of the same Christian name, survived him, for the will mentions a legacy of 3*l.* to the older man,— besides all the household goods which the latter brought with him when he came to live with his son. The composer also left 4*d.* to each of his pupils.

Far too little of Robert Whyte's music has been printed, and there is every reason for Nagel's suggestion being acted upon. Barnard printed the anthem, " The Lord bless us " (1641) and Burney reproduced " Lord, who shall dwell in Thy Tabernacle ? " Of more modern reprints, Mr. G. E. P. Arkwright's *Old English Edition* (*No.* XXI) contains the anthem printed by Barnard, and also " O how glorious " (both five-part) ; " O, Praise God in His Holiness " was edited by Mr. C. K. Scott (*Euterpe*,

Vol. 8, 1909), and the same anthem appeared under the editorship of Mr. J. E. West (Novello). A large number of manuscripts in various collections contain work by Robert Whyte which awaits publication : the British Museum, the Bodleian (Oxford), Christ Church (*Ib.*), the Music School (*Ib.*), the Royal College of Music (London), and several other libraries possess specimens of his composition. A few pieces for the lute are also known, and an organ composition is in the Christ Church (Oxford) library. A certain amount of difficulty presents itself when manuscripts are consulted. Several composers of the same surname are represented, and it is not always possible to determine with any degree of accuracy to which of them certain of the pieces are to be attributed.

WHYTHORNE (Thomas): Historically rather than musically Thomas Whythorne is an important figure in the story of English secular (vocal) music. The work which places him in this position is *Songs for three, fower, and five voyces, composed and made by Thomas Whythorne, Gent., the which songes be of sundrie sortes . . .,* published in 1571 from the press of John Day (*q.v.*). The seventy-six " songs " contained in the book are by no means comparable in quality with the excellent work of, say, Byrd (1588 set), but, at the same time, they do not merit the contempt that has been heaped upon them by many critics and historians from Burney onwards. It is not given to many musicians unless they be of William Byrd's stature, to write music in a form entirely new to them and produce work anything but uncertain and lacking in maturity. Whythorne's songs in spite of their " crudity " and " barbarity " stand as an important landmark in the history of English part-song writing. A second work of his, the *Duos, or Songs for two Voices,*—containing fifty-two compositions for treble and bass, two trebles, and two cornets (*v. Dic. O. E. Mus.*), in addition to some Canons, was published in 1590. Nothing is known of his life beyond the assumption that he was born in 1528. The late Dr. Cummings possessed a portrait of Whythorne as he was in 1569. Each part of the *Duos* contains

a portrait " aetatis suae anno XL ".

WIGHT (Robert), *see* WHYTE (Robert).

WILBYE (John): One of that band of Elizabethan madrigalists whose work brought to its highest state of florescence a form of composition that the English musicians made their own, and in which they ultimately equalled their Continental models. It is no exaggeration to say that Wilbye, the lutenist, teacher, and probably also violist, has left examples of the madrigal which have not been surpassed by the best writers of Italy or the Low Countries. In writing of the work of such men as Morley, Weelkes and Wilbye it is as difficult to avoid extravagance of language, as it is easy to hail each of them as the greatest writer in this particular form of composition. For each has proved himself to be a consummate master of his art in one or other respect, and together they,—in the company of another half-dozen only slightly inferior writers,—form a school of musicians of which any age and any country might well be proud. The peculiar features that help to make of Wilbye's vocal music the highly polished art-work it is, consiſt of a remarkable power of invention that discovers melodic material and harmonic treatment which fits the sense of the words without being unduly "programmatic"; an equally noteworthy reſtraint which prevents the dramatic inſtinꜩs of the writer from lowering the high artiſtic value of his work by a senseless prodigality in the employment of his resources ; a delicacy of touch and a deep appreciation of beauty in its pureſt form which allow the message of the often very fine poetry to be expressed without distortion ; and a technical skill in writing,—a workmanship that is maſterly from whichever angle it is viewed. These are some of the qualities that are the explanation for the faꜩ that Wilbye's madrigals have been sung continuously from the moment of their writing to the present day. His harmony is decidedly prophetic, and it may be that here we see a reason for his continued popularity. From Peacham (who, in 1622, considered Wilbye among the beſt musicians in Europe) to the hiſtorians of the present day,

all who have occasion to write of Wilbye have also spoken of him in terms of such high praise that in would be difficult to credit their accounts were none of his work available for examination and performance in modern reprints. There can remain, after an adequate performance of some of Wilbye's beſt madrigals, no doubt that he is entitled to recognition as one of the foremoſt half-dozen of English musicians.

In attempting to trace the life-ſtory of John Wilbye we are rather more fortunate in regard to material than in the case of many another musician of the period. A number of authentic documents are available that enable the hiſtorian to conſtruꜩ a fairly complete account of his life. Although Wilbye's will has been preserved at Somerset House since this building has been put to its present use, and although it has been accessible to all who desired to see it, the gratitude of all admirers of English music muſt be expressed to Dr. E. H. Fellowes for having followed up the clues to be derived from that intereſting document. His researches resulted in the narrowing of the field to be hunted, and after the discovery of Wilbye's name in parish registers, in his father's will, and in the papers connected with the establishments of Sir Thomas Kytson of Hengrave Hall and of Lady Rivers, the rest was easy. I was acquainted with Wilbye's will (which has been printed by Major Francis Skeet and Dr. Fellowes,— by the latter in the *Proceedings of the Musical Association*, February 16th, 1915), but was forestalled by the learned Doctor in my further quest. From the documents mentioned it appears that Wilbye was baptized on March 7th, 1573–4, that his father was Matthew Wilbye, and that he was born at Diss in Norfolk. He was the junior of three sons, and his father, who was a tanner and apparently in easy circumstances, bequeathed to him his household linen and silver (will of Matthew Wilbye, proved at Norwich on July 6th, 1605). It is quite possible that he inherited his musical talent from his father, for the latter seems to have been a lutenist, having left his instrument to John. Where the latter received his training in music we do not know, and until the last

decade of the sixteenth century, when he entered the service of Sir Thomas Kytson, we find no further trace of him. Until this knight's widow died in 1626 Wilbye remained at Hengrave Hall ; and the Household Books of Sir Thomas (which I have drawn upon so frequently in my *Dictionary of Old English Music*) are the only sources of information we possess of the madrigalist's activities at that period. In 1598 we know that Wilbye accompanied Sir Thomas to the latter's town residence in Austin Friars, for his first set of madrigals, published in that year, were sent into the world " from the Augustine Fryers ". Four years later Sir Thomas died, and Wilbye remained as musician in the household of Lady Kytson. As was usual in the case of a director of music resident with a member of the landed nobility, Wilbye had his own apartments, and in the Household Books of Hengrave an account is given of the furniture in " Wilbee's Chamber " Two such lists are given, one in 1602–3 and the other in an inventory made between 1621 and 1625. Wilbye received frequent rewards for his services, and in 1613 a lease of land (known as Sexten's Farm) was added. After the death of Lady Kytson, Wilbye filled a similar position in the household of Lady Rivers at Colchester, for "Wilbye's Chamber" is mentioned also in her will. He died in 1638 (probably in the autumn, for his will was proved on November 13th), and was buried at Colchester (Holy Trinity). Since the will has already been twice printed, and Dr. Fellowes's paper so easily accessible, a few extracts will suffice to serve our present purpose : " I John Wilby of Colchester doe this present daie . . . 10th of September, A.D. 1638 make and ordaine this my last Will and Testament ". Nearly all of his property and cash he left to nephews and a niece, and the fact that he could bequeath nearly five hundred pounds in money, exclusive of landed property, shows that he had amassed what was in those days a considerable fortune. " I doe give my best Vyall unto the most excellent and most illustrious Prince Charles, Prince of Wales." How " illustrious " this princeling could have been in 1638 when in

his eighth year is not clear ; but had the polished and artistic John Wilbye known what changes this prince was going to make in the trend of native music when he ascended the throne after the Restoration as King Charles II, he might possibly have left his " best Vyall " to someone else. The fact that all his property was left to nephews, and the circumstance that he spent almost the whole of his adult life in the two establishments named would seem to prove that he never married.

Wilbye's compositions are not numerous. His first published work was *The First Set of English Madrigals to 3, 4, 5 and 6 voices : Newly composed by John Wilbye at London* (1598), —this set, issued while at Austin Friars, contained thirty compositions. In 1601 he contributed the six-part madrigal, " The Lady Oriana was dight, *etc.*", to the *Triumphes of Oriana*. A further eight years elapsed before his *Second Set of Madrigales to 3, 4, 5 and 6 Parts, apt both for Voyals and Voyces* appeared in 1609,—this book containing thirty-four numbers. Both the first and the second sets are in the British Museum. One four-part composition and one for five voices appeared in Leighton's *Teares or Lamentacions*, etc. (1614). It will be seen that Wilbye's great reputation rests upon sixty-seven comparatively short pieces ; but their quality is so uniformly high, —especially that of the madrigals,—that they suffice to secure for him the fame he so richly merits. All of these published works have been reprinted, wholly or in part, by many editors. The latest and, to my mind, by far the best modern publication to contain Wilbye's work, is *Volume* VI of Dr. E. H. Fellowes's *English Madrigal School* (Stainer and Bell, 1914). This contains a facsimile of a letter from the composer (dated 1628), the first set of madrigals (1598), the *Oriana* madrigal, and the two motets from Leighton's collection (1614). *Volume* VII of the same series contains the second set of madrigals (1609).

Wilbye's sacred music is not of the same high standard as his secular work, but even in the former he exhibits occasional touches of exquisite beauty,—particularly in one of the motets (1614)—

" O God the Rock ". Two Latin motets are contained in *Volume* XXI of G. E. P. Arkwright's *Old English Edition* (one *à* 5, and one *à* 6). Thomas Myriell's collection (*Add.* 29372–7) and Part-Books in the Bodleian library (Oxford) contain manuscript sacred music of Wilbye's. Copies in manuscript of some of his printed works appear in the library of Christ Church (Oxford) and specimens of the madrigals are also in manuscripts kept at the British Museum. That he wrote instrumental music in known only from an Altus part-book (*Add.* 29427) which contains music for the viols, but which is, of course, quite useless unless the other parts are discovered. A book of lute lessons was in existence in the eighteenth century, but its present location is unknown.

WILDER (Philip Van): A number of musicians with the surname of Wilder, Weldre, or Wildroe appear to have come from the Netherlands and to have settled in England during the early Tudor era. Philip van Wilder (sometimes given as Veldre and Welter) was keeper of the instruments to Henry VIII (*v. Harl.* 1419 *A.*) and is entered in the State Papers as a "minstrel" in 1526 (*Annalen*). In 1538 he is given as a "Luter". In 1557 (Mary Tudor) his salary is mentioned as 38*l*. 5*s*. per annum. Edward VI granted this musician a warrant in 1550 empowering him "to take to the King's use, such and as many singing children and choristers, as he or his deputy should think good" (Rimbault, *Introduction* to the printed version of *C.B.C.R.*). He was then known as a "Gentleman of the Privy Chamber".

Music by Philip van Wilder was printed in foreign collections (Paris and Antwerp) of 1544, 1545, 1572, and 1597, but it does not follow, of course, that the composer was alive until the last of them appeared. Great confusion prevailed in the cataloguing of manuscript music by this composer, since many of the pieces are signed merely "Philip", or "Phillips", and a copyist adding "Mr." would soon cause the compositions to be attributed to Mr. (Peter) Philips (*q.v.*). This was the case in the British Museum printed catalogue of music manuscripts ; but the necessary corrections have now

been made in ink in the copy on the shelves of the Manuscript Department (Students Room). Compositions by Philip van Wilder may be seen in *Add.* 5059, *Add.* 11584, *Add.* 17802–5, *Add.* 29427, *Add.* 29372–7 (an anthem here signed "Peter Philips "), *Add.* 34071 (a madrigal signed "Philippe de Vuildre "), *Add.* 22597, *Add.* 30480–4 ("Phillip de Wildroe "), while *Add.* 29246–7 has lute arrangements signed "Phillip" which may also be his. The "Aspice Domine " (*à* 5) of *Add.* 5059 is also contained in *MSS. No.* 979–83 in the Christ Church (Oxford) collection.

With Philip van Wilder there is often mentioned a Peter van Wilder,—relationship not known. Peter is first given in February, 1519, as a lutenist and flautist to Henry VIII at 10*l*. per annum. He is entered in the State Papers until 1559 (*Annalen* and *L.C.R.*). A Matthew de Weldre is also given in 1516 as a "lewter" and player on the "veoldes" with a salary of twenty marks a year (Order of Henry VIII to John Heron, dated from Greenwich, 7*th Jan.* 8 *Hen. VIII*). A Henry Vanwilder's name is entered in the Lord

Chamberlain's Records as that of a " musician " to Mary Tudor (*Vol.* 791), in 1556–7 (*Vol.* 811), and 1558 (*Vol.* 1). WILDROE, *see* WILDER (Philip Van).
WILKES, *or* WILKS, *see* WEELKES (Thomas).
WILSON (John): A singer, lutenist, and composer who enjoyed a very great reputation among his contemporaries of the seventeenth century. As a vocalist and performer on the lute he won the admiration of many well-known men of his time who, like Henry Lawes, wrote very highly of his character and musical taste. Anthony Wood gives us much information upon the personal aspect of John Wilson, and during the Oxford days in the Commonwealth, the University historian and the musician often came in contact (*cf.* article on Baltzar). The identification of John Wilson with the " Jacke Wilson " of the stage direction to *Much Ado about Nothing* is still a procedure without complete justification. From Rimbault (*Who was Jack Wilson?* 1846) to Mr. G. E. P. Arkwright (*Grove*, Ed. 1914) there have been many writers who have sustained the theory very bravely. But, although

there is no evidence to make John Wilson and the Shakespearean singer two distinct personages with absolute certainty, there is also no evidence that identifies them to the exclusion of all doubt (*cf. also* the article on John Wilson in the *Dictionary of National Biography, Reprint*). Charles I was very fond of the performance of John Wilson, and when the latter sang to his own accompaniment at court, the king (no mean judge of music) would be a most interested and flattering listener.

Wilson was born on April 5th, 1595, and, according to Anthony Wood who knew him personally, was a native of Faversham, Kent. The source of his musical knowledge is not known, but he must have commenced composing at a very early age, for some work in his *Cheerfull Ayres* proves to be an arrangement of the music used in the *Masque of Flowers* (printed 1614) generally assigned to Coperario (*q.v.*). We hear nothing further of him until we read of his appointment as a musician to Charles I in 1635 (*L.C.R., Vol.* 739, and *Cal. S.P.*) and the years between the breaking of his voice and

1635 might well have been occupied in the manner suggested by the " Jack Wilson " theorists. The last entry in the Lord Chamberlain's Records referring to him, before the outbreak of the Civil War, is dated 1641, and alludes to him as a " musician for the lutes, violls, and voices ". He followed his master to Oxford, and while there took part in those genial " music meetings " so naively described by Wood. It was while at Oxford that Wilson rose in Wood's estimation to be " the greatest judge of musick that ever was " (*Diary of his Life, Ed.* 1772) and the best lutenist in all England. In 1644–5 also Wilson graduated as Doctor of Music at Oxford, royal favour probably assisting him on that occasion. After the surrender of the king to the Scottish army in 1646 the glory of Oxford was dimmed for a time, and Wilson retired to the residence of Sir William Walter and his wife, who were both well-known lovers of music and patrons of musicians (Wood). In 1656 Wilson was elected Choragus at Oxford (*v.* article on William Heather), and Wood tells us that at this time he had lodgings at Balliol College.

He remained at Oxford until 1661 when, the monarchy having been restored, he resigned his academic post and returned to the metropolis. He is mentioned already in a list of musicians to receive livery allowances (16*l.* 2*s.* 6*d.* per annum) in 1660 (*L.C.R., Vol.* 460). Nagel (*Annalen, p.* 50) speaks of a document dating from 1660 in which Dr. John Wilson petitions for a post in the royal service as was promised him at the death of Charles I. The Lord Chamberlain's entry of March 8th, 1660–1, shows that the musician obtained the place of Alphonso Bales, deceased. In 1662 he succeeded Henry Lawes as Gentleman of the Chapel Royal (*v.* Henry Lawes for the entry in the *C.B.C.R.*). He held these posts until 1673 when he died. Wilson was twice married, his second wedding taking place in 1670–1. During his later years he resided at the Horseferry, Westminster. His death was announced officially in the Cheque-Book : " Dr. John Wilson departed this life the 22nd day of February, 1673 " and in the Lord Chamberlain's Records we find the " Certificate of the burial of Dr. Wilson . . . in the

Cloyſter belonging to the Collegiate church of St. Peter's, Weſtminſter, on the 27th February, 1673. Signed Stephen Crespion, Chanter " (*L.C.R.*, *Vol.* 198). In the Private Musick of the king he was succeeded by Thomas Purcell. A portrait of Wilson hangs in the Music School, Oxford.

John Wilson is pre-eminently a writer of secular music, and though none of his work reaches the higheſt level, it is nevertheless tuneful and pleasant. But although the bulk of his music is secular, he did not forget the duties of an Oxford Professor of Music, and thus the firſt work of his to appear after the conferring of the doctorate was his *Psalterium Carolinum. The Devotions of His Sacred Majeſtie in his Solitudes and Sufferings*, rendered in Verse. *Set to Musick for three voices with an organ or Theorbo* (four part-books, 1657). The work contains passages from the Psalms for three voices with the inſtrumental accompaniment named. It is noteworthy that a work with such a title could appear in 1657, and it speaks volumes for Cromwell's indulgence ; it certainly shows what was the republican

attitude towards a censorship. Three years later he published at Oxford, *Cheerfull Ayres or Ballads. Firſt Composed for one Single Voice and since Set for 3 Voices* (three part-books ; 1660). The music contained is by Nicholas Lanier, Robert Johnson, and John Wilson, and the book was said to have been the firſt music ever printed at Oxford. Examples of Wilson's vocal music may be seen in Playford's *Select Musicall Ayres and Dialogues* (1652 and 1653), in *Catch that Catch Can* (1658), in *Select Ayres and Dialogues* 1659), in the *Musical Companion* (1672), the laſt containing nine of Wilson's moſt popular part-songs, and in many others. To Henry Lawes's *Second Book of Ayres and Dialogues* (1655) he contributed some complimentary verses, and in the *Choice Psalms* of the brothers Lawes (1648) he has " An Elegie to the memory of his Friend and Fellow, Mr. William Lawes ". Several modern reprints and arrangements of two or three of Wilson's songs have appeared. Rimbault names Wilson as the composer of music used in Richard Brome's *Northern Lass* (1632), fragments exiſting at the Oxford Music School. A good deal of Wilson's music is scattered among various manuscripts, the largeſt colleƈtion of which is probably that in the British Museum. Specimens of his work are to be found in : *Eg.* 2013 (songs), *Harl.* 7341 (Evening Service in G ; Tudway MS.), *Add.* 5337 (glee), *Add.* 10444 (ſtring duet), *Add.* 11608 (songs), *Add.* 29396 (songs), *Add.* 29481 (a fragment), *Add.* 31806 (" Where the bee sucks ", three-part), and *Add.* 36952 (Sir Henry Bishop's adaptation of a glee by Wilson to produce the popular " O, By Rivers ", for a production of *Twelfth Night*). The Bodleian library has works by Wilson in manuscript (settings of several Horatian odes and passages from other Latin writers).

WISE (Michael): An organiſt and composer of ecclesiaſtical music of the poſt-Reſtoration period. One of the children of the Chapel Royal almoſt immediately after the reconſtruƈtion of that eſtablishment, Wise was a contemporary of Pelham Humfrey, John Blow, and the reſt, and enjoyed the inſtruƈtion of Captain Henry Cooke (*q.v.*). Although by no means comparable with the beſt work of the preceding era, his compositions are perhaps more satisfying than those of his younger contemporaries ; for he looked back rather than forward. In the moſt successful of his sacred music he often exhibits beauties and shows feelings of a more deeply-rooted nature than do the majority of Charles the Second's composers.

Wise was a native of Wiltshire and was born probably at Salisbury. The date of his birth muſt be placed round about 1648, since in 1664 he had already left the Chapel Royal on account of the breaking of his voice (*L.C.R.*, *Vol.* 742). In 1678 (May 17th) we ſtill find an entry in the same records of the payment of 30*l.* per annum to Michael Wise " late child of the Chappell, whose voyce was changed, and was gon from the Chappell, which payment is to be continued during his Majeſty's pleasure " (*Id.*, *Vol.* 747). Exaƈtly what this means cannot be determined. It is not unusual to find such entries continued in the State Papers long after the events with which they deal ; this was no doubt due either to faulty book-keeping or to the non-payment of the grants at the time of the original warrants. But it may also mean that Charles liked the boy and wished to pay him what would to-day be called a retaining-fee until his voice had settled. In 1663 Wise filled a post at Windsor, and on leaving that Chapel he returned to his native county and in 1668 was appointed organist at Salisbury Cathedral. He retained this post until the year of his death, although he was re-appointed to the Chapel Royal in London as a Gentleman in 1675–6 in succession to Raphael Courteville I, who died on December 28th. The differences that cropped up between Wise and the Salisbury Dean and Chapter were probably occasioned by the former's frequent absences when serving in London. A deputy was engaged for the Salisbury post and his fees were deducted from Wise's salary. In 1684 (November 24th) he is given in the Lord Chamberlain's Records as a " Musician for the Cornets " with a salary of 20d. per day and the usual annual livery allowance of 16l. 2s. 6s., Dr. Child being mentioned as cornettist in the same warrant (L.C.R., Vol. 749).

At the accession of James II (1685), he was relieved of his Chapel Royal position. The reasons for this are not known, though it is supposed that they were political. More probably his dismissal was brought about by some hasty remark of his, for he was the possessor of a very uneven temper. In 1686–7 he was given the duties of Almoner and Master of the Choristers at St. Paul's Cathedral, and in the same year he died. It is said that he met his death at the hands of a night-watchman who felled the composer with his weapon for failing to give an account of himself when traversing the streets in a furious temper and " boiling with rage " after a quarrel with his wife. Hawkins relates the tale ; but there is no further evidence either in support or refutation. Even the place of his death is not known with certainty, and it can have taken place in London or Salisbury (v. footnote to p. 101, J. E. West, Cathedral Organists, Ed. 1921). Wise was twice married, his first wife (Jane) dying in 1682 at the age of thirty, and second (Barbara) surviving him. His three children were placed in the care of a guardian.

Not very much of his music has been printed. Boyce gave six anthems (including the beautiful " Thy beauty, O Israel " and " Awake up, my glory "), while others have been issued by Novello and Co. with the organ-parts of Vincent Novello. Of earlier published work, specimens may be seen in the *Musical Companion* (1667 ; Catches), in *Cantica Sacra* (1674), in *New Ayres and Dialogues* (1678), in Langdon's *Divine Harmony* (1774), while the two-part " Old Chiron thus preached " exists in several printed versions. Manuscript music by Wise is preserved in the books of the Chapel Royal (*v. L.C.R., Vol.* 745 ; August 1st, 1676), Ely Cathedral (Gloria and anthems), Christ Church, Dublin (Service), and Gloucester Cathedral (anthems). The British Museum possesses a good collection in *Harl.* 7338 (Morning and Evening Service in D Minor ; and anthems), *Harl.* 7339 ("verse evening service in E-flat " and anthems), *Add.* 30933 (Service in D), *Add.* 17784, *Add.* 17820, *Add.* 17840, *Add.* 29396–7, *Add.* 29481, *Add.* 30382, *Add.* 30478–9, *Add.* 30932, *Add.* 31404, *Add.* 31444–5, *Add.* 31460,

and *Add.* 31821 and 34203 (anthems or parts of the same). The duet " Old Chiron " is contained in *Add.* 29397, *Add.* 31455, *Add.* 31993, *Add.* 33234, and *Add.* 33351. Another duet,— " Man's life is but vain ", —is in *Add.* 22099. *Add.* 29386, and *Add.* 31462 contain Catches.

WITHIE (John): A composer of viol music who flourished at the middle of the seventeenth century. Nothing is known of his life. Nine short pieces by him are to be found in *Musick's Recreation on the Viol, Lyra-way* (1669), the last being a Saraband " with Divisions ". *Add.* 31423 (in the hand of John Jenkins) contains a Pavane, an Allemande, an Air, and a Courante in F, presumably for three viols ; while *Add.* 29283–5 contain seventeen pieces without names by Withie.

WOODSON (Leonard): A singing-man of St. George's Chapel, Windsor, who became instructor of the choristers there in 1605 (*Chapter Acts* of St. George's) and organist to Eton College in 1615. His name appears in the College Accounts until 1641 in which year he must have died, for Barnard's collection, dated 1641, includes a *Te Deum* of his, and the book contains no work by composers then living. The Oxford Music School collection of *In Nomines* has him represented, and a couple of Anthems are preserved in a manuscript at the Royal College of Music (London). Another Leonard Woodson (given in the *C.B.C.R.* as Wooddeson) was sworn a Gentleman of the Chapel Royal in succession to Alphonso Marsh in 1681, and died on March 14th, 1716–17. It is not known with certainty whether he was related to the Eton organist of the same name.

WOODSON (Thomas): Gentleman of the Chapel Royal and writer of ecclesiastical music. Of his early life we know nothing, and we do not come across his name until his appointment to the Chapel is entered : "1581. William Edney died of the plague the 13th of November, and Thomas Woodson of Poules sworne in his place the 25th of Decr. Ao. 24 " (*C.B.C.R.*), an entry which tells us that he was previously a chorister at St. Paul's Cathedral. His name is given as "Woodeson" in the list of Gentlemen who received mourning livery for the funeral of Queen Elizabeth in 1603 (*L.C.R., Vol.* 554). The last we hear of him is again from the Cheque-Book : "1605. Tho. Woodson solde his place to William West of Canterbury, who was sworn in his place the 20th of Marche." The date of his death is not known. A *Te Deum* of his is in *Add.* 29289 and also in *Add.* 30086. An organ solo intended to be "Forty wayes of two parts in one on the *Miserere*" is contained in *Add.* 29996, but only twenty of the versions are given in the manuscript. There is nothing to show that he was related to either of the Leonard Woodsons.

Y

YONGE (Nicholas): An Elizabethan musician who achieved immortality by the publication of two books of foreign madrigals which, with the exception of William Byrd's book and that of Thomas Whythorne of 1588, were the first works of that nature to be published in England. The first was : "*Musica   Transalpina*. Madrigales translated of foure, five, and sixe, parts, Chosen out of diuers excellent Authors, with the first and second Part of *La Verginella*, made by Maister *Byrd* upon two Stanz's of *Ariosto*, and brought to speak English with the rest . . . 1588." The book contains madrigals by Ferrabosco, Marenzio, Palestrina, Byrd, Donato, Lasso, and others. In the dedication Yonge explains how these compositions came to be translated by one whom he calls a "Counsellor of Estate" for the use of the circle of amateurs who foregathered in his house : " Since I first began to keep house in this city, a great number of gentlemen and merchants of good accompt (as well of this realm as of foreign nations) have taken in good part such entertainment of pleasure, as my poor ability was able to afford them, both by the exercise of music daily used in my house, and by furnishing them with books of that kind yearly sent to me out of Italy and other places." The second work was entitled: "*Musica   Transalpina*. The Second Booke of Madrigalles, to five and six Voices : translated out of Sundrie Italian Authors, and newly published by Nicholas Yonge. . . . 1597". This book contains work by Ferrabosco, Marenzio, Croce, Palavicino, Vecchi, Nanini, and other less-known writers.

Yonge came from Lewes in Sussex, and all that we know of his private life is that he lived in the parish of St. Michael's, Cornhill (London), that his wife's name was Jane, and that he had nine children. He is most probably to be identified with a contemporary Nicholas Young who sang in the St. Paul's choir. Yonge died in the latter part of October, 1619, for his will (dated the nineteenth of the month) was proved by his widow on November 12th. He was buried in the churchyard of St. Michael's parish on October 23rd, 1619. A complete re-issue of the eighty-one compositions in the two books was undertaken by G. W. Budd, but he proceeded no farther than the first half-dozen. Yonge does not appear to have composed any music himself.

YOULL (Henry) : An Elizabethan madrigalist,—or, rather, a writer of Canzonets, —who flourished towards the end of the sixteenth century. Of his life next to nothing is known. Judging by the dedication of the only work of his that is known to us to-day, he was musically active in the household of a certain Edward Bacon, whose four sons he appears to have instructed. The title-page to the *Canzonets to Three Voyces* (1608) tells us that he was a " Practitioner in the Art of Musicke ", and that these pieces were the " first fruits of my indevours ". The songs are all in three parts, and are chiefly marked by a fine sense of rhythm and a certain optimistic atmosphere; but, though they are well up to the average for the period, they cannot claim comparison with the works of the giants of that, the madrigalian, era.

Youll's publication contains twenty-four numbers, the last six being " Fa-las " (*v. Dic. O. E. Mus.*, *s.v.* Fa-La). The British Museum copy is the only one known to exist. " Pipe, Shepherds, pipe," from this work, was reprinted by C. K. Scott in 1909, and the complete set was published by Dr. E. H. Fellowes as *Volume* XXVIII of *The English Madrigal School* (Stainer and Bell). Rimbault, in the historical introduction to the Musical Antiquarian Society's edition of Purcell's *Bonduca*, says that Youll composed music to Ben Jonson's *Cynthia's Revels* (1600), but I have discovered no further trace of it.

YOUNG (John I): A bass-viol player who was appointed as gambist in the private music of the king on June 24th, 1673, at a salary of 40*l.* per annum, plus the usual 16*l.* 2*s.* 6*d.* for livery (*L.C.R.*, *Vol.* 744). In 1680 (July 22nd) he is given as " deceased " (*Id.*, *Vol.* 747). This latter date prevents us from identifying him with John Young the publisher (*q.v. inf.*) as some authorities suggest.

YOUNG (John II): A music-publisher whose productions are met with rather too late to come within the scope of the present volume ; but since he issued the work of several musicians mentioned in these pages, he should perhaps be included. The period of his activities lies between 1698, when he published John Banister's *Compleat Tutor to the Violin,* and about 1728, when he printed *The Third Volume of the Dancing Master.* Soon after this date he disappears. At his shop in St. Paul's Churchyard, London, he also sold musical instruments.

YOUNG (Nicholas), *see* YONGE (Nicholas).

YOUNG (William): An eminent violist, who, in 1653, was in the service of the Archduke Ferdinand Charles, when he published a set of twenty-one *Sonate à* 3, 4, 5 *voci con Allemande, Corranti, etc., à* 3 at Innsbruck. A copy of this work is preserved in the University library of Upsala. The late Sir Frederick Bridge had one of these " Sonatas " performed at a Gresham Lecture, and it proved to be a very interesting and technically advanced work. Playford advertised some three-part *Fantasies* in 1669, but whether these were ever published and whether they were identical with the Innsbruck set, I cannot say.

The Oxford Music School possesses manuscripts of his and he is represented in *Musick's Recreation on the Viol, Lyra-way* (1669 and 1682) and in the *Musical Banquet* of 1651 (*Part I*).

A William Young was appointed as violinist and flautist to Charles II in 1660. He was still active in 1670, but is given as " deceased " in 1671 (*L.C.R.*). Whether these two Youngs should be identified, as several authorities think, is very much open to doubt.

INDEX

Note :—Figures in heavy type refer to the pages in which the chief account of the subject is to be found.

M m

INDEX

Printed in Great Britain by Stephen Austin & Sons, Ltd., Hertford.